THE STUDENT'S GUIDE TO
SANSKRIT COMPOSITION

(Being a Treatise on Sanskrit Syntax)

By

VAMAN SHIVARAM APTE

Eastern Book Linkers

DELHI : : (INDIA)

Publishers :

EASTERN BOOK LINKERS

H. O.: 5825/7, New Chandrawal,
Jawahar Nagar, Delhi-110007
Ph.: 9811232913

Show Room: 4806/24, Bharat Ram Road,
Darya-Ganj, New Delhi-110002
Ph. 45797575, 9718887575
e-mail: eblindology@gmail.com
ebl.info76@gmail.com
Website: www.eblindology.com

Edition: **2024**

Rs.: ₹ **500.00**

ISBN: 978-81-7854-058-0

THE STUDENT'S GUIDE TO SANSKRIT COMPOSITION

By **VAMAN SHIVARAM APTE**

PREFACE.

A glance at the Table of Contents will show that this edition differs from the first in many respects. The additions and alterations that have been made both in *matter* and *arragement* require a few words of explanation.

The main body of the work is divided into four Parts. The first Part gives the general scope of *Syntax* and lays down the principal laws of *Concord*. The second Part deals with *Government* and gives principal rules in the *Káraka Prakarana*. In the third Part are considered the more important *Grammatical Forms*, the meaning and use of which require explanation; such as, several kinds of Participles, the Infinitive Mood, the ten Tenses and Moods. Particles, such as are most frequently used in Sanskrit Literature, are also treated and illustrated being alphabetically arranged and distributed over eight Lessons. Some peculiarities of the Parasmaipada and Atmanepada—certain roots taking the one or the other pada according as they are used in a particular sense or are preceded by certain prepositions—which were given in an Appendix in the first edition, have here been incorporated into the body of the work, and treated in two additional Lessons. The fourth Part gives matter not given in the first edition—the *Analysis* and *Synthesis of Sanskrit sentences.* I have tried to apply the system of English analysis to Sanskrit sentences, and in doing so I have illustrated the rules of English Grammar by examples from Sanskrit authors, making such additions and alterations as were necessitated by the peculiarity of the Sanskrit idiom. To some this portion may perhaps appear superfluous. But my experience is that a correct knowledge of the relations subsisting between the different parts of a sanskrit sentence is highly useful to the student, not only in translating from Sanskrit into English, but also in translating from English into Sanskrit, inasmuch as it clearly brings to his notice the difference in construction between the two languages, and in composing sentences. The general rules of Analysis are much the same in all languages, but their application is not easily understood. In Section II of this part some rules on the *order of words* have been given, mostly drawn from an examination of the construction of Sanskrit Sentences and comparison with Latin idiom. The third Section takes up the *Composition* of sentences, where the student has to frame some sentences so as to apply the rules of analysis given in the first Section. Several exercises have, with this view, been given in this Section. I am inclined to believe that these exercises, if carefully worked, will give the student considerable facility in writing a few sentences of *original* Sanskrit on a given subject. The student has also been shown how to *paraphrase* Sanskrit passages, and it is expected that, with the help of Analysis, he will be able to paraphrase in Sanskrit as he does in English. The fourth Section treats of Letter writing, in which are given with examples and exercises, some of the common forms of letters. On this subject I have derived considerable help from a number of manuscripts, dealing with प्रशस्थाय:—forms of writing—that were brought to my notice by Dr. Bhandarkar, and kindly placed at my disposal for some months.

This edition differs also in the arrangement of matter. Each Lesson here consists of three parts: the first gives the rules with illustrations; the second and third gives sentences for exercise. *Choice Expressions and Idioms* which were, in the former edition, given after the rules, and the *Sentences for Correction* which were given last, have here been given after the Notes. The *Idioms* have been arranged in the alphabetical order of the important words in their English equivalents, and a good many taken from standard authors have been added so as to increase the former number by over one-half. The *sentences for correction* have been promiscuously arranged, and they may be attempted after the rules have been fully mastered. There is one more material change in arrangement that will not fail to strike the reader. The Sanskrit sentences have been divided into two parts: those in large type for reading in class, and 'additional sentences for exercise' which may be read at home as additional reading. I have been obliged to make this division, not because I considered the number of sentences very large, as some of my critics did, but because the sentences, as they stood, were too many to be read by students in the ordinary course of class lessons. I myself felt the difficulty, while teaching the book ; and I thought it proper to do that which I myself did, and which other teachers also, who did me the honor of teaching it to their pupils, must have done, namely to effect a division of the Sanskrit sentences. This has, moreover, enabled me to add under the 'additional sentences' several passages from authors not previously drawn upon.

The lesson on the Nominative case in the first edition has been omited, as it was found to be superfluous, and that on Pronouns being out of place in Concord, has been transferred to Part III. The Appendix on the formation of the feminine of nouns and adjectives has been dropped.

Other improvements made in this edition are two *Glossaries*—Sanskrit English and English Sanskrit—which give the difficult words occurring in the excercises for translation, and an alphabetical *Index* of all the nouns, adjectives, roots, &c., which have given rise to syntactical or other rules. The want of the two Glossaries, more especially of the first, was much felt by students. The most ordinary words which the student must have come across in his elementary course of study, have not been included. The importance of the Index need not be much dilated upon, since it facilitates reference to a very remarkable degree and is now regarded as almost a *sine qua non* of such works. For this I must thank Professor Max Muller who was kind enough to suggest, among other things, this idea of giving an Index. The Notes, given after Part IV, retain much of their former character. They are mostly intended to be explanatory. Individual words, being included in the Glossaries, have not here been repeated.

There are the main additions and alterations made in this edition. Besides, the work has been most carefully revised throughout; indeed, it will be difficult to find a page which has not undergone careful revision. Several rules have been recast; and many more, drawn from a closer study of Sanskrit Grammar and the works of classical authors have been added to each Lesson. Throughout the book several Sanskrit passages have been added, either to the illustrative sentences, or to the sentences for exercise. The effect of this and the like additions has been to increase the matter by nearly one-half. Yet by a suitable arrangement of types, the volume of the work has not much increased and that it may be within the reach of all classes of students, the price has been reduced to *Re 1 as. 8.* The rapid sale of a large edition in less than three years shows that the book, in some measure, supplied a felt want; and it is hoped that the student of Sanskrit will find this edition more useful and a better guide to Sanskrit composition than the first on account of the improvements effected in it.

Before concluding I must not omit to tender my most sincere thanks to Dr. R. G. Bhandarkar, who was kind enough to spare time to go over the greater portion of the book with me, and to make several important suggestions which have been mostly acted upon; and scondly to Mr. Lee Warner, Acting Director of Public Instruction who, at the recommendation of Dr. Bhandarkar, was pleased to sanction the work for use in High Schools. My acknowledgments are also due to Dr. Morell, Professor Bain, and Mr. McMordie, whose works have been useful to me in writing Part IV; and lastly to Mr. M. Sheshagiri Prabhu of the Madras Presidency who was the first to suggest the addition of Analysis and Synthesis of sentences.

Poona, 24th December, 1885. V. S. APTE.

TABLE OF CONTENTS.

PART I.

		SECTIONS	PAGE.
	Introductory	1—8	1

Concord.

LESSON.			
I.	Concord of Subject and Verb	9—17	4
II.	Concord of Substantive and Adjective	18—22	9
	Concord of Relative and its Antecedent	23—25	11

PART II.

Government.

III.	The Accusative Case		15
	General uses	26—30	
	Particular uses	31—37	
IV.	Verbs governing two Accusatives	38—41	23
V.	The Causal	42—49	27
VI.	The Instrumental Case		35
	General uses	50—54	
	Particular uses	55—59	
VII.	The Dative Case		43
	General uses	60—65	
	Particular uses	66—71	
VIII.	The Ablative Case		51
	General uses	72—75	
	Particular uses	76—86	
IX.	The Locative Case		60
	General uses	87—92	
	Particular uses	93—100	

Lesson.		Sections.	Page.
X.	The Genitive Case		67
	General uses	101—105	
	Particular uses	106—119	
XI.	The Genitive and Locative absolutes...	120—125	78

PART III.

The use and meaning of Grammatical Forms & Words.

XII.	Pronouns		86
	Personal	126—129	
	Demonstrative	130—132	
	Relative	133	
	Interrogative, Indefinite, and Reflexive	134—140	
XIII.	Participles		93
	Introductory	141	
	Present Participles	142—147	
	Future	148	
	Perfect	149	
XIV.	Participles continued		99
	Past Participles	150—154	
	Potential Passive Participles	155—157	
XV.	Participles continued		105
	Gerunds	158—161	
	Namul or Gerund in अम्	162—171	
XVI.	The Infinitive Mood	172—181	114
XVII.	Tenses and Moods		121
	Introductory	182—184	
	Present Tense	185—190	
	The Imperative Mood	191—194	
	The Benedictive Mood	195	
XVIII.	The Potential Mood	196—206	128

LESSON.		SECTIONS	PAGE.
XIX.	Imperfect, Perfect and Aorist		135
	Imperfect	207—208	
	Perfect	209	
	Aorist	210—211	
XX.	The two Futures and the Conditional		139
	The two Futures	212—215	
	The Conditional	216	
	Additional remarks on the use of the Tenses and Moods	217—241	

Particles.

XXI.	अंग, अथ, अधिकृत्य, अपि, अयि, अये, अहह and अहो	242—251	150
XXII.	आ, आं, आः, इति, इव, उत, एव, एवं, and ओम्	252—262	157
XXIII.	कच्चित्, क्व—क्व, कामं, किं, किल, केवल, and खलु	263—271	165
XXIV.	च (च-च), जातु, तद्, ततः, तथा, तावत् and तु	272—279	172
XXV.	दिष्ट्या, न, नाम, नु, ननु and नूनं	280—287	179
XXVI.	पुनः, प्रायः, बत, बलवत्, मुहुः, यद् and यत्सत्यं.	288—295	185
XXVII.	यथा-तथा, and यावत्-तावत्	296—300	190
XXVIII.	वरं-न, स्थाने, हंत, हा and हि	301—307	198
XXIX.	Parasmaipada and Atmanepada		205
	Introductory	308—309	
	Roots of the first Conjugation	310—325	
XXX.	Roots of the remaining Conjugations and Causals	326—355	215

PART IV.

Analysis and Synthesis of Sentences

(With Exercises).

Section I.

	Sections	Page.
Analysis of Sentences		225
Introductory	346—349	
The Simple Sentence	350—376	
The Complex Sentence	377—391	
The Compound Sentence	392—398	

Section II.

On the order of words in Sentences	399—414	251

Section III.

On the Synthesis of Sentences		257
Simple Sentences	415—420	
Complex Sentences	421—423	
Compound Sentences and Paraphrasing	424—426	

Section IV.

Letter-writing.		268
Introductory	427—430	
Domestic letters	431—433	
Miscellaneous	434—438	
Notes		277
Choice Expressions and Idioms		316
Sentences for Correction		353
Sanskrit-English Glossary		358
English-Sanskrit Glossary		388
Index		401

LIST OF CONVENTIONAL ABBREVIATIONS USED IN THE BOOK.

N. B.—Where a Roman figure is followed by an Arabic figure the former signifies the canto or chapter (in the case of Mb., Râm. the Parva or Kâ*n*da), and the latter the number of the verse; a single Arabic figure in the case of dramas signifies the number of the act.

A. R. stands for Anarghyarâghava.

Bg.	„	Bhagavadgîtâ (Bombay Edition).
Bh.	„	Bhartrihari II denoting Nîtis'ataka and III Vairâgya-s'ataka (Bombay Edition).
Bk.	„	Bhattikâvya.
C.	„	Châṇakyas'ataka.
Dk.	„	Das'akumâracharita, I denoting the first part, and II the second and the Arabic figure the number of the story (Bom. Edition).
G. M.	„	Ganaratnamahodadhi.
H.	„	Hitopades'a, the Arabic figures denoting the four parts in their order (Bombay. Edition).
H. C.	„	Harshacharita.
K.	„	Bâṇâ's Kâdambari (Bombay Edition), Arabic figure signifying the number of the page.
Kâv.	„	Kâvyaprakâs'a.
Ki.	„	Kirâtârjuniyam.
Ku.	„	Kumârasambhava (Calcutta Edition)
M.	„	Mâlavikâgnimitra (Bombay Edition).
Mâl.	„	Mâlatimâdhava (Bombay Edition).
Mb.	„	Mahâbhârata.
Mbh.	„	Mahâbhâshya.

Me. stands for Meghadûta.
Mk. „ Mrichchakatika.
Mu. „ Mudrárákshasa.
Mv. „ Mahávîracharita.
Na. „ Naishadha.
Nág. „ Nágánanda.
P. „ Panchatantra, the Roman figure denoting the number of the Tantra, and Arabic figure the number of the story (Bombay Edition).
P. R. „ Prasannarághava.
R. „ Raghuvans'a (Bombay Edition).
Rám. „ Rámáyana.
Ratn. „ Ratnávali (Calcutta Edition).
S'. „ S'akuntalá (Bombay Edition).
S'. B. „ S'ánkarabháshya.
S'i. „ S'is'upálavadha.
S. K. „ Siddhánta Kaumudi.
S. M. „ S'ankarácharya's Mohamudgara.
Su. „ Subhashitaratnákara.
U. „ Uttararámacharita (Calcutta Edition).
V. „ Vikramorvas'îyam (Bombay Edition).
Vár. „ Vártika of Kátyáyana.
Vás. „ Vásavadatta.
V. B. „ Viddhas'álabhanjika.
Ve. „ Venisamhára (Calcutta Edition).
Y. „ Yájnavalkya, where II denotes the *Vyavahàra* chapter.

THE

STUDET'S GUIDE

TO

SANSKRIT COMPOSITION.

PART I.

INTRODUCTORY.

'SYNTAX' in English deals with the mode of arranging words in sentences, and lays down rules for the proper and correct arrangement of words. In Sanskrit and other languages that are rich in inflexions *Syntax* has not this definite scope. The grammatical inflexion itself shows the relation of one word to another, and no harm or inaccuracy occurs, if the student do not observe the usual order of words in a sentence. Take, for example, the English sentence, "Ràma saw Govinda." If the order of the words 'Ràma' and 'Govinda' be changed, there will be a very great difference in the meaning; it will, in fact, be a different sentence altogether. Take, however, the Sanskrit sentence for the same: रामो गोविन्दमपश्यत्. Here, even if the order of the words be changed, no difference occurs in the meaning; the sentences रामो गोविन्दमपश्यत्, गोविन्दं रामोऽपश्यत्, अपश्यद्रामो गोविन्दं &c., all mean the same thing. The *order* or *arrangement* of words in Sanskrit sentences is not, therefore, a point of great importance except in some cases, but this does not mean that perfect arbitrariness is allowed, and there are certain cases in which it is necessary to arrange words in a particular manner. In Sanskrit Grammars, rules on *Concord* and *Order* are rarely given. The "Kàraka Prakarana" in the *Siddhanta Kaumudî* is popularly, though not correctly, taken to represent Syntax in Sanskrit, but it represents only one of the parts of Syntax properly so called, *i. e., Government*. The use and meaning of particles and grammatical forms has also to be taken into account in the joining together of words into sentences. This portion of Grammar is usually considered in English Grammars under *Etymology*; while in Sanskrit Grammars, in explaining the formation of words in *Accidence*, the use of the words themselves is given; as in the Sútra लटः शतृशानचावप्रथमासमानाधिकरणे (Pàṇini III. 2. 124) which states how to form present participles as well as when to use them. In treating of 'Syntax' in Sanskrit, one has thus to look mainly to *Concord* and *Government* and the *Use and Meaning of Grammatical Forms and Words*, and the Lessons in this work are accordingly arranged.

As already remarked, the *order* of words is not so important a point in Sanskrit as in English; but there are a few cases in which it has to be carefully attended to. Some hints on this subject will be found in Part IV.

§ **2**. There are in Sanskrit, as in English and other languages, three persons and three genders. The use of *persons* is not practically different from what it is in English. As regards *genders* of nouns in Sanskrit, no definite rules can be laid down to distinguish one from another. The assignment of genders is purely arbitrary, except in those cases where the male and female sexes are indicated, and where the distinction is natural; as, चटकः 'a male sparrow,' चटका 'a female sparrow;' हंसः, हंसी; अजः, अजा &c. The arbitrariness of genders may well be seen from the fact that there are, in Sanskrit, three words of three different genders for one and the same thing; 'wife' is represented by दार (*masc.*), भार्या (*fem.*), and कलत्र (*neut.*); 'body' by कायः; तनुः, and शरीरं &c. Genders must, for the most part, be studied from the dictionary.

There are three *numbers*, instead of two, as in English or Latin, some peculiarities in the use of which are noted below.

§ **3**. The three numbers in Sanskrit are the singular, dual, and plural. The singular number denotes 'one' or a single individual, but often represents, as in English, the whole class; as नरः 'a man'; सिंहः सर्वश्वापदेषु बलिष्ठः 'the lion is the strongest of all beasts.'

Note.—To represent a class the singular or plural may be used: 'Bràhmaṇas must be respected' may be expressed by ब्राह्मणः पूज्यः, or ब्राह्मणाः पूज्याः.

§ **4**. The dual denotes 'two'; अश्विनौ 'the two Aśvins'; दंपती 'a pair' (husband and wife). But words meaning a 'couple' or 'pair', such as द्वय, द्वितय, युगल, युग, द्वंद्व, &c. are always singular, except when several pairs are indicated; as बाहुद्वयं 'a pair of arms'; सुकुमारचरणयुगलं 'a pair of delicate feet.'

(*a*) The dual form sometimes denotes a 'male' and a 'female' belonging to the same class, the form being an instance of the एकशेषद्वन्द्व compound; as जगतः पितरौ वन्दे पार्वतीपरमेश्वरौ (R. I. 1) 'I salute the parents of the universe, Pàrvatî and Parameśvara (S'iva)'.

§ **5**. Some words having a dual sense, that occur in the plural form in English ought, in Sanskrit, to be translated by the dual alone; as, 'he washed his hands and feet' हस्तौ पादौ चाक्षालयत्; 'she shut her eyes' सा लोचने न्यमीलयत्.

§ **6**. The plural denotes 'more than two', and may, like the singular, represent the whole class; शकुंताः 'birds,' or a 'class of birds'. But there are some words in Sanskrit which, though used in the plural are singular in sense; as, दाराः 'wife'; similarly अप्, वर्षा, सिकता, अक्षता, असु, प्राण &c.

(*a*) Sometimes the plural is used to show respect, or to speak of a person with reverence; as, इति श्रीशंकराचार्याः 'so says the revered Śankara.'

(*b*) In the first person the plural sometimes stands for the singular, if the speaker is a high personage; as, वयमपि भवत्यौ सखीगतं किमपि पृच्छामः (S. 1) 'we, too (*i. e.* I) ask your ladyships something regarding your friend'; वयमपि स्वकर्मण्यभियुज्यामहे (Mu. 3.) 'we, too, shall apply ourselves to our work'. But this condition is not absolutely necessary; *e. g.* किंत्वरण्यसदो वयमनभ्यस्तरथचर्याः (U. 5).

§ **7**. Names of countries are always in Sanskrit used in the plural because they are taken from the people themselves; as, अहं गतः कदाचित् कलिंगान् (D. K. II. 7) 'I once went to *Kalinga*' (the country of the Kalingas).

N. B.—When the words देश, विषय &c. are used with the names of countries, the singular must be used; as, मगधदेशे पाटलिपुत्रं नाम नगरं 'there is a town called Pataliputra in the country of the Magadhas'.

§ **8**. The plural of proper nouns not unfrequently denotes the family or race, as in English; as, रघूणामन्वयं वक्ष्ये (R, I. 9) 'I will describe the family (genealogy) of the race of Raghu; जनकानां रघूणांच संबन्धः कस्य न प्रियः (U. 1) 'to whom is a connection between the families of Raghu and Janaka not dear ?'

LESSON I.

§ **9**. "When two connected words are of the same gender, number, person or tense, they are said to agree with one another, or to be in **Concord**. Speaking of a man, we have to say *he*, of a woman *she*, of plurality of persons *they;* these are agreements or concords." —*Bain.*

The Concords that deserve notice in Sanskrit are three : (**1**) *Concord of Subject and Verb,* (2) *Concord of Substantive and Adjective* and (3) *Concord of Relative and its Antecedent.*

Concord of Subject and Verb.

§ **10**. That about which something is said or asserted is called the *subject* of a sentence, and is put in the nominative case. A verb, as in English, agrees with its subject in *number* and in *person;* as आसीद्राजा शूद्रको नाम (K. 5) 'there was a king named Śúdraka;' साधयामो वयं (S. I) 'we go (take our way)'.

§ **11.** The *predicate*, or that which is said about the subject, may be a finite verb, as in the above instances, or a substantive or adjective with अस् 'to be' expressed or understood. In such cases the substantive should be used in its natural gender, being made to agree with the subject only in *case*; as, सा कुलपतेरुच्छ्वसितमिव (S'. 3), 'she is, as it were, the life of the Kulapati;' ककुदं वेदविदां (Mk. 1) 'who is the hump (chief) of those who know of the Vedas.'

Obs.—The concord of the adjective is given in Lesson II.

(*a*) The verb, when used in such cases, always agrees with the subject; as तस्मात्सखा त्वमसि (U. 5) 'thou art, therefore, a friend.'

(*b*) When words like पात्र, आस्पद, स्थान, पद, प्रमाण, भाजन, are used as predicates, they are always in the singular number and neuter gender, though the subject be of any number or gender, and the verb agrees with the subject, and not with the predicative noun, whatever be its position; as, गुणाः पूजास्थानं गुणिषु (U. 4) 'with the meritorious, merits are the object of worship;' आर्यमिश्राः प्रमाणं (M. 1) 'your honour is an authority' (your opinion is accepted); संपदः पदमापदां (H. 1.) 'wealth is the abode of miseries;' त्वमसि महसां भाजनं (Mal. 1.) 'thou art the receptacle of light;' विविधमहमभूवं पात्रमालोकितानां (Mal. 1) 'in various ways did I become the object of (her) looks.'

Here it would be wrong to say 'गुणाः पूजास्थानमस्ति, अहं पात्रमभूव' though the words स्थानं and पात्रं be placed anywhere in the sentence.

§ **12.** The noun or adjective used to complete the sense of the so-called verbs of incomplete predication, such as, 'be,' 'become,' 'grow,' 'seem,' 'appear,' is put in the nominative case; as, यदि सर्ग एष ते (R. III. 51) 'if this *be* thy resolution;' प्रभुर्बुभूषुर्भुवनत्रयस्य (S'i. I. 49) 'wishing to *become* the lord of the three worlds;' so मदनक्लिष्टेयमालक्ष्यते (S'. 3.).

(*a*) The same rule holds good in the passive construction of the transitive verbs of incomplete predication, such as, 'call,' 'name,' 'make,' 'consider,' 'think,' 'choose,' 'appoint' &c.; as कुक्कुरो व्याघ्रः कृतः (H. 4) 'the dog was *made* a tiger;' नायं मूर्खो मन्तव्यः 'he should not be *considered* a fool' &c.

§ **13**. When the subject consists of two or more nouns connected by '*and*' the verb agrees with their *combined* number; as तयोर्जगृहतुः पादान्राजा राज्ञी च मागधी (R. I. 57) 'the king and the queen Mâgadhî seized their feet.'

(*a*) When the nouns are not taken together, but each is considered separately, or when they together form but one idea, the verb may be singular; as, न मां त्रातुं तातः प्रभवति न चांबा न भवति (Mal. 2) 'my father cannot save me, neither can my mother, nor yourself;' पटुत्वं सत्यवादित्वं कथायोगेन बुध्यते (H. 1.) 'skill and truth-speaking *is* known in conversation.'

(*b*) Sometimes the verb agrees with the nearest subject, and is left to be understood with the rest; as, अहश्च रात्रिश्च उभे च संध्ये धर्मोपि जानाति नरस्य वृत्तम् (P. I. 4) 'day and night, both the twilights, and Dharma also *knows* the action of man.'

So in Latin: (*a*) 'Tempus necessitaque *postulat*,' 'time and necessity demand;' (*b*) Filia et unus e filiis *captus est*,' 'a daughter, and one of the sons was taken prisoner.'

§ **14**. Singular subjects connected by 'or' will take a singular verb; as, रामो गोविन्दः कृष्णो वा गच्छतु 'let Râma, Govinda *or* Krishna go;' so शिशुत्वं स्त्रैणं वा भवतु ननु वन्द्यासि जगतः (U. 4).

(*a*) When the subjects are of different numbers, the verb will agree with the nearest subject; as ते वाऽयं वा पारितोषिकं गृह्णातु 'let them or this (person) take the reward.'

§ **15**. When two or more nominatives of different persons are connected by '*and*' the verb agrees with their combined *number;* and in *person*, agrees with the *first* person in preference to the *second* or *third*, and with the *second* in preference to the *third;* as, त्वं चाहं च पचावः (Mbh.) 'thou and I cook;' similarly ते किंकरा अहं च श्वो ग्रामं प्रतिष्ठेमहि 'those servants and myself shall start for the village to-morrow;' त्वं

चैव सोमदात्तश्च कर्णश्चैव...तिष्ठत (Mbh. VII. 87. 12) 'thou Somadatti, and Karṇa remain.'

So in Latin: 'Si tu et Tullia lux nostra *valetis*, ego et suavissimus Cicero *valemus*,' 'if thou and my darling Tullia are well, so am I and my sweetest Cicero.'

§ **16**. When two or more nominatives of different persons are connected by '*or*,' the verb agrees with the one *nearest* to it in *number* and *person*; as, 'he or you have done the work' **स वा यूयं वैतत्कर्माकुरुत;** 'either they or we can do this difficult work' **ते वा वयं वेदं दुष्करं कार्यं संपादयितुं शक्नुमः.**

§ **17**. When wo or more subjects are in apposition to some pronoun or noun, the predicate agrees with the latter; as **माता मित्रं पिता चेति स्वभावात्त्रितयं हितम्** (H. I.) 'the mother, the friend, and father, (these) three are naturally friendly.'

उर्वशी सुकुमारं प्रहरणं महेन्द्रस्य । प्रत्यादेशो रूपगर्वितायाः श्रियः । अलंकारः स्वर्गस्य । (V. 1.)

सर्वत्रौदरिकस्याभ्यवहार्यमेव विषयः । (V. 3)

हा कथं महाराजदशरथस्य धर्मधाराः प्रियसखी मे कौशल्या । क एतत्प्रत्येति सैवेयमिति । (U. 4)

सार्थवाहस्यार्थपतेर्विमर्दको बहिश्चराः प्राणाः । (D. K. II. 2)

ममापि दुर्योधनस्य शंकास्थानं पांडवाः । (Ve. 2.)

त्वं चाहं च वृत्रहन्नुभौ संप्रयुज्यावहै (Mbh.)

प्रवृद्धं यद्वैरं मम खलु शिशोरेव कुरुभि-

र्न तत्रार्यो हेतुर्न भवति किरीटी न च युवाम् । (Ve. 1)

त्वं जीवितं त्वमसि मे हृदयं द्वितीयं

त्वं कौमुदी नयनयोरमृतं त्वमङ्गे । (U. 3)

बलवानपि निस्तेजाः कस्य नाभिभवास्पदम् ।
निःशंकं दीयते लोकैः पश्य भस्मचये पदम् ॥ (H. 2)

तीर्थोदकं च वह्निश्च नान्यतः शुद्धिमर्हतः । (U. 1.)

इक्ष्वाकुवंश्यः ककुदं नृपाणां ककुत्स्थ इत्याहितलक्षणोऽभूत् । (R. VI. 71.)

ADDITIONAL SENTENCES FOR EXERCISE.

अस्ति तावदेकदा प्रसंगतः कथित एव मया माधवाभिधानः कुमारो यस्त्वमिव मामकीनस्य मनसो द्वितीयं निबन्धनम् । (Māl. 3.)

एकस्मिञ्जीर्णकोटरे जायया निवसतः पश्चिमे वयसि वर्तमानस्य कथमपि पितुरहमेवैको विधिवशात्सूनुरभवम् । (K. 25.)

देव काचिच्चंडालकन्यका शुकमादाय देवं विज्ञापयति । सकलभुवनतलसर्वरत्नानामुदधिरिवैकभाजनं देवः । विहंगमश्चायमाश्चर्यभूतो निखिलभुवनतलरत्नमिति कृत्वा देवपादमूलमागताहमिच्छामि देवदर्शनसुखमनुभवितुमिति । (K. 8.)

आयुः कर्म च वित्तं च विद्या निधनमेव च ।
पञ्चैतान्यपि सृज्यन्ते गर्भस्थस्यैव देहिनः ॥ (H. 1.)

रहस्यभेदो याञ्चा च नैष्ठुर्यं चलचित्तता ।
क्रोधो निःसत्यता द्यूतमेतन्मित्रस्य दूषणम् ॥ (H. 1.)

अदेयमासीत्त्रयमेव भूपतेः शशिप्रभं छत्रमुभे च चामरे (R. III. 16.)
निसर्गभिन्नास्पदमेकसंस्थमस्मिन्द्वयं श्रीश्च सरस्वती च (R. VI. 29.)

व्यतिकरितदिगन्ताः श्वेतमानैर्यशोभिः
सुकृतविलसितानां स्थानमूर्जस्वलानाम् ।
अकलितमहिमानः केतनं मंगलानां
कथमपि भुवनेऽस्मिंस्तादृशाः संभवन्ति ॥ (Māl. 2)

The king of the Vangas lost his life in battle.

When she saw that dreadful sight, her hands and feet began to tremble.

O Govinda, thou art my life, my joy, my object of pride, my all the world.

They became an object of suspicion without any fault of theirs.

Good wives are the prime cause of all religious actions.

Bhishma, Drona, Kripa, Karna, thyself, the powerful Bhoja, S'akuni, Drauni, and myself, constitute O king, your army.

When he fell down from his horse, Ràma, Gopàla and we two were present.

Why do you and Krishna not try to finish this work? Is it very difficult?

Obedience, truthfulness, want of pride, and assiduity in doing his work: these are the merits of a servant.

You, Ràma, and myself passed the time happily in the forest of Dandakà.

Riches are a source of innumerable miseries in this world.

Paras'uràma, the son of Hari, is the jewel of his class, and the ornament of his family.

Let that man or these boys take this fruit.

Hari and I, or you and Krishna, can do this work; neither Gopàla nor his younger brothers can do it.

You two, the three servants of Pushpàmitra, and two other men should go to the royal court.

LESSON II.

Concord of Substantive and Adjective.

§ **18.** In English an adjective is used with all genders, numbers and cases, in the same unaltered form; as a *good* man, *good* tables, I saw a *good* horse &c. In Sanskrit, however, all adjectives, whether participial, pronominal or qualitative, must take the same *gender*, *number*, and *case* as the noun which they qualify; as, गच्छन्ती मारी, का

तृप्ति:, तत्सुखं; शोभनानि गृहाणि '*good* houses'; शोभनेभ्यो गृहेभ्यः 'from *good* houses'; शोभनाभ्यो वापीभ्यः 'from *good* wells;' हरिं पश्यन् मुच्यते &c. The adjective in Sanskrit must, in fact, be treated like a noun capable of taking cases, genders and numbers.

Obs.—Numeral adjectives differ from ordinary adjectives. They have particular rules for their use, for which see *Grammar.*

§ **19**. When adjectives are used in Appositional or Bahuvrîhi compounds, they are used in their original unmodified form; as, कृष्णमृगः 'a black deer'; रक्तनेत्रा 'of red eyes' (fem.); रूपवद्भार्या 'a beautiful wife'; गृहीतधनुः 'a bow taken;' अन्यसंक्रांतहृदयो नरः 'a man whose heart is fixed on another (lady)' &c.

(*a*) There are a few exceptions. The sign of the feminine gender is retained, when the feminine is treated as an appellative, when an ordinal number in the feminine gender is the first member, or when the first member is regarded as a class-name; as, दत्ताभार्यः, पंचमीभार्यः, शूद्राभार्यः &c.; also सुकेशीभार्यः, स्रौघ्नीभार्यः. For further particulars, see *Sidhânta Kaumudi* on Pânini VI. 3. 34-41.

§ **20.** When participial adjectives, such as, past and potential passive, are used as predicates, and when the subject is followed by an appositional noun used predicatively, the participle agrees with the subject (see § 11); as, मालविका उपायनं प्रेषिता (M. 1) 'Mâlavikâ was sent (as) a present.'

§ **21.** When there are two or more substantives qualified by the same adjective, the latter is used in their combined *number*. As regards *gender*, when the substantives are masculine and feminine, the adjective will be *mesculine;* and when they are masculine or feminine and neuter, the adjective will be *neuter;* as, पक्षपातिनावनयोरहं देवी च (M.1) 'I and the Queen are (respectively) interested in these two'; तस्मिन्सत्यं धृतिर्ज्ञानं तपः शौचं दमः शमः। ध्रुवाणि पुरुषव्याघ्रे लोकपालसमे नृपे॥ (Mbh. III. 58. 10) 'truth, courage, knowledge, religious austerities, purity, self-control, and tranquillity, are firm in that king, pre-eminent among men and resembling the guardians of the worlds.'

Obs.—This rule is based on the principle involved in Pàṇini 1. 2, 72—त्यदादीनि सर्वैर्नित्यम्; on which a Vàrtika says: त्यदादितः शेषे पुंनपुंसकतो लिंगवचनानि; सा च देवदत्तश्च तौ; तच्च देवदत्तश्च यज्ञदत्ता च तानि; तच्च देवदत्तश्च ते.

So in Latin: 'Pater mihi et mater *mortui sunt*,' 'my father and mother are dead.'

§ **22.** But an adjective in Sanskrit often agrees with the substantive nearest to it; as, यस्य वीर्येण कृतिनो वयं च भुवनानि च (U. 1) 'by whose valour we are rendered happy, as also the three worlds' (भुवनानि कृतीनि); कामश्च जृंभितगुणो नवयौवनं च (Màl. 1) 'Love has displayed its power, as also the blooming youth.' Here we must follow what is called the लिंगविपरिणाम process; that is, the gender must be understood again to suit the next substantive.

Concord of Relative and its Antecedent.

§ **23**. The concord of the relative pronoun and its antecedent has no special peculiarities in Sanskrit. The relative pronoun agrees with its antecedent in *gender*, *number*, and *person*, the *case* of the relative being determined by its relation to its own clause. Like other pronouns in Sanskrit, it may stand by itself, or may be used adjectively. The relative pronoun generally precedes the noun to which it relates in the relative clause; or the relative may stand alone, the antecedent noun being used with the demonstrative pronoun; while sometimes the antecedent noun is not expressed at all; अंतर्यो मृग्यते स स्थाणुर्वो निःश्रेयसायास्तु (V. 1) 'may that Sthàṇu, who is inwardly sought, contribute to your supreme happiness;' बुद्धिर्यस्य बलं तस्य (P. I. 9) 'he who has intellect has strength'. (knowledge is power); धिगस्मान् सर्वान्ये एकाकिना बटुना सह युध्यामहे 'fie upon us all, who are fighting with a single-handed boy.'

§ **24**. When the relative has for its predicate a substantive differing in gender from the antecedent, the relative generally agrees with the predicate; as, शैत्यं हि यत् सा प्रकृतिर्जलस्य (R. V. 54) 'for what is coolness is the natural property of water;' so मातुस्तु यौतकं यत् स्यात् कुमारीभाग एव सः (Manu. IX. 131).

Obs.—It will be seen from these examples that the correlative pronoun agrees in gender with the noun it qualifies. But Pánini in I. 4. 32 says **कर्मणा यमभिप्रैति स** (not **तत्**) **संप्रदानम्.**

§ **25.** When the relative stands for a whole sentence, such as is represented by '*that*' in English, it is always used in the neuter gender singular (**यत्**); as **ननु वज्रिण एव वीर्यमेतद्विजयन्ते द्विषतो यदस्य पक्ष्याः ।** (V. 1) 'is it not indeed Indra's valour *that* his allies subdue their enemies?'; **मम तु यदियं याता लोके विलोचनचन्द्रिका। नयनविषयं जन्मन्येकः स एव महोत्सवः ।** (Mal. 1) 'But *that* she, the moon-light of my eyes, came within the range of my sight, is the only great festival (joyous occasion) in my whole existence'.

In such cases in the principal sentence, the gender of the demonstrative is the same as that of the antecedent noun (**महोत्सवः**) and not neuter because **यत्** is neuter.

तयैव देवतया तयोः कुशलवाविति नामनी प्रभावश्चाख्यातः (U. 2)

यदेते चंद्रसरोरक्षकास्त्वया निःसारितास्तदनुचितं कृतम् । (H. 3)

यस्मिन्नेवाधिकं चक्षुरारोपयति पार्थिवः ।
अकुलीनः कुलीनो वा स श्रियो भाजनं नरः ॥ (P. I. 8)

कृताः शरव्यं हरिणा तवासुराः
शरासनं तेषु विकृष्यतामिदम् । (S'. 6))

स सुहृद् व्यसने यः स्यात् स पुत्रो यस्तु भक्तिमान् ।
स भृत्यो यो विधेयज्ञः सा भार्या यत्र निर्वृतिः ॥ (P. I. 15.)

पांडवाश्च महात्मानो द्रौपदी च यशस्विनी ।
कृतोपवासाः कौरव्य प्रययुः प्राङ्मुखास्ततः (Mb. XVII. 1. 29.)

धर्मः कामश्च दर्पश्च हर्षः क्रोधः सुखं वयः ।
अर्थादेतानि सर्वाणि प्रवर्तन्ते न संशयः ॥ (Ram. VI. 62. 37)
उमावृषाङ्कौ शरजन्मना यथा यथा जयन्तेन शचीपुरन्दरौ ।
तथा नृपः सा च सुतेन मागधी ननन्दतुस्तत्सदृशेन तत्समौ ॥ (R. III. 23.)

ADDITIONAL SENTENCES FOR EXERCISE.

धन्या सा यार्यपुत्रेण बहु मन्यते या चार्यपुत्रं विनोदयन्त्याशानिबन्धनं जाता जीवलोकस्य। (U. 3.)

सोय पुत्रस्तव मदमुचां वारणानां विजेता
यत्कल्याणं वयसि तरुणे भाजनं तस्य जातः। (U. 3)
न प्रमाणीकृतः पाणिर्बाल्ये बालेन पीडितः।
नाहं न जनको नाग्निर्नानुवृत्तिर्न सन्ततिः॥ (U. 7)
यं ब्राह्मणमियं देवी वाग्वश्येवानुवर्तते।
उत्तरं रामचरितं तत्प्रणीतं प्रयुज्यते॥ (U. 1)
चतुर्दश सहस्राणि रक्षसां भीमकर्मणाम्।
त्रयश्च दूषणखरत्रिमूर्द्धानो रणे हताः॥ (U. 2)
रोगी चिरप्रवासी परान्नभोजी परावसथशायी।
यज्जीवति तन्मरणं यन्मरणं सोस्य विश्रामः॥ (H. 1)
मित्रं प्रीतिरसायनं नयनयोरानन्दनं चेतसः
पात्रं यत्सुखदुःखयोः सह भवेन्मित्रेण तद्दुर्लभम्।
ये चान्ये सुहृदः समृद्धिसमये द्रव्याभिलाषाकुला-
स्ते सर्वत्र मिलन्ति तत्त्वनिकषग्रावा तु तेषां विपत्॥ (H. 1)
यस्यार्थास्तस्य मित्राणि यस्यार्थास्तस्य बान्धवाः
यस्यार्थाः स पुमाँल्लोके यस्यार्थाः स हि पण्डितः॥ (H. 1)
हिंसाशून्यमयत्नलभ्यमशनं धात्रा मरुत्कल्पितं
व्यालानां पशवस्तृणाङ्कुरभुजः सृष्टाः स्थलीशायिनः।
संसारार्णवलंघनक्षमधियां वृत्तिः कृता सा नृणां
यामन्वेषयतां प्रयान्ति सततं सर्वे समाप्तिं गुणाः॥ (Bh. III. 10)
महिमानं यदुत्कीर्त्य तव संन्हियते वचः।
श्रमेण तदशक्त्या वा न गुणानामियत्तया॥ (R. X. 32)

यस्मिन् सत्यं च मेधा च नीतिश्च भरतर्षभे ।
अप्रमेयाणि दुर्धर्षे कथं स निहतो युधि ॥ (Mb. VI. 6. 26).

There are many good people in this city, but they are despised by some peevish, wicked, and narrow-minded men.

The king of Pàtaliputra and his queen are both very generous.

I saw yesterday, three beautiful lakes, six deep wells, and fifty-six extensive gardens.

He who speaks a lie in order to hide his fault, commits two faults.

That you should say so is certainly astonishing.

That a man should be always virtuous is the opinion of all philosophers, ancient and modern.

These sweet mangoes are sent (*use a participial adjective*) as a present by my younger brother.

That wicked people should hate the virtuous is but their inborn disposition.

Those persons who are ready-witted, can surmount difficulties.

On account of this incident I became (*adj.* from **जन्**) the object of their envy.

Patience, industry, and honesty are always commendable; but rashness, idleness and faithlessness are censurable.

PART II.

GOVERNMENT.

LESSON III.

The Accusative Case.

§ **26**. We now come to *Government*, the second general principle regulating the grammatical union of words in sentences. '*Government*' is the *power* which a word has to regulate the case of a noun or pronoun. The Lessons in this Part are intended to explain and illustrate this power.

§ **27**. 'Káraka' is the name given to the relation subsisting between a noun and a verb in a sentence. Thus any relation subsisting between words not connected with the verb will not be called a Káraka. There are six Kárakas in Sanskrit: कर्ता, कर्म, करण, संप्रदान, अपादान and अधिकरण. These relations belong to the first seven cases except the Genitive, which is not regarded as a Káraka case. कर्ता is principally the sense of the Instrumental, and means 'agent'. The nominative in Sanskrit, as in other languages, is simply the *naming* case, that which is concerned in अभिधान 'predication'. According to Pàṇini II. 3. 46 (प्रातिपदिकार्थलिंगपरिमाणवचनमात्रे प्रथमा) the nominative is used to denote the crude form or base of a word, gender, measure, and number only; as, नीचैः, कृष्णः, श्रीः, ज्ञानं, तटः-टी-टं, द्रोणो व्रीहिः, एकः, द्वौ, बहवः &c.

Note.—Several indeclinable words govern nouns in one or another of the Káraka cases, and such cases, are then called 'उपपदविभक्ति' i. e. cases governed by indeclinables &c., as distinguished from कारकविभक्ति; cases governed by verbs; as, नमो नृसिंहाय, मामन्तरा, ग्रामादुत्तरं &c. The latter predominate over the former, where both are possible (उपपदविभक्तेः कारकविभक्तिर्बलीयसी).

§ **28**. The person or thing, upon whom or which the *effect* of an action takes place, is called the *object* of that action. An object is put in the Accusative case, except in the *passive* voice; as, स हरिमपश्यत् 'he saw Hari;' ओदनं बुभुक्षुर्विषं भुंक्ते (S. K.) 'wishing to eat food he eats poison.' Here हरि and विष are objects of the verbs अपश्यत् and भुंक्ते. But in हरिः सेव्यते the *passive* form सेव्यते expresses the relation of object and verb which exists between हरि and सेव् and therefore हरि is not required to be in the Accusative case; but in हरिं सेवते there being no passive termination, the noun हरि is put in the Accusative case.

§ **29**. Verbs signifying '*to name*,' '*to choose*,' '*to make*,' '*to appoint*,' '*to call*,' '*to know*,' '*to consider*,' &c. and the like, govern a *factitive* or *indirect* object; besides a direct; object as, त्वामामनन्ति प्रकृतिं (Ku. II. 13) 'they consider thee to be Prakriti;' कामपि गणिकामवरोधमकरोत् (D. K. II. 6.) 'made a certain courtezan his wife;' जानामि त्वां प्रकृतिपुरुषं (Me. 6) 'I know thee (to be) the chief person (minister).

§ **30**. All verbs that show *motion* govern the Accusative case; as गतोहं कामदेवायतनं (Màl. 1) 'I had gone to the temple of Cupid.' अहमपि महीमटन् (D. K. II. 2) 'I also roaming over the earth;' यमुनाकच्छमवतीर्णः (P. I. 1) 'went down to the bank of the Jumna;' so विचचार दावं (R. II. 8). But this idea of *motion* is expressed in a variety of idiomatic expressions, where the motion is not *actual* but merely *conceived*; as, परं विषादमगच्छत् (P. I. 1) 'was greatly dejected;' अश्वत्थामा किं न यातः स्मृतिं ते (Ve. 3) 'was not As'vathàman thought of by you'; पश्चादुमाख्यां सुमुखी जगाम (Ku. I. 26) 'the fair-faced lady afterwards went by (acquired) the name Umá'; so नरपतिहितकर्ता द्वेष्यतां याति लोके (P. I. 2); न तृप्तिमाययौ (R. III. 3.)

(*a*) Generally intransitive roots, preceded by prepositions become transitive in sense, and then govern; this case; as, वृत् 'to be'; अनुवृत् 'to act according to,' 'to follow'; as, प्रभुचित्तमेव हि जनोऽनुवर्तते (S'i. XV. 41) 'the people, indeed, follow the will of their lord'; अचलतुंगशिखरमारुरोह (K. 120) 'ascended the lofty summit of the mountain';

similarly यन्ता गजस्याभ्यपतद्गजस्थं (R. VII. 37); नोत्पतति वा दिवं (K. 132) ऋषीणां पुनराद्यानां वाचमर्थोऽनुधावति (U. I.).

§ **31**. *The roots शी 'to lie down,' स्था 'to stand,' and आस् 'to sit,' when preceded by अधि govern the Accusative of the *place* where these actions are performed; as, चन्द्रापीडो मुक्ताशिलापट्टमधिशिश्ये (K. 206) 'Chandràpída lay down on a slab of pearl-stone'; अर्धासनं गोत्रभिदोऽधितष्ठौ (R. VI. 73) 'stood on (occupied) half the seat of Indra'; अध्यास्य पर्णशालां (R. I. 95) 'lying in a hut (made) of leaves.'

(*a*) † विश् with अभिनि governs the same case; as, अभिनिविशते सन्मार्गम् (S. K.) 'he resorts to a good path;' so भयं तावत्सेव्यादभिनिविशते सेवकजनं (Mu. 5).

§ **32**. ‡ The root वस् 'to dwell,' when preceded by the prepositions उप, अनु, अधि or आ, governs the Accusative case of that which forms the place of residence; as उप-अनु-आ-अधि-वसति वैकुंण्ठ हरिः (S. K.) 'Hari dwells in Vaikuntha (the heavens)'.

§ **33**. $ The words उभयतः, सर्वतः, धिक्, and the double forms उपर्युपरि, अधोधः, अध्यधि, when they have the sense of 'nearness' and प्रति '*to*,' govern the Accusative case; as, उभयतः कृष्णं गोपाः (S. K.) 'cowherds are on both sides of Krishna;' सर्वतः कृष्णं (*ibid*) 'on all sides of Krishna;' उपर्युपरि लोकं हरिः (*ibid*) 'Hari is just over the world;' अधोऽधो लोकं (*ibid*) 'just below the world;' धिग्जाल्मान् (U. 5.) 'fie upon the rogues;' न मे संशीतिरस्या दिव्यतां प्रति (K. 132.) 'I have no doubt as to her being heavenly;' so बुभुक्षितं न प्रति भाति किंचित् (Mbh.). When nearness is not indicated the Genitive may be used; as, उपर्युपरि सर्वेषामादित्य इव तेजसा (Mb.) 'higher and higher than all by means of his lustre, like the sun.'

---

* अधिशीङ्स्थासां कर्म (I. 4. 46).

† अभिनिविशश्च । (I. 4. 47).

‡ उपान्वध्याङ्वसः (4. 48).

$ उभसर्वतसोः कार्या धिगुपर्यादिषु त्रिषु ।
द्वितीयाम्रेडितान्तेषु ततोन्यत्रापि दृश्यते ॥ (Vár.)

(*a*) धिक् may sometimes be used with nominative or vocative; as, धिङ् मूढ 'fie upon thee, fool;' धिगियं दरिद्रता (P. II.) 'cursed be this poverty.'

§ **34.** *The words अभितः, परितः (both meaning '*round*'), समया, निकषा (both meaning '*near*') and हा '*woe be to*', govern the Accusative case; as परिजनो राजानमभितः स्थितः (M. 1) 'the attendants stood round the king;' रक्षांसि वेदीं परितो निरास्थत् (Bk. I. 12) 'destroyed the demons (seated) round the altar;' ग्रामं समया निकषा (S. K.) 'near the village;' so निकषा सौधभित्ति (D. K.) (पयोधिं) विलंघ्य लंकां निकषा हनिष्यति (S'i. I. 68); हा कृष्णाभक्तं (*ibid.*) 'woe be to a non-worshipper of Krishna.' हा is sometimes used with the Vocative; as, हा भगवत्यरुन्धति (U. 1) 'alas ! oh revered Arundhati.'

§ **35.** † The word अंतरेण meaning '*without*,' '*excepting*,' and '*with reference to, regarding*,' governs the same case; as, कोन्यस्त्वामंतरेण शक्तः प्रतिकर्तुं (Ve. 3) 'who else but thee is able to retaliate?' भवन्तमंतरेण कीदृशाऽस्या दृष्टिरागः (S'. 2) 'how is her eye-love regarding you?'

(*a*) So also अंतरा, meaning 'between;' अंतरा त्वां च मां च कमण्डलुः (Mbh.); पंचालास्तव पश्चिमेन त इमे वामा गिरां भाजनास्त्वद्दक्षिणतिर्पीभवन्तु यमुनां त्रिस्रोतसं चांतरा (B. R. 70.)

§ **36.** Words denoting *duration of time* and *space* are put in the Accusative case; as, न ववर्ष वर्षाणि द्वादश दशशताक्षः (D. K. II. 6) 'the thousand-eyed (Indra) did not rain for 12 years;' क्रोशं कुटिला नदी (S. K.) 'the river runs winding for 2 miles;' सभा वैश्रवणी राजन् शतयोजनमायता (Mb. II. 10. 1.) 'O king, the hall of Vis'ravana is 100 yojanas in length.'

§ **37.** The preposition अनु is sometimes found to be used by itself with nouns in the Accusative case, in the sense of '*after, in consequence of*,' or '*being indicated by*,' '*resembling*' or '*imitating*;' as जपमनु

---

* अभितःपरितःसमयानिकषाहाप्रतियोगेपि । (Vàr.)

† अन्तरान्तरेण युक्ते । (II. 3. 4.)

प्रावर्षत् (S. K.) 'it rained *after* the muttering of prayers;' **सर्वं मामनु ते** (V. 4) 'everything of thee is *after* mine (resembles mine).'

Obs. Pânini mentions **अभि** in the sense of 'before,' 'hard by,' 'in,' **उप** 'near,' 'inferior to,' **अति** 'superior to,' and **अनु** 'by the side of,' 'along,' 'inferior,' under the category of prepositions, which can be used by themselves and which govern the Accusative case (See Pân. I. 4. 84-5-6-7, 90-1-5); as, **हरिमभिवर्तते, भक्तो हरिमभि, उप हरिं सुराः, अति देवान् कृष्णः, नदीमन्ववसिता सेना, अनु हरिं सुराः**, &c. (S. K.). Prepositions, used by themselves and governing a noun in some case, are called *Karmapravachaniya* (**कर्मप्रवचनीय**).

धारिणीभूतधारिण्योर्भव भर्ता शरच्छतम् (M. 1.)

बिंदूत्क्षेपान् पिपासुः परिपतति शिखी भ्रान्तिमद्वारियन्त्रम् । (M. 2.)

मन्दौत्सुक्योऽस्मि नगरगमनं प्रति । (S'. 1.)

एषा मे मनोरथप्रियतमा सुकुसुमास्तरणं शिलापट्टमधिशयाना सखीभ्यामन्वास्यते । (S'. 3.)

सागरं वर्जयित्वा कुत्र वा महानद्यवतरति । क इदानीं सहकारमन्तरेणातिमुक्तलतां पल्लवितां सहते । (S'. 3.)

स राजर्षिरिमानि दिवसानि प्रजागरकृशो लक्ष्यते । (S'. 3.)

धिङ् मामुपस्थितश्रेयोऽवमानिनम् । (S'. 6.)

धिगिमां देहभृतामसारताम् । (R. VIII. 51.)

इष्टान्देशान्विचर जलद प्रावृषा संभृतश्रीः (Me. 118.)

कृतकार्यमिदं दुर्गं वनं व्यालनिषेवितम् ।'

यदध्यास्ते महाराजो रामः शस्त्रभृतां वरः । (Râm. II. 98. 13.)

धिक् प्रहसनम् । अयमृष्यशृंगाश्रमादरुन्धतीपुरस्कृतान् महाराजदशरथस्य दारानधिष्ठाय भगवान् वसिष्ठः प्राप्तः । तत्किमेवं प्रलपामि । (U. 4.)

तत्र च निखिलधरणितलपर्यटनखिन्नस्य निजबलस्य विश्रामहेतोः कतिपयान् दिवसानतिष्ठत्। (K. 119.)

अस्यां वेलायां किं नु खलु मामन्तरेण चिन्तयति वैशंपायन इति चिन्तयन्नेव स निद्रां ययौ। (K. 178.)

अमी वेदिं परितः क्लृप्तधिष्ण्याः समिन्द्धतः प्रान्तसंस्तीर्णदर्भाः।
अपघ्नन्तो दुरितं हव्यगन्धैर्वैतानास्त्वां वह्नयः पावयन्तु ॥ (S'. 4.)

शक्रस्य दिव्या सभा।
विस्तीर्णा योजनशतं शतमध्यर्द्धमायता।
वैहायसी कामगमा पंचयोजनमुच्छ्रिता ॥ (Mb. II. 7. 3.)

रम्यां रघुप्रतिनिधिः स नवोपकार्यां
बाल्यात्परामिव दशां मदनोऽध्युवास। (R. V. 63.)

तस्य पुत्रो महातेजाः संप्रत्येम पुरीमिमाम्।
आवसत्परमप्रख्यः सुमतिर्नाम दुर्जयः ॥ (Ràm. II. 47. 7.)

क्रमेण सुप्तामनु संविवेश सुप्तोत्थितां प्रातरनूदतिष्ठत्। (R. II. 24.)

ADDITIONAL SENTENCES FOR EXERCISE.

सकृत्कृतप्रणयोऽयं जनः। तदस्या देवीं वसुमतीमन्तरेण महदुपालम्भं गतोस्मि (S'. 5.)

कथय कथमियन्तं कालमवस्थिता मया विना भवती। (V. 4)

भाव प्रेषिता हि स्वगृहान्महाराजेन लंकासमरसुहृदो महात्मानः प्लवंगराक्षसा नानादिगंतागता ब्रह्मर्षयो राजर्षयश्च येषामाराधनायेयतो दिवसानुत्सव आसीत् (U. 1.)

विवक्षता दोषमपि च्युतात्मना
त्वयैकमीशं प्रति साधु भाषितम् (Ku. V. 81.)

धिग्विधातारमसदृशसंयोगकारिणम्। (K. 12.)

आर्य आर्य प्रणिपत्य देवश्चन्द्रगुप्तो विज्ञापयति क्रियान्तरान्तरायमन्तरेणार्यं द्रष्टुमिच्छामीति । (Mu. 3.)

मन्दोऽप्यमन्दतामेति संसर्गेण विपश्चितः ।
पङ्कच्छिदः फलस्येव निकषेणाविलं पयः ॥ (M. 2.)

भर्तुमित्रं प्रियमविधवे विद्धि मामम्बुवाहम् (Me. 102.)

अथाधिशिश्ये प्रयतः प्रदोषे रथं रघुः कल्पितशस्त्रगर्भम् (R. V. 28.)

मनुष्यवाह्यं चतुरस्रयानमध्यास्य कन्या परिवारशोभि ।
विवेश मंचांतरराजमार्गं पतिंवरा क्लृप्तविवाहवेषा ॥ (R. VI. 10.)

अभिन्यविक्षथास्त्वं मे यथैवाव्याहता मनः
तवाप्यध्यावसन्तं मां मा रौत्सीर्हृदयं तथा ॥ (Bk. VIII. 80.)

अर्थानामर्जने दुःखमर्जितानां च रक्षणे
आये दुःखं व्यये दुःखं धिगर्थाः कष्टसंश्रयाः ॥ (P. I. 4.)

हा हा धिक् परगृहवासदूषणं यद्वैदेह्याः प्रशमितमद्भुतैरुपायैः
एतत्तत्पुनरपि दैवदुर्विपाकादालर्कं विषमिव सर्वतः प्रसृप्तम् ॥ (U. 1.)

यत्र द्रुमा अपि मृगा अपि बान्धवो मे
यानि प्रियासहचरश्चिरमध्यवत्सिम् ।
एतानि तानि बहुनिर्झरकंदराणि
गोदावरीपरिसरस्य गिरेस्तटानि । (U. 3.)

को वीरस्य मनस्विनः स्वविषयः को वा विदेशस्तथा
यं देशं श्रयते तमेव कुरुते बाहुप्रतापार्जितम् ।
यद् दंष्ट्रानखलांगुलप्रहरणः सिंहो वनं गाहते
तस्मिन्नेव हतद्विपेन्द्ररुधिरैस्तृष्णां छिनत्त्यात्मनः ॥ (H. 1.)

धिक् सानुजं कुरुपतिं धिगजातशत्रुं
धिग्भूपतीन्विफलशस्त्रभृतो धिगस्मान् ॥
केशग्रहः खलु तदा द्रुपदात्मजाया
द्रोणस्य चाद्य लिखितैरिव वीक्षितो यैः ॥ (Ve. 3.)

जलानि सा तीरनिखातयूपा वहत्ययोध्यामनु राजधानीम् । (R. XIII. 61.)

प्रमदामनु संस्थितः शुचा नृपतिः सन्निति वाच्यदर्शनात् ।
न चकार शरीरमग्निसात्सह देव्या न तु जीविताशया ॥ (R. VIII. 72.)

A wife should always follow the will of her husband.

Here is another person coming to wait upon us with regard to another business.

Then she was made acquainted with (*use* अंतरेण) your immodesty by the girl when greatly importuned.

There is a beautiful garden round the city of Pushpapura.

Oh (हा) my misfortune! My only son also is reported to be dead!

He studied Nyàya for three years and seventy-five days, and has now become proficient in it.

For two miles from Avanti are to be seen beautiful gardens on all sides.

Has she not yet recovered her senses? I believe it is impossidle without the application of a better remedy.

What will the people of Ma*n*ipura think of (अंतरेण) my past adventures in that city?

It appears to (प्रति) us proper that we should now return to the subject of our discussion.

Fie upon those who wish to afflict others without any advantage to themselves!

Woe be to those who follow immoral paths!

Ràma dwelt on (वस् with अधि) the mountain Chitrakûta for several days.

The servant informed the Queen that His Majesty was sitting (आस् with अधि) on the pleasure-mountain, and that he had called her there without delay.

When she was herself again, she burnt the body of her dead brother, and then slept (शी with अधि) on a mat for the whole night.

That cow now resides (स्था with अधि) in the lower regions, the doors of which are closed by large serpents.

The vernal season does not appear splendid without the presence of mango-sprouts.

I do not remember what you said to me after (अनु) the departure of that young sage.

What do you say "There is no Kshatriya but our Emperor ?" Fie upon you, rogues ! Here I take away your banner; save it if you can.

LESSON IV.

Verbs governing two Accusatives.

§ **38**. There are some verbs in Sanskrit which take what is called an *akathita* object, in addition to their usual direct one. As its name indicates, it is that object which is not otherwise '*kathita*' or mentioned by way of any of the other case relations, such as **अपादान**, **अधिकरण** &c. and is, therefore, *optional.* If the noun capable of taking this *akathita* object be not intended for any other case, it is put in the Accusative case with such verbs; as, **धेनुं दोग्धि पयः** 'he milks the cow (her milk);' **व्रजमवरुणद्धि गां** 'he confines the cow to the fold.' Here **धेनुं** and **व्रजं** are *akathita* or optional objects. If the speaker do not intend to have this object, the words will be put in their natural cases; as, **धेन्वाः** (ablative) **पयो दोग्धि, व्रजे** (locative) **अवरुणद्धि गां.**

§ **39**. The roots that are capable of governing two accusatives are mentioned in the following *Kárikâ*:—

दुह्याच्पच्दण्ड्रुधिप्रच्छिचिब्रूशासुजिमन्थ्मुषाम् ।
कर्मयुक् स्यादकथितं तथा स्यान्नीहृकृष्वहाम् ॥

In the case of the roots **दुह्** 'to milk,' **याच्** 'to beg,' **पच्** 'to cook,' **दण्ड्** 'to punish,' **रुध्** 'to obstruct,' or 'to confirm,' **प्रच्छ्** 'to ask,' **चि** 'to collect,' **ब्रू** 'to tell,' **शास्** 'to instruct,' **जि** 'to win' (as a prize of wager), **मन्थ्** 'to churn,' **मुष्** 'to steal,' and also in the case of **नी, हृ, कृष्** and **वह्**, all meaning 'to take' or 'carry,' and others having the same signification, the noun which, besides the direct object, is affected by the verb, is put in the Accusative case; as, **गां दोग्धि पयः** (S. K.) 'he milks the cow;' **बलिं याचते वसुधां** (*ibid*) 'he begs the Earth of Bali'; similarly **तण्डुलानोदनं पचति, गर्गाञ्छतं दण्डयति, व्रजमवरुणद्धि गां, माणवकं पंथानं पृच्छति, वृक्षमवचिनोति फलानि, माणवकं धर्मं ब्रूते-शास्ति, शतं जयति देवदत्तं, सुधां क्षीरनिधिं मथ्नाति, देवदत्तं शतं**

मुष्णाति; ग्राममजां नयति-हरति-कर्षति-वहति-वा, are examples of the other roots in order. माणवकं धर्मं भाषते वक्ति वा, बलिं वसुधां भिक्षते, तां त्वां संवरणस्यार्थे वरयामि विभावसो (Mb. I. 171, 21) are instances of this kind of object, because भाष् or वच् and भिक्ष् or वृ have the same meaning as ब्रू and याच् the roots given in the Káriká.

Obs. The poots चि, मुष्, पच्, मन्थ्, रुध्, जि, कृष्, हृ and even वह् are of very rare occurrence, as governing two accusatives, in classical literature, though given in the above list.

§ **40.** The roots mentioned above and others having the same sense, thus take two objects. One of them is *principal* and the other, *secondary*. In the case of the first twelve roots from दुह् to मुष्, the nouns पयः, वसुधां, फलानि, सुधां, &c. are *principal* objects, and गां, बलिं, वृक्षं, क्षीरनिधिं, &c. are *secondary* objects; for they can, according to the speaker's volition, be put in other cases. And in the case of the last four roots, अजा is the *principal* object and ग्रामं, the *secondary*. Thus that which is necessarily put in the Accusative case in order to complete the idea of the verb, is the *principal* object, and, that which may be put in the Accusative case, depending upon the speaker's will, is called the *secondary* object.

§ **41.** *In the passive construction of roots governing two accusatives the *secondary* object in the case of the first twelve roots, and the *principal* object in the case of the last four, is put in the nominative case, the other object remaining the same as in the active construction: *e. g.*

Active construction.	Passive construction.
(स) धेनुं पयो दोग्धि।	(तेन) धेनुः (nom.) पयो (acc.) दुह्यते।
देवाः समुद्रं सुधां ममंथुः।	देवैः समुद्रः (nom.) सुधां (acc.) ममंथे।
सोऽजां ग्रामं नयति हरति कर्षति वहति वा।	तेनाजा (nom.) ग्रामं (acc.) नीयते ह्रियते कृष्यते उह्यते वा।

* गौणे कर्मणि दुह्यादेः प्रधाने नीहृकृष्वहाम्। लादयो मताः (S. K.)

आज्ञप्तास्मि देव्या धारिण्या अचिरप्रवृत्तोपदेशं चलितं नाम नाटयमंतरेण कीदृशी मालविकेति नाटयाचार्यमार्यगणदासं प्रष्टुम्। (M. 1.)

ह्यस्तत्रभवतीरावती देवीं सुखं प्रष्टुमागता। (M. 4.)

महाश्वेता कादंबरीमनामयं पप्रच्छ। (K. 192.)

हिमालयं सर्वशैला वत्सं परिकल्प्य
भास्वन्ति रत्नानि महौषधीश्च
पृथूपदिष्टां दुदुहुर्धरित्रीम् (Ku. I. 2.)

संकल्पितार्थे विवृतात्मशक्ति-
माखण्डलः काममिदं बभाषे। (Ku. III. 11.)

सोहं तृष्णातुरैर्वृष्टिं विद्युत्वानिव चातकैः।
अरिविप्रकृतैर्देवैः प्रसूतिं प्रतियाचितः। (Ku. VI. 27.)

किमत्र चित्रं यदि कामसूर्भूर्वृत्ते स्थितस्याधिपतेः प्रजानाम्।
अचिन्तनीयस्तु तव प्रभावो मनीषितं द्यौरपि येन दुग्धा॥ (R. V. 33.)

तमरण्यसमाश्रयोन्मुखं शिरसा वेष्टनशोभिना सुतः।
पितरं प्रणिपत्य पादयोरपरित्यागमयाचतात्मनः॥ (R. VIII. 12.)

अथ ज्येष्ठां गुराः सर्वे देवकार्यचिकीर्षया।
शैलेन्द्रं वरयामासुर्गङ्गां त्रिपथगां नदीम्। (Rám. I. 35. 16.)

ADDITIONAL SENTENCES FOR EXERCISE.

तमातिथ्यक्रियाशान्तरथक्षोभपरिश्रमम्।
पप्रच्छ कुशलं राज्ये राज्याश्रममुनिं मुनिः॥ (R. I. 58.)

तं क्रमेण जन्मभूमिं जातिं विद्यां कलत्रमपत्यानि विभवं वयःप्रमाणं प्रव्रज्याकारणं च स्वयमेव पप्रच्छ चन्द्रापीडः। (K. 228.)

कौशिकेन स किलक्षितीश्वरो राममध्वरविघातशांतये।
काकपक्षधरमेत्य याचितस्तेजसां हि न वयः समीक्ष्यते ॥ (R. XI. 1.)

तं तथा कृपयाविष्टमश्रुपूर्णाकुलेक्षणम् ।
विषीदन्तमिदं वाक्यमुवाच मधुसूदनः ॥ (Bg. II. 1)

भर्तुस्तथा कलुषितां बहुवल्लभस्य
मार्गे कथंचिदवतार्य तनूभवन्तीम् ।
सर्वात्मना रतिकथाचतुरेव दूती
गङ्गां शरन्नयति सिन्धुपतिं प्रसन्नाम् (Mu. 3.)

तामायुष्मन्मम च वचनादात्मनश्चोपकर्तुं
ब्रूया एवं तव सहचरो रामगिर्याश्रमस्थः।
अव्यापन्नः कुशलमबले पृच्छति त्वां वियुक्तः
पूर्वाभाष्यं सुलभविपदां प्राणिनामेतदेव ॥ (Me. 104.)

सोपृच्छल्लक्ष्मणं सीतां याचमानः शिवं सुरान् ।
रामं यथास्थित सर्वं भ्राता ब्रूते स्म विह्वलः ॥
संदृश्य शरणं शून्यं भिक्षमाणो वनं प्रियाम् ।
प्राणान्दुहन्निवात्मानं शोकं चित्तमवारुधत् ॥
गता स्यादवचिन्वाना कुसुमान्याश्रमद्रुमान् ।
आ यत्र तापसान् धर्मं सुतीक्ष्णः शास्ति तत्र सा ॥ (Bk. VI. 8-10.)

I asked him ten questions, but he did not answer any one of them.

The mendicant begged fifty rupees of a rich man, who was reported to be very liberal.

The king punished (दण्ड्) the culprit with a fine of three hundred and sixty rupees.

The preceptor instructs (शास्) these pupils in the principles of Nyáya and Vyákarana.

The king was begged (*pass.* of याच्) by the minister to pardon (क्षमा) the fault of his servant.

He tells (ब्रू) me that Gopála has milked his cows.

Sir, you were asked by me your name and family, and not how much wealth you have.

Fourteen jewels were churned out of the milk-ocean.

The shepherd took all the sheep to the market and sold them.

Yesterday the cows were milked by my youngest daughter.

The Gods went to Bramhan and asked (वृ) him for a deliverer from Tàraka.

LESSON V.

The Causal.

§ **42**. "The causal of a root conveys the notion that a person or thing causes or makes another person or thing to perform the action or to undergo the state denoted by the root" (Dr. Kielborn's Grammar § 416); *e. g.* **गम्** 'to go'; **गच्छति** 'he goes'; **गमयति** 'he causes to go'; **अश्** 'to eat'; **अश्नाति** 'he eats'; **आशयति** 'he causes to eat'.

§ **43**. That which is the *subject* of a verb in its primitive sense is put in the Instrumental case in the causal, the *object* remaining unchanged; *e. g.*

Primitive.	Causal.
देवदत्त ओदनं पचति Devadatta cooks food.	(स) देवदत्तेनौदनं पाचयति (He) causes Devadatta to cook food.
रामो भार्यां त्यजति Ràma abandons (his) wife.	(स) रामेण भार्यां त्याजयति (He) makes Ràma adandon (his) wife.

§ **44**. *In the case of roots that imply 'motion,' 'knowledge' or 'information,' or some kind of 'eating,' and other roots having a similar sense; also of roots that have some literary work for their object, and of intransitive roots, that which is the *subject* of the verb

---

* गतिबुद्धिप्रत्यवसानार्थशब्दकर्माकर्मकाणामणि कर्ता स णौ। (I. 4. 52)

in its primitive sense is put in the Accusative case in the causal, the *object* remaining unchanged; *e. g.*

Primitive.	Causal
शत्रवः स्वर्गमगच्छन्	शत्रून् स्वर्गमगमयत्
स्वे वेदार्थमविदुः	स्वान् वेदार्थमवेदयत्
देवा अमृतमाश्नन्	देवानमृतमाशयत्
विधिर्वेदमध्यैत	विधिं वेदमध्यापयत्
पृथ्वी सलिले आस्त	पृथ्वीं सलिले आसयत्*

But in **गमयति रामो गोविन्दं** (Ráma makes Govind go) if somebody else (**विष्णुमित्र**) prompts (Ràma) to do this, we shall have to say **विष्णुमित्रो रामेण गोविन्दं गमयति** 'Vishnumitra prompts Ràma to cause Govinda to go.' Here 'Ràma,' is not put in the Accusative case, because it is the subject of the verb, not in its *primitive*, but *causal*, sense.

Note.—Patañjali, in his Mahàbhàshya, adds this explanation on the meaning of the word **शब्दकर्म** in the Sútra **गतिबुद्धि** &c. **शब्दकर्म** may mean either **शब्दो येषां क्रिया** or **शब्दो येषां कर्म**. When we take the former interpretation, the roots **ह्वयति (ह्वे)**, **क्रन्दति (क्रन्द्)**, and **शब्दायते** denom. of (**शब्द**) have to be excluded from the rule; as, **ह्वयति देवदत्तः; ह्वाययति देवदत्तेन; क्रन्दति–शब्दायते–देवदत्तः; क्रन्दयति–शब्दाययति–देवदत्तेन**. And the roots **श्रु**, **ज्ञा** with **वि**, and **लभ्** with **उप**, must be included in the rule; as **शृणोति–विजानाति–उपलभते–देवदत्तः, श्रावयति-विज्ञापयति-उपलम्भयति-देवदत्तम्**. When we adopt the second interpretation, the roots **जल्प्**, **भाष्** with **आ**, and **लप्** with **वि**, must be included in the rule; **जल्पति–विलपति–आभाषते–देवदत्तः, जल्पयति–विलापयति–आभाषयति–देवदत्तं.**

§ **45**. There are several exceptions and counter-exceptions to the preceding rule, which are important:—

---

*These examples are put together in the following verse:—
शत्रूनगमयत्स्वर्गं वेदार्थं स्वामवेदयत्। आशयच्चामृतं देवान्वेदमध्यापयद्विधिम्। आसयत्सलिले पृथ्वीं यः स मे श्रीहरिर्गतिः ॥

(*a*) * The causals of नी 'to lead,' and वह् 'to carry,' do not govern the Accusative, but the Instrumental; *e. g.*

भृत्यो भारं नयति वहति वा	भृत्येन भारं नाययति वाहयति वा (S. K.)
A servant carries a load.	(He) causes a servant to carry a load.

But वह्, when it has for its subject in the causal a word signifying a 'driver,' obeys the general rule; as,

वाहा रथं वहन्ति Horses draw the chariot.	सूतो वाहान् रथं वाहयति (S. K.) The charioteer makes the horses draw the chariot.
वहन्ति यवान् बलीवर्दाः	वाहयति यवान् बलीवर्दान् (Mbh.)

(*b*) † The causals of the roots अद् and खाद्, 'to eat,' govern the instrumental case; *e. g.*

बटुरन्नमत्ति खादति वा The boy eats his food.	बटुनान्नमादयति खादयति वा (He) causes the boy to eat his food.

(*c*) ‡ भक्ष्, when it has not the sense of हिंसा 'injury to a sentient thing,' governs the Instrumental; as, भक्षयति पिंडीं देवदत्तः, भक्षयति पिंडीं देवदत्तेन; but भक्षयन्ति यवान् बलीवर्दाः, भक्षयति बलीवर्दान् यवान् (Mbh.)

(*d*) The roots स्मृ and घ्रा, which denote particular kinds of Knowledge' or 'perception,' are not used with the Accusative; as, स्मरति-जिघ्रति-देवदत्तः, स्मारयति-घ्रापयति-देवदत्तेन.

Sometimes, however, the Accusative also is used in the case of the root स्मृ, especially when it means 'to think of or remember with regret;' as, अपि चन्द्रगुप्तदोषा अतिक्रान्तपार्थिवगुणान् स्मारयन्ति प्रकृतीः (Mu. 1) see S'i. VI. 56 also.

---

* नीवह्योर्न (Vàr.) नियन्तृकर्तृकस्य वहेरनिषेधः । (Vàr.)

† आदिखाद्योर्न (Vàr.)

‡ भक्षेरहिंसार्थस्य न । (Vàr.)

(*e*) दृश् is construed with the Accusative in the causal; as भक्ता हरिं पश्यन्ति, दर्शयति भक्तान् हरिं (S. K.).

Obs. दृश् in classical literature is sometimes found used with the Dative, instead of the Accusative; as, प्रत्यभिज्ञानरत्नं च रामायादर्शयत् कृती। (R. XII. 64).

(*f*) † The subject of the verb in the primitive sense in the case of हृ and कृ, and of अभिवद् and दृश् when used in the Atmanepada, is either put in the Accusative or Instrumental case in the causal; *e. g.*

भृत्यः कटं करोति हरति वा	भृत्यं भृत्येन वा कटं कारयति हारयति वा (S.K.)
The servant makes or takes a mat.	(He) causes the servant to make or take a mat.

So अभिवादतये-दर्शयते-देवं-भक्तं भक्तेन वा (S. K.) (He) makes the devotee bow down to, or see, the God.

§ **46.** By 'intransitive' roots mentioned in § 44 is meant such roots as are not, by their nature, capable of governing an object other than that of 'time,' 'place' &c., and not those roots which, though transitive may sometimes be used intransitively according to the speaker's volition, or when their meaning is quite evident; as किंकरः पचति. Here पचति, though transitive, is used without an object, because it can be easily understood; hence किंकरेण पाचयति and not किंकरं; but मासमासयति देवदत्तं.

§ **47.** ‡ In forming the passive construction of causal verbs, the *principal* object in the causal, which is the *subject* (agent) of the verb in its primitive sense, is put in the Nominative case, and the other *object* remains unchanged; *e. g.*

---

* दृशेश्च । (Vàr.)

† हृक्रोरन्यतरस्याम् । (I. 4. 53.)

‡ बुद्धि भक्षार्थयोः शब्दकर्मणां च निजेच्छया ।
प्रयोज्यकर्मण्यन्येषां ण्यन्तानां लादयो मताः ॥ (S. K.)

Primitive.	Causal Active.	Causal Passive.
रामो ग्रामं गच्छति Ràma goes to a village.	रामं ग्रामं गमयति (He) causes Ràma to go to a village.	रामो ग्रामं गम्यते Ràma is caused to go &c.
भृत्यः कटं करोति The servant prepares a mat.	भृत्येन भृत्यं वा कटं कारयति (He) causes the servant to perpare a mat.	भृत्यः कटं कार्यते The servant is måde to prepare &c.
गोविन्दो मासमास्ते Govind sits for one month.	गोविन्दं मासमासयति (He) makes Govind sit &c.	गोविन्दो मासमास्यते Govind is made to sit &c.

(*a*) But in the case of roots that imply 'knowledge', 'eating', and those that have a literary work for their object the principal object is put in the Nominative case, and the secondary in the Accusative, or *vice versa*; *e. g.*

माणवकं धर्मं बोधयति 'he makes Manavaka know his duty;' माणवको धर्मं बोध्यते or माणवकं धर्मो बोध्यते 'M. is made to know duty,' or 'duty is made known to M.'; बटुमोदनं भोजयति 'he make the boy eat food;' बटुरोदनं भोज्यते or बटुमोदनो भोज्यते (S. K.)

§ **48**. The causal forms of roots of the tenth conjugation are the same as the primitive forms, and the meaning must be decided by the context; as, रामो धनं चोरयति 'Râma steals wealth;' रामो गोविन्देन धनं चोरयति 'Ràma causes Govinda to steal wealth.' In the latter sentence the verb has a causal sense.

§ **49**. With regard to roots that govern two accusatives, the rules mentioned in §43 and §44 hold good in their case also; *i. e.* those roots that imply motion &c., govern the Accusative of the subject of the primitive base, and others, the Instrumental case, subject to § 45; as, वामनो बलिं वसुधां याचते; (ईश्वरो) वामनेन बलिं वसुधां याचयति '(God) makes Vàmana ask Bali for Earth;' गोपोऽजां नगरं हरति; (स्वामी) गोपं गोपेन वाजां नगरं हारयति '(The master) makes the cowherd take the sheep to the town.'

अभिमन्युतनयं परीक्षितमुदरादुपरतमेव निर्गतमुत्तराप्रलापोपजनितकृपो भगवान् वासुदेवो दुर्लभानसून् प्रापितवान्। (K. 175.)

अयं शिशुर्न शक्नोति शिरोधरां धारयितुम्। तदेहि गृहाणेममवतारय सलिलसमीपमित्यभिधाय तेनर्षिकुमारेण मां सरस्तीरमनाययत्। उपसृत्य च जलसमीपं स्वयं मामादाय मुक्तप्रयत्नमुत्तानितमुखमङ्गुल्या कतिचित्सलिल-बिन्दूनपाययत्। (K. 38.)

काम इदानीं सकामो भवतु येनासत्यसंधे जने सखी पदं कारिता।
(S'. 4.)

महेन्द्रभवनं गच्छतोपाध्यायेन त्वमासनं प्रतिग्राहितः। (V. 3.)

तौ कुशलवौ भगवता वाल्मीकिना धात्रीकर्मवस्तुतः परिगृह्य पोषितौ परिरक्षितौ च। वृत्तचूडौ च त्रयीवर्जमितरा विद्याः सावधानेन परिपाठितौ। समनन्तरं च गर्भादेकादशे वर्षे क्षात्रेण कल्पेनोपनीय गुरुणा त्रयीविद्यामध्या-पितौ (U. 2.)

नलिनिके पायय कमलमधुरसं कलहंसान्। पल्लविके भोजय मरिचाग्रपल्ल-वदलानि भवनहारीतान्। (K. 178.)

आर्यो दापयतु मे वैशंपायनानयनाय गमनाभ्यनुज्ञां तातेन। नान्यथा मे दोषशुद्धिर्भवति। (K. 180.)

तौ दंपती स्वां प्रति राजधानीं
प्रस्थापयामास वशी वसिष्ठः। (R. II. 70.)

ततो द्रोणोऽर्जुनं भूयो रणशिक्षामशिक्षयत् (Mb. I. 130. 25.)

तौ दंपती बहु विलप्य शिशोः प्रहर्त्रा
शल्यं निखातमुदहारयतामुरस्तः। (R. IX. 78.)

वाल्मीकिस्तौ कुशलवौ
साङ्गं च वेदमध्याप्य किंचिदुत्क्रान्तशैशवौ ।
स्वकृतिं गापयामास कविप्रथमपद्धतिम् (R. XV. 33.)
स सेतुं बन्धयामास प्लवगैर्लवणांभसि ।
तेनोत्तीर्य पथा लंकां रोधयामास पिंगलैः ।
द्वितीयं हेमप्राकारं कुर्वद्भिरिव वानरैः ॥ (R. XII. 70-1.)

ADDITIONAL SENTENCES FOR EXERCISE.

एवं क्रियते युष्मद् देशः । किंतु या यस्य युज्यते भूमिका तां तथैव भावेन सर्वे वर्ग्याः पाठिताः । (Mal. 1.)

स कार्तान्तिकस्तां विलोक्य स्निग्धदृष्टिराचष्ट । भद्रे अस्ति कौशलं शालिप्रस्थेनानेन संपन्नमाहारमस्मानभ्यवहारयितुमिति । (D. K. II. 6.)

ततो मया पाटलिपुत्रं गत्वा श्रावितोऽमात्यसन्देशं वैतालिकः स्तनकलशः । (Mu. 4)

रजनीतिमिरावगुण्ठिते पुरमार्गे घनशब्दविक्लवाः ।
वसतिं प्रिय कामिनां प्रियास्त्वदृते प्रापयितुं क ईश्वरः (Ku. IV. 11.)
तामर्चिताभ्यः कुलदेवताभ्यः कुलप्रतिष्ठां प्रणमय्य माता ।
अकारयत् कारयितव्यदक्षा क्रमेण पादग्रहणं सतीनाम् ॥ (Ku. VII. 27.)
प्रियागुणैः सहस्राणामेकोन्मीलनपेशलैः ।
य एव दुःस्मरः कालस्तमेव स्मारिता वयम् ॥ (U. 6.)
शरैरुत्सवसंकेतान् स कृत्वा विरतोत्सवान् ।
जयोदाहरणं बाह्वोर्गापयामास किन्नरान् ॥ (R. IV. 78.)
अथानाथाः प्रकृतयो मातृबंधुनिवासिनम् ।
मौलैरानाययामासुर्भरतं स्तम्भिताश्रुभिः ॥ (R. XII. 12.)
त्वं रक्षसा भीरु यतोपनीता तं मार्गमेताः कृपया लता मे ।
अदर्शयन् वक्तुमशक्नुवत्यः शाखाभिरावर्जितपल्लवाभिः ॥ (R. XIII. 24.)
गुणानुरक्तामनुरक्तसाधनः
कुलाभिमानी कुलजां नराधिपः ।

परैस्त्वदन्यः क इवापहारये-
न्मनोरमामात्मवधूमिव श्रियम् ॥ (Ki. I. 31.)

यः पयो दोग्धि पाषाणं स रामाद्भूतिमाप्नुयात् ।
रावणं गमय प्रीतिं बोधयन्तं हिताहितम् ॥
प्रीतोऽहं भोजयिष्यामि भवतीं भुवनत्रयम् ।
किं विलापयसेऽत्यर्थं पार्श्वे शायय रावणम् ॥
आज्ञां कारय रक्षोभिर्मा प्रियाण्युपहारय ।
कः शक्रेण कृतं नेच्छेदधिमूर्धानमञ्जलिम् ॥ (Bk. VIII. 82-4.)

विद्यामथैनं विजयां जयां च रक्षोगणं क्षिप्नुमविक्षतात्मा ।
अध्यापयद्गाधिसुतो यथावद्विघातयिष्यन्युधि यातुधानान् ॥ (Bk. II. 21.)

We made him know (विद्) his duty, and sent (*caus.* of स्था with प्र) him home.

When the desire of independence enters the heart of a minister, he will make the king himself lose (त्यज्) his life.

Having vanquished his foe in the battle, he made his bards sing (गै) the glory of his warlike deeds.

He caused his servants to bring (नी or हृ) fuel from the market.

It is no wonder that the tributary princes are made by the Emperor to obey his commands.

These persons were told to get garlands prepared by those maid-servants.

When a student is made to know the theory of a subject, he is taught the practice of it.

Overcome your enemies and make them pay (दा) you tributes.

He caused a large *mandap* to be erected (कृ) by his servants for the marriage of his son.

He made the boy eat (अद् or खाद्) food against his will.

I showed (*caus.* of दृश्) my library to my distinguished guest.

He makes Ràma ask the pilgrims the way to Benares.

The sheep were caused by the master to be taken (वह्) to the village by his servant.

A lord should be made by a servant to give him rewards, by adapting himself to his will.

I caused them to stand round the king, and made them salute (*caus.* of वद् with अभि) him.

LESSON VI.

The Instrumental Case.

§ 50. *The Instrumental case in Sanskrit has two principal senses: it either denotes the *agent* of an action, or the *instrument* or *means* by which the action is done; as, ततो देव्या किमभिहितम् (Ve. 1) 'then what was said by the Queen ?'; संचूर्णयामि गदया न सुयोधनोरू (Ve. 1) 'shall I not reduce to powder the thighs of Suyodhana with my club ?' तामेव दिव्ययोषितं चक्षुषा पुनर्निरूपयामास (K. 131) 'again looked at that very celestial woman with his eye.'

§ 51. The instrumentality, which this case denotes, may be expressed by various relations:—

(*a*) The *manner* of doing an action, or an attribute which characterizes a noun; as, आत्मानुरूपां विधिनोपयेमे (Ku. I. 18) 'he married (her) worthy of himself according to the rite'; प्रकृत्या दर्शनीयः (Mbh.) 'lovely by nature'; माठरोस्मि गोत्रेण (*ibid.*) 'I am Màthara by my family name'; विषमेण धावति (*ibid.*) 'walks unevenly'; similarly द्विद्रोणेन धान्यं क्रीणाति, साहस्रेण पशून् क्रीणाति, शतेन शतेन पाययति वत्सान्, &c.

(*b*) The price at which a thing is bougtht; as, कियता मूल्येन क्रीतं पुस्तकं 'at what price was the book bought ?'

(*c*) With verbs indicating *motion*, the conveyance becomes the instrument; as, आत्मनः पदं विमानेन विगाहमानः (R. XIII. 1) passing through his own abode (the sky) in a balloon.'

---

* कर्तृकरणयोस्तृतीया । (II. 3. 18.)

(*d*) With verbs of *carrying* or *placing*, that on which a thing is carried or placed is put in the Instrumental; as, स श्वानं स्कन्धेनोवाह (H. 4) 'he bore the dog on his shoulder'; भर्तुराज्ञां मूर्ध्ना आदाय (Ku. III. 22) 'placing his master's order on his head.'

(*e*) With words of 'swearing,' that, in whose name the oath is taken, becomes the instrument; as, जीवितेनैव शपामि ते (K. 233) 'I swear to thee by my very life.'

(*f*) The direction or route followed to go to a particular place also becomes the instrument; as, कतमेन दिग्भागेन गतः स जाल्मः (V. 1) 'in what direction did the rogue go?'

§ **52**. With verbs implying '*excelling*' and '*resembling*' the Instrumental is used of the qualities in which the excellence consists, or the points or particulars referred to in the resemblance; as, पूर्वान्महाभाग तयातिशेषे (R. V. 14) 'O you fortunate one, you excel your ancestors in that (devotion)'; स्वरेण रामभद्रमनुहरति (U. 4) 'resembles Ráma in his voice.'

Obs. Sometimes the Locative is used in the same sense; as, धनदेन समस्त्यागे सत्ये धर्म इवापरः (Ráma I. 19) 'equal to Kubera in (point of) charity (munificence), and like another Dharma (a second Dharma) in truthfulness.'

(*a*) Words implying 'separation from', are usually construed with the Instrumental; as, अयमेकपदे तया वियोग उपनतः (V. 4.) 'there is this separation from her suddenly fallen to my lot'; so मा भूदेवं क्षणमपि च ते विद्युता विप्रयोगः (Me. 118).

(*b*) Words expressing '*likeliness*' or *equality*' are also used with this case; as, धनदेन समस्त्यागे 'equal to Kubera in munificence'; अस्य मुखं सीताया मुखचन्द्रेण संवदति (U. 4) 'his face corresponds to (is just similar to) the moonlike face of Sítá.' *See* under Genitive also.

§ **53**. * The Instrumental is used with words expressive of *time* or *place* when the accomplishment of the desired object is meant

---

अपवर्गे तृतीया। (II. 3. 6)

to be expressed; as द्वादशवर्षैर्व्याकरणं श्रूयते (P. I.) 'grammar is learnt in twelve years'; क्रोशेन पाठस्तेनाधीतः (S. K.) 'the lesson was learnt by him in (*i. e.* by going over) a *Koss.*'

§ **54**. * When a noun denotes the *cause* or *motive* of a thing or action, as distinguished from the *means* or *instrument*, it is put in the Instrumental case; as, गुरौ भक्त्या प्रीतास्मि ते (R. II. 63) 'I am pleased with thee for thy devotion to thy preceptor'; अतिदवीयस्तया च तस्य प्रदेशस्य न किंचिददर्शं (K. 126) 'the place being very far off, he could not see anything.

(*a*) The *object* or *purpose* also is put in the Instrumental case; as, अध्ययनेन वसति (S. K.) 'dwells with the view (for the purpose) of studying.'

Obs.—The Instrumental, which is used with verbs meaning 'to be satisfied', 'to rejoice at,' 'to be astonished at', 'to be ashamed of', is accounted for by this rule; as, कापुरुषः स्वल्पकेनापि तुष्यति (P. I. 1) 'a low person is pleased even with little'; उभयोर्न तथा लोकः प्रावीण्येन विसिष्मिये (R. XV. 68) 'the people did not so much wonder at the proficiency of both of them'; अनेन प्रागल्भ्येन लज्जे (K. 193) 'I am ashamed of this boldness.'

§ **55**. † Attributives, which show some defect of the body govern the (word expressive of the) defective limb in the Instrumental case; as, अक्ष्णा काणः (S. K.) 'blind of one eye'; so पादेन खञ्जः, कर्णेन बधिरः *&c.*

§ **56**. ‡ An attribute, which indicates the existence of a particular state or condition, is put in the Instrumental case to express this relation; as जटाभिस्तापसः (S. K.) 'he is an ascetic by (the fact of his having) matted hair.'

§ **57**. अलं and कृतं meaning '*enough*' govern this case; as अलमतिविस्तरेण (Ve. 1) 'enough of prolixity'; कृतमश्वेन (U. 4.) 'away with the horse'; तस्मात्कृतं चरणपातविडम्बनाभिः (P. IV. 1.)

---

* हेतौ । (II. 3. 23.)

† येनाङ्गविकारः । (II. 3. 20.)

‡ इत्थंभूतलक्षणे,। (II. 3 21)

(*a*) In this sense अलं is often used with a gerund; as, अलमन्यथा गृहीत्वा (M. 1) 'enough of misunderstanding (do not misunderstand).' In such cases it has a prohibitive force.

§ **58**. * Words like सह, साकं, सार्धं, समं &c. haveing the sense of 'companionship' govern the Instrumental case of that which expresses the accompaniment of the principle subject of assertion; as, त्वया सह निवत्स्यामि वनेषु (U. 2) 'I will dwell with thee in forests'; अमरोसधुः सार्धमस्मद्विधाभिः (U. 3) 'the heavenly river with persons like us'; आस्व साकं मया सौधे (Bk. VIII. 79) 'sit with me on the mansion.'

§ **59**. Words like किं, कार्यं, अर्थः, प्रयोजनं, गुणः &c. expressing *use* or *need*, and the root कृ with किं when used in this sense, govern the Intrumental of that which is used or needed and the Genitive of the user; as, देवपादानां सेवकैर्न प्रयोजनं (H. 1) 'your Majesty's feet have no need of servants'; तृणेन कार्यं भवतीश्वराणां (P. I. 1) 'of rich persons (even) some purpose is served by a blade of grass'; किं तया क्रियते धेन्वा (P. I.) 'what is to be done with that cow?'; किं तया दृष्टया (S'. 2) 'what is the good of seeing her'; अप्राज्ञेन सानुरागेण भृत्येन को गुणः (Mu. 1) 'what is the use of a devoted but foolish servant?'

Obs.—Pánini mentions दिवः कर्म च (I. 4. 43) *i. e.*, दिव् *to play* governs the acc. or instr.; as, अक्षैरक्षान्वा दीव्यति 'he plays at dice'; also संज्ञोऽन्यतरस्यां कर्मणि (II. 3. 22); पित्रा पितरं वा संजानीते 'he lives in harmony with his father.'

अलमलं बहु विकत्थ्य । राज्ञः समक्षमेवावयोरधरोत्तरव्यक्तिर्भविष्यति । (M. I.)

देवेन देव्या च परिगृहीतोऽहममुना हरदत्तेन प्रधानपुरुषसमक्षमयं न मे पादरजसा तुल्य इत्यधिक्षिप्तः । (M. I.)

---

* सहयुक्तेऽप्रधाने । (II. 3. 19.)

शापितासि मम लवंगिकावलोकितयोर्जीवितेन यदि वाचा न कथयसि । (Mal. 8.)

आगंतुकतयाऽश्रुतपूर्व आवाभ्यामेष वृत्तान्तः । (S'. 6.)

भगवति तमसे अयं (करिकलभकः) तावदीदृशः संपन्नः । तौ पुनर्न जाने कुशलवावेतावता कालेन कीदृशाविव भवतः । (U. 3.)

चन्द्रापीडस्य सहपांशुक्रीडिततया सहसंवृद्धतया च सर्वविश्रम्भस्थानं द्वितीयमिव हृदयं वैशंपायनः परं मित्रमासीत् । (K. 76.)

अलमतियन्त्रणया । कृतमतिप्रसादेन । भगवति प्रसीद विमुच्यतामयमत्यादर इति तामब्रवीत् । (K. 133.)

उषसि चोत्थाय तस्य जरद्द्रविडधार्मिकस्येच्छया निसृष्टैर्धनविसरैः पूरयित्वा मनोरथमभिमतमभिरमणीयेषु प्रदेशेषु निवसन्नल्पैरेवाहोभिरुज्जयिनीमाजगाम । (K. 229.)

अलमुपालम्भ्य । आर्य दैवेनेदमनुष्ठितं किमत्रार्यस्य । (Mu. 3.)

अयि पंचालतनये अलं विषादेन । किं बहुना । यत्करिष्ये तच्छ्रूयताम् ।

अचिरेणैव कालेन सुयोधनशोणितशोणपाणिस्तव कचान् भीम उत्तंसयिष्यति । (Ve. 1.)

स्वहृदयेनापि विदितवृत्तान्तेनामुना जिह्रेमि । (K. 233.)

प्रवातशयने निषण्णा देवी परिजनहस्तगृहीतेन चरणेन परिव्राजिकया कथाभिर्विनोद्यमाना तिष्ठति । (Mk. 4.)

मदनमपि गुणैर्विशेषयन्ती
रतिरिव मूर्तिमती विभाति सेयम् । (Mk. 4.)

शुद्धान्तदुर्लभमिदं वपुराश्रमवासिनो यदि जनस्य ।
दूरीकृताः खलु गुणैरुद्यानलता वनलताभिः। (S'I.)

शरीरसादादसमग्रभूषणा मुखेन सालक्ष्यत लोध्रपाण्डुना ।
तनुप्रकाशेन विचेयतारका प्रभातकल्पा शशिनेव शर्वरी ॥
(R. III. 2.)

यो मामजमनादिं च वेत्ति लोकमहेश्वरम् ।
असंमूढः स मर्त्येषु सर्वपापैः प्रमुच्यते ॥ (Bg. X. 5.)

किं तया क्रियते धेन्वा या न सूते न दुग्धदा ।
कोऽर्थः पुत्रेण जातेन यो न विद्वान् न भक्तिमान् ॥ (P. I.)

ADDITIONAL SENTENCES FOR EXERCISE.

अधुनाऽन्या गतिर्नास्ति । अकथ्यमाने च महाननर्थोपनिपातो जायते प्राणपरित्यागेऽपि रक्षणीयाः सुहृदसव इति कथयामि । (K. 152.)

तेषु तेषु रम्यतरेषु स्थानेषु तया सह तानि तान्यपरिसमाप्तान्यपुनरुक्तानि न केवलं चन्द्रमाः कादंबर्या सह कादंबरी महाश्वेतया सह महाश्वेता तु पुण्डरीकेण सह पुण्डरीकोऽपि चन्द्रमसा सह परस्परावियोगेन सर्व एव सर्वकालं सर्वसुखान्यनुभवन्तः परां कोटिमामन्दस्याध्यगच्छन् (K. 369.)

अवधूतप्रणिपाताः पश्चात्संतप्यमानमनसोऽपि ।
निभृतव्र्यपत्रपन्ते दयितानुनयैर्मनस्विन्यः (U. 1.)

कष्टं जनः कुलधनैरनुरञ्जनीयस्तन्नो यदुक्तमशिवं न हि तत्क्षमं ते ।
नैसर्गिकी सुरभिणः कुसुमस्य सिद्धा मूर्ध्नि स्थितिर्न चरणैरवताडनानि ॥ (U. 1.)

अथ दुर्लंघ्यशासनतया भगवतो मनोभुवो मंदजननतया च मधुमास्यातिरमणीयतया च तस्य प्रदेशस्याविनयबहुलतया चाभिनवयौवनस्य चंचलप्रकृतितया चेन्द्रियाणां दुर्निवारतया च विषयाभिलाषाणां तथा भवितव्यतया च तस्य तस्य वस्तुनः तमपि तरलतामनयदनगः । (K. 143.)

विनाप्यर्थैर्वीरः स्पृशति बहुमानोन्नतिपदं
समायुक्तोऽप्यर्थैः परिभवपदं याति कृपणः

स्वभावादुद्भूतां गुणसमुदयावाप्तिविषयां
द्युतिसैंहीं किं श्वा धृतकनकमालोऽपि लभते ॥ (H. 17.)

अलं महीपाल तव श्रमेण प्रयुक्तमप्यस्त्रमितो वृथा स्यात् ।
न पादपोन्मूलनशक्ति रंहः शिलोच्चये मूर्च्छति मारुतस्य (R. II. 34.)

कुलेन कांत्या वयसा नवेन गुणैश्च तैस्तैर्विनयप्रधानैः ।
त्वमात्मनस्तुल्यममुं वृणीष्व रत्नं समागच्छतु कांचनेन (R. VI. 79.)

लोभश्चेदगुणेन किं पिशुनता यद्यस्ति किं पातकैः
सत्यं चेत्तपसा च किं शुचि मनो यद्यस्ति तीर्थेन किम् ।
सौजन्यं यदि किं गुणैः स्वमहिमा यद्यस्ति किं मंडनैः
सद्विद्या यदि किं धनैरपयशो यद्यस्ति किं मृत्युना ॥ (Bh. II. 55.)

अयमार्यचाणक्यस्तिष्ठति—
यो नन्दमौर्यनृपयोः परिभूय लोक-
मस्तोदयौ प्रतिदिशन्नविभिन्नकालम् ।
पर्यायपातितहिमोष्णमसर्वगामि
धाम्नातिशाययति धाम सहस्रधाम्नः (Mu. 3.)

भूषणाद्युपचारेण प्रभुर्भवति न प्रभुः ।
परैरपरिभूताज्ञस्त्वमिव प्रभुरुच्यते ॥ (Mu. 3.)

आज्ञा कीर्तिः पालनं ब्राह्मणानां दानं भोगो मित्रसंरक्षणं च ।
येषामेते षड्गुणा न प्रवृत्ताः कोऽर्थस्तेषां पार्थिवोपाश्रयेण ॥ (Bh. II. 48)

न तेन सज्जं क्वचिदुद्यतं धनुः कृतं न वा कोपविजिह्ममाननम् ।
गुणानुरागेण शिरोभिरुह्यते नराधिपैर्माल्यमिवास्य शासनम् ॥(Ki. I. 21)

समुद्र इव गांभीर्ये स्थैर्ये च हिमवानिव ।
विष्णुना सदृशो वीर्ये क्षमया पृथिवीसमः । (Rám. 1. 178.)

स बाल आसीद्वपुषा चतुर्भुजो मुखेन पूर्णेन्दुनिभस्त्रिलोचनः ।
युवा कराक्रान्तमहीभृदुच्चकैरसंशयं संप्रति तेजसा रविः ॥ (S'. I. 70.)

A king should protect his subjects according to the rules laid down by Manu.

Morality says that one should save the life of his friend even at the cost of his own life.

This man is avarice incarnate; he will never be satisfied with hoarding money.

Are you not ashamed of your ignorance, and do you boast of your noble birth, not attended with knowledge?

This king excels all others in bravery, knowledge, and the desire to keep his subjects contented.

That your orders are borne by other kings on their heads is one great sign of your sovereignty.

The man took the lamb on his shoulder, and went by this road to the slaughter-house.

I swear by my tutelary deity that I have never before seen your ring.

I know my servants will come back within fifteen days: for what is the use of their staying there longer.

Even a sinner is freed from all his sins by repeating but once the syllable *Om* through ardent devotion.

What is the use of walking with this man? He is lame of his right leg and cannot walk swiftly.

Away with doubts in this respect. This matter is all but agreed to by my sister's husband.

Fie upon you, fool! What is the use of this burden of books to you if you do not read them?

Do not (अलं) censure me; this was not done by me.

Child, do not (अलं) weep; when thy mother comes here, I shall cause thee to be fed with food by her.

Śakuntalá did not notice the approach of Durvásas on account of her thinking of her lover.

O blind man, what is the use of this lamp to you?

LESSON VII.

The Dative Case.

§ **60.** The person to whom something is given is called संप्रदान. A noun denoting संप्रदान is put in the Dative case; as, किं वस्तु विद्वन् गुरवे प्रदेयं (R. V. 18) 'Oh learned Sir, what is to be given to the preceptor?' The person or thing with reference to whom or having in view which an action is done is also संप्रदान; as, युद्धाय संनह्यते (Mbh.) 'he prepares for battle'; तां नन्दनाय प्रार्थयते (Mâl.) 'he demands her for Nandana.

(*a*) * In the case of the root यज् 'to sacrifice' or 'to give as in a sacrifice,' the person to whom the sacrifice is offered is put in the Accusative, and the thing or means by which it is made is put in the Instrumental; as, पशुना रुद्रं यजते (S. K.) 'he sacrifices a bull to Rudra.'

§ **61.** † In the case of the root रुच् 'to like' and others having the same signification, the person or thing that is pleased or satisfied is put in the Dative case; as, यत्प्रभविष्णवे रोचते (S'. 2) 'what pleases your Lordship'; यज्ञदत्ताय स्वदतेऽपूपः (Kás'iká) Yajnadatta likes *Apupa*.

§ **62.** ‡ The person to whom something is due (the creditor) in the case of the root धृ (10 cl.) 'to owe' and the thing desired in the case of स्पृह्, are put in the Dative case ; as वृक्षसेचने द्वे धारयसि मे (S'. 1) 'thou owest me two sprinklings of trees'; परिक्षीणो यवानां प्रसृतये स्पृहयति (Bh. III. 45) 'an impoverished person desires a handful of barley-corn.'

Obs.—Derivatives from स्पृह् are sometimes construed with the Dative; as, भोगेभ्यः स्पृहयालवः (Bh. III. 64) 'desirous of enjoyments' ; कथमन्ये करिष्यन्ति पुत्रेभ्यः पुत्रिणः स्पृहां (Ve. 3); but generally with the Locative ; स्पृहावती वस्तुषु केषु मागधी (R. III. 5).

---

* यजेः कर्मणः करणसंज्ञा संप्रदानस्य च कर्मसंज्ञा । (Vár.)

† रुच्यर्थानां प्रीयमाणः । (I. 4. 33.)

‡ धारेरुत्तमर्णः । स्पृहेरीप्सितः (I. 4. 35-6.)

§ **63**. * The roots, क्रुध्, द्रुह्, ईर्ष्य्, असूय्, and others having the same sense, 'govern the Dative of the person against whom the feeling of anger, hatred, malice, &c., is directed, as, हरये क्रुध्यति-द्रुह्यति-ईर्ष्यति-असूयति वा (S. K.) 'he is angry with, or bears hatred towards, Hari.' But क्रुध् and द्रुह्, when preceded by prepositions, govern the Accusative; as, मच्छरीरमभिद्रोग्धुं (Mu. 1) 'to do injury to my person'; न खलु तामभिक्रुद्धो गुरुः (V. 3) 'did not the preceptor get angry with her ?'

§ **64**. † In the case of the root श्रु with प्रति or आ meaning 'to promise,' the person to whom something is promised, is put in the Dative case; as, प्रतिशुश्राव काकुत्स्थस्तेभ्यो विघ्नप्रतिक्रियां (R. XV. 4) Kákutstha promised them the removal of obstacles.'

§ **65**. ‡ The purpose for which an action is done, or that for making which another thing exists or is used (as a thing made for a certain purpose) is put in the Dative case; as काव्यं यशसे (Káv. 1) 'a poem (is composed) for fame'; यूपाय दारु (Mbh.) 'a piece of wood for (making a sacrificial) post'; कुंडलाय हिरण्यं (*ibid.*) 'gold is (used) for Kundala ornament'; अवहननाय उलूखलं (*ibid.*) 'a mortar for pounding down.'

(*a*) § When the sense of an infinitive of purpose is suppressed in a sentence, the object of this infinitive is put in the Dative case; as, फलेभ्यो याति=फलान्याहर्तुं याति 'he goes for fruits' *i. e.* 'to bring fruits'; वनाय गां मुमोच=वनं गन्तुं गां मुमोच 'he let loose the cow for (*i. e.* to go to) the forest.' Here फल and वन, the objects of the infinitives आहर्तुं and गन्तुं, are put in the Dative.

(*b*) $ The Dative of an abstract noun is often used to express the sense of the infinitive of purpose from the root; as, यागाय याति= यष्टुं याति 'he goes to offer a sacrifice'; so समिदाहरणाय प्रस्थिता वयं (S'. 1) यतिष्ये वः सखीप्रत्यानयनाय (V. 1).

---

* क्रुधद्रुहेर्ष्यासूयार्थानां यं प्रति कोपः । क्रुधद्रुहोरुपसृष्टयोः कर्म । (I. 4. 37-8.)

† प्रत्याङ्भ्यां श्रुवः पूर्वस्य कर्ता । (I. 4. 40.)

‡ तादर्थ्ये चतुर्थी वाच्या । (Vár.)

§ क्रियार्थोपपदस्य च कर्मणि स्थानिनः । (II. 3. 14.)

$ तुमर्थाच्च भाववचनात् । (II. 3. 15.)

§ **66**. *In the case of the root क्लृप् 'to be adequate to,' 'to bring about,' 'to tend to,' and roots having a similar sense, such as संपद्, भू, जन् the result brought about, or the end to which anything leads, is put in the Dative case; as, कल्पसे रक्षणाय (S'. 5) 'thou art adequate to bring about (our) protection'; मूत्राय कल्पते-जायते-संपद्यते यवागूः (Mbh.) 'grual tends to (produce) urine.' The Dative is frequently used in this sense without भू or अस्; as, यतस्तौ स्वल्पदुःखाय (P. I.) 'since they two cause very little pain.'

(*a*) † That which is foreboded by a portentous phenomenon is also put in the Dative case, as, वाताय कपिला विद्युत् (Mbh.) 'the twany lightning forebodes a hurricane;' मांसौदनाय व्याहरति मृगः (*ibid.*) 'the sound of a deer indicates (the getting of) food of flesh.'

(*b*) With the words हित and सुख the Dative is used; as, ब्राह्मणाय हितं-सुखं, (S. K.) 'good for a Bràhma*n*a'; हितमामयाविने (Mbh.) 'good for a sickly person.'

Obs.—हित in the sense of 'good in or to' is used with the Locative and Genitive also.

§ **67**. ‡ The words नमः, स्वस्ति, स्वाहा, स्वाधा, and वषट् (terms used in offering oblations to gods &c.), and अलं in the sense of '*a match for*', '*sufficient for*', govern this case; as नमो विश्वसृजे तुभ्यं (R. X. 16) 'a bow to you who created the universe'; स्वस्ति भवते (M. 2) 'good-bye to you'; अग्नये स्वाहा (S. K.) 'this offering to Agni'; similarly पितृभ्यः स्वधा, इन्द्राय वषट्; दैत्येभ्यो हरिरलं (S. K.) 'Hari is a match for the demons'; अलमेषा क्षुधितस्य (मे) तृप्त्यै (R. II. 39,) 'this (cow) is sufficient to satisfy me who am hungry.'

(*a*) Words having the sense of अलं 'sufficient for,' 'able to do', such as प्रभु शक्त and even the verb प्रभू, are used with the Dative; as, प्रभुर्मल्लो मल्लाय, शक्तो मल्लो मल्लाय, प्रभवति मल्लो मल्लाय (Mbh.) 'one wrestler

---

* क्लृपि संपद्यमाने च । (Vár.)

† उत्पातेन ज्ञापिते च । (Vár.)

‡ नमःस्वस्तिस्वाहास्वधालंवषड्योगाच्च । (II. 3. 16.)

is a matcn for another'; विधिरपि न येभ्यः प्रभवति (Bh. II. 94) 'over whom even the Creator does not prevail.'

(*b*) नमः joined to कृ generally governs the Accusative, but sometimes the Dative also; as, मुनित्रयं नमस्कृत्य (S. K.) 'saluting the three sages'; but नमस्कुर्मो नृसिंहाय (*ibid*) 'we salute Nrisimha.'

(*c*) Roots meaning 'to salute,' such as प्रणिपत्, प्रणम्, are construed with the Dative or Accusative; as, धातारं प्रणिपत्य (Ku. II. 3) 'saluting the creator'; also तस्मै प्रणिपत्य नन्दी (Ku. III. 60), आर्यं प्रणिपत्य (Mu. 1) ; so, तां भक्तिप्रवणेन चेतसा प्रणनाम (K. 228.); तां कुलदेवताभ्यः प्रणमय्य (Ku. VII. 27); प्रणम्य त्रिलोचनाय (K. 131).

Note.—Classical authors occasionally use the nouns also derived from these verbs with the Dative; as, मूर्ध्ना प्रणामं वृषभध्वजाय चकार (Ku. III. 62); अस्मै प्रणाममकरवम् (K. 142), तस्मै दण्डप्रणाममकरवम् (D. K. I. 2).

(*d*) In greeting and in expressing a blessing, the Dative is used with words like स्वागतं, कुशलं; as, देवदत्ताय कुशलं (Mbh.); स्वागतं देव्यै (M. 1) 'welcome to the Queen.' Words like कुशलं, भद्रं, सुखं, &c. are used with the Genitive also; *see* Lesson X.

§ **68**. The roots कथ्, ख्या, शंस्, and चक्ष्, all meaning '*to tell*' (contrary to the principle of दुह्याच्पच् &c.) the causal of विद् with नि (contrary to § 44), and other roots having the same sense, govern the Dative of the person to whom something is told; as, आर्ये कथयामि ते भूतार्थं (S'. 1) 'O worthy lady, I tell you the truth'; एहि इमां वनस्पतिसेवां काश्यपाय निवेदयावहः (S'. 4) 'come, let us communicate this service of the trees to Kásyapa;' so यस्मै ब्रह्मपारायणं जगौ (U. 4) 'to whom he sang (revealed) the Veda'; यस्मै मुनिर्ब्रह्म परं विवव्रे (Mu. 2).

§ **69**. Verbs meaning 'to send' or 'despatch' generally govern the Dative of the person, but Accusative of the place, to whom or which a thing is sent; as, भोजेन दूतो रघवे विसृष्टः (R. V. 39) 'a messenger was sent to Raghu by Bhoja; माधवं पद्मावतीं प्रहिण्वता देवरातेन (Mál. 1.) 'by Devaráta sending Mádhava to Padmávatí.'

§ **70** * The secondary or indirect object of the root **मन्** 'to think' cl. 4, which is not an animal, takes either the Accusative or Dative, when *contempt* is to be shown; as, **न त्वां तृणाय तृणं वा मन्ये** (S. K.) 'I do not consider thee to be worth a straw.'

Obs.—When no negation and contempt are meant, but mere *comparison*, the Accusative alone is used; as, **त्वां तृणं मन्ये** (Mbh.) 'I consider thee as a straw'; but **हरिमप्यमंसत तृणाय** (Ś. XV. 61.).

§ **71**. † In the case of roots implying *motion*, the place to which motion is directed is put in the Dative or Accusative case when physical motion is indicated; as **ग्रामं ग्रामाय वा गच्छति**; but **मनसा हरिं व्रजति** 'goes to Hari mentally' (contemplates him.)

Obs.—(1) **राधीक्ष्योर्यस्य विप्रश्नः** (I. 4. 39) *i. e.* the person, with regard to whom some questions as to good fortune or welfare are asked, is put in the Dative in the case of the roots **राध्** 'to propitiate' and **ईक्ष्** 'to look to the welfare of any one'; as, **कृष्णाय राध्यति ईक्षते वा गर्गः** (*i. e.* **पृष्टो गर्गः शुभाशुभं पर्यालोचयति**); (2) **परिक्रयणे संप्रदानमन्यतरस्यां** (I. 4. 44.) *i. e.* the price at which a person is empolyed on stipulated wages is put in the instr. or dat. case; as, **शतेन शताय वा परिक्रीतोऽयं दासः ।**

नैतन्न्याय्यम् । सर्वज्ञस्याप्येकाकिनो निर्णयाभ्युपगमो दोषाय ।
(M. 1.)

चपलोयं बटुः कदाचिदस्मत्प्रार्थनामन्तःपुरेभ्यः कथयेत् । (S'. 2.)

अहमपि वैतानिकं शान्त्युदकमस्यै गौतमीहस्ते विसर्जयिष्यामि ।
(S'. 3.)

स्पृहयामि खलु दुर्ललितायास्मै । मृगतृष्णिकेव नाममात्रप्रस्तावो मे विषादाय कल्पते । (S'. 7.)

मूर्ख नैष तव दोषः । साधोः शिक्षा गुणाय संपद्यते नासाधोः ।
(P. I. 19.)

---

* **मन्यकर्मण्यनादरे विभाषा प्राणिषु** । (II. 3. 17)

† **गत्यर्थकर्मणि द्वितीयाचतुर्थ्यौ चेष्टायामनध्वनि** (II. 3. 12.)

प्रसीद भगवति वसुंधरे शरीरमसि संसारस्य । तत्किमसंविदानेव जामात्रे कुप्यसि । (U. 7.)

मिथ्यामाहात्म्यगर्वनिर्भरा न प्रणमन्ति देवताभ्यो न मानयन्ति मान्यानात्मप्रज्ञापरिभव इत्यसूयन्ति सचिवोपदेशाय कुप्यन्ति हितवादिने ।

(K. 108.)

प्रतिश्रुतं तेन तस्मै स्वसुरवन्तिसुंदर्याः प्रदानम् । (D. K. II. 19.)

चन्द्रापीडः समुपसृत्य पूर्ववदेव तां महाश्वेताप्रणामपुरःसरं दर्शितविनयः प्रणनाम K. 219.)

प्रणिपत्य सुरास्तस्मै शमयित्रे सुरद्विषाम् ।
अथैनं तुष्टुवुः स्तुत्यमवाङ्मनसगोचरम् ॥ (R. X. 15.)

रविमावसते सतां क्रियायै सुधया तर्पयते सुरान् पितृंश्च ।
तमसां निशि मूर्च्छतां निहन्त्रे हरचूडानिहितात्मने नमस्ते । (V. 3.)

उमा वधूर्भवान् दाता याचितार इमे वयम् ।
वरः शंभुरलं ह्येष त्वत्कुलोद्भूतये विधिः ॥ (Ku. VI. 82.)

चरतः किल दुश्चरं तपस्तृणबिन्दोः परिशंकितः पुरा ।
प्रजिघाय समाधिभेदिनीं हरिरस्मै हरिणीं सुरांगनाम् (R. VIII. 97.)

वाताय कपिला विद्युदातपायातिलोहिनी ।
पीता भवति सस्याय दुर्भिक्षाय सिता भवेत् ॥ (Mbh.)

स्वस्त्यस्तु ते निर्गलितांबुगर्भं
शरद्घनं नार्दति चातकोऽपि । (R. V. 17.)

ताभ्यां तथागतमुपेत्य तमेकपुत्र-
मज्ञानतः स्वचरितं नृपतिः शशंस । (R. IX. 77.)

परित्राणाय साधूनां विनाशाय च दुष्कृताम् ।
धर्मसंस्थापनार्थाय संभवामि युगे युगे ॥ (Bg. IV. 8.)

ADDITIONAL SENTENCES FOR EXERCISE.

तदाकर्ण्य तामहं दंडवत्प्रणम्य तस्यै मद्वृत्तान्तमखिलमाख्याय विस्मयविकसिताक्षं जनकमदर्शयम् । (D. K. I. 4.)

सखि वासन्ति दुःखायेदानीं रामस्य दर्शनं सुहृदाम् । तत्कियच्चिरं त्वां रोदयिष्यामि । तदनुजानीहि मां गमनाय । (U. 3.)

स्वयमेवोत्पद्यन्त एवंविधाः कुलपांशवो निःस्नेहाः पशवो येषां क्षुद्राणां प्रज्ञा परामिसन्धानाय न ज्ञानाय पराक्रमः प्राणिनामुपघाताय नोपकाराय धनपरित्यागः कामाय न धर्माय किंबहुना सर्वमेव येषां दोषाय न गुणाय । (K. 288.)

श्रोत्रियायाभ्यागताय वत्सतरीं महोक्षं वा निर्वपन्ति गृहमेधिनः । (U. 4.)

दुदोह गां स यज्ञाय सस्याय मघवा दिवम् ।
संपद्विनिमयेनोभौ दधतुर्भुवनद्वयम् ॥ (R. I. 26.)

नमस्त्रिमूर्तये तुभ्यं प्राक्सृष्टेः केवलात्मने ।
गुणत्रयविभागाय पश्चाद्भेदमुपेयुषे ॥ (Ku. II. 4.)

स स्थाणुः स्थिरभक्तियोगसुलभो निःश्रेयसायास्तु वः । (V. 1.)

सर्वः कल्ये वयसि यतते लब्धुमर्थान्कुटुम्बी
पश्चात्पुत्रैरपहृतभरः कल्पते विश्रमाय । (V. 1.)

यदेवोपनतं दुःखात्सुखं तद्रसवत्तरम् ।
निर्वाणाय तरुच्छाया तप्तस्य हि विशेषतः ॥ (V. 3.)

शुद्धान्तसंभोगनितान्ततुष्टे न नैषधे कार्यमिदं निगाद्यम् ।
अपां हि तृप्ताय न वारिधारा स्वादुः सुगन्धिः स्वदते तुषारा ॥ (N. III. 95.)

किमित्यपास्याभरणानि यौवने धृतं त्वया वार्द्धकशोभि वल्कलम् ।
वद प्रदोषे स्फुटचन्द्रतारका विभावरी यद्यरुणाय कल्पते ॥ (Ku. V. 44.)

पुंसामसमर्थानामुपद्रवायात्मनो भवेत्कोपः ।
पिठरं क्वथदतिमात्रं निजपार्श्वमेव दहतितराम् ॥ (P. I. 14.)

पयःपानं भुजंगानां केवलं विषवर्द्धनम् ॥
उपदेशो हि मूर्खाणां प्रकोपाय न शांतये ॥ (H. 3.)

प्रतिवाचमदत्त केशवः शपमानाय न चेदिभूभुजे।
अनुहुंकुरुते घनध्वनिं न हि गोमायुरुतानि केसरी ॥ (Śi. XVI. 25.)
संतानकामाय तथेति कामं राज्ञे प्रतिश्रुत्य पयस्विनी सा।
दुग्ध्वा पयः पत्रपुटे मदीयं पुत्रोपभुंक्ष्वेति तमादिदेश ॥ (R. II. 65.)
तस्याः प्रसन्नेन्दुमुखः प्रसादं गुरुर्नृपाणां गुरवे निवेद्य।
प्रहर्षचिह्नानुमितं प्रियायै शशंस वाचा पुनरुक्तयेव ॥ (R. II. 68.)
ततो यथावद्विहिताध्वराय तस्मै स्मयावेशविवर्जिताय।
वर्णाश्रमाणां गुरवे स वर्णी विचक्षणः प्रस्तुतमाचचक्षे ॥ (R. V. 19.)
वसन् स तस्यां वसतौ रघूणां पुराणशोभामधिरोपितायाम्।
न मैथिलेयः स्पृहयांबभूव भर्त्रे दिवो नाप्यलकेश्वराय ॥ (R. XVI. 42.)
तस्यै स्पृहयमाणोऽसौ बहुप्रियमभाषत।
सानुनीतिश्च सीतायै नाक्रुध्यन्नाप्यसूयत ॥
संक्रुध्यसि मृषा किं त्वं दिदृक्षुं मां मृगेक्षणे।
ईक्षितव्यं परस्त्रीभ्यः स्वधर्मो रक्षसामयम् ॥
रावणाय नमस्कुर्याः स्यात् सीते स्वस्ति ते ध्रुवम्।
अन्यथा प्रातराशाय कुर्याम त्वामलं वयम् ॥ (Bk. VIII. 75–6, 98.)

Wretched man, do you like service in the house of a Châṇḍâla ?

Lady, do not misunderstand me, and do not get angry with me in vain.

I do not long for (स्पृह्) wealth, but immortal glory.

Having promised Lakshmaṇa to accompany him, why do you now tell him that you are unable to do so ?

Being greatly delighted at hearing the account, they communicated (विद् with नि) to him even their very secrets.

Even a sight of these pious men will bring about (क्लृप्) my purification ; I shall, therefore, wait upon them for the accomplishment of my desired object.

I told him (ख्या with आ) through my brother that I had nothing to do with seeing him.

Old lady, such sad thoughts will only result in greater sorrow; therefore compose yourself for a time.

The enjoyment of pleasures in this world only leads to disgust.

My subjects bear hatred towards (असूय्) me and plot against (द्रुह्) my life.

First salute (प्रणम्) your preceptor and then begin to learn your lesson.

A bow to the three-eyed God, who reduced Cupid to ashes with the fire of his third eye.

When a man gets a son, he pays off the debt due to his fathers.

You yourself are able to defeat (*use* अलं) a whole troop of the enemy.

When a man is doomed by fate, even a trifling cause is sufficient (अलं) to bring about his ruin.

I shall send a messenger to the king of Videha, and communicate to him this glad tidings.

LESSON VIII.

The Ablative Case.

§ **72**. The chief sense of the Ablative case is अपादान. That from which separation, whether actual or conceived, takes place is called अपादान, and is put in the Ablative case; as, ग्रामादायाति 'he comes from a village'; *i. e.* that from which the separation takes place is ग्राम. It has thus the sense of 'from' in English.

§ **73**. * A noun in the Ablative case frequently denotes the cause of an action or phenomenon, and has the sense of 'on account of', 'for', 'by reason of' &c.; as, सौहृदादपृथगाश्रयां (U. 1) 'not living apart (whose resort was not different) on account of affection.' A noun not of the feminine gender denoting the cause of an action is put in the Instrumental or Ablative; as, जाड्येन जाड्याद् वा बद्धः (S. K.)

* विभाषा गुणेऽस्त्रियाम्। (II. 3. 25).

'he was caught by reason of his dulness;' बुद्ध्या मुक्तः (S. K.) 'was set at liberty on account of his skill'; भक्त्या गुरौ मय्यनुकंपया च प्रीतास्मि ते (R. II. 63) 'I am pleased with thee for thy devotion to (thy) preceptor and compassion on me.'

Obs.—Sometimes a feminine noun also is used in the Ablative in this sense; as, नास्ति घटोऽनुपलब्धेः (S. K.).

(*a*) The Ablative often serves the purpose of a whole causative assertion in replying to, or advancing arguments in discussions; as, पर्वतो वह्निमान् धूमात् (Tarka.) 'the mountain has fire (in it), because there is smoke'; नेश्वरो जगतः कारणमुपपद्यते। कुतः वैषम्यनैर्घृण्यप्रसंगात् (S. B.) (A disputant says) 'God cannot be the efficient cause of the world. Why ? (Because) he is liable to (the two charges of) being partial and cruel.'

§ **74**. Words in the comparative degree, or such as have the sense of comparison, are used with the Ablative of that with reference to which the comparison is made; as, सत्यादप्यनृतं श्रेयः (Ve. 3) 'falsehood even is better than truth'; मोहादभूत्कष्टतरः प्रबोधः (R. XIV. 56) 'consciousness became more painful than swoon'; चैत्ररथादनूने वृंदावने (R. VI. 50) 'in Vrindávana not inferior to Chaitraratha'; अश्वमेधसहस्रेभ्यः सत्यमेवातिरिच्यते (H. 4) 'truth itself is superior to a thousand horse-sacrifices'; श्राद्धस्य पूर्वाह्णादपराह्णो विशिष्यते (Manu. III. 271) 'for a S'ráddha ceremony afternoon is preferrned to forenoon'.

§ **75**. *When the sense of an absolutive is suppressed in a sentence, the object of the absolutive is put in the Ablative case; as, प्रसादात्प्रेक्षते (S. K.)=प्रासादमारुह्य प्रेक्षते 'sees from a palace'; so श्वशुराज्जिहेति (S. K.)=श्वशुरं वीक्ष्य जिहेति

(*a*) The place where an action is performed is also put in the Ablative under the same circumstances; as, आसनात्प्रेक्षते *i. e.* आसने उपविश्य प्रेक्षते 'sees from a seat.'

---

* ल्यब्लोपे कर्मण्युपसंख्यानम्। अधिकरणे च। प्रभाख्यानयोश्च। (Vár.)

(*b*) In questions and answers also the Ablative is used; as, कुतो भवान्-पाटलिपुत्रात् (Mbh.)

§ **76**. * Words denoting जुगुप्सा 'abhorrence,' विराम 'cessation', 'refraining', and प्रमाद 'swerving', govern the Ablative case; as, पापाज्जुगुप्सते (Mbh.) 'he shrinks from sin'; वत्सैतस्माद्विरम (U. 1) 'desist from this, O child'; स्वाधिकारात्प्रमत्तः (Me. 1) 'swerving from his duty'; similarly प्राणाघातान्निवृत्तिः (Bh. II. 26) refraining from injury to life'; धर्मान्मुह्यति (Mbh.)

Obs.—प्रमद् is usually construed with the Locative in the sense of 'to be careless about'; as, न प्रमाद्यन्ति प्रमदासु विपश्चितः (Manu. II. 213) 'wise men are not careless about their women.'

§ **77**. † The teacher from whom something is learnt, the prime cause in the case of जन् 'to be born', and the 'source' in the case of भू, are put in the Ablative case; as उपाध्यायादधीते (S. K.) 'learns from the preceptor'; so मया तीर्थादभिनयविद्या शिक्षिता (M. I.) 'I learnt the art of dramatic representation from a teacher'; गोमयाद्वृश्चिको जायते (Mbh.) 'the scorpion is produced from cowdung'; प्राणाद्वायुरजायत (Rigveda X. 90) 'the wind was born from the breath'; हिमवतो गंगा प्रभवति (Mbh.) 'the Ganges has its source in the Himâlayas'; लोभात् क्रोधः प्रभवति (H: K.) 'anger proceeds from avarice'.

Obs.—Verbs meaning 'to be born' are often used with the Locative of the 'source'; as, परदारेषु जायेते द्वौ सुतौ कुंडगोलकौ (Manu. III. 174); जातोपि दास्यां शूद्रेण (Y. II. 133); शुकनासस्यापि रेणुकायां तनयो जातः (K. 73) सा तस्यामुदपादि (Ku. I. 22.)

§ **78**. ‡ In the case of words implying 'fear' and 'protection from danger', that from which the fear or danger proceeds is put in the Ablative case; as, न भीतो मरणादस्मि (Mk. 10) 'I am not afraid of death'; कपेरत्रासिषुर्नादात् (Bk. IX. II) 'were afraid of the monkey's

---

* जुगुप्साविरामप्रमादार्थानामुपसंख्यानम् । (Vâr.)

† आख्यातोपयोगे । जनिकर्तुः प्रकृतिः । भुवः प्रभवः । (I. 4. 29, 30-1).

‡ भीत्रार्थानां भयहेतुः (I. 4. 25)

sound'; तीक्ष्णादुद्विजते (Mn. 3) 'is afraid of (shrinks away from) a severe person'; भीमाद् दुःशासनं त्रातुं (Ve. 3) 'to save Duḥśâsana from Bhima'; so लोकापवादाद्भयं (Bh. II. 62), तृणबिन्दोः परिशंकितः (R. VIII. 79).

(*a*) * That from which a person is warded off or prevented, is also put in the Ablative; as, पापान्निवारयति) Bh. I. 72) 'wards off from sin'.

§ **79.** † In the case of the root जि with परा, that which becomes unbearable is put in the Ablative case; as, अध्ययनात्पराजयते (Mbh.) 'finds study unbearable'.

§ **80**. ‡ The point of time or space from which some 'distance or time or space, is measured, is put in the Ablative case. The word denoting the 'distance in space' is put either in the Nominative or Locative, and that denoting 'the distance in time', in the Locative; as, गवीधुमतः सांकाश्यं चत्वारि योजनानि चतुर्षु योजनेषु वा (Mbh.) 'S. is four yojanas from G.'; कार्तिक्या आग्रहायणी मासे (*ibid.*) 'A. is one month (at the interval of one month) from K.' So समुद्रात्पुरी क्रोशौ or क्रोशयोः.

§ **81**. $ Words meaning 'other than' or 'different from', such as अन्य, पर, इतर; आरात् 'near' or 'remote'; ऋते 'without'; words indicative of the 'directions' used also with reference to the 'time' corresponding to them; words expressive of 'directions' derived from अंच्; for instance प्राक्, प्रत्यक्; and such as end in आ and आहि; all these govern the Ablative case; as कृष्णादन्यो भिन्न इतरो वा (S. K.) 'different from, or other than, Krishna', आराद्ग्रामात् (S. K.) 'near the village, or away from it'; विविक्तादृतेऽन्यच्छरणं नास्ति (V. 2.) 'there

---

* वारणार्थानामीप्सितः। (I. 4. 27.)

† पराजेरसोढः। (I 4. 26.)

‡ यतश्चाध्वकालनिर्माणं तत्र पञ्चमी। तद्युक्तादध्वनः प्रथमासप्तम्यौ। कालात् सप्तमी च वक्तव्या। (Vâr.)

$ अन्यारादितरर्तेदिक्शब्दाञ्चूत्तरपदाजाहियुक्ते। (II. 3. 29.)

is no resort other than a retired spot'; ग्रामात्पूर्वं उत्तरो वा 'to the east or north of the village'; चैत्रात्पूर्वः फाल्गुनः (S. K.) 'the month of Fálguna is prior to (that of) Chaitra'; प्राक् प्रत्यग्वा ग्रामात् (*ibid*) 'to the east or west of the village'; दक्षिणा दक्षिणाहि वा ग्रामात् (*ibid*) 'to the south or in the southern direction, of the village'; प्राग्नाभिवर्धनात् (Manu. II. 29) 'before the navel is cut.'

§ **82**. The words प्रभृति, आरभ्य, बहिः, ऊर्ध्वं, परं, अनंतरं govern this case; as, शैशवात्प्रभृति पोषितां (U. 1) 'brought up ever since her childhood'; मालत्याः प्रथमावलोकदिवसादारभ्य (Màl. 6) 'from the day of first seeing Màlatí'; निवसन्नावसथे पुराद्बहिः (R. VIII, 14) 'residing in a dwelling out of the town'; पाणिपीडनविधेरनन्तरं (Ku. VIII. 1) 'after the espousing of her hand'; अस्मात्परं (S'. 6) 'after this person'; ऊर्ध्वं म्रिये मुहूर्ताद्धि (Bk. XVIII. 36) 'I shall die after a moment.'

Obs.—(*a*) The words प्रभृति and आरभ्य are often found used with adverbs of time in the same sense; as, यतः प्रभृति, ततः प्रभृति (S'. 3); अद्यप्रभृति तवास्मि दासः (Ku. V. 86).

(*b*) The sense of अनन्तरं, परं &c. is sometimes understood; as, बहोर्दृष्टं कालात् (U. 2) 'seen after a long time.'

§ **83**. *The words पृथक् 'different,' विना and नाना govern, besides this case, tha Accusative and Instrumental cases; as, रामाद्रामेण रामं वा विना पृथग् नाना वा (S. K.) 'without or different from Ràma'; नाना नारिं निष्फला लोकयात्रा (Vopadeva).

§ **84**. The preposition आ in the sense of '*till*,' '*as far as*,' and '*from*' governs the Ablative case; as, आपरितोषाद्विदुषां (S'. 1) 'till the satisfaction of the learned'; आमूलाच्छ्रोतुमिच्छामि (S'. 1) 'I wish to hear from the beginning'; आकैलासात् (Me. 11) 'as far as the Kailàsa.' Sometimes आ is joined to nouns to form Avyayíbháva compounds; as, आमेखलं संचरतां घनानां (Ku. I. 5.) 'of clouds sweeping as far as the girdle (middle part).'

---

* पृथग्विनानानाभिस्तृतीयाऽन्यतरस्याम् (II. 3, 32)

§ **85**. * When 'concealment' is indicated, the person whose sight one wishes to avoid is put in the Ablative case; as, मातुर्निलीयते कृष्णः (S. K.) 'Krishna hides himself from his mother.'

§ **86**. † The preposition प्रति in the sense of 'representative of' or 'in exchange for', governs the Ablative; as, प्रद्युम्नः कृष्णात्प्रति (S. K.) 'P. is the representative of K.'; तिलेभ्यः प्रतियच्छति माषान् (S. K.) 'exchange Máshas for sesamum'.

अनुष्ठितनिदेशोपि सत्क्रियाविशेषादनुपयुक्तमिवात्मानं समर्थये। (S. 7)

अलमलमाक्रन्दितेन । सूर्योपस्थानात्प्रतिनिवृत्तं पुरूरवसं मामुपेत्य कथ्यतां कुतो भवत्यः परित्रातव्या इति । (V. 1.)

रामः—एवमेतत् । एते हि हृदयमर्मभिदः संसारभावा येभ्यो बीभत्समानाः संत्यज्य सर्वान् कामान्मनीषिणोऽरण्ये विश्राम्यन्ति । (U. 1)

नास्ति जीवितादन्यदभिमततरमिह जगति सर्वजंतूनाम् । (K. 35)

नैव जानासि तं देवमैक्ष्वाकं यदेवं वदसि। तद्विरम्यतामतिप्रसंगात् । (U. 5)

कृतातिथ्यया महाश्वेतया परिपृष्टो दिग्विजयादारभ्य किन्नरमिथुनानुसरणप्रसंगेनागमनमात्मनः सर्वमाचचक्षे । (K. 144)

वत्से मालति जन्मनः प्रभृति वल्लभा ते लवंगिका । तत्किमुज्जिहानजीवितां वराकीं नानुकम्पसे । (Mál. 10)

चाणक्यः—वृशल वृशल अलमुत्तरोत्तरेण । यद्यस्मत्तो वरीयान् राक्षसोऽवगम्यते तदिदं शस्त्रं तस्मै दीयताम् । (Mu. 3)

---

* अन्तर्धौ येनादर्शनमिच्छति । (I. 4. 28)

† प्रतिनिधिप्रतिदाने च यस्मात् । (II. 3. 11).

तासां चतुर्दश कुलानि । एकं भगवतः कमलयोनेर्मनसः समुत्पन्नम् । अन्यद्वेदेभ्यः संभूतम् । अन्यदग्नेरुद्भूतम् । अन्यत् पवनात्प्रसूतम् । अन्यदमृतादुन्मथ्यमानादुत्थितम् । अन्यज्जलाज्जातम् । अन्यदर्ककिरणेभ्यो निर्गतम् । अन्यत्सौदामिनीतः प्रवृत्तम् । (K. 136)

मां तावदुद्धर शुचो दयिताप्रवृत्त्या
स्वार्थात्सतां गुरुतरा प्रणयिक्रियैव । (V. 4)

निशम्य चैनां तपसे कृतोद्यमां सुतां गिरीशप्रतिसक्तमानसाम् ।
उवाच मेना परिरभ्य वक्षसा निवारयन्ती महतो मुनिव्रतात् ॥

(Ku. V. 3)

प्रजां संरक्षति नृपः सा वर्द्धयति पार्थिवम् ।
वर्द्धनाद्रक्षणं श्रेयस्तदभावे सदप्यसत् ॥ (H. 3)

त्वचं स मेध्यां परिधाय रौरवी-
मशिक्षतास्त्रं पितुरेव मन्त्रवत् । (R. III. 31)

अनम्राणां समुद्धर्तुस्तस्मात्सिन्धुरयादिव ।
आत्मा संरक्षितः सुह्मैर्वृत्तिमाश्रित्य वैतसीम् ॥ (R. IV. 35)

ध्यायतो विषयान्पुंसः संगस्तेषूपजायते ।
संगात्संजायते कामः कामात्क्रोधोऽभिजायते ॥
क्रोधाद्भवति संमोहः संमोहात्स्मृतिविभ्रमः ।
स्मृतिभ्रंशाद्बुद्धिनाशो बुद्धिनाशात्प्रणश्यति ॥ (Bg. IV. 62-3)

हिमवद्विन्ध्ययोर्मध्यं यत्प्राग्विनशनादपि ।
प्रत्यगेव प्रयागाच्च मध्यदेशः प्रकीर्तितः ॥ (Manu. II. 12)

ADDITIONAL SENTENCES FOR EXERCISE,

जन्मकर्मतो मलिनतरजनं जनतो निस्त्रिंशतरलोकहृदयं लोकहृदयेभ्यो निर्घृणतरसर्वसंव्यवहारमपुण्यकर्मैकापणं पक्कणमपश्यम् । (K. 356)

सा कुसुमघटितशिलीमुखमनोहरान्मदनचापादिव प्रमदवनात्त्रस्यति जानकीव पीतरक्तेभ्यो रजनिचरेभ्य इव चंपकाशोकेभ्यो बिभेति । (K. 225.)

तं नृपं वसुरक्षितो नाम मन्त्रिवृद्ध एकदाऽभाषत । तात अत्रभवति सर्वैवात्मसंपदभिजनात्प्रभृत्यन्यूनैव लक्ष्यते । बुद्धिश्च निसर्गपट्वि तवेतरेभ्यः प्रतिविशिष्यते । (D.K.II.8)

अहो दुराराध्या राजलक्ष्मीरात्मविद्भिरपि राजभिः—

तीक्ष्णादुद्विजते मृदौ परिभवत्रासान्न संतिष्ठते
मूर्खान्द्वेष्टि न गच्छति प्रणयितामत्यन्तविद्वत्स्वपि ।
शूरेभ्योऽप्यधिकं बिभेत्युपहसत्येकान्तभीरूनहो
श्रीर्लब्धप्रसरेव वेशवनिता दुःखोपचर्या भृशम् ॥ (Mu. 3.)

सर्वद्रव्येषु विद्यैव द्रव्यमाहुरनुत्तमम् ।
अहार्यत्वादनर्घत्वादक्षयत्वा च सर्वदा ॥ (H. 1.)

प्रजानां विनयाधानाद्रक्षणाद्भरणादपि ।
स पिता पितरस्तासां केवलं जन्महेतवः ॥ (R. I. 24)

न नवः प्रभुराफलोदयात्स्थिरकर्मा विरराम कर्मणः ।
न च योगविधेर्नवेतरः स्थिरधीरापरमात्मदर्शनात् ॥ (R. VIII. 22)
रत्नैर्महार्हैस्तुतुषुर्न देवा न भेजिरे भीमविषेण भीतिम् ।
सुधां विना न प्रययुर्विरामं न निश्चितार्थाद्विरमन्ति धीराः ॥ (Bh. II. 80)
श्रेयान्स्वधर्मो विगुणः परधर्मात्स्वनुष्ठितात् ।
स्वधर्मे निधनं श्रेयः परधर्मो भयावहः ॥ (Bg. III. 35)
लोभान्मोहाद्भयान्मैत्र्यात् कामात्क्रोधात्तथैव च ।
अज्ञानाद्बालभावाच्च साक्ष्यं वितथमुच्यते । (Manu. VIII. 118)
पूर्वस्मादन्यवद्भाति भावाद्दाशरथिं स्तुवन् ।
ऋते क्रौर्यात्समायातो मां विश्वासयितुं नु किम् ॥
इतरो रावणादेष राघवानुचरो यदि ।
सफलानि निमित्तानि प्राक् प्रभातात्ततो मम ॥ (Bk. VIII. 105-6)

वृक्षाद्वृक्षं परिक्रामन्रावणाद्बिभ्यतीं भृशम् ।
शत्रोस्त्राणमपश्यन्तीमदृश्यो जनकात्मजाम् ॥
तां पराजयमानां स प्रीते रक्ष्यां दशाननात् ।
अंतर्दधानां रक्षोभ्यो मलिनां श्याममूर्धजाम् ॥ (अपश्यत्) (Bk. VIII. 70-1)
एतद्वोयं भृगुः शास्त्रं श्रावयिष्यत्यशेषतः ।
एतद्धि मत्तोधिजगे सर्वमेषोखिलं मुनिः ॥ (Manu. I. 59)
एकाक्षरं परं ब्रह्म प्राणायामाः परं तपः ।
सावित्र्यास्तु परं नास्ति मौनात्सत्यं विशिष्यते ॥ (Manu. II. 83)

A house without a house-wife surpasses a forest in dreariness.

Go in the northern direction (उत्तरं) of this tree, and I shall just follow you.

Do not desist from the work you have once promised to perform.

I have walked to this place from the hermitage of Vàlmiki to learn the Vedas from these ascetics.

He exposed himself to much trouble in saving that girl from danger.

He who wards off his friend's mind from sin and makes him set it on virtue, is called a real friend.

Do you not know that various kinds of miseries result from treading in the foot-steps of the wicked ?

This your illness arose (जन्) from your great exertions of yesterday. Is there now any change for the better ?

Who else but this powerful king can protect his realm as far as (आ) the regions of the Himàlayas ?

Before (प्राक्) beignning his studies he places his grammar and dictionary by him.

Five years ago I saw this very charming forest; but now it has undergone a vast change.

Ever since the day on which I happened to see her, my mind has become perturbed, and I do not think even of taking my food, on account of my constantly thinking of her.

I do not approve of the speech you made yesterdy after (ऊर्ध्वं (अनन्तरं) the excellent oration of the President.

Sitá was dearer to Ràma (*gen.*) than his very life.

Honesty is superior to all other virtues; without it one cannot inspire any one with confidence.

That wretched fowler did not see the little parrot on account of his body being contracted through fear

Revered Sir, we wished to hear from you the history of this parrot from (आ) the beginning.

Bombay is one hundred and twenty miles from Poona.

LESSON IX.

The Locative Case.

§ **87**. The place *in* or *on* which an action is represented as taking place is called अधिकरण and is put in the Locative case; as, स्थाल्यामोदनं पचति 'cooks food in a cooking utensil'; आसने उपविशति 'sits on a seat.'

(*a*) The Locative is used to denote the time when an action takes place; as, आषाढस्य प्रथमदिवसे (Me. 2) 'on the first day of Áshàdha'; so शैशवेऽभ्यस्तविद्यानां यौवने विषयैषिणाम् (R. I. 8).

§ **88**. The Locative has very often the sense of 'towards,' 'about', 'as to' &c.; as, मयि मा भूत्करुणा (Mál. 9) 'be not ruthless towards me'; विषयेषु विनाशधर्मसु निःस्पृहोभवत (R. VIII. 10) 'became free from desire for perishable objects.'

§ **89**. * With adjectives in the superlative degree, and in those cases where a distinction is made, as of an individual from his whole class, (generally expressed by 'of', or 'among' in English), the nouns with respect to which such pre-eminence or distinction is shown, are put in the Genitive or Locative; as, गवां गोषु वा कृष्णा बहुक्षीरा (S. K.) 'among cows the black one gives much milk'; so नृणां नृषु वा द्विजः श्रेष्ठः (*ibid.*)

---

* यतश्च निर्धारणम् । (II. 3. 41).

§ **90.** *Words expressive of the interval of time or space, are put in the Ablative or Locative; as, अस्मिन्दिने भुक्त्वाऽयं त्र्यहात् त्र्यहे वा भोक्ता (S. K.) 'having dined to-day, he will dine again after (the interval of) three days;' इहस्थोयं क्रोशात्क्रोशे वा लक्ष्यं विध्येत् (S. K.) 'standing here, he will hit a mark at (the distance of) one *Koss*.'

§ **91**. This case is used in lexicons to denote 'in the sense of'; as, बाणो बलिसुते शरे (Amara) बाण is used in the sense of 'the son of Bali', and 'an arrow'.

§ **92**. The Locative is sometimes used to denote the object or purpose for which anything is done; as, चर्मणि द्वीपिनं हन्ति दंतयोर्हन्ति कुंजरम्। केशेषु चमरीं हन्ति सीम्नि पुष्कलको हतः॥ (Mbh.) 'man kills the tiger for skin, the elephant for tusks, the Chamarí for hair, and the musk-deer for musk.'

§ **93**. Words meaning 'to act', 'to behave', 'to deal with', are construed with the Locative; as आर्योस्मिन्विनयेन वर्ततां (U. 6) 'let your honour act modestly towards this person;' कथं कार्यविनिमयेन व्यवहरति मय्यनात्मज्ञः (M. 1) 'Oh ! does the fool deal with me by an exchange of duties?'; कुरु प्रियसखीवृत्तिं सपत्नीजने (S. 4.) 'act the part of a dear friend towards the rival wives.'

§ **94**. Words signifying 'love', 'attachment', 'respect', such as स्निह्, अभिलष्, अनुरञ्ज्, &c., govern the Locative of the person or thing for whom or which the 'love' &c. is shown; as किं नु खलु बालेस्मिन् स्निह्यति मे मनः (Ś. 7) 'why indeed, does my mind love this child ?'; न तापसकन्यकायां शकुंतलायां ममाभिलाषः (Ś. 2) 'I cherish no love for Śakuntalá, the daughter of the sage'; स्वयोषिति रतिः (Bh. II. 62) 'attachment to one's own wife'; दण्डनीत्यां नात्यादृतोऽभूत् (D. K. II. 8)' had no great regard for politics'; देवे चन्द्रगुप्ते दृढमनुरक्ताः प्रकृतयः (Mu. 1) 'the subjects are firmly attached (devotedly loyal) to His Majesty Chandragupta'; अस्ति मे सोदरस्नेहोप्येतेषु (Ś. 1) 'I have also a sisterly affection for them.'

---

* सप्तमीपञ्चम्यौ कारकमध्ये। (II. 3, 7)

Obs.—Derivatives from अनुरञ्ज् are occasionally used with the Accusative; as, एषा भवन्तमनुरक्ता (Ś. 6); अपि वृषलमनुरक्ताः प्रकृतयः (Mn. 1). In such cases अनु must be taken separately, and understood as a कर्मप्रवचनीय governing the Accusative case. See § 37.

§ **95**. When a word indicating 'cause' is used, 'the effect' is often put in the Locative; as, दैवमेव हि नृणां वृद्धौ क्षये कारणं (Bh. II. 84) 'fate alone is the cause of the decline and prosperity (rise and fall) of men'.

§ **96**. The root युज् and its derivatives govern the Locative of the thing in the sense of '*to*' in English; as, असाधुदर्शी तत्रभवान् काश्यपो य इमामाश्रमधर्मे नियुंक्ते (Ś. 1) 'the revered Kàśyapa is not prudent as he appoints her to the duties of the hermitage.'

(*a*) With words expressive of 'fitness', 'suitableness' &c., the nouns regarding which the fitness is expressed are put in the Locative case; as, युक्तरूपमिदं त्वयि (Ś. 2) 'this is fit for thee'; त्रैलोक्यस्यापि प्रभुत्वं तस्मिन्युज्यते (H. 3) 'the sovereignty of even the three worlds suits him'; अथवोपपन्नमेतदृषिकल्पेऽस्मिन्राजनि (Ś. 2) 'or this is quite proper for this sage-like king'; ते गुणाः परस्मिन् ब्रह्मण्युपपद्यन्ते (Ś. B. 190) 'those attributes suit the Supreme Brahma.'

Obs.—The Genitive is not unfrequently used in the same sense; as, उपपन्नमिदं विशेषणं वायोः (V. 2) 'this epithet suits the wind.'

§ **97**. The Locative, strictly speaking, implies *place*, but in several cases it is used with the object of *recipient* to which anything is entrusted or imparted; as, शुकनासनाम्नि मंत्रिणि राज्यभारमारोप्य यौवनसुखमनुबभूव (K. 57) 'having entrusted the responsibilities of the kingdom to his minister Śukanásа (he) enjoyed the pleasures of youth'; वितरति गुरुः प्राज्ञे विद्यां यथैव तथा जडे (U. 2) 'a preceptor imparts instruction to a clever person in the same way as he does to a dull-headed one'; so योग्यसचिवे न्यस्तः समस्तो भरः (Ratn. 1).

Note.—तॄ with वि is used with the Dative also; as, मह्यं ते व्यतरन् (D. K. I. 1) 'gave him over to me'; so, मारीचस्ते दर्शनं वितरति (Ś. 7).

(*a*) Roots implying 'to seize' or 'to strike,' often govern the Locative of that which is caught hold of or struck; as, आर्तत्राणाय वः शस्त्रं न प्रहर्तुमनागसि (Ś. 1) 'your weapon is for protecting the distressed and not for striking the innocent'; केशेषु गृहीत्वा 'seizing by the hair.'

§ **98**. Words like क्षिप्, मुच्, अस्, having the sense of 'throwing' or 'darting', govern the Locative of that against which anything is thrown; as मृगेषु शरान्मुमुक्षोः (R. IX. 58) 'of him who wished to throw arrows at the deer'; न बाणः संनिपात्योऽस्मिन्मृगशरीरे (Ś. 1.) 'an arrow should not be discharged at this body of the deer.'

(*a*) Words implying 'belief', 'confidence', generally govern the Locative of that in which 'belief' is placed; as, पुंसि विश्वसिति कुत्र कुमारी (N. V. 100.) 'when does a virgin ever believe in man?'

Obs.—श्रद्धा governs the Accusative; as, कः श्रद्धास्यति भूतार्थं (Mk. 3) 'who will believe the real state (of things)?'

§ **99**. *Words like अधीतिन् 'who has learnt', गृहीतिन् 'who has comprehended', govern the Locative of that which forms their object; and साधु and असाधु, of that towards whom the goodness or otherwise is shown; as, अधीती चतुर्ष्वाम्नायेषु (D. K. II. 5) 'versed in the four Vedas'; गृहीती षट्स्वङ्गेषु (*ibid.*) 'who has mastered the six *angas*;' मातरि साधुरसाधुर्वा (S. K.) 'well-behaved or ill-behaved towards his mother'.

§ **100**. Words like व्यापृत, आसक्त, व्यग्र, तत्पर, having the sense of 'engaged in', 'intent on', and कुशल, निपुण, शौण्ड, पटु, प्रवीण, पण्डित, meaning 'skilful', and धूर्त and कितव 'a rogue', are used with the Locative; as, गृहकर्मणि व्यापृता व्यग्रा वा (P. II.) 'engaged in her house-hold duties'; रामोऽक्षद्यूते निपुणः-प्रवीणः (S. K.) 'Rāma is skilful in playing at dice.'

(*a*) † The words प्रसित and उत्सुक meaning 'greatly desirous of', 'longing for', govern the Locative or Instrumental; as, निद्रायां निद्रया वा उत्सुकः (S. K.) 'longing for sleep', so मनो नियोगक्रिययोत्सुकं मे (R. V. 11.).

---

* क्तस्येन्विषयस्य कर्मण्युपसंख्यानम् । साध्वसाधुप्रयोगे च (Vār.)

† प्रसितोत्सुकाभ्यां तृतीया च । (II. 3, 44)

Note.—**राध्** with **अप** in the sense of 'to offend' generally governs the Locative in the sense of the Accusative, and sometimes the Genitive; as, **कस्मिन्नपि पूजार्हेऽपराद्धा शकुंतला** (Ś. 4) 'Śakuntalā has offended (erred with respect to) some one deserving respect'; so **अपराद्धोऽस्मि तत्रभवतः कण्वस्य** (Ś. 7).

प्रथितयशसां भासकविसौमिल्लकविमिश्रादीनां प्रबन्धानतिक्रम्य वर्तमानकवेः कालिदासस्य क्रियायां कथं परिषदो बहुमानः । (M. 1)

यः पौरवेण राज्ञा धर्माधिकारे नियुक्तः सोहमविघ्नक्रियोपलम्भाय धर्मारण्यमिदमायातः । (S. 1)

दृढं त्वयि बद्धभावोर्वशी । न सेतोगतमनुरागं शिथिलयति । (V. 2)

एष देवो रघुपतिस्तिष्ठति । स च स्निह्यत्योवयोरुत्कण्ठते च युष्मत्सन्निकर्षस्य । (U. 6.)

दुर्जनत्वं च भवतो वाक्यादेव विज्ञातं यदनयोर्भूपालयोर्विग्रहे भवद्वचनमेव निदानम् । (H. 3)

एष धृष्टद्युम्नेन द्रोणः केशेष्वाकृष्यासिपत्रेण व्यापाद्यते । (Ve. 3.)

न जानामि केनापि कारणेनापहस्तितसकलसखीजनं त्वयि विश्वसिति मे हृदयम् । (K. 233.)

उपकारिषु यः साधुः साधुत्वे तस्य को गुणः ।
अपकारिषु यः साधुः स साधुः सद्भिरुच्यते ॥ (H. 2)

न मातरि न दारेषु न सोदर्ये न चात्मनि ।
विश्वासस्तादृशः पुंसां यावान्मित्रे स्वभावजे ॥ (H. 1)

क्षमा शत्रौ च मित्रे च यतीनामेवं भूषणम् ।
अपराधिषु सत्त्वेषु नृपाणां सैव दूषणम् ॥ (H. 2)

वाञ्छा सज्जनसंगमे गुणिगणे प्रीतिर्गुरौ नम्रता
विद्यायां व्यसनं स्वयोषिति रतिर्लोकापवादाद्भयम् ।
भक्तिः शूलिनी शक्तिरात्मदमने संसर्गमुक्तिः खले-
ष्वेते येषु वसन्ति निर्मलगुणास्तेभ्यो नरेभ्यो नमः ॥ (Bh. II. 62)

सन्तानार्थाय विधये स्वभुजादवतारिता ।
तेन धूर्जगतो गुर्वी सचिवेषु निचिक्षिपे ॥

भूतानां प्राणिनः श्रेष्ठाः प्राणिनां बुद्धिजीविनः ।
बुद्धिमत्सु नराः श्रेष्ठा नरेषु ब्राह्मणाः स्मृताः ॥ (Manu I. 19)

ADDITIONAL SENTENCES FOR EXERCISE.

अवैमि ते सारमतः खलु त्वां कार्ये गुरुण्यात्मसमं नियोक्ष्ये ।
व्यादिश्यते भूधरतामवेक्ष्य कृष्णेन देहोद्वहनाय शेषः ॥ (Ku. III. 13)

अशुद्धप्रकृतौ राज्ञि जनता नानुरज्यते । (P. I. 11)

जनकानां रघूणां च यत्कृत्स्नं गोत्रमङ्गलम् ।
तस्मिन्नकरुणे पापे वृथा वः करुणा मयि ॥ (U. 6)

निर्गुणेष्वपि सत्त्वेषु दयां कुर्वन्ति साधवः ।
न हि संहरते ज्योत्स्नां चन्द्रश्चांडालवेश्मनः ॥ (H. I)

इत्युक्तवन्तं जनकात्मजायां नितान्तरूक्षाभिनिवेशमीशम् ।
न कश्चन भ्रातृषु तेषु शक्तो निषेद्धुमासीदनुमोदितुं वा ॥ (R. XIV. 43)

परकर्मापहः सोऽभूदुद्यतः स्वेषु कर्मसु ।
आवृणोदात्मनो रन्ध्रं रन्ध्रेषु प्रहरन् रिपून् ॥ (R. XVII. 61)

भगवति कमलालये भृशमगुणज्ञासि ।
आनन्दहेतुमपि देवमपास्य नन्दं
रक्तासि किं कथय वैरिणि मौर्यपुत्रे (Mu. 2)

साक्षात्प्रियामुपगतामपहाय पूर्वं
चित्रार्पितां मुहुरिमां बहु मन्यमानः ।
स्रोतोवहां पथि निकामजलामतीत्य
जातः सखे प्रणयवान्मृगतृष्णिकायाम् ॥ (S'. 6)
पोतो दुस्तरवारिराशितरणे दीपोऽन्धकारागमे
निर्वाते व्यजनं मदान्धकरिणां दर्पोपशान्त्यै सृणिः ।
इत्थं तद्भुवि नास्ति यस्य विधिना नोपायचिन्ता कृता
मन्ये दुर्जनचित्तवृत्तिहरणे धातापि भग्नोद्यमः ॥ (H. 2)
चिरेणानुगुणं प्रोक्ता प्रतिपत्तिपराङ्मुखी ।
न मासे प्रतिपत्तासे मां चेन्मर्तासि मैथिलि ॥ (Bk. VIII. 95)
एतस्मान्मां कुशलिनमभिज्ञानदानाद्विदित्वा
मा कौलीनादसितनयने मय्यविश्वासिनी भूः । (Me. 115)
एवमाप्तवचनात्स पौरुषं काकपक्षकधरेऽपि राघवे ।
श्रद्दधे त्रिदशगोपमात्रके दाहशक्तिमिव कृष्णवर्त्मनि ॥ (R XI. 42)

The subjects of this king are all attached (रञ्ज् with अनु) to him.

He who shows pity towards helpless men, and he who performs sacrifices to gods, are considered equal in merit.

My husband does not love (स्निह्) me, does not believe in what I tell him, and appoints me to unworthy acts; will you, my friend, tell me what I should do under these circumstances ?

A sage becomes regardless (निःस्पृह) of the pleasure or pain of this wordly life.

Have no anxiety whatever as to the education of this boy.

He entrusted the burden of his family to his eldest son, and bidding farewell to all his friends and relations, betook himself to a forest residence.

He was seized by the hair and pulled down; and then all the spectators threw (क्षिप् or मुच्) stones at him.

The absent-minded woman did not cast even a look at what was taking place near her.

This news has all got abroad. Has it not reached your ears that the king has fixed his love on Ságariká ?

Kaikeyî was the prime cause of the banishment of Ráma for fourteen years.

He always spends his time in gambling with men expert in that art.

This is the tallest tree of all in this garden.

Of all persons, he who is intent on doing good to others, is most to be praised.

Among Indian poets Kálidása and Bhavabhûtî are the most renowned.

Rákshasa will not leave his family with men not equal to him in dignity.

LESSON X.

The Genitive Case.

§ **101**. The Genitive case, as observed in Lesson III, is not a Káraka case, and, strictly speaking, expresses the relation of one noun to another in a sentence. In the rules given in this Lesson the Genitive has one principal sense, *viz.* **संबन्ध**, and even in those cases where verbs are used with the Genitive, it is to be considered as having the sense of *relation* only. But in several instances this case is used by loose, and not unfrequently even classical, authors, to express relations pertaining to other cases; as, **तं च व्यसृजद्भरतस्य** (U. 4) 'sent it to Bharata' (**भरतस्य** being put for **भरताय**); **जयसेनायास्तावत्संवेद्य गच्छ** (M. 4) for **जयसेनायै** &c.; **स्त्रीणां विश्वासो नैव कर्तव्यः** (H. 1.) for **स्त्रीषु** &c. Such constructions should be considered as deviations from the usual practice, and should not be imitated.

§ **102.** Generally speaking, the Genitive case denotes the dependence of a substantive or pronoun upon another word, which is usually a substantive or adjective, but sometimes a verb.

(*a*) It is thus used to represent 'of' in English; but in several cases compounds are used instead of the Genitive; as, दशरथस्य पुत्रः or दशरथपुत्रः 'the son of Daśaratha.'

Obs. Mark that all the relations expressed by '*of*' in English cannot be expressed by the Genitive in Sanskrit; *e. g.* the *adjective* meaning and the *apposition* meaning; as, 'a pot of gold' is generally translated by a compound, हेमपात्रं, or by a derivative हैमं पात्रं, but not by हेम्नः पात्रं; 'a pot of clay' मृद्भाण्डं or मृण्मयं भाण्डं; 'a pearl of great price' महार्घं मुक्ताफलं; 'a man of strength' सबलो नरः, not बलस्य नरः. Similarly 'in the month of Vaiśākha' वैशाखे मासे or वैशाखमासे, but not वैशाखस्य मासे; 'the town of Bombay' मुंबापुरी or मुंबा नाम पुरी.

So in Latin: 'a man of talent' is ' homo ingeniosus' (धीमान्नरः); not 'homo ingenii'; but 'a man of great talent' is, unlike Sanskrit, 'homo magni ingenii.'

§ **103**. The Genitive denotes the *possessor*, or the person or thing whereto anything belongs, that which belongs or is possessed, being put in the Nominative case; as, यस्य नास्ति स्वयं प्रज्ञा (P. I.) 'he who himself possesses or has no talent'; इमे नो गृहाः (Mk. 1) 'this is our house'; 'to err belongs to men' स्खलनं मनुष्याणां धर्मः.

Obs.— This sense is often expressed by derivatives; as, पैतृकं रिक्थं ' property belonging to ancestors'; so अस्मदीयं गृहं &c.

§ **104**. The Genitive is used with substantives, and words used substantively, to denote the whole of which a part is taken and it is then called *'partitive genitive'*; as, जलस्य बिंदुः 'a drop of water'; अयुतं शरदां ययौ (R. X. 1) 'ten thousand years passed'; so गवां शतसहस्राणि, "thousands of cows."

So in Latin: 'Mille hominum valentium', 'a thousand of strong men.

(*a*) The Partitive Genitive is also found used with ordinals an. pronouns or adjectives implying a number; as, त्वमेव कल्याणि तयोस्तृतीया (R. VI. 39) 'blessed girl, you alone are their third'; गृह्यतामनयोरन्यतरा (M. 5) 'let one of the two be accepted'; तासामन्यतमा (Mâl. 1) 'one of those (girls).'

Compare Latin '*primi juvenum*,' and '*consulum alter*.'

(*b*) The Partitive Genitive is likewise used with superlatives and words having the force of superlatives; as, द्विजानां ब्राह्मणः श्रेष्ठः; धौरेयः साहसिकानामग्रणीर्विदग्धानां (K. 5) 'the foremost among the bold, and among the clever.

Obs. This use of the Genitive is already considered in § 89.

So in Latin: *Maxime principum*' 'greatest of princes'; '*orat rum praestantissimi*' 'the most eminent of orators.'

(*c*) Sometimes, मध्ये is used with the Genitive in the sense of '*of* or *among*'; as, एतेषां मध्ये केचिदरेः कोषदण्डाभ्यामर्थिनः (Mu. 5) 'of these some are desirous of the treasure and army of the enemy.'

§ **105**. When a certain period is represented to have elapsed after the occurrence of an action, the word expressing the occurrence is put in the Genitive case; as, अद्य दशमो मासस्तातस्योपरतस्य (Mu. 6.) 'it is to-day ten months since the death of my father'; कतिपये संवत्सरास्तस्य तपस्तप्यमानस्य (U. 4) 'several years have elapsed since he began to practise penance.'

§ **106**. Words having the sense of 'dear to' or the reverse, are used with this case; as, प्रकृत्यैव प्रिया सीता रामस्यासीत् (U. 6) 'Sítá was by her very nature dear to Ráma'; कायः कस्य न वल्लभः (P. I.) 'to whom is the body not dear?'

(*a*) This case also occurs in the construction of words signifying 'difference', such as, विशेषः, अंतरं; as एतावानेवायुष्मतः शतक्रतोश्च विशेषः (S'. 7) 'this is the only difference between the long-lived one (you) and Indra'; अत्रभवतो मम च समुद्रपल्वलयोरिवान्तरं (M. 1.) 'there is as much difference between this worthy person and myself as between the sea and a puddle.'

§ **107**. * In the case of potential passive participles, the *agent* of the action is put in the Genitive or Instrumental case; as, नास्ति असाध्यं नाम मनोभुवः (K. 157) 'indeed, there is nothing that cannot be accomplished by the mind-born (Cupid)'; so न वयमनुग्राह्याः प्रायो देवतानां (K. 61.); न वञ्चनीयाः प्रभवोऽनुजीविभिः (Ki. I. 4); राक्षसेन्द्रस्य संरक्ष्यं मया लव्यमिदं वन (Bk. VIII. 129) 'this forest fit to be preserved by the lord of the demons must be cut down by me.'

§ **108**. † With words meaning 'cause', 'sake', 'reason' the Genitive is used; as, अल्पस्य हेतोर्बहु हातुमिच्छन् (R. II. 47) 'wishing to give up (lose) much for the sake of little'; विस्मृतं कस्य हेतोः (Mu. I), for what reason is it forgotten?'

Obs. Patanjali says that the words meaning 'cause', 'reason' such as निमित्त, कारण, हेतु may be used in this sense in *any* case in agreement with pronouns. But this is not universally supported by the usage of classical authors. केन निमित्तेन-कारणेन-हेतुना and कस्मिन्निमित्तात्-कारणात्-हेतोः, are the usual constructions in this sense. We do not say को हेतुः वससि or कं हेतुं वससि in the same sense, nor even कस्मै हेतवे वससि which means 'for what object (purpose) in view do you dwell?' किंनिमित्तं-प्रयोजनं-कारणं-अर्थं is, however, not uncommon. Patanjali's rule must, therefore, be understood in a restricted sense.

§ **109**. ‡ With nouns, derived from roots by *Krit* affixes such as ति, तृ, अ, अन, &c., the Genitive is used in the sense of the *agent* and *object* of the action denoted by the nouns; in other words, the Genitive in Sanskrit is both *subjective* and *objective*; as क्रियामिमां कालिदासस्य (V. 1) 'this composition of Kálidása'; भर्तुः प्रणाशात् (R. XIV. 1) 'on account of death of their lord'; शास्त्राणां परिचयः (K. 18) 'the know-

---

* कृत्यानां कर्तरि वा । (II, 3. 71)

† षष्ठी हेतुप्रयोगे । (II. 3. 26)

‡ कर्तृकर्मणोः कृति । (II. 3. 65)

ledge of S'àstras'; आहर्ता क्रतूनां (K. 5) 'the performer of sacrifices'; दुःखायेदानीं रामस्य सुहृदां दर्शनं (U. 3) 'Ráma's seeing his friends now only contributes to (produce) sorrows'.

Obs. In the case of verbs governing two objects the ***secondary*** object is put in the Genitive or Accusative; as, नेता अश्वस्य स्रुघ्नं स्रुघ्नस्य वा (Mbh.) 'the taker of the horse to Srughna.' This construction, however, is very rare; the Genitive is more generally used with both objects (principal and secondary); गवां दुग्धस्य दोहनं; सागरस्य अमृतस्य मंथनं, where the first genitive has the sense of the ablative.

§ **110.** *When the *agent* and *object* of the action denoted by the nouns formed by *krit* affixes are both used in a sentence, the ***object*** is put in the Genitive case, and not the agent; as, आश्चर्यं गवां दोहोऽगोपेन (S. K.) 'the milking of cows without a cowherd is a wonder.'

(*a*) † When the agent and object are both used, the ***agent*** is put in the Instrumental or Genitive case, when as some say, the ***Krit*** terminations are of the feminine gender, or as others say, when the terminations are of any gender; as, विचित्रा जगतः कृतिर्हरेर्हरिणा वा (S. K.) 'the creation of the world by Hari is wonderful'; शब्दानामनुशासनमाचार्येण आचार्यस्य वा (S. K.); so शोभना खलु पाणिनेः (or पाणिनिना) सूत्रस्य कृतिः (Mbh.).

§ **111.** ‡ The words. आयुष्यं, मद्रं, भद्रं, कुशलं, सुखं, अर्थः, and हितं, govern the Dative or Genitive case, when a blessing is intended; as, कृष्णस्य-कृष्णाय-कुशलं, हितं, भद्रं भूयात् (S. K.) 'may happiness or good luck attend *Krishna*.'

§ **112.** $ Words ending in तस् showing direction, and other words such as उपरि, अधः, पुरः, पश्चात्, अग्रे, पुरस्तात् &c. having the same meaning as those ending in तस्, govern the Genitive of that with

---

* उभयप्राप्तौ कर्मणि । (II. 3. 66)

† शेषे विभाषा । स्त्रीप्रत्यय इत्येके । केचिदविशेषेण विभाषामिच्छन्ति (Vàr.)

‡ चतुर्थी चाशिष्यायुष्यमद्रभद्रकुशलसुखार्थहितैः । (II. 3. 73.)

$ षष्ठ्यतसर्थप्रत्ययेन । (II. 3. 30)

reference to which the direction is shown; as, ग्रामस्य दक्षिणतः–उत्तरतः (S. K.) 'to the south or north of the village'; गतमुपरि घनानां (S'. 7) 'going above the clouds'; तरूणामधः (S'. 1) 'under the trees'; तिष्ठन् भाति पितुः पुरो भुवि यथा (Nâg. 1) 'as one shines standing on the ground before his father; यः पुरस्ताद्यतीनां (M. 1) 'who is foremost among (is at the head of) ascetics.'

Obs. उपरि is often joined in a compound; as, प्रत्यारोपय रथोपरि राजपुत्रं (U. 5); चाणक्योपरि प्रद्वेषपक्षपातः (Mu. 3.).

(*a*) * Words expressive of 'direction' ending in एन such as दक्षिणेन, उत्तरेण &c., govern the Genitive or Accusative of the place with respect to which the direction is shown; as दक्षिणेन तु श्वेतस्य निषधस्योत्तरेण तु (Mb. VI. 3. 2) 'to the south of S'veta and to the north of Nishadha'; दक्षिणेन वृक्षवाटिकां (S'. 1)' to the south of the grove of trees'; धनपतिगृहादुत्तरेण (Me. 78) 'to the north of the house of Kubera.'

(*b*) † Words having the sense of दूर 'distant', and अंतिक 'near' govern either the Genitive or Ablative; as, ग्रामात् ग्रामस्य वा वनं दूरं निकटं समीपं &c. (S. K.) 'the forest is distant from or near the village.'

Obs. The Genitive, however, is more generally used; as, तस्याश्रमपदस्य नातिदूरे (K. 22); अतः समीपे परिणेतुरिष्यते (S'. 5); प्रयामि तस्याः सकाशं (K. 158) &c.

§ 113. ‡ Verbs implying 'to be master of', 'to rule' like ईश, भू with प्र, दय् 'to pity', 'to have compassion on,' and words implying 'remembering' (with regret), 'to think of' like स्मृ, with अधि, govern the object fo these actions in the Genitive case; as, ननु प्रभवत्यार्यः शिष्यजनस्य (M. 1) 'why, your honour has mastery over your pupil'; प्रभवति निजस्य कन्यकाजनस्य महाराजः (Mâl. 4); यदि प्रभविष्यामि आत्मनः (S'. 1); नायं गात्राणामीष्टे (K. 312) 'he cannot rule (control) his limbs';

---

* एनपा द्वितीया । (II. 3. 31)

† दूरान्तिकार्थैः षष्ठ्यन्यतरस्याम् (II. 3. 34)

‡ अधीगर्थदयेशां कर्मणि (II. 3. 52)

रामस्य दयमानोसावध्येति तव लक्ष्मणः (Bk. VIII. 191) 'Lakshmana, taking pity on Râma, remembers (thinks of) you'; स्मर्तुं दिशन्ति न दिवः सुरसुंदरीभ्यः (Ki. V. 28) 'do not persuade the heavenly nymphs to think of heaven'; so अस्मार्षीज्जलनिधिमंथनस्य शौरिः (S'i. VIII. 64.)

So in Latin: '*animus meminit paerteritorum*'; '*o virgo miserceremei.*'

Obs. (*a*) भू with प्र in the sense of 'to be able' is used with the infinitive (see the Lesson) and in the sense of to be 'sufficient for' governs the Dative; see § 67 (*a*).

(*b*) स्मृ in the ordinary sense of 'remembering' is used with the Accusative; as, स्मरसि तान्यहानि स्मरसि गोदावरीं वा. (U. 1). In this case the *object* is intended to be used (यदा कर्म विवक्षितं भवति तदा षष्ठी न भवति Mbh.)

(*c*) Adjectives signifying 'conscious' or 'knowing', 'mindful,' and their opposites, govern the Genitive of the *object*; as, अनभिज्ञो गुणानां यः स भृत्यैर्नानुगम्यते (P. 1, 1.) 'he who is not mindful of merits (does not appreciate merits) is not followed by his servants'; so अनभ्यंतरे आवां मदनगतस्य वृत्तान्तस्य (S'. 3). The Locative also is sometimes used; as यदि त्वमीदृशः कथायामभिज्ञः (U. 4); तत्राप्यभिज्ञो जनः (U. 5).

§ **114**. * Words showing 'so many times' or the numeral adverbs of frequency, such as द्विः, त्रिः, अष्टकृत्वः, शतकृत्वः &c. govern the Genitive of the *time* in the sense of the Locative; as, द्विरह्नो भोजनं (S. K.) 'taking meals twice (in) a day'; शतकृत्वस्तवैकस्याः स्मरत्यह्नो रघूत्तमः (Bk. VIII. 122) 'the best of the Raghus thinks of you alone a hundred times a day.'

§ **115**. † Past participles ending in त are used with the Genitive, when they are used in the sense of the present tense; as, अहमेव मतो महीपतेः (R. VIII. 8) 'I alone am regarded by the king'; विदितं तप्यमानं च तेन मे भुवनत्रयं (R. X. 39) 'I know that the three worlds are

---

* कृत्वोर्थप्रयोगे कालेधिकरणे । (II. 3. 64)

† क्तस्य च वर्तमाने । (II. 3. 67)

being tormented by him'; राज्ञां पूजितः (S. K.) 'is honoured by kings.'

(*a*) But when *past* time is meant to be indicated, the Instrumental alone is used; as, न खलु विदितास्ते चाणक्यहतकेन (Mu. 2) 'were they not discovered by the wretched Chà*n*akya.'

(*b*) When used as *abstract neuter nouns*, past participles are, of course, used with the Genitive; as, मयूरस्य नृत्तं (Mbh.) 'the dancing of a peacock'; कोकिलस्य व्याहृतं, नटस्य भुक्तं, छात्रस्य हसितं (*ibid.*).

§ **116**. कृते 'for,' 'for the sake of' and समक्षं 'in the presence of' govern the Genitive; as, अमीषां प्राणानां कृते (Bh. III. 36.) 'for this life'; राज्ञः समक्षमेव (M. 1.) 'in the presence of the king himself.'

Obs. कृते is often compounded with another word; as, काव्यमर्थकृते (Kàv. 1.).

§ **117**. ‡ Words having the sense of 'equal to', 'like', such as तुल्य, सदृश, सम, संकाश &c. govern the Genitive or Instrumental of that with which any object is compared; as कृष्णस्य तुल्यः-सदृशः &c. (S. K.). For the Instrumental see § 52 (*b*).

Obs. Pà*n*ini says that the words तुला and उपमा cannot be used with the Instrumental. But this is against good usage; as, तुलां यदारोहति दंतवाससा (Ku. V. 34); नभसा तुलां समारुरोह (R. VIII. 15); स्फुटोपमं भूतिसितेन शंभुना (S'i. I. 4.). Mallinàtha tries to reconcile these instances with Pà*n*ini's Sùtra; but the defence is eveidently lame.

(*a*) Adjectives implying 'worthy of', 'proper', 'befitting', are usually construed with the Genitive; as, सखे पुंडरीक नैतदनुरूपं भवतः (K. 146) 'friend, Pu*n*darikà, this is not worthy of you'; सदृशमेवैतत्स्नेहस्यानवलेपस्य (Ś. 6) 'this, indeed, befits the prideless love.' See also § 96 (*a*).

§ **118**. Nouns ending in तृ are used with the Accusative instead of the Genitive, when 'habit' or 'disposition' is intended to be expressed; as, पितरमाराधयिता भव (V. 5) 'always keep thy father pleased'; संभावयिता बुधान् न्यग्भावयिता शत्रून् (D. K. II. 8) 'whose habitual disposi-

‡ तुल्यार्थैरतुलोपमाभ्यां तृतीयाऽन्यतरस्याम् । (II. 3. 72.)

tion is to respect the wise and to humble his foes'; but जगतो निर्माता, घटस्य कर्ता &c.

(*a*) कृ with अनु 'to imitate', 'resemble', is often found used with the Genitive or Accusative of the *object*; as, ततोऽनुकुर्यात्तस्याः स्मितस्य (Ku. I. 44) 'then it might imitate (resemble) her smile'; श्यामतया भगवतो हरेरिवानुकुर्वतीं (K. 10) 'as if resembling the god Hari in point of sableness'; सर्वाभिरन्याभिः कलाभिरनुचकार तं वैशंपायनः (K. 76) 'V. imitated him in all other arts'; so शैलाधिपस्यानुचकार लक्ष्मीं (Bk. II. 8.)

§ **119**. *The roots व्यवहृ and पण् (I A.) in the sense of 'dealing in transactions', 'staking in gambling', govern the Genitive of the object; as, शतस्य व्यवहरणं-पणनं (S. K.) 'dealing in hundred' or 'staking hundred'; so प्राणानामपणिष्टासौ (Bk. VIII. 121). But the Accusative is more generally used; as, पणस्व कृष्णां पांचालीं (Mb. II, 65. 32).

(*a*) दिव्, when it has the same sense, is similarly used; as, शतस्य दीव्यति (S. K.); (but when it is preceded by a preposition, the Accusative or Genitive may be used; as, शतस्य शतं वा प्रतिदीव्यति (S. K.)

तस्याः पंडितकौशिक्या सहितायाः समक्षमेव न्याय्यो व्यवहारः । (M. 1).

श्वापदानुसरणैर्मम गात्राणामनीशोस्मि संवृत्तः । (S. 2)

कथं मामेकाकिनीं त्यक्त्वार्यपुत्रो गतः । भवतु कोपिष्यामि यदि तं प्रेक्षमाणात्मनः प्रभविष्यामि । (U. 7)

अयि भागीरथीप्रसादाद्वनदेवतानामप्यदृश्यासि संवृत्ता । (U. 6)

---

* व्यवहृपणोः समर्थयोः । दिवस्तदर्थस्य । विभाषोपसर्गे (II. 3. 57-9).

हा देवि स्मरसि वा तस्य प्रदेशस्य तत्समयविश्रंभातिशयप्रसंगसाक्षिणः ।

एवमवस्थिते यदत्रावसरप्राप्तमीदृशस्य चानुरागस्य सदृशमस्मदागमनस्य चानुरूपमात्मनो वा समुचितं तत्र प्रभवति देवीत्यभिधाय मन्मुखासक्तदृष्टिः कपिञ्जलस्तूष्णीमासीत् । (K. 158)

धिङ् मां दुष्कृतकारिणीं यस्याः कृते तवेयमीदृशी दशा वर्तते ॥
(K. 167)

हा दयित माधव परलोकगतोपि स्मर्तव्यो युष्माभिरयं जनः । न खलु स उपरतो यस्य वल्लभो जनः स्मरति । (Mal. 5)

कापि महती वेला वर्तते तवादृष्टस्य । तदनया सहैवागच्छ ।
(K. 246)

अहं हि संमतो राज्ञो य एवं मन्यते कुधीः ।
बलीवर्दः स विज्ञेयो विषाणपरिवर्जितः । (P. I.10)

शरीरस्य गुणानां च दूरमत्यन्तमन्तरम् ।
शरीरं क्षणविध्वंसि कल्पान्तस्थायिनो गुणाः । (H. I)

अर्थानामीशिषे त्वं वयमपि च गिरामीश्महे यावदर्थम् ।
(Bh. III. 30.)

समरशिरसि चञ्चत्पञ्चचूडश्चमूना-
मुपरि शरतुषारं कोप्ययं वीरपोतः (किरति) ।

ADDITIONAL SENTENCES FOR EXERCISE.

स राजा मनसि धर्मेण कोपे यमेन प्रतापे वह्निना सुखे शशिना प्रज्ञायां सुरगुरुणा तेजसि सवित्रा च वसता सर्वदेवमयस्य प्रकटितविश्वरूपाकृतेरनुकरोति भगवतो नारायणस्य । (K. 6)

नियतमिह सर्वात्मना कृतावस्थितिना भगवता परिभूतकलिकालविलसितेन धर्मेण न स्मर्यते कृतयुगस्य । (K. 44)

उदेति पूर्वं कुसुमं ततः फलं घनोदयः प्राक् तदनन्तरं पयः ।
निमित्तनैमित्तिकयोरयं क्रमस्तव प्रसादस्य पुरस्तु संपदः ॥ (S'. 7)

शंबूको नाम वृषलः पृथिव्यां तप्यते तपः ।
शीर्षच्छेद्यः स ते राम तं हत्वा जीवय द्विजम् ॥ (U. 2.)
अपीप्सितं क्षत्रकुलांगनानां
न वीरसूशब्दमकामयेताम् (R. XIV. 4)
वाच्यस्त्वया मद्वचनात्स राजा वह्नौ विशुद्धामपि यत्समक्षम् ।
मां लोकवादश्रवणादहासीः श्रुतस्य किं तत्सदृशं कुलस्य । (R. XIV. 61)
देव्या शून्यस्य जगतो द्वादशः परिवत्सरः ।
प्रनष्टमिव नामापि न च रामो न जीवति ॥ (U. 3.)
अयं मैथिल्यभिज्ञानं काकुत्स्थस्यांगुलीयकः ।
भवत्याः स्मरतात्यर्थमर्पितः सादरं मम ॥ (Bk. VIII. 118)
पुरः प्रवेशमाश्चर्यं बुद्ध्वा शाखामृगेण सा ।
चूडामणिमभिज्ञानं ददौ रामस्य संमतम् ॥
रामस्य शयितं भुक्तं जल्पितं हसितं स्थितम् ।
प्रक्रान्तं च मुहुः पृष्ट्वा हनूमन्तं व्यसर्जयत् ॥ (*ibid.* 124-5)
तं दृष्ट्वाऽचिन्तयत्सीता हेतोः कस्यैष रावणः ।
अवरुह्य तरोरारादेति वानरविग्रहः ॥
उत्तराहि वसन् रामः समुद्राद्रक्षसां पुरम् ।
अवैल्लवणतोयस्य स्थितां दक्षिणतः कथम् ॥ (*ibid.* 104, 107)

The women looking intently at the young man could, with great difficulty, control (ईश्) themselves.

What difference is there between men and beasts if the former imitate (कृ with अनु) the latter in their actions ?

Friend, do not despair; she, for (कृते) whom you are so much afflicted, will herself soon come to you.

There is no pleasure equal to (तुल्य) that enjoyed by those who, devolving their house-hold duties upon their sons, reside in forests.

Is this your act suitable to the dignity of the high family in which you are born?

The order of my elders will only have power (भू with प्र) over my body, but not over my mind and its workings.

The child being long kept away (दूर) from its mother, remembers (स्मृ) her often and often.

To the north (उत्तरत:) of this mountain is an extensive plain, covered all over with verdant grass, which almost enchants the beholder's eye.

The story, which the attendant narrated to the king in the presence of (समक्षं) all his ministers, went home to his heart.

Here I see before (पुर:) me a large heap of bones; there a number of bits of flesh under (अध:) the trees. What may it be?

In the reign of Sushena every one out of his subjects thought that he was respected (पूज्) and liked (मन्) by the king.

Be thou worthy of thy father by reason of thy qualities liked by the people!

A long time has elapsed since the venerable lady went to see Málaviká.

This king is fit to be waited upon (सेव्य) by servants; and the epithet 'protector of men' quite becomes him.

There is nothing in this world like (सदृश) friendship with the good.

Good books are dearer to clever students than fine clothes.

A devout Bráhmana should perform his Sandhyá adoration thrice a day, and eat only once in a day before sunset.

Ráma was dearer to Sitá than her very life.

LESSON XI.

The Genitive and Locative Absolutes.

§ **120**. 'When the participle agrees with a subject, different from the subject of the verb, the phrase is said to be in the absolute construction.' (Bain). The phrase is unconnected with the general structure of the clause in which it stands; as, 'the wind being favourable, the ship set sail.' The Absolute case differs in different language; in English, it is the nominative; in Latin, the ablative; and in Sanskrit, the genitive and locative. If it be found that the nominative of the subordinate sentence be not a noun occurring in the principal sentence, or a pronoun representing such a noun, the absolute construction may be used. Take the sentence: Ráma, after he had taken Lanká, returned to Ayodhyá.' Here the subjects of both the sentences are the same, and no absolute contruction can be used. The sentence may be translated by लंकां गृहीत्वा (or गृहीतलंकः) रामोऽयोध्यां निवदृते. But the sentence 'Ráma, after the monkeys had taken Lanká, returned to Ayodhyá, may be translated by कपिभिर्गृहीतायां लंकायां (or कपिषु लंकां गृहीतवत्सु) रामोऽयोध्यां निवदृते.

Note.—To form these absolutes, the subject of the participle must be put in the Genitive or Locative case, and the participle made to agree with it in *gender* and *number*.

§ **121**. *A noun or pronoun which expresses a thing, the action done or suffered by which indicates the *time* of another action is put in the Locative case, *i. e.* the time of the first action is supposed to be known, and that of the second which is unknown, is determined with reference to it; as, कः पौरवे वसुमतीं शासति अविनयमाचरति (S'. 6) 'who, while Paurava is ruling the Earth, acts immodestly ?'; वचस्यवसिते तस्मिन् ससर्ज गिरमात्मभूः (Ku. II. 53) 'that speech being finished, the Self-existent (Brahmà) uttered the words'. क एष मयि स्थिते चन्द्रगुप्तमभिभवितुमिच्छति (Mu. 1) 'who, while I am still living, wishes to overcome Chandragupta ?'.

Obs. The Locative absolute in Sanskrit is used in the sense of the nominative absolute in English.

§ **122**. When 'contempt' or 'disregard' is to be shown, the Genitive absolute is used; as, नन्दाः पशव इव हताः पश्यतो राक्षसस्य (Mu.3) 'the Nandas were killed like (so many) beasts, Rákshasa looking on (notwithstanding that Rákshasa was looking on). Thus, where clauses or sentences introduced by 'notwithstanding,' 'in spite of'

*यस्य च भावेन भावलक्षणम् । (II. 3. 37)

'for all' &c. occur in English, the Genitive absolute may be used; as 'in spite of (for all) my looking on, the child was snatched away by a hawk' पश्यतोपि मे श्येनेनापहृतः शिशुः (P. 1. 21).

§ **123**. The Genitive, like the Locative absolute, is frequently used to express the sense of the English particles '*when*', '*while*', &c., it not conveying its usual meaning; as, एवं तयोः परस्परं वदतोः स राजा शयनमासाद्य प्रसुप्तः (P. 1. 9) 'while they two were thus speaking, the king coming to his bed slept down'.

Obs. When the participle of an absolute construction is '*being*', it is omitted in Sanskrit, and two substantives or a substantive and adjective, are put together in the absolute case; as, नाथे कुतस्त्वय्यशुभं प्रजानां (R. V. 13) 'you (being) the lord, how can any mishap befall the subjects ?'

So in Latin: *M. Tullio Cicerone et Antonio consulibus.*

§ **124**. Sometimes both the Genitive and Locative absolutes are used to show 'disregard', 'in spite of' &c.; as, रुदति पुत्रे रुदतो वा पुत्रस्य पिता प्राव्राजीत् (S. K.) 'the father turned out a recluse, in spite of his son's weeping.'

(*a*) The sense of '*as soon as*', '*no sooner—than*', '*scarcely—when*', '*the moment that*' &c. is expressed by the Locative absolute, with the word एव used with the locative, or मात्र joined to the participle, and the compound word is put in the locative, with or without एव; as, अनवसितवचन एव मयि महानाशीविष उदैरयच्छिरः (D. K. II. 4) 'the moment I had finished my speech (scarcely had I finished etc. when) a large serpent lifted up its hood'; अप्रभातायामेव रजन्यां (Mu. 1) 'when it had scarcely dawned (scarcely had the night dawned)'; प्रविष्टमात्र एव तत्रभवति निरुपप्लवानि नः कर्माणि संवृत्तानि (S. 3) 'no sooner had his honour stepped in, than our actions were left without any obstruction.'

Note. मात्र with or without एव, joined to other cases gives the same meaning; as, जातमात्रं न यः शत्रुं व्याधिं च प्रशमं नयेत् (P. III. 1) 'he who does not quell an enemy and a disease as soon as that is born (arises).'

(*b*) Sometimes the word agreeing with the participle is an indeclinable, such as, एवं, इत्थं, तथा, इति, &c.; as, एवं गते (S'. 4) 'such being the case'; तथानुष्ठिते (H.) 'it being so done' &c.

§ **125**. The *subject* or *object* of an absolute construction is not repeated in the principal sentence, in any case except the Genitive, either in its own form, or when it is represented by a demonstrative pronoun. When instances occur in which the subject or object, or the pronoun representing it, is to be used in the principal sentence, the absolute construction should not be used; the whole should be treated as one sentence, and translated by the use of participles; *e. g.*, instead of saying गोषु दुह्यमानासु ता जलमपाययत्, we should say दुह्यमाना गा जलमपाययत्; similarly, आगतेषु विप्रेषु तेभ्यो दक्षिणां देहि is not so idiomatic as आगतेभ्यो विप्रेभ्य &c., or आपणात्पात्रे समानीते तस्मिन्नन्नं पचामि, as आपणात् समानीते पात्रेऽन्नं पचामि. So also सारंगे एवं विचारयति स (सारंगः) व्याधेन हतः is not so idiomatic as एवं विचारयन् सारंगो व्याधेन हतः; and ताडयतोऽपि स्वामिनस्तस्मै भृत्या न कुप्यन्ति is not so idiomatic as ताडयतेऽपि स्वामिने भृत्या न कुप्यन्ति। But मदने हरेण दग्धे तस्य पत्नी विवशा बभूव, or मृतेऽस्मिन् राज्ञि तस्य पुत्रो राज्यमधिगमिष्यति is perfectly idiomatic.*

---

* This is a point on which grammarians are silent; still I think it may be said to be definitely settled (1) by the very definition of an absolute construction, (2) the overwhelming evidence furnished by the best Sanskrit writers, and (3) the analogy of the classical languages, *e. g.*, Latin. The definition distinctly implies that the subject of the absolute phrase must not be a noun occurring in the principal sentence, and hence it cannot be repeated in any case. Secondly, in the several instances of absolute constructions that we find in Sanskrit authors, we find very few, or hardly any, cases in which the subject or object is repeated in the principal assertion in any case except the Genitive. And just as we should not say महानदी in the sense of 'hav-

अलमलमुपालम्भेन। पत्तने विद्यमानेऽपि ग्रामे रत्नपरीक्षा। (M. 1.)

इदमवस्थान्तरं गते तादृशेऽनुरागे किं वा स्मारितेन। (Ś. 5)

मा तावदनात्मज्ञे। देवेन प्रतिषिद्धे वसन्तोत्सवे त्वमाम्रकलिकाभङ्गं किमारभसे। (Ś. 6)

अभिव्यक्तायां चन्द्रिकायां किं दीपिकापौनरुक्त्येन। (V. 3)

आर्ये आत्रेयि अथ तस्मादरण्यात्परित्यज्य गते लक्ष्मणे सीतादेव्याः किं वृत्तमित्यस्ति काचित्प्रवृत्तिः। (U. 2)

हा कष्टमरुन्धतीवसिष्ठाधिष्ठितेषु रघुकदंबकेषु जीवन्तीषु च प्रवृद्धासु राज्ञीषु कथमिदमापतितम्। (U. 2)

---

ing much strength', but merely **महाबलः** the same meaning being more compactly expressed by this word; so also constructions like **दुह्यमाना गा जलमपाययत्** are more *compact* than **गोषु दुह्यमानासु** &c. and have, therefore, become more *idiomatic.* Thirdly, the nature of an absolute case in Latin is precisely the same. "When a substantive or pronoun together with a participle or an adjective, form a clause by themselves and are not under the Government of, or in agreement with, any other words, they are put in ablative absolute"; as 'Pythagoras *Tarquinio Superbo regnate* in Italiam venit.' Thus though Sanskrit grammarians are silent on this point the three circumstances above alluded to lead to the conclusion that what is more *compact* and idiomatic is more *correct* than that which grammarians by their silence do not condemn. A friend from the South draws my attention to a work called "Náyaníyam"—an abridgment of Śrî-Bhágavata Puráṇa—in which the writer does not invariably observe the rule given above. My friend quotes two or three instances in support of his statement. I, for my part, should consider such instances inaccurate and unidiomatic, if not positively incorrect, constructions, rather than modify the rule, by relying on insufficient evidence.

अत्रान्तरे शक्तिखंडामर्षितेन गांडीविनैवं भणितम् । अरे दुर्योधनप्रमुखाः कुरुबलसेनाप्रभवः अरे अविनयनदीकर्णधार कर्ण युष्माभिर्मम परोक्ष एकाकी पुत्रकोऽभिमन्युर्व्यापादितः । अहं पुनर्युष्माकं प्रेक्षमाणानामेनं कुमारवृषसेनं स्मर्तव्यशेषं नयामि । (Ve. 4.)

कुतो धर्मक्रियाविघ्नः सतां रक्षितरि त्वयि ।
तमस्तपति धर्मांशौ कथमाविर्भविष्यति ॥ (Ś. 5)

मनोरथस्य यद्बीजं तद्दैवेनादितो हतम् ।
लतायां पूर्वलूनायां प्रसूनस्यागमः कुतः ॥ (U. 5)

सा सीतामङ्कमारोप्य भर्तृप्रणिहितेक्षणाम् ।
मामेति व्याहरत्येव तस्मिन्पातालमभ्यगात् ॥ (R. XV. 84)

ADDITIONAL SENTENCES FOR EXERCISE.

राजा देवीमुखेन दुहितरमुवाच । पुत्रि त्वयि दुहितरि स्थितायां किमेवं युज्यते यत्सर्वे पार्थिवा मया सह विग्रहं कुर्वन्ति । (P. I. 5)

अथ कदाचिदवसन्नायां रात्रावस्ताचलचूडावलम्बिनि भगवति कुमुदिनीनायके चन्द्रमसि लघुपतनको नाम वायसो व्याधमपश्यत् । (H. 1.)

विकारहेतौ सति विक्रियन्ते
येषां न चेतांसि त एव धीराः । (Ku. I. 59.)

अनपायिनि संश्रयद्रुमे गजभग्ने पतनाय वल्लरी । (Ku. IV. 31.)

यस्मिन्जीवति जीवन्ति बहवः सोऽत्र जीवति ।
वयांसि किं न कुर्वन्ति चञ्च्वा स्वोदरपूरणम् । (P. I. 1.)

दर्शितभयेऽपि धातरि धैर्यध्वंसो भवेन्न धीराणाम् ।
शोषितसरसि निदाघे नितरामेवोद्धतः सिंधुः ॥ (P. I. 11.)

गुणवत्तरपात्रेण छाद्यन्ते गुणिनां गुणाः ।
रात्रौ दीपशिखाकान्तिर्न भानावुदिते सति ॥ (P. I. 16.)

संतानवाहीन्यपि मानुषाणां दुःखानि सद्बन्धुवियोगजानि ।
दृष्टे जने प्रेयसि दुःसहानि स्रोतः सहस्रैरिव संप्लवन्ते ॥ (U. 4)
पञ्चभिर्निर्मिते देहे पञ्चत्वं च पुनर्गते ।
स्वां स्वां योनिमनुप्राप्ते तत्र का परिदेवना ॥ (H. 4)
सर्वत्र नो वार्तमवेहि राजन्नाथे कुतस्त्वय्यशुभं प्रजानाम् ।
सूर्ये तपत्यावरणाय दृष्टेः कल्पेत लोकस्य कथं तमिस्रा ॥ (R. V. 13)
तस्मिन् ह्रदः संहितमात्र एव क्षोभात्समाविद्धतरंगहस्तः ।
रोधांसि निघ्नन्नवपातमग्नः करीव वन्यः परुषं ररास ॥ (R. XVI. 78)
जीवत्सु तातपादेषु नवे दारपरिग्रहे ।
मातृभिश्चिन्त्यमानानां ते हि नो दिवसा गताः ॥ (U. 1)
त्वय्युत्कृष्टबलेऽभियोक्तरि नृपे नन्दानुरक्ते पुरे
चाणक्ये चलिताधिकारविमुखे मौर्ये नवे राजनि ।
स्वाधीने मयि मार्गमात्रकथनव्यापारयोगोद्यमे
त्वद्वाञ्छान्तरितानि संप्रति विभो तिष्ठन्ति साध्यानि वः ॥ (Mu. 4)
अस्त्रज्वालावलीढप्रतिबलजलधेरन्तरौर्वायमाणे
सेनानाथे स्थितेऽस्मिन्मम पितरि गुरौ सर्वधन्वीश्वराणाम् ।
कर्णालं संभ्रमेण व्रज कृप समरं मुञ्च हार्दिक्य शङ्कां
ताते चापद्वितीये वहति रणधुरां को भयस्यावकाशः ॥ (Ve. 3)

N. B.—The following sentences should be translated by using the absolute construction only.

Men commit misdeeds, though gods see them.

The tree of self-respect being cut down by the wild elephant of poverty, all the birds of merits fly away.

When calamities are closely impending, even friends become enemies.

The moment the picture is finished by the painter, come to call me.

Scarcely had the sage uttered these words, when the lovely nymph was transformed in a moment into a stone.

The cause of danger being so distant, why do you, under colour of illness, say that you will be unable to accompany us ?

When this sad news reached their ears, they were excessively distressed.

I do not know what became of the boy after he had been ruthlessly abandoned by his mother.

His mind being engrossed by these and the like perplexing thoughts, he passed a sleepless night.

No sooner was an arrow discharged at the object than he heard a plaintive cry in that direction.

Damayanti wishes to have Nala for her husband, though there are the resplendent guardians of the worlds.

Fie upon ye, ye base vaunters ! Who is able to cross even the shadow of my brother, while we, hundred brothers, are yet alive ?

The mass of darkness being dispelled by the rising moon, the eastern direction attracts my eyes.

Notwithstanding my entreaties for the prisoner's life, the king ordered him to be executed.

Since death is certain, why do you sully your fame by having recourse to retreat ?

PART III.

THE USE AND MEANING OF GRAMMATICAL FORMS AND WORDS.

LESSON XII.

Pronouns.

Personal Pronouns.

§ **126**. The use of the personal pronouns is not peculiar. They are subject to the same rules as nouns, when under the government of verbs or prepositions; as, अहं त्वां प्रार्थये 'I pray to thee'; त्वया विना सोऽपि समुत्सुको भवेत् (V. 1.).

§ **127**. *But the short forms of अस्मद् and त्वद्, *i. e.* मा, मे, नौ, नः, त्वा, ते, वां, and वः deserve notice. They are never used at the beginning of a sentence and immediately before the particles च, वा, एव and हा (rarely अह or ह), and at the beginning of a foot of metre; as, मे मित्रं; नः पाहि वां सख्यं &c. are wrong; तस्य च मम (not मे) च वैरमस्ति 'there is enmity betwixt him and me'; तस्य मम वा गृहम् (not मे वा); 'इदं पुस्तकं ममैव' (not मे एव); हा मम मंदभाग्यं (not मे); वेदैरशेषैः संवेद्योऽस्मान् (not नः); कृष्णः सर्वदाऽवतु (S. K.) 'may K*r*ish*n*a, fit to be known by all the Vedas, always protect us!'

(*a*) When the particles do not connect these forms, the short forms may be used with them; as, हरो हरिश्च मे स्वामी (S. K.) 'Hara and Hari are my lords'; किं वा मे पुत्री करोतु 'what, indeed, will my daughter do?'

---

* न चवाहाहैवयुक्ते । (VIII. 1. 24); पदात् ।-अपदादौ । युष्मदस्मदोः षष्ठीचतुर्थीद्वितीयास्थयोर्वांनावौ । (VIII. I, 17, 18, 20).

(*b*) Similarly these short forms are not used immediately after Vocative forms; as, वयस्य मम गृहमेतत् (not मे); देवास्मान् (not नः) पाहि सर्वदा (S. K.) 'O God, always protect us.' The Vocative is, in fact, an abridged sentence.

(*c*) If a qualifying adjective follows the Vocative forms the short forms may be used; as, हरे दयालो नः पाहि (S. K.) 'Oh, kind Hari, protect us.'

§ **128**. भवत् is often used with reference to the person addressed, as a courteous form of expression, not necessarily implying respect; it is to be regarded as a pronoun of the third person, and the verb must agree with the third person; as, अथवा कथं भवान्मन्यते (M. 1) 'or how do you think ?'; वयमपि भवत्यौ किमपि पृच्छामः 'I, too, ask you something.'

§ **129**. When respect is to be shown, भवत् (भवती *f.*) is preceded by अत्र and तत्र or स,* the former referring to a person that is near, the latter to one who is at a distance, or absent, from the speaker; as, क्व तत्रभवती कामन्दकी 'where is the worshipful Kamandaki ?' आदिष्टोस्मि तत्रभवता काश्यपेन (S'. 4) 'I am ordered by the worthy Kás'yapa'; अपेहि रे अत्रभवान्प्रकृतिमापन्नः (S'. 2) 'begone, this worthy person is himself again'; मां सभवान् नियुंक्ते (Mál. 1) 'His honour appoints me.'

Demonstrative Pronouns.

§ **130**. There are three demonstrative pronouns; इदम् or एतद् 'this', तद् 'that', and अदस् 'this', or 'that'; they are used along with the nouns they refer to, or are used without them; as, एष नृपः; स पुरुषः; तद्गृहं; स आह; एष मे किंकरः; इदं नो गृहं; असौ विद्याधरः.

§ **131**. The forms of इदम् and एतद् are sometimes used in the sense of '*here*' in sentences like '*here* I come'; '*there* comes the boy', usually in conjunction with the 1st or 3rd persons, and agreeing with the subject of the sentence like an ordinary adjective; as, आर्यपुत्र इयमस्मि (S'. 1) 'lord, here am I;' इयमहमारोहामि (U. 1.) 'here I mount;' अयमागच्छामि (S'. 3) 'here I come' ; so इयं सा जातिः परित्यक्ता (Ve. 3).

* This is an inaccuracy. स is not prefixed to भवत् like अत्र or तत्र; we do not find such forms as सभवता &c. in use. In the instance cited it must be read separately.

§ **132**. तद् is often used in the sense of *celebrated* or *well-known*; as, सा रम्या नगरी (Bh. III. 37) 'that celebrated charming city'; सामंतचक्रं च तत् (*ibid.*) 'and that well-known circle of tributary princes.'

Compare the use of *ille* in Latin.

(*a*) तद् is often used in the sense of '*very*', '*same*', with एव generally expressed or implied from the context; as, तानीन्द्रियाणि सकलानि (Bh. II. 40) 'all the organs are the same'; तदेव नाम (*ibid.*) 'the name is the same'; एते त एव गिरयः (U. 3) 'these are those very mountains'; तदेव पंचवटीवनं (U. 3) 'the forest of Panchavatî is the same.'

(*b*) When तद् is repeated, it has the sense of '*several*,' '*various*;' as, तेषु तेषु स्थानेषु (K. 369) 'in various places.'

Relative Pronouns.

§ **133**. When the relative pronoun is repeated, it has the sense of '*totality*', '*whatever*', and the correlative pronoun is generally repeated; as, क्रियते यद्यदेषा कथयति (U. 1) 'I shall do all that she says'; यो यः शस्त्रं बिभर्ति......क्रोधान्धस्तस्य तस्य स्वयमिह जगतामन्तकस्यान्तकोऽहं (Ve. 3) 'whoever bears a weapon, of him, even the destroyer of the worlds, I become the destroyer'; so यं यं पश्यसि तस्य तस्य पुरतो मा ब्रूहि दीनं वचः। (Bh. II. 51).

(*a*) Sometimes the idea of '*whatever*' or '*any whatever*', is expressed by joining the relative with the interrogative pronoun, with or without the particles अपि, चित्, or चन; as, एतादृशी रूपवती कन्या यस्मै कस्मैचिन्न दातव्या 'a girl, so beautiful as this, should not be given to any person whatsoever'; यो वा को वा भवाम्यहं (Ve. 3) 'whoever I may be'; यत्रकुत्रापि स्वपिति 'he sleeps anywhere'.

Interrogative, Indefinite and Reflexive Pronouns.

§ **134**. Interrogative pronouns and their derivatives are used in asking questions; as, कः पुनरसौ जामाता (U. 1) 'but who is this son-in-law'; कतमेन दिग्भागेन गतः स जाल्मः (V. I) 'in what direction is the rogue gone?' किं करोमि क्व गच्छामि (U. 1.) 'what shall I do? where shall I go?'

§ 135. चित्, चन, अपि and sometimes स्विद् are added to interrogative pronouns and adverbs to give them the sense of indefinite pronouns; as, कश्चिद्यक्षो वसतिं चक्रे (Me. 1) 'a certain Yaksha made his abode;' कदाचित्-चन-अपि 'at some time'; कास्विदवगुण्ठनवती नारी (S'. 5) 'some veiled lady.'

(*a*) अपि sometimes has the sense of "indescribable" (अनिर्वाच्य); as, कोपि हेतुः (U. 6) 'some indescribable motive'; so तत्तस्य किमपि द्रव्यं यो हि यस्य प्रियो जनः (U. 2.)

(*b*) क्वचित्-क्वचित्, कदाचित्-कदाचित्, are used in the sense of *in some place—in another place* (here—there) and *at one time—at another time*, (*sometimes—sometimes, now—now*); as, क्वचिद्वीणावाद्यं क्वचिदपि च हा हेति रुदितं (Bh. III. 12) 'in one place is the playing on the lute; in another the cry of 'alas' (here you hear the flute—there you hear the cries of 'alas')'; कदाचित्काननं जगाहे कदाचित् कमलवनेषु रेमे (K. 58). 'sometimes (now) he plunged into a forest, and sometimes (now) he sported in lotus-forests.'

(*c*) क्वचित्—क्वचित् has rarely a reference to *time* also; as, क्वचिद् घनानां पततां क्वचिच्च (R. XIII. 19) 'now of clouds, now of birds.'

§ 136. The pronoun अन्य—अन्य or पर—पर is used in the sense of—*one—another*; as, अन्यः करोति अन्यो भुंक्ते 'one does, another suffers'; मनस्यन्यद्वचस्यन्यत्कार्यमन्यद्दुरात्मनां (P. I.) 'wicked people have one thing in mind, another in speech, and another in action.'

§ 137. More generally एक—अपर or अन्य is used in the sense of *the one—the other* with reference to two objects that are before specified; as, एको ययौ चैत्ररथप्रदेशान् सौराज्यरम्यानपरो विदर्भान् (R. V. 60) 'the one went to the regions of Chaitraratha, the other to the country of the Vidarbhas (which was) happy on account of a good king.'

§ 138. When एक—अपर or अन्य is used in the plural, it has the sense of *some—others*; as, विधवानां पुनरुद्वाहः शास्त्रप्रतिषिद्ध इत्येके मन्यन्ते शास्त्रविहित

इत्यपरे (or **अन्ये**) 'some think that widow-marriage is prohibited by the Śástras, others that it is ordained by them.'

(*a*) In this sense **केचित्** sometimes takes the place of **एके**; as, **मदुक्तं केचिदन्वमन्यन्त । अपरे पुनर्निनिन्दुः** (D. K. II. 4.) 'some approved of my speech, others, however, censured (it).'

§ **139**. **स्व, स्वकीय, आत्मीय** and **निज** are used reflexively; as, **स्वं नाम कथय** 'tell your own name'; **निजं धैर्यमदर्शयत्** 'he showed his (own) courage.'

(*a*) **स्वयं** meaning '*of one's self*' is a reflexive adverb; as, **सा स्वयमेव तत्र जगाम** 'she herself went there.'

§ **140**. The word more commonly used as a reflexive pronoun is **आत्मन्** (=self). It is always used in the masculine gender and singular number, though the noun to which it refers be in any gender or number; as, **का स्त्री अनेन प्रार्थ्यमानमात्मानं विकत्थते** (V. 2) 'what woman boasts of herself being sought after by him?'; **आत्मानं बहुमन्यामहे वयं** (Ku. VI. 20) 'we think highly of ourselves'; so **गुप्तं ददृशुरात्मानं सर्वाः स्वप्नेषु वामनः** । (R. X. 60).

तस्य च मम च पौरधूर्तैर्वैरमुदपाद्यत । (D. K. II. 2)

न नः कुतूहलमस्ति सर्पदर्शने । (Mu. 2)

श्रीशस्त्वाऽवतु मापीह दत्ता ते मेऽपि शर्म सः ।
स्वामी मे तेऽपि स हरिः पातु वामपि नौ विभु ॥
सुखं वां नौ ददात्वीशः पतिर्वामपि नौ हरिः ।
सोऽव्याद्वो नः शिवं वो नो दद्यात्सेव्योऽत्र वः स नः ॥

एवमत्रभवन्तो विदांकुर्वन्तु अस्ति तत्रभवान् काश्यपः श्रीकण्ठपदलाञ्छनो भवभूतिर्नाम जातुकर्णीपुत्रः । (U. 1)

एषोस्मि कार्यवशादायोध्यिकस्तदानींतनश्च संवृत्तः । (U. 1)

तदेव पंचवटीवनम् । सैव प्रियसखीवासन्ती । त एव जातनिर्विशेषाः पादपाः । मम पुनर्मन्दभाग्यायाः सर्वमेवैतद् दृश्यमानमपि नास्ति । (U. 3)

आयुष्मन्नेष वाग्विषयीभूतः स वीरः । (U. 5)

राजा—आर्य बहु प्रष्टव्यमत्र । चा०—वृषल विश्रब्ध ब्रूहि । ममापि बह्वाख्येयमत्र । रा०—एष पृच्छामि । चा०—अहमप्येष कथयामि ।
(Mu. 3)

अमुना व्यतिकरेण कृतापराधमिव त्वय्यात्मानमवगच्छति कादम्बरी ।
(K. 203)

केचित् संपद्भिः प्रलोभ्यमाना रागावेशेन बाध्यमाना विह्वलतामुपयान्ति । अपरे तु धूर्तैः प्रतार्यमाणाः सर्वजनस्योपहास्यतामुपयान्ति ।
(K. 108)

साहसकारिण्यस्ताः कुमार्यो याः स्वयं संदिशन्ति समुपसर्पन्ति वा ।
(K. 237)

अनयत्प्रभुशक्तिसंपदा वशमेको नृपतीनन्तरान् ।
अपरः प्रणिधानयोग्य या मरुतः पंच शरीरगोचरान् ॥ (R. VIII. 19)

कामैस्तैस्तैर्हृतज्ञानाः प्रपद्यन्तेऽन्यदेवताः ।
तं तं नियममास्थाय प्रकृत्या नियताः स्वया । (Bg. VII. 20)

ADDITIONAL SENTENCES FOR EXERCISE.

अयमसौ मम ज्यायानार्यः कुशो नाम भरताश्रमात्प्रतिनिवृत्तः । (U. 6.)

लक्ष्म्योन्मादिता व्यसनशतशरव्यतामुपगता वल्मीकतृणाग्रावस्थिता जलबिन्दव इव पतितमप्यात्मानं नावगच्छन्ति । (K. 107.)

तस्य तरुषंडस्य मध्ये मणिदर्पणमिव त्रैलोक्यलक्ष्म्याः क्वचित् त्र्यंबकवृषभविषाणकोटिखण्डिततटशिलाखण्ड क्वचिदैरावतदशनमुसलखण्डितकुमुददण्डमच्छोदं नाम सरो दृष्टवान् । (K. 123)

इति नरपतिरत्नं यद्यदाविश्चकार
  क्रमविदथ मुरारिः प्रत्यहंस्तत्तदाशु (Si. XX. 76)
तानीन्द्रियाणि सकलानि तदेव नाम
  सा बुद्धिरप्रतिहता वचनं तदेव ।
अर्थोष्मणा विरहितः पुरुषः स एव
  त्वन्यः क्षणेन भवतीति विचित्रमेतत् ॥ (Bh. II. 4)
एते त एव गिरयो विरुवन्मयूरा-
  स्तान्येव मत्तहरिणानि वनस्थलानि ।
आमञ्जुमञ्जुललतानि च तान्यमूनि
  नीरन्ध्रनीलनिचुलानि सरित्तटानि ॥ (U. 2.)
योत्ति यस्य यदा मांसमुभयोः पश्यतान्तरम् ।
एकस्य क्षणिका प्रीतिरन्यः प्राणैर्विमुच्यते ॥ (H. I)
वज्रं च राजतेजश्च द्वयमेवातिभीषणम् ।
एकमेकत्र पतति पतत्यन्यत्समंततः ॥ (H. I.)
विश्वंभरात्मजा देवी राज्ञा त्यक्ता महावने ।
प्राप्तप्रसवमात्मानं गंगादेव्यां विमुञ्चति ॥ (U. 7.)
काप्यभिख्या तयोरासीद् व्रजतोः शुद्धवेषयोः ।
हिमनिर्मुक्तयोर्योगे चित्राचन्द्रमसोरिव ॥ (R. I. 46)
कोप्येष एव पिशुनोग्रमनुष्यधर्मः ।
कर्णे परे स्पृशति हन्ति परं समूलम् ॥ (P. I. 11)
रूपं तदोजस्वि तदेव वीर्यं तदेव नैसर्गिकमुन्नतत्वम् ।
न कारणात्स्वाद्बिभिदे कुमारः प्रवर्तितो दीप इव प्रदीपात् ॥ (R. V. 37)

The worshipful Gautama has ordered me to do this work.

What does your reverence intend to speak on this auspicious occasion?

Dear Gopál, do not weep; here come thy two brothers whom thou regardest as dead.

Here comes the mother of this child with fruits in her hand.

There is some indescribable pleasure in the company of the wise.

They saved themselves with great difficulty at that perilous time.

These two boys were brought up by me just like my own children; the one was very clever, but the other extremely dull.

She thought herself most unfortunate at hearing that news.

There goes a report that in the temple of Bhadrakáli lives an old woman. At one time she begins to rave, at another to speak sensibly.

Some philosophers believe that God created the whole Universe; others hold that it sprang up of itself.

Some men accomplish their own good, some the good of the people alone, while others try to accomplish both.

The sons of Yajnadatta have become proficient in various arts and sciences.

It is the very man I saw on the road, dressed in tattered rags.

He studies anywhere, goes out with any body, dines in any body's house, and sleeps anywhere.

Whoever is strong-minded, will try to take revenge for any insults given to him.

Speak sweetly with all those persons that may come to your house.

LESSON XIII.

Participles.

§ 141. All participles in Sanskrit, except the so-called indeclinable past participles or absolutives, are to be regarded as *adjectives*, agreeing with the nouns they qualify, in gender, number, and case. They are called 'participles' from the supposed *participation* or sharing in the functions of the verb, the adjective, and the noun. The principal kinds of participles in Sanskrit are these : Present, Past

Future, Perfect, Potential, Passive, and Indeclinable Past Participles; (for the rules of formation see *Grammar*). These participles obey the same rules for governing cases that *may* have been laid down regarding the roots from which they are derived. Present, Future and Perfect Participles are treated in this lesson.

Presnt Partioiples.

§ **142**. The present participle in Sanskrit (for rules of formation see Dr. Kielhorn's Grammar § 490-2) corresponds to the participle in English ending in '*ing.*' It is used when contemporaneity of action is indicated; as, इति विचारयन्नेव तुरगादवततार (K. 125) 'while thinking in this manner, he dismounted from his horse'; विवाहकौतुकं बिभ्रत एव तस्य वसुधां हस्तगामिनीमकरोत् (R. VIII. 1) 'he made over the earth to him while (yet) wearing the marriage-string'; व्रजंश्च समर्थयामास (K. 141) 'and going, he thought.'

The sense of '*while*', '*whilst*' is thus inherent in this participle which serves to express an idea expressed in Fnglish by a whole sentence.

Obs. (*a*) The Sanskrit participle must never be confounded with the participial substantive or gerund in English which also ends in *ing*.

(*b*) When no contemporaneity of action is indicated, this participle cannot be used; as, 'ascending the mountain, they rested for some time'; पर्वतमारुह्य ते कंचित् कालं व्यश्राम्यन् and not पर्वतमारोहन्तः &c. unless the sentence implies that both actions are performed at the same time.

(*c*) The persent participle is not used in the nominative case as a predicative adjective. We do not say स कुर्वन्नस्ति 'he is doing', though we say कार्यं कुर्वन् स क्रीडति.

§ **143**. * The present participle (Atm.) is often used to denote 'disposition' or 'habit', 'some standard of age', and 'ability' or

* ताच्छील्यवयोवचनशक्तिषु चानश् । (III. 2. 129.)

'capacity to do a thing'; as, भोगं भुञ्जानः (S. K.), 'habituated to enjoy'; कवचं बिभ्राणः (*ibid.*) 'wearing an armour' (of the age at which armour may be worn); शत्रुं निघ्नानः (*ibid*) 'able to destroy his foe.'

Compare with the second example: सम्यग्विनीतमथ वर्महरं कुमारं (R. VIII. 94) where वर्महरः=कवचधारणार्हवयस्कः.

§ **144**. * The present participle is used to denote an attendant circumstance or attribute, and the cause of an action; as, शयाना भुञ्जते यवनाः (S. K.) 'the Yavanas take their meals, (by) lying down;' so तिष्ठन् मूत्रयति (Mbh.); गच्छन् भक्षयति (*ibid*); हरिं पश्यन् मुच्यते (S. K.) 'by (reason of) seeing Hari he gets absolution.' The first sentence is an answer to the question कथं भुञ्जते, and the last to केन मुच्यते.

(*a*) This participle also *defines* the agent of an action; as, योऽधीयान आस्ते स देवदत्तः (Mbh.) 'he is Devadatta who sits studying'; so य आसीनोऽधीते स देवदत्तः (*ibid*).

Obs. This use corresponds to the *restrictive* use of the participle in English; 'students, *preparing* their lessons, will be rewarded' पाठानधीयानाः शिष्याः पारितोषिकाणि लप्स्यन्ते.

(*b*) This participle is also used to state a general truth; as, शयाना वर्धते दूर्वा (Mbh.) 'the Durvá grass grows (when) in a recumbent position'; आसीनं वर्धते बिसं (*ibid.*) 'a lotus-stalk grows (when) in an upright position.

§ **145**. The roots आस् 'to sit,' स्था 'to stand' and rarely भू and अस्, are used with the present participles of roots to show the *continuity* of the action denoted by them; as, वल्मीकाग्राणि विदारयन्प्रगर्जंश्चास्ते (P. I. 1) 'kept on pulling down the tops of ant-hills and bellowing loudly;' गीतसमाप्त्यवसरं प्रतीक्षमाणस्तस्थौ (K. 132) 'continued to await the time of the conclusion of the song.'

§ **146**. Verbs like लज्ज्, ह्री, त्रप् 'to be ashamed' are usually used with the present participle of roots in the sense of '*to*' in English. एवं निर्घृण प्रहरन् लज्जसे (K. 247) 'art thou not ashamed to strike

---

* लक्षणहेत्वोः क्रियायाः । (III. 2. 126)

so mercilessly'; स्वयं साहसं संदिशन्ती बाला जिह्रेमि (K. 237) 'I, a young girl, am ashamed to communicate a rash thing myself.'

§ **147**. The present participle is rarely used with the prohibitive participle मा to imply a curse; as, मा जीवन् यः परावज्ञादुःखदग्धोऽपि जीवति (Śi. II. 45) 'cursed be he (*lit.* may he not live) who, though smitten by the pain of the contempt of others, still lives.'

Future Partciples.

§ **148**. The future participle which ends in स्यत् (or ष्यत्) (pass मान) denotes that a person or thing is going, or is about, to do the action, or to undergo the state, expressed by the root; as, करिष्यन् 'going to do' or 'about to do'; मोक्ष्यन् 'going to loose'; करिष्यमाण 'being about to be done.'

(*a*) Besides showing *simple futurity*, it denotes *intention* or *purpose*; as, वन्यान्विनेष्यन्निव दुष्टसत्त्वान्स दावं विचचार (R. II. 8) 'he ranged over the forest as if wishing to tame the wild beasts;' करिष्यमाणः सशरं शरासनं (R. III. 52) 'intending to fit an arrow to his bow.' This participle thus corresponds, to the English *prospective form.*

Note. Such sentences as '*before* taking his departure, he drank a little water' are translated by means of the future participle made to qualify the subject; as, प्रयाणं करिष्यन् स किंचिज्जलं पपौ. 'Before' has here the sense of 'going' or 'about to take' &c.

Perfect Participles.

§ **149**. The perfect participle (ending in वस् or आन) is less frequently used. It has the sense of 'who or what has or has been done'; as, श्रेयांसि सर्वाण्यधिजग्मुषस्ते (R. V. 34) 'of thee who hast obtained all good things (blessings)'; निषेदुषीमासनबन्धधीरः (R. II. 6) firmly maintaining his seat when she had sat down.'

सा टिट्टिभी स्वाण्डभङ्गाभिभूता प्रलापान् कुर्वाणा न कथंचिदातिष्ठत्।
(P. I. 15)

अथ द्वावपि तौ पुष्पितपलाशप्रतिमौ परस्परवधकांक्षिणौ दृष्ट्वा करटको दमनकमाह । भो मूढमते अनयोर्विरोधं वितन्वता त्वया न साधु कृतम् ।
(P. I. 16

राजा विस्फारितेन स्निग्धेन चक्षुषा पिबन्निवालपन्निव स्पृशन्निव मनोरथसहस्रप्राप्तदर्शनं सस्पृहमीक्षमाणस्तनयाननं मुमुदे कृतकृत्यं चात्मानं मेने । (K. 72.)

साहित्यसंगीतकलाविहीनः साक्षात्पशुः पुच्छविषाणहीनः ।
तृणं न खादन्नपि जीवमानस्तद्भागधेयं परमं पशूनाम् ॥ (Bh. II.

सज्जीभूतं साधनम् । प्रयाणाभिमुखः सकलः स्कंधावारस्त्वां प्रतिपालयन्नास्ते । तत्किमद्यापि विलंबितेन । (K. II. 77.)

राजाधिराजनन्दन नगरन्ध्रगतस्य ते गतिं ज्ञास्यन्नहं च गतः कदाचित्कलिंगान् । (D. K. II. 7.)

अनुयास्यन्मुनितनयां सहसा विनयेनवारितप्रसरः ।
स्थानादनुच्चलन्नपि गत्वेव पुनः प्रतिनिवृत्तः ॥ (Ś. 1.)

वामनाश्रमपदं ततः परं पावनं श्रुतमृषेरुपेयिवान् ।
उन्मनाः प्रथमजन्मचेष्टितान्यस्मरन्नपि बभूव राघवः ॥
(R. XI. 22.)

ADDITIONAL SENTENCES FOR EXERCISE.

आसीच्च मे मनसि। शांतात्मन्यस्मिञ्जने मां निक्षिपता किमिदमनार्येणासदृशमारब्धं मनसिजेन। (K. 142.)

अग्रजन्माऽब्रवीत् । महाभाग सुतानेतान् मातृहीनाननेकैरुपायै रक्षन्निदानीमस्मिन्देशे भैक्ष्यं संपाद्य दददेतेभ्यो वसामि शिवालयेऽस्मिन्निति । (D. K. I. 3.)

विवादे दर्शयिष्यन्तं क्रियासंक्रान्तिमात्मनः ।
यदि मां नानुजानासि परित्यक्तोस्म्यहं त्वया ॥ (M. I.)

अविदित्वात्मनः शक्तिं परस्य च समुत्सुकः ।
गच्छन्नभिमुखे वह्नौ नाशं याति पतंगवत् ॥ (P. I. 8.)

अन्तर्लीनस्य दुःखाग्नेरद्योद्दामं ज्वलिष्यतः ।
उत्पीड इव धूमस्य मोहः प्रागावृणोति माम् ॥ (U. 3.)

आदिदेशाथ शत्रुघ्नं तेषां क्षेमाय राघवः ।
करिष्यन्निव नामास्य यथार्थमरिनिग्रहात् ॥ (R. XV. 6.)

कदा वाराणस्याममरतटिनीरोधसि वसन्
वसानः कौपीनं शिरसि निदधानोऽञ्जलिपुटम् ।
अये गौरीनाथ त्रिपुरहर शंभो त्रिनयन
प्रसीदेत्याक्रोशन्निमिषमिव नेष्यामि दिवसान् ॥ (Bh. III. M. 10.)

तं तस्थिवांसं नगरोपकण्ठे तदागमारूढगुरुप्रहर्षः ।
प्रत्युज्जगाम क्रथकैशिकेन्द्रश्चन्द्रं प्रवृद्धोर्मिरिवोर्मिमाली ॥ (R. V. 61.)

N. B.—In the following sentences use participles for the italicised words.

I saw many men on the road *bearing* loads of corn on their heads and *walking* gently, *talking* with each other.

While *going* to England in a ship, one may see several beautiful scenes.

Oh the beauty of this picture! The painter has fully shown his skill in *making* the several parts so charming to the eye.

Is he not ashamed (ह्री) to communicate such a message to me through you?

Rati, *looking* at the dead body of her husband and *remembering* his diverse good qualities, kept on (स्था) weeping for a long time.

When Chandrápída *was about to be crowned* (सिच् with अभि) as heir-apparent to the throne, S'ukanása advised him, *directing* his attention to many important things.

Wishing to become proficient in Nyáya, he went to Benares and studied there for several days.

Before giving (दा) Gopál the reward I had promised him to give I asked him if he would consider it unworthy of his exertions.

Reeds, *because they bow down* to a stronger foe, are saved, while huge oak trees, proudly *standing up*, are swept away by the current of water.

The lion kept on *killing* the beasts of the forest in their turn.

You should not bear hatred towards (द्रुह्) this Bráhmana who *has studied* (इ with अधि) the four Vedas, *mastered* completely the six Angas, and *has seen* the end of (fully mastered) the four S'ástras.

Janaka, gave his daughter Sítá to Ráma who *had broken* the bow of S'iva, and *attracted* the minds of the beholders by his uncommon strength and skill.

LESSON XIV

Past Participles.

§ 150. There are two kinds of past participles: one is *passive* formed by the addition of त or न to the root, and the other *active* formed by adding वत् to the passive participle; as, तेनेदमुक्तं 'this was said by him'; स इदमुक्तवान् 'he said this'. They are both used in the sense of the *past* tense. In later Sanskrit it became more usual to use participles than verbs. We generally find मया तत्कृतं or अहं तत्कृतवान् instead of अहं तदकरवम्, and many purposes of the predicate are served by this participle.

§ 151. Many intransitive verbs have past passive participles and they, as well as the past participles of transitive verbs used intransitively, are often used *impersonally* with an instrumental construction; as, प्रतिबुद्धमिदानीं मकरंदपूर्णचन्द्रेण (Mál. 4) 'the full-moon-like Makaranda has now recovered his consciousness'; जितमपत्यस्नेहेन (U. 7) 'victorious (all-powerful) is the affection for children.'

Obs. This kind of construction is not restricted to past participles alone; it occurs in the passive voice of verble tenses also; as, मध्याह्नेऽपि वनराजिषु आहिण्ड्यते (S'. 2) 'it is wandered (*i. e.* I wander) through rows of forests even at midday.'

आपदां कथितः पन्था इन्द्रियाणामसंयमः ।
तज्जयः संपदां मार्गो येनेष्टं तेन गम्यताम् ॥ (C. 74)

Non-restraint of the senses is regarded as the path to miseries; victory over them, as the road to riches (prosperity); go by whatever way you please.

§ **152**. *The past passive participles of roots implying *motion*, of intransitive roots generally, and of the roots श्लिष् 'to embrace,' शी, स्था, आस्, वस् 'to dwell,' जन्, रुह्, and जॄ, 'to grow old' cl. 4, have an active sense; as, गतोहं कलिंगान् (D. K. II.) 'I went to Kalinga'; जलं पातुं यमुनाकच्छमवतीर्णः (P. I. 1) 'he went down to the bank of the Jumna to drink'; लक्ष्मीमाश्लिष्टो हरिः (S. K.) 'Hari embraced Lakshmí'; शेषमधिशयितः 'sat on the serpent'; शिवमुपासितः 'served S'iva'; विश्वमनुजीर्णः 'grew old after the world'; उपरते भर्तरी (K. 173) 'the husband being dead'; so वैकुंठमधिष्ठितः, हरिदिनमुपोषितः, वृक्षमारूढः, सुतो जातः &c.

Obs. Kálidása construes the past passive participle of स्मृ in an active sense; as, मधुकर विस्मृतोस्येनां कथं (S'. 5.) अन्यसंगात् पूर्ववृत्तं विस्मृतो भवान् (*ibid*); अहो विस्मृतं मे हृदयं (V. 2).

§ **153**. †Past passive participles ending in त have sometimes the sense of *neuter abstract nouns*; as, जल्पितं 'speech,' शयितं 'sleeping,' हसितं 'laugh'; so गतं, स्थितं; कस्येदमालिखितं 'whose is this picture ?'

Obs. In such cases the forms lose their *passive* force, and are not used with the instrumental; as, 'her gait is graceful' तस्याः (not

* गत्यर्थाकर्मकश्लिषशीङ्स्थासवसजनरुहजीर्यतिभ्यश्च । (III. 4. 72).
† नपुंसके भावे क्तः । (III. 3. 114.)

तया) गतं सविलासं; नृत्तादस्याः स्थितमतितरां कांतं (M. 2) 'her (motionless) posture is far more charming than the dancing.'

§ **154.** The past passive participle of the roots मन् 'to think,' 'to wish,' बुध् 'to know,' and पूज् 'to adore', and others having the same signification, are used in the sense of the present tense and are then construed with the Genitive. See § 115.

Obs. There are other words which are similarly used. They are given in the following verses:—

शीलितो रक्षितः क्षांत आक्रुष्टो जुष्ट इत्यपि ।
रुष्टश्च रुषितश्चोभावभिव्याहृत इत्यपि ॥
हृष्टतुष्टौ तथा कांतस्तथोभौ संयतोद्यतौ ।
कष्टं भविष्यतीत्याहुरमृताः पूर्ववत्स्मृता ॥ (Mbh.)

Potential Passive Participles.

§ **155.** There are three ways in which potential passive participles are formed in Sanskrit:—(1) by तव्य; (2) by अनीय, and (3) by य; (for the rules of formation *vide* Dr. Kielhorn's Grammar § § 519-529); as कर्तव्य, करणीय, and कार्य. They perform a very useful function in the economy of the Sanskrit tongue, and enable it to express in one word an idea which would require many words in English; as, 'he should be killed'=हंतव्यः. They denote that 'the action or the state expressed by the root or derivative base, *must* or *ought* to be done or undergone;' as, वक्तव्यं-वाच्यं-वचनीयं 'what *ought to be said.*' The sense thus conveyed by them is that of *fitness*, *obligation*, or *necessity*; *e. g.*, 'I have to go there' मया तत्र गंतव्यं; 'I must do it' मया तत्कर्तव्यं.

§ **156.** These participles are used in sentences in the same way as the passive of the roots from which they are derived; as, मद्वचनात्स राजा त्वयेदं वाच्यः (R. XIV. 61) 'the king should be told this in my behalf'; अजा ग्रामं नेतव्याः 'the sheep ought to be taken to the village;' so असौ दुहितुः पत्या परिग्रहप्रियमस्माभिः श्रावयितव्यः (S'. 7) 'he should be made to hear the good fortune in the form of the acceptance of his daughter by her husband.' They are used with the Instrumental or Genitive of the agent of the action denoted by them; see § 107.

§ **157.** The *impersonal* use of this participle is not very peculiar. It is used in the neuter gender singular, taking the place of the verb; as **अभिज्ञानशकुंतलाख्येन नाटकेनोपस्थातव्यमस्माभिः** (Ś. 1) 'we must wait upon (the audience) with the drama (represent before them &c.)'; **तत्रभवता तपोवनं गंतव्यं** (V. 5) 'his honour should go to a penance grove.'

(*a*) The impersonal use of the forms **भवितव्यं** and **भाव्यं** deserves notice. They are used impersonally in their literal sense of '*being*', or in the sense of '*must be*', '*in all probability is*', showing some uncertainty &c., and in both cases the noun or adjective coming after 'be' must agree with the agent like an ordinary adjective; as, **स्वेषु स्वेषु पाठेष्वसंमूढैर्भवितव्यं** (**युष्माभिः**) (V. 1.) 'you should be careful of your respective parts'; **तयाऽस्मिँल्लतामंडपे संनिहितया भवितव्यं** (S'. 3.) 'she must be (is most probably) present in this bower of creepers'; **अस्य शब्दानुरूपेण पराक्रमेण भाव्यं** (**भवितव्यं**) (P. I. 1) 'his strength must (in all likelihood) be corresponding to his bellowing'.

(*b*) Sometimes the participle is used in the sense of the future with certainty; as, **लुब्धकेन मृगमांसार्थिना गंतव्यं** (H. 1.) 'the fowler is sure to go (will surely go) seeking after the deer's flesh'; **ततस्तेनापि शब्दः कर्तव्यः** (H. 3) 'then he also will surely make a noise'.

(*c*) Sometimes the potential passive participle merely denotes a future time; as, **युवयोः पक्षबलेन मयापि सुखेन गंतव्यं** (H. 4) 'I, too, shall go at ease by the strength (support) of your wings'.

अत्रभवतोः परस्परेण ज्ञानसंघर्षो जातः । तदत्रभवत्या प्राश्निकपदमध्यासितव्यम् । (M. 1.)

तयोर्बद्धयोः किन्निमित्तोऽयं मोक्षः किं देव्या परिजनमतिक्रम्य भवान्संदिष्ट इत्येवमनया प्रष्टव्यम् । (M. 4.)

विश्रांतेन भवता ममाप्येकस्मिन्ननायासे कर्मणि सहायेन भवितव्यम् । (S.' 2.)

नास्मि भवत्योरीश्वरनियोगप्रत्यर्थी । स्मर्तव्यस्त्वयं जनः । (V. 2.)

तत्किं मन्यसे राजपुत्रि मृषोद्यं तदिति ! न हीदं सुक्षत्रियेऽन्यथा मंतव्यम् । भवितव्यमेव तेन । (U. 4.)

सर्वथा निष्प्रतीकारेयमापदुपस्थिता । किमिदानीं कर्तव्यं कां दिशं गंतव्यमित्येते चान्ये च विषण्णहृदयस्य मे संकल्पाः प्रादुरासन् ।
(K. 157.)

सततमतिगर्हितेनाकृत्येनापि परिरक्षणीयान्मन्यन्ते सुहृदसून्साधवः । तदतिहेपणमकर्तव्यमप्येतदस्माकमवश्यकर्तव्यतामापतितम् । (K 158.)

चाणक्यः—भद्र प्रथमं तावद्वध्यस्थानं गत्वा घातकाः सरोषं दक्षिणाक्षिसंकोचसंज्ञां ग्राहयितव्याः । तेषु गृहीतसंज्ञेषु भयापदेशादितस्ततः प्रद्रुतेषु शकटदासो वध्यस्थानादपनीय राक्षसं प्रापयितव्यः । (Mu. 1)

आः क्षुद्राः समरभीरवः । कथमेवं प्रलपतां वः सहस्रधा न दीर्णमनया जिह्वया । (Ve. 3.)

आपदि येनोपकृतं येन च हसितं दशासु विषमासु ।
उपकृदपकृदपि च तयोर्यस्तं पुरुषं परं मन्ये ॥ (P. I. 15)

ADDITIONAL SENTENCES FOR EXERCISE.

आपन्नस्य विषयवासिनो जनस्यार्तिहरेण राज्ञा भवितव्यमित्येष वो धर्मः । (S'. 3)

अंतरिते तस्मिन्शबरसेनापतौ स जीर्णशबरस्तं वनस्पतिमामूलादपश्यत् । उत्क्रांतमिव तस्मिन्क्षणे तदालोकभीतानां शुककुलानामसुभिः । (K. 33.)

अहं तच्छ्रुत्वा चेतस्यकरवम् । मयाधुना म्लेच्छजातिभिरपि दूरतः परिहृतप्रवेशं पक्कणं द्रष्टव्यम् । चंडालैः सहैकत्र स्थातव्यम् । चंडालबालकजनस्य च कीदृशेनायेन भवितव्यमिति ।
(K. 355.)

कार्यव्यग्रत्वान्मनसः प्रभूतत्वाच्च प्रणिधीनां कोयमिति विस्मृतम् । इदानीं स्मृतिरुपलब्धा व्यक्तमाहितुण्डिकच्छद्मना कुसुमपुराद्गतेन विराधगुप्तेन भवितव्यम् । (Mu. 2)

आः दुरात्मन् कुरुकुलपांसुल एवमतिक्रांतमर्यादे त्वयि निमित्तमात्रेण पांडवक्रोधेन भवितव्यम् । (Ve. 1.)

वत्से सांप्रतिकमेवैतत् । कर्तव्यानि दुःखितैर्दुःखनिर्वापणानि ।

पूरोत्पीडे तडागस्य परीवाहः प्रतिक्रिया ।
शोकक्षोभे च हृदयं प्रलापैरेव धार्यते ॥ (U. 3)

तेनाधीतं श्रुतं तेन तेन सर्वमनुष्ठितम् ।
येनाशाः पृष्ठतः कृत्वा नैराश्यमवलंबितम् ॥ (H. 1)

आरूढमद्रीनुदधीन्वितीर्णं भुजंगमानां वसतिं प्रविष्टम् ।
ऊर्ध्वं गतं यस्य न चानुबन्धि यशः परिच्छेत्तुमियत्तयालम् ॥ (R. VI. 77.)

अवसितं हसितं प्रसितं मुदा विलसितं ह्रसितं स्मरभासितम् ।
न समदाः प्रमदा हतसंमदाः पुरहितं विहितं न समीहितम् ॥ (Bk. X 6.)

शार्ङ्गरव त्वया मद्वचनात्स राजा शकुंतलां पुरस्कृत्य वक्तव्यः—

अस्मान्साधु विचिन्त्य संयमधनानुच्चैःकुलं चात्मन-
स्त्वय्यस्याः कथमप्यबान्धवकृतां स्नेहप्रवृत्तिं च ताम् ।
सामान्यप्रतिपत्तिपूर्वकमियं दारेषु दृश्या त्वया
भाग्यायत्तमतः परं न खलु तद्वाच्यं वधूबन्धुभिः ॥ (S'. 4.)

स्वमर्हतां प्राग्रसरः स्मृतोऽसि मः शकुंतला मूर्तिमती च सत्क्रिया ।
समानयस्तुल्यगुणं वधूवरं चिरस्य वाच्यं न गतः प्रजापतिः ॥ (S'. 5)

N. B. Use participles for the words italicised.

Kártikeya *defeated* Táraka though he was *guarded* by strong armies.

Dear child, in doing this you have *offended* (राध् with अप) Jámadagnya, and not *done* him any good (कृ with उप).

His army being completely defeated by the enemy, some of his soldiers *mounted* (रुह् with अधि) hills, some *descended* to seas, while others *entered* (विश्) solitary caves.

You *will surely become* an object of contempt if you slight your intimate friends.

Who may this man be, that calls me by my name? Oh yes, he is *most probably* my old friend, Mitravarman.

Wait for me a little; I, too, *have to be* present at the meeting.

As soon as he gets up, *instead of beginning* his studies he goes out to play.

Do not give way to sorrow; your child *must have* by this time *come* home directly.

I have *wandered* (भ्रम्) over several countries, suffering many difficulties, but *have not obtained* (लभ् or आसद् *caus.*) my desired object.

He appears to be bent on ruining you, but I tell you he is *sure to be defeated* in his attempts.

How *should* he *sustain* his life in that country if you were not to assist him?

These things *should be taken* (प्रापय्) by you to the owner of that large palace.

I *have* yet to *read* (वाचय्) many books; so I shall not be able to accompany you.

This great reward indicates that the ring *must have been* greatly *liked* (मन्) by the king.

Nothing is difficult to be accomplished (दुःसाध्य) by wise men.

Since he had much, he *must have had* many wives.

How long *should* we *remain* with our armies ready for battle?

LESSON XV.

Part I

Indeclinable Past Participles or Gerunds.

§ **158.** The indeclinable past participle, in Sanskrit, commonly called 'absolutive' or 'gerund,' always denotes a *prior* action, or an action *completed* before another, and corresponds to the perfect participle, or the participle in *ing* having the sense of the perfect participle, in English; as, प्रतीहारी समुपसृत्य सविनयमब्रवीत् (K. 8) 'the female door keeper, drawing near or having drawn near, modestly said;' वैशंपायनो मुहूर्तमिव ध्यात्वा सादरमब्रवीत् (K. 18) 'Vais'ampáyana, as if contemplating for a moment, respectfully said'.

But in the sentence 'going to a village, he touches a blade of grass on his way,' we must say, ग्रामं गच्छन् पथि तृणं स्पृशति.

§ **159**. Indeclinable past participles in Sanskrit are formed by त्वा or by य (changed to त्य) when a preposition precedes a root (for rules *vide* Dr. Kielhorn's Grammar § § 505—516). They are, as before stated, used to denote a *past* or *prior* action and must have *the same agent* as the main verb; as, तुरासाहं पुरोधाय धाम स्वायंभुवं ययुः (Ku. II. 1) 'having placed Indra at their head they went to the abode of Brahman'. Here the agent of 'placing' and 'going' is the same, and hence the gerund can be used; but स तं हत्वाहमागच्छम् is wrong. In such cases the gerund cannot be used; the Locative absolute construction will have to be used to express the same sense; as, तस्मिंस्तेन हतेहमागच्छम्. So सर्वैः पशुभिर्मिलित्वा सिंहो विज्ञप्तः (H. 2), 'the lion was entreated by all the beasts, having assembled together;' स एनं दोषं प्रख्याप्य नगरान्निर्वास्यताम् (Mu. 1) 'let him be expelled the city (by thee) having proclaimed this crime.'

§ **160**. The Sanskrit gerunds are very useful to economize the use of conjunctions and verbal forms in describing or narrating events. In translating constructions introduced by *'after having,' 'when'* or *'after'*; 'when,' 'after' &c., need not be translated, the gerund of the verb being alone used; as, रावणं हत्वा 'after having killed Rávaņa;' 'when he went there, he did not find anything' स तत्र गत्वा न किमपि लेभे.

An English sentence containing several clauses introuduced by 'having' would look awkward; but in Sanskrit several gerunds can be strung together to express those ideas which would be expressed in English by a verbal tense and the copulative conjunction; as, मां रुधिरेणालिप्य वृक्षस्याधः प्रक्षिप्य गम्यतां पर्वतमृष्यमूकं प्रति (P. III.) 'having besmeared me with blood, and thrown me under the tree, go to the mountain Rishyamûka,' *i. e.*, *besmear* me &c. *and go* &c.; अथ स ब्राह्मणस्तं पशुं राक्षसं मत्वा भयाद्भूमौ प्रक्षिप्य दैवं निर्भर्त्स्य गृहमुद्दिश्य प्रस्थितः (H. 4) 'then, the Brâhma*n*a thinking the beast to be a demon, threw it on the ground with fear, and censuring Fate, set off for his home'. When there are copulative assertions in English, the gerunds may be conveniently used in translating them into Sanskrit.

Obs. The natural sequence of events must be observed in the use of these gerunds; as, पक्त्वा भुक्त्वा स्वपिति 'having cooked and taken his food he sleeps'; but not भुक्त्वा पक्त्वा स्वपिति.

§ **161**. Some Sanskrit gerunds may often have the sense of prepositions and prepositional phrases; as, मुक्त्वा 'except', आदाय 'with', उद्दिश्य 'towards', अधिकृत्य 'with reference to'.

PART II.

Namul or Gerund in अम्.

§ **162**. There is another kind of gerund in Sanskrit formed by the addition of अम् immediately to the root or derivative base, and making the same changes as before the इ of the passive Aorist (see Dr. Kielhorn's Grammar § 397); as, क्षेपं 'having thrown' from क्षिप्; वादं 'having spoken'; भोजं 'having dined'.

§ **163**. When this gerund is repeated, it denotes a repetition or recurrence of the action or state expressed by the root; as, स्मारं स्मारं नमति शिवं (S. K.) 'having often and often called to mind S'iva', he bows to him'. कलिंगनाथो मयि बद्धवैर इति श्रावं श्रावं चंडवर्मा युद्धायोद्यतो बभूव (D. K. II. 3) 'having repeatedly heard that the lord of the Kalingas was hostilely inclined towards himself, Cha*n*davarman became ready to fight'; so also पायं पायं, दर्शं दर्शं 'having repeatedly drunk or seen'.

§ **164**. * With the words अग्रे, प्रथमं and पूर्वं this gerund or the ordinary one in त्वा is used; as, अग्रे-प्रथमं पूर्वं-वा भोजं भुक्त्वा वा व्रजति 'having first eaten he goes'.

---

* विभाषाग्रेप्रथमपूर्वेषु । (III. 4. 24)

(*a*) * With the words अन्यथा, एवं, कथं, and इत्थं this gerund of कृ 'to do' is used, provided the whole word thus formed retains the same meaning as the words themselves; as, एवंकारं भुंक्ते (S. K.) 'he eats *thus*'; कथंकारं भुंक्ते 'in what manner does he eat'; but शिरोऽन्यथा कृत्वा भुंक्ते.

(*b*) † With the words यथा, तथा, when an angry reply is given; as, यथाकारं भोक्ष्ये किं तवानेन (S. K.) 'I will eat *that way*; what have you to do with it ?'

§ **165.** ‡ With the words implying 'sweet' or 'seasoned' this gerund of कृ is used; as, स्वादुंकारं-लवणंकारं-भुंक्ते 'he eats, having made his food sweet or seasoned.'

§ **166.** § In the case of the roots दृश् and विद् 'to know' this gerund is joined with their *object* to denote the *whole* or *collection* of that object; as कन्यादर्शं वरयति (S. K.) 'he chooses as many girls as he sees'; *i. e. all* the girls seen; ब्राह्मणवेदं भोजयति 'he feeds as many Bràhmanas as he knows', *i. e. all.*

(*a*) †† विद् 'to get' and जीव 'to live' are combined with यावत् in the same sense; as, यावेद्वेदं भुंक्ते 'he eats *as much as* he gets'; यावज्जीवमधीते 'he studies *as long as* he lives' *i. e.* throughout his life.

(*b*) $ With the words चर्मन् and उदर this gerund of पूर् is used with the *object*: as, उदरपूरं भुंक्ते 'eats so as to fill his belly', so चर्मपूरं स्तृणाति 'spreads so as to cover the skin.'

§ **167.** ‖ With the words शुष्क, चूर्ण and रूक्ष this gerund of पिष् is used like the cognate accusative in English, *i. e.*, the gerund of the root and the root itself are used to signify the sense denoted by the

---

* अन्यथैवंकथमित्थंसु सिद्धाप्रयोगश्चेत् । (III. 4. 27)

† यथातथयोरसूयाप्रतिवचने । (III. 4. 28)

‡ स्वादुमि णमुल् । (III. 4. 26)

§ कर्मणि दृशिविदोः साकल्ये । (III. 4. 29)

†† यावति विन्दजीवोः । (III. 4. 30)

$ चर्मोदरयोः पूरेः (III. 4. 31)

‖ शुष्कचूर्णरूक्षेषु पिषः (III. 4. 35)

root; as, चूर्णपेषं पिनष्टि 'he grinds something till it is reduced to powder', *i. e.* he grinds it *to powder*; so शुष्क-रूक्ष-पेषं पिनष्टि.

(*a*) * With the words समूल, अकृत, जीव, the roots हन्, कृ, and ग्रह् are respectively used in a cognate sense; as, समूलघातं हन्ति 'he destroys so as to tear up by the roots, *i. e.* he totally extirpates; अकृतकारं करोति 'he does a thing which was not done before'; तं जीवग्राहं गृह्णाति 'captures him so as to preserve his life', *i. e.*, *captures* him *alive*.

(*b*) In the same way this gerund of हन् and पिष् is used with a noun to denote that it is the *instrument* of the action; as, पादघातं हन्ति=पादेन हन्ति he strikes *with* the foot;' उदपेषं पिनष्टि=उदकेन पिनष्टि 'he grinds *with* water'; similarly, तं हस्तग्राहं गृह्णाति 'he takes him by the hand'; so पाणिग्राहं; करग्राहं &c. हस्तवर्तं वर्तयति=हस्तेन &c. Other examples are:—जीवनाशं नश्यति 'perishes so that his life perishes,' *i. e.*, dies away; ऊर्ध्वशोषं शुष्यति वृक्षः 'the tree is dried up while it is still standing'; so ऊर्ध्वपूरं पूर्यते.

§ **168.** † Sometimes this gerund is used to denote similitude or likeliness, such as would be ordinarily expressed by इव; as, अजनाशं नष्टः 'he perished like a goat'; पार्थसंचारं चरति 'he walks like Pártha;' घृतनिधायं निहितं जलं 'water was kept as ghee (would be kept).'

§ **169.** ‡ Roots having the sense of हिंस् 'to strike,' such as हन्, तड् &c. are used in this gerundive form with nouns, when the *object* of this gerund is the same as the object of the main verb, and when the noun with which it is compounded would have stood in the instrumental case if the ordinary gerund had been used; as दंडोपघातं गाः कालयति 'he collects together the cows, beating (*them*) *with* a club.'

(*a*) Similarly, व्रजोपरोधं गाः स्थापयति 'he stations the cows so that they are all in the fold'; पार्श्वोपपीडं शेते=पार्श्वाभ्यामुपपीडयन् &c.

(*b*) ग्रह् is joined with हस्त, केश, and words having the same sense, when immediate contiguity is intended; as, केशग्राहं युध्यन्ते 'hav-

---

* समूलाकृतजीवेषु हन्कृञ्ग्रहः । (III. 4. 36)

† उपमाने कर्मणि च । (III. 4. 45)

‡ हिंसार्थानां च समानकर्मकाणाम् । (III. 4. 48)

ing closely caught (each other) by the hair they fight' (=केशेषु गृहीत्वा). Also हस्तग्राहं=हस्तेन गृहीत्वा, यष्टिग्राहं 'taking a stick,' (यष्टिं गृहीत्वा) so लोष्टग्राहं.

§ **170**. *With words signifying 'limbs of one's own body' this gerund is used, when the limb is not kept steady; as, भ्रूविक्षेपं कथयति (वृत्तान्तं) 'he narrates (the account) throwing his eyebrows (glances) about in all directions.'

(*a*) † In the same way when a part of the body is completely hurt or afflicted in the action, this gerund is used with that part in the sense of the accusative; as, उरःप्रतिपेषं युध्यन्ते 'they fight so as to afflict their *whole* bosom' (कृत्स्नमुरः पीडयन्तः); स्तनसंबाधमुरो जघान च (Ku. IV. 26) 'and she struck her bosom so as to hurt her breasts.'

§ **171**. ‡ The roots दिश् with आ and ग्रह् are joined in their gerundive form with नामन् in the sense of the accusative; as, नामादेशमाचष्टे 'he mentions (it) telling his name'; नामग्राहं मामाह्वयति 'he calls me by taking my name' (*i. e. by my name*).

Obs. This gerund is used with nouns to form compound words; as ब्राह्मणवेदं not ब्राह्मणान् वेदं; जीवग्राहं, not जीवं ग्राहं &c.

स दुष्टाशयो बकः क्रमेण तान्पृष्टमारोप्य जलाशयस्य नातिदूरे शिलां समासाद्य तस्यामाक्षिप्य स्वेच्छया भक्षयित्वा भूयोपि जलाशयं समासाद्य जलचराणां मिथ्यावार्तासंदेशकैर्मनांसि रञ्जयन्नाहारवृत्तिमकरोत्। (P. I. 7)

ततो भ्रातृशरीरमग्निसात्कृत्वा पुनर्नवीकृतवैधव्यदुःखया मया त्वदीयं देशमवतीर्येमे काषाये गृहीते। (M. 5)

प्रवृत्ते प्रदोषसमये चन्द्रापीडश्चरणाभ्यामेव राजकुलं गत्वा पितुः समीपे

---

* स्वांगेऽध्रुवे। (III. 4. 54)

§ परिक्लिश्यमाने च। (III. 4. 55)

‡ नाम्न्यादिशिग्रहोः। (III. 4. 58)

मुहूर्तं स्थित्वा दृष्ट्वा च विलासवतीमागत्य स्वभवनं शयनतलमधिशिश्ये ।
(K. 68)

ते हिमालयमामन्त्र्य पुनः प्राप्य च शूलिनम् ।
सिद्धं चास्मै निवेद्यार्थं तद्विसृष्टाः खमुद्ययुः ॥ (Ku. VI. 94)

अहं येनेष्टिपशुमारं मारितः सोऽनेन स्वागतेनाभिनन्द्यते । (S'. 6)

सा कुबेरभवनान्निवर्तमाना समापत्तिदृष्टेन केशिना दानवेन चित्रलेखाद्वितीया बन्दीग्राहं गृहीता । (V. I.)

मगधराजः प्रक्षीणसकलसैन्यमंडलं मालवराजं जीवग्राहमभिगृह्य दयालुतया पुनरपि स्वराज्यं प्रतिष्ठापयामास । (D. K. I. 1)

मत्तकालो नाम लाटेश्वरो वीरकेतोस्तनयः कामलोचनां नाम तरुणीरत्नमसामान्यलावण्यं श्रावं श्रावमवधूतदुहितृप्रार्थनस्य तस्य पाटलीं नाम्ना नगरीमरौत्सीत् । (D. K. I. 3)

अनन्तरं सूत्रधारो दारुवर्मा वैरोधकपुरःसरैः पदातिलोकैर्लोष्टघातं हतः । (Mu. 2)

संप्राप्य राक्षससभां चक्रन्दं क्रोधविह्वला ।
नामग्राहमरोदीत्सा भ्रातरौ रावणान्तिके ॥ (B. K. V. 5)

ADDITIONAL SENTENCES FOR EXERCISE.

लतानुपातं कुसुमान्यगृह्णात्स नद्यवस्कंदमुपास्पृशच्च ।
कुतूहलाच्चारुशिलोपवेशं काकुत्स्थ ईषत्स्मयमान आस्त ॥ (B. K. II.)

स्नेहात्सभाजयितुमेत्य दिनान्यमूनि
नीत्वोत्सवेन जनकोऽथ गतो विदेहान् ।

देव्यास्ततो विमनसः परिसान्त्वनाय
धर्मासनाद्विषति वासगृहं नरेन्द्रः ॥ (U. 1)

विश्वासप्रतिपन्नानां वञ्चने का विदग्धता ।
अंकमारुह्य सुप्तं हि हत्वा किन्नाम पौरुषम् ॥ (H. 4.)

तामिन्दुसुंदरमुखीं सुचिरे विभाव्य
चेतः कथं कथमपि व्यपवर्तते मे ।
लज्जां विजित्य विनयं विनिवार्य धैर्य-
मुन्मथ्य मन्थरविवेकमकाण्ड एव ॥ (Mál. 1)

श्रुत्वा वार्तां जलदकथितां तां धनेशोऽपि सद्यः
शापस्यान्तं सदयहृदयः संविधायास्तकोपः ।
संयोज्यैतौ विगलितशुचौ दंपती हृष्टचित्तौ
भोगानिष्टानविरतसुखान् प्रापयामास शश्वत् ॥ (Me. 119.)

निमित्तानि च पश्यामि विपरीतानि केशव ।
न च श्रेयोऽनुपश्यामि हत्वा स्वजनमाहवे ॥ (Bg. I. 31)

राजवाहनो रसालतरुषु कोकिलादीनां पक्षिणामालापाञ्श्रावं श्रावं विकसितानि सरांसि दर्शं दर्शममंदलीलया ललनासमीपमवाप । (D. K. I. 5)

तेनैव दीपदर्शितेन बिलपथेन गत्वा स्थितेऽर्धरात्रे वासगृहं प्रविष्टो विश्रब्ध प्रसुप्तं सिंहघोषं जीवग्राहमग्रहीषम् । (D. K. II. 4)

तं विप्रदर्शं कृतघातयत्ना यान्तं वने रात्रिचरी डुढौके ।
जिघांसुवेदं धृतभासुरास्त्रस्तां ताडकाख्यां निजघान रामः ॥ (Bk. II. 23)

विद्युत्प्रणाशं स वरं प्रनष्टो यद्वोर्ध्वशोषं तृणवद्विशुष्कः ।
अर्थे दुरापे किमुत प्रवासे न शासनेऽवास्थित यो गुरूणाम् । (Bk. III. 14)

यो नष्टानपि जीवनाशमधुना शुश्रूषते स्वामिन-
स्तेषां वैरिभिरक्षतः कथमसौ संधास्यते राक्षसः ।
इत्थं वस्तुविवेकमूढमतिना म्लेच्छेन नालोचितं
दैवेनोपहतस्य बुद्धिरथवा पूर्वं विपर्यस्यति ॥ (Mu. 6)

N. B.—Use participles for the words italicised.

Seeing the fowler *coming* towards them, all the animals *becoming* frightened, ran away in different directions.

When did you come back, *acquainting* the lord of the Vangas with this news?

Becoming of one accord and *forming* a strong resolution not to desist from the work undertaken, begin your business.

A jackal, *roaming* at will near the precincts of a town, accidentally fell into an indigo vat, and *being* unable to get up, remained there, *feigning* himself to be dead.

The Bràhmana, *hearing* the words of the rogue, placed the goat on the ground, looked at it again, and again, placed it once more on his shoulder, and took his way home, *thinking* over the rogues' words.

Then he was respectfully dismissed by the minister, *having called* him to court, *honoured* him with suitable presents, and *communicated* to him the message of the king.

N. B.—Use Namul forms for the words italicised

He chose *as many girls as* he *saw* (दृश) suitable to himself.

He *reduced* (पिष्) the medicine *to powder*, and placing it on fire and boiling it, drank it up.

He *was pelted to death* (हन्) by the followers of the king for having killed their master.

I fell upon my enemy all at once, and routing all his followers *caught* (ग्रह्) him *alive*.

The king of Pátaliputra captured the town of Vasudurga, and *took* its inhabitants *prisoners*.

Who calls me *by my name*?

LESSON XVI.

The Infinitive Mood.

§ **172**. When one action is represented as being done for another action, the latter is, in Sanskrit, expressed by the Infinitive, which is formed by the addition of the termination तुम् to the root in the same way as the third person singular of the Periphrastic Future. It has the sense of '*in order to*,' '*for the purpose of*,' '*for*' and thus corresponds to that form of the English Infinitive which is called 'infinitive of purpose' or 'gerund.' The Sanskrit Infinitive has thus a dative sense, and may, if necessary, be replaced by the dative case of the verbal noun derived from the root; as, पारसीकांस्ततो जेतुं प्रतस्थे (R. IV. 60) 'he then set out *to conquer* the Persians,' *i. e.* for the purpose of conquering &c.' Here जेतुं=जयाय, and the sentence may stand thus: पारसीकानां जयाय प्रतस्थे; so स्वेदसलिलस्नातापि पुनः स्नातुमवातरम् (K. 147) where स्नातुं=स्नानाय.

Obs. (*a*) Like the English infinitive, the Sanskrit Infinitive is a remnant of an old inflexion. In Vedic times the verbal noun formed from a root by the termination तु (गंतु, यातु) was regularly declined. We find such forms as गंतुं, गंतवे, गंतोः, as if गंतु was a regular noun. In course of time the use of the forms गंतोः, गंतवे, became less and less frequent, and the form that was chiefly used was the accusative inflection. It was subsequently considered to have a dative sense, and hence the present Infinitive form in Sanskrit has always the sense of the dative.

(*b*) The Sanskrit Infinitive corresponds in Latin to the Supine in *um* (*datum*=दातुं) which is properly the accusative of a verbal substantive, just as in Sanskrit; 'Themistocles Argos *habitatum* (स्थातुं) concessit' 'Themistocles retired *to live* at Argos.' The same sense is expressed, as in Sanskrit, by the dative of the gerundive participle; 'Decemviri *legibus scribundis*' (विधिनिर्माणाय) 'Decemvirs *for framing* laws.'

§ **173**. It follows from the definition that the Infinitive in Sanskrit cannot stand as the *subject* or *object* of a verb. It has no connection with any words in the sentence, except that it may, where possible, govern a noun in the same case as the root from which it is derived. Where the Infinitive occurs in English as the *subject* or *object* of a verb an abstract noun from the root must be used in Sanskrit; as, '*to get up* early in the morning is wholesome' प्रातरेव उत्थानं (not उत्थातुं) आरोग्यावहं; 'I learn *to sing*' अहं गानमधीये.

(*a*) The Infinitive after verbs of '*seeing*,' '*hearing*' is, as in Latin, translated by the present participle; as 'I heard him *speak*' भाषमाणं तमश्रौषं; so अधीयानं ददर्श तं 'he saw him *study*.'

§ 174. The strict sense of the Sanskrit Infinitive is *motive* or *purpose* of an action; but there are some cases, as in English, where the Infinitive is used with *nouns* and also *adjectives*; as, 'fit *to do*,' 'able *to go*,' 'time *to read*.' Such cases are, however, limited by Sanskrit idiom. Some of the principal cases of this nature are given below.

§ 175. * The Infinitive is used with verbs and substantives meaning '*to wish*' or '*desire*', provided the agents of the infinitive and the verb are the same; as, पिनाकपाणिं पतिमाप्तुमिच्छति (Ku. V. 53) 'desires to obtain for her husband the Pináka-handed god (S'iva)'; so अत्तुं वान्छति शांभवो गणपतेराखुं क्षुधार्तः फणी (P. 1. 3); but not त्वां गंतुमहमिच्छामि 'I wish thee *to go*', where the agents of गम् and इष् are not the same.

§ 176. † It is used with verbs meaning *to be able*, *to make bold*, *to know*, *to be wearied*, *to strive*, *to begin*, *to get*, *to set about*, *to bear*, *to be*

---

* समानकर्तृकेषु तुमुन् । (III. 3. 158.)

† शकधृषज्ञाग्लाघटरभलभक्रमसहार्हास्त्यर्थेषु तुमुन् (III. 4. 65)

This Sutra presents a knotty point. Bhattoji Dîkshita says अर्थग्रहणमस्तिनैव संबध्यते अनंतरत्वात् *i. e.* the Sutra gives roots from शक् to अर्ह् and roots having the same sense as अस् 'to be.' But this is hardly consistent with the almost overwhelming evidence of usage. According to Dîkshita's interpretation, पारय् 'to be able' cannot be used with the infinitive; but न पारयामि निवेदयितुं (S'. 4), पारयिष्यस्यत्रभवत्या अपराद्धुं (M. 3)

pleased or *to condescend*, and *to be*; *as*, न शक्नोसि हृदयमवस्थापयितुं (U. 4) 'I am not able to compose my heart'; वक्तुं मिथः प्राक्रमतैवमेनं (Ku. III. 2) 'thus proceeded to speak to him privately'; जानासि देवीं विनोदयितुं (U. 1) 'you know (how) to entertain my queen'; अस्ति-भवति-विद्यते-वा भोक्तुमन्नं (S. K.) 'there is food to eat'; न विषहे विपत्तिमवलोकयितुं (Ve. 3) 'I cannot bear to see the distress.'

§ **177**. *It is used with words meaning *'sufficient, strong, able,'* and substantives meaning *ability, power*, or *skill*; *as*, लिखितमपि ललाटे प्रोज्झितुं कः समर्थः (H. 1) 'who is able to avoid that which is written on his forehead?' लोकानलं दग्धुं हि तत्तपः (Ku. II. 56) 'his penance is able (sufficient) to burn the worlds'; अस्ति मे विभवः सर्वं परिज्ञातुं (V. 2) 'I have power to know everything'; कोन्यो हुतवहाद्दग्धुं प्रभविष्यति (S'. 4) 'who else than fire has power to burn?'; भोक्तुं प्रवीणः कुशलः पटुर्वा (S. K.) 'skilful in eating' (knowing how to eat).

§ **178**, † It is used with words meaning *'time'* with reference to the work of the time; as, अवसरोऽयमात्मानं प्रकाशयितुं (S'. 1) 'this is, indeed, the time to show myself'; समयः खलु स्नानभोजने सेवितुं (V. 2) 'It is time to bathe and take food.'

Note.—As in Latin, some verbs in Sanskrit are of the nature of *deponents, i. e.* passive in form, but active in sense; as, शक्, युज्, अर्ह् and their derivatives; as, न शक्यास्ते दोषाः समाधातुं (H. 3) 'those faults cannot be corrected or remedied'; न युक्तं अशोको वामपादेन ताडयितुं (M. 3) the As'oka does not deserve to be kicked with the left foot.'

are instances from a standard author; similarly विद् 'to know' cannot be used with the infinitive; but न च वेद सम्यग् द्रष्टुं न सा (R. VI. 30) is as good an instance. We must therefore, suppose that the Sútra indicates the existence of an interpretation connecting अर्थग्रहण with all the preceding roots; otherwise we shall have to condemn as wrong all such constructions as those given above. Taking this view I have interpreted the Sútra, connecting अर्थग्रहण with all roots.

* पर्याप्तिवचनेष्वलमर्थेषु । (III. 4. 66)

† कालसमयवेलासु तुमुन् । (III. 3. 167)

§ **179**. The Sanskrit Infinitive has no *passive* form, the same form being used to denote both *active* and *passive* senses. In turning a sentence involving an Infinitive into the passive voice, the words governed by the Infinitive remain unaffected; as, स मित्राय द्रोग्धुमिच्छति तेन मित्राय द्रोग्धुमिष्यते; रामो ग्रामं गन्तुमारेभे; रामेण ग्रामं गन्तुमारेभे. Where the object of the Infinitive and the verb is the same, it is, in the passive voice, put in the nominative case, leaving it to be *understood* with the Infinitive; as स ग्रन्थं पठितुमिच्छति; तेन ग्रन्थः पठितुमिष्यते, the object of पठितुं being तं, if necessary. In this case it will not do to say ग्रन्थं पठितुमिष्यते, for this would be an *impersonal* construction, though इष् is not an intransitive verb.

In the case of roots like those referred to in the Note to § 178, both constructions will be faultless; पत्रनमालिंगितुं शक्यते or पवनः आलिंगितुं शक्यते, though the latter looks more elegant and classical.

§ **180**. The use of the root अर्ह् 'to deserve' deserves to be marked. It is frequently combined with the Infinitive in the sense of '*prayer*' or '*respectful entreaty*' or in those sentences where '*be pleased*' or '*I pray*' or '*beg*' occurs in English, and in this sense it is generally used with the 2nd and 3rd persons; as, न मां परं संप्रतिपत्तुमर्हसि (Ku. V. 39) '(I) pray, do not consider me to be a stranger'; अवहितस्तावच्छ्रोतुमर्हति कुमारः (Mu. 4) 'be pleased, O Prince, to hear it attentively' (I beg that you will hear &c.); प्रिये जानकि न मामेवंविधं परित्यक्तुमर्हसि (U. 3) 'dear Jánaki, be pleased not to forsake me who am in this plight.'

§ **181**. The infinitive with the final म् omitted is used with the words काम and मनः in the sense of '*wishing*' or '*desiring*,' or '*having a mind*', to do that indicated by the root; as पुनरपि वक्तुकाम इवार्यो लक्ष्यते (S'. 1) your honour appears desirous of speaking again.

मध्यस्था भवती नौ गुणदोषतः परिच्छेत्तुमर्हति। (M. 1)

न युक्तं ते तथा पुराश्रमपदे स्वभावोत्तानहृदयमिमं जनं समयपूर्वं प्रतार्य ईदृशैरक्षरैः प्रत्याचष्टुम् । (S.' 5.)

नार्हति तातो गुजपुंगवधारितायां धुरि दम्यं नियोजयितुम् । (V. 5.)

न शक्यं दैवमन्यथा कर्तुमभियुक्तेनापि । यावत्तु मानुष्यके शक्यमुपपादयितुं तावत्सर्वमुपपाद्यताम् । (K. 62.)

का गणना सचेतनेषु । अपगतचेतनान्यपि संघट्टयितुमलमयं मदनः (K. 157.

अचिराधिष्ठितराज्यः शत्रुः प्रकृतिष्वरूढमूलत्वात् ।
नवसंरोहणशिथिलस्तरुरिव सुकरः समुद्धर्तुम् ॥ (M. 1)

घातयितुमेव नीचः परकार्यं वेत्ति न प्रसाधयितुम् ।
पातयितुमेव शक्तिर्नाखोरुद्धर्तुमन्नपिटम् ॥ (P. I. 15)

शब्दादीन्विषयान् भोक्तुं चरितुं दुश्चरं तपः ।
पर्याप्तोसि प्रजाः पातुमौदासीन्येन वर्तितुम् ॥ (R. X. 25)

वृत्तं रामस्य वाल्मीकेः कृतिस्तौ किन्नरस्वनौ ।
किं तद्येन मनो हर्तुमलं स्यातां न शृण्वताम् । (R. XV. 64)

व्यपदेशमाविलयितुं किमीहसे जनमिमं च पातयितुम् ।(S'. 5.)

व्यालं बालमृणालतंतुभिरसौ रोद्धुं समुज्जृम्भते
छेत्तुं वज्रमणीञ् शिरीषकुसुमप्रान्तेन सन्नह्यते ।
माधुर्यं मधुबिन्दुना रचयितुं क्षारांबुधेरीहते ।
नेतुं वाञ्छति यः खलान् पथि सतां सूक्तैः सुधास्यन्दिभिः॥ (Bh. II. 6)

ADDITIONAL SENTENCES FOR EXERCISE.

अलमनया कथया। संह्रियतामियम्। अहमप्यसमर्थः श्रोतुम्। अतिक्रांतान्यपि संकीर्त्यमानान्यनुभवसमां वेदनामुपजनयन्ति सुहृज्जनस्य दुःखानि। तन्नार्हसि कथं कथमपि विधृतानिमानसुलभानसून् पुनः पुनः स्मरणशोकानलेन्धनतामुपनेतुम्। (K. 169)

अमात्य कुमारो विज्ञापयति। यद्यपि स्वामिगुणा न शक्यन्ते विस्मर्तुं तथापि मद्विज्ञापनां मानयितुमर्हत्यार्यः। (Mu. 2)

न खलु न खल्वमंगलानि चिन्तयितुमर्हन्ति भवन्तः कौरवाणाम्। सन्धेयास्ते भ्रातरो युष्माकम्। (Ve. I)

शमयति गजानन्यान्गन्धद्विपः कलभोऽपि सन्
भवति सुतरां वेगोदग्रं भुजंगशिशोर्विषम्।
भुवमधिपतिर्बालावस्थोऽप्यलं परिरक्षितुं
न खलु वयसा जात्यैवायं स्वकार्यसहो भरः॥ (V. 5)

अतोऽत्र किञ्चिद्भवतीं बहुक्षमां द्विजातिभावादुपपन्नचापलः।
अयं जनः प्रष्टुमनास्तपोधने न चेद्रहस्यं प्रतिवक्तुमर्हसि॥ (Ku. V. 40

तमर्थमिव भारत्या सुतया योक्तुमर्हसि।
अशोच्या हि पितुः कन्या सद्भर्तृप्रतिपादिता॥ (Ku. VI. 79)

न पृथग्जनवच्छुचो वशं वशिनामुत्तम गन्तुमर्हसि।
द्रुमसानुमतां किमन्तरं यदि वायौ द्वितयेऽपि ते चलाः॥ (R. VIII. 90)

अयि सुतपराक्रमानभिज्ञे
धर्मात्मजं प्रति यमौ च कथैव नास्ति
मध्ये वृकोदरकिरीटभृतोर्बलेन।
एकोपि विस्फुरितमण्डलचापचक्रं
कः सिन्धुराजमभिषेणयितुं समर्थः॥ (Ve. 2)

He strove as far as possible to effect the good of his countrymen.

Why do you wish to appropriate to yourselves the property of your brother?

I told him to do the work, which he did most reluctantly.

To take revenge appears at first pleasant to a man, but in the end it results in ruin to himself.

I do not bear to see even poor men disrespectfully treated.

Be pleased, O Kr̥ishṇa, to clear (छिद्) this doubt.

It is now time for you to begin to study your lessons.

Even an insignificant enemy does not deserve (अर्ह्) to be slighted.

I desired them to go to Bombay, but they did not like to do accordingly.

How is it possible (शक्य) to go to another country, leaving you here alone?

Not to mention the poor, even rich persons find it difficult to live honourably in times of famine.

This villain deserves (युज्) to be punished for his crimes.

Let all the prisoners be ordered to be released on this auspicious day.

To expose one's self to danger is sometimes preferable to remaining idle in the house, being deterred by calamities.

In Alakà the splendid palaces will be able (अलं) to equal (तुल्) you in those various particulars.

He was greatly desirous of doing good to others, but has not been able to accomplish his object to any extent.

I beg your honour to grant this request; it will ever be my duty to remember it with gratitude.

LESSON XVII.

Tenses and Moods.

§ **182.** In Sanskrit there are altogether ten Tenses and Moods: Present, Imperfect, Perfect, Aorist, Periphrastic Future, Simple Future, Imperative, Potential, Conditional and Benedictive. The ten *lakaras* given by Pánini are—**लट्, लङ्, लिट्, लुङ्, लुट्, लृट्, लोट्, लिङ्, लृङ्**, and **लेट्**.* Of these the last **लेट्** is found only in the Veda, and has the sense of the subjunctive, and it is generally termed the 'Vedic subjunctive.' The remaining nine respectively correspond to the tenses and moods given above, the Benedictive being in Sanskrit included in **लिङ्** and distinguished from the Potential (विधिलिङ्) as **आशीर्लिङ्**.

§ **183.** Every verb in Sanskrit, whether in a primitive, causal, desiderative, or frequentative form, may be conjugated in the ten tenses and moods, though the last two derivative forms of verbs are very rarely used except in the Present tense. The senses conveyed by them are usually expressed by other forms or combinations of words; as जिगमिषति=गन्तुमिच्छति; अटाट्यते=भृशमटति.

§ **184.** Some of the tenses and moods in Sanskrit exactly correspond to the tenses and moods in other languages, and some are peculiar to Sanskrit. In this and the next three Lessons are given their uses and meanings. The Present tense and the Imperative and Benedictive moods are considered in this Lesson.

---

* The terminology of Pánini is artificial, and is not based on any particular principle. Other grammarians have adopted a somewhat rational nomenclature. The names of the several tenses and moods, according to them, are in the above order as follows:—**भवन्ती (वर्तमाना), ह्यस्तनी, परोक्षा, अद्यतनी, श्वस्तनी, भविष्यन्ती, पंचमी, सप्तमी**, (these two alone being quite artificial) **क्रियातिपत्तिः** and **आशीः**—The feminine is used, because the word **वृत्तिः** is understood after each.

Present Tense.

§ **185**. The Present tense is used to denote an action taking place, or a fact existing, at the *Present* time; as, जगतः पितरौ वन्दे (R. I. 1) 'I salute the parents of the Universe.'

Obs. Strictly speaking, the present tense in Sanskrit corresponds to the present progressive, imperfect or incomplete form, which expresses the *continuance of an action which is begun.* Patanjali says 'प्रवृत्तस्याविरामे शासितव्या भवन्ती ' which indicates that the action denoted by a verb in the Present tense is yet continuing and has not stopped; as, वहति जलमियं पिनष्टि गंधानियं (Mu. I) 'this lady *brings* (is bringing) water ; this (another) *grinds* (is grinding) odorous substances'; एतास्तपस्विकन्यका इत एवाभिवर्तन्ते (S'. 1) (these ascetic-girls *come* (are coming) in this very direction.' There is no distinct form in Sanskrit to express this *continuous* action; hence its usual signification.

It must, however, be remembered that it is only by a special adverb or by the context, that the Present tense can be confined to mean a *present act solely*; as देवदत्तो गच्छति (*i. e.* अधुना); or संप्रत्यधीयावहे. The prinicipal use of the Present indefinite is, as observed by Bain (*Grammar page* 185) ' to express *what is true at all times.*' It expresses present time only as representing *all* time. The permanent arrangements and laws of nature, the peculiarities and propensities of living beings, and whatever is constant, regular, and uniform, have to be represented by the present indefinite; as सत्संगतिः कथय किं न करोति पुंसां ((Bh. II. 23)'say what the company of the good does not do to men'; अस्त्युत्तरस्यां दिशि हिमालयो नाम नगाधिराजः (Ku. I. 1) 'there is (stands) in the northern direction the lord of mountains called Himâlaya';-so नास्ति जीवितादन्यदभिमततरमिह सर्वजंतूनां (K. 35); ऋषीणां पुनराद्यानां वाचमर्थोऽनुधावति (U. 1.); न खलु बहिरुपाधीन् प्रीतयः संश्रयन्ते (Mâl. 1.) &c.

§ **186**. Besides these general senses, the Present tense in Sanskrit has like the English present, the following senses:—

(*a*) It has sometimes the menaning of *immediate future;* as, अयमहमागच्छामि (S'. 3) 'here *I come* (shall come)'; कदा गमिष्यसि—एष गच्छामि (S. K.); नन्वयं न भवसि (Mâl. 5).

(*b*) When an action has just taken place, the Present may be used to denote the *recent* past action; as, कदा त्वं नगरादागतोसि—अयमागच्छामि (S. K.) 'when did you come from the village ?—here I *come* (*I have just come*).

(*c*) In fables and in recounting past events it is used as if the narrator saw them passing before his eyes; as, हस्ती ब्रूते कस्त्वं (H. 2) 'the elephant *asks* (asked) who art thou ?'

(*d*) With words meaning *till, as far as, before, when &c.*, it has the sense of the Future perfect; as, तद्यावन्न परापतति तावदपसर्पतानेन तरुगहनेन (U. 4.) 'therefore, *before* he *returns* (or till he shall have not returned) walk away through this thicket of trees.'

(*e*) Sometimes the Present denotes a *habitual action* such as is represented in English by the past habitual '*used to*' or '*would*'; as, पातुं न प्रथमं व्यवस्यति जलं (S'. 4) 'did not think of drinking water first' (was not in the *habit* of drinking &c.); so हिरण्यको भोजनं कृत्वा बिले स्वपिति (H. I).

§ **187**. The Present is sometimes used for the Future in conditional sentences, or such as imply condition; as, योन्नं ददाति (दाता दास्यति वा); स स्वर्गं याति (याता यास्यति वा) (S. K.) 'he who *offers* (will offer) food; *goes* (will go) to heaven.'

§ **188**. When joined with the particle स्म the Present has the sense of the Past; as, कस्मिंश्चिद्वने भासुरको नाम सिंहः प्रतिवसति स्म (P. I. 8) 'there lived in a forest a lion named Bhâsuraka' क्रीणन्ति स्म प्राणमूल्यैर्यशांसि (S'i. XVII. 15) 'bought fame at the cost of their lives.'

§ **189**. With interrogatives, the Present often conveys the sense of the Future with reference to a desire; as, किं करोमि क्व गच्छामि (U. I.) 'what shall I do, where shall I go'; कं भोजयसि (S. K.); so किं गच्छामि तपोवनं (Mu. 6.).

(*a*) When an answer is given to a question, the Present is used in the sense of the Past with the word ननु; as, कटमकार्षीः किम्—ननु करोमि भोः (S. K.).

§ **190.** *With the words पुरा and यावत् when used as adverbs, it has the sense of the Future, when *certainty* is indicated; as, आलोके ते निपतति पुरा (Me. 88) 'will surely fall in the range of your sight'; यावदस्य दुरात्मनः समुन्मूलनाय शत्रुघ्नं प्रेषयामि (U. 1) 'I shall send S'atrughna to exterminate this wretch.'

Obs. 'Certainty' need not be necessarily meant.

The Imperative Mood.

191. This mood is used in the 2nd person in the sense of *command*, *entreaty* or *gentle advice*, as in English; शृणुत रे पौराः (Mk. 10) 'Listen, ye citizens'; परित्रायध्वं परित्रायध्वं! 'help! help!'; हा प्रियसखि क्वासि देहि मे प्रतिवचनं (U. 1) 'alas, my beloved, where art thou? Give me response'; तृष्णां छिन्द्धि भज क्षमां जहि मदं (Bh. II.) 'leave off ambition (greedy desire); have forbearance; give up pride.'

(*a*) The Imperative in the passive voice is often used as a polite way of expression; as, एतदासनमास्यतां (V. 2.) 'here is a seat, please sit down.'

§ **192.** The second and third person Imperative is frequently used to express benediction or blessings; as प्रत्यक्षाभिः प्रपन्नस्तनुभिरवतु वस्ताभिरष्टाभिरीशः (S'. 1) 'may S'iva, endowed with those eight visible forms, protect you!'; पर्जन्यः कालवर्षी भवतु जनमनोनन्दिनो वान्तु वाताः (Mk. 10) 'may rain pour down in season! may winds blow pleasant to the people's mind'; पुत्रमेवंगुणोपेतं चक्रवर्तिनमाप्नुहि (S.' 1) 'may you get a son posssessed of these qualities, who will be a sovereign ruler!'; पुत्रं लभस्वात्मगुणानुरूपं (R. V. 34) 'may you get a son worthy of yourself'; तात मे चिरं जीव (U. 4) &c.

§ **193.** The Imperative is used in commands and exhortations extending to the future as well as to the present, and is generally used

---

* यावत्पुरानिपातयोर्लट्। (III. 3. 4)

in laws and in laying down precepts, just as the Potential mood is used in the same sense. See Lesson XVIII.

§ **194**. There is a use of the second person Imperative, which deserves notice. When 'frequency' or 'repetition of acts' is indicated the imperative second person (Parasm. and Atm.) is repeated, though the subject of the main verb be different and the verb be in any tense; as, **याहि याहीति याति** (S. K.) 'he goes often and often'; so **यात यातेति याथ; अधीष्व अधीष्वेति अधीते.**

Obs. This corresponds to the use of the Imperative mood in Maráthi and other languages derived from Sanskrit; as, '**हा गृहस्थ खा खा खातो**'; '**बोल बोल बोलतो**'; '**पंतोजीनें मुलांना मार मार मारिलें.**'

(*a*) The Imperative is similarly used (without being repeated) when several acts are spoken of as being done by one person; as, **सक्तून् पिब धानाः खादेत्यभ्यवहरति** (S. K.) 'he takes his meals, eating barley and tasting fried corn.'

Compare Maráthi:—'**शेंगा खा, दाणे चाव, पाणी पी, अशा रीतीनें हा सकाळीं चरत असतो;**' **कुठें झाडेंच उपट, कुंड्याच फोड, फुलेंच तोड, फांद्याच मोड, असा त्या दुष्टानें बागेचा अगदीं नाश करून सोडिला.**'

The Benedictive Mood.

§ **195**. The Benedictive mood (**भूयात्-भविषीष्ट**) is always used in giving blessings, and in the first person expresses the speaker's wish; as, **तत्किमन्यदाशास्महे केवलं वीरप्रसवा भूयाः** (U. 1) 'so what else shall we say as a blessing ? May you give birth to a warrior'; **विधेयासुर्देवाः परमरमणीयां परिणतिं** (Mál. 6) 'may the gods make the end very pleasant ! **कृतार्था भूयासं** (*ibid.*) 'may I become successful !'

क नु खलु संस्थिते कर्मणि सदस्यैरनुज्ञातः श्रमक्लान्तमात्मानं विनोदयामि
(S.' 3.)

किमधुना करोमि । क गच्छामि । कथं मे शान्तिर्भविष्यति । अथवा

तमेव पिंगलकं गच्छामि कदाचिच्छरणागतं मां रक्षति न प्राणैर्वियोजयति ।
(P. 1.)

ततो दिनेषु गच्छत्सु पक्षिशावकानाक्रम्य कोटरमानीय प्रत्यहं खादति स मार्जारः । (H. I.)

तारापीडो देवीमवदत् । अफलमिवाखिलं पश्यामि जीवितं राज्यं च । अप्रतिविधेये धातरि किं करोमि । तन्मुच्यतां देवि शोकानुबन्धः । आधीयतां धैर्ये च धर्मे च धीः । (K. 15)

शुश्रूषस्व गुरून् कुरु प्रियसखीवृत्तिं सपत्नीजने
भर्तृर्विप्रकृतापि रोषणतया मास्म प्रतीपं गमः ।
भूयिष्ठं भव दक्षिणा परिजने भाग्येष्वनुत्सेकिनी
यान्त्येवं गृहिणीपदं युवतयो वामाः कुलस्याधयः ॥
पातुं न प्रथमं व्यवस्यति जलं युष्मास्वपीतेषु या
नादत्ते प्रियमण्डनापि भवतां स्नेहेन या पल्लवम् ।
आद्ये वः कुसुमप्रवृत्तिसमये यस्या भवत्युत्सवः
सेयं याति शकुन्तला पतिगृहं सर्वैरनुज्ञायताम् ॥ (S'. 4)

ADDITIONAL SENTENCES FOR EXERCISE.

अये उदितभूयिष्ठ एष भगवानशेषभुवनद्वीपदीपकस्तपनः । तमुपतिष्ठे ।(Mál. 1.)

अनन्यभाजं पतिमाप्नुहीति सा तथ्यमेवाभिहिता हरेण ।
न हीश्वरव्याहृतयः कदाचित्पुष्णन्ति लोके विपरीतमर्थम् ॥ (Ku. III. 63)

पुरीमवस्कन्द लुनीहि नन्दनं मुषाण रत्नानि हरामरांगनाः ।
विगृह्य चक्रे नमुचिद्विषा बली य इत्थमस्वास्थ्यमहर्दिवं दिवः ॥ (S'i. I. 51)

सन्तः सन्तु निरन्तरं सुकृतिनो विध्वस्तपापोदया
राजानः परिपालयन्तु वसुधां धर्मे स्थिताः सर्वदा ।
काले संततवर्षिणो जलमुचः सन्तु स्थिराः पुण्यतो
मोदन्तां घनबद्धबान्धवसुहृद्गोष्ठीप्रमोदाः प्रजाः (Mal. 10.)

तृष्णां छिन्धि भज क्षमां जहि मदं पापे रतिं मा कृथाः
सत्यं ब्रूह्यनुयाहि साधुपदवीं सेवस्व विद्वज्जनम् ।
मान्यान्मानय विद्विषोऽप्यनुनय प्रच्छादय स्वान्गुणान्
कीर्तिं पालय दुःखिते कुरु दयामेतत्सतां चेष्टितम् ॥ (Bh. II. 77)

कश्चैकान्तं सुखमुपगतो दुःखमेकांततो वा
नीचैर्गच्छत्युपरि च दशा चक्रनेमिक्रमेण । (Me. 112)

जाड्यं धियो हरति सिञ्चति वाचि सत्यं
मानोन्नतिं दिशति पापमपाकरोती ।
चेतः प्रसादयति दिक्षु तनोति कीर्तिं
सत्संगतिः कथय किं न करोति पुंसाम् ॥ (Bh. II. 23)

The serpent having climbed the tree used to eat the young ones of crows.

Arjuna, having strung his bow, says to Karna:—'Are you now ready to fight with me?'

There is a tortoise being carried by two birds on their shoulders.

Why do you abandon me here ? What shall I do ? To whom shall I go for protection ?

I shall just wait for her (*use* यावत्) sitting under the shade of this tree.

I have just come back from a long travel; and do you tell me to work so soon ?

May you both get sons resembling you in all good qualities !

Obey your parents; respect the learned; never speak one word of censure to others; and be content with your position.

May cows give (*Ben.* of दा) much milk! May the Earth be furnished with all sorts of corn by clouds pouring down in season!

Let spies, disguised as ascetics, be sent all over his dominions to find out the real state of his kingdom.

He desolated the whole country pulling down houses, driving away the people, and burning down their possessions.

LESSON XVIII.

The Potential Mood.

§ **196**. The Potential mood in Sanskrit correponds to the Subjunctive mood in English and Latin, but it has not all the senses and uses of the English Subjunctive, nor the wide application of the Latin Subjunctive. In English the Subjunctive mood is not used in independent clauses; in Latin, it is used without any preceding verb to express a *wish* but it is generally used in dependent assertions; but in Sanskrit the Potential mood is used both in *independent* and *dependent* assertions; नीचैराख्यं गिरिमधिवसेः (Me. 26); कृत्यं घटेत सुहृदो यदि तत्कृतं स्यात् (Mál. 1). We shall now see in what senses it is used in Sanskrit.

§ **197**. The Potential expresses (A) probability, command, wish, prayer, hope, and capability; (B) it is used in dependent clauses in which the above senses are implied; and (C) it is used in conditional or hypothetical sentences, in which one statement depends upon another as its reason, or condition.

A.

§ **198**. The senses of 'probability,' 'command' &c. expressed by the Potential are expressed, in English, by '*may*' '*shall*', or '*should*,' and often by '*will*', '*would*', '*could*,' '*might*,' as used in direct assertions; as लभेत सिकतासु तैलमपि यत्नतः पीडयन् (Bh. II. 5) 'one may even get oil from sand, by diligently squeezing it together'; मौर्ये भूषणविक्रयं नरपतौ को नाम संभावयेत् (Mu. 5) who, indeed, would think it probable that the Maurya king would sell ornaments?;' जेतारं कार्तिकेयस्य

विजयेय (Mv. 3) 'may I conquer the conqueror of Kártikeya'; **मनसिजतरुः कुर्यान्मां फलस्य रसज्ञं** (M. 4) 'may the tree of Love make me taste the flavour of its fruit;' **कुर्यां हरस्यापि पिनाकपाणेर्धैर्यच्युतिं** (Ku. III. 10) 'I could make even the Pináka-weaponed God lose his strength of mind;' **भो भोजनं लभेय** (S. K.) 'I pray that I get food.'

(*a*) The most general application of the Potential is in giving commands, in laying down precepts or rules for guidance, and in showing obligations of duty, as expressed by *shall* or *should* in English; as, **ऊनद्विवर्षं निखनेत्** (Y. III. 1) 'one shall bury a child that is less than two years old'; **आपदर्थे धनं रक्षेत्** (C. 29) 'one should save wealth against (in order to meet) bad time'; **सहसा विदधीत न क्रियां** (Ki. II. 30) 'one should not do any act rashly.'

Obs.—Pâṇini lays down that the Potential, as well as the Imperative, is used in *directing* (a subordinate &c.), *giving invitation, expressing permission* (to do a thing), *speaking of an honorary office or duty in asking questions, and in prayers* (**विधिनिमन्त्रणामन्त्रणाधीष्टसंप्रश्नप्रार्थनेषु** III. 3. 161), and that in the case of *direction, premission* and *proper* (particular) *time* the Potential, the Imperative and the Potential passive participles may be equally used (**प्रैषातिसर्गप्राप्तकालेषु कृत्याश्च** III. 3. 163); as **इह भुंजीत-भुंक्तां भवान्; इहासीत भवान्** or **इहास्यतां आसितव्यं भवता** 'you may sit here'; **नीचैराख्यं गिरिमधिवसेः** (Me. 26) 'you may dwell on the mountain' &c.; **पुत्रमध्यापयेद्भवान्** 'you will teach the son as an honorary duty'; **किं भो वेदमधीयिय उत तर्कं** 'Sir, what shall I learn, the Veda or Logic ?' ; **भोजनं लभेय** or **लभै**...(S. K.).

The use of the Potential is, however, more common in these senses than that of the Imperative or the participle.

§ **199.** When *fitness* is implied, the pontential passive participle or this mood may be used; and sometimes the noun in **तृ** also; as, **त्वं कन्यां वहेः, त्वं कन्याया वोढा**, or **त्वया कन्या वोढव्या** (S. K.) 'thou art fit to marry the girl.'

(*a*) When '*capability*' is implied, the Potential or the Potential passive participle may be used; as, **भारं त्वं वहेः** or **भारस्त्वया वोढव्यः** (S. K.) 'you can carry the load.'

§ **200.** *With interrogative words such as, किं, कतर &c. the Potential or Simple Future is used to imply censure; as, कः कतरो वा हरिं निन्देद्व निन्दिष्यति वा 'who will censure Hari ?'

(*a*) †When wonder is implied, the Simple Future is used in preference to the Potential, when यदि is not used; as, आश्चर्यमन्धो नाम कृष्णं द्रक्ष्यति (S. K.) 'it is a wonder that the blind man should see Kr̥ishna !'; but आश्चर्यं यदि सोऽधीयीत 'a wonder if he study.'

B.

§ **201.** The Potential mood is used in dependent sentences implying the senses of *hope, prayer,* &c. stated in § 197; as, आशंसेऽधीयीय (S. K.) 'I hope I shall learn'; आशंसा न हि नः प्रेते जीवेम दशमूर्धनि (Bk. XIX. 5) 'we had no hopes that we should live' &c.

(*a*) With words implying '*wish*' the Potential is used in the sense of the infinitive mood when the agents of both the actions are the same; as, भुंजीयेति इच्छति (S. K.)=भोक्तुमिच्छति 'wishes that he will eat', or 'wishes to eat.'

§ **202.** In dependent sentences, the Potential is often used with relative words to denote '*result* or *purpose*'; as, दोषं तु मे कंचित्कथय येन स प्रतिविधीयेत (U. 1.) 'but tell me some fault of mine so that (in order that) it may be rectified.'

§ **203.** ‡When a *hope* is expressed except by the word कच्चित्, the Potential is generally used; as, कामो मे भुञ्जीत भवान् 'it is my hope that you will eat'; but कच्चिज्जीवति 'I hope he lives'; कच्चिद्भर्तुः स्मरसि रसिके त्वं हि तस्य प्रियेति (Me. 88) 'I hope you remember your master, O pleasing bird, because you are his favourite.'

(*a*) ‖ When '*expectation*' is implied by such words as, संभावय्, अपि, or अपि नाम, the Potential or Simple Future is used except when

---

* किंवृत्ते (गर्हायां) लिङ्लृटौ (III. 3. 144)

† (चित्रीकरणे) शेषे लृडयदौ । (III. 3. 151)

‡ कामप्रवेदनेऽकच्चिति । (III. 3. 153)

‖ विभाषा धातौ संभावनावचनेऽयदि (III. 3. 155)

the word यद् is used; as, संभावयामि भुञ्जीत भोक्ष्यते वा भवान् (S. K.) 'I expect you will eat'; अपि नाम भगवतीनीतिर्विजेष्यते (Mál. 7) 'would (I wish) that the plans of the revered lady become successful'; अपि जीवेत् स ब्राह्मणशिशुः (U. 2) 'may I expect that the Bráhmana boy comes to life?' (Would that he comes to life). But संभावयामि यद्भुञ्जीथास्त्वम् 'I expect that you will eat.'

(*b*) *When words expressing '*wish*' such as इष्, कम्, प्रार्थ्, &c., are used, the Potential or Imperative is used; as, इच्छामि सोमं पिबेत् पिबतु वा भवान् (S. K.) 'I wish your honour will drink Soma.'

§ **204.** † With the words काल, वेला, समय, the Potential is used when the word यद् occurs in the sentence; as, कालः-समयो-वेला वा यद् भवान्भुञ्जीत 'it is time that your honour should take your meals.'

C.

§ **205.** In conditional sentences in which one statement is made to depend upon another as its reason or ground, the Potential is used in both the *antecedent* and the *consequent* clauses, (otherwise called the *protasis* and *apodosis*), the former containing the condition or ground of argument, and the latter the conclusion based upon it. The place of '*if*' whether expressed or understood, is taken by यदि or चेद्; as यद्यत्र तातः सन्निहितो भवेत् ततः किं भवेत् (S'. 1.) 'if our papa were here today—then what would happen'; दैवात्पश्येर्जगति विचरन्निच्छया मत्प्रियां चेद् आश्वास्यादौ तदनु कथयेर्माधवीयामवस्थां (Mál. 9) 'if you, roaming at will over the world, happen to see my beloved, first comfort her, and then relate the state of Mádhava'; so कृत्यं घटेत सुहृदो यदि तत्कृतं स्यात् &c.

Obs.—Mark that चेद् never stands at the beginning of a sentence.

§ **206.** In conditional sentences the Present of Simple Future is often used instead of the Potential; as, यदि स्थित्वा द्रक्ष्यति कुप्यति प्रभुः (Bh. III. 97) 'if the lord get up and see (you), he will be angry'; न चेद्ब्रवीषि प्रश्नानश्नामि त्वां (D. K. II. 6) 'if you do not answer my ques-

---

* इच्छार्थेषु लिङ्लोटौ । (III. 3. 157)

† (कालसमयवेलासु) लिङ् यदि । (III. 3. 168)

tions, I shall eat you'; कृष्णं नंस्यति चेत्सुखं यास्यति (S. K.) 'if he bow down to Krishna he will go happily.'

Obs.—(*a*) Sometimes the Present is used in the protasis and the Potential in the apodosis; as, यदि तस्य प्राणविपत्तिरुपजाते तदपि महदेनो भवेत् (K. 160) 'if his death take place, that also will be a great sin'; so क्षणमप्यवतिष्ठते श्वसन्यदि जंतुर्ननु लाभवानसौ (भवेत्) (R. VIII. 87).

(*b*) The Imperative is used instead of the Potential, in the apodosis as a polite way of speaking; as, न चेदन्यकार्यातिपातो गृह्यतामातिथेयसत्कारः (S'. 1) 'if any other duty should not suffer thereby, you might enjoy the hospitality shone to guests.'

(*c*) When the conditional clause is *affirmative* and *certain* as expressed by the indicative mood of the verb, or when both Members of the sentence deal with *facts*, the Present must be used instead of the Potential; as, if 'it *rains*, we cannot go out'; यदि देवो वर्षति तर्हि वयं बहिर्गन्तुं न शक्नुमः; not देवो वर्षेत् &c.

वयस्य किं परमार्थत एव देव्या व्रतनिमित्तोऽयमारंभः स्यात् ।

(V. 3)

यदि त्वामीदृशमैक्ष्वाको राजा रामभद्रः पश्येत्तदास्य हृदयं स्नेहेनाभिष्यन्देत् । (U. 5)

देव यदि चन्द्रमस्युष्मा दहने वा शीतलत्वमंशुमालिनि वा तमः संभाव्यते ततो युवराजेऽपि दोषः । (K. 286)

यदि मे सहसा दर्शनपथान्नापयाति नारोहति वा कैलासशिखरं नोत्पतति वा गगनतलं ततः सर्वमेतदेनामुपसृत्य पृच्छामि । (K. 132)

लभेत वा प्रार्थयिता न वा श्रियं
श्रिया दुरापः कथमीप्सितो भवेत् ! (S'. 3)

परोक्षे कार्यहन्तारं प्रत्यक्षे प्रियवादिनम् ।
वर्जयेत्तादृशं मित्रं विषकुम्भं पयोमुखम् ॥ (C. 18)

अलब्धं चैव लिप्सेत लब्धं रक्षेदवक्षयात् ।
रक्षितं वर्द्धयेत्सम्यग् वृद्धं तीर्थेषु निक्षिपेत् ॥ (H. 2)

उत्सीदेयुरिमे लोका न कुर्यां कर्म चेदहम् ।
संकरस्य च कर्ता स्यामुपहन्यामिमाः प्रजाः ॥ (Bg. III 24)

भवेदभीष्ममद्रोणं धृतराष्ट्रबलं कथम् ।
यदि तत्तुल्यकर्मात्र भवान् धुर्यो न युज्यते ॥ (Ve. 3)

तन्नो देवा विधेयासुर्येन रावणवद्वयम् ।
सपत्नांश्चाधिजीयास्म संग्रामे च मृषीमहि ॥ (Bk. XIX. 2)

आददीध्वं माहाहार्णि तत्र वासांसि सत्वराः ।
उद्धुनीयात सत्केतून् निर्हरेताग्र्यचन्दनम् ॥ (Ibid. 8)

नावकल्प्यमिदं ग्लायेद्यत्कृच्छ्रेषु भवानपि ।
न पृथग्जनवज्जातु प्रमुह्येत् पन्डितो जनः (Ibid. 17)

ADDITIONAL SENTENCES FOR EXERCISE.

अपि नामोर्वशी—

गूढा नूपुरशब्दमात्रमपि मे कांतं श्रुतौ पातयेत्
पश्चादेत्य शनैः करांबुजहृते कुर्वीत वा लोचने ।
हर्म्येऽस्मिन्नवतीर्य साध्वसवशान्मन्दायमाना बला-
दानीयेत पदात्पदं चतुरया सख्या ममोपान्तिकम् ॥ (V. 3)

इति ध्रुवेच्छामनुशासती सुतां शशाक मेना न नियन्तुमुद्यमात् ।
क ईप्सितार्थस्थिरनिश्चयं मनः पयश्च निम्नाभिमुखं प्रतीपयेत् ॥ (Ku. V. 5)

फलार्थी नृपतिर्लोकान्पालयेद्यत्नमास्थितः ।
दानमानादितोयेन मालाकारोऽङ्कुरानिव ॥ (P. I. 8)

कौर्मं संकोचमास्थाय प्रहारानपि मर्षयेत् ।
प्राप्तकालं तु नीतिज्ञ उत्तिष्ठेत्कृष्णसर्पवत् ॥ (H. 3)

किं वा तवात्यन्तवियोगमोघे कुर्यामुपेक्षां हतजीवितेऽस्मिन् ।
स्याद्रक्षणीयं यदि मे न तेजस्त्वदीयमन्तर्गतमन्तरायः ॥ (R. XIV. 65)

प्रसह्य मणिमुद्धरेन्मकरवक्त्रदंष्ट्रांकुरात्
समुद्रमपि संतरेत्प्रचलदूर्मिमालाकुलम् ।
भुजंगमपि कोपितं शिरसि पुष्पवद्धारये-
न्नतु प्रतिनिविष्टमूर्खजनचित्तमाराधयेत् ॥ (Bh. II 4)

अप्राज्ञेन च कातरेण च गुणः स्यात्सानुरागेण कः
प्रज्ञाविक्रमशालिनोऽपि हि भवेत्किं भक्तिहीनात्फलम् ।
प्रज्ञाविक्रमभक्तयः समुदिता येषां गुणा भूतये
ते भृत्या नृपतेः कलत्रमितरे संपत्सु चापत्सु च ॥ (Mu. 1)

स्रगियं यदि जीवितापहा हृदये किं निहिता न हन्ति माम् ।
विषमप्यमृतं क्वचिद्भवेदमृतं वा विषमीश्वरेच्छया ॥ (R. VIII. 46)

While he was thinking how he should accomplish his desired object, the whole night passed away.

How possibly will he be at ease, being plunged into this great ocean of sorrow ?

May it be that her agony proceeds from the influence of love ?

You should obey your parents and teachers, speak the truth, keep company with the good, and always think of the greatness of God.

If you go out in this pitchy darkness, and bring me flowers from the garden, I shall consider you to be of a fearless mind.

Even if his heart were made of stone, he would be moved to pity at seeing this heart-rending state of the woman.

Having heard that strange account I was at a loss what to say or do next.

One should win over a covetous man by giving him wealth and a fool by acting according to his humour.

Who but the sun can clear the sky of the pollution of nocturnal darkness?

I might overtake even Garuda if he has started before me with this speed of the chariot.

Would that the wretched Cháṇakya were won over to the side of the Nanda family.

I hope (*use* कच्चित्) your religious austerities are being carried on without any obstruction.

LESSON XIX.

Imperfect, Perfect, and Aorist.

§ **207.** 'In English there is only one tense referring to *past* time; it is the *past indefinite* or *Aorist*' (Howard's *Note on English verb* P. 12); as, 'I walked.' In Sanskrit there are three tenses referring to a past time: *Imperfect, Perfect* and *Aorist.* Each of these had originally a peculiar signification. In ancient works, or works composed at a time when, we have reason to believe, Sanskrit was a spoken language, they are found to be used in their exact senses; later on, as Sanskrit became less and less a spoken language, writers began to use these three tenses promiscuously. The senses in which they were originally used are as follows:—

The *Imperfect* is, according to Páṇini, अनद्यतने लङ्, *i. e.*, it denotes past action done previous to the current day, hence at a time removed from this day. The *Perfect* is परोक्षे लिट् *i. e.*, it denotes past action done previous to this day, and which was not witnessed by the speaker. The *Aorist* is merely भूतार्थे लुङ्., *i. e.*, it has reference to a past time indefinitely or generally, without reference to any particular time. An action done before to-day is expressed by the Perfect or Imperfect; what remains for the Aorist is, therefore, to express a past action done very *recently*, say, in the course of the current day or having reference to a present act. Aorist, therefore, merely implies the completion of an action at a past time *generally*, and also an action done at a very recent time, as during the course of this day. The Imperfect and Perfect are used in narrating events of past occurrence, generally in remote past time; the Aorist in used is dialogues and conversations which refer to recent past actions; but it is not used to denote past *specified* time, or to narrate events.* Thus in the whole of the *Purusha-Sukta* (Rigveda X. 90) the Imperfect or Perfect alone is used, the events narrated referring to a past time, and in Aitareya Brahmana recent actions are shown by the Aorist; as, स भूमिं विश्वतो वृत्वा अत्यतिष्ठद्दशांगुलं, गावो ह जज्ञिरे तस्मात् &c.; अजनि ते वै पुत्रो यजस्व मामनेनेति. But later Sanskrit writers lost sight of this difference between the Imperfect, Perfect, and Aorist, and the three are found to be promiscuosly used to denote merely *a past action*, whether recent, remote or not witnessed by the speaker; as, तदाहं किमकरवं क्वागमं किं व्यलपमिति सर्वमेव नाज्ञासिषम् (K. 166).

§ **208**. The *Imperfect*, besides its general use, is sometimes used to ask a question referring to a recent time; as, अगच्छत्किं स ग्रामं '*has* he *gone* to the village?'; but when a remote time is implied, the Perfect alone should be used; as, कंसं जघान किं (S. K.) 'did he kill Kamsa?'

§ **209**. *The Perfect*—In the first person the Perfect denotes some distraction or unconscious state of the mind: it should not, therefore, be used in the first person, except in this sense; as, बहु जगदपुरस्तात्तस्य मत्ता किलाहं (S'i. XI. 39) 'being frenzied, I forsooth prated much before him.'

(*a*). It is also used in the first person to conceal the truth from somebody by affirming the opposite of that which is alleged against

---

* For a fuller explanation of the difference between these three tenses, see Prof. R. G. Bhandarkar's *Second Book of Sanskrit*, Preface to the First Edition.

him; as कलिंगेष्ववात्सीः किं 'didst thou dwell in the country of the Kalingas ?'; नाहं कलिंगाञ्जगाम (S. K.) 'I did not (so much as) go to the Kalingas.'

§ **210.** The *Aorist*—* This tense, besides its general meaning of a *recent*, indefinite past time, also implies the idea of *continuousness*. The Imperfect cannot be used in this sense; as, ब्राह्मणेभ्यो यावज्जीवमन्नमदात् (not अददात्) 'he gave food to Brahma*n*as throughout his life.'

(*a*) In the case of पुरा 'formerly, not joined with स्म, the Imperfect, Perfect, Aorist or Present may be used; as, वसन्तीह पुरा छात्रा अवात्सुरवसन्नूषुर्वा 'here formerly dwelt pupils.' But with पुरास्म the Present alone is used; as, यजति स्म पुरा 'he formerly sacrificed.'

§ **211.** The augment of the Aorist is usully cut off after the particle मा or मास्म. In the second person this tense with the augment so cut off has the sense of the imperative mood, and in the first and third, that of the English *that*' with '*may*' or '*might*' or simply of '*may*'; as, वयस्य मा कातरो भूः (M. 4) 'friend, be not afraid'; भर्तुर्विप्रकृतापि रोषणतया मास्म प्रतीपं गमः (S'. 4) 'though wronged (ill-treated), do not through anger, go against (the will of) thy husband'.

मा मूमुहत्खलु भवन्तमनन्यजन्मा
मा ते मलीमसविकारघना मतिर्भूत् ।
इत्यादि नन्विह निरर्थकमेव (Mál. 1)

'May the Self-born (Cupid) not infatuate thee; may thy mind be not infested with dark thoughts (emotions)—it is but vain to say this or some such thing in this case.'

तपोवनवासिनामुपरोधो मा भूत् । (S'. 1)

नरपतिराहारं निर्वर्त्यास्थानमंडपमगयासीत् । तत्र चावनिपतिभिरमात्यैर्मित्रैश्च सह तास्ताः कथाः कुर्वन् मुहूर्तमिवासांचक्रे । (K. 17)

---

* क्रियाप्रबंधसामीप्ययोः । (III. 3. 135)

शुकनासोऽपि महान्तं कालं तं राज्यभारमनायासेनैव प्रज्ञाबलेन बभार । यथैव राजा सर्वकार्याण्यकार्षीत्तद्वदसावपि द्विगुणितप्रजानुरागश्चकार ।

(K. 58)

आविर्भूतज्योतिषां ब्राह्मणानां
ये व्याहारास्तेषु मा संशयो भूत् ॥ (U. 4)

जुगोपात्मानमत्रस्तो भेजे धर्ममनातुरः ।
अगृध्नुराददे सोऽर्थमसक्तः सुखमन्वभूत् ॥ (R. I. 17)

अधिगतपरमार्थान्पण्डितान्मावमंस्था-
स्तृणमिव लघुलक्ष्मीर्नैव तान्संरुणद्धि । (Bh. II. 17)

ADDITIONAL SENTENCES FOR EXERCISE.

चंडवर्मा प्राणैरेनं न व्ययूयुजत् । अपि त्वमीनयदपनीताशेषशल्यमकल्पसंधो बंधनगृहमजीगणच्च गणकसंघैरद्यैव क्षपावसाने विवाहमीया राजदुहितेति । (D. K. II. 1)

दिशः प्रसेदुर्मरुतो ववुः सुखाः प्रदक्षिणार्चिर्हविरग्निराददे ।
बभूव सर्वं शुभशंसि तत्क्षणं भवो हि लोकाभ्युदयाय तादृशाम् ॥ (R. III. 14)

मा भूदाश्रमपीडेति परिमेयपुरःसरौ ।
अनुभावविशेषात्तु सेनापरिवृताविव । (R. I. 14)

भूयस्तपोव्ययो मा भूद्वाल्मीकेरिति सोऽत्यगात् ।
मैथिलीतनयोद्गीतनिस्पन्दमृगमाश्रमम् ॥ (R. XV. 37)

क्लैब्यं मास्म गमः पार्थ नैतत्त्वय्युपपद्यते ।
क्षुद्रं हृदयदौर्बल्यं त्यक्त्वोत्तिष्ठ परंतप ॥ (Bg. II. 3)

When I knew that my friends had heard me prate in my sleep, I felt ashamed.

Do not be (भू) anxious on this point; my father will take care of (चिन्त्) your son in your absence.

He spent the whole day in the company of his friends now by conversing with them on scriptural points, and now by engaging in drawing pictures.

Why have you spoilt my book?—No, Sir, I did not even look (दृश्) at it.

When I went to see him I did not find him at home.

Our father has divided the whole ancestral property that we might not afterwards quarrel with one another.

The king has stationed (स्थापय् *aor.*) his guards arround all hermitages that the ascetics might not be disturbed (*aor. pass.* of the *caus.* of अर्द्) in their penances.

I am glad to find that your attempts at improving the condition of the poor have been crowned with success.

The witnesses of the plaintiff have all come; let, therefore, the hearing of the case be proceeded with.

Having spent his life in hunting for many years he at last accidentally fell a victim into the jaws of a fierce tiger.

LESSON XX.

The two Futures and the Conditional.

§ **212.** In English *futurity* is expressed by *will* or *shall*; in Sanskrit there are two different tenses to denote a future action; the the First or Periphrastic Future, and the Second or Simple Future. The original distinction between the two is nearly the same as between Imperfect and Aorist, except this, that the latter refer to a *past* time, the former to a *future* one; in other words, the First Future denotes an action which is not to take place in the course of the current day, while the Second Future refers to a future time generally or indefinitely, as also to a recent future action. Thus the First Fututre denotes a remote future time not of to-day; while the Second Future is employed to denote indefinite future time, to-day's future time, and recent and future continuous time; as, पंचषैरहोभिर्वयमेव तत्र गंतारः (Mu. 5) 'we ourselves shall go there in five or six days;' एते...उन्मूलितारः कपिकेतनेन (Ki. III. 22) 'they will be extirpated by Arjuna (the monkey-bannered)'; यास्यत्यद्य शकुंतला (S'. 4) S'akuntal will depart (departs) to-day'; सेविष्यन्ते नयनसुभगं खे भवन्तं बलाकाः (Me. 9) 'cranes will wait (at some future time) upon thee, lovely to behold, in the sky.' Writers are not so loose in the use of these two tenses, as in the use of the three past tenses. The Periphrastic Future is far less frequently used; and where it is used, it *generally* denotes a *remote* (not to-day's) future action; while the Simple Future is used to denote *any* indefinite future action.

§ **213.** When the close proximity of future action is intended, the Present or the Future may be used; as कदा गमिष्यसि—एष गच्छामि गमिष्यामि वा (S. K.) 'when will you go? I shall just go.'

§ **214.** *When hope is expressed in a conditional form, the Aorist, the Present, or Simple Future is used in both the clauses to denote a future time; as देवश्चेदवर्षीद् वर्षति वर्षिष्यति वा धान्यमवाप्स्म वपामो वप्स्यामो वा (S. K.) 'if it were to rain we should sow corn.'

§ **215**. Sometimes the Simple Future is used in the sense of the Imperative as a courteous way of telling one to do a thing; as, तदां मम पाशांश्छेत्स्यसि (H. I) 'afterwards cut my bonds'; so पश्चात्सरः प्रति गमिष्यसि मानसं तत् (V. 4) this corresponds to the polite form of expression in English; as, 'you *will see* me at the station to-morrow at twelve noon.'

§ **216**. The *Conditional* is used in those conditional sentences in which the *non-performance* of the action is implied, or 'where the falsity of the antecedent is implied *as a matter of fact*'. It usually corresponds to the English pluperfect Conditional and must in

* आशंसायां भूतवच्च (III. 3. 132.)

Sanskrit be used in *both* the antecedent and the consequent clause; as, यदि सुरभिमवाप्स्यस्तन्मुखोच्छ्वासगन्धं तव रतिरभविष्यत्पुंडरीके किमेस्मिन् (V. 4) 'if you had felt (which you clearly have not) the fragrant smell of her breath, would you have had any liking for this lotus ?'

Bhaṭṭi's use of the Conditional (Canto 21) is much wider, but it is not supported by classical usage.

N. B.—The Sanskrit Conditional should not be used in those conditional sentences, where it is merely implied that under a supposed condition, such a consequence would follow; as, 'if he were here, he would defend his country bravely;' 'if I could agree to this your plan I would rather die than live.' In translating such sentences the Potential is used; as, यदि सोऽत्र सन्निहितो भवेत्तर्हि स्वदेशं वीरवद्रक्षेत्.

Additional Remarks on the use of the Tenses and Moods.

§ **217.** The intricacies and details of the several forms of the Present, Past, and Future are not found in Sanskrit. There is one principal tense, and the different forms are usually expressed by that tense. Even in English forms like the future progressive passive, future progressive passive continuous, are of a modern growth, and are not of frequent occurrence. Hence it is that a student of Sanskrit generally finds it difficult to translate the multifarious forms of these tenses into their corresponding Sanskrit equivalents. Some hints on this point are given in the following sections, stating in more detail what has been given in the three preceding lessons.

Present, Past, and Future.

§ **218.** As before observed, the Present tense in its simple form (called the *present indefinite*) has in Sanskrit most of the senses which it has in English (§ 186). The English Past tense has according to the usage of classical authors at least, come to be expressed by any of the three tenses referring to a past action, and future time is generally denoted by the two Future forms in Sanskrit, and sometimes by the Potential mood (§ 198). But the several forms of the different tenses are not considered by Sanskrit writers; if they are to be translated into Sanskrit, other forms have to be used for them.

§ **219.** The *continuous* forms, called 'present continuous', 'past continuous,' and 'future continuous,' may be generally translated into Sanskrit by merely putting the simple forms of the tenses, as, 'he *is studying* his lesson' **स पाठमधीते**, and not **अधीयानोऽस्ति**; for the progressive or continuous form is a *true or strict present tense* (Bain's *Grammar* P. 186); the boys *are* now *playing*' **बालका अधुना क्रीडन्ति**; 'the sun was shining' **रविरतपत्** (not **तपन् आसीत्**); 'he *will be preparing* his lesson' **स पाठमध्येष्यते.**

Obs. The present participle with **आस्** is used in those cases where a regular continuity of action is intended to be expressed, such as is stated in § 145. When these continuous forms occur in subordinate sentences, the locative absolute of the present participle may be conveniently used; as, 'while the minister *was speaking,* a messenger entered the assembly,' **भाषमाणेऽमात्ये कश्चिद्दूतः सभां प्राविशत्.**

§ **220.** The *emphatic* forms, which exist only for the Present and Past, may be translated by **एव**, **नूनं**, **खलु**, or some such word expressing *certainty,* with the simple forms; as, 'I *do consider* thee guilty' **अहं त्वामपराधिनं मन्ये खलु—एव**, or **नूनं त्वां...मन्ये**; 'he *did tell* a lie' **सोऽसत्यमभाषतैव** or **अभाषत खलु.**

Perfect and its continuous Forms.

§ **221.** The *Present Perfect* is more strictly expressed by the *Aorist,* or by the past participle of the root; as, 'what sin I *have committed* by day' **यदह्ना पापमकार्षम्**; 'I *have done* my work' **अहं मम कार्यं संपादितवान्**; or sometimes by the *Imperfect,* and the *Perfect* also; as 'he *has finished* his speech' **भाषणमवसितवान्**; or **भाषणाद्व्यरंसीत्** or **व्यरमत्** or **विरराम.**

§ **222.** The *Past Perfect* or *Pluperfect* may in dependent sentences be translated by the locative absolute or ground; as, 'when he *had departed* I came back' तस्मिन्नपक्रान्तेऽहं प्रत्यागच्छम्; 'after I *had prepared* my lessons, I went to school' पाठानदीत्य शालामगच्छम्; or sometimes by the past participle alone; as, "I said to him who *had* thus *spoken* 'go now' " इत्युक्तवन्तं व्रज साधयेत्यहमब्रवम्; 'he cured him who *had been wounded* क्षतमचिकित्सत.

§ **223.** The *Future Perfect* may be expressed by the Potential of भू with the past part. of the verb; or better, by the passive or impersonal construction; as, 'he *will have gone* there by this time' अनेन समयेन स तत्र गतो भवेत, or तेन तत्र गंतव्यं.

§ **224.** The *Perfect continuous* forms 'I have been doing', 'I had been doing,' 'I shall have been doing,' may be translated by (*a*) the simple tense with words of time ; as, तौ चिरान्निवसतः (H. I. 2.) (*b*) by present participles with the corresponding tenses of आस्, वस्, or स्था (§ 145) ; or (*c*) more idiomatically, by the genitive of the present participle, made to qualify the subject, with words expressive of time; as, 'I *have been* doing it for 3 days' इदं कुर्वतो मम दिनत्रयं जातं; 'how long *had* he *been staying* there ?' तस्य तत्र स्थितस्य कियान् कालो व्यतीतः.

§ **225.** The *prospective* or *intentional* forms, *i. e.* 'he is going or is about to do', 'he was about to do' and 'he will be about to do ' may be expressed by the words काम or मनः joined to the Infintive of the verbs (§ 181); as, कर्तुकामोऽस्ति बभूव-भविष्यति वा; and in subordinate sentences, they may be translated by the future participles also; as 'when he *was about to go* I spoke to him thus ' गमिष्यन्तं-गंतुकामं तमहमेवमवोचम्.

Will and Shall.

§ **226.** *Shall* in the 1st person and *will* in the 2nd and 3rd persons expressing mere futurity, may be translated by the Simple Future or Potential; as, 'I shall do it' अहं तत्कुर्यां or करिष्यामि; 'he *will* go there' स तत्र गच्छेत् or गमिष्यति.

§ **227**. *Will* in the 1st person showing 'intention or resolution on the part of the agent' may be expressed by the Present tense of verbs meaning 'to wish', or more generally by the Simple Future with एव or similar words showing *certainty*; as 'I *will* do it' अहं तत्कर्तुमिच्छामि, or generally अहं तत्करिष्यामेव; 'even if death be the result, I *will* do it', 'यद्यपि तन्मृत्युपर्यवसायि भवेद् तथाप्यहं तत्करिष्यामेव.

§ **228**. *Shall* in the 2nd and 3rd persons, showing (1) *command* or *threat* or *self-determination* on the part of the speaker, may be translated by the Potential mood, or by some word meaning 'to command', such as आज्ञापय्, or by the Future of the causal of the verb, the subject of the causal being the speaker; as, 'the son *shall* obey his father' पुत्रः पितुराज्ञामनुरुध्येत; 'thou *shalt* go to the castle' *i. e.* 'I *command* thee to go' &c. दुर्गं गंतुं त्वामाज्ञापयामि; 'he shall do it' अहं तं तत्कारयिष्यामि, अहं तं गमयिष्यामि &c.; or sometimes by the use of the potential passive participle with or without एव, अवश्यं &c.; as, 'thou *shalt* not kill him' त्वया स नैव हंतव्यः; 'thou *shalt* not move even a step from this place' त्वयास्मात्स्थानात्पदात्पदमपि न दातव्यं. (2) When *shall* shows *promise*, it may be translated by the Potential or Simple Future of the verb with a word expressing 'certainty'; as, 'he *shall* be my prime minister' स मम प्रधानसचिवो भवेत् (भविष्यति) इत्यहं निश्चयेन कथयामि or तं प्रधानसचिवं करिष्याम्येव.

§ **229**. *Shall* in *indirect* speeches, expressing futurity in all persons, may be expressed by the simple Future or Potential; as, 'you say you *shall* do it' वयं तत्करिष्यामः (कुर्याम) इति यूयं भणथ. *Will* showing *determination* on the part of the agent and used in all persons, may be translated as in § 227. 'He says he *will* write' अहमवश्यं लेखिष्यामीति स वदति ।

§ **230**. *Will* and *shall* occuring in interrogative sentences in all persons except the 1st, and expressing *will* or *wish* on the part of the person interrogated, may be translated by the Potential or Imperative when referring to another's will, and by roots meaning 'wish' when referring to the will of the subject of the sentence; as, '*shall* I or he go?' गच्छेयं or गच्छामि किं, गच्छेत् (गच्छतु) किं; '*shall* you go?' गच्छेत किं or गन्तुं शक्नुयात किं; '*will* you or he go?' गन्तुमिच्छथ or इच्छति किं; but when *will*, interrogatively used, merely refers to futurity, the Simple Future is used; as, '*will* he go there?' तत्र गमिष्यति किं; '*will* you come to my house' मम गृहमागमिष्यथ किं.

Should and Would.

§ **231.** *Should* expressing contingent futurity, obligation or duty, is translated by the Potential mood (§ 198), or by the potential passive participle; when it shows some doubt or diffidence, as in 'I should think so', we may say; इति मे वितर्कः or मतिः.

§ **232.** *Would* showing *contingency* or *wish* is expressed by the Potential (§ 198) ; when it shows *habitual* action it may be translated by the Present tense alone; as, कालं नयति '*would* pass his time'; पातुं न प्रथमं व्यवस्यति जलं (S'. 4) 'she *would* not drink water first'; '*would* that he were present' यदि सोऽत्र सन्निहितः स्यात् तर्हि अहो शोभनं भवेत्.

(*a*) In interrogative sentences, *would* and *should* are translated much in the same way as 'will,' and 'shall'; as, '*should* I or he go out?' बहिर्गच्छेयं-गच्छानि किं (गच्छेत् or गच्छतु) '*would* you do this?' यूयमेतत्करिष्यथ or कर्तुमिच्छथ किं, according to the sense.

May (might) and Can (could).

§ **233.** *May* in its senses of 'possibility', 'permission,' 'purpose' is expressed by the Potential, as, अक्षैर्दीव्येयमिति प्रत्यहमत्रायामि 'I come here every day that I *may* play at dice'; but when it expresses a *wish*, it is translated by the Potential, the Imperative, or Benedictive.

§ **234.** *Can* (*could*) always shows *power*, and not *permission*, and is expressed in Sanskrit by words meaning 'to be able' with the Infinitive of the main verb; as, 'I *can* do it' तत्कर्तुं शक्नोमि, समर्थः, पारयामि &c.

§ **235.** *Might* is usually expressed by the Potential; as, 'it *might* be so' एवं स्यात्; or sometimes by using the potential passive participle; as 'he *might* be my friend' कदाचिदनेन मम मित्रेण भवितव्यं.

(*a*) *Might* used with the Perfect tense may be expressed by the potential or past passive participle when it denotes '*possibility*'; as 'he *might* have done it' तेनैतत्कृतं स्यात्—कर्तव्यं; so also 'I *could have* done it' मयैतत्कर्तुं शक्यमासीत् (किन्तु न कृतं).

Must and Ought.

§ **236.** *Must* in its senses of 'necessity', 'force from without', 'certainty or necessary inference' is always expressed by the potential passive participle; as 'you *must* go' त्वया गंतव्यं; 'he *must* obey me' अहं तेनानुरोद्धव्यः.

§ **237.** *Ought* is expressed in the same way; as, 'you *ought* to learn it' त्वयेदं (अवश्यं) अध्येतव्यं, and sometimes by the Infinitive with अर्ह्. Used with the Perfect tense, *must* and *ought* may be translated by the Potential with a past participle or by the potential passive participle; 'he *must* have come home' स गृहमागतो भवेत् or तेन गृहमागंतव्यं; एवमनया प्रष्टव्यं (M. 4) 'she *ought* to have asked you so'; 'you *ought* to have told me this' इदं त्वया मह्यं कथयितव्यम्.

The Subjunctive Mood.

§ **238.** There are three principal forms in which the Subjunctive mood occurs in English; the present, past, and pluperfect. When the Subjunctive mood is used in the present in dependent clauses governed by verbs of 'command', 'advise' &c., is used after verbs of hoping, praying &c. and after *lest,* it should be translated in Sanskrit by the Potential mood or Imperative; as, 'I order that he *be* hanged' स शूलमारोप्येत or आरोप्यतां इत्यहमाज्ञापयामि; 'I hope I *come out* successful in this affair' अस्मिन्कार्ये विजयी भवेयमित्याशंसे, or अपि नाम विजयी भवेयं (§ 203); 'save her, *lest* her indisposition increase' परित्रायतामेनां भवान् । मा अस्या विकारो वर्धताम्.

§ **239.** In conditional sentences where the Subjunctive is expressed by the Present tense in both the clauses, it may be translated according to § 206; as, 'if you *go* I go' **यदि यूयं गच्छथ (गमिष्यथ** or **गच्छेत) तर्हि अहं गच्छामि (गमिष्यामि** or **गच्छेयं**); 'if it *rains* we shall not be able to go out' **यदि देवो वर्षेत् (वर्षति वर्षिष्यति वा) तर्हि वयं बहिर्गन्तुं न शक्नुयाम (शक्ष्यामः)** &c.

§ **240.** When the Subjunctive mood occurs in conditional sentences with the Past tense, the Potential mood is used in both the clauses; 'if he *were* here, he *would* accompany me' **यद्यत्र स भवेत्तन्मया सहागच्छेत्.** But when the past subjunctive implies a denial or falsity of the antecedent, the Pontential cannot be used, but the Conditional (§ 216); as, 'if the book *were* in the library (as it is not), it should be given to you' **यदि तत्पुस्तकं ग्रन्थालयेऽभविष्यत्तर्हि तद्युष्मभ्यं अदास्यत.** Thus in translating the three sentences 'if the book *is* (as I know it is) in the library, you may take it', 'if it *be* (I am uncertain) there, you may take it', and 'if it *were* (as I know it is not) you might take it,' the Present or Potential may be used in the first two, and the Conditional in the last.

§ **241.** The Pluperfect Conditional is always expressed by the Sanskrit Conditional (§ 216).

तदाकर्ण्य दमनकश्चिन्तयामास । युद्धाय कृतनिश्चयोऽयं दृश्यते दुरात्मा तद्यदि कदाचित्तीक्ष्णशृंगाभ्यां स्वामिनं प्रहरिष्यति तन्महाननर्थः संपत्स्यते । (P. I.)

युवराज किं न जितं देवेन तारापीडेन यज्जेष्यसि । कानि द्वीपान्तराणि नात्मीकृतानि यान्यात्मीकरिष्यसि । कानि रत्नानि नोपार्जितानि यान्युपार्जयिष्यसि । (K. 117.)

तौ चेद्राजपुत्रौ निरुपद्रवाववर्धिष्येतामियता कालेन तवेमां वयोवस्थाम-स्प्रक्ष्येताम् (D. K. II. 3)

तया देवतयास्मै स्वप्ने समादिष्टम्। उत्पत्स्यते तवैकः पुत्रो जनिष्यते चैका दुहिता। स तु तस्याः पाणिग्राहकमनुजीविष्यति। (D. K. II. 6)

गामधास्यत्कथं नागो मृणालमृदुभिः फणैः।
आ रसातलमूलात्त्वमवालंबिष्यथा न चेत्॥ (Ku. VI. 68)

राजन्प्रजासु ते कश्चिदपचारः प्रवर्तते।
तमन्विष्य प्रशमयेर्भवितासि ततः कृती॥ (R. XV. 47)

अकरिष्यदसौ पापमतिनिष्करुणैव सा।
नाभविष्यमहं तत्र यदि तत्परिपन्थिनी॥ (Mal. 9)

सिध्यन्ति कर्मसु महत्स्वपि यन्नियोज्याः
संभावनागुणमवेहि तमीश्वराणाम्।
किं वाऽभविष्यदरुणस्तमसां विभेत्ता
तं चेत्सहस्रकिरणो धुरि नाकरिष्यत्॥ (S'. 7)

ADDITIONAL SENTENCES FOR EXERCISE.

भागुरायणः—कुमार न कदाचिदपि शकटदासोऽमात्यराक्षसस्याग्रतोऽयं लेखो मया लिखित इति प्रतिपत्स्यते। अतोऽन्यल्लिखितमानीयतामस्य यतो वर्णसंवाद एवैतत्सर्वं विभावयिष्यति। (Mu. 5)

रात्रिर्गमिष्यति भविष्यति सुप्रभातं
भास्वानुदेष्यति हसिष्यति चक्रवालम्।
इत्थं विचिन्तयति कोषगते द्विरेफे
हा हंत हंत नलिनीं गज उज्जहार॥ (Su.)

परस्परेण स्पृहणीयशोभं न चेदिदं द्वंद्वमयोजयिष्यत्॥
अस्मिन्द्वये रूपविधानयत्नः पत्युः प्रजानां विफलोऽभविष्यत्॥
(Ku. VII. 66.)

यदा ते मोहकलिलं बुद्धिर्व्यतितरिष्यति ।
तदा गन्तासि निर्वेदं श्रोतव्यस्य श्रुतस्य च ॥
श्रुतिविप्रतिपन्ना ते यदा स्थास्यति निश्चला ।
समाधावचला बुद्धिस्तदा योगमवाप्स्यसि ॥ (Bg. II. 52-3)
भयाद्रणादुपरतं मंस्यन्ते त्वां महारथाः ।
येषां च त्वं बहुमतो भूत्वा यास्यसि लाघवम् ॥ (Bg. II. 35)
मच्चित्तः सर्वदुर्गाणि मत्प्रसादात्तरिष्यसि ।
अथ चेत्त्वमहंकारान्न श्रोष्यसि विनंक्ष्यसि ॥ (Bg. XVIII. 58)
परिणेष्यति पार्वतीं यदा तपसा तत्प्रवणीकृतो हरः ।
उपलब्धसुखस्तदा स्मरं वपुषा स्वेन नियोजयिष्यति ॥ (Ku. IV. 42)

Let all the subjects be informed that Chandragupta himself will henceforth look to the affairs of the state.

You will get your desired object, if you only attempt to get it.

'All this,' said the sage, 'will happen (पद् with सं) in the Kali age yet to come, and men will commit various sins.'

If that boy had been brought up with care from his childhood, I am sure he would have now grown as old as this boy.

Friends will swarm round a man by hundreds in days of prosperity, but in adversity they will leave him.

If a king were not prompt in inflicting punishment on defaulters, the stronger would prey upon the weaker.

If you and Gopâla were here, you could hardly bear to see the dreadful sight.

A stag once proudly said to himself that if his legs had been similar to his horns, no animal on the earth would have been able to equal (तुल्) him in beauty.

If Râma has not gone there just at the moment, the whole house would have been burnt down.

Had I not then remained quite indifferent, I should have incurred the displeasure of the king.

That he would now come back and joyfully spend his days with us, is next to impossible.

Had I but served my God with half the zeal I served my King, he would not have given me over naked to my enemies.

LESSON XXI.

Particles.

अग, अथ, अधिकृत्य, अपि, अयि, अये, अहह & अहो.

§ **242** There are several particles given under the head of '*Avyayas*' in Pánini, Amarakosha and in the *Ganaratnamahodadhi* of Vardhamána. Some of them are very useful as short connecting words and, as such, their meaning must be accurately understood. Some of the more common of such particles are considered in this and the next seven lessons.

§ **243** *अंग by itself is used as a vocative particle; as, तन्मन्ये क्वचिदंग भृंगतरुणेनास्वादिता मालती (G. M.) 'hence, Sir, I think the Málati flower was somewhere tasted by a young bee'; अंग कच्चित्कुशली तातः (K. 221); प्रभुरपि जनकानामंग भो याचकस्ते (Mv. 3); or as a particle showing respect or reverence; as, अंग विद्वन्माणवकमध्यापय (G. M.) 'learned Sir, teach Mánavaka.'

(*a*) It is sometimes used with किं and means much the same as किमुत or किंपुनः 'how much more', 'how much less'; as, तृणेन कार्यं भवतीश्वराणां किमंग वाग्घस्तवता नरेण (P. 1. 1) 'rich persons (even) have need of a blade of grass; much more of a man possessed of speech and hands.'

---

* अंग पूजासंबोधनयोः । (ग. म.)

§ **244.** * अथ is used in these senses:—(1) As a sign of auspiciousness; अथातो ब्रह्मजिज्ञासा (S. B.) 'henceforth the inquiry about Brahma'; (2) marking the beginning of a statement; अथेदमारभ्यते द्वितीयं तंत्रं (P. II.) 'now (here) begins the second Tantra (book)'; (3) '*afterwards*', '*then*'; अथ प्रजानामधिपः प्रभाते वनाय धेनुं मुमोच (R. II. 1) 'afterwards the lord of men in the morning let loose the cow to go to the forest'; often used as a correlative of यदि or चेद् in this sense; न चेन्मुनिकुमारोयमथ कोस्य व्यपदेशः (S'. 7); (4) asking a question; अथ शक्नोसि भोक्तुं (G. M.); often with the interrogative word itself अथ सा किमाख्यस्य राजर्षेः पत्नी (S'. 7); (5) '*and*', '*also*'; भीमोऽथार्जुनः (G. M.) 'Bhima and (as well as) Arjuna'; गणितमथ कलां कौशिकीं (Mk. 1) 'Mathematics as also the Kaus'iki art'; (6) '*if*', '*supposing that*', '*in case*'; अथ कौतुकमावेदयामि (K. 144) 'if you have a curiosity, I shall relate (it)'; अथ मरणमवश्यमेव जंतोः (Ve. 3.) 'in case (but if) death is certain to befall man'; (7) '*totality*', '*entirety*'; अथ धर्मं व्याख्यास्यामः (G. M.) 'we shall explain the whole Duty (duty in its entirety)'; (8) '*doubt*', '*uncertainty*'; शब्दो नित्योऽथानित्यः (G. M.).

Obs. Lexicons mention also अधिकार; ' अथ समासः'; but (1) and (2) and अधिकार are identical, in as much as they all mark the beginning of a statement; so also अन्वादेश (re-employment of the same word in a subsequent part of the sentence) and प्रतिज्ञा (affirmation, proposition).

§ **245.** अथ joined with किं means '*what else*', '*yes*', '*exactly so*'; as, शकारः—चेट प्रवहणमागतं । चेटः—अथ किं (Mk. 8) 'S'akâra—has the carriage arrived ? Servant—yes, (exactly)'.

(*a*) अथ वा is used like the disjunctive '*or*' in English; but more generally it is used to correct or modify a former statement in the sense of '*or why*', '*or rather*'; as, दीर्घे किं न सहस्रधाहमथ वा रामेण किं

* मंगलानन्तरारंभप्रश्नकार्त्स्न्येष्वथो अथ । (अ)
अथोथ स्यातां समुच्चये ।
मंगळे संशयारंभाधिकारानन्तरेषु च ।
अन्वादेशे प्रतिज्ञायां प्रश्नसाकल्ययोरपि ॥ (है)

दुष्करं (U. 6) 'why am I not shattered to thousands of pieces ?—or why (I should not say so) what is impossible to be done by Ráma ?'

§ **246.** The gerundive participle अधिकृत्य is used in the sense of '*regarding*' '*with respect to*', '*referring to*', and governs the Accusative; as, अथ कतमं पुनर्ऋतुमधिकृत्य गास्यामि (S'. 1) 'but referring to which season shall I sing ?' उद्दिश्य is used in the same way in the sense of '*with reference to*', '*towards*'; as स्वपुरमुद्दिश्य प्रतस्थे (H. 4) 'he set out towards his town'; किमुद्दिश्यामी ऋषयो मत्सकाशं प्रेषिताः स्युः (S'. 5) 'with what object (with reference to what) may these sages have been sent to me ?'

§ **247.** *अपि has the following senses:—(1) '*Though*', '*even if*'; पातितोपि कराघातैः (Bh. II. 85) 'though made to fall down by the strokes of the hand'; (2) '*even*'; इयमधिकमनोज्ञा वल्कलेनापि तन्वी (S'. 1) 'this slender-bodied girl appears more charming even by means of the bark-garment'; (3) '*also*', '*and also*', '*on one's part*'; राजापि मुनिवाक्यमंगीकृत्यातिष्ठत् (D. K. I. 1) 'the king, on his part, (and the king also) accepted the words of the sage and remained (quiet)'; विष्णुशर्मणापि राजपुत्राः पाठिताः (P. I.) 'Vishnus'arman, on his part, taught the Princes'; अपि सिंच अपि स्तुहि (S. K.) 'sprinkle and pray'; अस्ति मे सोदरस्नेहोप्येतेषु (S'. 1) 'I have also a sisterly affection for them'; (4) In asking questions, in which case it is used first; अपि तपो वर्धते (S'. 1) 'is your penance-prospering ?'; अप्येतत्तपोवनं (U. 2) 'can (may) this be the penance-forest ?'; (5) '*Doubt*' or '*uncertainty*'; अपि चोरो भवेत् (G. M.) 'may he be a thief ? (I am not certain about it); (6) '*Hope*', '*expectation*'; अपि जीवेत्स ब्राह्मणशिशुः (U. 2) 'I hope the Bráhma*n*a boy will come to life'.

Obs. In the last sense अपि is generally joined with नाम; तदपि नाम रामभद्रः पुनरपीदं वनमलंकुर्यात् (U. 2) 'then I expect that Ráma will again grace this forest (with his presence)'.

---

* गर्हासमुच्चयप्रश्नशंकासंभावनास्वपि (अ)
अपि संभावनाप्रश्नशंकागर्हासमुच्चये ।
तथायुक्तपदार्थेषु कामचारक्रियासु च ॥ (वि.)

Note. Other senses are also mentioned ; as गर्हा 'censure'; धिग्देवदत्तमपि स्तुयाद्वृषलं (S. K.) 'fie upon Devadatta, he will even praise a S'udra' (so culpable is he) ; पदार्थ 'the sense of a word understood'; सर्पिषोपि स्यात् (S. K.) 'even a drop of clarified butter' ; and कामचारक्रिया or अन्ववसर्ग 'permission to do as one likes'; आप स्तुहि 'you may pray, (if you like)' so अपि स्तुह्यपि सेधास्मांस्तथ्यमुक्तं नराशन (Bk. VIII. 92).

(*a*) After words expressing *number* अपि has the sense of 'totality'; as, सर्वैरपि राज्ञां प्रयोजनं (P. I. 1) 'kings have need of all (not excluding *even* one)'; so चतुर्णामपि वर्णानाम्.

(*b*) Joined to interrogative pronouns and their derivatives, it has the sense of '*any*', and sometimes that of 'indescribable', see § 135.

(*c*) यद्यपि—तथापि are correlatives, and mean 'though—yet, still or nevertheless.'

§ **248.** *अयि is used (1) as a gentle address in the sense of, '*friend, prythee*', as, अयि विवेकविश्रांतमभिहितं (M. *v*) 'friend, you have said something void of judgment', अयि मातर्देवयजनसंभवे देवि सीते (U. 4) 'O darling Sîtá, born from the sacrifice to the gods' ; (2) In asking a gentle question; अयि जीवितनाथ जीवसि (Ku. IV. 3) 'lord of my life, art thou alive?'

§ **249.** अये is principally used to express (1) 'surprise', 'wonder'; अये भगवत्यरुन्धती (U. 5) 'Oh ! it is the revered Arundhati; as अये मय्येव भ्रुकुटीधरः संवृत्तः (U. 5) ; (2) 'grief', 'dejection', 'fear'; अये देवपादपद्मोपजीविनोवस्थेयम् (Mu. 2) 'alas ! this is the state of a servant of the lotus-like feet of His Majesty'.

§ **250.** † अहह is used to denote (1) joy, astonishment, or amazement, and (2) grief or excessive torment ; अहह महतां निःसीमानश्चरित्रविभूतयः (Bh. II. 35) 'Oh, the greatness of the life of the great is, indeed, infinite !' ; अहह दारुणो वज्रनिर्घातः (U. 2) 'Oh ! it is a terrible

---

* अयि प्रभानुनययोस्तथां संबोधनेपि च (मे.)

† अहहेत्यद्भुते खेदे परिक्लेशप्रकर्षयो (मे.)

thunder-stroke'; **अहह कष्टमपंडितता विधेः** (Bh. III. 110) 'Oh, the folly of the creator!'

§ **251.** * **अहो** (1) is a vocative particle; as, **अहो राजानः** 'O kings'; (2) it is very generally used with adjectives and nouns in the sense of '*Oh*' '*O how*' expressive of joy, grief, or sorrow; as, **अहो मधुरमासां कन्यकानां दर्शनं** (S'. 1) 'O how pleasing is the sight of these girls!'; **अहो सर्वास्ववस्थास्वनवद्यता रूपस्य** (M. 2) 'Oh! the faultlessness of beauty in all states!' (how faultless is beauty &c.); **अहो विपाकः** (U. 4) 'Oh this change of state!' **अहो उन्मीलन्ति वेदनाः** (U. 4); (3) it sometimes denotes *surprise* as caused by meeting with some person or thing unexpectedly; as, **अहो बकुलावलिका** (M. 1) 'Oh, it is Bakulávaliká!'

अहो सर्वास्ववस्थासु चारुता शोभां पुष्यति। (M. 2.)

सर्वः कान्तमात्मीयं पश्यति। अहं तु तामेवाश्रमललामभूतां शकुन्तलामधिकृत्य ब्रवीमि। (S'. 2.)

अहो दीप्तिमतोऽपि विश्वसनीयतास्य वपुषः। अथवोपपन्नमेतदस्मिन्नृषिकल्पे राजनि। (S'. 2.)

अपि ज्ञायते कतमेन दिग्भागेन गतः स जाल्म इति। (U. 1)

अयि जात कथयितव्यं कथय। (U. 4.)

कथमीदृशेन सह वत्सस्य चन्द्रकेतोर्द्वंद्वसंप्रहारमनुजानीयाम्। अथ वा इक्ष्वाकुगृहवृद्धा वयम्। प्रत्युपस्थिते च का गतिः। (U. 4.)

अतिप्रबलपिपासावसन्नानि गन्तुमल्पमपि मे नालमंगकानि। अलमप्रभु-

---

* अहो धिगर्थे शोके च करुणार्थे विषादयोः।
संबोधने प्रशंसायां विस्मये पादपूरणे ॥ (मे.)

रस्यात्मनः । सीदति मे हृदयम् । अंधकारतामुपयाति चक्षुः । अपि नाम खलो विधिरनिच्छतोऽपि मे मरणमद्यैवोपपादयेत् । (K. 36.)

अहो प्रभावो महात्मनाम् । अत्र शाश्वतं विरोधमपहायोपशांतान्तरात्मानस्तिर्यञ्चोऽपि तपोवनवसतिसुखमनुभवन्ति । (K. 45)

अपि नाम तयोः कल्याणिनोर्भूरिवसुदेवरातापत्ययोर्मालतीमाधवयोरभिमतः पाणिग्रहः स्यात् । (Mal. 1.)

अहो मे मूर्खतायाः प्रकारः । अहो यत्किंचनकारितायामादरः । अहो निरर्थकव्यापारेष्वभिनिवेशः । अहो बालिशचरितेष्वासक्तिः । (K. 120)

चा०—भद्र उपवर्णयेदानीं कुसुमपुरवृत्तांतम् । अपि वृषलमनुरक्ताः प्रकृतयः । चरः—अथ किम् । आर्येण तेषु तेषु विरागकारणेषु परिहृतेषु देवे चन्द्रगुप्ते दृढमनुरक्ताः प्रकृतयः । (Mu. 1)

अये अश्वमेध इति विश्वविजयिनां क्षत्रियाणामूर्जस्वलः सर्वक्षत्रियपरिभावी महानुत्कर्षनिकषः । (U. 4)

ताः स्वचारित्र्यमुद्दिश्य प्रत्याययतु मैथिली ।
ततः पुत्रवतीमिनां प्रतिपत्स्ये त्वदाज्ञया ॥ (R XV. 73)

ADDITIONAL SENTENCES FOR EXERCISE.

भगवति मदीयेषु लेखेषु तत्र भवते त्वामुद्दिश्य सभाजनाक्षराणि पातयिष्यामि । (M. 5.)
हा कथं सीतादेव्या ईदृशं जनापवादं देवस्य कथयिष्यामि । अथ वा नियोगः खल्वीदृशो मंदभाग्यस्य । (U. 1)

चाणक्यः—अपि प्रचीयन्ते संव्यवहाराणां लाभा वः । चं.—आर्य अथ किम् । (Mu. 1)

अथ धर्मानुरोधादितरपक्षावलंबन द्वारेण मृत्युमंगीकरोमि एवमपि प्रथमं तावत्स्वय मागतस्य तत्रभवतः कपिंजलस्य प्रणयप्रसरभंगः । पुनरपर यदि तस्य जनस्य मत्कृतादाशा भंगात्प्राणविपत्तिरुपजायते तदपि मुनिजनवधजनितं महदेनो भवेत् । (K. 160)

चाणक्यः—अगृहीते राक्षसे किमुत्खातं नन्दवंशस्य किं वा स्थैर्यमुत्पादितं चन्द्रगुप्तल क्ष्म्याः । अहो राक्षसस्य नंदवंशे निरतिशयो भक्तिगुणः । स कस्मिंश्चिदपि जीवति नन्दान्व यावग्रत्रे वृषलस्य साचिव्यं ग्राहयितुं न शक्यते । (Mu. 1)

यदि यथा वदति क्षितिपस्तथा त्वमसि किं पितुरुत्कुलया त्वया ।
अथ तु वेत्सि शुचिव्रतमात्मनः पतिकुले तव दास्यमपि क्षमम ॥ (S'. 5.)
अप्यग्रणीर्मन्त्रकृतामृषीणां कुशाग्रबुद्धे कुशली गुरुस्ते । (R. V. 4.)
विललाप स बाष्पगद्गदं सहजामप्यपहाय धीरताम् ॥
अभितप्तमयोपि मार्दवं भजते कैव कथा शरीरिषु ॥ (R.VIII. 43)
अपि क्रियार्थं सुलभं समित्कुशं जलान्यपि स्नानविधिक्षमाणि त ।
अपि स्वशक्त्या तपसि प्रवर्तसे शरीरमाद्यं खलु धर्मसाधनम् ॥
(Ku. V. 33)

अथ चैनं नित्य जातं नित्यं वा मन्यसे मृतम् ।
तथापि त्वं महाबाहो नैनं शोचितुमर्हसि ॥ (Bg. II. 26)
सरसिजमनुविद्धं शैवलेनापि रम्यं
मलिनमपि हिमांशोर्लक्ष्म लक्ष्मीं तनोति ।
इयमधिकमनोज्ञा वल्कलेनापि तन्वी (S'. 1)

Even a fool should not be disrespected; much less a learned man.

But suppose you take me there perforce, my mind will still be directed to my beloved, the sole object of my love.

Master—Have you done the work I told you to do? Servant—Yes; it is long since I did it.

This King deserves praise for protecting his subjects well; or why, it is the very duty of kings to do so.

The boy, about whom I am speaking, is very sharp.

He who gets angry for a definite cause is appeased as soon as that cause is removed.

At this the God Vishnu went to the house of Garuda. He, in his turn, came out hastily to receive his worthy master.

Is it likely that my desires will be fulfilled ?

How pitiable is the condition of those distressed persons !

It will make even a heart of stone relent.

Oh the serene beauty of this lovely garden !

How full of obstacles is the accomplishment of one's desired object ?

Alas ! I have spent away my whole time in gambling, and whom have I to blame but myself ?

Oh ! it is my own ring; I have been searching for it these eight days. Where did you find it ?

I am tired of walking; prythee, let us now go home.

I hope you remember the man regarding whom I spoke to you a month back.

LESSON XXII

आ, आं, आः, इति, इव, उत, एव, एवं, ओम्.

§ **252.** * आ besides its meanings of '*till*' and '*from*' (see § 84), has the sense of '*a little, somewhat*', and is equivalent to the English *ish* in 'blackish' *&c.* It is prefixed to adjectives; as, आपिंगल 'a little tawny'; आमत्तानां कोकिलानां कूजितैः (M. 3.) 'with the warblings of cuckoos somewhat drunk with passion'.

The use of आ with verbs is well-known.

(*a*) † आ is somtimes used in recollecting past events; as, आ एवं किल तदासीत् (U. 6) 'ah ! such indeed was then the case'; and sometimes, merely as an expletive; as, आ एवं मन्यसे (G. M.)

---

*आङीषदर्थेऽभिव्याप्तौ सीमार्थे धातुयोगजे ।

† आ प्रगृह्यः स्मृतौ वाक्ये । (अ.)

§ **253.** *आं is used in recollecting a past occurrence, and is sometimes used as an enclitic particle, showing determination; as किं नाम दण्डकेयं—(सर्वतो विलोक्य)=आं (U. 2) 'is this surely the Daṇḍaka forest ? ' (looking all around) 'Oh yes,' (I now recollect); आं चिरस्य प्रतिबुद्धोस्मि (G. M.) 'indeed, I have awakened after a long time.'

(*a*) Occasionally it is used in giving answers in the sense of 'yes'; as, आं देव्याः पार्श्वगतोसौ जनश्चित्रे दृष्टः (M. 1.) 'yes, that person standing near the queen, was seen in a picture.'

§ **254.** † आः is used to denote 'pain' or 'anger'; as, आः शीतं (G. M.) 'Oh, how chill it is !'; आः, कथमद्यापि राक्षसत्रासः (U. 1) 'ah ! is there still disturbance from demons ?'

§ **255.** The particle इति is most generally used to report the very words spoken or supposed to be spoken by some one as expressed by the *direct construction* in English. It takes the place of the quotation marks or '*that*' occurring in oblique narrations, and is used at the end of the words of a speaker which are quoted; as, आज्ञप्तोस्मि राजश्यालकेन । स्थावरक प्रवहणं गृहीत्वा जीर्णोद्यानमागच्छेति (Mk. 6) 'I have been ordered by the king's brother-in-law—Sthâvaraka, come with the carriage to the old garden'; तयोर्मुनिकुमारकयोरन्यतरः कथयति अक्षमाला-मुपयाचितुमागतोस्मीति (K. 151) 'one of the two young sages says, 'I have come to ask for the rosary of beads' , or 'says, *that* he has come to ask ' &c.

Obs. In translating oblique constructions into Sanskrit, the words as they would stand in the *direct* construction are translated with इति at the end of the words quoted; 'Râma said to me that he would give me money whenever I wanted it. रामो मामुवाच । यदा यदा धनेन तव प्रयोजनं स्यात् तदा तदाहं तत्तुभ्यं दद्यामिति or दद्यामीति रामो मामुवाच.

(*a*) The particle इति, being in this sense used to indicate an assertion, requires that all the conditions of a distinct assertion or

---

* आं स्मृतौ चावधारणे । (वि.)

† आस्तु स्यात्कोपपीडयोः । (अ.)

proposition should be fulfilled, *i. e.*, there must be at least a *subject* and a *verb* in the sentence quoted; as, क्रमादमुं नारद इत्यबोधि सः (S'i. 1.3) 'he by degrees recognized him *to be* Nárada'; अवैमि चैनामनघेति (R. XIV. 40) 'I know her *to be* innocent (guiltless).' Here it would be wrong to say क्रमादमुं नारदमित्यबोधि सः or एनामनघामित्यवैमि. If इति be not used, the accusative may be used.

§ **256.** * Besides this general sense, इति has the following senses:—(1) '*cause*', as expressed in English by '*because*', '*since*', '*on the ground that*'; वैदेशिकोऽस्मीति पृच्छामि कः पुनरसौ जामाता (U. 1) 'I ask you *because* I am a stranger, who is this son-in-law'; लब्धास्पदोऽस्मीति विवादभीरोः (M. 1) 'of him who is afraid of (shrinks from) a contest *on the ground* that he has secured a footing'; (2) '*purpose*' or '*motive*', शरीरस्य मा विनाशो भूदिति मयेदमुत्क्षिप्य समानीतं (K. 320) 'I brought the body up that it should not be destroyed' (*lest* it be destroyed); (3) '*thus*', to mark the conclusion; इति तृतीयोऽङ्कः '*thus* (ends) the third act'; पृथिव्यापस्तेजो वायुराकाशं कालो दिगात्मा मन इति द्रव्याणि 'earth, water......these are the *dravyas*'; (4) 'so', '*in this manner*', '*of this description*'; इत्युक्तवन्तं परिरभ्य दोर्भ्यां (Ki. II. 80) 'having clapsed in his arms him who had said so'; गौरश्वो हस्तीति जातिः '*Jati* (kind) is of this nature or description, as, a cow, a horse, an elephant'; (5) '*as follows*', '*to the following effect*', in denoting what is related afterwards; रामाभिधानो हरिरित्युवाच (R. XIII. 1) 'Hari by name (in the form of) Ráma, said as follows'; (6) '*in the capacity of*', '*as regards*', '*as for*' to show the capacity in which a thing is considered; as, पितेति स पूज्यः, अध्यापक इति निन्द्यः 'as a father, he must be respected, as a teacher, censured'; शीघ्रमिति सुकरं निभृतमिति चिन्तनीयं भवेत् (S'. 3) 'as for (doing it) quickly, it is easy; as for (doing it) secretly, it is a question (must be thought of)'; (7) 'an opinion accepted'; इत्यापिशलिः (G. M.) 'such is the *opinion* of A'pis'ali'; (8) 'an illustration'; इन्दुरिन्दुरिव श्रीमानित्यादौ तदनन्वयः (Chandráloka).

---

* इति स्वरूपे सान्निध्ये विवक्षानियमे मते ।
हेतौ प्रकारप्रत्यक्षप्रकाशेष्ववधारणे ॥
एवमर्थे समाप्तौ स्यात् । (हे.)

Obs. The senses स्वरूप and प्रकार are allied to each other; while प्रत्यक्ष, प्रकाश, and अवधारण are very rare.

(*a*) इति is joined to किं to form a strong question, 'why indeed', 'why to be sure'; किमित्यपास्याभरणानि यौवने धृतं त्वया वार्धकशोभि वल्कलं (Ku. V. 44) 'why indeed, have you cast off ornaments, and put on, in your youth, a bark garment befitting (only) old age ?'

§ **257.** * इव is generally used to show comparison and is put after the standard of comparison; as वैनतेय इव विनतानन्दजननः (K. 5) 'he was like Vainateya who gave delight to Vinata' (or 'those who submitted to him'); so संसारः अर्णव इव 'the ocean-like worldly existence.'

Obs. The words connected by इव must be in the same case; महीमिव जलभृतदेहां कन्यकां ददर्श (K. 131) 'he saw a girl who was like the earth, whose surface is filled with water (who supported her body by means of water)'; दिवसेनेव मित्रानुवर्तिना विलासिजनेनाधिष्ठिता (K. 51) 'inhabited by amorous people who followed their friends like day following the sun.'

(*a*) Its other senses are:—(1) '*a little*', '*somewhat*'; कडार इवायं (G. M.) 'he is somewhat tawny'; (2) '*as if*', '*as it were*'; मृगानुसारिणं पिनाकिनमिव पश्यामि (S'. 1) 'I, as it were, see (before me) Pinákin following a deer'; यो जहासेव वासुदेवं (R. 5) 'who, as if, laughed at (ridiculed) Vásudeva.'

(*b*) इव is added to interrogative pronouns and their derivatives, in the sense of '*possibly*', '*I should like to know*', '*indeed*'; as, विना सीतादेव्या किमिव हि न दुःखं रघुपतेः (U. 5) 'what possibly (I should like to know) will not be distressful to the lord of the Raghus separated from the queen Sîtá'; परायत्तः प्रीतेः कथमिव रसं वेत्तु पुरुषः (Mu. 3) 'how possibly should a dependent person know the taste of happiness ?'

§ **258.** † उत is generally used in the sense of '*or*', to express

---

* ईषदर्थोपमोत्प्रेक्षावाक्यभूषणयोरिव । (G. M.)

† उत प्रश्ने वितर्के स्यादुतात्यर्थविकल्पयोः । (वि.)

different alternatives, and is, in this sense, usually the correlative of किं '*whether*', the place of उत being also taken by आहो, उताहो, आहोस्वित्; as, न जाने किमिदं वल्कलानां सदृशमुताहो जटानां समुचितं किं तपसोनुरूपमाहोस्विद्धर्मोपदेशांगमिदं (K. 151) 'I know not whether this is worthy of your bark garments, or suitable to your matted hair; whether it befits your penance, or forms part of your religious instructions.'

(*a*) उत when repeated, has the sense of '*either—or*'; as, एकमेव वरं पुंसामुतराज्यमुताश्रमः (G. M.) 'one thing only is preferable to men, either a kingdom (sovereignty) or a hermitage.'

§ **259**. Used by itself उत has these senses:—(1) '*doubt*,' '*uncertainty*', '*guess*'; स्थाणुरयमुत पुरुषः (G. M.) 'may it be a post or a human being'; (2) in asking a question; उत दंडः पतिष्यति (*ibid.*) 'will the stick fall ?'

Obs.—The sense अत्यर्थ is very rare.

§ **260**. एव is most frequently used to strengthen and emphasize the idea expressed by a word. In this sense it may be variously rendered by 'just', 'same', 'very', 'only', 'alone', 'already', 'the very moment', 'scarcely'; as, एवमेव 'exactly so', 'just so'; अर्थोष्मणा विरहितः पुरुषः स एव (Bh. II. 49) 'that very man (the same man), devoid of the warmth of wealth'; सा तथ्यमेवाभिहिता भवेन (Ku. III. 63) 'she was told by S'iva only the truth' (nothing but the truth); नाम्नैव निर्भिन्नारातिहृदयः (K. 5) 'who broke through the hearts of his enemies only by his name'; उपस्थितेयं नाम्नि कीर्तित एव यत् (R. I. 87) 'since she is here the moment her name was uttered' (immediately on mentioning her name); भवितव्यमेव तेन (U. 4.) 'it *will* take place.'

§ **261**. *एवं is most frequently used in the sense of '*so*,' '*thus*', '*in this manner*,' either with reference to what precedes or follows, or in giving directions to do a certain thing; as, एवमुक्तः कपिञ्जलः प्रत्यवादीत् (K. 151) 'Kapinjala, thus addressed (by me) replied.'

---

*एवं प्रकारोपमयोरंगीकारेऽवधारणे । † (वि.)

(*a*) It is also used to show '*assent*' (yes, indeed); as, **एवमेतत्** (U. 1) 'quite so, yes, you are right'; **एवं कुर्मः** 'yes, we shall do so.'

Obs.—**एवं** is rarely used to show 'likeness' or 'determination.'

§ **262**. ***ओम्** is not a particle of frequent occurrence. It is generally used to mark an auspicious beginning; as **ओं अग्निमीडे पुरोहितं**; or to mark the conclusion of a sacred ritual or prayer, in the sense of '*amen*'; **ब्रह्म भूः भुवः स्वरोम्.**

(*a*) It occurs in classical literature in the sense of '*yes*,' '*very well*,' signifying 'assent' or 'approbation'; as, **ओमित्युच्यताममात्यः** (Màl. 6) let the minister be told, 'I shall do so (very well)'; **द्वितीयश्चेदोमिति ब्रूमः** (S. D. 1).

भर्तृदारिके आर्यायाः पण्डितकौशिक्या इव स्वरसंयोगः श्रूयते । (M. 5)

उत्खातिनी भूमिरिति मया रश्मिसंयमनाद्रथस्य मंदीकृतो वेगः । (S'. 1)

प्रथममिति प्रेक्ष्य दुहितृजनस्यैकोऽपराधो भगवता मर्षयितव्यः । (S'. 4)

अतिभूमिं गतेन रणरणकेनार्यपुत्रशून्यमिवात्मानं पश्यामि । (U. 1)

सखे करटक किमित्ययमुदकार्थी स्वामी पानीयमपीत्वा सचकितो मन्दं मन्दमवतिष्ठते । (H. 2)

सखे पुण्डरीक सुविदितमेतन्मम केवलमिदमेव पृच्छामि यदेतदारब्धं भवता किमिदं गुरुभिरुपदिष्टमुतधर्मशास्त्रेषु पठितमुत मोक्षप्राप्तियुक्तिरियमाहोस्विदन्यो नियमप्रकारः । (K. 155)

सीता—एते चत्वारो भ्रातरो विवाहदीक्षिता यूयम् । अहो जाने तस्मिन्नेव प्रदेशे तस्मिन्नेव काले वर्त इति ।

रामः—एवम् ।

---

* **ओमित्यनुमतौ प्रोक्तं प्रणवे चाप्युपक्रमे** । (वि.)

पुराणमित्येव न साधु सर्वं न चापि काव्यं नवमित्यवद्यम् ।
सन्तः परीक्ष्यान्यतरद्भजन्ते मूढः परप्रत्ययनेयबुद्धिः (M. 1)

यदभावि न तद्भावि भावि चेन्न तदन्यथा ।
इति चिन्ताविषघ्नोऽयमगदः किं न पीयते ॥ (H. 1)

प्रकृत्यैव प्रिया सीता रामस्यासीन्महात्मनः ।
प्रियभावः स तु तया स्वगुणैरेव वर्धितः ॥
तथैव रामः सीतायाः प्राणेभ्योऽपि प्रियोऽभवत् ।
हृदयं त्वेव जानाति प्रीतियोगं परस्परम् ॥ (U. 6)

ययातेरिव शर्मिष्ठा भर्तुर्बहुमता भव ।
पुत्रं त्वमपि सम्राजं सेव पूरुमवाप्नुहि ॥ (S'. 4)

लिम्पतीव तमोऽङ्गानि वर्षतीवाञ्जनं नभः ।
असत्पुरुषसेवेव दृष्टिर्विफलतां गता ॥ (Mk. 5)

ADDITIONAL SENTENCES FOR EXERCISE.

किमिव दुष्करमकरुणानां यतः सोऽयमनेनैव पादपमधिरुह्यैकैकशः फलानीव तस्य वनस्पतेः शाखासन्धिभ्यः कोटरान्तरेभ्यः शुकशावकानग्रहीदपगतासूंश्च कृत्वा क्षितावपातयत् (K. 33)

स मद्वचनानन्तरमेव न वेद्मि किमसह्यवृत्तेर्मदनज्वरस्य वेगादुत सद्योविपाकस्यात्मनो दुष्कृतस्य गौरवादाहोस्विन्मद्वचस एव सामर्थ्यादाच्छिन्नमूलस्तरुरिव क्षितावपतत् ।
(K. 312)

पात्रविशेषन्यस्तं गुणान्तरं व्रजति शिल्पमाधातुः ।
जलमिव समुद्रशुक्तौ मुक्ताफलतां पयोदस्य ॥ (M. 1)
सर्वोपमाद्रव्यसमुच्चयेन यथाप्रदेशं विनिवेशितेन ।
सा निर्मिता विश्वसृजा प्रयत्नादेकस्थसौन्दर्यदिदृक्षयेव ॥ (Ku. 1. 49)
का कथा बाणसंधाने ज्याशब्देनैव दूरतः ।
हुंकारेणेव धनुषः स हि विघ्नानपोहति ॥ (S'. 3)
गत एव न ते निवर्तते स सखा दीप इवानिलाहतः ।
अहमस्य दशेव पश्य मामविषह्यव्यसनेन धूमिताम् ॥ (Ku. IV. 30)
स्वशरीरशरीरिणावपि श्रुतसंयोगविपर्ययौ यदा ।
विरहः किमिवानुतापयेद्वद बाह्यैर्विषयैर्विपश्चितम् ॥ (R. VIII. 89)
प्रयान्तीव प्राणाः स्फुटतु हृदयं ध्वंसत इव ।
ज्वलन्तीवांगानि प्रसरति समंतादिव तमः । (Mal. 9)
किमात्मनिर्वादकथामुपेक्षे जायामदोषामुत सन्त्यजामि ।
इत्येकपक्षाश्रयविक्लवत्वादासीत्स दोलाचलचित्तवृत्तिः ॥ (R. XIV. 34)

A wicked person is not to be trusted because he speaks sweet words.

He has been staying here for the last two months that he might be acquainted with the learned men of the city.

He, hastily coming up to me, as if enraged, said that I had greatly offended him.

That misfortunes never come single is a wise saying often realized by men in this world.

When the enemies fell upon us like so many hail-stones, we did not know what to do.

Not being fed with food for a long time, he became, as it were, ready to die.

The whole world considers me to be powerless because I do not harm anybody.

Immediately on hearing my words, the rash man, with only one attendant, became ready to run the risk.

I do not know what to do next; whether I should stay in this town, or leave it.

He remained thinking whether the person standing before him was his enemy, or some spy disguised as an ascetic, or actually some beggar needing protection.

LESSON XXIII.

कच्चित्, क्व–क्व, कामम्, किं, (किमु, किमुत, किंपुनः), किल, केवलं & खलु.

§ **263.** * कच्चित् implies some hope expressed by the speaker, and has the sense of 'I hope that' &c. It is interrogative in form, in which the expected answer is '*yes*' or '*no*' according to the form of the question; as, शिवानि वस्तीर्थजलानि कच्चित् (R. V. 8) 'are your holy waters undisturbed ?' (I hope they are &c.); कच्चिन्न वाय्वादिरुपप्लव आश्रमपादपानां (*ibid.*) 'I hope no accident, such as a hurricane, befalls the trees in the hermitage' (no, it does not).

§ **264.** † क्व means 'where'; and when it is repeated with two or more assertions, it denotes *great difference*, or *excessive incongruity* or *unfitness;* as, क्व सूर्यप्रभवो वंशः क्व चाल्पविषया मतिः (R. I. 2) 'where the race born from the Sun, and where (my) intellect of a limited scope' (there is a very great *distance* between the two, the intellect being quite unable to describe the race); तपः क्व वत्से क्व च तावकं वपुः (Ku. V. 4) 'what a great incongruity is there between penance and thy body' (thy delicate body is unfitted to practise penance.)

§ **265.** ‡ कामं means 'at will', 'to one's satisfaction'; but its most general use in classical literature is in the sense of '*granted that,*' '*admitting*', '*supposing for a moment*', being usually followed by तु or तथापि or a similar word as its correlative; as, कामं न तिष्ठति मदाननसंमुखी सा भूयिष्ठमन्यविषया न तु दृष्टिरस्याः (S'. I) 'granted (admitting)

---

* कच्चित् कामप्रवेदने । (अ.)

† द्वौ क्वशब्दौ महदन्तरं सूचयतः । (Mallinatha on R. I. 2)

‡ कामं प्रकामेऽनुमतावसूयायुगमेऽपि च । (वि.)

that she does not stand facing me, still her glance is for the most part not directed to anything else.'

§ **266**. * किं is mostly used in asking questions in the sense of '*why*', '*wherefore*'; as, तत्रैव किं न चपले प्रलयं गतासि (Mu. 2), 'wherefore, O fickle goddess, wert thou not destroyed at that very place?' sometimes it enters into compounds in the sense of '*bad*'; as, स किंसखा साधु न शास्ति योधिपं (Ki. I. 5) 'is he a friend (*i. e.* he is a bad friend), who does not properly advise his lord?'

§ **267**. किं when followed by वा, उत, or आहो &c. (*or*) has the sense of '*whether*'; as, ज्ञायतां किमेतदारण्यकं ग्राम्यं वेति (P. I. 1) 'let it be ascertained whether this (animal) is wild or domesticated.' For the use of किं with उत &c. see § 258.

(*a*) † किं is usually joined to उ, उत, or पुनः in the sense of '*how much more*' ,'*how much less*', '*much more*', '*much less*'; as, एकैकमप्यनर्थाय किमु तत्र चतुष्टयं (H. 1) 'even one of these taken singly will cause ruin, how much more, all the four'; चाणक्येमाहूतस्य निर्दोषस्यापि शंका जायते किमुत सदोषस्य (Mu. 1) 'suspicion (fear) is aroused in even an innocent person (when) summoned by Cháṇakya, much more then, in a guilty person'; मयि नांतकोपि प्रभुः प्रहर्तुं किमुतान्यहिंस्राः (R. II. 62) 'even the Destroyer is not able to strike (hurt) me, much less other wild animals'; स्वयं रोपितेषु तरुषु उत्पद्यते स्नेहः किंपुनरंगसंभवेष्वपत्येषु (K. 291) 'affection is felt even for trees planted by oneself much more for one's own children'; भवादृशस्य त्रैलोक्यमपि न क्षमं परिपन्थीभवितुं किं पुनर्युधिष्ठिरबलं (Ve. 3) 'even the three worlds dare not come in the way of a person like you, much less the army of Dharma.'

Obs.—किमु is also used to denote 'uncertainty', or 'doubt'; as, किमु विषविसर्पः किमु मदः (U. 1) 'may it be the spreading of poison (over the body), or excessive delight?'

§ **268**. The general sense of किल is '*verily*', '*indeed*', '*assured-*

---

* किं पृच्छायां जुगुप्सने । (अ.)

† किमु संभावनायां स्यात् विमर्शे चापि दृश्यते (मे.)
किमुतातिशये प्रश्ने विकल्पे च प्रयुज्यते (वि.)

(c) and it follows the word on which it lays stress; as, अर्हति किल कितव उपद्रवं (M. 4) 'the rogue does deserve annoyance'; प्रगृहः सर्वसिद्धीनामुत्तापः प्रथमः किल (H. 3) 'previous over-excitement is verily an obstacle to all accomplishments (of desired objects).'

§ **269**. * किल is also used (1) in the sense of 'as is reported', 'as they say'; as, बभूव योगी किल कार्तवीर्यः (R. VI. 38) 'there was, as is reported, a Yogin, Kârtavîrya'; जघान कंसं किल वासुदेवः (Mbh.); (2) to express a feigned action; as, प्रसह्य सिंहः किल तां चकर्ष (R. II. 27) 'a false lion seized her with violence'; पयस्यगाधे किल जातसंभ्रमा (Ki. VIII. 48); (3) to express hopes or expectations; as, पार्थः किल विजेस्यते कुरून् (G. M.) 'I hope Pártha will conquer the Kurus.'

Obs.—The senses अरुचि 'dislike' and 'न्यक्करण 'contempt' (एवं किल केचिद्वदन्ति and त्वं किल योत्स्यसे) given by Vardhamána, are found when किल is joined with किं; as, न श्रद्दधे किं किल त्वं शूद्रान्नं भोक्ष्यसे (S. K.) 'I cannot believe that you will eat the food of S'údras.'

The sense हेतु is very rare.

§ **270**. केवलं is an adverb meaning 'only', 'merely', but it is sometimes used as an adjective also; as, निषेदुषी स्थंडिल एव केवलं (Ku. V. 12) 'sitting on the bare altar' (without any coverlet.)

(*a*) The combination of न केवलं with अपि or किंतु in the sense of '*not only—but*' is very common; as, वसु तस्य विभोर्न केवलं गुणवत्तापि परप्रयोजना (R. VIII. 31) 'not only his wealth but even his possession of good qualities, was for the sake of others.'

(*b*) प्रत्युत sometimes takes the place of अपि; as, अयं वत्सो न केवलं ध्रियते प्रत्युत प्राञ्जलिना गरुडेन पर्युपास्यमानस्तिष्ठति (Nág. 5) 'not only is my child alive, but (on the contrary) he is waited upon by Garuda with folded hands.'

§ **271**. † खलु is used in the following senses:—(1) '*indeed*'

---

* वार्तासंभाव्ययोः किल। (अ.)
किल इत्यागमारुचिन्यक्करणसंभाव्यहेत्वलीकेषु। (ग. म.)

† निषेधवाक्यालंकारजिज्ञासानुनये खलु। (अ.)
खलु इति निषेधवाक्यालंकारजिज्ञासानुनयनियमनिश्चयहेतुविषादेषु। (ग. म.)

'surely,' 'verily', for the sake of emphasis, or as an expletive; **मार्गे पदानि खलु ते विषमीभवन्ति** (S'. 4) 'thy footsteps do, indeed, fall uneven (trip) on the way'; (2) *'conciliation'*, as an entreating word; **न खलु न खलु बाणः सन्निपात्योयमस्मिन्** (S'. 1) 'pray, let not the arrow be discharged at this'; so **न खलु न खलु मुग्धे साहसं कार्यमेतत्** (Nâg.); (3) *'an inquiry'*, as a softened question; **न खलु तामभिक्रुद्धो गुरुः** (V. 3) 'I should like to know if the preceptor did not get angry with her' (was he not angry with her ?); (4) with gerunds, having a *prohibitive* sense like **अलं** (see §57); **निर्धारितेऽर्थे लेखेन खलूक्त्वा खलु वाचिकं** (Śi. II. 70) 'when any matter is determined (decided) by a letter, do not, indeed, add a verbal message' (it is unnecessary); (5) 'reason' (for); **न विदीर्ये कठिनाः खलु स्त्रियः** (Ku. IV. 5); 'I am not shattered to pieces, for women are hard' (this is given by Vardhamána as an instance of **विषाद** ' dejection '); so **विधिना जन एष वञ्चितस्त्वदधीनं खलु देहिनां सुखं** (Ku. IV. 10); (6) it is sometimes used merely as an expletive or to add grace to the sentence.

Obs.—The senses **नियम** and **निश्चय** in G. M. are nearly identical.

विकारं खलु परमार्थतोऽज्ञात्वाऽनारम्भः प्रतीकारस्य । (S'. 3)

न खलु विदितास्ते तत्र निवसन्तश्चाणक्यहतकेन—अथ किम् ।

(Mu. 2)

भर्तृगतया चिन्तयात्मानमपि नैषा विभावयति किं पुनरागंतुकम् ।

(S'. 4)

द्वावपि किलागमिनौ प्रयोगनिपुणौ च । किंतु शिष्यागुणविशेषेण गणदास उन्नमितोपदेशः । (M. 3)

अनुत्सेकः खलु विक्रमालंकारः । (V. 1)

भो न केवलं रूपे शिल्पेऽप्यद्वितीया मालविका । (M. 2)

वत्से सीते स्वहस्तावचितैः पुष्पैः सवितारं देवमुपतिष्ठस्व । न च त्वामवनिपृष्ठचारिणीमस्मत्प्रभावाद्वनदेवता अपि द्रक्ष्यन्ति किं पुनर्मर्त्याः ।
(U. 3)

गर्भेश्वरत्वमभिनवयौवनत्वमप्रतिमरूपत्वममानुषशक्तित्वं चेति महतीयं खल्वनर्थपरंपरा । सर्वाविनयानामेकैकमप्येषामायतनं किमुत समवायः ।
(K. 103)

भोः कामं धर्मकार्यमनतिपात्यं देवस्य । तथापीदानीमेव धर्मासनादुत्थितस्य पुनरुपरोधकारि कण्वशिष्यागमनमस्मै निवेदयितुं नोत्सहे । (S'. 5)

एवं कदलीदलेनानवरतं वीजयतः समुदभून्मे मनसि चिन्ता । नास्ति खल्वसाध्यं मनोभुवः । क्वायं हरिण इव वनवासनिरतः स्वभावमुग्धो जनः क्व च विविधविलासरसराशिर्गन्धर्वराजपुत्री महाश्वेता ॥ (K. 157)

निवार्यतामालि किमप्ययं बटुः पुनर्विवक्षुः स्फुरितोत्तराधरः ।
न केवलं यो महतोऽपभाषते शृणोति तस्मादपि यः स पापभाक् ॥
(Ku. V. 34)

किमपेक्ष्य फलं पयोधरान्ध्वनतः प्रार्थयते मृगाधिपः ।
प्रकृतिः खलु सा महीयसः सहते नान्यसमुन्नतिं यया ॥ (Ki. II. 31)

कच्चिदेतच्छ्रुतं पार्थ त्वयैकाग्रेण चेतसा ।
कच्चिदज्ञानसंमोहः प्रनष्टस्ते धनंजय ॥ (Bg. XVIII. 72)

कामं नृपाः सन्तु सहस्रशोऽन्ये राजन्वतीमाहुरनेन भूमिम् ।
नक्षत्रताराग्रहसंकुलापि ज्योतिष्मती चन्द्रमसैव रात्रिः ॥ (R. VI. 22)

क्व वयं क्व परोक्षमन्मथो मृगशावैः सममेधितो जनः ।
परिहासविजल्पितं सखे परमार्थेन न गृह्यतां वचः ॥ (S'. 2)

ADDITIONAL SENTENCES FOR EXERCISE.

वयस्य मया न साधु समर्थितमापत्प्रतीकारः किल प्रमदवनोद्यानप्रवेश इति। (V. 2)

भगवन्तं जाबालिमवलोकयाहमचिन्तयम्। तपस्विनां प्रतनुतपसामपि तेजः प्रकृत्या दुःसहं भवति किमुत सकलभुवनवन्दितचरणानां मुनीनाम्। एवंविधानामघक्षयकारिणां पुण्यानि नामग्रहणान्यपि महामुनीनां किं पुनर्दर्शनानि। (K. 43)

आजन्मनः शाठ्यमशिक्षितो यस्तस्याप्रमाणं वचनं जनस्य।
परातिसन्धानमधीयते यैर्विद्येति ते सन्तु किलाप्तवाचः (S'. 5)

यदृच्छया त्वं सकृदप्यवन्ध्ययोः पथि स्थिता सुंदरि यस्य नेत्रयोः।
त्वया विना सोऽपि समुत्सुको भवेत्सखीजनस्ते किमु रूढसौहृदः (V. 1)

न केवलं दरीसंस्थं भास्वतां दर्शनेन वः।
अन्तर्गतमपास्तं मे रजसोऽपि परं तमः (Ku. VI. 60)

न केवलं तद्गुरुरेकपार्थिवः।
क्षितावभूदेकधनुर्धरोपि सः (R. III. 31)

सुखश्रवा मंगलतूर्यनिस्वनाः प्रमोदनृत्यैः सह वारयोषिताम्।
न केवलं सद्मनि मागधीपतेः पथि व्यजृम्भन्त दिवौकसामपि (R. III. 19))

रघुमेव निवृत्तयौवनं तममन्यन्त नवेश्वरं प्रजाः।
स हि तस्य न केवलां श्रियं प्रतिपेदे सकलान्गुणानपि (R. VIII. 5)

मेघालोके भवति सुखिनोप्यन्यथावृत्ति चेतः।
कंठाश्लेषप्रणयिनि जने किं पुनर्दूरसंस्थे (Me. 3)

दृष्टे सूर्ये पुनरपि भवान् वाहयेदध्वशेषं।
मन्दायन्ते न खलु सुहृदामभ्युपेतार्थकृत्याः॥ (Me. 39)

स्त्रीणामशिक्षितपटुत्वममानुषीषु
संदृश्यते किमुत याः प्रतिबोधवत्यः।
प्रागंतरिक्षगमनात्स्वमपत्यजात-
मन्यैर्द्विजैः परभृताः खलु पोषयन्ति (S'. 5)

क रुजा हृदयप्रमाथिनी क च ते विश्वसनीयमायुधम्।
मृदुतीक्ष्णतरं यदुच्यते तदिदं मन्मथ दृश्यते त्वयि (M. 3)

कामं प्रिया न सुलभा मनस्तु तद्भावदर्शनाश्वासि।
अकृतार्थेपि मनसिजे रतिमुभयप्रार्थना कुरुते। (S'. 2)

It is reported that the king has become exceedingly angry with us for our carelessness.

I shall not forget a person who may be but once seen; much less an old friend.

Even inanimate things in this penance-forest appear to be possessed of a purifying power; how much more objects possessed of life.

When I went to him, he reviled not only me, but the preceptor himself.

Not only do no people hate me, but on the contrary they feed me with food.

I hope it has not reached the king's ears that it was I who ordered the *kaumudi* festival to be at once stopped.

We find that even persons that are born rich are not completely happy in this world; much less are those who have to gain their livelihood by various kinds of troublesome occupations.

I earnestly hope that you will spare the life of this helpless creature. Good men hesitate to kill their very enemy; much less an innocent creature like this child.

I hope you are all going on uninterruptedly with your religious austerities.

Granted that you are possessed of all good qualities, still I consider it my duty to advise you, because youth is subject to temptations.

True that I do not remember to have married her; nevertheless my mind is greatly affected at seeing her.

Is there any congruity between thy sacred learning and this fickle state of heart ?

The acts of kings naturally unfathomable, cannot be sounded by men like me whose knowledge is very limited. (*use* क्व-क्व).

LESSON XXIV.

च (च–च), जातु, तत्, ततः, तथा, तावत्, & तु.

§ **227.** * च is, by pre-eminence, a copulative conjunction, and joins words or assertions together. It does not stand in the same place as '*and*' in English or '*et*' in Latin. It is used with each of the words or assertions which it joins together, or is used after the last of the words or assertions so joined, but it can never stand first in a sentence; as, रामश्च गोविंदश्च or रामो गोविंदश्च 'Râma *and* Govinda'; तंडुलानानयति च तान् पचति चौदनं भुंक्ते च or तंडुलानानयति तान् पचत्योदनं भुंक्ते च 'he brings rice, cooks them, and eats the cooked food.' But it is generally better to use च last, rather than repeat it after each connected word; as, कुलेन कान्त्या वयसा नवेन गुणैश्च तैस्तैर्विनयप्रधानैः (R. VI. 79).

(*a*) Not unfrequently च is admitted to any other part of a sentence than the first word; as, अथ गजस्तं प्रणम्य प्रस्थितः शशकाश्च तद्दिनादारभ्य सुखेन तिष्ठन्ति (P. III. 1) 'then the elephant, bowing down to him, went away, and the hares lived happily from that day.'

(*b*) च when used with न has sometimes the sense of '*neither*,' '*nor*'; as, न च न परिचितो न चाप्यगम्यः (M. 1) 'neither is he unknown nor unapproachable.'

(*c*) Sometimes it has a disjunctive force, and may be translated by '*but*', '*still*', '*nevertheless*'; as, शांतमिदमाश्रमपदं स्फुरति च बाहुः (S'. 1) this hermitage is tranquil, still my arm throbs.

Obs.—In this sense च is generally repeated; see the next section.

(*d*) Rarely it has also the sense of 'indeed,' 'verily,' having the force of एव; as अतीतः पंथानं तव च महिमा वाङ्मनसयोः (G. M.) 'your greatness, indeed, transcends the range of speech and mind.'

(*e*) It is sometimes used to denote 'condition' (=चेद् or यदि); as, जीवितं चेच्छसे मूढ हेतुं मे गदतः शृणु (Mb.), *i. e.*, जीवितमिच्छसे चेद् &c.

---

* चान्वाचये समाहारेऽप्यन्योन्यार्थे समुच्चये
पक्षान्तरे तथा पादपूरणेऽप्यवधारणे ॥ (वि.)

(*f*) Or it may be used as an expletive; as, भीमः पार्थस्तथैव च (G. M.).

Obs.—Lexicographers give as the sense of च, अन्वाचय, समाहार, इतरेतर, समुच्चय, which are included in the general idea of 'conjunction' or 'copulation' denoted by च. अन्वाचय means 'connecting a subordinate fact with a principal one'; as, भिक्षामट गां चानय 'go to beg and (while doing so) bring the cow'; समाहार is 'collective combination'; as, पाणी च पादौ च पाणिपादं; इतरेतर is 'mutual connection'; as प्लक्षश्च न्यग्रोधश्च प्लक्षन्यग्रोधौ; समुच्चय is 'aggregation'; as, पचति च पठति च.

§ **273.** च is frequently repeated with two assertions (1) in the sense of '*on the one hand—on the other hand*', '*though yet*' to denote antithesis; as, न सुलभा सकलेन्दुमुखी च सा किमपि चेदमनंगविचेष्टितम् (V. 2) 'on the one hand that full-moon-faced woman is not easy to obtain; and on the other hand there is this unaccountable working of Love'; or 'that full-moon-faced lady &c...and yet' &c.; (2) or to express *simultaneous* or *undelayed* occurrence of two events, as denoted by 'no sooner than' or 'as soon as' &c. in English; as, ते च प्रापुरुदन्वन्तं बुबुधे चादिपूरुषः (R. X. 6) 'no sooner did they reach the ocean than the Supreme Being (Vishnu) awoke.'

§ **274.** जातु means '*at all*', '*possibly*', '*perhaps*'; as, किं तेन जातु जातेन (P. I. 1) 'what possibly is the use of him being born'; न जातु बाला लभते स्म निर्वृतिं (Ku. V. 55) 'the maiden did not at all enjoy (never enjoyed) pleasure.'

Obs.—Pàṇini lays down that जातु is used with the Potential in the sense of 'not allowing', 'not suffering'; as, जातु यत्वादृशो हरिं निन्देन्न-मर्षयामि (S. K.) 'I do not suffer (allow) that a person like you should censure Hari.'

§ **275.** तद् is a pronoun (see § 132 for its uses) and an adverb. In the latter case it means (1) '*for that reason*,' '*therefore*', '*consequently*'; as, राजपुत्रा वयं तद्विग्रहं श्रोतुं नः कुतूहलमस्ति (H. 3.) 'we are princes; therefore, we have a desire to hear of war'; (2) '*then*.' '*in that case*' often as the correlative of यदि; as, तर्हेहि विमर्दक्षमां भूमिमवतरावः

(U. 5) 'come, then, let us go to a place fit for our combat', तथापि यदि महत्कुतूहलं तत्कथयामि (K. 136) 'still if you have a great curiosity, (then) I shall relate.'

§ **276**. ततः is often used for the ablative forms of तद्, such as तस्मात्, तस्याः, ततोन्यत्रापि दृश्यते (S. K.)=तस्मादन्यत्रापि; but it is oftener used as an adverb. It primarily means 'thence,' 'from that place'; and generally, '*then*', *afterwards*', '*thereupon*'; as, ततः कतिपयदिवसापगमे (K. 110.) 'afterwards (then) some days having elapsed'. It also means (1) '*for that reason*', '*therefore*', '*consequently*', as a correlative of यतः; (2) '*then*', '*in that case*' serving as a correlative of यदि; as, यदि गृहीतमिदं ततः किम् (K. 120) 'if this be caught, then what would happen ?'; (3) sometimes '*beyond that*', '*further*', '*moreover*', ततः परतो निर्मनुष्यमरण्यं (K. 121) 'beyond that is a tenantless (dreary) forest.'

(*a*) ततस्ततः (ततः—ततः) is used in dialogues in the sense of '*what next*,' '*go on*', '*proceed*'; as, राक्षसः—उभयोरप्यस्थाने प्रयत्नः । ततस्ततः (Mu. 2) 'Ràkshasa—The attempt of both was out of place—Well what (happened) next (proceed)'.

§ **277**. *तथा means '*so*', '*thus*', '*in that manner*'; as, तथा मां वञ्चयित्वा (S'. 5) 'having deceived me in that manner'; सूतस्तथा करोति (V. 1) 'the charioteer does so (accordingly)'; तथा च श्रुतिः (S. B.) 'and so says the Veda.'

(*a*) It is also used in the following senses:—(1) '*and also*', '*so also*,' '*in like manner*'; as, अनागतविधाता च प्रत्युत्पन्नमतिस्तथा (P. I. 13) 'he who provides for the future *and also* he who is ready-witted '; (2) '*yes*', '*be it so*', '*so it shall be*', signifying 'assent', 'promise ', &c. and followed by इति; *as* राजा—एनं तत्रभवतः सकाशं प्रापय । प्रतीहारी—तथेति निष्क्रान्ता 'King—Take him to his Honour.' 'Prutihàri—Yes, so it shall be, (your commands will be obeyed), so saying *exit*; (3) in forms of adjurations, '*as surely as*' (preceded by यथा); as यथाहमन्यं न चिन्तये तथायं पततां परासुः 'as surely as I do not think of any other man, so surely let this person fall dead.'

---

*तथाऽभ्युपगमे पृष्टप्रतिवाक्येसमुच्चये ।
सदृशे निश्चयेपि स्यात् । (मे.)

For some of the meanings of **तथा** as correlative of **यथा** see Lesson 27.

Obs.—**तथाहि** means 'for', 'so it has been said', 'for instance'; **तथा च** 'and likewise.' Both are often used in introducing quotations.

§ **278**. **तावत्**, as a particle, is used (1) in its literal sense of '*first*,' 'before doing any thing else;' as, **प्रिये इतस्तावदागम्यतां** (S'. 1) 'my dear, just (first) come here'; **आह्लादयस्व तावच्चन्द्रकरश्चन्द्रकांतमिव** (V. 5) 'first gladden me as a lunar ray does the moon-stone'; (2) '*on one's part*', '*in the meanwhile*'; or '*while*'; as, **सखे स्थिरप्रतिबन्धो भव । अहं तावत्स्वामिनश्चित्तवृत्तिमनुवर्तिष्ये** (Ś. 2) 'friend, be firm in your opposition'; 'I, on my part (while I) shall act up to the will of my master'; (3) '*just*', '*now*'; as, **गच्छ तावत्** 'go now'; (4) to emphasize a statement, in the sense of '*indeed*', '*really*'; as, **त्वमेव तावत्प्रथमो राजद्रोही** (Mu. 1) 'thou (*indeed*) thyself art the first traitor'; (5) '*as for*', '*with respect to*' *&c.*; as, **एवं कृते तव तावत्प्राणयात्रा क्लेशं विना भविष्यति** (P. I. 8) 'this being done, as far as you are concerned (with respect to yourself) your maintenance will be secured (to you) without any trouble'; **विग्रहस्तावदुपस्थितः** (H. 3) 'as for war, it is imminent.'

For the other senses of **तावत्** as a correlative of **यावत्** see Lesson 27.

§ **279**. *.**तु** 'is most frequently used as an adversative particle meaning '*but*', '*on the contrary*', '*however*', '*on the other hand*'; as, **स सर्वेषां सुखानां प्रायोऽन्ते ययौ । एकं तु सुतमुखदर्शनसुखं न लेभे** (K. 59) 'he completely enjoyed all pleasures, only he did not enjoy the pleasure of seeing the face of a son.' In this sense it is often added to **किं** and **परं**.

Note.—**तु** is never used at the beginning of a sentence, while **परंतु** and **किंतु** always stand first.

(*a*) **तु** is frequently used in the sense of '*and now*', '*now*,' '*on one's part*', '*as to*,' without any adversative force; as, **एकदा तु नातिदूरोदिते सहस्रमरीचिमालिनि प्रतीहारी समुपसृत्याब्रवीत्** (K. 8) 'now once upon a time, when the thousand-rayed god had not risen high enough, the door-keeper, drawing near, said'; **अवनिपतिस्तु तामनिमेषलोचनो ददर्श** (K. 11)

* **तु पादपूरणे भेदे समुच्चयेऽवधारणे । (वि.)**

'the lord of the earth, on his part, looked at her with a stead-. gaze'; **यत्तु आसनशब्दस्यासन्नादेश इति काशिकायामुक्तं तत्प्रामादिकं** (S. K.) o. **निर्वापितं तु परिरभ्य वपुर्न नाम** (Mál. 8).

(*b*) Sometimes **तु** marks a 'difference or superior quality'; as, **मृष्टं पयो मृष्टतरं तु दुग्धं** (G. M.) 'pure is water, purer still is milk'; and sometimes it is used as an emphatic particle ; as, **भीमस्तु पांडवानां रौद्रः** (*ibid*) 'Bhîma alone is the fiercest of the Pándavas.'

तद्यदि नातिखेदकरमिव ततः कथनेनात्मानमनुग्राह्यमिच्छामि । (K. 134)

अपसृते च तस्मिन् स विहंगराजो राजाभिमुखो भूत्वा राजानमुद्दिश्यार्यामिमां पपाठ । राजा तु तां श्रुत्वा संजातविस्मयोऽमात्यमब्रवीत् । (K. 12)

आर्य ततः किं विलम्ब्यते । त्वरितं (तं) प्रवेशय । (U. 1)

अनेन क्रमेण तस्य सर्वेष्वरण्यवासिष्वाधिपत्यं बभूव । ततस्तेन स्वज्ञातिभिरावृतेनाधिकं प्रभुत्वं साधितम् । (H. 3)

आर्ये कृतपरिश्रमोस्मि चतुःषष्ठ्यंगे ज्योतिःशास्त्रे । तत्प्रवर्त्यतां भगवतो ब्राह्मणानुद्दिश्य पाकः । चन्द्रोपरागं प्रति तु केनापि विप्रलब्धासि । (Mu. 1)

भगवन् कुसुमायुध त्वया चन्द्रमसा च विश्वसनीयाभ्यामतिसन्धीयते कामिजनसार्थः । (Ś. 3)

तात लताभगिनीं वनज्योत्स्नां तावदामन्त्रयिष्ये । (S . 4)

करटक उवाच । भद्र किं कृतं तत्र भवता । दमनक आह । मया तावन्नीतिबीजनिर्वापणं कृतं परतो दैवविहितायत्तम् ।

दृष्ट्वा मेघनादं दूरत एव कृतनमस्कारं तमप्राक्षीत् । तिष्ठतु तावत्पुरस्तात्पत्रलेखागमनवृत्तांतप्रश्नो वैशंपायनवृत्तांतमेव तावत् पृच्छामि । (K.314)

अयमेकपदे तया वियोगः सहसा चोपनतः सुदुःसहो मे ।
नववारिधरोदयादहोभिर्भवितव्यं च निरातपत्वरम्यैः ॥ (V. 4)

प्रतिगृहीतुं प्रणयिप्रियत्वात्त्रिलोचनस्तामुपचक्रमे च ।
संमोहनं नाम च पुष्पधन्वा धनुष्यमोघं समधत्त बाणम् ॥
(Ku. III. 66)

न जातु कामः कामानामुपभोगेन शाम्यति ।
हविषा कृष्णवर्त्मेव भूय एवाभिवर्धते ॥ (Manu. II. 94)

ADDITIONAL SENTENCES FOR EXERCISE.

अत्रभवत्याप्रसवादस्मद्गृहे तिष्ठतु। कुत इदमुच्यत इति चेत्त्वं साधुभिरुपदिष्टः प्रथममेव चक्रवर्तिनं पुत्रं जनयिष्यसीति। स चेत्तल्लक्षणोपपन्नो भविष्यति अभिनन्द्य शुद्धान्तमेनां प्रवेशयिष्यसि। विपर्यते तु पितुरस्याः समीपनयनमवस्थितमेव। (S'. 5)

कथारंभकाले राजपुत्रा ऊचुः। आर्य मित्रलाभः श्रुतस्तावदस्माभिः। इदानीं सुहृद्भेदं श्रोतुमिच्छामः। (H. 2)

सुखमापतितं सेव्यं दुःखमापतितं तथा।
चक्रवत्परिवर्तन्ते दुःखानि च सुखानि च ॥ (H. 1)

लब्धान्तरा सावरणेपि गेहे योगप्रभावो न च लक्ष्यते ते।
बिभर्षि चाकारमनिर्वृतानां मृणालिनी हैममिवोपरागम् ॥ (R. XVI. 7)

मुनिसुताप्रणयस्मृतिरोधिना मम च मुक्तमिदं तमसा मनः।
मनसिजेन सखे प्रहरिष्यता धनुषि चूतशरश्च निवेशितः ॥ (S'. 6)

देव परावृत्तेषु कण्वशिष्येषु

सा निन्दन्ती स्वानि भाग्यानि बाला बाहूत्क्षेपं क्रन्दितुं च प्रवृत्ता।
स्त्रीसंस्थानं चाप्सरस्तीर्थमारादुत्क्षिप्यैनां ज्योतिरेकं जगाम ॥ (S'. 5)

धनं तावदसुलभं लब्धं कृच्छ्रेण रक्ष्यते।
लब्धनाशो यथा मृत्युस्तस्मादेतन्न चिन्तयेत् (H. 1)

सर्वस्य चाहं हृदि संनिविष्टो मत्तः स्मृतिर्ज्ञानमपोहनं च।
वेदैश्च सर्वैरहमेव वेद्यो वेदान्तकृद्वेदविदेव चाहम् ॥ (Bg. XV. 15)

न खलु न खलु बाणः सन्निपात्योऽयमस्मिन्
मृदुनि मृगशरीरे तूलराशाविवाग्निः ।
क्व बत हरिणकानां जीवितं चातिलोलं
क्व च निशितनिपाता वज्रसाराः शरास्ते ॥ (S'. 1)
आपूर्णश्च कलाभिरिन्दुरमलो यातश्च राहोर्मुखं
संजातश्च घनाघनो जलधरः शीर्णश्च वायोर्जवात् ।
निर्वृत्तश्च फलग्रहिर्द्रुमवरो दग्धश्च दावाग्निना
त्वं चूडामणितां गतश्च जगतो यातश्च मृत्योर्वशम् ॥ (Mál. 9)

Those, who act in a virtuous way and are devoted to doing good to others, alone become the objects of God's mercy.

I have brought from Bombay eight silken clothes, five silver pots, and several other useful things.

On the one hand I have never before seen him; on the other, there is his speech as hard as the stroke of a thunderbolt; who may this man be ?

As soon as these brave soldiers desert their master's side, I shall provoke revolts in his territories.

You have made very good preparations for war; nothing will therefore, be wanting to you.

Duryodhana:—Oh the bravery of that youthful warrior ! I think all warriors must have for a time stood still with amazement, to see his extraordinary exploits.—Well, proceed.

Having imposed upon me in that manner by your honeyed sentences, are you not ashamed to cast me off now ?

You are so much afflicted with even a temporary separation from your mate, and yet you are so averse to giving a love-lorn man like me, information regarding his lost beloved.

The moment he placed his foot within the threshold of the house three men rushed upon him and made him their prisoner.

You have now got wealth, honour, children and everything else desired by men; what else do you want?—or why, it is truly said 'there is no knowing how far human desires may extend.'

Go thou to Yajnas'arman and ask him why he has tarried so long; while I shall go and call the other Brâhmanas.

Ráma getting up early in the morning, begins to study; whereas thou sleepest snoring in the bed.

As far as the eldest son of Mitragupta is concerned, he may certainly be relied upon, but I do not know anything about his other sons.

If this be done, you yourself will go on uninterruptedly with your work; and we also shall be enabled to do our own.

LESSON XXV.

दिष्ट्या, न, नाम, नु, ननु, & नूनं.

§ **280.** दिष्ट्या is a particle expressive of joy or gladness and may be translated by '*I am glad*', '*happily*, '*thank God*'; as, दिष्ट्या प्रतिहतं दुर्जातं (Mál. 4) 'I am glad the evil is averted'; दिष्ट्या कोपव्याजेन देव्या परित्रातो भवान् (M. 1) 'thank God (that) you are saved by the Queen under the pretext of anger.'

(*a*) दिष्ट्या is often used with the root वृध् and दिष्ट्या वृध् may be translated by '*to congratulate* (one) *upon*', the *subject* of वृध् being the person congratulated, and the matter of congratulation being put in the instrumental case; as, दिष्ट्या महाराजो विजयेन वर्धते (V. 1) 'I congratulate your Majesty upon your success'; दिष्ट्या सुहृद्धृद्ध्या वर्धितोसि (Mál. 4) 'you are to be congratulated upon your friend's recovery (from the swoon)', or 'I congratulate you &c.'

§ **281.** न '*not*' is used like an adverb; न दृष्टोयं मया 'he was *not* seen by me.' '*No*' as applied to nouns is expressed by न with any one of the indefinite forms; as, 'no man came to me' न कोपि नरो मामा-

यातः; योगिनां न किमपि भयं 'Yogins have no fear.' In negative sentences the indefinite forms mark the exclusion of all; as, मरणान्न कोपि बिभेति 'no one whatever is afraid of death.'

(*a*). In several cases न-न is used to express an assertion emphatically positive; as, नेयं न वक्ष्यति मनोगतमाधिहेतुं (S'. 3) 'she will *certainly* mention the secret cause of her agony' (lit. *not* that she will *not* mention &c.).

§ **282.** *नाम is most frequently used in the sense of '*by name*' '*called*' '*named*', '*known as*'; as, रावणो नाम लंकेशः 'the lord of Lanká by name Rávana'; पुष्पपुरी नाम नगरी 'a town called Pushpapurí'

Obs. The noun before नाम must in this sense be in the same case as the noun of which it may be an attribute; as, मेघनादो नाम मित्रं (P. I. 15) 'a friend called Meghanáda'; तत्रान्दिनीं सुवृत्तां नामोपयम्य (D. K. I. 1); अस्ति पाटलिपुत्रे नाम नगरे बलभिन्नाम वणिक् (D. K. II. 6). This नाम does not enter into any compound, and should not be confounded with नामन् which is compounded; thus दशरथनाम राजा is wrong; it should be either दशरथो नाम राजा or दशरथनामा राजा (दशरथो नाम यस्य सः).

§ **283**. Another most general sense of नाम is '*indeed*', '*to be sure*', '*verily*,' '*forsooth*'; as, मया नाम जितं (V. 1) 'I have indeed conquered' (become victorious); विनीतवेषेण प्रवेष्टव्यानि तपोवनानि नाम (S'. 1) 'hermitages should, indeed (to be sure), be entered with a modest (humble) dress.'

Obs. When नाम is used with कः, किं, कथं, &c., the meaning expressed is that of '*possibility*' or '*I should like to know*' (*cf.* इव § 257); as, को नाम राज्ञां प्रियः (P, I. 3) 'who possibly is a favourite of kings'; को नाम पाकाभिमुखस्य जन्तुर्द्वाराणि दैवस्य पिधातुमीष्टे (U. 7) 'what creature, I should like to know, is able to shut the doors of Fate, when disposed to show its power'; अयि कथं नामैतत् (D. 6) 'O, how indeed is this ?'

---

* नाम प्राकाश्यसंभाव्यक्रोधोपगमकुत्सने । (अ.)
नाम प्राकाश्यकुत्सयोः ।
संभाव्याभ्युपगमयोरलीके विस्मये क्रुधि । (हे.)

§ **284.** **नाम** is also used (1) to express a '*pretence*' or a feigned action; as, **कार्तान्तिको नाम भूत्वा** (D. K. II. 6) 'pretending to be an astrologer'; (with imperatives, in the sense of '*granted*', '*it may be that*', "*if you like*'; as, **यत्खल्वनालोचितावधि दुःखावसानमेव दुःखं तन्मरणभीरोर्भवतु नाम शोकावेगाय** (K. 328); 'granted (it may be) that that calamity which being of indefinite duration, will end in sorrow, will create emotions of grief in one afraid of death'; **एवमस्तु नाम** 'well, be it so' (if you like); (3) '*wonder*'; **अन्धो नाम पर्वतमारोहति** (G. M.) 'it is a wonder that a blind man ascends a mountain'; (4) '*anger*' and rarely '*censure*'; **किं नाम विस्फुरन्ति शस्त्राणि** (U. 4.) 'Oh ! do missiles gleam forth !'; **ममापि नाम दशाननस्य परैः परिभवः** (G. M.) 'What ! Should I, Das'ánana, be defeated by others ?'

§ **285.** * **नु** has an interrogative force involving some 'doubt' or 'uncertainty'; as, **स्वप्नो नु माया नु मतिभ्रमो नु** (S'. 6) 'was it a dream, an illusion, or an infatuation of the brain ?'

(*a*) **नु** is very often compounded with the interrogative pronoun and its derivatives, in the sense of '*possibly*', '*indeed*' (*cf.* **इव** § 257); as, **किं न्वेतत्स्यात्किमदन्यदितोथवा** (Mál. 1.) 'what may this possibly be ?—or what else than this'; **कथं नु गुणवद्विन्देयं कलत्रं** (D. K. II. 6) 'how, indeed, shall I get a virtuous wife ?'

§ **286.** † The most general combination of **नु** is with the word **न**, and **ननु** is now treated as a separate word. It is used in the following senses:—(1) '*is it not indeed that*', '*surely it is*'; as **यदामेधाविनी शिष्योपदेशं मलिनयति तदाचार्यस्य दोषो ननु** (M. 1) 'when a dull-witted pupil spoils the instruction (given), is it not indeed (surely it is) the fault of the preceptor ?'; (2) it is used as a corrective word like '*why*' in English; as, **ननु पदं परिवृत्य भण** (M. 5) 'I say, say (it) changing the words'; **ननु भवानग्रतो मे वर्तते** (S'. 2) 'why you yourself are before me' (is it not, indeed, that &c.); **ननु विचिनोतु भवांस्तदस्मिन्नुद्याने** (V. 2) (well, why do you stand) 'you should look for it in this garden'; (3) in

---

* **नु पृच्छायां विकल्पे च।** (**अ.**)

† **प्रश्नावधारणानुज्ञानुनयामन्त्रणे ननु।** (**अ.**)

propitiatory expressions, in the sense of *'pray'*, *'be pleased'* &c.; as ननु मां प्रापय पत्युरन्तिकं (Ku. IV. 32) 'be pleased to take me to my husband'; (4) as a vocative particle used in addressing persons, meaning *'Oh'*, *'ah'* &c.; as राजवाहनोऽभाषत । ननु मानव अत्र भवानेकाकी किमिति निवसति (D. K. I. 2) 'Rajaváhana said:—O man, why do you live here alone?'; ननु मूर्खाः पठितमेव युष्माभिस्तत्काण्डे (U. 4) 'ah fools, you have already learnt it in that chapter'; (5) in asking questions; as, ननु समाप्तकृत्यो गौतमः (U. 4) 'has Gautama accomplished his object?'

(*a*) In argumentative discussions ननु is very often used to head an objection or advance a contrary proposition, and उच्यते, with or without अत्र, is used with the statement that answers the objection raised, or refutes the proposition asserted; as, ननु एकाधिकं हरेज्ज्येष्ठ इति वचनेन विषमो विभागो दर्शित इति । अत्रोच्यते । सत्यमयं विषमो विभागः शास्त्रस्तथापि लोकविद्विष्टत्वान्नानुष्ठेयः (Mitákshara) 'now it may be objected that the division (of the ancestral property) is declared to be uneven, by the precept 'the elder shall take 2 parts'.—To this we reply, true this unequal division *is* ordained by S'ástras, but it is not to be followed being opposed to practice; so ननु अचेतनान्येव वृश्चिकादिशरीराण्यचेतनानां गोमयादीनां कार्याणीति उच्यते (S'. B. 428); other examples of the use of ननु in this sense are:—ननु चेतनमपि कार्यकारणं स्वामिभृत्यन्यायेन भोक्तुरुपकरिष्यति । न । (S'. B. 423); ननु जगदप्यप्रकृतमसंशब्दितं च । सत्यमेतत् । (*ibid.* 383).

Obs. कथं तर्हि (then how is this), इति चेत् (if any were to say so), are sometimes used in raising objections; as, कथं तर्हि 'क्वासि हे सुभ्रु'—प्रमाद एवायमिति भागुरिः (S. K.) 'now one may ask how is it सुभ्रु (voc.)', (we say) 'Bhaguri thinks that it is a mistake.'

§ **287.** The chief sense of नूनं is *'certainly'*, *'indeed'*, *'positively'*; as, स नूनं तव पाशांच्छेत्स्यति (H. I) 'he will certainly cut your bonds;' अद्यापि नूनं हरकोपवह्निस्त्वयि ज्वलति (S.' 3) 'surely (indeed) the fire of the anger of Hara is still burning in you.'

ननु समानेऽपि ज्ञानवृद्धभावे वयोवृद्धत्वाद्रणदासः पुरस्कारमर्हति । (M. 2)

मया नाम मुग्धचातकेनेव शुष्कघनगर्जितेऽन्तरिक्षे जलपानमिष्टम् ।
(M. 2)

अनियन्त्रणानुयोगो नाम तपस्विजनः । (S'. 1)

अलं रुदित्वा। ननु भवतीभ्यामेव स्थिरीकर्तव्या शकुन्तला । (S'. 4)

दिष्टया धर्मपत्नीसमागमेन पुत्रमुखदर्शनेन चायुष्मान्वर्धते । (S'. 7)

निशम्यैतन्नियतिबलान्नु तत्पाटवान्नु स्वबुद्धिमांद्यान्नु स्वनियममनादृत्य तस्यामसौ प्रासजत् । (D. K. II. 2)

एतद्वचनं श्रुत्वा बद्धकलकले महाजने पितुरंगे प्रदीप्तशिरसमाशीविषं न्याक्षिपम् । अहं च भीतो नामावप्लुत्य तातस्य विषं क्षणादस्तम्भयम् ।
(D. K. II. 4)

इमं ललनाजनं सृजता विधात्रा नूनमेषा घुणाक्षरन्यायेन निर्मिता । नोचेदब्जभूरेवंविधनिर्माणनिपुणो यदि स्यात् तर्हि समानलावण्यामन्यां तरुणीं किं न करोति । (D. K. I. 5)

यदि गर्जति वारिधरो गर्जतु तन्नाम निष्ठुराः पुरुषाः ।
अयि विद्युत्प्रमदानां त्वमपि च दुःखं न जानासि ॥ (Mk. 5.)

प्रश्चोतनं नु हरिचन्दनपल्लवानां
निष्पीडितेन्दुकरकंदलजो नु सेकः ।
आतप्तजीवनमनःपरितर्पणो मे
संजीवनौषधिरसो नु हृदि प्रसिक्तः ॥

ADDITIONAL SENTENCES FOR EXERCISE.

नन्वार्यमिश्रैः प्रथममेवाज्ञप्तमभिज्ञानशाकुन्तलं नामापूर्वं नाटकं प्रयोगेणाधिक्रियतामिति । (S'. 1)

अनुपपन्नं खल्वीदृशं त्वयि । न कदाचित्सत्पुरुषाः शोकपात्रात्मानो भवन्ति । ननु प्रवातेपि निष्कंपा गिरयः । (S'. 6)

सखि लवंगिके दिष्ट्या वर्द्धसे । ननु भणामि प्रतिबुद्ध एव ते प्रियवयस्यः प्रतिपन्नचेतनो महाभागो मकरन्द इति । (Mal. 4)

आर्य ननु रामभद्र इत्येव मां प्रत्युपचारः शोभते तातपरिजनस्य । तद्यथाभ्यस्तमभिधीयताम् । (U. 1)

स शक्तिकुमारो नाम श्रेष्ठिपुत्रोऽष्टादशवर्षदेशीयश्चिन्तामापेदे । नास्त्यदाराणामननुगुणदाराणां वा सुखं नाम । तत्कथं नु गुणवद्विन्देयं कलत्रमिति । अथ परप्रत्ययाहृतेषु दारेषु याहच्छिकीं संपत्तिमनभिसमीक्ष्य कार्तान्तिको नाम भूत्वा भुवं बभ्राम । (D. K. II. 6)

विधिप्रयुक्तां परिगृह्य सत्क्रियां परिश्रमं नाम विनीय च क्षणम् ।
उमां स पश्यन्नृजुनैव चक्षुषा प्रचक्रमे वक्तुमनुज्झितक्रमः ॥ (Ku. V. 32)

नियमयसि विमार्गप्रस्थितानात्तदण्डः
प्रशमयसि विवादं कल्पसे रक्षणाय ।
अतनुषु विभवेषु ज्ञातयः सन्तु नाम
त्वयि तु परिसमाप्तं बन्धुकृत्यं प्रजानाम् ॥ (S.' 5)

वपुषा करणोज्झितेन सा निपतन्ती पतिमप्यपातयत् ।
ननु तैलनिषेकबिन्दुना सह दीपार्चिरुपैति मेदिनीम् । (R. VIII. 38)

अस्याः सर्गविधौ प्रजापतिरभूच्चन्द्रो नु कांतिप्रदः
शृंगारैकरसः स्वयं नु मदनो मासो नु पुष्पाकरः ।
वेदाभ्यासजडः कथं नु विषयव्यावृत्तकौतूहलो
निर्मातुं प्रभवेन्मनोहरमिदं रूपं पुराणो मुनिः ॥ (V. 1)

There lived a rich merchant by name Dhanamitra in a town called Ma*n*ipura.

What mortal can possibly know the greatness of God, which baffles the imagination even of great sages ?

He, possessed of inauspicious features, was, indeed, crowned king notwithstanding that there were other qualified princes.

Who is there who will try to bring down ruin on his head with his own hands ?

I congratulate you all on the accomplishment of your desired objects.

Thank God that thou art again seen by me after a long separation.

Friend, please do this much for me; I shall put on a female dress and profess myself to be your daughter; you will then take me to the king and speak to him thus.

May it be a real tiger, or some other animal dressed in a tiger's skin?

Govinda:—Ráma, when will you go to wait upon the *Guru* ? Râma—Why, it is your turn to-day to wait upon our preceptor.

You say Govinda is very lavish in spending money; why, you yourself resemble him in this and several other respects.

If then that friend demand 'why Brutus (Gopala) rose against Cæsar (Vish*n*u)', this is my answer:—'Note that I loved Cæsar less, but that I loved Rome (Suvar*n*apura) more.'

LESSON XXVI.

पुनः, प्रायः (प्रायेण), बत, बलवत्, मुहुः, यत् & यत्सत्यं.

§ **288**. **पुनः** usually means 'again'; as, **पुनर्विवक्षुः** (Ku. V. 83) 'wishing to speak again'; but it has often the sense of '*whereas,*' '*while,*' '*on the other hand*'; as, **तदेव पंचवटीवनं स एव आर्यपुत्रः। ममपुनर्मन्दभाग्याया दृश्यमानमपि सर्वमेवैतन्नास्ति** (U. 3) 'it is the same Panchavatî forest, and my lord is the same; but (on the other hand, however) to me an unlucky being, all this, though before the eye, is as if nothing.'

(*a*) पुनः पुनः is stronger than पुनः and means '*over and over again*', '*repeatedly*'; as, स्वपाठान्पुनः पुनर्वाचय 'read thy lessons over and over again.' The use of पुनः with किं is already given (*vide* § 267).

§ **289.** प्रायः or प्रायेण means '*generally*,' and is used in laying down a general rule or statement; as, प्रायो भृत्यास्त्यजन्ति प्रचलितविभवं स्वामिनं सेवमानाः (Mu. 4.) 'generally (as a general rule) servants, waiting upon their lord, leave him when his prosperity declines (fades away)'; प्रायेणैते रमणविरहेष्वंगनानां विनोदाः (Me. 87) 'generally these are the amusements of women during their separation from lovers.'

§ **290.** *बत is used in the following senses:—(1) '*alas*,' to express pity or sorrow; as, अहो बत महत्पापं कर्तुं व्यवसिता वयं (Bg. I. 45) 'alas! what a great sin are we going to commit!' (2) '*joy*' or '*surprise*', and it is generally found in conjunction with अहो in these senses; as, अहो बतासि स्पृहणीयवीर्यः (Ku. III. 20); 'oh! how enviable thy valour'; so अहो बत महच्चित्रं (K. 154); हता बत वराकी सा (G. M.) as a vocative particle; as, बत वितरत तोयं तोयवाहा नितान्तं (G. M.) 'clouds give plentiful water'; त्यजत मानमलं बत विग्रहैः (R. IX. 47).

§ **291.** बलवत् meaning 'having strength' is used as an adverb in the sense of '*strongly*', '*excessively*', '*very much*'; as, शिव इन्द्रियक्षोभं बलवन्निजग्राह (Ku. III. 69) 'S'iva strongly (perforce) curbed (quieted) the agitation of his senses'; बलवदस्वस्थशरीरा शकुन्तला (S'. 3) 'S'akuntalá is very severely indisposed.'

§ **292.** मुहुः means 'often'; as, बालो मुहु रोदिति 'the child often weeps'; and in this sense it is generally repeated. It also means '*at one time—at another time*', '*now—now*', and is used with each clause; as मुहुर्भ्रश्यद्बीजा मुहुरपि बहुप्रापितफला अहो चित्राकारा नियतिरिव नीतिर्नयविदः।(Mu.5) 'at one time (now) its seed appears to disappear; at another (now) it yields many fruits; oh, how varied is the policy of a politician, like Fate!'

§ **293.** यत् introduces a direct assertion with or without इति at the end; as, सत्योयं जनप्रवादो यत्संपत्संपदमनुबध्नातीति (K. 73) 'the popular

---

* खेदानुकम्पासंतोषविस्मयामन्त्रणे बत। (अ.)

saying is true *that* one fortunate thing follows another'; तस्य कदाचिच्चिन्ता समुत्पन्ना यदर्थोत्पत्युपायाश्चिन्तनीयाः कर्तव्याश्च (P. 1) 'a thought once occurred to him *that* means for acquiring wealth should be devised and executed.'

(*a*) यत् has the force of ' that ' in such sentences as 'art thou mad *that* thou speakest so incoherently ?' किं त्वं मत्तोसि यदेवमसम्बद्धं प्रलपसि; or *'because*, or *'since'*; as, किं शेषस्य भरव्यथा न वपुषि क्ष्मां न क्षिपत्येष यत् (Mu. 2) 'does not the serpent, S'esha, feel the heaviness of the load on his body because he does not throw down the Earth (from his head) ?'; प्रियमाचरितं लते त्वया मे यदीयं पुनर्मया दृष्टा (V. 1) 'O creeper, you have done me a service, since she has been once more seen by me.'

Obs. In translating sentences having the sense of 'since—therefore', 'because—hence', *'therefore'*, *'hence'*, may be translated by तत् or ततः; or the whole sentence may be expressed by using यत् or यतः; as अहं भ्रातरं गृहान्निष्कासयामि यत् (यतः) सोऽतीव दुर्वृत्तः 'I shall drive my brother out of the house *because* he is exceedingly ill-behaved'.

§ **294.** यतः means 'from which place', being used for यस्मात्; as, यतस्त्वया ज्ञानमशेषमाप्तं (R. V. 4) 'from whom (your preceptor) complete knowledge has been obtained by you'; or it means *'for'*, *'because'*, *'since'*, when a reason is assigned; as, किमेवमुच्यते महदन्तरं यतः कर्पूरद्वीपः स्वर्ग एव (H. 3) 'why do you say so ? There is a great difference; for the Karpura island is heaven itself'.

§ **295.** यत्सत्यं, regarded as one word, is used in the sense of *'to be sure'*, *'to own'* or *'to speak the truth'*, *'verily'*; as अमंगलाशंसयास्य वो वचनस्य यत्सत्यं कम्पितमिव मे हृदयं (Ve. 1) 'by the ominous nature of this your speech, my heart, to speak the truth, trembles.'

यद्वेतसः कुब्जलीलां विडम्बयति तत्किमात्मनः प्रभावेण ननु नदीवेगस्य । (S'. 2)

इदं तत्प्रत्युत्पन्नमति स्त्रैणमिति यदुच्यते । (S'. 5)

निराकरणविक्लवायाः प्रियायाः समवस्थामनुस्मृत्य बलवदशरणोस्मि । (S'. 6)

सर्वथा न कश्चिन्न खलीकरोति जीविततृष्णा यदीदृगवस्थमपि मामायासयति जलाभिलाषः । (K. 35)

पुण्यभाजः खल्वमी मुनयो यदहर्निशमेनं भगवन्तं पुण्याः कथाः शृण्वन्तः समुपासते । (K. 43)

कस्मान्मया निष्प्रयोजनमिदमश्वमुखद्वयमनुसृतमिति विचार्यमाणे यत्सत्यमात्मैव मे परिहासमुपजनयति । (K. 120)

अहं तं समादिशम् । सैषा सज्जनाचरिता सरणिर्यदणीयसि कारणेऽनणीयानादरः संदृश्यते । (D. K. II. 7)

अलमन्यथा गृहीत्वा न खलु मनस्विनि मया प्रयुक्तमिदम् ।
प्रायः समानविद्याः परस्परयशःपुरोभागाः ॥ (M. 1)

अयि कठोर यशः किल ते प्रियं किमयशो ननु घोरमतः परम् ।
किमभवद्विपिने हरिणीदृशः कथय नाथ कथं बत मन्यसे ॥ (U. 3)

यत्सत्यं काव्यविशेषवेदिन्यां परिषदि प्रयुञ्जानस्य ममापि चेतसि सुमहान् परितोषः प्रादुर्भवति । यतः

चीयते बालिशस्यापि सत्क्षेत्रपतिता कृषिः ।
न शालेः स्तंबकरिता वप्तुर्गुणमपेक्षते ॥ (B. Ve. I)

ADDITIONAL SENTENCES FOR EXERCISE.

अथ तेषां मध्यात् काकः प्रोवाच । स्वामिन्वयं तावत्सर्वत्र पर्यटिताः परं न किंचित्समासादितं दृष्टं वा । तदद्य मां भक्षयित्वा प्राणान्धारयतु स्वामी येन देवस्याप्यायना भवति । मम पुनः स्वर्गप्राप्तिरिति (P. I. 11)

इह (पंचमे प्रकोष्ठे) गंधर्वसुरगणैरिव विविधालंकारशोभितैर्गणिकाजनैर्बंधुलैश्च यत्सत्यं स्वर्गायत इदं गेहम् (Mk. 4)

आपरितोषाद्विदुषां न साधु मन्ये प्रयोगविज्ञानम् ।
बलवदपि शिक्षितानामात्मन्यप्रत्ययं चेतः ॥ (S'. 1)
ज्वलति चलितेन्धनोऽग्निर्विप्रकृतः पन्नगः फणां कुरुते ।
प्रायः स्वं महिमानं क्षोभात्प्रतिपद्यते जंतुः ॥ (S'. 6.)
अदूरवर्तिनीं सिद्धिं राजन्विगणयात्मनः ।
उपस्थितेयं कल्याणी नाम्नि कीर्तित एव यत् ॥ (R. I. 87)
अथवा मम भाग्यविप्लवादशनिः कल्पित एष वेधसा ।
यदनेन तरुर्न पातितः क्षपिता तद्विटपाश्रिता लता ॥ (R. VIII. 47)
खल्वाटो दिवसेश्वरस्य किरणैः संतापितो मस्तके
वाञ्छन्देशमनातपं विधिवशात्तालस्य मूलं गतः ।
तत्राप्यस्य महाफलेन पतता भग्नं सशब्दं शिरः
प्रायो गच्छति यत्र भाग्यरहितस्तत्रैव यान्त्यापदः ॥ (Bh. II. 90)

I do not think it proper to speak on this subject, because I am not conversant with its details.

Since you broke open my house last night, I take you prisoners, and shall take you to the Court for inquiry.

In matters concerning girls, householders generally see with the eyes of their wives.

Oh the unparallelled splendour of this place! To own the truth, it will vie even with the garden of Indra in point of beauty.

Is the place, from which you have come, supplied with plenty of corn?

I am going to execute my master's command, but where are *you* going?

Thus the wood-cutter saved his life and wealth, while the evil spirit was engaged in employment for whole twelve years.

Suvadaná tells me that Chandralekhá, her mistress, has been very ill since the day of her dancing in the temple of Durgá; I must now go to inquire how she is doing.

As a general rule the regard shown by masters to their servants, varies as the nature of the work intended to be accomplished through them.

Do you think the sun is not exhausted simply because, he never remains stationary in his celestial path?

Friend, cut of my snares very soon and save me; for it is truly said that 'adversity is the touchstone of friendship.'

LESTON XXVII.

यथा-तथा & यावत्-तावत्.

§ **296.** यथा by itself means (1) '*as*', '*in the manner mentioned*'; as, यथाज्ञापयतिदेव: (S'. 1) 'just as your Majesty orders,' *i. e.*, your orders will be obeyed; (2) '*namely*' '*as follows*', '*so*'; as, तद्यथानुश्रूयते (P. I) 'it is as stated below, (as follows); it is namely reported'; (3) '*like*', '*as*', showing 'comparison' like इव; as, आसीदियं दशरथस्य गृहे यथा श्री: (U. 4) 'she was in the house of Das'aratha like the Goddess of wealth'; (4) it is used to introduce a direct assertion, to report words or speeches, occuring in the direct construction in English; as, विदितं खलु ते यथा स्मर: क्षणमप्युत्सहते न मां विना (Ku. IV. 36) 'it is already known to you that Cupid does not feel at ease, without me even for a moment.' यथा in this sense is usually followed by इति at the end; as, संदिष्टोस्मि तातेन यथा वत्स मित्रावसो जीमूतवाहनाद्योग्यतरो वरो न लभ्यते । तस्मादस्मै मलयवती प्रतिपाद्यतामिति (Nág. 2) 'I am entrusted with a message by my father (to this effect);—O Mitrávasu, a better bridegroom than Jîmûtawáhana cannot be found; so give him Malayavatî'; (5) '*as*' '*for instance*'; as, यत्र यत्र धूमस्तत्र तत्र वह्निः यथा महा-

नसे (Taraka.) 'wherever there is smoke, there is fire; for instance in the kitchen'; (6) '*so that*' where येन often takes the place of यथा; as, त्वं दर्शय तं चौरसिंहं यथा व्यापादयामि (P. I. 8) 'show thou that rogue of a lion so that I may kill (him)'; स्वामिन्मम प्राणैः प्राणयात्रा विधीयतां येन ममोभयलोकप्राप्तिर्भवति (P. I. 11) 'Lord, maintain yourself by my life, so that I may secure both the worlds.'

§ **297.** यथा and तथा, when used as correlatives of each other, have the following senses:—(1) '*as—so*,' in which case तद्वत् sometimes takes the place of तथा; as, यथा वृक्षस्तथा फलं 'as the tree, so the fruit'; यथा बीजांकुरः सूक्ष्मः प्रयत्नेनाभिरक्षितः। फलप्रदो भवेत्काले तद्वल्लोकः सुरक्षितः (P. I. 8) 'as a small sprout growing from a seed, carefully tended, will yield fruits at the proper time, so (will) people when properly protected'; (2) '*so—that*,' where तथा stands for *so*, and यथा for *that*; as, यदि वामनुमतं तथा वर्तेथां यथा तस्य राजर्षेरनुकंपनीया भवामि (S'. 3) 'if you approve of it, so act that I shall be favoured by the royal sage'; अहं स्वामिनं विज्ञाप्य तथा करिष्ये यथा स वधं करिष्यति (P. I. 11) 'I, requesting his Majesty, shall so manage that he will kill him.'

Obs. The words ईदृश, तादृश, तावत्, एतावत्, इयत् &c., are similarly used for तथा, and forms of the relative pronoun (generally येन) are used with the second clause for यथा; as, ईदृशी अहं मन्दभागिनी यस्या न केवलमार्यपुत्रविरहः पुत्रविरहोपि (U. 3) 'I am *so* unfortunate *that* not only am I separated from my lord, but even from my children'; मम चैतावान् लोभविरहो येन स्वहस्तगतसुवर्णकंकणमपि यस्मै कस्मैचिद्दातुमिच्छामि (H. 1) 'my absence of greed (desire) is *such that* I wish to give to any body this golden bracelet, though actually in my hands'; (3) '*since—therefore*'; '*because* (*as*)—*so*'; as, यथायं चलितमलयाचलशिलासंचयः प्रचंडो नभस्वांस्तथा तर्कयामि आसन्नीभूतः पक्षिराजः (Nág. 4) 'since (as) this wind is terrible, shaking the collection of stones on the Malaya mountain, (therefore) so I think that the lord of the birds has approached'; (4) '*if—then*' used like यदि-तर्हि; or as a strong form of adjuration, 'as surely as—so surely'; as,

वाङ्मनःकर्मभिः पत्यौ व्यभिचारो यथा न मे।
तथा विश्वंभरे देवि मामन्तर्धातुमर्हसि॥ (R. XV. 81)

'*If* (as surely as) there is no unchastity in my conduct with regard to my husband, in word, thought, or deed, *then* (so surely), O all-pervading Goddess (Earth), be pleased to take me in'; (5) '*as much—as*', '*so much—as*' where तथा stands for 'as much' or 'so much' and यथा for 'as', when the sense intended is that of 'equality of relation'; as, न तथा बाधते शीतं यथा बाधति बाधते (Su.) 'cold does not pain me so much as dose the (form) *Bàdhati*.' In this sense एव is often used with यथा and तथा, or with one of them, to make the equality more emphatic, and then they may be translated by '*as—as*'; as, वधूचतुष्केपि यथैव शांता प्रिया तनूजास्य तथैव सीता (U. 4) 'among the four daughters-in-law, Sitá was as dear to him as his daughter S'ántá.'

(*a*) यथा and तथा are repeated (यथा यथा—तथा तथा) in the sense of *the* used with adjectives in the comparative degree, the adjectives themselves being translated by their Sanskrit equivalents, or in the sense of '*the more—the more*,' '*the less—the less*'; as, '*the older* he grew, *the stronger* became his torment (anxiety) caused by want of issue' यथा यथा यौवनमतिचक्राम तथा तथा अनपत्यताजन्मा महानवर्द्धतास्य संतापः (K.59); so '*the less* you think of your lost son, *the less* will be your sorrow' यथा यथा मृतपुत्रं न चिन्तयिष्यसि तथा तथा तव दुःखं शममेष्यति, or यथा यथा अल्पीयसि पुत्रचिन्ता तथा तथा अल्पीयो दुःखम्.

§ **298.** *यावत्, used by itself, is used in the sense of '*as far as*,' '*till*,' '*for*' showing duration of time or space and governs the Accusative case; as, स्तन्यत्यागं यावत्पुत्रयोरवेक्षस्व (U. 7) 'take care of (these) sons till they are weaned'; कियन्तमवधिं यावदस्मच्चरितं चित्रकारेणालिखितं (U.1) 'till what limit (how far) has our life been painted by the painter?'

(*a*) यावत् sometimes has the sense of '*just*', '*then*' denoting an action that is intended to be done immediately (*vide* § 190); as, तद्यावद् गृहिणीमाहूय संगीतकमनुतिष्ठामि (S'. 1) 'therefore calling my wife, I shall begin the concert'; यावदिमां छायामाश्रित्य प्रतिपालयामि तां (S'. 3) 'having resorted to this shade, I shall then wait for her.'

---

* यावत्तावच्च साकल्येऽवधौ मानेऽवधारणे । (अ)

§ **299.** Used as correlatives यावत् and तावत् have these senses:—(1) *'as much—as,'* तावत् standing for 'as much,' and यावत् for 'as, both being used like nouns or adjectives; as, पुरे तावन्तमेवास्य तनोति रविरातपम् । दीर्घिकाकमलोन्मेषो यावन्मात्रेण साध्यते । (Ku. II. 33) 'the sun sheds as much light only, in his city, as causes the bursting open of lotuses in his ponds'; (2) *'all'*, where the two together have the sense of totality; as, यावद्दत्तं तावद् भुक्तं (G. M.) 'I have eaten all that was given'; यावन्मानुष्यके शक्यमुपपदायितुं तावत्सर्वमुपपादितं (K. 62); (3) *'as long as'—'so long'*, where यावत् stands for 'as long as' and तावत् for 'so long'; as, यावद्वित्तोपार्जनशक्तस्तावन्निजपरिवारो रक्तः (Mohamudgara) - 'as long as one is able to acquire wealth, so long is his retinue attached to him'.

Obs. (*a*) Where in English *'as long,' 'so long as'*, or *'till,' 'until'* &c., are used, both यावत् and तावत् will have to be used in Sanskrit, यावत् with the clause introduced by *'as long as'*, *'till'* &c., and तावत् with the principal clause; as, '*as long as* the responsibility of the kingdom is entrusted to me, I shall keep the subjects contented' यावद्राज्यभारो मयि विन्यस्तस्तावदहं प्रजा अनुरक्ताः करिष्यामि; 'charioteer, stop the chariot *till* I get down' सूत तावद्रथं स्थापय यावदहमवतरामि.

(*b*) In translating sentences introduced by *'before'* यावन्न will have to be used for *'before,'* it being equivalent to *till not*; as, यावदेते सरसो नोत्पतन्ति तावदेतेभ्यः प्रवृत्तिरवगमयितव्या (V. 4) 'I must obtain information from them *before* they fly up from the lake.'

§ **300.** Sometimes यावत्—तावत् have simply the force of *'when—then'*; as यावदसौ पान्थ उत्थ योर्ध्वं निरीक्षते तावत्तेनावलोकितो हंसः काण्डेन हतो व्यापादितश्च (H. 3) 'when the traveller having got up, looked upwards, (then) the flamingo, being observed by him, was struck with an arrow and killed'; and sometimes the sense of *'as soon as'*, *'no sooner—than'*, *'scarcely—when'* &c. where यावत् stands for 'no sooner', 'scarcely' &c., and तावत् for 'than' 'when' &c.; as, एकस्य दुःखस्य न यावदन्तं गच्छामि...... तावद् द्वितीयं समुपस्थितं मे (H. I.) 'scarcely had I gone (before I had gone) to the end one of calamity, (when) another has befallen me again !'

भगवन्संकल्पयोने प्रतिबन्धवत्स्वपि विषयेष्वभिनिवेश्य तथा प्रहरसि यथा जनोयं कालान्तरक्षमो न भवति । (M. 3)

अकथितोपि ज्ञायत एव यथायमाभोगस्तपोवनस्येति । (S'. 1)

आश्रमवासिनो यावदवेक्ष्याहमुपावर्ते तावदार्द्रपृष्ठाः क्रियन्तां वाजिनः । (S'. 1)

बहुवल्लभा राजानः श्रूयन्ते । तद्यथा नो प्रियसखी बन्धुजनशोचनीया न भवति तथा निर्वाहय । (S'. 3)

संजीवक आह । भो मित्र कथं ज्ञेयो मयासौ दुष्टबुद्धिरिति । इयन्तं कालं यावदुत्तरोत्तरस्नेहेन प्रसादेन चाहं दृष्टः । (P. I. 15)

यद्येवं नकुलस्य बिलद्वारात्सर्पकोटरं यावन्मत्स्यमांसशकलानि प्रक्षिप यथा नकुलस्तन्मार्गेण गत्वा तं दुष्टसर्पं विनाशयति । (P. I. 20)

अयि मातर्देवयजनसंभवे देवि सीते ईदृशस्ते निर्माणभागः परिणतो येन लज्जया स्वच्छन्दमाक्रन्दितुमपि न शक्यते । (U. 4)

ततो यावदसौ पान्थस्तद्वचसि प्रतीतो लोभात्सरसि स्नातुं प्रविशति तावन्महापंके निमग्नः पलायितुमक्षमः । (H. 1,

यथा यथेयं चपला दीप्यते तथा तथा दीपशिखेव कज्जलमलिनमेव कर्म केवलमुद्वमति । (K. 105)

यावत्संबन्धिनो न परापतन्ति तावद्वत्सया मालत्या नगरदेवतागृहं गन्तव्यमित्यादिशन्ति भगवतीनिदेशवर्तिनोऽमात्यदाराः । (Mál. 6)

यथेतोमुखागतैरपि महान्कलकलः श्रुतोऽस्माभिस्तथा तर्कयामि अन्यदपि पारक्यं बलमुपगतमिति । (Mál. 8)

क्रोधं प्रभो संहर संहरेति यावद्गिरः खे मरुतां चरन्ति ।
तावत्स वह्निर्भवनेत्रजन्मा भस्मावशेषं मदनं चकार ॥ (Ku. IV. 72)

यथैव श्लाघ्यते गंगा पादेन परमेष्ठिनः ।
प्रभवेण द्वितीयेन तथैवोच्छिरसा त्वया ॥ (Ku. VI. 70)

अर्थेन तु विहीनस्य पुरुषस्याल्पमेधसः ।
क्रियाः सर्वा विनश्यन्ति ग्रीष्मे कुसरितो यथा ॥ (H. 1)

यावतः कुरुते जन्तुः संबन्धान्मनसः प्रियान् ।
तावन्तोपि विलिख्यन्ते हृदये शोकशंकवः ॥ (H. 4)

स तावदभिषेकान्ते स्नातकेभ्यो ददौ वसु ।
यावतैषां समाप्येरन् यज्ञाः पर्याप्तदक्षिणाः ॥ (R. XVII. 17)

ADDITIONAL SENTENCES FOR EXERCISE.

यावत्तत्रभवान्वयस्यः कार्यासनादुत्तिष्ठति तावदेतस्मिन्विरलजनसंपाते विमानोत्संगपरिसरे स्थास्यामि । (V. 2.)

तदेवंप्रायेऽतिकुटिलकष्टचेष्टासहस्रदारुणे राज्यतंत्रेऽस्मिन् महामोहान्धकारकारिणि च यौवने कुमार तथा प्रयतेथा यथा नोपहस्यसे जनैर्नोपालभ्यसे सुहृद्भिर्नाक्षिप्यसे विषयैर्न विकृष्यसे रागेण नापह्रियसे सुखेन । (K. 109)

यथा यथा चलितजलयन्त्रविगलिताभिरंबुधाराभिराहन्यते सा तथा तथा वैद्युतानलसहोदर इव स्फुरति मदनपावकः । (K. 251)

चन्द्रापीडः प्रातरेव किंवदंतीं शुश्राव यथा किल दशपुरीं यावत् परागतः स्कंधावार इति । (K. 262)

वत्स यावदयं संसारस्तावत्सिद्धैवेयं लोकयात्रा यत्पुत्रैः पितरो लोकद्वयेऽप्यनुवर्तनीया इति। (Ve. 3)

अपि दृष्टवानसि मम प्रियां वने कथयामि ते तदुपलक्षणं शृणु।
पृथुलोचना सहचरी यथैव ते सुभगं तथैव खलु सापि वीक्षते॥ (V. 4)

वितरति गुरुः प्राज्ञे विद्यां यथैव तथा जडे
न तु खलु तयोर्ज्ञाने शक्तिं करोत्यपहन्ति वा।
भवति च पुनर्भूयान्भेदः फलं प्रति तद्यथा
प्रभवति शुचिर्बिम्बोद्ग्राहे मणिर्न मृदां च यः॥ (U. 2.)

यथा कालकृतोद्योगात्कृषिः फलवती भवेत्।
तद्वन्नीतिरियं देव चिरात्फलति न क्षणात्॥ (H. 3)

क्रोडीकरोति प्रथमं यथा जातमनित्यता।
धात्रीव जननी पश्चात्तथा शोकस्य कः क्रमः॥ (Nâg. 4)

यथा काष्ठं च काष्ठं च समेयातां महोदधौ।
समेत्य च व्यपेयातां तद्वद्भूतसमागमः॥ (H. 4)

उभयोर्न तथा लोकः प्रावीण्येन विसिष्मिये।
नृपतेः प्रीतिदानेषु वीतस्पृहतया यथा॥ (R. XV. 68)

यावत्स्वस्थमिदं कलेवरगृहं यावच्च दूरे जरा
यावच्चेन्द्रियशक्तिरप्रतिहता यावत्क्षयो नायुषः।
आत्मश्रेयसि तावदेव विदुषा कार्यः प्रयत्नो महान्
प्रोद्दीप्ते भवने तु कूपखननं प्रत्युद्यमः कीदृशः। (Bh. III. 88)

यथा प्रदीप्तं ज्वलनं पतंगा विशन्ति नाशाय समृद्धवेगाः।
तथैव नाशाय विशन्ति लोकास्तवापि वक्त्राणि समृद्धवेगाः॥ (Bg. XI. 29)

A hundred schemes have been devised by me for his ruin, in consultation with my friends, they are as follows:—

I suppose you have already heard that in the heavens dwells a class of nymphs called Apsarases.

He is like Bhîma in heroism, but in wickedness of heart, he surpasses the cruellest of demons.

Rávana so pleased S'ankara by his austere penance, that the God granted him several boons.

This king governs his country so well that not one of his numerous subjects is disloyal to him.

Since all the preparations of war have been completed, I do not think it proper to treat with the enemy.

The more I think about this world, the more does my mind become disgusted with it.

The moment he stepped into his house, his wife rushed to him exclaiming 'a serpent has bitten my child.'

I hope you will stay here till Govinda comes back from his pilgrimage.

As long as I breathe, I shall defend my dear country even at the cost of my life, so that I may not die with a name sullied with disgrace.

He took the doctor's medicine for (यावत्) 21 days, but finding no change for the better, he ceased to take it.

The teacher beat the child with a stick so severely that he fell down senseless on the ground.

The more do philosophers think about God, the less do they know him.

He is as much distinguished by the purity of his conduct as by his talents, and as intent upon restraining his senses as upon doing good to others.

Do you not know that all carnivorous animals are provided with claws (*use* यावत्—तावत्).

The more diligently you study, the fewer will be your chances of failure, and the greater the probability of improvement.

LESSON XXVIII.

वरं-न, वा, स्थाने, हंत, हा, & हि.

§ **301.** वरं with न generally followed by च, तु or पुनः is used in the sense of '*better—than*,' '*better—but not*,' to express preference, वरं being used with the clause containing the thing preferred (which is put in the nominative case) and न च, न तु or न पुनः with the clause containing the thing to which the first is preferred (this also being put in the nominative case) ; as, वरं कन्या जाता न चाविद्वांस्तनयः (P. I. 1.) 'better (that) a girl (be) born rather than a foolish son'; वरं प्राणत्यागो न पुनरधमानामुपगमः (H. 1) 'better to lose life, but not the vicinity to (contact with) the base.'

(*a*) Sometimes न is used without च, तु or पुनः ; as, याच्ञा मोघा वरमधिगुणे नाधमे लब्धकामा (Me. 5) 'better (that) a request to a worthy person (should even be) unheeded, than that it being made to a base man should be gratified'; वरं भ्रांतं वनचरैः सह न मूर्खजनसंपर्कः (Bh. II. 14) 'it were better to roam with wild ones than (to keep) company with foolish people.'

§ **302.** *वा is an alternative conjunction meaning '*or*'; but its position is different in Sanskrit, being similar to that of च, see § 272; 'Ráma *or* Govinda' रामो गोविंदो वा or रामो वा गोविंदो वा.

(*a*) It has also these senses:—(1) '*and*,' '*as well*,' '*also*'; as, पत्रलेखे कथय महाश्वेतायाः कादंबर्याश्च कुशलं कुशली वा सकलः परिजन इति (K.230) 'Patralekhá, tell me whether Mahás'vetá and Kádambarî are doing well, and also whether the whole retinue is doing well'; (2) '*like*', '*as*', having the sense of इव; as, जातां मन्ये तुहिनमथितां पद्मिनीं वान्यरूपां (Me. 86) 'I consider her to be changed in form (appearance) like a lotus blighted by frost'; (3) '*optionally*,' mostly in grammatical rules; as, दोषो णौ । वा चित्तविरागे (Pán. VI. 4. 90-91) in the causal the उ of दुष् is lengthened; but optionally, when it means to pervert the mind.'

(*b*) वा is added to the interrogative pronoun and its derivatives

---

* वा समुच्चय एवार्थे उपमानविकल्पयोः । (हे.)

in the sense of 'possibly' like इव, or नाम (see § 257); as, मृतः को वा न जायते (P. I. 1) 'who possibly, that is dead, is not born again'; कस्य वान्यस्य वचसि मया स्थातव्यं (K. 156) 'whose words else should I possibly act up to?'; कथं वा गम्यते (U. 3) 'how, indeed, can you go?'

§ **303**. वा, when repeated, has the sense of '*either—or*' '*whether—or*'; as, उभे एव क्षमे वोढुमुभयोर्बीजमाहितं। सा वा शंभोस्तदीया वा मूर्तिर्जलमयी मम। (Ku. II. 60) 'two only are able to bear the seed of us two; either she (Pârvatî) of S'ambhu, or his watery form, mine'; तत्र कविपरिश्रमानुरोधाद्वा उदात्तकथावस्तुगौरवाद्वा नवनाटकदर्शनकुतूहलाद्वा भवद्भिरवधानं दीयमानं प्रार्थये। (Ve. 1) 'I solicit your attention being paid to it whether out of regard to the poet's labour, or the importance of the sublime subject-matter, or a desire to see a new drama represented.'

§ **304**. स्थाने is used as an adverb in the sense of '*justly*,' '*properly*,' '*it is quite proper that*'; as, स्थाने प्राणाः कामिनां दूत्यधीनाः (Me. 3) 'it is proper (it is justly said) that the life of lovers is in the hands of (depends upon) messengers'; स्थाने तपो दुश्चरमेतदर्थमपर्णया पेलवयापि तप्तं (Ku. VII. 65) 'it is quite proper that Aparnâ, though delicate, practised very austere penance for his sake.'

(*a*) अस्थाने means 'inopportune', 'out of place'; as, अस्थाने द्वयोरपि प्रयत्नः (Mu. 2) 'the attempt of both was out of place.'

§ **305**. *हंत is used in the following senses:—(1) '*joy*,' '*surprise*', '*flurry*', such as is expressed by '*oh*' in English; as, हंत प्रवृत्तं संगीतकं (M. 1) 'oh! the concert has commenced'; (2) '*compassion*', '*pity*'; as, पुत्रक हंत ते धानाकाः (G. M.) 'it is a pity, child, that you have only Dhánákas'; (3) '*oh*', '*alas*', showing grief; as, हंत धिङ् मामधन्यं (U. 1) 'alas, fie upon me, an unhappy being!'; (4) it is sometimes used as an inceptive particle; as, हंत ते कथयिष्यामि (Rám. I. 48, 14) 'well, now I shall tell you.'

§ **306**. † हा most frequently denotes 'grief', 'dejection', 'pain', as expressed by 'ah,' 'alas,' 'woe me'; as, हा प्रिये जानकि (U. 3) 'alas!

---

*हंत हर्षेऽनुकंपायां वाक्यारंभविषादयोः। (अ.)

† हा इति विस्मयविषादशुग्जुगुप्सार्तिषु। (ग. म.)

oh beloved Jánakí' ; हा हा देवि स्फुटति हृदयं (U. 3) 'alas ! alas ! queen, my heart bursts.' It is sometimes used to express 'surprise' as, हा कथं महाराजदशरथस्य धर्मदाराः प्रियसखी मे कौसल्या (U. 4) 'oh! indeed, she is Kausalyá, my dear friend, the duly married wife of king Das'aratha.'

For the use of हा with the accusative see § 34.

Obs. The sense of जुगुप्सा 'reproach' is very rare.

§ **307**. *हि, never used at the beginning of a sentence, has these senses:—(1) *'for,' 'because'*, expressing a strict or logical reason; as, अग्निरिहास्ति धूमो हि दृश्यते (G. M.) 'here is fire, for there appears smoke'; अपि महर्षिणा त्वं गृहायानुमतः। कालो ह्ययं संक्रमितुं द्वितीयमाश्रमं (R. V. 10) 'have you been permitted by the great sage to become a householder; for it is now time to enter upon the second stage of life.'

Obs. In general statements with reference to a particular case, this sense of हि 'for' is understood.

(2) *'Indeed'*, *'surely'*; as, देव प्रयोगप्रधानं हि नाट्यशास्त्रं किमत्र वाग्व्यवहारेण (M. 1) 'my lord, the science of acting, indeed, consists principally of representation; what is the use of oral discussion in this case?'; न हि कमलिनीं दृष्ट्वा ग्राहमवेक्षते मतंगजः (M. 3) 'surely an elephant, having seen a lotus-plant, cares not for the shark'; (3) it has often the sense of *'for instance,'* (स्फुटार्थ) 'as is well-known', when a fact is stated to illustrate a foregoing assertion, in the sense of तथा च; as, प्रजानामेव भूत्यर्थं स ताभ्यो बलिमग्रहीत्। सहस्रगुणमुत्स्रष्टुमादत्ते हि रसं रविः (R. I. 18) 'he took taxes from his subjects only for the sake of doing good to them; (for instance) the sun drinks up water in order to give it back increased a thousand-fold'; (4) *'only'*, *'alone'* to emphasize an idea; as, मूढो हि मदनेनायास्यते (K. 155) 'a fool only is troubled by Cupid'; (5) sometimes as an expletive.

शकुन्तला—सखि कस्य वान्यस्य कथयिष्यामि । किंत्वायासयित्रीदानीं वां भविष्यामि ।

---

*हि पादपूरणे हेतौ विशेषेप्यवधारणे. (वि.)

उभे—अत एव खलु निर्बन्धः। स्निग्धजनसंविभक्तं हि दुःखं सह्यवेदनं भवति। (S'. 3)

हंत भोः शकुन्तलां पतिकुलं विसृज्य लब्धमिदानीं स्वास्थ्यम्। (S'. 4)

स्थाने खलु प्रत्यादेशविमानिताप्यस्य कृते शकुन्तला क्लाम्यति। (S'. 6)

अविनीत किं नोऽपत्यनिर्विशेषाणि सत्त्वानि विप्रकरोषि। हंत वर्धते ते संरम्भः। स्थाने खलु ऋषिजनेन सर्वदमन इति कृतनामधेयोसि। (S'. 4)

स्थाने खलु नारायणमृषिं विलोभयन्त्यस्तदूरुसंभवामिमां दृष्ट्वा व्रीडिताः सर्वा अप्सरस इति। (V. 1)

भवादृशा एव भवन्ति भाजनान्युपदेशानाम्। अपगतमले हि मनसि स्फटिकमणाविव रजनिकरगभस्तयो विशन्ति सुखमुपदेशगुणाः। (K. 103)

तदेषा भवतः कांता त्यजैनां वा गृहाण वा।
उपपन्ना हि दारेषु प्रभुता सर्वतोमुखी॥ (S'. 5)

अनन्तरत्नप्रभवस्य यस्य हिमं न सौभाग्यविलोपि जातम्।
एको हि दोषो गुणसन्निपाते निमज्जतीन्दोः किरणेष्विवाङ्कः॥
(Ku. I. 3)

बहूनामप्यसाराणां समवायो हि दुर्जयः।
तृणैरावेष्टयते रज्जुर्यया नागोपि बध्यते॥ (P. I. 14)

कुसुमान्यपि गात्रसंगमात्प्रभवन्त्यायुरपोहितुं यदि।
न भविष्यति हंत साधनं किमिवान्यत्प्रहरिष्यतो विधेः॥
(R. VIII. 44)

सेवां लाघवकारिणीं कृतधियः स्थाने श्ववृत्तिं विदुः । (Mu. 3)

वरं मौनं कार्यं न च वचनमुक्तं यदनृतं
वरं क्लैब्यं पुंसां न च परकलत्राभिगमनम् ।
वरं प्राणत्यागो न च पिशुनवाक्येष्वभिरुचि-
र्वरं भिक्षाशित्वं न च परधनास्वादनसुखम् ॥ (H. 1)

ADDITIONAL SENTENCES FOR EXERCISE.

वरमावाभ्यां कतिपयदिवसाननयोरप्यदर्शनकृताः क्लेशा अनुभूता न पुनरस्य वैशंपायनानवलोकनदुःखदीनं दिने दिने मुखमीक्षितम् । (K. 294)

असंशयं क्षत्रपरिग्रहक्षमा यदार्यमस्यामभिलाषि मे मनः ।
सतां हि संदेहपदेषु वस्तुषु प्रमाणमन्तःकरणप्रवृत्तयः ॥ (S'. 1)

सुतनु हृदयात्प्रत्यादेशव्यलीकमपैतु ते
किमपि मनसः संमोहो मे तदा बलवानभूत् ।
प्रबलतमसामेवंप्रायाः शुभेषु हि वृत्तयः
स्रजमपि शिरस्यन्धः क्षिप्तां धुनोत्यहिशंकया (S'. 7)

राजा—एवमादिभिरनुपक्रम्योऽयमातंकः । पश्य
कुसुमशयनं न प्रत्यग्रं न चन्द्रमरीचयो
न च मलयजं सर्वांगीणं न वा मणियष्टयः ।
मनसिजरुजं सा वा दिव्या ममालमपोहितुं
रहसि लघयेदारब्धा वा तदाश्रयिणी कथा ॥ (V. 3)

स्थाने त्वां स्थावरात्मानं विष्णुमाहुस्तथाहि ते ।
चराचराणां भूतानां कुक्षिराधारतां गतः । (Ku. VI. 67)

आलोके ते निपतति पुरा सा बलिव्याकुला वा
मत्सादृश्यं विरहतनु वा भावगम्यं लिखन्ती ।
पृच्छन्ती वा मधुरवचनां सारिकां पंजरस्थां
कच्चिद्भर्तुः स्मरसि रसिके त्वं हि तस्य प्रियेति ॥ (Me. 88)

अरुन्धती—हा वत्से

शिशुर्वा शिष्या वा यदसि मम तत्तिष्ठतु तथा
विशुद्धेरुत्कर्षस्त्वयि तु मम भक्तिं द्रढयति ।

शिशुत्वं स्त्रैणं वा भवतु ननु वंद्यासि जगतो
गुणाः पूजास्थानं गुणिषु न च लिङ्गं न च वयः ॥ (U. 4)

स्थाने भवानेकनराधिपः सन्नकिंचनत्वं मखजं बिभर्ति ।
पर्यायपीतस्य सुरैर्हिमांशोः कलाक्षयः श्लाघ्यतरो हि वृद्धेः ॥ (R. V. 16)

प्रेष्यभावेन नामेयं देवीशब्दक्षमा सती ।
स्नानीयवस्त्रक्रियया पत्रोर्णं वोपयुज्यते । (M. 5)

नृपतेः प्रतिषिद्धमेव तत्कृतवान् पंक्तिरथो विलंघ्य यत् ।
अपथे पदमर्पयन्ति हि श्रुतवन्तोपि रजोनिमीलिताः । (R. IX. 74)

तमवेक्ष्य रुरोद सा भृशं स्तनसंबाधमुरो जघान च ।
स्वजनस्य हि दुःखमग्रतो विवृतद्वारमिवोपजायते ॥ (Ku. IV. 26)

व्यतिषजति पदार्थानान्तरः कोपि हेतु-
र्न खलु बहिरुपाधीन्प्रीतयः संश्रयन्ते ।
विकसति हि पतंगस्योदये पुण्डरीकं
द्रवति च हिमरश्मावुद्गते चन्द्रकांतः ॥ (Mál. 1)

अर्हस्येनं (दावाग्निं) शमयितुमलं वारिधारासहस्रै-
रापन्नार्तिप्रशमनफलाः संपदो ह्युत्तमानाम् । (Me. 54)

स्थाने हृषीकेश तव प्रकीर्त्या जगत्प्रहृष्यत्यनुरज्यते च ।
रक्षांसि भीतानि दिशो द्रवन्ति सर्वे नमस्यन्ति च सिद्धसंघाः ॥ (Bg. XI. 36)

राक्षसः—अहो सुश्लिष्टोऽभूदयं प्रयोगः ।
लेखोयं न ममेति नोत्तरमिदं मुद्रा मदीया यतः
सौहार्दं शकटेन खण्डितमिति श्रद्धेयमेतत्कथम् ।
मौर्ये भूषणविक्रयं नरपतौ को नाम संभावयेत्
तस्मात्संप्रतिपत्तिरेव हि वरं न ग्राम्यमत्रोत्तरम् ॥ (Mu. 5)

स्वसुखनिरभिलाषः खिद्यसे लोकहेतोः
प्रतिदिनमथवा ते वृत्तिरेवंविधैव ।
अनुभवति हि मूर्ध्ना पादपस्तीव्रमुष्णं
शमयति परितापं छायया संश्रितानाम् ॥ (S'. 5)

उचितः प्रणयो वरं विहन्तुं बहवः खंडनहेतवो हि दृष्टाः ।
उपचारविधिर्मनस्विनीनां न तु पूर्वाभ्यधिकोपि भावशून्यः ॥ (M. 3)

It is far better to support one's self by begging from door to door than to be always fawning upon the haughty rich.

Either he is able to do it, or his two brothers, but not any body else.

It is but just that he gives you this warning to spend money economically, for the marriage of your daughter is every day drawing near.

When calamities befall a man, discrimination is the real wisdom; for those who act without discrimination have their miseries multiplied.

The poet that said 'one fault merges in a collection of good qualities,' did not properly observe human nature; for, generally poverty destroys even a group of good qualities.

Who indeed, except this magnanimous person, would risk his life to save that of others?.

Be sure, O woman, that you will ere long be united with your husband; is it not a fact that a river, the water of which is dried up in summer, is again united with its current in the rainy season?

I worship all gods with the same devotion, whether they belong to the Yavans or Bráhma*n*as.

I shall even prefer (*use* वर-न) a dreary forest haunted by tigers and wolves, to a life led in poverty amongst one's kinsmen.

Woe me that have survived all that I held dearest on this earth!

Oh! I have found the ring that I had lost.

Oh! how delightful is the appearance of this man? It is just that the author of the **Râmaya*n*a** used divine speech to describe his manifold deeds.

Out of hundreds of kings, she chose only this king for her husband; for the mind is conscious of its former associatior

Who possibly, that has fallen into the snares of the wicked, has safely escaped? And what week person has not failed in his attempts at contending with the strong?

LESSON XXIX.

PARASMAIPADA AND ATMANEPADA.

(*N. B.*—In this and the next lesson the unspecified references are to Siddhánata Kaumudí; and Bk. means the eight canto of Bhatti Kávya.)

§ **308.** There are two Padas in Sanskrit: the Atmanepada and Parasmaipada. The Atmanepada ('voice for one's self') denotes that the fruit of the action accrues to the agent (**कर्तृगामि फलं**); as, **कुरुते** 'does for himself.' The Parasmaipada ('voice for another') denotes that the fruit of the action accrues to another; **गच्छति** 'goes for another.' This distinction is scarcely, if ever, observed in practice. It is the original meaning of the terms, but cannot be consistently followed in all cases. Sanskrit writers use both the Padas promiscuously; as, **निदेशमिदानीं श्रोतुमिच्छामि** (M. I.) 'I wish now to here the message'; **उत्कंठासाधारणं परितोषमनुभवामि** (S'. 4); **यावद्यते साधयितुं त्वदर्थं** (R. V. 15.).

If it be supposed that this distinction is meant to be observed when a root admits of both the Padas, this is also not borne out by usage; as, **राजा स्वसूनोश्चन्द्रापीड इति नाम चकार शुकनासोपि विप्रजनोचितं वैशंपायन इति नाम चक्रे** (K. 74), where the two Padas are used in the same sense.

§ **309.** Some roots are conjugated in one Pada only, as **नम्**, **भ्रम्**, **रुच्**, **भाष्**, &c; some in both the Padas, as **कृ**, **चि**, **चुर्**, **दुह्** &c., while some are restricted to one Pada or the other, according as certain prepositions are prefixed to them, or they are used in particular senses; as, **गम्** is Parasmaipada; but **संगम्** is Atmanepada; **शास्** 'to rule' is Parasmaipada, but **आशास्** 'to bless' is Atm. Some roots of this nature are given in this and the next lesson.

Roots of the First Conjugation.

§ **310.** The root क्रम्*, when not preceded by a preposition, takes both the Padas. But it is used in the Atm. by itself when the sense of 'continuity', or 'want of interruption', 'energy,' and 'development', or 'increase' is indicated; as क्रममाणोरिसंसदि (Bk. 21) 'moving unobstructed in the enemy's assembly'; अध्ययनाय क्रमते 'shows energy for studying'; क्रमन्तेस्मिञ् शास्त्राणि 'the S'astras are developed in him.'

(*a*) Preceded by उप and परा, it is Atm. in the same senses; as, इत्युक्त्वा खे पराक्रंस्त (Bk. 22) 'so saying he showed his might in the sky'; परीक्षितुमुपाक्रंस्त राक्षसी तस्य विक्रमं (*ibid.* 23) 'made bold to test &c.'

(*b*) When preceded by आ, it is Atm. in the sense of '*ascending*' or '*rising*' of a luminary; as, आक्रमते सूर्यः (Mbh.) 'the sun rises'; दिवमाक्रममाणेव (Bk. 23). But आक्रामति धूमो हर्म्यतलात् 'the smoke issues from the surface of the terrace'; or आक्रमति धूमो हर्म्यतलं (Mbh.) 'covers the terrace.'

(*c*) With वि in the sense of 'walking', 'placing the footsteps'; विष्णुस्त्रेधा विचक्रमे 'Vishnu took three steps'; वाजी विक्रमते; but विक्रामति संधिः 'the joint splits.'

(*d*) With प्र and उप in the sense of 'beginning'; as, वक्तुं मिथः प्राक्रमतैवमेनं (Ku. III. 2) 'thus began to talk with him privately.' But प्रक्रामति 'goes'; उपक्रामति 'comes.'

§ **311.** The root † क्रीड् 'to play' is usually Paras., but when preceded by the prepositions अनु, सं, परि, and आ, it is Atm.; अनु-परि-आ-क्रीडते माणवकः; संक्रीडन्ते मणिभिः यत्र कन्याः (Me. 70) 'play with jewels.' But माणवकमनुक्रीडति (Mbh.) 'plays with Mánavaka.'

---

*वृत्तिसर्गतायनेषु क्रमः । उपपराभ्याम् । आङ उद्गमने । वेः पादविहरणे । प्रोपाभ्यां समर्थाभ्याम् । अनुपसर्गाद्वा । (I. 3. 38-43:)

†क्रीडोऽनुसंपरिभ्यश्च । (I. 3. 21)

(*a*) With सं, it is Paras. in the sense of 'making a noise'; as संक्रीडन्ति शकटानि (Mbh.) 'the carts creak.'

§ **312.** *गम् with सं is Atm. in the sense of 'communicate with', 'unite with,' 'join'; as, अक्षधूर्तैः समगंसि (D. K. II. 2) 'I joined gamblers.' So ऋ or ऋच्छ् with सं; as, समारन्त ममाभीष्टाः (Bk. 16).

§**313.** The root † चर् 'to walk,' when preceded by उद्, is Atm., when used transitively; as, पानशौण्डाः पथः क्षीबा वृन्दैरुदचरन्त च (Bk. 31) 'drunkards, being intoxicated, strayed away from the paths in crowds'; so धर्ममुच्चरते 'transgresses duty.' But बाष्पमुच्चरति 'vapour goes up.'

(*a*) With सं, it is Atm. when used with the instrumental of a conveyance; as, यानैः समचरन्तान्ये (Bk. 32) 'others went in vehicles'; क्वचित्पथा संचरते सुराणां (R. XIII. 19) 'now passes through the path of gods (sky).'

§ **314.** ‡ जि, when preceded by वि and परा, in the sense of 'to conquer', or 'to be victorious', and 'to defeat' respectively is Atm.; as, चक्षुर्मेचकमंबुजं विजयते (V. B. 1) 'her (blue) eye surpasses the blue lotus'; विजयतां देवः (M. 1) 'victory to your Majesty !'; खं पराजयमानोसौ (Bk. 9) 'defeating (completely overstriding) the sky.'

§ **315.** When § तप् 'to heat', preceded by वि or उद्, is intransitively used, or has 'a limb of the body' for its object, it is Atm.; as, रविर्वितपतेत्यर्थं (Bk. 14) 'the sun is shining very hot'; तीव्रमुत्तपमानोयमशक्यः सोढुमातपः (*ibid.* 15) 'this excessively scorching heat is unbearable'; उत्तपते वितपते-पाणी (Mbh.) 'he warms his hands.' But उत्तपति सुवर्णं सुवर्णकारः (Mbh.) 'a goldsmith heats (causes to melt) gold'; so चैत्रो मैत्रस्य पाणिमुत्तपति.

Obs. तप्, by itself, is intransitive; as, तमस्तपति घर्मांशौ कथमाविर्भविष्यति (S'. 5) 'how will darkness manifest itself, when the sun is shining?'

---

* समो गम्यृच्छिभ्याम् । (I. 3. 29)

† उदश्चरः सकर्मकात् । समस्तृतीयायुक्तात् (I. 3. 53-4)

‡ विपराभ्यां जेः (I. 3. 19)

§ उद्विभ्यां तपः (I. 3 27); स्वांगकर्मकाच्चेति वक्तव्यम् ।

§ **316.** * नी 'to lead or carry', without a preposition or with the prepositions उद्, उप, or वि is Atm. in the following senses:—(1) instructing (lit. honouring); as, शास्त्रे नयते 'gives instructions in S'âstra'; (2) 'lifting up'; as, दंडमुन्नयते 'lifts up a stick'; (3) initiating into sacred rites'; माणवकमुपनयते 'invests Mánavaka with the sacred thread'; (4) 'knowledge', 'investigation'; तत्त्वं नयते 'investigates the truth'; (5) 'employing on wages', 'hiring'; कर्मकरानुपनयते 'employs labourers as hired servants'; (6) 'paying off, as a tribute, debt, &c.'; करं विनयते 'pays the tax due to the king'; (7) 'spending', 'applying to use'; शतं विनयते 'spends a hundred (for charity).'

(*a*) नी with वि is Atm., only when the object is something else than 'a part of the body'; as विनेष्ये क्रोधमथवा (Bk. 28) 'or I shall remove (restrain) my anger'; but गंडं विनयति 'turns away his cheek.'

Obs. विनी in the sense of 'teaching', 'taming', 'domesticating', is Paras.; वन्यान्विनेष्यन्निव दुष्टसत्वान् (R. II. 8) 'as if wishing to tame the wicked animals of the forest'; so विनिन्युरेनं गुरवो गुरुप्रियं (R. III. 27)

§ **317.** † यम् preceded by आ is Atm., either when it is intransitively used, or has 'a limb of the body' for its object, or anything other than a work of composition; as, आयच्छते 'spreads'; पाणिमायच्छते 'stretches his hand'; वस्त्रमायच्छते 'spreads the cloth.'

(*a*) Preceded by सं, and उद् it is Atm., when the object is not 'a literary work'; as, व्रीहीन्संयच्छते 'gathers rice'; भारमुद्यच्छते 'lifts up a load' but उद्यच्छति वेदं 'tries hard to learn the Vedas.'

(*b*) यम्, with उप, is Atm., in the sense of 'marrying,' 'espousing', or 'accepting' in general; as, सीतां हित्वा दशमुखरिपुर्नोपयेमे यदन्यां (R. XIV. 71) 'that the enemy of the ten-mouthed (Rávana), having abandoned Sîta, did not marry another.'

§ **318.** ‡ रम् 'to sport' is usually Atm., but preceded by the

---

* संमाननोत्सञ्जनाचार्यकरणज्ञानभृतिविगणनव्ययेषु नियः। (I. 3. 36)

† आङो यमहनः (I. 3. 28); समुदाङ्भ्यो यमोऽग्रन्थे (I. 3. 75); उपाद्यमः स्वकरणे (I. 3. 56)

‡ व्याङ्परिभ्यो रमः। विभाषाऽकर्मकात्। (I. 3. 83-85)

prepositions वि, आ, or परि it is Paras; as, विरम विरम वह्ने (Ratn. 4) 'stop, stop, O fire'; आरमति उद्याने 'takes rest in a garden'; क्षणं पर्यरमतस्य दर्शनात् (Bk. 53) 'was for a time pleased at his sight.'

(*a*) With उप, when intransitively used, रम् takes either Pada; as उपारंसीच संपश्यन् वानरस्तं चिकीर्षितात् (Bk. 54) the monkey, seeing him, desisted from what he meant to do'; नात्र सीतेत्युपारंस्त 'he stopped seeing there was no Sita'.

§ **319.** *वद् 'to speak', by itself is Atm., in the following senses:—(1) 'showing brilliance or proficiency in'; as, शास्त्रे वदते; (2) 'pacifying or coaxing' (generally preceded by उप in this sense); as, भृत्यानुपवदते 'conciliates or cajoles his servants'; (3) 'knowledge'; as, शास्त्रे वदते 'knows S'astra'; (4) 'toil,' 'effort'; as, क्षेत्रे वदते 'toils in the field'; (5) 'difference of opinion', 'quarrel' (generally) preceded by वि in this sense); as, परस्परं विवदमानानां शास्त्राणां (H. 1) 'of mutually conflicting scriptures'; (6) 'flattering', 'requesting'; as, दातारमुपवदते 'coaxes the donor'; [this sense is analogous to (2.)].

(*a*) With संप्र it is Atm., in the sense of 'loud and distinct speaking' (as that of men &c.); as, संप्रवदन्ते ब्राह्मणाः 'the Brahmanas are speaking loudly together'; but वरतनु संप्रवदन्ति कुक्कुटाः (Mbh.) 'O beautiful lady, the cocks are crowing.'

(*b*) With अनु, वद् is Atm., under the same circumstances as (*a*), when it is intransitively used; as अनुवदते कठः कलापस्य 'Katha imitates Kalapa'; but उक्तमनुवदति 'recapitulates or reproduces what is said'; अनुवदति वीणा 'the lute resounds.'

(*c*) With विप्र, in the sense of 'disputing', 'wrangling', it takes either Pada; as, विप्रवदन्ते-न्ति वैद्याः 'the doctors are at variance' (are disputing); ऐद्विप्रवदमानैस्तां संयुक्तां ब्रह्मराक्षसैः (Bk. 42) 'went to it filled with wrangling evil demons.'

(*d*) With अप it is Atm., in the sense of 'reviling', 'reproaching'; as, न्यायमपवदते; नृभ्योऽपवदमानस्य (Bk. 53).

---

* भासनोपसंभाषाज्ञानयत्नविमत्युपमन्त्रणेषु वदः । व्यक्तवाचां समुच्चारणे । अनोरकर्मकात् । विभाषा विप्रलापे । (I. 3. 47–50)

§ **320.** * स्था is Atm., by itself in the sense of 'disclosing one's intentions'; as गोपी कृष्णाय तिष्ठते; or 'accepting as umpire'; as, संशय्य कर्णादिषु तिष्ठते यः (Ki. III. 14) 'who, when he is in doubt, has recourse to Karna as his judge or umpire.'

(*a*) With सं, अव, प्र and sometimes वि it is Atm., as, दारिद्र्यात्पुरुषस्य बान्धवजनो वाक्ये न संतिष्ठते (Mk. 1) 'on account of a man's poverty, his relations do not act up to his words'; क्षणमप्यवतिष्ठते श्वसन् यदि जंतुः (R. VIII. 12) 'if a being breathes on, though only for a moment'; हरिर्हरिप्रस्थमथ प्रतस्थे (S'i. III. 1) 'then Hari set out for Hariprastha'; so अत्रापरे प्रत्यवतिष्ठन्ते (S'. B. 45); अग्रेर्ज्वलतः विस्फुलिंगा विप्रतिष्ठेरन् (*ibid*).

(*b*) With आ it is Atm., only in the sense of 'solemn declaration' (प्रतिज्ञा); as, जलं विषं वा तव कारणादास्थास्ये (Mb.) 'for thee I shall surely have recourse to water or poison.'

§ **321.** With † उद् in its literal sense of 'getting up', it is Paras.; but in a figurative sense, it is Atm.; as, उत्तिष्ठमानं मित्रार्थे कस्त्वां न बहुमन्यते (Bk. 12) 'who does not esteem you, who strive for your friend'; मुक्तावुत्तिष्ठते 'raises himself up (aspires) to absolution'; see Ki. XI. 13, and S'i. XIV. 17; but पीठादुत्तिष्ठति; ग्रामाच्छतमुत्तिष्ठति 'a hundred is yielded by a village.'

§ **322.** ‡ With उप it is Atm., in the sense of 'waiting upon in a religious manner', 'worshipping' (as a deity); as, ये सूर्यमुपतिष्ठन्ते मन्त्रैः (Bk. 13) 'those who wait upon the sun according to religious *mantras*'; ; न त्र्यंबकादन्यमुपास्थितासौ (Bk. I. 3).

Obs. In this sense of 'waiting upon' in general, the root is found in literature taking either pada; as, उपतस्थुर्महात्मानं धर्मपुत्रं युधिष्ठिरं (Mb. II. 47.); स्तुत्यं स्तुतिभिरर्थ्याभिरुपतस्थे सरस्वती (R. IV. 6) $

---

* समवप्रविभ्यः स्थः । प्रकाशनस्थेयाख्ययोश्च । (I. 3. 22-3)

† उदोऽनूर्ध्वकर्मणि । (I. 3. 24)

‡ उपान्मन्त्रकरणे । (I. 3. 25)

$ On this the Mahábhashya has the following:—

बहूनामप्यचित्तानामेको भवति चित्तवान् ।
पश्य वानरसैन्येऽस्मिन्यदर्कमुपतिष्ठते ॥

§ **323.** With *उप it is Atm., also in the following senses:—(1) 'uniting', 'joining'; as, गंगा यमुनामुपतिष्ठते 'the Ganges joins the Jumná'; (2) forming 'friendship with'; as, रथिकानुपतिष्ठते (Mbh.) 'forms friendship with charioteers;' (3) 'lead to' (as a way); as, अयं पन्थाः साकेतमुपतिष्ठते (Mbh.) 'this way leads to Sàketa (Ayodhyá)'.

(*a*) With उप it takes either Pada when 'a desire to get a thing' is implied; as, भिक्षुको ब्राह्मणकुलमुपतिष्ठते·ति (Mbh.) 'a beggar waits at the palace of a Bráhma*n*a (with the desire of getting something)'; also when it is intransitively used; as भोजनकाले उपतिष्ठते 'stands ready at the time of dinner.'

§ **324.** † हृ with अनु is Atm., in the sense of 'constantly practising'; as, पैतृकमश्वा अनुहरन्ते 'horses always practise the gait of their progenitor'; but in the sense of 'resembling' it is Paras.; as, रामभद्रमनुहरति (U. 4.)

§ **325.** ‡ ह्व preceded by आ is Atm., in the sense of 'challenging'; as, कृष्णश्चाणूरमाह्वयते (Sk.) आह्वत चेदिराण्मुरारिं (S'i. XX. 1); but इत एवाह्वयैनमप्यायुष्मन्तं (U. 6) 'call this long-lived boy also here.'

राज्यं नाम शक्तित्रयायत्तम्। शक्तयश्च मन्त्रप्रभावोत्साहाः परस्परानुगृहीताः कृत्येषु क्रमन्ते। (D. K. II. 8)

असौ पापः क्रमेण शाखान्तरैः सञ्चरमाणः कोटरमागत्य तातमपगतासुमकरोत्। (K. 133)

एवं भोः सन्ततिविच्छेदनिरवलम्बानां मूलपुरुषावसाने संपदः परमुपतिष्ठन्ति। (S'. 6)

मैवं मंस्थाः सचित्तोऽयमेषोऽपि हि यथा वयम्।
एतदप्यस्य कापेयं यदर्कमुपतिष्ठति॥

* उपाद्देवपूजासंगतिकरणमित्रकरणपथिष्विति वाच्यम्।

† हरतेर्गतताच्छील्ये।

‡ स्पर्धायामाङः। (I. 3. 31)

उषसि स्नात्वा कृतमङ्गलो मन्त्रिभिः सह समगच्छे। (D. K. II. 3)

अये वनदेवतेयं फलकुसुमपल्लवार्घ्येण मामुपतिष्ठते। (U. 2)

विजयेतां रामलक्ष्मणौ कुम्भकर्णमेघनादौ। (A. R. 6)

ततः प्रतस्थे कौबेरीं भास्वानिव रघुर्दिशम्। (R. IV. 66)

वक्तुं धीरः स्तनितवचनैर्मानिनीं प्रक्रमेथाः। (Me. 101)

बलिर्बबन्धे जलधिर्ममन्थे जह्रेऽमृतं दैत्यकुलं विजिग्ये।
कल्पान्तदुःस्था वसुधा तथोहे येनैष भारोऽतिगुरुर्न तस्य॥
(Bk. II. 39.)

उत्तिष्ठमानस्तु परो नोपेक्ष्यः पथ्यमिच्छता।
समौ हि शिष्टैराम्नातौ वर्त्स्यन्तावामयः स च॥ (S'. II. 10)

अयमपि च गिरं नस्त्वत्प्रबोधप्रयुक्ता-
मनुवदति शुकस्ते मञ्जुवाक् पञ्जरस्थः। (R. V. 74)

यावत्प्रतापनिधिराक्रमते न भानु-
रह्नाय तावदरुणेन तमो निरस्तम्। (R. V. 71)

अथ सर्वस्य धातारं ते सर्वे सर्वतोमुखम्।
वागीशं वाग्भिरर्थ्याभिः प्रणिपत्योपतस्थिरे॥ (Ku. IV. 3)

स मानसीं मेरुसखः पितॄणां कन्यां कुलस्य स्थितये स्थितिज्ञः।
मेनां मुनीनामपि माननीयामात्मानुरूपां विधिनोपयेमे॥
(Ku. I. 18)

पटुर्धारावाही नव इव चिरेणापि हि न मे
निकृन्तन्मर्माणि क्रकच इव मन्युर्विरमति। (U. 4)

फलान्यादत्स्व चित्राणि परिक्रीडस्व सानुषु ।
साध्वनुक्रीडमानानि पश्य वृन्दानि पक्षिणाम् ॥ (Bk. VIII. 10)
किंचिन्नोपावदिष्टासौ केनचिद् व्यवदिष्ट न ।
शृण्वन् संप्रवदमानाद्रावणस्य गुणाञ् जनात् ॥ (Ibid. 28)

ADDITIONAL SENTENCES FOR EXERCISE.

एते भगवत्यौ भूमिदेवानां मूलमायतनमन्तर्वेदिं पूर्वेण कृष्णागरुमलयजरसमंगरागमन्योन्यस्य कुर्वाणे कलिन्दकन्यामन्दाकिन्यौ संगच्छेते । (A. R. 7)

इत्युक्त्वा शुकनासो हेमंतकालोत्पलिनीमिवोद्बाष्पां दृष्टिमुद्वहन्नुद्वेपिताधरश्च बहिरलब्धनिर्गमेण स्फुटन्निवान्तर्मन्युपूरेण निश्वसन्नेवावतस्थे । (K. 289.)

वयोवेषविसंवादि रामस्य च तयोस्तदा ।
जनता प्रेक्ष्य सादृश्यं नाक्षिकम्पं व्यतिष्ठत ॥ (R. XV. 67)
तत्रैनं हेमकुंभेषु संभृतैस्तीर्थवारिभिः ।
उपतस्थुः प्रकृतयो भद्रपीठोपवेशितम् ॥ (R. XVII. 10)
इति दर्शितविक्रियं सुतं मरुतः कोपपरीतमानसम् ।
उपसान्त्वयितुं महीपतिर्द्विरदं दुष्टमिवोपचक्रमे ॥ (Ki. II. 25)
पारसीकांस्ततो जेतुं प्रतस्थे स्थलवर्त्मना ।
इन्द्रियाख्यानिव रिपूंस्तत्त्वज्ञानेन संयमी ॥ (R. IV. 60)
विनयन्ते स्म तद्योधा मधुभिर्विजयश्रमम् ।
आस्तीर्णाजिनरत्नासु द्राक्षावलयभूमिषु ॥ (R. IV. 65)
श्रुतमप्यधिगम्य ये रिपून् विनयन्ते न शरीरजन्मनः ।
जनयन्त्यचिराय संपदामयशस्ते खलु चापलाश्रयम् ॥ (Ki. II. 41)
प्रियप्राया वृत्तिर्विनयमधुरो वाचि नियमः
प्रकृत्या कल्याणी मतिरनवगीतः परिचयः ।
पुरो वा पश्चाद्वा तदिदमविपर्यासितरसं
रहस्यं साधूनामनुपधि विशुद्धं विजयते ॥ (U. 2)
क्षणं भद्रावतिष्ठस्व ततः प्रस्थास्यसे पुनः ।
न तत्संस्थास्यते कार्यं दक्षेणोरीकृतं त्वया ॥ (Bk. VIII. 11)
द्रष्टुं प्रक्रममाणोसौ सीतामम्भोनिधेस्तटम् ।
उपाक्रंस्ताकुलं घोरैः क्रममाणैर्निशाचरैः ॥ (*Ibid.* 25)

जल्पितोत्कुष्टसंगीतप्रनृत्तस्मितवल्गितैः ।
घोषस्यान्ववदिष्टेव लंका पूतक्रतोः पुरः ॥ (*Ibid.* 29)
व्यरमत्प्रधनाद्यस्मात्परित्रस्तः सहस्रदृक् ।
क्षणं पर्यरमत्तस्य दर्शनान्मारुतात्मजः ॥ (*Ibid.* 53)
यावदर्थपदां वाचमेवमादाय माधवः ।
विरराम महीयांसः प्रकृत्या मितभाषिणः ॥ (S'i. II. 13)
विपक्षमखिलीकृत्य प्रतिष्ठा खलु दुर्लभा ।
अनीत्वा पंकतां धूलिमुदकं नावतिष्ठते ॥ (S'. II. 34)
समगध्वं पुरः शत्रोर्मोदयध्वं रघूत्तमम् ।
नोपयध्वं भयं सीतां नोपायंस्त दशाननः ॥
ततः प्रास्थिषताद्रीन्द्रं महेद्रं वानरा द्रुतम् ।
सर्वे किलकिलायन्तो धैर्यं चाधिषताधिकम् ॥ (Bk. VII. 101-2)

At midnight, while I was sleeping soundly in my bed I was awakened by a noise proceeding from persons quarrelling (वद् with वि) with one another.

Having entrusted the protection of his family to his eldest son, the old man started off (स्था with प्र,) for a holy place.

The French, commanded by their ablest General, began (क्रम् with उप) to storm the citadel, but the Chinese easily defeated (जि with परा) them.

From high words the two young men came to blows, and the more fiery-tempered of the two challenged (ह्वे with आ) the other to a single combat.

Fie upon those who wait upon (स्था with उप) rich men and flatter them, simply with desire of getting wealth from them !

The Jumna joins (गम् with सं) the Ganges at Prayága, and this place is held very sacred by the Hindus.

Cease (रम् with वि) from anger and forsake avarice; fret not thyself in any way to do evil.

While Paras'uráma was riding out (चर् with सं) on a high-mettled palfrey, it shied at a pool of water, and the rider was violently thrown down.

The heir-apparent to the throne of England has married (यम् with उप) the daughter of the king of Denmark.

He who initiates (नी with उप) a boy into the sacred ceremonies and teaches him sacred learning, is called an Âchârya.

This way leads (स्था with उप) directly to the river; while the other is rather circuitous; choose which you will.

When the heat of the sun is so scorching (तप् with उत्), how can you go out without an umbrella ?

The light of Brahman is naturally gentle; and, though it be for a time disturbed, it soon resumes (स्था with अव with *loc.*) its wonted nature.

Expectant of favours, we have long put up with the taunts of the wicked, and tamely submitted to the insults of the proud; when, then, O Hope, wilt thou cease to work ?

S'ukanàsa waited upon (स्था with उप) Chandrápída, and having advised him on several important matters, returned home with a delighted heart.

LESSON XXX

RootS of the Second Conjugation.

§ **326.** विद् 'to know' with सं is Atm., in the sense of '*recognizing*'; as, पितरावपि मां न प्रतिसंविदाते (D. K. II. 3) 'even my parents do not recognize me.'

(*a*) It is also Atm., when used intransitively, in the sense of '*knowing*,' '*to be aware of*;' as, के न संविद्रते वायोर्मैनाकाद्रिर्यथा सखा (Bk. 17) 'who do not know that the Mainàka mountain is the friend of the wind.

§ 327. शास् with आ in the sense of '*blessing*' and with प्र in the sense of '*praying for*' is Atm.; ऋक्छंदसाशास्ते (S'. 4) 'blesses her by means of a *Rik* metre'; इदं प्रशास्महे (U. I.) 'we pray for this.'

§ 328. हन् is usually Paras.; but when preceded by आ it is Atm., when used intransitively and referring to one's own body; as, आघ्नान इव संदीप्तैरलातैः सर्वतो मुहुः (Bk. 15) 'as if striking with blazing firebrands, in all directions.'

But परस्य शिर आहन्ति (S. K.)

Obs. This restriction is not always observed; आजघ्ने विषमविलोचनस्य वक्षः (Ki. XVII. 63).

Roots of the Third, Fourth, and Fifth Conjugations.

§ 329. The root दा 'to give' by itself takes either Pada; but when preceded by आ it is Atm., in the sense of '*taking*'; as, नादत्ते भवतां स्नेहेन या पल्लवं (S'. 4) 'who out of affection, would not take (pluck) your foliage'; but मुखं व्याददाति 'opens his mouth'; also विपादिकां व्याददाति 'opens the pimple on his foot'; नदी कूलं व्याददाति; but व्याददते पिपीलिकाः पतंगस्य मुखं (Mbh.)

§ 330. नह् with सं, in the sense of '*preparing*', '*being ready for*' is Atm., as, छेत्तुं वज्रमणीन् संनह्यते (Bh. II. 6) 'is ready to cut adamants'; युद्धाय संनह्यते (Mbh.) 'prepares for battle.'

§ 331. श्रु with सं, when transitively used, is Paras.; as, मद्वचनं न संशृणोति 'does not listen to my words'; but used intransitively, it is Atm.; as संशृणुष्व कपे (Bk. 16) 'listen, O monkey.'

Roots of the Sixth Conjugation.

§ 332. कृ 'to scatter, with अप, in the sense of '*throwing up*,' '*scratching*' (with joy) for maintenance or making an abode is Atm.; as, छायापास्किरमाणविष्किर (U. 2) 'the animals scratching (the ground) for food under the shade'; so अपास्किरते कुक्कुटो भक्ष्यार्थी, श्वा आश्रयार्थी.

But अपकिरति कुसुमं 'scatters a flower.'

§ **333.** गृ 'to eat' is Atm., when preceded by अव; as, अवगिरते ग्रासं 'swallows a mouthful.'

(a) With सं in the sense of *'promising,' 'pledging one's word'*; as, संगिरते शब्दं 'pledges his word'; but संगिरति ग्रासं.

§ **334.** प्रच्छ् with आ is Atm.; in the sense of *'taking leave of,' 'bidding adieu to'*; as, आपृच्छस्व प्रियसखममुं (Me. 10) 'take leave of this your dear friend.'

§ **335.** विश् with नि is Atm., as, किष्किन्धाद्रिं न्यविशत (Bk. VI. 143) 'entered the Kishkindha mountain.'

(a) With अभि also; as, भयं तावत्सेव्यादभिनिविशते सेवकजनं (Mu. 4) 'in the first place the fear of the person to be served enters (the mind of) a servant.'

Roots of the Seventh Conjugation.

§ **336.** *भुज् is Atm., except in the sense of 'protecting'; as ओदनं भुंक्ते 'eats food'; सदयं बुभुजे स मेदिनीं (R. VIII. 7) 'he tenderly enjoyed the earth'; वृद्धो जनो दुःखशतानि भुंक्ते 'old people suffer hundreds of miseries'; but भुनक्ति स्वराज्यं (A. R. 3) 'governs his own country.'

§ **337.** The root †युज् when preceded by प्र and उप, or generally by any preposition beginning or ending with a vowel, is Atm., except with reference to sacrificial vessels; as, प्रयुञ्जानः प्रिया वाचः (Bk. 39) 'employing agreeable words'; आश्रमधर्मे नियुंक्ते (S'. 1); तमन्वयुंक्त (R. VIII. 18); षण्बन्धमुखान् गुणानजः षडुपायुंक्त (*ibid.* 21) 'Aja employed the six expedients beginning with peace.'

Roots of the Eighth Conjugation.

§ **338.** ‡कृ 'to do' by itself admits of either Pada, but it is Atm., generally with prepositions, in the following senses:—(1) *'do-*

---

* भुजोऽनवने (I. 3. 66)

† प्रोपाभ्यां युजेरयज्ञपात्रेषु । (I. 3. 64); स्वराद्यन्तोपसर्गादिति वक्तव्यम् (*Vârtika*).

‡ गन्धनावक्षेपणसेवनसाहसिक्यप्रतियत्नप्रकथनोपयोगेषु कृञः । (I. 3. 32)

ing an injury to'; as उत्कुरुते 'informs against'; (2) '*censure*,' '*blame*', '*overcoming*'; as, श्येनो वर्तिकामुदाकुरुते 'the hawk overcomes a snail'; (3) '*serving*,' '*attending upon*'; as, हरिमुपकुरुते 'serves Hari'; (4) '*acting violently*', '*outraging*'; परदारान् प्रकुरुते 'outrages another's wife'; (5) '*preparing*,' '*dressing*'; as, एधो दकस्योपस्कुरुते 'fuel prepares (boils) water'; (6) '*reciting*'; as, गाथाः प्रकुरुते 'recites stories'; (7) '*employing*,' '*applying to use*'; as, शतं प्रकुरुते 'devotes a hundred' (to sacred purposes); so उपकुर्वन्तमत्यर्थं प्रकुर्वाणोऽनुजीविवत् (Bk. 18).

(a) कृ with उप in the sense of '*doing good to*' is used in both the Padas; as, न हि दीपौ परस्परस्योपकुरुतः (S'. B.) 'two lamps do not, indeed, help each other'; किं त्वां भूयः प्रियमुपकरोमि (Mu. 7) ; सा लक्ष्मीरुपकुरुते यया परेषां (Ki. VII. 28) 'that is wealth by means of which the possessor does good to others.

(b) With *अनु and परा, the root is Paras.; as, पराकरोति दानं 'rejects a gift'; अनुकरोति भगवतो नारायणस्य (K. 6.)

§ **339.** † कृ with अधि is Atm., in the sense of '*bearing*,' '*enduring*,' or '*overpowering*'; as, शत्रुमधिकुरुते 'forgives or overpowers his enemy'; but मनुष्यानधिकरोति शास्त्रं (S'. B.) 'Scripture authorizes men.'

§ **340.** With ‡ वि it is Atm., in the sense of '*uttering*' (having 'sounds' for its object); as, स्वरान् विकुरुते 'produces sounds' but चित्तं विकरोति कामः 'Love affects the mind.'

(a) When intransitively used, it is Atm., with वि; as, विकुर्वे नगरे तस्य (Bk. 21) 'I shall act at will in his city'; विविधं (चेष्टे).

Roots of the Ninth Conjugation.

§ **341.** The root क्री§ 'to buy' is Atm., when preceded by परि, वि, and अव; as, कृतेनोपकृतं वायोः परिक्रीणानं (Bk. 8) 'requiting by deeds the obligations of the wind'; यस्तानि विक्रीणीते (Y. II.) 'he who sells them.'

---

* अनुपराभ्यां कृञः। (परस्मैपदं) (I. 3. 79)

† अधेः प्रसहने। (I. 3. 33)

‡ वेः शब्दकर्मणः। अकर्मकाच्च। (I. 3. 34, 5)

§ परिव्यवेभ्यः क्रियः। (I. 3. 18)

§ **342**. *ज्ञा, used by itself, admits of both the Padas, as जानासि विनोदयितुं (U. 1); जानीते हि भवान् (V. 2) ; with अप it is Atm. in the sense of '*denying*, '*concealing*;' as, शतमपजानीते 'denies a hundred.'

(*a*) With सं and प्र it is Atm. except in the sense of '*thinking of*'; as शतं संजानीते 'looks for a hundred'; हरचापारोपणेन कन्यादानं प्रतिजानीते (P. R. 4) 'promises the hand of his daughter by (on condition of) stringing the bow of Hara. But मातरं मातुर्वा संजानाति 'thinks of his mother.'

(*b*) ज्ञा with अनु takes either Pada; as अनुजानीहि मां गमनाय (U. 3); ततोनुजज्ञे गमनं सुतस्य (Bk. III. 23) 'then consented to the departure of his son.'

(*c*) The desiderative of ज्ञा is always Atm.; as, जिज्ञासमानानुचरस्य भावं (R. II. 26) 'desirous of knowing the devotion of her follower.'

Roots of the Tenth Conjugation and Causals.

§ **343**. Roots of the tenth conjugation and causals generally admit of either Pada. But there are exceptions.

(*a*) † When the causals of transitive verbs are used reflexively or when the object in the primitive sense becomes the agent in the causal, the Atmanepada is used, except in the sense of remembering with tenderness'; as, भक्ता भवं पश्यन्ति 'devotees see Bhava'; भवो भक्तान् दर्शयते 'Bhava shows himself to his devotees'; दर्शयते नित्यं मनुष्यान् (Mb. II. 5. 86); but स्मरयति वनगुल्मः कोकिलं=उत्कंठापूर्वकस्मृतौ विषयो भवति (S. K.). This, it will be easily seen, is quite different from the ordinary use of the causal; भक्तान् भवं दर्शयति देवदत्तः.

(*b*) In general, the causal takes Atm., when the fruit of the action accrues to the agent; as कटं कारयते 'gets the mat prepared for himself'; स्वार्थं कारयमाणाभिः (Bk. 48) 'accomplishing their own good.'

§ **344**. ‡ The causals of बुध्, युध्, नश्, जन्, इ (with अधि), प्रु, द्रु, स्रु, take Parasmaipada; as, बोधयति पद्मं, नाशयति दुःखं, जनयति सुखं &c.

---

* अपह्नवे ज्ञः । संप्रतिभ्यामनाध्याने । (I. 3. 44, 46)

† णेरणौ यत्कर्म णौ चेत्स कर्ताऽनाध्याने । (I. 3. 67)

‡ बुधयुधनशजनेङ्प्रुद्रुस्रुभ्यो णेः (I. 3. 86.)

(*a*) Roots having the sense of 'eating' or 'swallowing' and 'shaking' take Paras. **अद्** is an exception except when the act is not for the agent.

§ 345. The causals of **पा**, 'to drink', **दम्**, **यम्** with **आ**, **यस्** with **आ**, **मुह्** with **परि**, **रुच्**, **नृत्** and **वद्** (with **अभि**) are used in the Atm., when the fruit of action accrues to the agent; as, **पिबत्यसौ पाययते च सिन्धुः** (R. XIII. 9).

(*a*) **मन्त्र** with **आ** is Atm., in the sense of '*addressing*' and '*bidding adieu to*' as; **आमन्त्रयस्व सहचरं** (S'. 3) 'bid farewell to your companion.'

सा दूरस्थितैव पाणिना वेणुलतामादाय नरपतिप्रबोधनार्थं संक्रुत्सभाकुट्टिममाजघान। (K. 10)

सखे सीरध्वज हृदयमेवामन्त्रयस्व किमर्थं कृतार्थमसीति। (A. R. 3)

सखे सैव धन्या गणिकादारिका यामेवं भवन्मनोभिनिविशते।
(D. K. II. 2)

इयमतिक्रम्य स्वकुलधर्ममर्थनिरपेक्षा गुणेभ्य एव स्वं यौवनं विचिक्रीषते। (Ibid.)

राज्ञा च तथानुशिष्टा सत्यप्यनाश्रवैव सा यदासीत्तदास्याः स्वसा माता च निर्बन्धेन राज्ञे समगिरेताम्॥ (D. K. II. 2.)

मानी मानसारो महेश्वरं समाराध्यास्माद्भयदां गदां लब्ध्वा आत्मानमप्रतिभटं मन्यमानो महाभिमानो भवन्तमभियोक्तुमुद्युंक्ते। (D. K. I. 1)

ततः प्रवृत्तासु प्रीतिसंकथासु सुहृदां वृत्तान्तं श्रोतुं कृतप्रस्तावस्तांश्च तदुक्तावन्वयुंक्त। (D. K. II. 1)

तथास्मासु प्रतिविधाय तिष्ठत्सु राजापि विज्ञापितोदन्तो जातानुतापः पारग्रामिकान् प्रयोगान् प्रायः प्रायुंक्त। (D. K. II. 4)

मदसिक्तमुखैर्मृगाधिपः करिभिर्वर्तयते स्वयं हतैः।
लघयन् खलु तेजसा जगन्न महानिच्छति भूतिमन्यतः॥
(Ki. II. 18)

उज्झत्सु संहार इवास्तसंख्यमह्नाय तेजस्विषु जीवितानि।
लोकत्रयास्वादनलोलजिह्वं न व्याददात्याननमत्र मृत्युः॥
(Ki. XVI. 16)

मृदुव्यवहितं तेजो भोक्तुमर्थान् प्रकल्पते।
प्रदीपः स्नेहमादत्ते दशयाभ्यन्तरस्थया॥ (S'i. II. 85)

षाड्गुण्यमुपयुञ्जीत शक्त्यपेक्षी रसायनम्।
भवन्त्यस्यैवमङ्गानि स्थास्नूनि बलवन्ति च (S'i. II. 93)

कृतसीतापरित्यागः स रत्नाकरमेखलाम्।
बुभुजे पृथिवीपालः पृथिवीमेव केवलाम्॥ (R. XV. 9)

कुलभार्यां प्रकुर्वाणमहं द्रष्टुं दशाननम्।
यामि त्वरावान् शैलेंद्र मा कस्यचिदुपस्कृथाः॥

योऽपचक्रे वनात्सीतामधिचक्रे न यं हरिः।
विकुर्वाणः स्वरानद्य बलं तस्य निहन्म्यहम्॥ (Bk. VIII. 19-20)

आत्मानमपजानानः शशमात्रोऽनयद्दिनम्।
ज्ञास्ये रात्राविति प्राज्ञः प्रत्यज्ञास्त कियापटुः॥

सञ्ज्ञानानान् परिहरन् रावणानुचरान् बहून् ।
लंकां समाविशद्रात्रौ वदमानोऽरिदुर्गमम् ॥ (*Ibid.* 26-27)

ADDITIONAL SENTENCES FOR EXERCISE.

अथ कुपितोऽर्थपतिर्व्यवहर्तुमर्थगर्वादभियोक्ष्यते । तं च भूयश्चित्रैरुपायैः कौपीनावशेषं करिष्यावः । (D. K. II. 2)

प्रजाभिस्तु बन्धुमन्तो राजानो न ज्ञातिभिः । तदुत्तिष्ठ कुरुष्व पुरेव सर्वाः क्रियाः । कृताहारे त्वय्यहमपि सुखमुपभोक्ष्ये पथ्यमित्येवमभिहितस्यास्य दिधक्षन्निव हृदयमतितरां शोकानलः संदुधुक्षे । (H. C. 5)

सभाजने मे भुजमूर्ध्वबाहुः सव्येतरं प्राध्वमितः प्रयुंक्ते । (R. XIII. 43)
स किंसखा साधु न शास्ति योऽधिपं हितान्न यः संशृणुते स किंप्रभुः ।
सदानुकूलेषु हि कुर्वते रतिं नृपेष्वमात्येषु च सर्वसंपदः । (Ki. I. 5)
सखीनिव प्रीतियुजोऽनुजीविनः समानमानान् सुहृदश्च बंधुभिः ।
स सततं दर्शयते गतस्मयः कृताधिपत्यामिव साधु बंधुताम् ॥ (Ki. I. 10)
मदमानसमुद्धतं नृपं न वियुंक्ते नियमेन मूढता ।
अतिमूढ उदस्यते नयान्नयहीनादपरज्यते जनः (Ki. II. 49)

स राजलोकः कृतपूर्वसंविदारंभसिद्धौ समयोपलभ्यम् ।
आदास्यमानः प्रमदामिषं तदावृत्य पन्थानमजस्य तस्थौ ॥ (R. VII. 31)
असंविदानस्य ममेश संविदां तितिक्षितुं दुश्चरितं त्वमर्हसि ।
विरोध्यमोहात्पुनरभ्युपेयुषां गतिर्भवानेव दुरात्मनामपि ॥
(Ki. XVIII. 42)

तत्प्रतीपपवनादि वैकृतं प्रेक्ष्य शान्तिमधिकृत्य कृत्यवित् ।
अन्वयुंक्त गुरुमीश्वरः क्षितेः स्वन्तमित्यलघयत्स तद्व्यथाम् ॥ (R. XI. 62)
नृपतिः प्रकृतीरवेक्षितुं व्यवहारासनमाददे युवा ।
परिचेतुमुपांशु धारणां कुशपूतं प्रवयास्तु विष्टरम् ॥ (R. VIII. 18)
समनद्ध किमङ्ग भूपतिर्यदि संधित्सुरसौ सहामुना ।
हरिराक्रमणेन सन्नतिं किल बिभ्रीत भियेत्यसंभवः (Si. XVI. 34)
न्यस्ताक्षरामक्षरभूमिकायां कार्त्स्न्येन गृह्णाति लिपिं न यावत् ।
सर्वाणि तावच्छ्रुतवृद्धयोगात् फलान्युपायुंक्त स दंडनीतेः (R. XVIII. 46)

नैतच्चित्रं यदयमुदधिश्यामसीमां धरित्री-
मेकः कृत्स्नां नगरपरिघप्रांशुबाहुर्भुनक्ति ।
आशंसन्ते समितिषु सुराः सक्तवैरा हि दैत्यै-
रस्याधिज्ये धनुषि विजयं पौरुहूते च वज्रे ॥ (S'. 2)
यन्मां विधेयविषये सभवान्नियुंक्ते
स्नेहस्य तत्फलमसौ प्रणयस्य सारः । (Mâl. 1)
अवाद्वायुः शनैरस्यां लतां नर्तयमानवत् ।
नायासयन्त संत्रस्ता ऋतवोऽन्योन्यसंपदः ॥
ज्योत्स्नामृतं शशी यस्यां वापीर्विकसितोत्पलाः ।
अपाययत संपूर्णः सदा दशमुखाज्ञया ॥
प्रादमयन्त पुष्पेषु यस्यां वन्यः समाहृताः ।
परिमोहयमाणाभी राक्षसीभिः समाहृताः ॥
यस्यां वासयते सीतां केवलं स्म रिपुः स्मरात् ।
न त्वरोचयतात्मानं चतुरो बुद्धिमानपि ॥ (Bk. VIII. 61-4)
उत्क्षिप्तगात्रः स्म विडम्बयन्नभः समुत्पतिष्यन्तमगेन्द्रमुच्चकैः ।
आकुञ्चितप्रोहनिरूपितक्रमं करेणुरारोहयते निषादिनम् ॥ (S'i. XII. 5)

Rishyas'ringa blessed (शास् with आ) Sitâ with the words 'mayest thou give birth to a warrior.'

When you prepare (नह् with सं) for this mortal combat, take (दा with आ) with you your best weapons.

Listen, my lord. You may oppress me, you may deprive (युज् with वि) me of all my property; but you cannot take away from me my attachment to the cause of Truth.

The ass, dressed in a tiger's skin, inspired fear (*caus.* of भी) in the animals that grazed about in the field.

Out of the six exedients always use (युज् with प्र) conciliation first; if that should fail, have recourse to others.

The cowherd made his cow drink (पा) the clear water of the pools and then took his way home, as the sun was about to set.

When a man has to go to a distant place, he takes leave of (प्रच्छ् with आ) his elders and bows down to his tutelary deities.

The elephant, afflicted by the scorching heat of the sun, at once plunged into (विश् with नि) the deep pool of water.

The king, who protects (भुज्) his subjects as if they were his own children, himself enjoys (भुज् with उप) unending happiness, and secures the loyal attachment of his people to the throne.

The king of the Drupadas promised (ज्ञा with प्रति) the hand of his daughter to any one who would shoot through a fish hung above a basin of water, by looking at its image below.

The sons of Sagara, while searching the sacrificial horse, fell in with the sage Kapila, and accused (युज् with अभि) him as the stealer of the horse.

Unluckily it fell out that the mother in her precipitate flight, blinded with haste, dashed (हन् with आ) her favourite child's head against a stone and killed it.

The crow picks up (कृ with अप) crumbs of cakes or other bits of eatables, and thus maintains himself.

A king of Persia once asked (युज् with अनु) a philosopher 'what do you value most in kings? 'Absence of greed' was his reply.

In this Kali age parents often sell (क्री with वि) their girls for money and wed them to persons bent double with age! Is this not monster-like?

PART IV.

ANALYSIS AND SYNTHESIS OF SENTENCES.

§ **346.** In the first three Parts we have dealt with some of the chief principles that regulate the joining together of words in sentences. We have also explained the meanings and uses of the more important grammatical forms and useful connective particles, which, as observed by Prof. Bain, 'belonging alike to all subjects and all styles, are the very hinges of composition.' The explanation of such forms and words is the more necessary in the case of Sanskrit, as in the existing Sanskrit Grammars that subject is rarely or very imperfectly treated, though, perhaps, in doing so a writer may seem to trench a little on the province of the lexicographer.

To render the rules of Syntax more simple and intelligible it is necessary to consider the **analysis of sentences.** This will enable the student to ascertain the different parts of sentences and the relation in which they stand to one another. The *analysis of sentences* will also facilitate Sanskrit composition, and help the student in translating from Sanskrit into English and *vice versa.*

SECTION 1.

ANALYSIS OF SENTENCES.

§ **347.** A *sentence* is the expression in language of a complete thought.

The expression of a single idea is a *word* (पद) ; the aggregation of two or more *words* without a subject or predicate is a *phrase* (पद-

समुच्चय) ; and the collection of words containing a finite and complete idea is a *sentence* (वाक्य); as,

रामः, सुवर्णं, नीतिः (words); रामविवासनं, अभितप्तं सुवर्णं, जनहितावहा नीतिः (phrases); and रामविवासनं कैकेय्या अभिमतं, अग्नितप्तं सुवर्णं विलिनाति, जनहितावहा नीतिः राज्ञा अनुरुध्यते (sentences).

N. B.—A sentence, whether indicative, imperative, optative, or interrogative in *form*, is the same in *essence*.

§ **348.** Every sentence consists of two parts: the *Subject* and the *Predicate*. That about which something is said or asserted is the *Subject*, and that which is said about the subject is the *Predicate* ; as, सविता उदेति '*the sun rises*.' Here सविता is the *subject* and उदेति the *Predicate*.

§ **349.** Sentences are of three kinds : *Simple*, *Complex*, and *Compound*.

A *simple* sentence contains one subject and one finite verb or whatever serves as a predicate (see further on) ; as, अहं पापकारिणी महाभागमद्राक्षं (K. 166); धिक् तां (Bh. II. 2).

A *complex* sentence is one which, while containing but one principal subject and one principal predicate, has two or more finite verbs ; as, यां चिन्तयामि सततं मयि सा विरक्ता (Bh. II. 2); यदि गर्जति वारिधरो (स) गर्जतु (Mk. 5).

A *compound* sentence is one which contains two or more principal sentences ; as, दुदोह गां स यज्ञाय शस्याय मघवा दिवं (दुदोह च) (R. I. 26).

THE SIMPLE SENTENCE.

§ **350.** The simple sentence contains one subject and one finite verb.

This is the most elementary form of a simple sentence; the enlarged and complicated forms may be considered as growing out of this by means of the processes afterwards given.

§ **351.** The primary elements of the simple sentence, Subject and Predicate, may be enlarged by one or more secondary elements or *adjuncts* attached to them, which, in their turn, may undergo further expansions.

Subject.

§ **352.** The *Subject* may be a noun, simple or compound, or a pronoun;

'आत्मा' तपस्यायोजितः (K. 173); 'शुकनासः' सविस्तरमुवाच (K. 102); 'भरतशत्रुघ्नौ' द्वंद्वं बभूवतुः (R. X. 81); 'त्रैलोक्यं' अपि पीडितं; पटुत्वं कथायोगेन बुध्यते (H. 1); 'मरणं' प्रकृतिः शरीरिणां (R. VIII. 87); 'सः' अप्याचचक्षे (D. K. II. 8).

Obs. (*a*) As the inflexion of the verb itself shows the number and person of the subject, it is very frequently not expressed at all; as, (भवान्) अपनयतु नः कुतूहलं (K. 18); कथं मंदभाग्यः करोमि (अहं) (U. 3); (त्वं) ब्रूहि रामचरितं (U. 2).

(*b*) An adjective is often used without the noun qualified by it; as, 'विद्वान्' सर्वत्र पूज्यते; 'द्वावपि' आगामिनौ (M. 3).

(*c*) The numeral substantives often stand as the subject of a sentence; शरदां 'अयुतं' ययौ (R. X. 1); 'शतं' अनूच्यमायुष्कामस्य.

§ **353.** The simple subject may be enlarged by the various means of qualifying the noun or pronoun:—

(1) By an adjective—pronominal or participial, qualitative or quantitative.

'स' राजा किमारंभः संप्रति (U. 2); का 'इयमन्या' बिभीषिका (U. 4); 'त्र-जेश्च' (स) समर्थयामास (K. 133); एवं 'अभिधीयमानः' स प्रत्यवादीत् (K. 147); पदपंक्तिर्दृश्यते 'अभिनवा' (S'. 3); 'चतुर्दश' सहस्राणि रक्षसां भीमकर्मणां हतानि (U. 2).

(2) By a noun or pronoun in the genitive case;

'रामस्य' करुणो रसः (U. 3); अपि कुशली 'ते' गुरुः (R. V. 4); अन्यविषया न तु दृष्टिः 'अस्याः' (S'. 3).

(3) By a noun in apposition;

तस्मिन् 'भोजवंशभूषणं' 'संभावयिता बुधान्' पुण्यवर्मा नामासीत् (D. K. II. 8).

Obs. Participial adjectives, if derived from transitive verbs, may govern an object;

'आसेदिवान्' रत्नवत् 'आसनं' सः गुहेमोपमेयकान्तिरासीत् (R. VI. 4); 'अनुयास्यन् मुनितनयां' (अहं) विनयेन वारितप्रसरः (S'. 1); 'रसिकमनांसि समुल्लासयन्' वसंतसमयः समाजगाम (D. K. I. 5).

N. B.—Indeclinable past participles in Sanskrit are of the nature of *adverbs* showing *time*, and will be considered in treating of the *extension* of the predicate.

§ **354.** The most general and frequent means of enlargement in Sanskrit is the use of *compounds*. They are the very essence of Sanskrit, and it will be difficult to find a passage where no compound is used. No limits have been set by grammarians to the length of these compounds, and to what extremity (absurd in some cases) this latitude is carried by writers, will be seen from the works of Da*n*din, Subandhu, Bá*n*a, and even Bhavabhûti (see Lavangiká's speeches in Mál. Act. III. and the well-known Da*n*daka metre in Act V). Compounds of moderate length add beauty to a sentence, and play a very important part in the economy of words.

§ **355.** The compounds most frequently used in the enlargement of the noun or pronoun are the Tatpurusha (Inflectional and Appositional) and Bahuvrîhi.

(I) Instead of the simple adjective may be used the Inflectional Tatpurusha, Karmadháraya, Upapada Tatpurusha and Bahuvrîhi;

क्षपिता 'तद्विटपाश्रिता' लता (R. VIII. 47); 'अबलाविप्रयुक्तः' 'कनकवलयभ्रंशरिक्तप्रकोष्ठः' स कामी (Me. 2); 'उटजद्वारविरूढं' नीवारबलिं (S'. 4); 'तांबूल-

करंकवाहिनी' तरलिका (K. 148); 'ग्रहीतप्रातिमुक्तस्य' तस्य (R. IV. 43); कुल्यां भोभिः 'पवनचपलैः' (S'. 1).

The Genitive Tatpurusha is mostly used for the possessive case;

कौत्सः प्रपेदे 'वरतंतुशिष्यः' (R. V. 1); नष्टाशंका 'हरिणशिशवः' चरन्ति (S'. 1).

§ **356.** The subject may be further enlarged by a repetition or combination of two or more of the above modes, and the adjuncts themselves, if they be nouns or pronouns, may be enlarged by other adjuncts:—

एकदा तत्रस्थ एव मृगयानिर्गतो विचरन् (adj.) काननं किंनरमिथुनमद्राक्षीत् (K. 119); तनयश्च (Gen. Tat.) हारीतनामा (adj.) तापसकुमारकः (noun in apposition) सनत्कुमार इव सर्वविद्यावदातचेताः (adj. Bahu. comp.) सिस्नासुः (adj.) उपागमत् (K. 37); ताभिरष्टाभिः प्रत्यक्षाभिः (adj. to तनुभिः) तनुभिः प्रपन्नः (adj. of Subj.) ईशो वः अवतु (S'. 1); मदम्बा पूर्णभद्रबोधितार्था (adj.) तादृशेपि व्यसने (adv. to the next) नातिविह्वला (adj.) कुलपरिजनानुयाता (adj.) मत्पितुरुत्तमांगं उत्संगेन धारयन्ती (part. adj. with obj. and adv.) राज्ञे समादिदेश (D. K. II. 4); so 'तस्य' 'त्रयः' 'पुत्राः' 'परमदुर्मेधसो' 'वसुशक्तिरुग्रशक्तिरनेकशक्तिश्चेतिनामानो' बभूवुः (P. I.); दुःखेन तप्यन्ते 'त्रयो' 'नः' पितरः 'अपरे' (U. 5).

Obs. This idea of enlarging the noun has been carried to excess by writers like Báṇa, Daṇḍin, and Subandhu in their descriptions of persons, places, towns, rivers, &c. Enlargement should be carried on so long as the sense does not become complicated or unintelligible. When there is danger of the sense being complicated, the sentence should be split up into two or more sentences.

Object or Completion of Predicate.

§ **357.** If the Predicate be a transitive verb, or a verb of motion, or any verb becoming transitive by the force of prepositions, it is *completed by means of an object.* The *object* may be a noun, or a pronoun, or whatever else may serve the purpose of a noun;

'जाबालिं' अपश्यं (K. 42); 'आखंडलः 'क्षममिदं' बभाषे (Ku. III. 11); याति 'अस्तशिखरं' पतिरोषधीनां (S'. 4); विचचार 'दावं' (R. II. 8) पत्तिः 'पदातिं' अभ्यपतत् (R. VII. 37).

§ **358.** The object, being of the same nature as the subject, may be enlarged in the same way (see § § 353-6.):—त्रियम्बकं 'संयमिनं' ददर्श (Ku. III. 44); 'विलपन्तं' कपिञ्जलमश्रौषं (K. 165); तं 'तस्थिवांसं' 'नगरोपकण्ठे' (adv. to adj.) प्रत्युज्जगाम क्रथकैशिकेंद्रः (R. V. 61); प्रकृतिवक्रः स 'कस्य' अनुनयं प्रतिगृह्णाति (S'. 4) 'इदं' 'अव्याजमनोहं' वपुः 'तपःक्षमं' साधयितुं य इच्छति (S'. 1); मेघं 'आश्लिष्टसानुं' 'वप्रक्रीडापरिणतगजप्रेक्षणीयं' ददर्श (Me. 2); अवनिपतिस्तु 'प्रतीहार्या निर्दिश्यमानां' 'तां' 'प्राट्षमिव घनकेशजालां' 'अलकोद्भासिनीं' 'अचिरोपरूढयौवनां' 'अतिशयरूपाकृतिं' 'अनिमेषलोचनो ददर्श' (K. 11).

§ **359.** Verbs of 'making,' 'naming,' 'calling,' 'thinking,' 'considering,' 'appointing' &c., govern a *factitive* object, besides the principal one; as,

तमात्मजन्मानं 'अजं' चकार (R. V. 36); आज्ञामपि 'वरप्रदानं' मन्यन्ते, दर्शनप्रदानमपि 'अनुग्रहं' गणयन्ति (K. 108); प्रत्याख्यानमपि 'ईर्षां' संभावयति, आक्रोशमपि 'परिहासं' आकलयति, दोषसंकीर्तनमपि 'स्मरणोपायं' अवगच्छति, अवज्ञानमपि 'अनियन्त्रणं प्रणयं' उत्प्रेक्षते (K. 235)

§ **360.** In the case of verbs governing two objects, such as, दुह् याच्, शास् and नी &c. there is a *principal* and a *secondary* object, or a *direct* and an *indirect* object. See § 40.

§ **361.** Sometimes verbs, transitive in *sense*, govern, by virtue of special rules, a noun or a pronoun in the dative, ablative, genitive or locative case. Such cases may be regarded as *completions* of the predicate, for without them the sense is not complete; स्पृहयामि दुर्ललिताय 'अस्मै' (S'.7); कुप्यन्ति हितवादिने (K. 108); असूयन्ति 'मह्यं' प्रकृतयः (V. 4); 'पापात्' जुगुप्सते (Mbh.); स्मरसि वा 'तस्य प्रदेशस्य' (U. 6); स स्निह्यति 'आवयोः' (U. 6).

§ **362.** Verbs of 'giving', 'telling', 'promising,' 'sending' govern a dative of the person to whom something is given, told &c.; this dative may be regarded as an *indirect object* ;

'विप्राय' गां प्रतिशृणोति, भोजेन दूतो 'रघवे' विसृष्टः (R. V. 30); 'तस्मै' प्रस्तुतमाचचक्षे (R. V. 19).

Obs. From another point of view, they may be regarded as *extensions* of the Predicate, answering to the question 'to whom,' 'whither.'

The Predicate.

§ **363.** The Predicate may be a single, finite verb; as, 'आज्ञापयतु' भवान् (S'. 4); त्वया सह गौतमी 'यास्यति' (*ibid.*).

§ **364.** The Predicate may also be a substantive or adjective, with the verb अस् 'to be' expressed or understood ;

अविवेकः परमापदां 'पदं' (Ki. II. 30); त्वं 'असि' महतां 'भाजनं' (Māl. 1); वत्से किमेवं 'कातरा' 'असि' (S'. 4) ; 'गृहीतः' संदेशः (*ibid*) ; 'अत्रहितोस्मि' (S'. 7); तेन हि श्रेयांसि 'अनतिक्रमणीयानि' (S'. 7); 'दूषिताः स्थ' 'परिभूताः स्थ' रामहतकेन (U. 1); व्यावर्तिततुरगश्च पुनः 'चिंतितवान्' (K. 121).

(*a*) The root अस् is, by pre-eminence, the verb of incomplete predication, and hence it requires a noun or adjective after it to complete its sense, as in the above instances. But when it denotes '*existence*', it may stand by itself; as,

हिमालयो नाम नगाधिराजः अस्ति (Ku. I. 1)

So also भू when it implies mere 'existence' and not 'becoming' 'बभूव' योगी किल कार्तवीर्यः (R. VI. 38).

(*b*) Sometimes the predicate (अस्, विद्, वृत्) is not expressed at all; मातले कतमस्मिन्प्रदेशे मारीचाश्रमः (S'. 7), *i. e.* अस्ति, विद्यते &c.

§ **365.** There are other verbs of incomplete predication, such as, भू, वृत् 'to become,' जन् 'to become,' or 'grow' भा, दृश् or लक्ष् *pass.* to 'appear,' to 'seem' &c., which require a noun or adjective to make a complete predicate:

तेपि 'यथोक्ताः' 'संवृत्ताः' (P. 1); तव प्रजासु बिडौजाः 'प्राज्यवृष्टिर्भवतु' (S'. 7) (become the pourer of copious showers); ईदृशानां विपाकोपि 'परमाद्भुतो जायते' (U. 3); स्वात्यां सागरशुक्तिसंपुटगतं (पयः) 'सन्मौक्तिकं जायते' (Bh. II. 67) (*becomes or grows a good pearl*) ; अयं पांड्यः 'अद्रिराजः' इवाभाति (R. VI. 60); 'मदनक्लिष्टा' इयमालक्ष्यते (S'. 3) (*appears or seems afflicted by love.*)

(*a*) The same is the case in the passive construction of verbs like मन् 'to consider,' 'deem,' 'think,' कृ 'to change into,' &c.;

नलिनी 'पूर्वनिदर्शनं मता' (R. VIII. 45); व्याघ्रः 'कुक्कुरः कृतः' (H. 4); so स 'सेनापतिर्नियुक्तः'.

Hence the predicate, if a noun or adjective, agrees in case with the subject, or is in the nominative case.

§ **366.** Sometimes, as in English, a sentence is expressed in a contracted form, by the use of particles or interjections, when the Subject and Predicate, or both, are not expressed, but have to be evolved out of the particles; as,

'धिक्' तां च तं च='सा' च 'स' च 'निन्द्यौ' स्तः; शिवाय 'नमः'=शिवः प्रणम्यते; 'अलं' प्रयत्नेन=प्रयत्नेन न ' किमपि ' साध्यं &c.

§ **367.** An indeclinable not unfrequently serves the purpose of the predicate; as,

विषवृक्षोपि छेत्तुं 'असांप्रतम्' (Ku. II. 55)=न युज्यते; पवनः आलिंगितुं 'शक्यं' (S'. 3)=शक्यते; ' कष्टं ' खलु अनपत्यता .(S'. 6); मनसिजरुजं सा वा दिव्या मम ' अलं ' अपोहितुं (V. 3)

Extension of the Predicate.

§ **368.** The Predicate is enlarged—is more accurately defined or determined—by an adverb or whatever has the force of, or is equivalent to an adverb. Such are adverbs of time, place, manner &c. particles and interjections, the several case inflectional forms (except those of the nominative, accusative, genitive, and vocative); and combinations of prepositions or adverbs with nouns; मया सार्धं, रामाद्विना, वृक्षाणामधः, राज्ञः समक्षं &c.

§ **369.** The enlargements or extensions of the Predicate may be classified under four heads:—

(1) Those relating to time.
(2) Those relating to place.
(3) Those relating to manner.
(4) Those relating to cause and effect.

Adjuncts of Time.

§ **370.** Adverbial adjuncts of *Time* are used to show one of the following conditions:—

(1) *Point* or *period* of time, answering to the question 'when ? '.

द्वयं गतं 'संप्रति' शोचनीयतां (Ku. V. 71); 'ततः' प्रविशति कंचुकी (S'. 5) यास्यति 'अद्य' शकुंतला (S'. 4) ; आषाढस्य 'प्रथमदिवसे' मेघं ददर्श (Me. 2); 'अनुदिवसं' परिहीयसे अंगैः (S'. 3); गिरिशमुपचचार 'प्रत्यहं' सा सुकेशी (Ku. I. 60); 'अस्मात्परं' को नः कुले निवपनानि नियच्छति (S'. 6).

Obs. (*a*) Locative absolute constructions generally signify *time* and may be regarded as adverbs of *time* under this head.

'अंतर्हिते शशिनि' सैव कुमुद्वती मे दृष्टिं न नन्दयति (S'. 4)
i. e. 'the moon having disappeared or *when* the moon is hid &c.';

'गते च केयूरके' चन्द्रापीडसुनात्त (K. 181).

(*b*) Similarly indeclinable past participles in त्वा (changed to य or त्य) are adverbial adjuncts showing *point* or *period* of time. If derived from transitive verbs, they may govern an object;

प्रतिनिवृत्य तं प्रदेशं व्यलोकयम् (K. 125); महाश्वेता 'तच्छ्रुत्वा' सुचिरं 'विचार्य' केयूरकं प्राहिणोत् (K. 181.); 'अचिरात् पावनं तनयं प्रसूय' मम विरहजां शुचं न गणयिष्यसि (S'. 4).

(2) *Duration* of time or space answering to the question 'How long':—

'इयन्ति दिवसानि' प्रजागरकृशो लक्ष्यते (S'. 3); दत्तदृष्टिः 'सुचिरं' व्यचरम् (K. 152); 'क्रोशं' कुटिला नदी (S. K.); 'स्तन्यत्यागं यावत् अवेक्षस्व' (U. 7).

(3) *Repetition* of time, answering to the question, 'How often':—

'वारंवारं' तिरयति दृशोरुद्गमं बाष्पपूरः (Mál. 1) ; अह्नो 'द्विः' भुंक्ते (S. K.) ताम्यन्मूर्तिः श्रयति 'बहुशः' चन्द्रपादान् (Mál. 3).

Adjuncts of Place.

§ **371.** Adverbial adjuncts of *place* specify three relations:—

(1) *Rest* in a place, answering to the question 'Where';

अस्ति 'अवंतीषु' उज्जयिनी नाम नगरी (K. 48) ; 'कस्मिंश्चिदधिष्ठाने' कौलिकः रथकारौ प्रतिवसतः स्म (P. I. 5); एष कण्वस्य महर्षेः 'उपमालिनीतीरं' आश्रमो दृश्यते (S'. 1); अस्ति 'उत्तरस्यां दिशि' नगाधिराजः (Ku. I. 1); निर्मलनखलग्नमूर्तिः 'पादयोः' पतति (K. 193).

(2) *Motion to* a place, answering to the question 'Whither';

सा तरलिका 'क्व' गता (K. 176); 'नीचैः' गच्छति 'उपरि' च दशा. (Me. 112); 'गृहाभिमुखं' प्रतस्थे (H. 4); मदोद्धताः 'प्रत्यनिलं' विचेरुः (Ku. III. 31).

(3) *Motion from* a place, answering to the question, 'whence;' 'from what' (the general sense of the ablative); यदि मे 'दर्शनपथात्' नापयाति (K. 132); 'वनस्पतिभ्यः' कुसुमान्याहरत (S'. 4); 'कुतः' इदं सौधमागतं (D. K. II 5).

Obs. The general senses of the ablative, except *cause* or *motive*, are expressed by this relation ;

'तीक्ष्णात्' उद्विजते (Mu. 3); 'दिवाकरात्' अंधकारं रक्षति (Ku. I. 12).

Adjuncts of Manner.

§ **372.** Adjuncts of *mode* or *manner* specify the following relations:—

(1) *Manner* or *mode* of an action (how);

चन्द्रापीडः 'सविनयं' अवादीत् (K. 134); माधवः 'सलज्जं' अधोमुखस्तिष्ठति (Mál. 1); को वा दुर्जनवागुरासु पतितः 'क्षेमेण' यातः पुमान् (P. I. 2); तदिदं 'कणशो' विकीर्यते (K. IV. 27); 'त्वरितं' अपसर्पतां तरुगहनेन (U. 4); अथवा 'कथं' भवान् मन्यते (M. 1); 'अयत्नेनैव' उपहासास्पदतामीश्वरो नयति जनं (K. 151); 'प्रकृत्या यद्वक्रं' (S'. 1);

(2) *Degree*;

तमवेक्ष्य सा 'भृशं' रुरोद (Ku. IV. 26); स राज्यं गुरुणा दत्तं प्रतिपद्य 'अधिकं' बभौ (R. IV. 1.); 'यावच्छक्यं' सुहृदसवो रक्षणीयाः (K. 151).

Obs. The ablative of comparison may be brought under this head;

'मोहात्' प्रबोधः कष्टतरोभूत् (R. XIV. 56); गृहं 'कांतारात्' अतिरिच्यते (P. IV. 1).

(3) *Instrument of an action*;

संचूर्णयामि 'गदया' न सुयोधनोरू (Ve. 1); कच्चित् 'पथा' संचरते सुराणां (R. XIII. 19); विसृजति 'हिमगर्भैर्मयूखैः' अग्निमिन्दुः (S'. 3).

Obs. The instrumental denoting the 'agent' of an action may be considered under this head for all practical purposes;

जनहितकर्ता त्यज्यते 'पार्थिवेन' (P. I. 2); 'त्वया' 'चंद्रमसा' च अतिसंधीयते कामिजनसार्थः (S'. 3); इदं 'अशरणैः' अद्याप्येवं रुद्यते (U. 3).

Or, it may be put under the subject, being regarded as the *agent* of the action.

(4) *Attendant circumstances;*

'त्वया सह' निवत्स्यामि (U. 2); रत्नं समागच्छतु 'काञ्चनेन' (R. VI. 79); 'जटाभिः' तापसः (भवति or ज्ञायते); 'महत्या सेनया' निर्जगाम; स्मरः क्षणमप्युत्सहते न 'मां विना' (Ku. IV. 36).

Adjuncts of Cause and Effect.

§ **373.** Adverbial adjuncts of this sort specify these relations:–

(1) The *ground, reason,* or *motive* of an action, (the senses conveyed by the instrumental and ablative);

'दौर्मंत्र्यात्' नृपतिर्विनश्यति (Bh. II. 42); 'भर्तृगतचिन्तया' आत्मानमपि नैषा विभावयति (S'. 4); 'आवेगस्खलितया गत्या' प्रभ्रष्टं मे पुष्पभाजनं (*ibid*); कापुरुषः 'स्वल्पकेनापि' तुष्यति (P. I. 1); लज्जेहं 'अनेन प्रागल्भ्येन' (K. 187); 'त्वया' जगन्ति पुण्यानि (U. 1); नाथवन्तः 'त्वया' लोकाः (*ibid*);

(2) The final *cause* or *purpose* of an action, as indicated by the dative case and the infinitive mood;

'समिदाहरणाय' प्रस्थिता वयं (S'. 1); श्रयति बहुशो 'मृत्यवे' चंद्रपादान् (Mál. 3); प्रवर्ततां 'प्रकृतिहिताय' पार्थिवः (S'. 7); 'अमीषां प्राणानां कृते' किं नास्माभिर्व्यवसितं (Bh. III. 36); तद्गच्छ 'सिद्धयै' (Ku. III. 18); 'लोकान्दग्धुं' तत्तपोऽलं (Ku. II. 56); यावद्यते 'साधयितुं तदर्थं' (R. V. 25); छेत्तुं 'वज्रमणीन्' शिरीषकुसुमप्रान्तेन संनह्यते (Bh. II. 6).

(3) *Condition, Concession* ;

'तथापि' घटिष्ये (M. 1); मन्दा हताः 'पश्यतो राक्षसस्य' (Mu. 3).

§ **374.** The particles considered in Lessons 21—28 are some of them, of a purely enclitic or exclamatory character, such as, एव, खलु, किल, हंत, अहो, बत, ननं, नाम. They may be either left out in analysis, or may be considered as adjuncts of *manner*.

§ **375.** The predicate may be further enlarged by a combination of two or more of the four circumstances above mentioned ; and these adjuncts may be enlarged by other adjuncts in any of the ways specified in § § 353-6:—

'दिष्ट्या' 'धर्मपत्नीसमागमेन' 'पुत्रमुखदर्शनेन' चायुष्मान्वर्धते (S'. 7) ; अयं च 'मन्दाकिनीचित्रकूटवनविहारे' 'सीतादेवीमुद्दिश्य' रघुपतेः श्लोकः (U. 6); 'नियतं' 'स्वयमेव' इयं 'अतिविनीततया' 'कतिपयैरेव दिवसैः' कुमारमाराधयिष्यति (K. 101); 'प्रत्यूषे' 'उत्थाय' 'तेनैव क्रमेण' 'अनवरतप्रयाणकैः' 'प्रतिप्रयाणकं उपचीयमानेन सेनासमुदायेन' जर्जरयन्वसुंधरां प्रातिष्ठत । (K. 118); 'अथ' राजवाहनः 'पुष्पोद्भवेन

सह' 'स्वमंदिरमुपेत्य' 'सादरं' 'बालचंद्रिकामुखेन' 'निजवल्लभायै' 'संगमोपायं वेदयित्वा' कौतुकाकृष्टहृदयः अतिष्ठत् (D. K. I. 5).

Analysis of Simple Sentences.

§ 376. In analysing simple sentences the manner of proceeding is as follows :—

1. First set down the *subject* of the sentence.
2. Then set down the *enlargements* or *attributive adjuncts* of the *subject*.
3. Give the *Predicate*.
4. State the *object*, if the Predicate be a transitive verb.
5. State the *enlargements of the object*.
6. Lastly, state the *adverbial adjuncts* of the Predicate.

Examples.

(1) विश्वंभरात्मजा देवी राज्ञा त्यक्ता महावने ।
प्राप्तप्रसवमात्मानं गंगादेव्यां विमुञ्चति ॥ (U. 7)

(2) एवं क्रमेण समारूढयौवनारंभं परिसमाप्तसकलकलाविज्ञानमवगम्यानुमोदितमाचार्यैश्चन्द्रापीडमानेतुं राजा बलाधिकृतं बलाहकनामानं बहुतुरगबलपदातिपरिवृतं प्राहिणोत् । (K. 77)

(3) पौरस्त्यानेवमाक्रामंस्तांस्ताञ्जनपदाञ्जयी ।
प्राप तालीवनश्याममुपकंठं महोदधेः । (R. IV. 34)

(4) पुराणस्य कवेस्तस्य चतुर्मुखसमीरिता ।
प्रवृत्तिरासीच्छब्दानां चरितार्था चतुष्टयी । (Ku. II. 17.)

(5) एवंगते मंत्रिणि राजनि च कामवृत्ते चन्द्रपालितोऽभ्येत्य विविधाभिः क्रीडाभिर्विहारभद्रमात्मसादकरोत् । (D. K. II. 8)

(6) कौशिकेन स किल क्षितीश्वरो
राममध्वरविघातशान्तये ।
काकपक्षधरमेत्य याचितः (R. XI. 1)

(7) धिक् सानुजं कुरुपतिं (Ve. 3)

Form of Analysis.

Subject.	Enlargements of subject.	Predicate.	Object.	Enlargements of object.	Adverbial adjuncts of Predicate.
I. देवी.	विश्वंभरात्मजा (noun in app.), राज्ञा महावने त्यक्ता (adj.)	विमुञ्चति.	आत्मानं	प्राप्तप्रसवं	गंगादेव्यां (*place.*)
I. राजा.		प्राहिणोत्	बलाधिकृतं	बहुतुरंगबलपदातिपरिवृतं (*adj.*), बलाहकनामानं	एवं क्रमेण समा-विज्ञानमवगम्य (*time.*), आचार्यैरनुमोदितं चन्द्रापीडमानेतुं (*purpose.*)
III. जयी.	तांस्तान् पौरस्त्यान् जनपदानेवमाक्रामन्. part. with object.	प्राप	उपकंठं	तालीवनश्यामं (adj. comp.), महोदधेः gen. of relation.	
IV. प्रवृत्तिः	शब्दानां, चतुष्टयी, तस्य पुराणस्य कवेश्चतुर्मुखसमीरिता (*a*)	चरितार्था आसीत्			
V. चंद्रपालितः		आत्मसात् अकरोत्	विहारभद्रं		एवं अभ्येत्य (*time*) विविधाभिः क्रीडाभिः (*means.*)
VI. क्षितीश्वरः कौशिकेन (agent)	स pron. adj.	याचितः	रामं (Secondary obj.)	काकपक्षधरं	एत्य (*time*), किल (*manner*), अध्वरविघातशांतये (*purpose.*)
VII. कुरुपतिः	सानुजः	धिक्=निंद्यः			

THE COMPLEX SENTENCE.

§ **377.** A complex sentence, while consisting of one principal subject and predicate, contains two or more finite verbs.

'यस्यार्थाः' तस्य मित्राणि (H. 1); 'इतश्चेतश्च निर्गतो युवराजः इति' आकर्ण्य आचकम्पे मेदिनी (K. 113).

The part containing the principal subject and predicate is called the *principal* clause, and the other part the *subordinate* clause.

§ **378.** Subordinate clauses are of three kinds:—the *noun clause*, the *adjective clause*, and the *adverbial clause*.

Strictly speaking, a complex sentence is only a simple sentence in an enlarged form; the noun clause being representative of the *noun*, the adjective clause of the *adjective*, and the adverbial clause of the *adverb* or extension of the predicate.

The Noun clause.

§ **379.** The noun clause occupies the place of the noun; that is it may be the (1) *subject* or (2) *object* of the principal predicate; (3) it may be in apposition to some noun in the principal clause; or (4) it may be the object of some verbal form in the principal clause:—

(1) 'अयं पुनरविरुद्धः प्रकार इति' वृद्धेभ्यः श्रूयते (U. 4.) (Subject of श्रूयते); 'स स पापादृते तासां दुष्यन्तः' इति घुष्यतां (S'. 6.), (subject of घुष्यतां).

(2) प्रकाशं निर्गतस्तावदवलोकयामि 'कियदवशिष्टं रजन्या इति' (S'. 4) (object of अवलोकयामि).

(3) 'अप्रतिष्ठे रघुज्येष्ठे का प्रतिष्ठा कुलस्य नः' । इति दुःखेन तप्यन्ते त्रयो नः पितरोपरे ॥ (U. 5) (in apposition to दुःखेन); तस्य कदाचित् चिन्ता समुत्पन्ना यदर्थोत्पत्युदुपायाश्चिन्तनीयाः (P. I. 1) (in apposition to चिन्ता).

(4) 'तथापि सुहृदा सुहृदसन्मार्गप्रवृत्तो यावच्छक्तितो निवारणीय इति' मनसा अवधार्य अब्रवम् (K. 155) (object of अवधार्य).

§ **380.** Noun clauses are principally denoted by इति, or introduced by यथा, यद्, with or without इति at the end.

अकथितोपि ज्ञायत एव 'यथायं तपोवनस्याभोग' इति (S'. 1); सत्योयं जनप्रवादो यत्संपत्संपदमनुबध्नातीति (K. 73); अविज्ञातमदनवृत्तान्ता 'क गच्छामि इति' नाज्ञासिषं (K. 147).

Obs. Sometimes इति is not used;

कथय 'सत्संगतिः पुंसां किं न करोति' (Bh. II. 28)

एतत्कल्याणाभिनिवेशिनः श्रुतिविषयमापतितमेव 'यथा विबुधसद्मन्यप्सरसो नाम कन्यकाः सन्ति' (K. 136).

The Adjective Clause.

§ **381.** An adjective clause is used to qualify a noun or pronoun, and is of the nature of an adjective. It is introduced by some forms of the relative pronoun यद् (यावत्, यादृश &c.).

An adjective clause may be used:—

(1) *With the subject*; 'यदालोके सूक्ष्मं' व्रजति सहसा तद्विपुलतां (S'. 1) तत्तस्य किमपि द्रव्यं 'यो हि यस्य प्रियो जनः' (U. 2) 'अहेतुः पक्षपातो यः' तस्य नास्ति प्रतिक्रिया (U. 5) (qualifying तस्य the adjunct of the subject).

(2) *With the object*; 'यस्यागमः केवलजीविकायै' तं ज्ञानपण्यं वणिजं वदन्ति (M. 1); स तावदभिषेकान्ते स्नातकेभ्यो ददौ वसु। यावत्तेषां समाप्येरन् यज्ञाः पर्याप्तदक्षिणाः ॥ (R. XVII. 17).

(3) *With adjuncts of the predicate*; 'युगांतकालप्रतिसंहृतात्मनो जगन्ति यस्यां सविकाशमासत'। तनौ ममूस्तत्र न कैटभद्विषस्तपोधनाभ्यागमसंभवा मुदः॥ (S'i. I. 23) (qualifying तनौ the adjunct of ममुः)

Obs. Mark the position of the adjective clause. It either stands *before* or *after* the principal clause, and not where '*who*,' '*which*', '*where*' &c. stand in English.

§ **382.** Adjective clauses are often expressed by compounds of the character of the *adjective, i. e.*, inflectional and appositional Tatpurusha and Bahuvrîhi; and also by participles (past, potential passive, and perfect);

तत्रान्दिनीं सुवृत्तां नामैतस्मात् द्वीपादागतो रत्नोद्भवो नाम रमणीयगुणालयो भ्रांतभूव-

लयो व्यवहारी उपयेमे (D. K. I. 1.), where आगत: and भ्रान्तभूवलय: represent the adjective clauses (यो द्वीपादागच्छत् and यो भूवलयं बभ्राम).

The Adverbial Clause.

§ **383.** An adverbial clause is the equivalent of an adverb, and modifies the verb. It occupies the place, and follows the construction, of an adverb, and like it, specifies the conditions of time, place manner, and cause and effect.

§ **384.** Adverbial clauses of *time* specify an event which takes place after, or at the same time with, that which is expressed in the principal clause.

सत्वरं निवेदय 'यावद् दंष्ट्रान्तर्गतो न भवसि' (P. I. 8); अत्रैव तावद्रथं स्थापय; 'यावदवतरामि' (S'. 1); 'यदा हर: पार्वतीं परिणेष्यति' तदा स्मरं स्वेन वपुषा नियोजयिष्यति (Ku. IV. 42.): 'यावदसौ पांथ: सरसि स्नातुं प्रविशति' तावन्महापंके निमग्न: (H. 1).

Obs. Adverbial clauses of time are often contracted by changing the particle and verb into a participle, or by using the locative absolute construction.

§ **385.** Adverbial clauses denoting *place* show only one relation, *i. e. rest in or motion to* a place.

'यत्र यत्र धूम:' तत्र तत्र वह्नि:.

§ **386.** Adverbial clauses relating to *manner* are used to denote:—

(1) *Likeness* or *analogy*, as expressed by इव, यथा (correl. तथा, तद्वत्); as, पुत्रं लभस्वात्मगुणानुरूपं 'भवन्तमीड्यं भवत: पिता इव' (अलभत) (R. V. 34); आसीदियं दशरथस्य गृहे 'यथा श्री:' (अस्ति) (U. 4); 'यथा काष्टं च काष्टं च समेयातां महोदधौ समेत्य च व्यपेयातां' तद्वत् भूतसमागम: (H. 4).

Obs. The clauses introduced by यथा or इव are often contracted.

(2) *Degree* or *relation* (equality, intensity, &c.)

'वितरति गुरु: प्राज्ञे विद्यां यथैव' तथा जडे (वितरति) (U. 2); 'यथा यथा अंबुधाराभिराहन्यते' तथा तथा स्फुरति मदनपावक: (K. 252).

§ **387.** Adverbial clauses of *manner* are often expressed by adjectival or Bahuvrîhi compounds used adverbially ; as,

राजा 'सविलक्षस्मितं' आह='यथा विलक्षस्मितं स्यात्' तथा आह; 'उद्द्योतिताम्बरदिगंतरं अंशुजालैः' शक्तिः पपात हृदि तस्य महासुरस्य (Ku. XVII. 51).

§ **388.** Adverbial clauses relating to *cause* and *effect* are used to denote the following relations:—

(1) *Ground* or *reason* (because, since, as) ;

'वत्से कठोरगर्भेति' नानीतासि (U. 1); ममापि तर्हि धर्मतस्तथैव 'यतः प्रियवयस्य इत्यात्थ' (U. 5); इत्यादि नन्विह निरर्थकमेव 'यस्मात्कामो जृंभितगुणः' (Mál. 1); कमपरमवशं न विप्रकुर्युः 'विभुमपि तं यदमी स्पृशन्ति भावाः' (Ku. VI. 95); कच्चिद्भर्तुः स्मरसि रसिके 'त्वं हि तस्य प्रियेति' (Me. 88).

(2) *Condition* or *supposition* ;

श्रूयतां 'यदि कुतूहलं' (K. 49); 'अथ तु वेत्सि शुचि व्रतमात्मनः' पतिगृहे तव दास्यमपि क्षमं (S'. 5); 'जात्या चेदवध्योहं ' एषा सा जातिः परित्यक्ता (Ve. 3).

(3) *Concession*:

'काममननुरूपमस्या वपुषो वल्कलं' न पुनरलंकारश्रियं न पुष्यति (S'. 1); 'नेत्रे पुनर्यद्यपि रक्तनीले ' तथापि सौभाग्यगुणः स एव (U. 6).

(4) *Purpose ;*

दोषं तु मे कञ्चित् कथय 'येन स प्रतिविधीयेत' (U. 1); तदागच्छ यथा दर्शयामि (P. I. 8); भो धीरं गच्छ 'मा खलु (lest) तत्रभवती धारिणी विसंवदिष्यति' (M. 1.); 'अस्य शरीरस्य मा विनाशो भूदिति' मयेदमुत्क्षिप्य समानीतं (K. 320).

(5) *Consequence, result;*

कुमार तथा प्रयतेथाः 'यथा नोपहस्यसे जनैः' (K. 110); स ऋत्विजस्तथानर्च 'यथा साधारणीभूतं नामास्य धनदस्य च' (R. XVII. 80); सा वेणुलतामादाय सभाकुट्टिममाजघान 'येन सकलमेव तद्राजकं तदभिमुखमासीत्' (K. 10).

§ **389.** A complex sentence may be enlarged by repeating the noun, adjective, or adverbial clauses, in which case the sentence will strictly speaking, be *compound*, each member of which is *complex*;

'कथं स त्वया दृष्टः' 'किं किमभिहितासि तेन ' 'कियन्तं कालमवस्थितासि तत्र' 'कियदनुसरत्रस्मानसावागतः' इति पुनः पुनः पर्यपृच्छम् (K. 150); 'यस्य चेन्द्रियाणि सन्ति' 'यः पश्यति वा' 'श्रुतमवधारयति वा' स खलूपदेशमर्हति (K. 156).

§ **390.** Again, two or more of the subordinate kinds of clauses may be used in the same complex sentence;

क्रोधं प्रभो संहर संहरेति (noun) यावद्गिरः खे मरुतां चरन्ति । (adv.) तावत्स

वह्निर्भवनेत्रजन्मा भस्मावशेषं मदनं चकार ॥ (Ku. III. 72); राष्ट्रमुख्यमाहूयाख्यातवान्। योसौ अनंतसीरः प्रहारवर्मणः पक्ष इति (adv.) निनाशयिषितः (adj.) सोपि पितरि मे प्रकृतिस्थे किमिति नश्येतेति (noun) (D. K. II. 3.).

Particles used to introduce subordinate clauses:—

- *Noun clause.* — इति, यथा, यद् with or without इति.
- *Adjective clause.* — Forms of यद्.
- *Adverbial Clause.*
  - *Time.* — यदा, यावत्, यावन्न (followed by तावत्), यदा यदा.
  - *Place.* — यत्र, यत्र यत्र.
  - *Manner* — इव, यथा (followed by तथा or तद्वत्) यथैव (तथैव), यथा यथा.
  - *Cause & Effect.* —
    (1) इति यतः (fol. by ततः), यद्, यथा (fol. by तथा), हि;
    (2) यदि (fol. by तर्हि, तद्, ततः), चेद्, अथ.
    (3) यद्यपि, कामं (तु, पुनः).
    (4) येन, इति, यथा, मा (with future or imperative).
    (5) यथा, येन.

Analysis of Complex Sentences.

§ 391. Complex sentences are to be analysed in the first place as if each subordinate clause were a single word or phrase. When this is done, the subordinate clauses may be separately analysed, like simple sentences.

Examples.

(1) अथ स निःश्वस्य लज्जाविशीर्यमाणविरलाक्षरं सखे कपिंजल विदितवृत्तांतोपि किं मां पृच्छसीति कृच्छ्रेण शनैः शनैरवदत्। (K. 155)

(2) एष नामानुगृहीतः यः शूलादवतार्य हस्तिस्कन्धे प्रतिष्ठापितः (S'. 6)

(3) अन्वेषमाणश्च यथा यथा नापश्यं तं तथा तथा सुहृत्स्नेहकातरेण मनसा तत्तदशोभनमाशंकमानो निपुणमितस्ततो दत्तदृष्टिः सुचिरं व्यचरम् (K. 152)

Form of Analysis.

Subject.	Enlargements of subject.	Predicate.	Object.	Enlargements of object.	Adverbial adjuncts of Predicate.
I. स	,,	अवदत्	सखे कपिंजल ...पृच्छसीति (*a*)	,,	अथ (*time*), निःश्वस्य (*time*), लज्जाविशीर्यमाण-विरलाक्षरं (*manner*), कृच्छ्रेण शनैः शनैः (*manner*)
(*a*) (त्वं) सखे कपिंजल (to be taken with subject).	आदितवृत्तांतोपि (adj.)	पृच्छसि		मां (indir.) किं (dir.)	
II एष	यः—प्रतिष्ठापितः (*a*)	अनुगृहीतः			नाम (*manner*)
(*a*) यः		प्रतिष्ठापितः			हस्तिस्कंधे (*place*) शूलादवतार्य (*time.*)
III (अहं)	सुहृत्स्नेह-शंकमानः (part. adj.) निपुणं इतस्ततो दत्तदृष्टिः (adj.)	व्यचरम्			तथातथा (*degree.*) यथायथा अन्वेषमाणो मापश्यं तं (*a*) (*degree.*) सुचिरं (*time.*)
(*a*) (अहं)	अन्वेषमाणः (part. adj.)	अपश्यं (न)	तं		यथायथा (*degree*)

THE COMPOUND SENTENCE.

§ **392.** A compound sentence contains two or more sentences, simple or complex, which are co-ordinate to each other.

The members may (1) be *simple* sentences, or (2) some may be *simple* and some *complex*, or (3) all may be *complex*;

(1) तथाप्येष प्राणः स्फुरति न तु पापो विरमति । U. 6)
मनो निष्ठाशून्यं भ्रमति च किमप्यालिखति च ॥ (Mál. 1)
(each being a simple-sentence).

(2) दाक्षिण्यं नाम बिंबोष्ठि बैंबिकानां कुलव्रतम् ।
तन्मे दीर्घाक्षि ये प्राणास्ते त्वदाशानिबंधनाः ॥ (M. 4).
(the second member being a complex sentence).

(3) यदि यथा वदति क्षितिपस्तथा त्वमसि किं पितुरुत्कुलया त्वया ।
अथ तु वेत्सि शुचि व्रतमात्मनः पतिकुले तव दास्यमपि क्षमम् ॥ (S'. 5.)
(both members being complex sentences).

In these examples the separate sentences are not in any away *dependent* upon each other. Either assertion might have been made independently of the other, while a complex sentence cannot be broken up into sentences having independent meaning.

§ **393.** There are three principal relations in which the parts of a compound sentence may stand to each other: (1) *Cumulative relation*, as expressed by the cumulative conjunctions च, तथा, अपिच &c.; in which two or more assertions are coupled together; (2) *adversative relation*, as expressed by the adversative conjunctions वा, तु, पुनः, परंतु etc., in which the second sentence is placed in some kind of opposition to the preceding; and (3) *Illative relation*, as expressed by the illative conjunctions अतः, तद्, ततः, in which an effect or consequence is said to be produced from what precedes.

Cumulative Relation.

§ **394.** The coupling of assertions together in the cumulative relation may take place in three different senses:—

(1) When equal stress is laid upon the assertions;

तटस्थः स्वानर्थान् घटयति 'च' मौनं ' च ' भजते (Mál. 1).

त्रिलोचनस्तां प्रतिगृहीतुमुपचक्रमे 'च' पुष्पधन्वा धनुष्यमोघं बाणं स ... ' (Ku. III. 66).

तृणमिव वने शून्ये (सा) त्यक्ता न 'वाप्य ' नुशोचिता (U. 3).

(2) When greater stress is laid upon the second clause;

न केवलं तातनियोग एव 'अस्ति मे सोदरस्नेहोऽप्येतेषु' (S'. 1)
पुण्यानि नामग्रहणान्यपि महामुनीनां 'किं पुनर्दर्शनानि ' (K. 33).

(3) When there is a progressive rise of the ideas;

उदेति पूर्वं कुसुमं 'ततः' फलं (S'. 5);
जगज्जीर्णारण्यं भवति हि विकल्पव्युपरमे
कुकूलानां राशौ 'तदनु' हृदयं पच्यत इव । (U. 6).

Obs. Several co-ordinate sentences follow one another in this relation, being merely placed side by side, without any connecting links, the sense of which, however is implied;

शुश्रूषस्व गुरून् कुरु प्रियसखीवृत्तिं सपत्नीजने...
भूयिष्ठं भव दक्षिणा परिजने भाग्येष्वनुत्सेकिनी (S'. 4)
(here there are four assertions);

जाड्यं धियो 'हरति ' ' सिंचति ' वाचि सत्यं
मानोन्नतिं 'दिशति ' पापं 'अपाकरोति' ।
चेतः 'प्रसादयति ' दिक्षु 'तनोति ' कीर्तिं (सत्संगतिः) (Bh. II. 23)
दारिद्र्याद्ध्रियमेति ह्रीपरिगतः प्रभ्रश्यते तेजसो
निस्तेजाः परिभूयते परिभवान्निर्वेदमापद्यते ।
निर्विण्णः शुचमेति शोकपिहितो बुद्ध्या परित्यज्यते
निर्बुद्धिः क्षयमेत्यहो निधनता सर्वापदामास्पदं ॥ (Mk. 1)

Adeversative Relation.

§ 395. The adversative relation is expressed in three ways:—

(1) By means of the exclusive conjunctions, which imply the exclusion of the first circumstauce:

प्रज्ञाहीनोयं राजा 'नोचेत्' नीतिशास्त्रकथाकौमुदीं वागुल्काभिः कथं तिमिरयति।
(H. 3)

व्यक्तं नास्ति कथं 'अन्यथा' वासंत्यपि तां न पश्येत्। (U. 3)
अद्यापि हरकोपवह्निस्त्वयि ज्वलति। 'अन्यथा' त्वं भस्मावशेषाः कथमित्थमुष्णः।
(S'. 3)

(2) By means of alternative conjuctions; वा-वा, किं-अथवा, उत आहो, or आहोस्वित्;

तदेषा भवतः कांता त्यजैनां 'वा' गृहाण 'वा'। (S'. 5);
सूतो 'वा' सूतपुत्रो 'वा' यो 'वा' को 'वा' भवाम्यहं। (Ve. 3);
किं धर्मोपदेशांगमिदं 'उत' मोक्षप्राप्तिरियं आहोस्विदन्यः कश्चिन्नियमप्रकारः।
(K. 150).

(3) By means of arrestive conjuctions तु, किंतु, परं (तु), पुनः तथापि; and (sometimes) केवलं;

दैवायत्तं कुले जन्म मदायत्तं 'तु' पौरुषं (Ve. 3); (अयं कथाप्रविभागः) प्रणीतो न 'तु' प्रकाशितः (U. 4); सखे पुंडरीक सुविदितमेतन्मम 'किंतु' इदमेव पृच्छामि (K. 155); न च न परिचितो न चाप्यगम्यः चकितमुपैमि 'तथापि' पार्श्वमस्य (M. 1); लौकिकानां हि साधूनामर्थं वागनुवर्तते। ऋषीणां 'पुनः' आद्यानां वाचमर्थोनुधावति॥ (U. 1); अनुदिवसं परिहीयसे अंगैः 'केवलं' लावण्यमयी छाया त्वां न मुञ्चति (S'. 3).

Illative Relation.

§ **396.** The illative relation is expressed by words or expressions like अतः, तस्मात्, ततः, तद्, अनेन हेतुना, एवं च तेन हि;

सतीमपि ज्ञातिकुलैकसंश्रयां भर्तृमतीं जनोन्यथा विशंकते 'अतः' प्रमदा स्वबंधुभिः परिणेतुः समीपे इष्यते (S'. 5) भो उपस्थितं नयनमधु संनिहिता च मक्षिका। 'तद्' अप्रमत्त इदानीं पश्य (M. 2); जनकोद्य गतो विदेहान्। 'ततो' विमनसो देव्याः परिसांत्वनाय नरेन्द्रो वासगृहं विशति (U. 1); अत्यद्भुतादपि गुणातिशयात्प्रियोसि 'तस्मात्' सखा त्वमसि (U. 5); मध्यस्था नौ गुणदोषतः परिच्छेत्तुमर्हति । 'तेन हि' प्रस्तूयतां विवादवस्तु (M. 1)

§ **397.** Very often in Sanskrit, as in English, when the coordinate parts of a compound sentence have the same subject, the same predicate, or any other part in common, the common part is not repeated, and thus the sentence is *contracted*;

(1) तटस्थः स्वानर्थान् 'घटयति च मौनं च भजते' (Mál. 1);
हृदयमशरणं मे पक्ष्मलाक्ष्याः कटाक्षैः
'अपहृतं' 'अपविद्धं' 'पीतं' 'उन्मूलितं' च (*ibid.*)

(2) दिष्ट्या न केवलं 'उत्संगः' चिरात् 'मनोरथोपि' मे 'पूर्णः' (U. 4)
न मां त्रातुं 'तातः' 'प्रभवति' न 'चांबा' न 'भवती' (Mál. 2)

Classification of particles used to connect co-ordinate sentences.

Cumulative Relation.	(1) च, च-च, तथाच, अपि, अपिच, अपरंच, अन्यच्च. (2) केवलं-अपि, किमुत, किंपुनः. (3) अथ, तदनु, पूर्वं-ततः अनंतरं-ततः परं, ततश्च अनंतरंच.
Adversative Relation.	(1) अन्यथा, न (नो) चेत्. (2) वा, वा-वा, न वा. (3) तु, किंतु, परं (तु), तथापि, पुनः केवलं.
Illative Relation.	तद्, तस्मात्, अतः, ततः, तथा, एवं च, एवं, तेन हि.

Analaysis of Compound Sentences.

§ **398.** In analysing a compound sentence first indicate the relation existing between the several co-ordinate sentences, and then the latter, according as they are simple or complex, may be separately analyzed.

Examples.

(1) वर्ष वा गर्ज वा शक्र मुंच वा शतशोशनिम् (Mk. 5)

(2) उचितः प्रणयो वरं विहंतुं बहवः खंडनहेतवो हि दृष्टाः । उपचारविधिर्मनस्विनीनां न तु पूर्वाभ्यधिकोपि भावशून्यः ॥ (M. 3)

(3) दृष्टा खलु मया तत्रभवत्या मालविकायाः प्रियसखी बकुलावलिका श्राविता च तमर्थं भवता यः संदिष्टः (M. 3)

I. शक्र (त्वं) वर्ष वा (A). Principal sentence.

(त्वं) गर्ज वा (B.) Principal, co-ordinate to A.

(त्वं) शतशोऽशनिं मुंच वा (C) Principal, co-ordinate to A and B.

The relation is adversative.

	Subject	Predicate	Object	Adverbial adjunct
A	(त्वं) शक्र	वर्ष (वा)		
B	(त्वं)	गर्ज (वा)		
C	(त्वं)	मुंच (वा)	अशनिं	शतशः (*manner.*)

II. उचितः प्रणयो विहंतुं वरं बहवः खंडनहेतवो दृष्टाः हि (A)
न तु पूर्वाभ्यधिकोपि भावशून्यो मनस्विनानामुपचारविधिः वरं (B)

The relation is *adversative* (arrestive.).

Analysis of (A) which is a complex sentence.

Subject	Predicate	Object	Adverbial adjuncts
A प्रणयः	वरं		विहंतुं (purpose)
(उचितः adj.)			बहवः दृष्टाः (*a*) *reason*
(*a*) खंडनहेतवः			
बहवः (adj.)	दृष्टाः		हि (*reason*).
B उपचारविधिः			
मनस्विनीनां (gen.)			
पूर्वाभ्यधिकोपि न (वरं)			
भावशून्यः (adj.)			

III. The first is a simple sentence. The second is a complex sentence, which may be analysed as above. The relation is *cumulative.*

Miscellaneous Examples for practice.

Analyse the following sentences, according to the methods before explained and illustrated, stating whether they are *simple*, *complex*, or *compound.*

1. महत्येव प्रत्युषे दास्याः पुत्रैः शकुनिलुब्धकैर्वनग्रहणकोलाहलेन प्रतिबोधितोऽस्मि। (S'. 2)

2. कुतो धर्मक्रियाविघ्नः सतां रक्षितरि त्वयि। (S'. 5)

3. प्रमाणादधिकस्यापि गंडश्याममदच्युतेः।
पदं मूर्ध्नि समाधत्ते केसरी मत्तदंतिनः॥ (P. I.)

4. लघुहृदयां मां लोकः कलयिष्यतीति निह्नक्रिया मया नाकलितम्। (K. 197)

5. दर्शनादारभ्य शरीरस्याप्ययमेव प्रभुः किमुत भवनस्य विभवस्य वा। (K. 196)

6. स चानुयुक्तो धूर्तः सविनयमावेदयत्। विदितमेव खलु वो यथाहं युष्मदाज्ञया पितृवनमभिरक्ष्य तदुपजीवी प्रतिवसामि। (D. K. II. 6)

7. यदा किंचित् किंचिद् बुधजनसकाशादवगतं।
तदा मूर्खोऽस्मीति ज्वर इव मदो मे व्यपगतः। (Bh. II. 8)

8. अहमतिमृदुनि पुलिनवति सरस्तीरेऽवरोप्य सस्पृहं निर्वर्णयंस्तां मत्प्राणैकवल्लभां राजकन्यां कंदुकावतीमलक्षयम्। (D. K. II. 6)

9. एवमेतत्। किंतु न कदाचिदार्यस्य निष्प्रयोजना प्रवृत्तिरित्यस्ति नः प्रश्नावकाशः। (Mu. 3)

10. विचिंतयन्ती यमनन्यमानसा तपोधनं वेत्सि न मामुपस्थितम्। स्मरिष्यति त्वां न स बोधितोऽपि सन् कथां प्रमत्तः प्रथमं कृतामिव॥ (S'. 4)

11. अये महाराजेति निष्प्रणयमामन्त्रणपदं सौमित्रिमात्रे च बाष्पस्खलिताक्षरः कुशलप्रश्नः। तथा मन्ये विदितसीतावृत्तान्तेयमिति॥ (U. 3)

12. वपुषु यद्बालमृगाक्षि मृग्यते तदस्ति किं व्यस्तमपि त्रिलोचने (Ku. V. 72)

13. तद् ब्रूत वत्साः किमितः प्रार्थयध्वं समागताः।
मयि सृष्टिर्हि लोकानां रक्षा युष्मास्ववस्थिता॥ (Ku. II. 28)

14. कामं भवान् प्रकृत्यैव धीरः पित्रा च महता प्रयत्नेन समारोपितसंस्कारः। तथापि भवद्गुणसंतोषो मामेवं मुखरीकृतवान् (K. 109)

15. वध्ये मयि मत्तहस्ती मृत्युविजयो नाम हिंसाविहारी राजगोपुरोपरितलाधिरूढस्य पश्यतः उत्तमामात्यस्य शासनाज्जनकंठरवद्विगुणितघंटारवो मंडलितहस्तकांडं समभ्यधावत् (D. K. II. 4)

16. यज्ञोपवीतं नाम
अमौक्तिकमसौवर्णं ब्राह्मणानां विभूषणम्।
देवतानां पितॄणां च भागो येन प्रदीयते॥ (Mk. 10)

17. अत्रान्तरे ब्राह्मणेन मृतं पुत्रमुत्क्षिप्य राजद्वारे सोरस्ताडनमब्रह्मण्यमुद्घोषितम् । ततो न राजापराधमन्तरेण प्रजास्वकालमृत्युश्चरतीत्यात्मदोषं निरूपयति करुणामये रामभद्रे सहसैवाशरीरिणी वागुदचरत् (U. 2)

18. अथ कदाचित् पिंगलको नाम सिंहः सर्वमृगपरिवृत्तः पिपासाकुल उदकग्रहणार्थं यमुनातटमवतीर्णः संजीवकस्य गंभीरतरशब्दं दूरादेवाशृणोत् । (P. I.)

19. यदि समरमपास्य नास्ति मृत्योर्भयमिति युक्तमितोऽन्यतः प्रयातुं ।
अथ मरणमवश्यमेव जंतोः किमिति मुधा मलिनं यशः कुरुध्वे ॥ (Ve. 3)

20. प्रायो गच्छति यत्र भाग्यरहितस्तत्रैव यान्त्यापदः । (Bh. II. 90)

21. यावत्स्वस्थमिदं कलेवरगृहं यावच्च दूरे जरा
आत्मश्रेयसि तावदेव विदुषा: कार्यः प्रयत्नो महान् (Bh. III. 88)

22. यथा तिरश्चीनमलातशल्यं प्रत्युप्तमन्तःसविषश्च दंशः ।
तथैव तीव्रो हृदि शोकशंकुर्मर्माणि कृन्तन्नपि किं न सोढः ॥ (U. 3)

23. परस्परविरोधिन्योरेकसंश्रयदुर्लभम् ।
संगतं श्रीसरस्वत्योर्भूतयेऽस्तु सदा सताम् ॥ (V. 5)

24. सर्वैरस्त्रैः समग्रैस्त्वमिव नृपगुणैर्दीप्यते सप्तसप्तिः (M. 2)

25. अस्त्वमर्शो मा भूद्वा । एतत्तु पृच्छामि दान्तं हि राघवं राजानं शृणुमः । स किल नात्मना दृप्यति न चाप्यस्य प्रजा ईदृशो जायन्ते तत् किमस्य मनुष्या राक्षसीं वाचं वदन्ति । (U. 5)

26. यथा नौ प्रियसखी बन्धुजनशोचनीया न भवति तथा निर्वाहय । (S'. 3)

27. अथ स विषयव्यावृत्तात्मा यथाविधि सूनवे
नृपतिककुदं दत्त्वा यूने सितातपवारणम् ।
मुनिवनतरुच्छायां देव्या तया सह शिश्रिये
गलितवयसामिक्ष्वाकूणामिदं हि कुलव्रतम् ॥ (R. III. 70)

As a further exercise the student may select sentences from the preceding Lessons, and analyse them.

LESSON II.

On the Order of Words in Sentences.

§ **399.** It has already been observed in the introductory section of Part I, that the *order* of words in a Sanskrit sentence is not a material point for consideration. In Sanskrit every word (except adverbs and particles) is inflected, and the grammatical inflexion itself shows the relation in which one word stands to another. Thus *grammatically* speaking, there is no order as such that need be much attended to. A sentence like कथमपि तत्याज वने सीतां लक्ष्मणः कठोरगर्भां may look very awkward but it is not grammatically *incorrect*. But if there is no *grammatical* order, there is a sort of *logical* sequence of ideas, which must follow one another in a paticular order. If we examine the pages of any Sanskrit prose work, we shall find that there is some order in the arrangement of words; *e. g.* first comes the subject expressed or understood, with its adjuncts, then the object, (if any), and lastly, the verb or predicate;

सा तु महाश्वेताया एव मुखमवलोकितवती (K. 307);
महीपतिस्तं विशेश्वरं सबहुमानं विससर्ज (D. K. I. 25).

Even in Kávyas and Dramatic poetry, which are aknowledged to be exempt from the rules of ordinary prose, this order is many times strictly followed;

रघूणामन्वयं वक्ष्ये (R. I. 8);

तृष्णां छिंद्धि पापे रतिं मा कृथाः (Bh. II. 77); वदनकमलकं शिशोः स्मरामि (U. 4); असिर्गात्रं गात्रं स पदि लवशस्ते विकिरतु (Mál. 5) &c.

We shall now lay down some principles regulating the *order* of words in sentences.

§ **400.** The best rule for the student to follow in arranging words in a prose sentence is this:—First place the *subject* with all its adjectives and adjectival phrases, then the *object* with its adjuncts, and lastly the *predicate* (verbal, nominal, or adjectival). Adverbs and adverbial phrases may occupy any place except the last; while conjunctions (except a few) stand first before the subject. Thus the student would give a very awkward sentence if he were to say.

'सकाशं गुरोः आशिषं राज्ञे अग्रजन्मा प्रयुज्य प्रतीयायेत्थं' instead of saying 'इत्थं राज्ञे आशिषं प्रयुज्याग्रजन्मा गुरोः सकाशं प्रतीयाय' (R. V. 35).

§ **401.** When a verse is construed and put in its prose order, the above sequence will be found to be generally observed. Take, for instance, the following verse:

अथ प्रजानामधिपः प्रभाते जायाप्रतिग्राहितगंधमाल्याम् ।
वनाय पीतप्रतिबद्धवत्सां यशोधनो धेनुमृषेर्मुमोच ॥ (R. II. 1)

The prose order will be as follows:—

अथ (conj.) यशोधनः (adj.) प्रजानां (gen.) अधिपः (subject) प्रभाते (exten. of the adjunct of object) जायाप्रतिग्राहितगंधमाल्यां (adj.) पीतप्रतिबद्धवत्सां (another adj.) ताम् ऋषेः (adjuncts of object) धेनुं वनाय गंतुं (adv.) मुमोच (predicate). Similarly अभिहंति हंत कथमेष माधवं सुकुमारकायमनवग्रहः स्मरः (Mål. 1); हंत, कथमेषोऽनवग्रहः स्मरः सुकुमारकायं माधवमभिहन्ति, or हंत एष.........कथमभिहन्ति.

The general rule may be now split into particular cases and we shall show what the positions of the several parts of speech should be relatively to one another.

§ **402.** The first principle to be learnt from the general rule is that words must be so arranged that the ideas will follow one another in their natural order, and the words in their natural connection, observing the laws of the dependence of words upon one another; in other words, the *governed* and *dependent* words generally stand before the words on which they *depend* or by which they are *governed.*

Thus an adjective and the substantive qualified by it, the transitive verb and its object, adverbs modifying verbs, prepositions and the words governed by them etc., should be kept as near as possible in a Sanskrit sentence.

§ **403.** When a sentence has a simple subject and a verb, the former stands first; रघुपतिस्तिष्ठति (U. 6). Adjectives precede the subject;

' देवो' रघुपतिस्तिष्ठति (U. 6). ' उपात्त विद्यो' ' गुरुदक्षिणार्थी ' कौत्सस्तं प्रपेदे (R. V. 1); ' अपगतश्रमः', चाभिमतं दिगन्तरमयासीत् (K. 32).

(*a*) Adjectives, of course, follow the substantives they qualify when they are used predicatively.

(*b*) When pronominal and qualitative adjectives are both used, the former usually precede; तस्यां अतिदारुणायां हतनिशायां (K. 169) 'on *that* accursed and dreadful night'; but sometimes stand after the adjectives of quality; as विचक्षणो वर्णी सः (Malli. on R. V. 19); पुना 'अनेन' पार्थिवेन सह (Malli. on R. VI. 32).

§ **404**. A noun in apposition should precede the word which it is intended to explain;

आसीदशेष नरपतिशिरःसमभ्यर्चितशासनः 'आदर्शः सर्वशास्त्राणां' 'उत्पत्तिः कुलानां' 'कुलभवनं गुणानां' राजा शूद्रको नाम (K. 5); अथ 'मीनकेतनसेनानायकेन' दक्षिणानिलेन मन्मथानलमुज्ज्वलयन् (D. K. I. 5);

§ **405.** The genitive generally stands before the word to which it relates, 'जगतः' पितरौ वंदे (R. I. 1); so

'अर्थानां' ईशिषे (Bh. III. 30).

(*a*) When the substantive is qualified by an adjective, the order is generally the adjective, genitive, and substantive: अयं अस्या देव्याः संतापः (K. 61); तस्य एवंविधस्य पद्मसरसः पश्चिमे तीरे (K. 23).

§ **406.** The vocative, should be placed at the head of a sentence; 'तात' एष बालः (D. K. II. 8); 'सखे पुंडरीक' नैतद्भवतोनुरूपं (K. 151); 'आर्यपुत्र इयमस्मि' (S'. 1).

§ **407.** The predicate (verbal or nominal) always stands last in a sentence; it *finishes* the idea intended to be expressed by a sentence, and hence, the last is its best position.

(*a*) In narratives the verb अस् '*to be*' and sometimes भू stands first, in the sense of '*there is,*' '*there was*';

'अस्ति' गोदावरीतीरे विशालः शाल्मलीतरुः (H. 1) 'अस्ति' मगधदेशशेखरीभूता पुष्पपुरी नाम नगरी (D. K. I. 1) 'अभूत्' अभूतपूर्वो राजा चिन्तामणिर्नाम (Vas. 3).

(*b*) Sometimes the predicate stands first for the sake of emphasis;

'भवेयुः' तावत्प्राणादयः पञ्च जना माध्यंदिनानां (S'. B. 371) ; 'आस्तां' तावत्सर्वमेवेदं (K. 18) ; 'उत्सर्पिणी' खलु महतां प्रार्थना (S'. 7) ; 'कृतं' त्वया रामसदृशं कर्म (U. 2.) 'विरलाः' हि तेषामुपदेष्टारः (K. 109) 'भवितव्यमेव' तेन (U. 4).

(*c*) The same happens in interrogative sentences when the interrogative particle is not used; as, जात 'अस्ति' ते माता 'स्मरसि' वा तातं (U. 4); 'स्मरसि' च तदुपान्तेष्वावयोर्वर्तनानि (U. 1)

§ **408.** Prepositions in Sanskrit—the so-called *Upasargas*—are usually prefixed to roots, and do not stand by themselves, except when they are used as कर्मप्रवचनीय (governing cases). In the latter case they follow the words they govern, according to the general law;

इति मन्दमतीन् 'प्रति' भायात् (S'. B.) ; अयोध्यां 'अनु' जलानि वहति (R. XIII. 61).

(*a*) Words like सह, ऋते, विना, अलं &c. which govern nouns or pronouns, mostly follow the words they govern.

रामेण सह, ईश्वरादृते, मां विना, संतोषायालं &c.

§ **409.** The term *indeclinable* in Sanskrit is of wider application than '*adverbs*' in English. It includes all words which are not declined ; *i. e.* adverbs, prepositions, conjunctions, particles or interjections. The several case-inflexions of nouns and pronouns—except those of the nominative and accusative cases, which serve the purpose of the subject and object of verbs, and the genitive, which expresses the relation of one word to another—may be regarded as 'adverbs' for all practical purposes. The following rules for the position of adverbs will thus apply to the case-inflexions also, which are so many 'extensions of the predicate,' showing time, place, manner or cause and effect.

§ **410.** Adverbs of time, place, manner or cause and effect, are usually placed near the words they modify ;

'हंसधवलशयनतले' निषण्णं पितरमपश्यम् (K. 92). Here तले modifies निषण्णं, and hence must be placed before it ; so 'आलोकमार्गेणैव' (adv. of cause) अपगतश्रमो मनसि (adv. of place) एवं (adv. of manner) अक-

रोद् (K. 124). 'इति मनसावधार्य' अब्रवम् (K. 155) ; 'तमवेक्ष्य' (adv. of time) सा 'भृशं' रुरोद (Ku. VI, 26). Here भृशं cannot be placed first, for it would alter the sense.

§ **411.** When adverbs modify the predicate they may stand before the subject, after the subject, or after the object (if any), but not last; अनेकवारं (time) अपरिश्लथं (manner) मां परिष्वजस्व (U. 6); प्रजानामेव भूत्यर्थं (purpose) स ताभ्यो (place) बलिमग्रहीत् (R. I. 18); सर्वं सौदामिन्यां (place) संभाव्यते (Mál 1.); दारिद्र्याद् (cause) ह्रियमेति (Mk. 1); हरिणा (agent) असुरास्तव शरव्यं कृताः (S'. 6) ; शिवाभ्यो (purpose, strictly indir. obj.) मांसबलिपिंडं अनुदिनं निशि (time) समुत्ससर्ज (K. 65); गुरौ भक्त्या मय्यनुकंपया (cause) च प्रीतास्मि (R. II. 63).

N. B. If the subject or object have any adjuncts, the adverb should be placed *after* the object to avoid ambiguity.

(*a*) The absolute clauses, being in sense adverbs of time or (sometimes) cause, are generally placed first.

'चन्द्रिकायामभिव्यक्तायां' किं दीपिकापौनरुक्त्येन (V. 3)
'युष्माकं प्रेक्षमाणानां' एनं स्मर्तव्यशेषं नयामि (Ve. 4)

Obs. Adverbs of *time* and *place* usually stand at the head of a sentence, next to the conjunctions, if any.

§ **412.** Of conjunctions, च, वा, तु, हि, चेत् never stand first, while अथवा, अथ, अपिच, किंच, usually stand first; and the correlative conjunctions यथा-तथा, यावत्-तावत्, यद्-तद्, यतः-ततः are used at the beginning in the clauses which they connect. For examples see the respective sections.

§ **413.** Of particles, the interrogatives usually stand first;

'अपि' एतत्तपोवनं; 'अपि' कुशली ते गुरुः; 'कथं' शास्त्राणां परिचयः; 'कियद्वा' वयः etc. (K. 18).

(*a*) The particles of emphasis, such as एव, नाम, किल, खलु, हि, are joined to the words which they emphasize. Particles like इव, तु, अपि are used with the words which the modify.

(*b*) Interjections, such as हा, हंत, अहह, and vocative particles, such as अहो, अये, अयि, usually head a sentence.

§ **414.** A repeated word or a word akin to the one already used in the sentence, is generally put as near that word as possible; as गुणी गुणं वेत्ति न वेत्ति निर्गुणः.

Obs. From the preceding sections it will be seen that the arrangement of words in a Sanskrit sentence is much the same as in Latin. The most general rule in Latin is that "in simple narrative, after the conjunctions comes the *subject* (nom. case), then the *governed* cases with *adverbs* and expressions of *time, place, manner, &c.* and last of all, the *verb.*" (Arnold.)

SECTION III.

On the Synthesis of Sentences.

§ **415.** Having explained the Analysis of Sanskrit sentences and laid down some principles regulating the order of words, we shall now take the student one step further—the *composition* of sentences.

He has already seen that a sentence must contain at least one subject and one predicate; that the subject or object may be enlarged by an adjective, a noun in the possessive case, a noun in apposition, by compounds, or by combining all these modes together; and that the predicate may be enlarged by circumstances of time, place, manner, and cause and effect. Let him now try to compose sentences.

Simple Sentences.

§ **416.** Take the words राम and गम्. They may be combined to form a sentence, रामो जगाम. Now the sentence रामो जगाम is in its elementary form. The subject may be thus enlarged:—

(1) दशरथस्य पुत्रः or दशरथपुत्रो रामो जगाम,

(2) कौसल्यानंदवर्धनः अखिलजनप्रियो दशरथपुत्रो etc.

(3) भरताग्रजः कौसल्यानंदवर्धनः etc. etc.

(4) भरताग्रजः कौसल्यानंदवर्धनोऽखिलजनप्रियो दशरथपुत्रो रामः ससीतालक्ष्मणो रम्याण्युपवनानि पश्यन् जगाम.

It will be seen how the last sentence has grown out of the simple elements, राम and गम्.

Ex. 1.

Frame sentences, using अर्जुन, हनुमान्, गंगा, and हरि as subjects, and enlarge them successively in the manner above indicated.

Ex. 2.

Frame sentences, using the roots कृ, वच्, पत्, रम् as predicates, and the subject enlarged in any two ways.

Ex. 3.

Take these pairs of words and write sentences enlarging the subject by an adjective and a noun, in the genitive case: शुक and ह्री, अंगना and या, सैनिक and युध्, गज and हन् *pass.* भृत्य and तड् *pass.*

Ex. 4-5

Take the sentences रावणः सीतां जहार and सारमेयोऽम्रियत, and enlarge the subject in all the ways of enlargement.

§ **417.** The predicate, if a transitive verb, is *completed* by means of an *object* which, being a noun or pronoun, may be enlarged in the same way as the *subject*; *e. g.*

अहं प्रासादमपश्यम्. Here the object may be thus enlarged अहं विशालं प्रासादमपश्यं; अहं वंगाधिपस्य विशालं प्रासादमपश्यम्; अहं सौख्यनिकेतनं नगरभूषणं च अनेकरक्षिपरिवृतं वंगाधिपस्य विशालं प्रासादमपश्यं. In the same manner राजा अमात्यं प्रोवाच may become, in its enlarged form, राजा शास्त्राध्ययनकठोरधियं अनुरंजितसकलप्रजाजनं सुरगुरोः प्रत्यादेशं स्वममात्यं प्रोवाच.

Ex. 6.

Find appropriate subjects (enlarged by adjectives) and predicates, and frame sentences in which each of the following will stand as the object:—

ऋ (क) तूनां शतं, अजाकुलं, मद्रात्रं, सभृंगाणि कमलानि, स्वं माम, शुष्कपर्णानि, महागजं, ह्रं लकणान्, हिमाद्रेः शिखरं and विपुलधनं.

Ex. 7.

Frame sentences using the following roots, and supplying objects enlarged by participial adjectives: श्रु, ग्रह्, सृज्, चुर्, पा 'to drink,' अद्, दा *with* प्र, व्यध्, रुध्, and नी.

Ex. 8.

Take the following words as subjects, and complete the sentences enlarging the subject and object: सर्प, धृतराष्ट्र, कंचुकिन्, यति, पथिक, इन्द्र, राज्ञी, पाठशाला, पुत्र, and पितृ.

Ex. 9-10.

Frame sentences, finding out an appropriate subject and object to each of the roots given below, and enlarging the subject and object in any two ways:—तृ, लिह् *with* अभि, भ्रम् *with* परि, आप्, प्रछ्, विष्, कृ, क्री, मन् and तड्.

Ex. 11.

Write six sentences, in which the subject is enlarged by a participial adjective, and the predicate completed by means of an object enlarged by a participial adjective.

Ex. 12.

Write six sentences in which the subject and object are both enlarged by a noun or pronoun in the genetive case and a participial adjective.

§ **414.** The predicate may be enlarged by circumstances of time, place, manner, and cause and effect. Take the sentence त्वं यासि. The predicate may be thus enlarged :—

त्वं 'अधुना' यासि (time); त्वं अधुना 'कुत्र' यासि (time, and place); त्वमधुना 'सत्वरं' कुत्र यासि (time, place and manner); त्वमधुना 'समिदाहरणाय' सत्वरं 'किमिति' पद्भ्यामेव यासि (time, manner, purpose, and cause); त्वमधुना समिदाहरणाय गुरुमपृष्ट्वा सत्वरं किमिति etc. यासि. Similarly सखे मां प्रतिपालय may be thus variously enlarged : सखे 'विरचितायां प्रयाणसंविधायां पि-

तत्रावापृच्छय द्वारे क्षणं' मां प्रतिपालय; स 'निशितेन शरेण मध्याह्नाहारार्थं' कमपि विलोलनेत्रं हरिणशिशुं 'नितंबदेशे' विव्याध; 'पश्यतोपि पितुः' त्वं 'श्वः स्ववेश्मनः निष्क्रम्य किंकरेण सार्धं अतिचटुलया गत्या कुत्र खलु' अगच्छः.

Ex. 13.

Join appropriate adverbial adjuncts of *time* and *manner* to the verbs in the following sentences; (1) विहगा हयन्ते; (2) पुस्तकं वाचय; (3) अहं गामानयम्; (4) गुरूननुरुध्यस्व; (5) त्वया रुद्यते; (6) आपणं याति; (7) सैनिकाः युयुधिरे; (8) कृषीवलः क्षेत्रमकृषत्; (9) प्रमदा उद्यानं जग्मुः; (10) संपदुद्यममनुगच्छति.

Ex. 14.

Frame sentences using the following adverbial adjuncts, the subject being enlarged in more than two ways:—सहसा, वारंवारं, त्रीन् संवत्सरान्, सपदि, कदा, पुनः, कल्याणाय, पूर्वं (with abl.), तदानीं, प्रत्यनलं, प्रतिदिनं, उपनदि, द्विक्रोशं, रात्रिंदिवं.

Ex. 15.

Use the following in sentences, the subject being enlarged by an adjective or a possessive case:—सेनया सह, श्रमाहते, अनेन हेतुना, कस्य हेतोः, मित्रं सान्त्वयितुं, जठरस्यार्थे, अपवादश्रवणात्, तथानुष्ठिते, पाठमधीत्य, गृहस्योपरि, मामंतरेण, दुर्दैवात्, अरण्ये, प्रबलवेदनया, अनुगंगं.

Ex. 16.

Take the following pairs of words, and enlarge the predicate by adverbial adjuncts of *time* and *place*: मुनि and वस्; राजन् and रक्ष्; पुत्र and सेव्; कोकिल and रु *with* वि; हरि and क्रुध्; शिष्य and नम् *with* प्र.

Ex. 17.

Frame sentences, using the following roots and enlarging the predicate by adverbial adjuncts of *manner* and *cause* and *effect*; मृ, या *with* प्र, स्था *with* प्र (Atm.), मृज्, वह् *with* उत्, याच्, पा 'to protect', स्निह्, ईश्, इ *with* अधि.

Ex. 18.

Take the following subjects and enlarge the predicate by

means of indeclinable past participles or gerunds: भृगाः नरः, देवाः, अमी, राक्षसैः (agent), भीमः, सामाजिकाः, दूतः, अधिराजः, अश्वत्थामा, सुभद्रा, and यवनाः.

Ex. 19.

Enlarge the predicate, by means of the absolute constructions, using the following roots:—भाष्, दह्, प्रच्छ्, कृ (past part.), स्पृह्, वद्, हन् (past part.), पठ्, मंत्र् *with* सं, and या.

Ex. 20.

Enlarge the predicate, by adjuncts of *time* and *manner* and by gerunds derived from the following roots:—बंध्, कथ्, क्षुद्, शास्, ज्ञा, स्तु, ग्रह्, दा *with* आ, श्वस् *with* वि, आस् *with* उप, सृ, and नी *with* परि.

Ex. 21.

Write twelve sentences in which the predicate is enlarged by adverbial adjuncts of time, place, manner, cause and effect.

§ **419**. When along with the predicate, the subject and object (if any) are also enlarged, the sentence assumes its fullest form, रविरुदगच्छत् is a sentence in its simplest form. Enlarging the subject and predicate we may have a sentence like the following:

'अरुणपुरःसरो' रविः 'तमोजालं निरस्य जनक्रियाप्रवृत्तये प्राच्यां दिशि झटिति' उदगच्छत्. In like manner the simple sentence स पदवीमन्वयात् may become, when enlarged, 'गुरुभिरुपदिष्टः' स 'प्रथमे वयसि वर्तमानोपि संसारादुद्विजमानः' 'अनेकयतिप्रतिपन्नां परमसुखदायिनीं' साधुपदवीं 'निवारयतोपि पितुः पारत्रिकसुखावाप्तये प्रशांतचेतसा' अन्वयात्; so also पांथः भुजंगं ददर्श may be enlarged into अथ 'असौ' पांथो 'ग्रामांतरं गच्छन् अध्वश्रमार्तः कथमपि पदानि न्यस्यन्' 'अनाक्रांते एवार्धपथे' 'कंचिद् बृहत्कायं प्रसारितफणं श्यामदेहं' भुजंगं 'यदृच्छया तरुतले' ददर्श. Other examples are:—इति परिकलय्य किंचिदुन्नमितकंधरो भयचकितया दृशा दिशोवलोक्य तृणेपि चलति पुनः प्रतिनिवृत्तं तमेव पदे पदे पापकारिणमुत्प्रेक्षमाणो निष्कम्य तस्मात्तमालतरुमूलात्सलिलसमीपमुपसर्तुं प्रयत्नमकरवम्। (K. 35); अनुबध्यमानश्च तया तां सर्वामतिथिसपर्यामतिदूरावनतेन शिरसा सप्रश्रयं प्रतिजग्राह (K. 133); किंनिमित्तं वा अनेकसिद्धसाध्यसंबाधानि सुरलोकसुलभान्यपहाय दिव्याश्रमपदानि एकाकिनी वनमिदममानुषमधिवससि। (K. 135).

Ex. 22.

Write six sentences in which the subject and predicate are enlarged by all the methods of enlargement. Use the verbs: धाव्, प्रकाश्, स्था with उत्, पत्, आस्, and भ्रम्.

Ex. 23.

Write six sentences in which the predicate and object are enlarged: Use the roots भू, स्तु, मन्, दुह्, चि and विद् 'to obtain.'

Ex. 24.

Write six sentences in which the subject, predicate and object are all enlarged in more than one way.

§ **420**. In simple sentences the expression may be varied by changing the *voice* of the verb, without altering the meaning: दासी पुष्पाण्यानयत् has the same meaning as दास्या पुष्पाण्यानीयन्त. Sometimes the expression may be varied by a change of phrases; कस्माद्धेतोरत्र निवससि, पिता सपुत्रो ग्रामं गतः are the same in sense, as, किमर्थमत्र निवससि and पिता पुत्रेण सह (or सहितः) ग्रामं गतः But very often in Sanskrit we may vary the expression of a sentence by expressing the same idea in different words. Take the sentence उद्यमात् विभवः प्रभवति. This sentence may be thus variously expressed, without altering the sense:—

उद्यमाद्विभव उत्पद्यते-संजायते.
उद्यमो विभवाय कल्पते-भवति-जायते.
उद्यमो विभवस्य कारणं-हेतुः.
उद्यमप्रभवो विभवः.
उद्यमेन नरो विभवं याति-विभवयुतो भवति.
उद्यमी नरो विभवसंपन्नो भवति.
उद्यममवलंब्य नरो विभवं याति.
उद्यमपरेण नरेण (प्रायः) विभवयुतेन भाव्यम्.
(or figuratively) उद्यमबीजाद्विभवांकुरः प्ररोहति.

Ex. 25.

Taking the above as a model express in different ways the ideas the following sentences:—

(1) निर्धनता सर्वापदामास्पदं; (2) अस्य कोपः सनिमित्तः; (3) मूर्खाणामुपदेशः प्रकोपाय भवति; (4) अविवेकः आपदां परं पदं; (5) न धर्मवृद्धेषु वयः समीक्ष्यते; (6) विद्वान्सर्वत्र पूज्यते; (7) दैवपरा नरा विनश्यन्ति; (8) सुतो लालनाद्विनश्यति; (9) त्वमेव नः परमा गतिः; (10) पराभवोपि मानिनामुत्सव एव.

Complex Sentences.

§ **421**. From the nature of a complex sentence it is clear that there is one principal assertion and at least one subordinate assertion. The principal clause is independent, while the subordinate clauses are dependent in *construction* on the principal. Thus take the sentence दूतो राज्ञे वार्तां न्यवेदयत्.

It is simple and may be made complex by taking on to it any one of the three kinds of subordinate clauses. Thus

सामंता महाराजमभिद्रोग्धुमहर्निशं यतन्ते इति वार्तां दूतो राज्ञे न्यवेदयत् (noun clause.)

यः पौरजानपदानपसर्पितुं प्रयुक्तः स दूतो &c. (adj. clause).

काले उपायश्चिन्त्येतेति हेतोः दूतो &c. (adv. clause).

§ **422.** We shall now give a few exercises in the composition of complex sentences. The student should, as far as possible, aim at variety in matter as well as expression. He should refer to the table given on page 243, which gives the particles used to introduce subordinate clauses.

Ex. 26-28.

Write five complex sentences in which the noun clause will be (I) the subject or object; (II) be in apposition to the subject or object of principal clause; (III) be governed by some participle in the principal clause.

Ex. 29.

Write one complex sentence about each of the following: सुवर्णकार, गुरु, विद्या, सुशिष्य, बाजीनृप and शिवराज.

Ex. 30.

Construct four complex sentences in which the adjective clause will respectively qualify the subject, the object, some adverbial *adjunct*, and any adjunct of the subject, object, or predicate.

Ex. 31-34.

Construct six complex sentences (I) having an adverbial clause denoting time; (II) place; (III) manner; and (IV) cause, condition, purpose etc. Use such verbs as the following:—स्वप्, स्था *with* उप, हन्, लभ्, पद्, आ-राध् *caus.*

Ex. 35.

Write six complex sentences having an adverbial clause denoting point of time, motion to a place, analogy, manner, consequence, and condition, respectively.

§ **423.** We have given exercises in complex sentences having *one* kind of subordinate clause. We shall now take sentences where two or more of such clauses occur. Take this sentence वृषल: समाज्ञापयति । य एष क्षपणको जीवसिद्धिर्नाम राक्षसप्रयुक्तो विषकन्यया पर्वतकं घातितवान् स एनमेव दोषं प्रख्याप्य सनिकारं नगरान्निर्वास्यतामिति (Mu. 1). Here the object of समाज्ञापयति is the clause स...इति, the subject of this clause being qualified by an adjective clause य...घातितवान्. So in the sentence यदैव मयायं देवस्योज्जयिनीगमनवृत्तांतो निवेदितस्तदैव सनिर्वेदमेवमेतदित्युक्त्वा उत्थाय महाश्वेता पुनस्तपसे स्वमाश्रमपदमाजगाम, the principal predicate is modified by an adverbial clause of *time* यदैव...निवेदित: and a noun clause is joined to one of its extensions (एवमेतत् being the object of उक्त्वा). In this manner we can combine two or more kinds of the subordinate clauses in one complex sentence; यदा अतितृष्णा नराणां हृदये पदं करोति तदा ते यदीश्वरेणात्मने स्थित्यनुरूपं दत्तं तेनापरितुष्टाः संतस्ततोधिकतरमीहमाना यत्तैः सुखेन भोक्तुं शक्यं तदपि तृष्णातिरेकात् प्रायो हापयन्तीति असकृद्वयमस्मिञ्जगति प्रतीमः. In this complex sentence there is one adverbial clause यदा......करोति modifying हापयन्ति, two adjective clauses यत्...दत्तं and यत्...शक्यं, and one noun clause तत्ते...हापयन्ति.

Ex. 36-40.

Construct five complex sentences each (1) with one adjective and one noun clause; (2) one adverbial and one adjective clause; (3) one noun and one adverbial clause; (4) one adverbial and one noun clause, each qualified by an adjective clause; and (5) all the three clauses used together.

Compound Sentences.

§ **424.** In a compound sentence, as we have already seen, there are two or more principal assertions. These assertions may be all *simple* or *complex*, or simple and complex combined. This holds good in all the three relations, cumulative, adversative and illative.

Take a simple sentence यात्रिकः काशीमगच्छत्. To turn this into a compound sentence, showing the three relations, we may say,

(1) यात्रिकः काशीमगच्छत्, गंगायाः पावने सलिलेऽस्नात् सकलानि च तत्रत्यानि तीर्थानि दृष्ट्वा स्वं ग्रामं न्यवर्तत.

(2) यात्रिकः काशीमगच्छत् किंतु गंगासलिले स्नानार्थमवतीर्णः केनचिन्महानक्रेण सहसा गृहीत्वाऽभक्ष्यत.

(3) यात्रिकः काशीमगच्छत् तेनात्मानं परिपूतं मेने.

The several members of the compound sentence are here *simple*; they may be made complex, if necessary. Thus taking (2)

यात्रिकः काशीमगच्छत् किंतु यावत्स्नानार्थं गंगासलिलेऽवतरति तावत्केनचिन्महानक्रेण सहसा गृहीत्वा भक्षितः.

Here the second member is a complex sentence and the first, simple, which may also be turned into a complex one, thus: श्रीविश्वेश्वरदर्शनेनात्मानं निर्धौतकल्मषं करोमीति यदा गाढाभिलाषो मनसि पदं चकार तदा स यात्रिकः etc.

Ex. 41—42.

On the above model construct (1) five compound sentences, having *simple* sentences for their members, and (2) five, having *complex* sentences for their members.

Ex. 43.

Write a compound sentence descriptive of each of the following:—(1) वर्षाकालः; (2) पाणिनिः; (3) अराजको जनपदः; (4) राजधर्मः; (5) धनं; and (6) कालिदासः.

§ **425.** In English, we can combine or contract several simple sentences into one sentence, by means of participial, prepositional or other phrases, and by means of subordinate or co-ordinate clauses. The sentence so formed may be simple, complex, or compound. Take for instance, the sentence:—'With these thoughts I came near the place. Just then I heard sounds of loud lament. I, therefore, eagerly pressed forward. Then I could clearly distinguish Kapinjala's voice upbraiding Pu*nd*arîka for his cruelty. The cruelty lay in leaving his friend to live without him.' These assertions may be thus combined into one sentence:—With these thoughts as I came near the place, I heard sounds of loud lament; and pressing eagerly forward, I could clearly distinguish Kapinjala's voice upbraiding Pu*nd*arîka for his cruelty in leaving his friend to live without him.' This, it will be seen, is a compound sentence, the first member of which is a complex sentence. In Sanskrit, the use of participles and participial phrases for the purpose of combining or contracting simple sentences is much more liberal, and this is largely supplimented by the use of adjectival compounds (Tatpurusha and Bahuvrîhi). By their aid simple sentences can be combined into one sentence, which may be either simple, complex, or compound. एकदा सा गंभिरध्वनिं शुश्राव। तमाकर्ण्य तस्याः कुतूहलमुपजातम्। अतः सा तस्यां दिशि दृष्टिं प्रेरितवती महान्तं च शबरगणं ददर्श. These may be thus combined into one simple sentence: एकदा श्रुते गंभीरे ध्वनौ सा तदाकर्णनोपजातकुतूहला तद्दिशि प्रेरितदृष्टिः महांतं शबरगणं ददर्श. So अथैकदा राजा दुष्यंतो मृगयार्थं वनामियाय। तं तस्य सैनिका अमात्याश्चानुजग्मुः। वने स बहून् मृगाञ्जघान। एकं मृगं पलायमानमनुससार। मार्गे दिव्याश्रमपदं ददर्श।

These sentences may be combined into one complex sentence thus:—

सैनिकैरमात्यैश्चानुगतो यदैकदा राजा दुष्यंतो मृगयार्थं वनमियाय तदा स तत्र बहून् मृगान् हत्वैकं मृगं पलायमानमनुसरन् मार्गे दिव्याश्रमपदं ददर्श। Or shorter still ससैनिकामात्यो राजा दुष्यंतो मृगयार्थं वनं गतः बहून् मृगान् etc.

Ex. 44.

Combine the following groups of sentences into a single sentence which may be simple, complex or compound.

(1) एवं महाश्वेता आहारं परिसमाप्य संध्योचिताचारान्निर्वर्तयामास। पश्चात्सा एकस्मिन् शिलातले विश्रब्धमुपाविशत्। तथा स्थितां तां चंद्रापीडो निभृतमुपससार। मुहूर्तमिव स्थित्वा च तां स सविनयमवादीत्॥

(2) तस्मिन्दिव्याश्रमपदे दुष्यंतः कामपि कन्यकामपश्यत्। सा कन्या चारुसर्वांगी आसीत्। स कण्वमुनेराश्रमः तं राजा प्राविशत्। तदा तत्सत्कारार्थं शकुन्तला आश्रमाद्बहिराजगाम। शकुंतला कण्वस्य कृतिका दुहितासीत्। सा सप्रश्रयं दुष्यंतं स्वागतं व्याजहार।

(3) पेशवे इति ख्यातानां महाराष्ट्राधिकारिणां मध्ये चरमो बाजीराज इत्येको बभूव। स पुण्यपत्तनमधितस्थौ। स किल बहुगुणोपपन्न आसीत्। किंतु तस्य राजकार्यावेक्षणविषयेऽतीव मंदादर आसीत्। अतः कर्मसचिवस्थाने बहवो नर्मसचिवा एव तं पर्यवारयन्। तैस्तस्य मनो विषयभोगेषु सुतरामाकृष्यत। एवं कामाधीने राजनि तच्छंदानुवर्तिनि चामात्यगणे महाराष्ट्रदेशोऽनायासेनैव रंध्रान्वेषणदक्षाणां शत्रूणामामिषतां गतः।

§ **426.** We have shown in the preceding section how to combine a given number of sentences into one sentence. We shall, as a further exercise to the student, now show how to resolve a given passage into a number of different sentences. This will enable him to acquire practice in paraphrasing Sanskrit passages, by varying the construction of the original passage to a considerable extent. This system will facilitate the work of paraphrasing by one-half; and if the student, after having split up a passage into different sentences, substitute equivalents for the words and expressions in the original, he will have given a free translation or *paraphrase* of the passage. Take, for instance, the verse: गुणदोषौ बुधो गृह्णन्निंदुक्ष्वेडाविवेश्वरः । शिरसा श्लाघते पूर्वं परं कंठे नियच्छति ॥ This may be thus expressed by different sentences, or *paraphrased:—*

शिवः इंदुं विषं च द्वावपि स्वीकरोति किंतु इंदुं शिरोधारणपूर्वकं प्रशंसति विषं च स्वकंठे नियच्छति । एवं प्राज्ञो नरः कस्यचिन्नरस्य गुणं दोषमुभावपि गृह्णाति । किंतु गुणं ग्रीवांदोलनपूर्वकं श्लाघते दोषं तु स्वकंठे नियम्य तन्नाममात्रमपि विलोपयति ।

This is no doubt, a free paraphrase of the original, but it makes the sense quite clear. Take another instance ;

संग्रामनिर्विष्टसहस्रबाहुरष्टादशद्वीपनिखातयूपः ।
अनन्यसाधारणराजशब्दो बभूव योगी किल कार्तवीर्यः ॥

This may be thus resolved into sentences: पुरा किल कार्तवीर्यो नाम योगी समाजयत । तस्य युद्धेषु (एव) बाहुसहस्रं परैरनुभूतम् (अन्यत्र स द्विभुज एव) तेन अष्टादशसु द्वीपेषु यज्ञस्तंभाः स्थापिताः । तथा च तस्य राजशब्दो नान्यसामान्य आसीत् । Similarly श्रुतिसुभगं गीतध्वनिं श्रुत्वा संजातकुतुको ध्वनिप्रभवजिज्ञासया कृतगमनबुद्धिर्दत्तपर्याणमिंद्रायुधमारुह्य प्रियगीतैः प्रथमप्रस्थितैर्वनहरिणैरुपदिश्यमानवर्त्मा पश्चिमया सरस्तीरवनलेखया निमित्तीकृत्य तं गीतध्वनिमभिप्रतस्थे may be thus expanded: यदा स सुखश्रवं गीतशब्दमशृणोत् तदा संजातकुतूहलस्तत्प्रभवमुपलब्धुं स ऐच्छत् । तदनुरोधात् गमनाय मतिं विधाय इंद्रायुधपृष्ठे पर्याणं समारोप्य तमारुरोह । तन्मार्गोपदेशाय इव सदाप्रियगीतरवा वनहरिणास्तस्मात्पूर्वमेव तदभिप्रेतां दिशं प्रस्थिताः । ताननुसरन् स पश्चिमेन सरस्तीरप्रांतेन तं गीतध्वनिमुद्दिश्य ययौ ।

On the above models and with the assistance of § 420, the student may select passages from authors and paraphrase them.

LESSON IV.

Letter-Writing.

§ **427.** Letter-writing is not a subject to which Sanskrit writers seem to have devoted much attention. We find very few instances of letters in the existing Sanskrit works, probably because our forefathers did not much resort to that system. Naturally, therefore, letter-writing in Sanskrit does not present the difficulty which a letter in English, with its various forms—private, commercial, official &c.—usually presents. Letters written in Sanskrit are mostly of one type. There are certain settled forms in which they should be begun. There is also a variety in these *forms* according to the position of the person to whom they are addressed. But beyond this difference there is nothing to distinguish a purely private letter, (say, from a father to his son) from the official or demi-official letter sent by a minister to his sovereign, or by any person to another person officially. We propose in this Section to give some of the common forms of letter-writing in Sanskrit, with examples.

§ **428.** We shall first give two specimens before asking the student to study the details:—

1. स्वस्ति। महेंद्रद्वीपात्परशुरामो लंकायाममात्यं माल्यवंतमभ्यर्हयति। अत्रैव परममाहेश्वरं लंकेश्वरमभिनंद्य ब्रवीति। विदितमेतद्वो यदस्माभिर्दण्डकारण्यतीर्थोपासकेभ्यस्तपोधनेभ्यः प्रतिज्ञातमभयम्। तत्र विराधदनुकबंधप्रभृतयः केप्यभिचरन्तीति श्रुतम्। तत्तान्प्रतिषिध्य सद्वृत्तिमस्मद्धितां च माहेश्वरप्रीतिमनुरुध्यन्तां भवन्तः।

ब्राह्मणातिक्रमत्यागो भवतामेव भूतये।
जामदग्न्यश्च वो मित्रमन्यथा दुर्मनायते॥ इति

Expressed in the form of an English letter the above will stand as follows:—

Mahendradvîpa.

My dear Mályavat,

\+ + + +

With kind regards, I remain,

Yours sincerely,

Paras'uráma.

Give my best compliments to the Lord of Lanká.

To

H. E. Mályavat, Minister of Rávana, King of Lanká.

II. Another specimen of a more modern form :

स्वस्ति । श्रीमत्संस्कृताद्यनेकविद्याविनयाविराजमाना राजमान्याः* श्रीयुतगोखले उपनामधारिणः कृष्णरावाख्याः शतशः साष्टांगप्रणामपुरस्सरं विज्ञाप्यन्ते । यत्काशीतो भवदर्थं आनीतस्य मानवधर्मशास्त्रग्रन्थस्य वार्ताहरदेयभागेन सहितं मूल्यं सार्धदशरूपकपरिमितमिमां पत्रिकां भवद्धस्तं प्रापयतो गोविंदस्य हस्ते दीयतामिति एषा विज्ञप्तिः ।

पुण्यपत्तने,
मार्गशीर्षसुदि १९, १८०७ संवत्सरे } पटवर्धनकुलोत्पन्नस्य हरिसूनोर्नारायणस्य.

§ **429.** We now call the attention of the student to the following points :

1. Every letter begins with the word स्वस्ति.

2. The *place* where the letter is written is stated †first, as in English, and is put in the ablative case, being construed with the main predicate. It is sometimes put last in the locative case, as in letter II.

3. The *address* ('my dear,' 'dear Mr.' etc.) is not actually expressed but is represented by some word expressive of that relation; as, आयुष्मत् indicating a younger relative, मित्र friendship etc.

4. The name of the *writer*, which is, in English, usually coupled with a word expressive of the relationship between him and the person addressed, is not usually written at the end, but at the beginning, being made the *subject* of the first introductory sentence. The degree of relationship is expressed in the *predicate* of the first sentence ('अभ्यर्हयति' 'pays his respects to', which indicates that the writer is a friend of the person addressed ; 'विज्ञाप्यन्ते' that they are mere acquaintances; 'परिष्वज्य दर्शयति' that the writer is a near relation, a father, husband &c.)

---

* These adjectives are merely complimentary. It is, however, usual to put in one or two as a graceful introduction. They may be omitted in a purely business letter.

† When letters pass between persons in the same town the place is usually omitted, as also the date.

N. B.—In modern forms the writer's name is put at the end (as in specimen II), in the genitive case, going with some word like विज्ञप्तिः, प्रार्थना in the body of the letter. It should be noted that this style is more *formal*, and should be used when the writer does not know, or is not familiar with, the person addressed.

5. The commencement, or the *form* proper, of the letter is in the third person, though other *persons* may occur in the body of the letter itself.

6. The *name* of the person *addressed* which, in English, is sometimes written at the end, near the left corner of the paper, and is written in full on the envelope, is, in Sanskrit, given in the introductory sentence together with the *place of his residence*, being made the object or the *subject* (as in letter II) of the predicate or connected with it in any other way. This gives the superscription or *address* of a letter.

7. It is not usual in Sanskrit to specify the *date* of writing: but when required, it is generally put in the locative case, being used as an adverbial adjunct of the predicate, or put last at the left-hand corner of the letter; as, सुभानुसंवत्सरे वैशाखवदि १३ भौमे ।

§ **430.** For the sake of convenience, letters may be divided into two classes:—

I. *Domestic*, or those passing between members of a family.

II. Other letters written by a person to his friend, a pupil to his preceptor, a minister to his sovereign, or in general by one person to another. These we shall call *Miscellaneous*.

I. Domestic Letters.

§ **431.** In a letter from a father to his son, or from an elder to a younger relation, or from a husband to his wife, the degree of relationship is expressed by such words as स्नेहात्परिष्वज्य, उत्तमांगे चुंबन, सस्नेहमालिंग्य etc.

We shall give a few examples.

(*a*) A letter from a father to his son.

स्वस्ति। यज्ञशरणात्सेनापतिः पुष्पमित्रो वैदिशस्थं पुत्रमायुष्मंतमग्निमित्रं स्नेहात्परिष्वज्य अनुदर्शयति। विदितमस्तु। योसौ राजसूययज्ञे दीक्षितेन मया राजपुत्रशतपरिवृतं वसुमित्रं गोप्तारमादिश्य निरर्गलस्तुरगो विसृष्टः स सिंधोर्दक्षिणरोधसि चरन्नश्वानीकेन यवनानां प्रार्थितः। ततः उभयोः सेनयोर्महानासीत्संमर्दः। किंतु वसुमित्रेण प्रसह्य ह्रियमाणो मे वाजिराजो निवर्तितः। सोहमिदानीं पौत्रेण प्रत्याहृताश्वो यक्ष्ये। तदिदानीमकालहीनं विगतरोषचेतसा भवता वधूजनेन सह यज्ञसंदर्शनायागंतव्यमिति।

(*b*) स्वस्ति। उज्जयिनीतः परममाहेश्वरो महाराजाधिराजो देवस्तारापीडः सर्वसंपदामायतनं चंद्रापीडमुत्तमांगे चुंबन्नंदयति। कुशलिन्यः प्रजाः। किंतु कियानपि कालो भवतो दृष्टस्य। बलवदुत्कंठितं नो हृदयम्। देवी च सहांतःपुरैर्म्लानिमुपनीता। अतो लेखवाचनविरतिरेव प्रयाणकालतां नेतव्येति।

(*c*) A letter of a more modern form will be as follows:—

स्वस्ति। पंचवटीतो गोविंदशर्मा पुण्यपत्तने पुत्रं विश्वनाथं (or आयुष्मन्तं विश्वनाथं) सोत्कंठं सस्नेहं निर्भरमालिंग्य कुशलं वार्तयति यथा। कार्यं च। कुशलमिहास्माकं सर्वेषाम्। भवदीया कुशलवती वार्ता सर्वदा प्रहेया। अद्यैव भवदर्थेऽस्मन्मित्रस्य परशुरामस्य हस्ते विंशती रूपका दत्ताः। तेषां विनियोगः कथं कृत इति यथावसरं निवेदनीयमिति।

शके १८०७ मार्गशीर्षवदि १४ भौमेऽहनि।

§ **432.** A father writing to his son, an elder to a younger brother, and generally an elderly relation writing to a younger one, will also use such a form as the following:—

स्वस्ति। श्रीमच्चिरंजीविषु अमुकशर्मसु प्राणाधिकतरेषु अमुकस्य (पितुः, भ्रातुः &c. as the case may be) सस्नेहा आशिषः कोटिशः स्फुरन्तु। विदितमस्तु &c.; or

स्वस्ति। अमुकस्थानात् अमुकस्थानवासिनं चिरंजीविनं or आयुष्मन्तं अमुकशर्माणं अमुकशर्मा सस्नेहमाशीःसहस्रपूर्वकं कुशलं वार्तयति; or सोत्कण्ठं सस्नेहं समालिंग्य कुशलं वार्तयति यथा। etc.

(*a*) From a husband to his wife.

स्वस्ति। अमुकस्थाने पालितपरमपातिव्रत्यगुणां सौभाग्यशालिनीं भार्याममुकनाम्नीं अमुकः सस्नेहं समालिंग्य कुशलं वार्तयति यथा। कार्यं च। कुशलमिहास्माकं। तत्रस्थसमस्तमानुषाणां कुशलवती वार्ता प्रहेया। or एवंगुणासु प्राणेभ्योपि प्रियतरासु नितांतालिंगनपूर्वकस्नेहसमूहाः। etc.

§ **433**. The following forms should be used when a younger writes to an elder relative, or a wife to her husband:

1 From a son to his **father**:—

(1) स्वस्ति । अमुकस्थाने अनेकगुणालंकृतस्नेहगुणभूषितपुत्रवत्सलपूज्यपितृपादारविन्दान् अमुकस्थानात्सदा विनीतः सुतः (or सदाज्ञाविधायी पितृभक्तितत्परः सुतः) अमुको महाभक्त्या सबहुमानं क्षितितलनिहितमौलिना साष्टांगं प्रणम्य सविनयं विज्ञापयति । ....सर्वाभ्यो मातृप्रभृतिभ्यो मदीयः प्रणामो वाच्यः । कार्यादिकं च सदादेष्टव्यमिति ।

(2) स्वस्ति । श्रीमत्पितृचरणेषु अकिंचित्करकिंकरस्य सुतस्य (sometimes मम) बद्धकरसंपुटं प्रणतिततिसहस्रमजस्रम् । कार्यं च &c.

(3) स्वस्ति श्रीजन्मकर्मार्थयशेषु जनकेष्वितः ।

स्नेहार्द्रभावसहिताः स्फुरन्तु नतयः पराः ॥

N. B. A younger writing to an elder brother, or a son to his mother, should make the necessary changes.

II. From a wife to her husband.

स्वस्ति । यथास्थाने सकलपूज्यतमगुणगणालंकृतभर्तुः पादान् (the name is sometimes given) अमुकस्थानात्सदाज्ञाविधायिनी अमुका पतिसेवातत्परा कंठाश्लेषपूर्वकं सस्नेहं सोत्कंठं सविनयं प्रणम्य विज्ञापयति यथा । कार्यं च ।

II. Miscellaneous.

§ **434**. We shall now turn to the class of letters which we have called *Miscellaneous*. One writing to his friend will generally use words of compliment ; such as, अमुकं अर्हयति, अभिनन्दयति, अभिनन्द्य ब्रवीति, सस्नेहं अनुदर्शयति, प्रणतिपुरःसरं निवेदयति &c.

The student has already been shown a form of such a letter from a classical author (see specimen letter I). He may take that as his model when writing to a friend.

Here are some modern forms:—

(1) स्वस्ति । यथास्थाने विद्वत्त्वदाक्षिण्यौदार्यादिगुणालंकृतशरीरं परमप्रेमनिधानं

वयस्यं अमुकं अमुकस्थानादमुकः सोत्कंठं सस्नेहं गाढमालिंग्य कुशलं वार्तयति यथा। कार्यं च।

(2) स्वस्ति। अस्मदेकाश्रयीभूतेषु विद्याविनयादिमण्डितेषु पूज्यतमेषु अमुकस्थाननिवासिषु अमुकशर्मसु अमुकस्थानवासिनः अमुकस्य प्रणतिसहस्रमजस्रम्।

§ **435**. Persons who are not familiar with or do not know each other, may use the following general form:—

स्वस्ति। अमुकस्थाननिवासी अमुकनामकः श्रीमतः सकलविद्यावदातचेतसः अमुकान् अनेकप्रणामपूर्वकं विज्ञापयति। or अमुकाः एवंगुणोपेताः (some complimentary adjective) अमुकेन प्रणामपुरःसरं विज्ञाप्यन्ते or निवेद्यन्ते (the conclusion in this case to be like that in specimen letter II.); or श्रीमतां अमुकनाम्नां—समक्षं (संनिधौ) अमुकस्थानवासिनः अमुकनाम्नः सविनया विज्ञप्तिः।&c.

Taking this as a model one may write to the author of a book, requesting him to send a copy by post:—

स्वस्ति। आंग्लभौमगीर्वाणादिभाषासु परां प्रतिष्ठां गताः कलिकातानगरस्थमहापाठशालाधिकृताः श्रीतर्करत्नवागीशाख्याः प्रणामपुरःसरं विज्ञाप्यन्ते। यत् भवत्प्रणीतं अलंकारदर्पणाख्यं ग्रंथं अधिकृत्य काचित् विज्ञप्तिपत्रिका मया मित्रहस्ते अद्य दृष्टा। तदवलोकनेन तं ग्रंथं क्रेतुं मन्मनसि बलवतीच्छा प्रादुर्भवति तदनुरोधात् राजशासनपत्रद्वारेण* वार्ताहरभागसहितं मूल्यं रूप्यकसार्धचतुष्टयं इतः प्रेषितम्। तद्यावच्छ्रयं सत्वरं तद्ग्रन्थस्य प्रेषणेनानुग्राह्यमात्मानमिच्छामि। ग्रंथश्च निम्नलिखितब्राह्मनामा प्रेषणीय इति विज्ञप्तिः।

पुण्यपत्तने संस्कृतपाठशालायां संवत् १९३९ श्रावणवदि ११ शनौ	अभ्यंकरोपनामकस्य गोविंदसूनोः रामशास्त्रिणः

N. B. In all these letters it is not unusual to put in some prayer or wish for the addressee's good health. It is put at the end in this way: शमिह भावत्कं भव्यमनुदिनमेधमानमाशास्महे or very shortly इति शम्.

§ **436**. A pupil will write to his teacher in the following way:—

स्वति। अमुकस्थाने (if in a different place) अनेकतीर्थावगाहनपवित्रीकृतमानसान् परमाराध्यपरमपूज्यश्रीगोविंदाचार्यपादारविंदान् अमुकस्थानात्सदादेशवर्ती अमुकनामकः परमभक्त्या क्षितितलनिहितमौलिना साष्टांगं प्रणम्य सविनयं विज्ञापयति; or

*By a Money Order.

एवंगुणोपेताः श्रीमदुपाध्यायपादा भक्तिसत्परेण अमुकनाम्ना शिष्येण सविनयप्रणामपूर्वकं विज्ञाप्यन्ते; or इति विज्ञप्तिः अमुकशर्मणः &c.

According to this form a pupil may thus write to his teacher asking for sick leave:—

स्वस्ति। सकलविद्यावगाहनविशदीकृतमानसाः परमपूज्याः गोपालरावाख्याः अनेकप्रणामपूर्वकं सविनयं विज्ञाप्यन्ते। यन्मम गेहे मातापितरावुभावपि ज्वरपीडितौ संतौ शय्याग्रस्तौ। तौ तथा परित्यज्य पाठशालां गंतुं नाहमुत्सहे। मामपि च बलवती शिरोबाधा पीडयति। अतः अद्य मम अनुपस्थितिं मर्षयितुमर्हन्ति आचार्यपादाः इति सविनया विज्ञापना सदाभवदादेशवर्तिनः शिष्यस्य.

खिस्ताब्दे दशममासस्य द्वादशवासरे १८८९ } काळेकुलोत्पन्नस्य गोविंदसूनोर्हरेः.

§ **437.** We shall conclude this Section with a few more forms:—(स्वस्ति may be repeated with each form.)

(1) From a minister or other official to a king:

श्रीसमस्तसामंतसेनानिर्वाहकेषु परोपकारसत्कारनिपुणेषु निजकीर्तिधवलितदिगंतरेषु महाराजाधिराजचरणेषु, आदेशवर्तिनो महाराजकिंकरस्य समस्ताशीराशीः सहस्रमजस्रम् or °काः °णाः °राः °णाः आशीःसहस्रपूर्वकं निवेद्यन्तेः or अमुकस्थाने देवं विनयनतशिराः अमुकः पादद्वंद्वारविंदे भक्त्या मूर्ध्नि अंजलिं रचयति। कार्यं च लिख्यते। etc.

(2) From a superior to an inferior:

अमुकस्थानात् अमुकः अमुकस्थाने अमुकं सप्रसादं समादिशति यथा (कार्यं च) etc.

(3) From an inferior to a superior:

पूज्यपरमाराध्यस्वामिअमुकपादान् अमुकस्थानात्सदादेशकारी अमुकः साष्टांगप्रणामपूर्वकं विज्ञापयति।

(4) To an ascetic:

श्रीमत्परमहंसपरिव्राजकाचार्यवेदभूदेवनरदेवपूजितेषु श्रीपादेषु अमुकस्य प्रपंचविस्मरणपूर्वकं नारायणस्मरणप्रणामसहस्रमजस्रं विज्ञप्तिश्च।

§ **438.** We shall now ask the student to write a few letters according to the directions in the preceding pages. It will be found that with these directions he will be able to write letters from one person to another in any capacity. There will be considerable variety in the matter, but the forms given will generally do.

Ex. 45–52.

1. A letter to your father, describing your progress at school.

2. From a father to his son, sending him books and some presents.

3. To your friend, asking him to give you the pleasure of his company at a dinner party or some religious ceremony.

4. To a book-seller, requesting him to send you the books you want.

5. To your teacher, asking for leave of absence on private affairs.

6. To a friend, asking of him some pecuniary assistance.

7. A note to one of your fellow-students asking him to lend you his Sanskrit Grammar for a few days.

8. From the head-master of a Páthas'ála to the eductional officer of the district asking for more assistants.

NOTES.

LESSON I.

P. 7. l. 17. Said by Pururavas with reference to Vidúshaka when he compared the moon to a *modak*. 'With a glutton food becomes in every case his proper scope or province,' *i. e.* even his similes and metaphors are derived from food.

—l. 19 'Who can assure himself (believe for certain) that she is the same,' there is such a vast change in her appearance.

—l. 20. अर्थपति a proper name (lord of wealth); the meaning is—'Vimardaka forms the external life, as it were of अर्थपति'; he holds him as dear as his own life which is अंतश्चरा: प्राणा:.

—l. 21. A question; 'are the Pándavás an object of dread' etc.

—ll. 23-24. Bhima says to Sahadeva: 'neither my worthy brother (Dharma), nor Arjuna, nor you two, are the cause' etc. मम शिशोरेव 'of me, while yet a boy, when a mere child.'

—l. 25. द्वितीयं हृदयं 'a second heart.' thou formest a part and parcel of myself.

P. 8. l. 2. निस्तेजा: 'void of spirit or pluck' and 'wanting *fire*,' having no power to burn. It refers to भस्मचय also, which though very big, is easily trodden under the foot, because there is no *fire* in it.

—l. 5. आहितलक्षण: 'was given the characteristic name *Kákutstha*,' became known as Kákustha, or 'noted for his good qualities' (according to Amara).

—l. 8. 'Who, like yourself, is the second tie of my mind.' Said by Kámandakî to Málatî, when she related to her who Mádhava was.

l. 9. पश्चिमे वयसि वर्तमानस्य 'being in his last (declining, old) age', who was far advanced in age.

P. 8. ll. 11-13. शुकमादाय 'bringing with her a parrot,' आश्चर्यभुत 'an object of wonder', a prodigy. इति कृत्वा 'so thinking,' with this thought.' देवपादमूलमागता 'come to your Majesty's feet.'

—l. 15. गर्भस्थस्यैव 'while he is yet in the womb', *i. e.* all these five are *born* with him.

—l. 18. भूपतेः=भूपतिना; only three things could not be given away by him because they were the essential insignia of royalty.

—l. 19. The line means that, though Wealth and Learning occupy, by their nature, different stations, yet in this king they live together; the combination of wealth and learning, which is very rare, is found in this king. एकसंस्थं=एका संस्था यस्य.

—ll. 20-23. व्यतिकरितदिगंताः 'who have pervaded (completely filled) the ends of quarters.' सुकृत etc. 'Who are the abode of mighty manifestations (displays) of good actions', who have done many meritorious deeds.

LESSON II.

P. 12. l. 16. चंद्रसरोरक्षकाः 'guardians of the moon-lake,' *i. e.* the hares.

—ll. 17. 'On whom the king fixes more his eye,' *i. e.* who is looked upon with a more favourable eye than others.

—ll. 19-20. The meaning is: 'The demons are fit marks for your arrows; so let your bow be bent against them.'

—l. 21. स सुहृद् व्यसने यः स्यात् 'he is a friend who is so in adversity,' or 'a friend in need is a friend indeed.'

P. 13. l. 4. 'In like manner the king and Mágadhî (Sudakshiná) who were like them (S'iva and Umá and Indra and S'achi) were pleased with their son (who was) like them (Kártikeya and Jayanta).

—ll. 6-7. बहु मन्यते 'is esteemed,' 'highly thought of'. आशानिबन्धनं etc. 'became the tie of the hope of the whole world.' Sítá means to say: 'Happy, indeed, is that woman who, having conti.lrted to divert my lord, the has caused the hopes of the people * be concentrated upon herself.'

P. 13. ll. 8-9. Said by Ráma with reference to the cub of elephant tenderly reared by Sítá. यत् कल्याणं &c. 'He has become the receptacle of what is good in youthful age.' *i. e.*, is possessed of youthful freshness and vigour.

—ll. 10-11. *Prithvî* means to say that **Ráma**, in abandoning Sítá was not swayed by these considerations, any of which would have decied against him.

—l. 15. Dúsha*n*a, Khara, and Trimùrdhan are names of demons killed by Ráma.

—l. 17. 'That he lives is death (really speaking), and death is rest to him,' *i. e.* the existence of such a man is a living death, and actual death only is his final rest.

—ll. 19-21. This is a rather doubtful line. It appears to mean—'that which may become a fit object both in joy and sorrow (prosperity and adversity), equally with a friend, is difficult to be found,' *i. e.* none but a *friend* will keep company with us in good and bad days. For ये मिलन्ति *cf.* Samson Agonists: 'In prosperous days they swarm; in adverse, withdraw their heads, not to be found though sought.' तत्त्वनिकष &c. 'But adversity is their touch-stone (on which their *true* character may be tested).'

—ll. 24-27. हिंसाशून्यं 'void of injury,' got without injuring any one; *cf.* Goldsmith: 'And from the mountain's grassy side, a *guiltless* feast I bring.' अशनं goes with व्यालानां समाप्तिं प्रयान्ति 'are spent away', 'are all exhausted', in trying to earn their livelihood.

—ll. 28-29. An address to the God Vish*n*u. 'That (our) words, having extolled thy greatness, are curtailed (fall short) is either through our exhaustion or inability (to describe), and not because thy merits are limited.'

LESSON III.

P 19. l. 12. बिंदूत्क्षेपान्, 'the drops of water thrown out' by the revolving wheel.

—ll. 16-17. Priyamvada means to say: 'Who else but Dushyanta can support (the life of) her who has exhibited signs of deep love ?

—l. 21. प्रावृषा संभृतश्री: 'whose splendour is enhanced by the rainy season.'

—ll. 22-23. कृतकार्यं predicate of वनं, 'having its object accomplished,' blessed. यद् object of अध्यास्ते.

—l. 25. अधिष्ठाय 'becoming the leader or conductor', becoming the guide.

P. 20. ll. 5-6. अमी goes with वह्नयः. क्लृप्तधिष्ण्याः 'whose places have been fixed or assigned.'

—ll. 8-9. Give the dimensions of the hall. शतमध्यर्द्धं 'one hundred and fifty.'

—ll. 10-11. रघुप्रतिनिधिः 'the representative (son) of Raghu' *i. e.* Aja—l. 24. 'Like Cupid assuming a state* other than boyhood.'

—l. 13. संप्रत्यावसत् 'has recently dwelt.'

—l. 14. 'He slept after she had slept, and rose in the morning after she had risen from sleep.'

—l. 16. अयं जनः generally refers to the speaker. Dushyanta means to say: 'This person (*i. e.* I) once made love (to her, *i. e.* Hamsapadiká); and hence have I been subjected to a great taunt with reference to the Queen Vasumati.'

—l. 21. दोषं विवक्षता त्वया 'by thee intending to imply a fault.'

P. 21. l. 1. क्रियांतरांतरायमंतरेण 'without interfering with your other duties' *i. e.* at a time when you have no other matters to attend to.

—l. 6. कल्पितशस्त्रगर्भे 'in the interior of which were weapons kept ready.'

---

* Or rather—the state next to childhood (*i. e.* youth.)

P. 21. ll. 7-8. चतुरस्रयानं 'a conveyance having four corners,' *i. e.* a palanquin. चतस्रः अश्रयो यस्य तत्. मंचांतरराजमार्ग 'the high (royal) road formed by the (rows of) sofas'. क्लृप्तविवाहवेषा 'decked in her wedding dress.'

—ll. 9-10. Said by Râvana to Sìtá.

—l. 12. कष्टसंश्रयाः 'attended with miseries.'

—ll. 13-14. यत् 'since'. The meaning is that, like the poison of a mad dog, this scandal about Sîtá has spread every-where, though it was removed before by miraculous means.

—l. 16. प्रियासहचरः 'the companion of my beloved', *i. e.* accompanied by my beloved.

—ll. 17-18. गोदावरीपरिसरस्य 'in the vicinity of which is the river Godávarî.'

—ll. 21-22. दंष्ट्रा &c.—'having for his weapons his jaws, claws and tail'. तृष्णां छिनत्ति 'slakes or quenches his thirst.'

—ll. 23-26. अजातशत्रुः 'Dharma', who had no enemies. लिखितैरिव 'as if drawn in a picture', as if we were so many pictures devoid of the power of movement, and retaliation.

—l. 27. 'It (the river Sarayù) on the banks of which are erected sacrificial posts, carries off its waters flows along the capital Ayodhyá.'

—l. 18. वाच्यदर्शनात् 'perceiving the censure' (to which he would be exposed). नृपतिः सन् 'lord of men as he was'.

LESSON IV.

P. 25. ll. 1-2. अचिरप्रवृत्तोपदेशं 'instruction in which has not been long commenced,' she being but recently made over to her master, कीदृशी मालविका 'how Málaviká fares or progresses,' what degree of proficiency she has attained.

—l. 3. कुशलं प्रष्टुं 'to ask how she is doing.'

P. 25 l. 7. पृथुपदिष्टां 'pointed out by the king Prithu' as capable of yielding several precious things when properly milked.

—l. 8. Who had shown his power with regard to the work aimed at by Indra, who had proved his capacity to do the work intended.

—l. 10. सोऽहं 'I therefore,' 'hence I.'

—ll. 12-13. Said by Kautsa when he found that Raghu had made Kubera pour down treasure from the heavens. वृत्ते स्थितस्य 'of him who acts according to the duty (right policy)' of kings. मनोपित्तं &c., 'even the heaven has been made to yield your desired object.'

—ll. 16-17. ज्येष्ठा 'the eldest daughter of Himavat.' त्रिपथगा 'running in three streams,' through Heaven, Earth, and Pátála.

—l. 20. राज्याश्रममुनिं 'the king who was, as it were, a Muni in the hermitage in the form of a kingdom.'

P. 26. l. 2. काकपक्षधरं 'who wore (graceful) side-locks of hair' *i. e.* who was quite a boy; a Gen. Tat. compound. तेजसां &c. 'age is not considered in the case of those who are possessed of lustre.' *Cf.* Bhartrihari 'न खलु वयस्तेजसो हेतुः.'

—l. 3. कृपयाविष्टं 'overcome by (the feeling of) pity'.

—ll. 5-8. The S'arat season is here compared to a clever messenger who takes her friend (the Ganges) to her lord (the ocean) in a perfectly pleased mood (with its extremely pure waters) after having, with great difficulty, brought her to the right path (having brought the river to its usual course), who has grown lean (which has shrunk within its bed), and who was much enraged at her husband's having many wives (which had turbid water in the rains, the ocean too, having several wives, the rivers).

—ll. 9-12. मम वचनात् 'at my instance, in my name'. पूर्वाभाष्यं &c. ' This (कुशलप्रश्न) is the only mode of address (to be used) by those beings who are easily subject to miseries'.

—ll. 13-18. सः ' Râma'. याचमानः शिवं सुरान् ' begging a blessing of the gods', praying to gods to wish well of Sitâ, यथास्थितं सर्वं 'everything as it stood'. भिक्षमाणो वनं प्रियां 'asking the forest (any information about) his beloved'. l. 21. 'As if squeezing out life from himself, he confined sorrow to his mind', *i. e.* became very desperate and hence was sad at heart. l. 17 throws out a conjecture. आ is a particle meaning 'yes, perhaps it may be.'

LESSON V.

P. 32. l. 4. अनांगयत्, *i. e.* हारितः, when he found the little parrot in that helpless state. मुक्तप्रयत्नं 'who had left off struggling.'

—l. 7. येन &c. 'By whom my friend was made to rely on that person false to his promise'.

—l. 9. आसनं प्रतिग्राहितः 'you were made to carry the (Guru's) seat.'

—l. 10. धात्रीकर्मवस्तुतः परिगृह्य 'having taken charge (of them) commencing with the duty of a nurse,' *i. e.* doing all that a nurse would have done under the same circumstances. Perhaps the sentence may be read as धात्रीकर्म वस्तुतः परिगृह्य 'having *actually* undertaken a nurse's duties'. वृत्तचूडौ 'after the tonsure ceremony was over.' त्रयीवर्जं 'excepting the three Vedas.'

—l. 16. Said by Chandrápîda to S'ukanasa, when requesting him to persuade his father to allow him to go to bring back Vais'ampayana.

—l. 18.-19. They two, having lamented, made the killer of their child extract from his heart the dart therein implanted'.

P. 33. ll 2-3. सांगं 'with its *angas*, which are six: Siksha, Chhandas, Vyákarana, Nirukta, Kalpa and Jyotisha'. उत्क्रांतशैशवौ who had passed their (state of) childhood.' कविप्रथमपद्धतिं 'the first path or road of (to be followed by) poets,' who first showed poets the way. He is 'आद्यः कविः' and hence the epithet.

—l. 8. भावेन 'by your honour', referring the Sûtradhara.

—ll. 13-14. Said by Rati to Cupid after he had been reduced

to athes by S'iva रजनी...मार्गे may be simply locative, or locative absolute. Enveloped in nocturnal darkness.'

P. 33, ll. 15-16. तां कुलप्रतिष्ठां प्रणमय्य-'making her, who was the glory or strength (source of stability) of the family, bow down to the tutelary deities. कारयितव्यदक्षा 'knowing well what others should be made to do'. सतीनां पादग्रहणमकारयत् 'made her seize (fall at) the feet of the chaste (matronly) women'.

—l. 17. एकोन्मीलनपेशल: 'calculated to at once unfold (recall to memory).'

—ll. 19-20. उत्सवसंकेतान् name of a people. जयोदाहरणं 'declaration or announcement of his victory' i. e. verses declaratory of the success of his arms.

—l. 21. अथ 'after the death of Das'aratha.' अनाथा: 'without a lord' owing to the king's death.'

—ll. 23-24. Said by Ráma to Sîtá रक्षसा 'by Rávana.'

—l. 25.—P. 34. l. 2. Said by Draupadî to Yudhisthira. 'What other king than yourself, who has all means favourable to him and who is proud of his family, will allow others to take away his wealth like his own wife, attached to him by virtue of good qualities, and born of a noble family'. क इव 'who possibly.'

P. 34. ll. 3-6. These four lines and the next two are addressed by Rávana to Sîtá, when he was endeavouring to win over her mind to himself. य: etc. 'he who extracts milk from a stone, will alone derive happiness from Ráma', meaning that it is simply impossible. बोधयंतं हिताहितं 'who (Rávana) is telling you what is good and bad.' किं विलापयसे 'why make me talk much.'

—ll. 7-8. 'Employ the demons and myself in rendering you service.' l. 25. 'who will not wish for the reverential bow made by Indra by folding his hands on his head,' i. e. as Indra, my conquered vassal, bows down to me, so will he bow down to you, my dear beloved. मूर्धानमधिगतः, or अधिगतो मूर्धा येन तमधिमूर्धानं.

P. 34. ll. 9-10. एनं *i. e.* रामं रक्षोगणं क्षिप्तुं 'calculated to disperse (destroy) the multitude of demons.' गाधिसुत: Vis'vámitra.

LESSON VI.

P. 38. l. 24. अधरोत्तरव्यक्तिर्भविष्यति 'it will be manifest who is inferior and who is superior.'

—ll. 26-27. अहं-अयं Ganadása, who complained to the king about Haradatta.

P. 39. l. 1. 'I conjure you by the life of' &c. if you do not say it in words. Said by Mádhava, when Málatî simply nodded replies to his questions.

—ll. 10-11. जरद्द्रविडधार्मिक: 'an old Dravida ascetic.' इच्छया goes with निसृष्ट:, and means 'to the satisfaction of.' अभिमतं goes with मनोरथं 'wished for,' 'cherished.'

—l. 14. किं बहुना 'why say much,' to be brief.

—l. 17. 'I am ashamed of my very heart, now that it knows the whole affair.'

P. 40. ll. 1-2. जनस्य *scil.* अस्ति 'belongs to,' 'is possessed by.' l. 21 'Then garden-creepers are, indeed, distanced, by wild creepers in point of excellence,' *i. e.* 'nature unadorned adorns the most.'

—ll. 3-4. Describe the state of Sudakshiná when pregnant. असमग्रभूषणा 'not having put on *all* her ornaments,' but only a few necessary ones, such as मंगलसूत्र, कंकण &c. मुखेन=मुखेनोपलक्षिता. तनुप्रकाश 'of dim lustre'. विचेयतारका the night 'the stars in which have to be searched out,' being very few, as it is nearly day-break.

—l. 6. मर्त्येषु असंमूढ: 'he, among all men, who, undeluded, knows me' etc.

—l. 10. अकथ्यमाने *i. e.* पुण्डरीकवृत्तांते.

—ll. 16-17. Translate :- 'Proud women, though they, having first slighted a prostration, are subsequently stung with remorse, ar nevertheless secretly (at heart) ashamed of propitiating their beloved ones, *i. e.* do not like to openly conciliate them.

P. 40. ll. 18-19. Said by Râma to Sîtâ, when Lakshamana said 'यावदार्याया हुताशने विशुद्धिं ' 'till the *purification* of Sîtá by fire.' Ráma means to say: 'Pity it is that people have to be propitiated by those whose wealth consists in their noble (*untarnished*) family, and hence that step (purification) was taken simply to please the people; and therefore what ill we have said of you, does not indeed befit you.' नः=अस्माभिः.

—ll. 20-21. Every instrumental is to be construed with the noun following it. अविनयबहुलतया etc. 'because blooming youth abounds in immodest acts.' तमपि=पुंडरीकं.

—l. 24—P. 41. l. 2. स्पृशति पदं 'attains to a position.' गुण etc. 'being connected with (arising from) the possession of a number of qualities', which are not found in the dog.

P. 41. l. 3. इति=मयि.

—l. 5. विनयप्रधानैः—विनयः प्रधानः येषां 'amongst which modesty stands foremost'.

—ll. 12-15. नंदमौर्यनृपयोः goes with अस्तोदयौ अविभिन्नकालं 'simultaneously'. These lines show the superiority of Chánakya to the sun: 'Who surpasses, by his lustre, the lustre of the thousand-rayed god, which is not all-pervading, and which causes cold and heat in *alternate succession*, (and not at one and the same time as did Chánakya).

—ll. 20-21. Describe the qualities of Duryodhana. उद्यतं 'uplifted' or drawn against enemies. His orders are most respectfully obeyed by kings. गुण also means 'a thread'.

—ll. 24-25. Refer to S'is'upála, as described by Nárada to Vishnu. बालः 'while yet a boy'. मुखेन etc. 'in face, being like the full moon, he was like the three-eyed god.' l. 20 'Now he, being a youth (grown-up man), who has made kings subject to tributes, is, to be sure, pre-eminently like the sun (who occupies the mountains with his rays).'

LESSON VII.

P. 47. l. 20. सर्वज्ञस्य has the sense of the instrumental. 'Undertaking to decide by only one person, howsoever omniscient, is liable to be faulty'.

—l. 23. अस्मै scil. बालकाय.

—l. 25. साधोः 'given to a good person.'

P. 48. l. 1. Said by Gangá to Earth when she was angry with Rama for having abandoned her daughter, Sítá. शरीरमसि संसारस्य 'you are the very body (main stay) of wordly life.'

—ll. 3-4. मिथ्या...निर्भरः 'full of pride of pretended (false) greatness.' आत्मप्रज्ञा etc. 'they hate the minister's advice thinking that it (following the advice) is degrading (derogatory to) their own wisdom'.

—l. 6. महाश्वेताप्रणामपुरःसरं 'first making his salutation (paying his respects) to Mahás'vetá.'

—l. 9. अवाङ्मनसगोचरं 'who is beyond the reach (range) of speech and mind', *i. e.* who can neither be described nor conceived.

—ll. 10-11. An address to the moon. The Amavasya (new moon day) occurs when the moon enters (आवसति) the body of the sun, but for which, there being no Dars'a day, there would be no performance of sacred rites by the pious. सुधया &c. *cf.* पर्यायपीतस्य सुरैर्हिमांशोः कलाक्षय श्लाघ्यतरो हि वृद्धे (R. V. 16.), the waning of the moon from day to day being ascribed to his being drunk up, digit by digit, by the Gods and Manes.

—ll. 12-13. Said by the seven sages to Himálaya when they asked Umá in marriage for S'iva. त्वत्कुल etc. 'this manner (collection of circumstances) is sufficient to elevate your family'.

P. 48. ll. 14-15. तृणबिंदोः परिशंकितः 'Indra afraid of Trinabindu' who was practising austere penance. Gods, and especially Indra, are always afraid of the penance of others; cf. S'ákuntala Act I.—'अस्त्येतदन्यसमाधिभीरुत्वं.' हरिणी name of a nymph.

—ll. 18-19. Said by Kautsa, when he found Raghu almost penniless, and wished to take his departure. निर्गलितांबुगर्भं etc. 'even the Chátaka does not trouble (press with request) an autumnal cloud, whose watery contents have been poured out or emptied.'

—ll. 20-21. 'The king having approached that only son* (of his parents) who was in that condition, told them both his deed done through ignorance.' उपेत्य, according to some means उद्दिश्य.

P. 49. l. 4. दंडवत्प्रणम्य 'falling quite prostrate on the ground,' like a stick lying horizontally down.

—l. 6. रामस्य दर्शनं सुहृदां 'the seeing of friends by Râma; Ráma's seeing his friends.'

—l. 8 कुलपांशव 'a disgrace to the family' who sully the honour of their family.

—ll. 12-13. स=दिलीपः. यज्ञाय 'for the performance of sacrifices' which keep gods contented. Indra sent down rain (*lit.* milked the heaven) for corn to grow; thus they two reciprocated services and supported the two worlds. गां दुदोह 'milked the earth' (took taxes).

—ll. 14-15. An address to Brahman. केवलात्मन् 'who was single, undivided.' गुणत्रय—'Rajas, Satva, and Tamas.' Bráhma was afterwards divided at the time of creation, the three qualities appearing respectively at the times of creation, preservation, and destruction.

—l. 16. दुःखात्सुखमुपनतं 'that happiness which falls to one's lot after (suffering) misery,' the savouriness of the pleasure arising from contrasted enjoyment.

—l. 24. अरुणाय कल्पते 'is fit to receive Aruna' the harbinger of the sun, which indicates the close of night.

P. 50. l. 2. अनुहुंकुरुते 'roars in return.'

* Better translate—The king having, approached them, told them of the condition their only son was in and his own deed etc.

P. 50. ll. 3-4. तथेति saying 'yes'. संतानकामाग 'who longed for issue or progeny.'

—ll. 5-6. तस्याः goes with प्रसादं.. l. 6. 'Communicated to his beloved the favour of the cow, inferred from the signs of delight (on his face), in words which were, as it were, superfluous, as the very appearance of delight informed the queen of the auspicious event.

—ll. 9-10. पुराणशोभां &c. 'restored to its former grandeur or magnificence.' न स्पृहयांबभूव etc. 'did not at all envy the happiness of either, because he already enjoyed it in his capital.'

—l. 12. सानुनीतिः=सानुनयः 'assuming a conciliatory tone.'

—ll. 13-16. दिदृक्षुं—त्वं शुभा न वेति द्रष्टुमिच्छन्तं. l. 14. 'It is the very character of demons that they should make inquiries about others' wives.' नमुस्कुर्याः scil. यदि.

LESSON VIII.

P. 56. l. 1. सत्क्रियाविशेषात् 'on account of the distinguished reception' (on the part of Indra); the king means to say that he has done nothing to merit such a grand reception at Indra's hands.

—l. 9. सूर्योपस्थानात् प्रतिनिवृत्तं 'returned after having served, or waited upon, the sun'.

—l. 18. उज्जिहानजीविता 'whose life is departing, or leaving her.'

—l. 20. उत्तरोत्तरं 'more following more,' 'talking more and more.'

P. 57. l. 1. तासां=अप्सरसां.

—ll. 5-6. Said by Purûravas to the swan. तावत् 'first,' 'before doing anything else.' l. 6. 'To the good the business of a supplicant is more weighty (important) than their own interest'.

—ll. 7-8. तपसे कृतोद्यमां 'who had made up her mind to practise penance.' मुनिव्रतं=तपश्चरणरूपं.

P. 57. l. 10. तदभावे &c.—In its absence (there being no protection) even that which exists becomes non-existing, *i. e.* there is no security of person or property.

—ll. 11-12. स=रघुः. अस्त्रं 'the science of missiles.' His father himself was his *guru.*

—ll. 13-14. तस्मात् 'from the conqueror, Raghu.' आत्मा संरक्षितः 'the Suhmas saved themselves.' वैतसीं वृत्तिमाश्रित्य 'following the course of reeds', which bend down to the current of water ; hence, 'yielding to a stronger enemy.'

—ll. 19-20. Describe the position of 'Madhyades'a.'

P. 58, ll. 2-3. जन्मकर्मतो मलिनतरजनं 'the people in which were dirtier than their birth and deeds.' निर्घृणतर etc. 'all whose practices were more abominable than their hearts.'

—ll. 4-5. She considers the pleasure-garden to be the bow of Cupid, which is lovely on account of having arrows made of flowers, and the garden is also lovely on account of bees clinging to the flowers. शिलीमुख 'arrow,' and 'bee.' पीतरक्ताः—पीताश्च ते रक्ताश्च, Champaka and As'oka being yellow and red respectively; and पीतं रक्तं यैस्ते when taken with रजनिचर.

—l. 6. आत्मसंपद् 'self-excellence.' आभिजनात्प्रभृति 'beginning with noble descent.'

—l. 13. लब्धप्रसरा 'who has got room for free or unhampered conduct,' 'grown ascendant.' दुःखोपचर्या 'served or propitiated with difficulty.'

—l. 16. विनयाधानं 'imparting moral training,' 'teaching good manners'.

—ll. 18-19. नवः=अजः ; नवेतरः=रघुः. l. 19. 'He, of firm resolve, did not desist from his practice of meditation till he had seen the Supreme Being.'

—l. 22. स्वनुष्ठित 'well-observed.'

P. 58. ll. 26-29. Said by Sîta, when she found Máruti near her in the As'oka garden. पूर्वस्मात् &c. 'he appears to be different from the former (*i. e.* Râvana), since he devoutly glorifies Rama; or is it that he has come here to inspire confidence in me, without any cruelty?' प्रभातात् प्राक् scil. दृष्टानि स्वप्नदर्शनादीनि शुभनिमित्तानि.

—l. 30. P. 59. l. 3. स=मारुतिः; तां=सीतां. प्रीतेः पराजयमानां 'who found (Rávana's) addresses to be unbearable.'

P. 59. ll. 6-7. एकाक्षरं 'the one syllable' ओम्. सावित्र्यास्तु परं नास्ति 'there is nothing superior to Sávitrî,' the celebrated Gayatri Mantra (which has to be silently repeated or *muttered.*)

LESSON IX.

P. 64. l. 6. वर्तमानकवि 'a *living* or contemporary poet.'

—l. 10. बद्धभाव 'has fixed her affection' on you. त्वद्गतं=त्वयि आहितं.

—ll. 11-12. Said by Lava to Kus'a.

P. 65. l. 5. संसर्गमुक्तिः खलेषु=खलसंसर्गमुक्तिः, 'shunning the company of wicked people.'

—l. 7. संतानार्थाय विधये 'for (the performance of) some rite having for its object progeny.'

—ll. 12-13. Said by Indra to Cupid, when entrusting to him a great mission. आत्मसमं 'you who are like myself;' भूधरतामवेक्ष्य 'seeing his capacity to hold up the earth.'

—l. 15. कृत्स्नं गोत्रमंगलं 'Sítá who formed the entire auspiciousness' of both the families.

ll. 19-20. ईशां 'their lord.' *i. e.* Rama. नितांत &c. 'who entertained a very cruel thought with respect to Sîta,' *i. e.* of abandoning her.

—ll. 21-22. परकर्मापहः 'destroying the works of his enemies.' l. 22. 'Striking his foes in their weak points, he covered his own weak ones.'

P. 65. ll. 23-27. Said by Rákshasa to Lakshmî with reference to the want of appreciation of merits shown by her in leaving Nanda and falling in love with Chandragupta.

P. 66. ll. 1-3. Said to Vidûshaka by Dushyanta who was pleased with the *picture* of S'akuntalá, though he had himself first repudiated her when she came to him *in person*.

—ll. 9-10. Said by Rávana to Sîtâ, when she contemptuously spurned all his supplications. प्रतिपत्तिपराङ्मुखी 'not inclined to acknowledge me' as your lord.

—ll. 13-14. स=जनकः. आप्तवचनात् 'from the words of the trust-worthy sage.' At these words of the sage, Janaka became assured of the manly heroism existing in Rághava though he appeared to be but a boy.' त्रिदशगोपमात्रके 'of the size of an Indragopa insect,' as small as etc.

LESSON X.

P. 75. l. 23. विश्रंभातिशयप्रसंगसाक्षिणः' 'bearing testimony to the occurrences (incidents) of much familiarity' between us two.

P. 76. l. 1. एवमवस्थिते 'under these circumstances.'

—l. 2. तत्र प्रभवति देवी 'your ladyship has full power to do that' etc.

—ll. 5-6. अयं जनः *i. e.* Málatî. न खलु etc. 'that being is surely not dead, who is remembered by his beloved.'

—l. 13. समरशिरसि 'in the front of battle,' 'in the thickest of the fight.'

—ll. 16-18 सर्वदेवमयस्य 'he was like Náráyana, who represents all gods, because he had the several deities dwelling in himself.' Dharma in the mind. *i. e.* he was as straightforward or righteous as Dharma, etc.

—ll. 19-20. Certainly Dharma staying here in his entirety, setting at naught the sports of Kali age (being not influenced by its effects) does not think of the (good old) Kr*i*ta age,' the age proper for Dharma; so good is the life of those who dwell in this hermitage.

P. 76. l. 22. तव प्रसादस्य etc. 'but with you, the blessings have preceded your favour', against the general course of cause and effect

P. 77. l. 2. शीर्षच्छेद्यः 'to be decapitated.' ते=त्वया.

—ll. 3 4. अकामयेतां scil. '2 two mothers, Kausalyâ and Sumitrâ.

—ll. 5-6. Said by Sîtá to Lakshma*n*a, when she was ruthlessly abandoned. मद्वचनात् 'in my name.'

—l. 7. द्वादशः परिवत्सरः 'it is now 12 years since the world was made destitute of the queen.'

—l. 9. मैथिल्यभिज्ञानं=मैथिलि अभिज्ञानं

—ll. 12-13. सा=सीता. etc. ' Knowing the entry of the monkey into the (impregnable) city Lanká to be a miraculous occurrence'.

—ll 15-18. Reflections of Sîtá, at her first seeing Máruti alighting in the garden. She first believes him to be Râva*n*a. ll. 17-18 state why she does not believe that the person had been sent by Râma. 'Dwelling to the north of this sea, how could Râma know this city situated to the south of the salt ocean ?'

LESSON XI.

P. 82. l. 1. Said by Parivrájika, when she was told to sit as a judge to decide the quarrel between the two dancing preceptors. पत्तने etc.—a question; 'is a jewel examined in a village there being a town (hard by)', meaning the king alone was fit to do the duty asked of her.

—l. 3. मा तावत् 'oh, do not do so', 'hold, hold.'

—l. 5. किं दीपिकापौनरुक्त्येन 'why the superfluity of lights' 'why want these lights', they are superfluous.

P. 82. l. 7. किं वृत्तं 'what became of her', 'how it fared with her.'

—l. 8. रघुकदंबकेषु 'the pre-eminent among Raghus'.

P. 83. l. 4. स्मर्तव्यशेषं नयामि 'make him only remain in memory', *i. e.* kill him,

—ll. 7-8. बीजं Sítá herself, who, when she was pregnant, was cast off.

—ll. 9-10. सा Prithví. मा त्यात व्याहरत्येव 'just as he (the lord) was saying 'oh, do not, do not take her away'.

—l. 18. पतनाय वल्लरी 'a creeper (dependent on the tree) tends (is sure) to fall down'.

—ll. 21-22. The strong-minded are not deterred by the appearance of danger.

P. 84. l. 1. संतानवाहीनि 'continuously flowing', 'incessantly working.'

—l. 2. स्रोतः सहस्रैरिव संप्लवन्ते 'flow together, as it were, in thousands of currents,' find out thousands of new channels to vent themselves.

—l. 3 पंचभिः 'the five constituent elements.' पंचत्वं गते 'reduced to the state of five', resolved or decomposed into its component members.

—ll. 7-8. तस्मिन्=अस्त्रे, the missile which was used by Kus'a against Vásuki to get back his golden bracelet. समाविद्ध etc. 'with its hands in the form of waves tossed about through agitation.' रोधांसि निघ्नन् 'violently dashing against the sides'.

—ll. 11-14. Rákshasa says to Malayaketu that everything is ready for action, and every circumstance is favourable to them. त्वद्वाञ्छांतरितानि 'obstructed by your desire,' *i. e.* 'only *desire* to march onward and everything else is ready.' The several locative absolutes show the favourable circumstances. चलिताधिकारविमुखे 'indifferent, being dismissed from his authority.' मार्ग etc.—योग is superfluous; 'whose business is only pointing out the way'.

P. 84. ll. 15-18. Said by As'vatthaman. l. 15. Who acted like the submarine fire in the ocean consisting of the enemy's forces lapped by the flames of the missiles hurled against them.

LESSON XII.

P. 90. ll. 20-23. The four lines give the use of all the short forms वः-नः in the sense of the instrumental; 'fit to be served *by* you or us.'

—l. 26. कार्यवशात् 'for my purpose', that I might understand and realise the events of that time.

P. 91. ll. 1-2. Said by Sítá. जातनिर्विशेषाः 'just like my children.'

—l. 3. वाग्विषयीभूतः 'who formed the subject of our talk.'

—l. 10. संदिशन्ति 'send love-messages'. समुपसर्पन्ति 'draw near their beloved ones.'

—ll. 12-13. एकः—अपरः Aja and Raghu. प्रभुशक्तिसंपदा 'by the excellence of his sovereign power'. प्रभुशक्ति consisting of कोष, दंड and बल. प्रणिधानयोग्यया 'by the practice of concentration (meditation)'. शरीरगोचरान् 'visible (existing) in (pervading) the body.'

—ll. 14-15. Krishna says to Arjuna: 'Those who are deprived of their discerning power by various desires, look up to other gods, performing various rites and controlled (guided) by their own nature.'

—ll. 18-19. Describe the state of those who are puffed up with the possession of riches. व्यसनशत &c. 'though become the mark of hundreds of calamities', though exposed to hundreds of miseries, they do not perceive that their fall is imminent like that of the drops of water on the ends of grass growing on ant-hills.

—l. 20. मणिदर्पणमिव etc.—on account of its lucid and transparent water, it served, as it were, as a mirror for the Goddess of Splendour to see her face in.

P. 92. ll. 1-2. नरपतिः the Chedi king. आविश्चकार 'put forth', 'exhibited.'

—l. 5. अर्थोष्मणा विरहितः 'devoid of the warmth of wealth'; *cf.* the English phrase 'a *warm* man.'

l. 18. 'As is seen in Chitrâ and the moon in their conjunction when freed from mists.'

ll. 19-20. The peculiarity of a slanderer is that he poisons the ears of *one* and destroys *another* (by reason of his backbiting), unlike the ordinary course of bites, which kill only him who is bitten.

—ll. 21-22. Describe the qualities of Aja. l. 22. 'The prince did not differ from his (generating) cause, his father, just as a lamp lighted from another, does not differ from it' (in flame or light).

LESSON XIII.

P. 97. l. 12. ते गतिं ज्ञास्यन् 'wishing to know your fate,' what had become of you.

—l. 14. वारितप्रसरः 'prevented from advancing.'

—ll. 16-17. श्रुतमृषेः 'learnt from the sage', of which he had heard from the sage. l. 17. Rághava became excited though he was not conscious of the acts of his former existence (in the Dwarf incarnation).

—ll. 20–21. Said by Máhas'vetá, when her mind was drawn by Cupid towards the holy sage Pu*nd*arîka.

P. 98. ll. 3-4. Said by Ga*n*adása, when Dhârinî wasn ot willing to allow him to exhibit his skill in acting in the person of his pupil Málviká. क्रियासंक्रांति 'the power of transferring or imparting to another what one knows or can do.'

—ll. 9-10. क्षेमाय 'for security', to ensure their safety. शत्रून् हन्तीति शत्रुघ्नः and hence the significance of his name.

P. 98. l. 16. क्रथकैशिकेन्द्रः=भोजः, the king of the Vaidarbhas. चंद्रं &c. 'like the sea, with its surging waves, going to meet the moon', which occurs at the phenomenon known as Tides.

LESSON XIV.

P. 102. l. 24. अत्रभवतोः of Haradatta and Ga*n*adása. ज्ञानसंघर्षः 'a literary contest', 'a contention for superiority in knowledge.'

—ll. 26-27. Said by Agnimitra to Vidushaka when the latter told him how he had made Mádhaviká set at liberty the two girls, Málaviká and Bakulávaliká.

P. 103. l. 1. Said by Purûravas to Chitralekha and Urvaśî, when they were called up to execute an order of their lord, Indra.

—l. 7. अवश्यकर्तव्यतामापतितं has become such as must be done', has become an imperative necessity.

—l. 8. दक्षिणाक्षि &c. 'should be made to take the hint given by the contraction (winking) of the right eye'; you should wink at them in such a manner that they will at once understand what you mean.

—ll. 13-14. I consider him to be the best man who respectively obliges and retaliates upon him who has helped and laughed at him in adversity.'

—l. 16. 'The king should remove the afflictions of a person who is distressed and who dwells in his dominions.'

—l. 17. उत्क्रांतमिवासुभिः 'their life left them, as it were.'

—ll. 22-23. Said by Ràkshasa, when he was told that a person desired to see him on urgent business.

P. 104. ll. 1-2 'When you have thus completely filled the measure of your sins, the anger of the Pa*nd*avas will act only as a trifling cause to lead you to your doom.'

—l. 5. 'A heart, agitated by grief, is eased (disburdened) only by lamentations.'

P. 104. l. 7. पृष्ठतः कृत्वा 'putting in the back ground,' repressing.

—ll. 8-9. Describe the fame of Raghu. अनुबन्धि 'ever continuous', eternal. इयत्तया परिच्छेत्तुं नालं 'cannot be circumscribed within any limits.' *i. e.* no determinate limit can be set to it.

—ll. 10-11. हसितं मुदा प्रसितं 'laughter delightfully continued.' विलसितं etc. 'joyous sports, enlivened by love' decreased. हतसंमदाः 'destitute of exhilerating passions.' पुरहितं etc. 'and what was beneficial to, and desired by, the town was not done.'

—ll. 12-16. Said by Kanva, when sending Dushyanta a message. संयमधनान् 'whose only wealth is their restraint of passions.' कथमप्यबांधवकृतां 'not in any way brought about by her relatives.' ll. 15-16 'She should be looked upon by you as one of your wives with a respect common to all. Further than this rests with fate; it should not be uttered (referred to) by the relatives of the bride.'

LESSON XV.

P. 110. l. 21. मिथ्यावार्तासंदेशकैः 'by false accounts and messages.'

P. 111. l. 5. इष्टिपशुमारं मारितः 'slaughtered like a sacrificial victim.' सः=मातलिः.

—l 6. चित्रलेखाद्वितीया 'having Chitralekhá for her companion.'

—ll. 15-16. कोधविह्वला scil. शूर्पणखा. भातरौ Khara and Dûshana.

—ll. 18-19. लतानुपातं 'repeatedly bending down the creepers.' नद्यवस्कंदं etc.—'would sip water, troubling the (waters of) rivers.' चारुशिलोपवेशं 'seating himself on some charming rock.'

P. 112. l. 3. विश्वासप्रतिपन्नानां 'who have entered into confidence.

—ll. 7-8. 'Overcoming (all sense of) shame, warding off decorum, and at once rooting out strength of mind.' मंथरविवेकं 'slow in (forming) judgment.'

—l. 16. अमंदलीलया 'with graceful agility.'

P. 112. l. 17. स्थिते अर्धरात्रे 'when it was midnight.'

—ll. 19-20 विप्रदर्शं...यत्ना 'who made an attempt at killing whomsoever she considered (saw) to be a Bráhmana.' जिघांसुवेदं...क्षः 'who took resplendant missiles to kill whomsoever he knew to be murderous.'

—ll. 22-23. 'Better that he dies or is dried up &c who does not abide by his elders' order in the case of a difficult thing (to do which is an arduous duty); how much more so when he is told to travel abroad' (a compratively easy work.)

—ll. 25-28. Rákshasa blames Malayaketu for suspecting his conduct without any ground. 'How' says he, 'did it not occur to his mind that he, who even now served his master's cause though they themselves were dead and gone, would not certainly ally himself with his professed enemies, so long as he *lived* safe and sound ?'

LESSON XVI.

P. 117. l. 29. नो गुणदोषतः परिच्छेत्तुं 'to examine or test us with regard to our merits and demerits,' so as to ascertain our excellences and defects.

P. 118. l. 1. समयपूर्वं 'attended with promises or agreements.

—l. 3. Said by the son of Purûravas, when he was about to be entrusted by his father with the serious responsibility of governing the kingdom.'

—l. 6. का गणना 'what need we say of,' 'much more is it true in the case of.'

—ll. 8-9. अचिराधिष्ठितराज्यः 'who has newly acquired sovereignty,' whose sovereignty is newly established. अरूढमूलत्वात् 'not having struck deep roots in (the minds of) his subjects,' and who, therefore, resembles a tree which is loose on account of its being newly planted (when it has not struck its roots deep in the soil).

—ll. 14-15. 'The life described was Ráma's; the work belonged to Vâlmîki, and they themselves had voices like those of Kinnaras; so what was there which was not calculated to enchant the hearer's mind?'

P.119. l. 4. अनुभवसमां वेदनां 'an agony equal to that when (they are) experienced', *i. e.* the same grief as that when the miseries are actually suffered. स्मरण etc. 'Be, therefore, pleased, not to make your life the fuel (prey) of the fire of sorrow caused by the recollection (of past incidents).

—ll. 9-10. Said sarcastically by Bhîma.

—ll. 11-14. वेगोदग्रं 'deadly by reason of its quickness of circulation,' 'deadly in its effect.' अयं भरः 'this pre-eminence or superiority' exists in them naturally (जात्या).

ll. 15-16. Said by S'iva disguised as an ascetic. बहुक्षमा 'possessed of much patience.

—l. 18. Said by the seven sages to Himâlaya: 'join your daugther with him, like meaning with words.'

ll. 20-21. शुचो वशं गंतुं नार्हसि 'be pleased not to give way to sorrow.'

—ll. 23-26. यमौ 'the twins' *i. e.* Nakula and Sahadeva कथैव नास्ति 'no account need be taken of' विस्फारित etc. 'who has drawn (made to vibrate) his circular bow' (or perhaps his bow and wheel).

LESSON XVII.

P. 126. ll. 8-11. भर्तुः goes with प्रतीपं l. 11 'In this way young women attain to the position of house wives; those of an opposite character are the banes of their families.'

—ll. 18-19. अनन्यभाजं 'not devoted to any one else' तथ्यमेव for she *did* afterwards obtain a husband of that description in Hara. l. 19. 'The words of the great (lords) never bear a contrary meaning in this world', *i. e.* never turn out false

—ll. 21-22. The might of Rávana is here described. Who night and day disturbed the heaven, by contending with the enemy of Namuch (Indra)' by doing the various things given in line 21. पुरी=अमरावती.

P. 127. ll. 3-4. धनबद्ध &c. 'May the people rejoice, deriving delight from the close (familiar) talks with their friends and relations.'

—l. 11. There are ups and downs in the state of man as in the course of the wheel.

LESSON XVIII.

P. 132. ll. 19-20. Said by S'ukanása in vindication of Chandrápídá's conduct.

—ll. 23-24. 'One who longs to secure S'rî may or may not get her; how can he, who is desired by S'rî herself, be unobtainable ?'

P. 133. l. 1. कार्यहंतारं 'marring the interests.'

—ll. 5-6. Krishna here describes the importance of religions actions.

—ll. 7-8. कथं भवेत् 'what will be its state ?' तत्तुल्य=भीष्मद्रोणतुल्य.

—ll. 17-20. The king names the several things he hopes Urvas'i will do. गूढा 'being herself hidden or invisible'. बलादानीयेत पदात्पदं 'may be forcibly brought (as it were) step by step', so unwilling is she, through fear, to advance.

—ll. 21-22. ध्रुवेच्छां 'of resolute will. ' l. 22 'who can turn back in the contrary direction (thwart) the mind which is firmly resolved upon securing its desired object, and water flowing towards a lower ground ?'

P. 134. ll. 5-6. Said by Sitâ. 'Or I should certainly be reckless of this wretched life of mine, fruitless on account of (my) ever-lasting separation from you (*i. e.* would gladly abandon it), if your seed implanted in my womb, and which must be preserved, were not an obstacle in my way.'

P. 134. दंष्ट्रांकुरात् 'from the pointed (sharp) jaws'.

—l. 13. भूतये goes with नृपतेः in the next line.

—l. 14. They are (real) servants of the king; others are like wives, who follow their husbands for *their* own good.

—l. 15. जीवितापहा 'mortal; fatal to life.'

LESSON XIX.

P. 138. l. 3. आविर्भूतज्योतिषां 'to whom the Supreme Light has manifested itself.'

—ll. 10-11. प्राणैः etc. 'did not deprive him of his life.' अपि तु etc. But he, whose will was inconceivable, caused him, when all his wounds had been healed, to be led to the prison and caused it to be estimated or calculated by astrologers' etc.

—ll. 13-14 प्रसेदुः 'brightened up.' प्रदक्षिणार्चिः etc. 'the fire accepted oblations (thrown into it) with its flames on the right.

—ll. 16-17. परिमेयपुरःसरौ 'with a limited (very small, which could be counted) retinue.' अनुभावविशेषात् 'by reason of their superior lustre.'

—ll. 18-19. अत्यगादाश्रमं 'passed by the hermitage' without stopping there for fear of obstructing the sage's penance.'

LESSON XX.

P. 147. ll. 25-26. 'If the two princes had grown up without any harm, they should have, by this time, attained to your age.'

P. 148. ll. 3-4. Said by the seven sages to Himalaya. How could the serpent have sustained the Earth with his tender hoods, if you had not supported it from its very depths.'

ll. 7-8. असौ *i. e.* Kapálakun*d*alá. पापं *i. e.* killing Málatí.

—ll. 9-10. 'That servants succeed even in great works is the result of the honour paid to them by their masters in assigning to them those duties.'

P. 148. l. 15. **अन्यल्लिखितं** 'any other document or paper' written by him.

—ll. 21-22. **स्पृहणीयशोभं** 'whose beauty was enviable.' **परस्परेण** goes with **द्वंद्वं** 'had not intended these two as a couple.'

P. 149. ll. 1-4. **मोहकलिलं** 'confusion or taint caused by ignorance,' **निर्वेदं गंतासि** etc. 'will become indifferent to all that you have heard or will hear;' **श्रुतिविप्रतिपन्ना** 'confused by what you have heard.'

—ll. 5-6. Masters of great cars (great chariot-warriors) will think that through fear, you desisted from the fight; then you, having been once highly thought of by them, will fall to littleness.'

LESSON XXI.

P. 154. l. 14. **कांतमात्मीयं पश्यति** 'considers his own as beautiful.'

—ll. 20-21. **द्वंद्वसंप्रहारं** 'mutual conflict.' **प्रत्युपस्थिते** 'when it has come to this pass.'

—l. 22.—P. 155. l. 2. **अलमप्रभुः** 'altogether powerless.' **अंधकारता-मुपयाति** 'grows dim.'

P. 155. l. 13. **उत्कर्षनिकषः** 'a test or criterion of superiority.'

—ll. 14-15. Said by Ràma to Válmíki. **ताः=प्रजाः.**

—ll. 17-18. **सभाजनाक्षराणि पातयिष्यामि** 'I shall drop a few words of compliments' as proceeding from you.

P. 156. ll. 1-3. Mahás'vetá means that if she, acting in pursuance of the dictates of propriety, were to become ready to die, she would reject the request of Kapinjala and at the same time incur the sin of having caused Pu*nd*aríka's death.

—l. 4. **अगृहीते राक्षसे** 'so long as Rákshasa is not won over.'

—ll. 7-8. Said by the enraged S'àrngarava to S'akuntalá, when he found the king denying all knowledge of having ever before married her. **तथा त्वमसि** *i. e.* **जारिणी.**

—l. 12. **क्रियार्थं** 'for religious rites.'

P. 156. l. 15. एनं 'the soul' नित्यजातं-नित्यं मृतं 'ever born, ever dead
—l. 18. लक्ष्मीं तनोति 'adds to, enhances, the lustre.'

LESSON XXII.

P. 192. l. 12. स्वरसंयोग: 'combination of notes,' voice.

—l. 15. अतिभूमिं गतेन 'having reached its climax,' excessive.

—l. 21. अहो जाने 'who, I fancy.'

P. 163. l. 3. 'The wise accept the one or the other after a careful examination (for themselves); a fool only has his mind guided (influenced) by the convictions of others.'

—l. 4. चिंताविषघ्न: 'antidote against anxiety.'

—l. 12. On account of the pitchy darkness 'the sight has become useless, like service rendered to a wicked man.'

—ll. 17-18. न वेद्मि etc. 'he fell down on the ground whether through the force of love etc.........I do not know.' सद्योविपाकस्य 'which reaped its fruit immediately.'

—ll. 20-21. पात्रविशेषन्यस्तं 'placed in, imparted to, an excellent material.' गुणान्तरं 'a higher excellence.'

P. 164. ll. 3-4. स सखा 'Cupid, your friend.' l. 4. 'I am, as it were, the wick of the lamp, all covered with smoke in the form of this unbearable calamity.'

—ll. 5-6. Since even one's own body and soul are known to be subject to separation (or subject to union and separation), say why separation from external objects (such as wife, children etc.) should trouble a wise man.'

—ll. 9-10. 'Said by Râma, when his mind was vacillating as to whether he should abandon the innocent Sîta, or turn a deaf ear to scandals about himself. एकपक्षाश्रय etc. 'being at a loss to follow any *one* alternative, his mind was swaying backwards and forwards, like a swing.'

LESSON XXIII.

P. 168. l. 21. भर्तृगतया 'about her husband'. गतया=संबन्धिन्या.

—l. 24. उन्नमितोपदेशः गणदासः 'Ganadása's instruction was found to be superior'.

P. 169. ll. 6-7. देवस्य *i. e.* of Dushyanta. Said by the Chamberlain when he was going to report the arrival of Kanva's pupils. उपरोधकारि 'causing trouble or disturbance, troublesome'.

—l. 11. Said by Párvatî to her friend. स्फुरितोत्तराधरः=स्फुरणभूयिष्ठः अधरो यस्य सः 'whose lip was greatly throbbing,' making a movement to speak; or better still 'whose upper and lower lips were throbbing'.

—l. 12. तस्मात्=महतोऽपभाषमाणात्.

—ll. 19-20. परोक्षमन्मथः 'who has had no percept nor experience of love', who is out of the reach of the influence of love. l. 20. 'Let not, O friend, that (which was simply uttered in jest,) be taken in earnest'.

P. 170. ll. 6-7. Said by S'árngarava to Dushyanta when he said he could not believe S'akuntalá's words. शाठ्यमशिक्षितः 'untrained to guile'. अप्रमाणं 'is not (regarded as) an authority', 'is not held trustworthy.' विद्या इति 'considering it to be a regular branch of learning'

—ll. 8-9. त्वं यस्य नेत्रयोः पथि स्थिता 'in whose range of sight you stood' by chance, and whose eyes, therefore, became अवंध्य (not useless, having reaped their fruit). दृढसौहृदः 'of deep-rooted friendship'.

—ll. 10-11. Said by Himálaya to the seven illustrious sages. रजसोपि परं 'even higher than (transcending) the *Rajas* quality'.

—ll. 12-13. Raghu's father was not only the sole Emperor, but also the sole (unrivalled) archer in the land.

—ll. 14-15. सुखश्रव 'pleasant to hear'. दिवौकसां पथि आकाशे

P. 170. ll. 18-19. अन्यथावृत्ति 'changed', 'perturbed'. कंठाश्लेषप्रणयिनि 'longing for a close embrace of the neck'.

—l. 22. अशिक्षितपटुत्वं 'untaught guile or cunning'.

—ll. 26-27. Agnimitra means to say that the severe pangs caused by Cupid seem hardly consistent with his weapon which is apparently so harmless, being only made of flowers; therefore the saying that 'the softer it is, the harder (to bear)', is realised in Cupid.

—ll. 28-29. ०दर्शनाश्वासि 'derives encouragement or consoles itself by seeing the manifestations of her love'. रतिं etc. 'the desire of both of us produces satisfaction', the very idea that we love each other contributes to make me happy.

LESSON XXIV.

P. 176. ll. 15-16. Said by the Sùtradhára to his wife when she was making grand preparations for a banquet in honour of Bráhmanas in view of the coming lunar eclipse, which, in his opinion, could not then take place.

—l. 22. तिष्ठतु पुरस्तात् 'let it stand over'.

P. 170. l. 2. भवितव्यं च etc. 'and the days are sure to become pleasant on account of the absence of heat'.

—l. 3. प्रणयिप्रियत्वात् 'on account of his affection (kind feeling) for his devotees or worshippers'. तां=मालां.

—ll. 9-11. The plan suggested by the family-priest when the king refused to acknowledge S'akuntalá as his wife. अत्रभवती=शकुंतला. उपदिष्ट 'told', 'foretold'. तल्लक्षणोपपन्नः 'endowed with the signs (of an emperor)'. विपर्यये 'if the result be otherwise.'

—ll. 16-17. Said by Kus'a to the presiding Goddess of Ayodhyá when she had found her way into the king's palace, though closely bolted. लब्धांतरा 'having got an access to.'

P. 176. ll. 21-22. बाहूत्क्षेपं 'throwing up her arms.' स्त्रीसंस्थानं ज्योतिः 'a flash of light in female shape.' अप्सरस्तीर्थं 'name of a holy place'.

P. 171. l. 4. निशितनिपाताः 'of sharp decent,' 'sharp-falling.'

—ll. 5-8. च-च in every line has the sense of 'scarcely-when.' घनाघनः 'compact and condensed.'

LESSON XXV.

P 182. l. 31. ज्ञानवृद्धभावः 'being advanced (grown old) in knowledge,' *i. e.* 'though both equally learned.' पुरस्कारमर्हति 'is entitled to precedence.'

P. 183. l. 1. Said by Vidùshaka who had expected to get a *vàyana* from the preceptor of dancing.

—l. 3. अनियंत्रणानुयोगः 'can be freely (without any reserve or restraint) questioned.'

—ll. 6-7. तत्पाटवात् the skill of Kámamanjarî who had entirely fascinated his mind.

—ll. 8-9. बद्धकलकले 'who had set up a loud uproar.' प्रदीप्तांशरसं 'with his hood expanded.' भीतो नाम 'pretending to be afraid,' 'like one afraid.'

—l. 11. घुणाक्षरं 'an incision in wood or in the leaf of a book caused by an insect or book-worm and resembling somewhat the form of a letter.' ०न्यायेन 'in a fortuitous and unexpected manner,' 'by a happy chance.'

—ll. 16-19. Said by Ráma when he felt the balmy touch of Sîtá's hand.

P. 184. l. 2. प्रयोगेणाधिक्रियतां 'should be made the subject of representation,' 'should be brought out on the stage.'

—ll. 8-9. Said by Ráma when the old Chamberlain addressed the newly-crowned king in his usual familiar way as 'Rámabhadra' and stopped short, discovering the impropriety. तात-परिजनस्य 'the servants of my father,' hence old enough to call Ráma

Rámabhadra instead of Máharája. यथाभ्यस्त 'as is your wont,' you are accustomed to do '

P. 184. l. 10. अष्टादशवर्षदेशीयः 'about 18 years old,' 'whose a; bordered on 18.'

—l. 14. अनुज्झितक्रमः 'not leaving the bounds of propriety.'

—ll. 15-18. आत्तदंडः 'having assumed the sceptre.' अतनुषु etc 'There may be kinsmen in affluent circumstances (when there ar abundant means of income), but in you is summed up (comprehended the whole duty of a kinsman towards your subjects,' *i. e.* there may b found many parasitical gluttons in days of prosperity, but you are th real kinsman of the people in good as well as bad days.

—ll. 19-20. करणोज्झितेन 'forsaken by the senses' of perceptior touch etc., *i. e.* grown senseless. तैलनुनिषेकबिंदुना with the drop of dripping oil.'

—ll. 21-22. कांतिप्रदः 'giver of lustre' मासो etc., 'the month o Vais'akha,' spring-time, when the trees are laden with flowers.

LESSON XXVI.

P. 187-28. कुब्जलीला 'the gait of a hump-backed person,' or 'the manner of the Kubja plant,' a bent gait.

—l. 30. प्रत्युत्पन्नमति 'possessed of ready wit,' 'having presence of mind.'

P. 188. l. 3. खलीकरोति 'makes one act wickedly.'

—ll. 9-10. यदणीयसि etc. 'that a great regard is shown (to a person) even for a small cause or occasion'.

—l. 11. अलमन्यथा गृहीत्वा 'do not misunderstand me.'

—l. 12. Generally persons, equally learned, are jealous of each other's renown.'

—l. 17. चीयते 'is attended with fruit, becomes fruitful.'

P. 189. l. 12. कल्याणी 'the sacred cow.'

P. 189. ll. 13-14. Said by Aja, when the celestial garland dropping on Indumatī's bosom, deprived her of life, but did him no harm,

---

LESSON XXVII.

P. 194. ll. 3-4. अभिनिवेश्य 'directing (the mind) to objects.' कालांतरक्षमो न भवति 'is unable to brook delay.'

—ll. 14-15. ईदृश: etc. 'such has turned out to be the lot (fate) of your being created.'

—ll. 18-19. The meaning is that, the more the desire for wealth is cherished, the more it leads one to commit *dark* deeds. The simile is taken from a lamp, which gives out more and more soot as the flame is made brighter and brighter.

P. 195. l. 4. भस्मावशेषं चकार 'reduced to ashes.'

—ll. 5-6. Just as the Ganges is revered for having taken its rise from thef oot of the Supreme Being (Vishnu), so also is it revered for having derived its second source from your high head. Said with reference to the Himálaya mountain personified. उच्छिरसा 'whose head (speaks) has gone up' into the sky.

—ll. 11-12. अभिषेकांते 'at the conclusion of the coronation ceremony.' l. 12. By which their own sacrifices, with complete gifts, would be completed,' *i. e.* wealth sufficient to enable them to complete their sacrifices

—ll 14-15. विरलजनसंपाते 'frequented by a few people.' विमानोत्संग name of the king's palace.

P. 196. l. 1. लोकयात्रा सिद्धा 'this course of life is settled.'

—l. 11. Since transitoriness *first* claps to the bosom one that is born, and *then* the mother like a nurse, what ground is there for lamentation ?'

—ll. 15-16. उभयो:=कुशलवयो:; 'the people wondered not so much at their skill in music as at their thorough disregard to the free-will gifts offered by the king.'

P. 196. l. 20. A salutary advice to those **who are in the habit doing things at the** eleventh hour.

LESSON XXVIII.

P. 201. ll. 9-10. Said by S'ukanása to Chandrápíd'a **सुखं विशां** 'easily find access to.'

—ll. 11-12. **सर्वतोमुखी** 'in every respect,' 'unlimited,' 'complet

—ll. 13. **यस्य** refers to Himálaya.

—ll. 16-17. The idea of the lines is best expressed by 'Uni is strength.'

P. 202. ll. 7-8. Said by Chandrápíd'a's mother to Manoramá the time of allowing him to go to bring back Vais'ampáyana.

—ll. 9-10. **असंशयं** etc. scil. **शकुंतला**. l. 10. The meaning is that t secret prompting (the inner voice) of the heart of good men is a sa guide for them to follow, since it can never think of an illegitima object.

—ll. 11-14. Said by Dushyanta to S'akuntalá. **एवंप्राया** etc. For suc for the most part, is the behaviour of those, over whom darkne (of infatuation) exercises mastery, in auspicious (good) matte (on auspicious occasions.)

—ll. 15-19. **एवमादिभिः** *i. e.* **उपायैः. सा=उर्वशी. तदाश्रयिणी** ' relatir to her.'

—ll. 20-21. 'They call you who are immovable (another Vishnu, for your belly (interior) (like Vishnu's) has become tl support of beings, movable and immovable.'

—ll. 22-25. Describe the position in which the cloud messeng will probably find the Yaksha's wife. **भावगम्यं** 'conceived by the mind

P. 203. l. 3. **मखजं** 'caused by the great Vis'vajit sacrifice,' i which Raghu had given away all his wealth.

P. 203. ll. 5-6. इयं Málaviká. प्रेष्यभावेन 'in the capacity of a servant.' वा 'like'

—ll 7-8. पंक्तिरथः=दशरथः, पंक्ति meaning '10'. What Das'aratha, transgressing the rules, did, was, indeed, forbidden to the king; (how, then, did he, a wise king, do it ?) for even learned persons, when blinded by (the quality of) darkness (passion) set foot on the wrong road.'

—ll. 20-23. Said by Rákshasa when he found the plot most cleverly laid against him by the wily Chánakya. शकटेन=शकटदासेन his bosom friend.

—ll. 28-29. Said by Agnimitra when he found it difficult to conceal any longer from Irávatì his ardent love for Málaviká. खंडन-हेतवः 'occasions or pretexts to disappoint her.'

—l. 29. 'But not a form of courtesy (polite behaviour) towards proud or intelligent women, though (it be) greater than before, but wanting in sincerity.'

LESSON XXIX.

P. 211. ll. 18-19. शक्ति 'regal power' which has three constituent elements: प्रभाव 'the majesty or pre-eminence of the king himself'; मंत्र 'the power of good counsel', and उत्साह 'the force of energy'.

—ll. 22-23. 'Oh! the property of those who are bereft of support through the failure of issue (lineal descendants) passes over to another, at the decease of the original progenitor (from whom in a direct line the family is descended).

P. 212. ll. 6-7. These lines refer to Vishnu. कल्पांतदुःस्था 'being in a distressed state at the end of the *Kalpa* (the time of general deluge).' ऊढे 'was uplifted or drawn out'.

—ll. 9-10. परः 'enemy.' l. 10. 'For he (an enemy) and a disease, when growing, are regarded by the wise, as the same' (in their fatal effects). i. e. if their growth be not checked in time, they will prove very injurious.

P. 212. ll. 11-12. Said by the bards to Aja, at the time of announcing to him the time of rising. त्वत्प्रबोधप्रयुक्तां 'employed to rouse you from sleep.'

—l. 15. सर्वतोमुखं 'having faces in all directions', because he was चतुर्मुख.

—ll. 17-18. स=हिमालय. पितॄणां मानसीं कन्यां 'the girl was a mental creation of the Fathers' (created by virtue of their desire, and not by the ordinary means.)

—l. 19. नव इव चिरेणापि 'my grief is, as it were, new, although so many (12) years have since then elapsed.

P. 213. l. 3. असौ Hanumat.

—ll. 6-7. The Jumna and the Ganges, having respectively black and white waters, seem to provide for each other black aloe and sandal ointment.

—l. 9. स्फुटन्निव etc. 'as if bursting out on account of the flood (excess) of internal excitement.'

—ll. 10-11. वयो etc. 'the resemblance between Ráma and the two (Lava and Kus'a) differing only in age and dress' i. e. they two and Ráma resembled in every respect except age and dress. नाक्षिकंपं व्यतिष्ठत 'stood without the twinkling of their eyes', stood fixing upon them a steadfast gaze.

—l. 14. मरुतः सुतं Bhima. दर्शितविक्रियं 'who had shown a change in mind', i. e. emotion of anger.

—ll. 18-19. तद्योधाः 'his warriors'. l. 19 'On grounds covered over with excellent hides of antelopes and surrounded by vines.'

—l. 20 श्रुतमधिगम्य 'having acquired a sound knowledge'. शरीरजन्मनः रिपून् Desire, Anger, Avarice etc., the six passions.

—l. 21. 'They soon bring upon Wealth the stigma (ill-repute) of unsteadiness,' *i. e.* wealth leaves such persons and becomes liable to be called चपला.

P. 213. ll. 22-25. प्रियप्रायाः 'for the most part kind. l. 25 'the flavour (interest) of which is unchanged (unabated) either before or afterwards,' *i. e.* which is at all times equally pleasing.

—l. 27. न संस्थास्यते 'will not stop,' will be accomplished.

—ll. 28-29. सीतां obj. of द्रष्टुं. उपाक्रंस्त 'proceeded towards the sea-shore.'

P. 214. ll. 1-2. The past participles are used as abstract nouns. l. 2. Lankâ (with so many jumbled noises) produced a noise resembling that in the city of Indra.'

—ll. 3-4. The son of the Wind was for a time pleased at the sight of Rávana of whom, being afraid, the thousand-eyed (Indra) ceased from fight.'

—ll. 5-6. यावदर्थपदां 'having words just enough to convey the meaning,' not using many words.

—l. 7. अखिलीकृत्य 'without having made powerless.'

—ll. 9-12. मोपयध्वं भयं 'do not entertain fear.' महेंद्र name of a mountain. धैर्यमाधिषत 'their hearts took courage.'

LESSON XXX.

P. 220. l. 11. नरपतिप्रबोधनार्थं *i. e.* to turn the eyes of the Princes which were fixed upon the king, to the Chándála girl who was being ushered in.

—ll. 18-19. अनाश्रवासीत् 'did not mind it', turned a deaf ear. समगिरंतां 'pledged their word', 'vowed.'

P. 221. l. 1. प्रतिविधाय तिष्ठ:स्व 'having adopted measures against the possible schemes of the king.'

—ll. 3-4. वर्तयते 'maintains himself', lives on elephants killed by himself. l. 4. 'A great person, who, by his prowess, humbles the world, does not forsooth wish for his own sustenance from others.'

P. 211. ll. 6-7. अस्तसंख्यं 'so as to be beyond calculation', in countless numbers. अत्र 'in this battle.'

—l. 9. The idea is that a warrior, having recourse to mild or soft means (such as forgiveness) should accomplish his object, just as a lamp sucks oil by means of the soft wick which intervenes, but for which the flame would be at once extinguished.

—l. 11-12. शक्ति 'strength'; had 'the three regal powers.' षाड्गुण्यं 'the six expedients ' अंगानि 'limbs' and 'component members of a State.'

—l. 16. मा कस्यचिदुपस्कृथाः 'do not prepare (for me) any articles of food' such as condiment, spices, etc. (दृष्यपेयभोज्यादिकं किमपि मा कुरु).

P. 222. l. 2. वद्मानः 'shining forth ' (भासमानः).

—ll. 4-5. व्यवहर्तुमभियोक्ष्यते 'will endeavour to go to a court of law'. कौपीनावशेषं etc. 'reduce him to absolute indigence.'

—l. 9. He with his (left) arm (always) raised up, lifts his right arm in this direction conformably to greet me'.

—ll. 12-13. "He, void of pride, always shows (to the world) his servants, as if they were his dear friends, treats his friends with a respect common to his nearest relations, and his relations as if they were vested with important authority.'

—ll. 16-17. कृतपूर्वसंविद् &c. 'who had previously formed a plot for the accomplishment of their scheme.' समयोपलभ्यं 'to be got at the time' of the departure of Aja.

—ll. 18-19. Said by Arjuna to S'iva. संविदामीष 'lord of faculties. l. 19. विरोध्यं etc. ' Of those who, through folly, become hostile, but afterwards become submissive.'

—ll. 21-22. शांतिमधिकृत्य asked the preceptor 'with reference to some expiatory rite for averting the evil.' स्वंतं 'resulting in good.'

—ll. 25-26. भूपति 'the Chedi king.' l. 26 'It is not probable that the lion (Krishna) will humbly crouch for fear of an attack.'

—ll. 27-28. He had scarcely mastered the characters of the

alphabet written on the writing-tablet, when he enjoyed all the fruits of political instruction from association with men advanced in knowledge.'

P. 223. ll. 1-2. उदधिश्यामसीमां 'having the ocean for its dark boundary' *i. e.* as far as the very ocean. नगर etc. 'having arms as loug as the bar of a city-gate', which is both long and massive, and hence indicative of great muscular strength.

—ll. 7-14 Describe the As'oka garden of Rávana लतां नर्तयमानवत् 'as if making the creeper dance to the breeze.' संत्रस्ताः 'afraid of Rávana.' नायासयन्त ' did not interfere with or affect' each coming round in *due* rotation. स्मरात् 'being love-smitten'

—ll. 15-16. The elephant, with his body tossed up, and hence imitating the lord of mountains about to dart up into the sky, made the driver get on himself, who placed his foot on the foot of the elephant slightly bent.

CHOICE EXPRESSIONS AND IDIOMS

A.

स दैवाधीनः कृतः, यद्भावि तद्भवतु इत्युक्त्वा परित्यक्तः 'he was *abandoned* to his fate.'

तव निर्णये स्थास्यामि, तव निर्णयः प्रमाणं 'I shall *abide* by (bow to) your decision.' प्रतिज्ञां-अभिसंधां-पालयति '*abides* by his promise.'

यथाशक्ति, यावच्छक्यं 'to the best (utmost) of one's *ability,*' all that one can do, as far as possible.

बहुकौतुकः स देशः 'the country *abounds* in curiosities.'

पंचवर्षदेशियः '*about* five years old. मध्याह्नप्रायः-कल्पः समयः ' it is *about* noon.' किं कर्तुमुद्यतोसि, किं कार्यव्यग्रोसि, किमारंभस्त्वं 'what are you *about*'.

स सर्वेषां मूर्ध्नि तिष्ठति 'he stands *above* (at the head of) all.' अदत्तावकाशो मत्सरस्य '*above* envy.'

सा दारुणा प्रतिज्ञा लोके प्रकाशतां गता-प्रकाशीभूता 'the dreadful vow became known *abroad*.'

शून्यमनस्क, शून्यहृदय, हृदयेनासंनिहित, विगतचेतन '*absent-minded.*'

कृतमेतादृशेन असंगतेन प्रलापेन 'do not talk so *absurdly.*'

मनोरथानामगतिर्न विद्यते 'nothing is *inaccessible* to desire.'

मरणं प्रकृतिः विकृतिर्जीवितमुच्यते 'death is *nature*, life is but an *accident.*'

भावमनुप्रविश् '*accommodate* oneself to the will of.'

एकचित्तीभूय 'with one *accord.*' यदृच्छया, स्वयं, स्वेच्छातः 'of one's own *accord.*' तद्वचनानुसारेण-अनुरोधेन 'in *accordance* with his words.' अनुज्येष्ठं '*according* to seniority.'

राजेति का मात्रा-गणना मम 'of what *account* (consideration) is a king to me' (I defy him).

AFF.

दैवहतकं, दग्धदैव, हतदैवं '*accursed* or wretched fate.'

बलवती शिरोवेदना मां बाधते 'I am suffering from a strong (bad) *headache*.'

भवतोऽविनयमंतरेण परिगृहीतार्था कृतादेवी 'the queen was made *acquainted* with your immodesty.'

ते स्वकर्म साधु निरवाहयन्-आचरन् 'they *acquitted* themselves well.'

शासने तिष्ठ भर्तुः '*act* up to your master's orders. लक्ष्मीभूमिकायां वर्तमाना '*acting* the part of Lakshmî.' कुरु प्रियसखीवृत्तिं सपत्नीजने '*act* the part of a dear friend towards your rivals.' मनोवाक्कायकर्मभिः 'in *action*, thought and speech' (in thought, words and deed.)

कुशाग्रबुद्धिः '*acuteness* (sharpness) of intellect.'

यथाकालं व्यवहर '*adapt* your conduct to circumstances. तस्यैकदेशः अभिनेयार्थः कृतः 'a portion of it has been *adapted* to the stage.

लक्ष्मीं तनोति '*adds* to the lustre.' गंडस्योपरि पिटिका संवृत्ता, अयमपरो गंडस्योपरि स्फोटः 'this is another evil to *add* to the first' (*lit.* 'a pimple has grown upon a boil').

मधुरालाप, प्रियंवद 'of agreeable *address*.' अदत्तबाह्यनामा लेखः 'a letter without any *address* upon it.' दत्त-लिखित मद्बाह्यनाम पत्रं प्रेषय 'send the letter to my *address*.'

आमंत्रयस्व-आपृच्छस्व सहचरं 'bid *adieu* to (take leave of, bid farewell to) your friend.'

सर्वविश्रमेष्वभ्यंतरीकरणीया 'she should be *admitted* to all confidential matters.' तस्या विकारो विलंबाक्षमः 'her illness *admits* of no delay.'

वयोवृद्ध, प्रवयस 'advanced in age.' ज्ञानवृद्ध '*advanced* in knowledge.'

मम छिद्रेण लब्धावकाशः 'taking *advantage* of my weak point.'

वसंतसमयावतारः, मधुप्रवृत्तिः '*advent* or setting in of spring.'

क्लेशलेशैरभिन्न 'not *affected* by the slightest fatigue.' वेतालोपहत '*affected* by a devil.' अनेकव्याध्युपसृष्ट '*affected* by many diseases.' न नः किंचिच्छिद्यते 'our position is not in the least *affected* (it does not *affect* us in the least).' कृतककलहं कृत्वा '*affecting* a quarrel.' मम वचसा तस्य हृदयं

AMO

द्रवीभूतं, मम वचस्तस्य हृदये दृढं पदं लेभे 'my words deeply *affected* his heart'. पंडितंमन्योसौ 'he *affects* learning'.

द्वौ नञौ प्रकृतार्थं गमयतः 'two negatives make one *affirmative*.'

इति वार्ता प्रसृता 'such a rumour' was *afloat*.'

अनुपूर्वशः 'one *after* another.' वृक्षं वृक्षं सिंचति 'waters tree *after* tree.' स पितामहनाम्नाऽभिधीयते-आहूयते 'he is called *after* his grandfather.'

प्राप्तव्यवहारदश 'come of *age*.' षोडशवर्षवयोवस्थामस्पृशत् 'he reached the 16th year of his *age*.'

अस्मिन्विषये सर्वेषां तेषामैकमत्यम् 'they all *agree* (there is a unanimity) on this point.'

शरसंधानं कुर्वन् 'taking *aim* with his arrow.' क्वानिर्दिष्टकारणं गम्यते 'where are you going without any definite *aim*.'

वातमासेव् 'to take the *air*.' प्रकाशतां गम् 'take *air*.' अवलेपमुद्रा 'an *air* of conceit.' निकृतमिवात्मानं संदर्श्य 'with the *air* of one who is offended.' गगनकुसुमानि-खपुष्पाणि-चि, मनोराज्यविजृंभणं कृ 'to build castles in the *air*.'

अकस्मात्, सहसा, एकपदे '*all* of a sudden.' एतावान्मे विभवो भवन्तं सेवितुं 'this is *all* I can do to serve you.' जीवितसर्वस्वं *all*-in-*all* of one's life.' एवं पिंडीकृत्य मह्यं विंशतिं रूपकान्देहि 'give me 20 rupees in *all*.' सर्वे मिलित्वा सप्त वयं 'we are 7 in *all*.'

इयं कथा मामेव लक्षीकरोति 'this story *alludes* to myself.'

क्षीणभूयिष्ठायां क्षपायां 'when the night had *almost* worn away.' अधुना प्रभातप्राया-कल्पा रजनी 'it is *almost* dawn now.' मृतप्राय-कल्प '*almost* dead (all but dead).'

अन्या गतिर्नास्ति, अन्यच्छरणं नालोक्यते 'there is no other *alternative* (course, help).'

एष तव वचसो निष्कर्षः—पिंडितोर्थः 'your whole speech *amounts* to this' (this is the purport or sum and substance of your speech).

अराजके जनपदे 'when the country is in a state of *anarchy*.'

जन्मदिवस: '*anniversary* of birth' मृततिथि. '*anniversary* of death.'

भवतु तथा इति स प्रत्युवाच 'he *answered* very well,' इदं मे इष्टसिद्धये कल्पेत 'this will *answer* my purpose', will do for me.

चिंताविषघ्नोऽगद: 'an *antidote* against anxiety'. विषवैद्य:, जांगुलिक: 'a dealer in *antidotes*.'

व्याजस्तुति: '*apparent* praise.

अस्मिन्नर्थेऽत्रभवंतं प्रमाणीकरोमि, अत्र भवान् प्रमाणं 'I *appeal* to your honour in this case'.

साक्षी नोपतस्थौ 'the witness did not *appear*.' शोभनाकृति, सुभगाकृति, चारुदर्शन, प्रेक्षणीय 'good in *appearance*', तव कथा सत्येव प्रतिभाति-अवभासते 'your story has an *appearance* of truth.'

सुखार्थे विषयशब्दं न प्रयुंजते 'they do not *apply* the word विषय to happiness'. द्वितीयगामी न हि शब्द एष न: 'this our title does not *apply* to any one else'. कोपरो नियोगोनुष्ठीयतामिति प्रार्थयामास 'he *applied* for further orders'. वयं स्वकर्मण्यभियुज्यामहे 'we *apply* ourselves to our work.'

संकेतं-समयं अनुरुध्यस्व: अनुपालय 'keep your *appointment* or engagement'. देवि सामायिका भवाम: 'Queen, let us keep (to) our *appointment* or engagement', let us be punctual.

तीक्ष्णमति 'of quick *apprehension*.' मंदधी, स्थूलबुद्धि 'of dull *apprehension*,' 'dull-headed'.

प्रस्तावसदृशं, प्राप्तकालं, कालोचितं, समयानुरूपं '*appropriate* to (fit for) the occasion.'

न ते वचोऽभिनन्दामि 'I do not *approve* of your speech' (your speech does not commend itself to me).

युवानो विस्मरणशीला: 'youths are *apt* to forget' अतिस्नेह: पापशंकी 'over-affection is *apt* to suspect evil.'

लोके गुरुत्वं विपरीतां वा स्वचेष्टितान्येव नरं नयांति 'man is the *architect* of his own fortune' (the fortunate circumstances of our lives are of our own making.)

ATT.

बध्नाति मे चक्षुश्चित्रकूटः 'the Chitrakûta mountain *arrests* my eye'.

अव्याजमनोहरं-अकृत्रिमलावण्यं-निसर्गरमणीयं वपुः 'an *artlessly* (naturally) lovely body'.

गुणास्तावत्तस्य नैव विद्यन्ते '*as* for merits, he has none'. शीघ्रमिति सुकरं '*as* for doing it quickly, it is easy'. पितेति मां स मानयति '*as* a father he respects me'.

वेलोपलक्षणार्थं 'to *ascertain* the time.'

कस्मिन् दोषं निक्षिपामि, कं दोषपक्षे स्थापयामि 'to whom shall I *ascribe* the blame' (on whom shall I lay the blame). पापकर्म तस्य संभाव्यते 'a sinful deed is *ascribed* to him.'

भस्मी-भस्मसात् कृ 'to reduce to *ashes*,' भस्मीभू 'to be reduced to *ashes*.'

तस्य वदनं हर्षोत्फुल्लं बभौ 'he had a cheerul *aspect*.' सर्वं विपर्यासं यातं 'all things wore a different *aspect*,' उदगभिमुखं मे गृहं 'my house has a northerly *aspect*.'

कवियशः प्रार्थी '*Aspiring* to the fame of a poet'. दूरारूढाः-दूराधिरोहिणः-उत्सर्पिणः खलु एते मनोरथाः 'these are, indeed, high *aspirations*' (ambitions, high soaring desires).

मृगा मृगैः संगमनुव्रजन्ति 'deer *associate* with deer.'

कृतकं-मिथ्या-मौनं '*assumed* silence.'

इति मे निश्चयः, इदं मन्ये 'I *assuredly* feel,' 'I feel *assured*.'

उपचारातिक्रमं-प्रणिपातलंघनं-प्रमार्ष्टुमयमारंभः 'this is an act to *atone* (make amends) for the slighting of prostration.'

लोकापवादो बलवान्मतो मे 'I *attach* great importance to public censure'. नृपं सुदृढमनुरक्ताः प्रजाः 'subjects are firmly *attached* to the king.'

युवतयो गृहिणीपदं यान्ति 'young women *attain* to the position of house-wives.'

उदार-आर्य-नेपथ्यभृत् 'richly or splendidly *attired*.'

BEN.

वैरभावः, विपक्षवृत्तिः 'hostile *attitude*.'

आत्मन्यारोपितालीकाभिमानाः '*attributing* to themselves false greatness.'

राजदर्शनं लेभे 'had an *audience* of (interview with) the king.' दर्शनानुग्रहमिच्छामि 'I wish to be favoured with an *audience*.'

विपदुत्पत्तिमतामुपस्थिता, जातस्य हि ध्रुवो मृत्युः 'destruction (death) *awaits* those that are born.'

चकितं नृपस्य पार्श्वमुपैमि 'I approach the king with *awe*.

B

परोक्षे-क्षं 'behind one's *back*' (in one's absence). उर्वशी प्रत्यादेशः श्रियः 'Urvas'î throws Lakshmî into the *back-ground*' (obscures, eclipses her).

सकलवचनानामविषयं-वर्णनविषयातिक्रांतं-मोघवर्णनप्रयत्नं-तत्स्थानं 'the place *baffles* description'.

ते कुलस्याधयः 'they are a *bane* to the family.'

इति समयः कृतः 'such a *bargain* was struck.' अपि च, अपरंच 'into the *bargain*.'

तस्मिन्नवसरे तेन धीरं विक्रांतं 'he *bore* himself bravely on the occasion.' चित्ते अवधृ, मनसि कृ, अनुस्मृ '*bear* in mind'. शोकवशं मा गमः '*bear up* under grief.' गर्भेश्वरः 'rich from his *birth*.'

सीतादेव्याः किं वृत्तं 'what *became* of the queen Sitâ,' what was Sitâ's fate?

आपतंति हि संसारपथमवतीर्णानामेते वृत्तांताः 'such incidents *befall* worldly persons.'

अश्रुतपूर्वं 'not heard *before*'.

लतांतरित-लताव्यवहित विग्रहः 'concealing or hiding his body *behind* creepers'

भ्रूभंगं कृ 'to *bend* the brow.' स पुनरपि स्वकार्ये मनो बबंधन्यवेशयत् 'he *bent* his mind again to his task'. भवंति नम्रास्तरवः फलागमैः 'trees *bend*

BY.

down under the load of fruits'. कृतनिश्चय, दृढनिश्चय, कृतसंकल्प, विहितप्रतिज्ञ '*bent* on'. परस्परवधोद्यतौ '*bent* on (killing) each other'.

आनंदपरवशः, आनंदेन विगतचेतन इव भूत्वा *beside* oneself with joy'. अप्रास्ताविकं, अप्रस्तुतं, अप्रासंगिक, अप्रकृतं एतत् 'this is *beside* the question, irrelevant, does not bear on the matter in question'.

अस्ति मे विशेषोऽद्य 'I am (feel) *better* to-day'. अभिभू-अति रिच् *pass.* 'to get the *better* of'.

दुर्गम, दुर्ज्ञेय, दुर्बोध '*beyond* comprehension'. आयाधिकं व्ययं करोति 'he lives *beyond* his means'. स श्रुतिपथ आतक्रांतः-व्यतीतः 'he went *beyond* hearing'.

न मनागपि न स्तोकांशेनापि 'not a *bit*, not in the least'.

मृत्पिंडबुद्धिः 'a *block-head*, clod-pated'.

समेत, संहत 'in a *body*'; आसन्नपरिचारकः 'a *body*-guard'.

भिन्नोऽष्टधा विप्रससार वंशः 'the family *branched* off into 8 parts'.

साहसे श्रीः प्रतिवसति 'fortune favours the *brave*'.

प्रभाता रजनी 'the day *broke*, it was day-break (dawn)'. विच्छेदमाप कथाप्रबंधः 'the story has suffered a *break*'. सभ्याः स्वं स्वं स्थानं प्रतिजग्मुः 'the assembly *broke* up'. तस्याक्ष्णोः प्रभातमासीत् 'the day *broke* upon his eyes'.

किं बहुना 'to be *brief*, in short'.

हर्षरोमांचित-पुलकित-कंटकित-तनुः 'his body *bristling* or thrilling with joy'.

तस्याः सहसा प्रावर्तताश्रुधारा 'she *burst* into tears'. संभूय प्रशंसागिर उदतिष्ठन् 'there was a *burst* of applause'.

अप्रस्तुतं किमिति अनुसंधीयते 'why do you beat about the *bush*.' ध्रुवाणि परित्यज्य अध्रुवनिषेवणं नेष्टं; अध्रुवाद् ध्रुवं वरं; वरमद्य कपोतो न श्वो मयूरः or वरं तत्कालोपनता तित्तिरी न पुनर्दिवसांतरिता मयूरी 'a bird in the hand is worth two in the *bush*'.

अनुदिवसं-दिनं, दिने दिने 'day *by* day.' शतशः '*by* hundreds.' एकैकशः आनुपूर्व्येण 'one *by* one'.

C

COM.

प्रयत्नसंवर्धितः 'brought up with *care*'. निपुणमन्विष्य 'searching with *care*. अधुनाहं वीतचिन्तः 'I do not *care* now'. न कामवृत्तिर्वचनीयमीक्षते 'a self-willed person *cares* not for blame.' प्रतिपात्रमाधीयतां यत्नः 'let *care* be taken of each character.'

प्रस्तुतविषये, प्रकृते in the *case* before us, in the present *case*'. तेन हि 'if such be the *case*', well then.

किं मिष्टमन्नं खरसूकराणां 'why *cast* pearls before swine'.

ज्वलनमुपगतं-अग्निदीप्तं-गेहं 'the house *caught* fire.' कर्मगृहीत, रूपाभिग्राहित, लोप्त्रेणगृहीत '*caught* in the act (red-handed).'

किन्नरमिथुनं यदृच्छयाद्राक्षीत् '*chanced* to see two Kinnaras.' घुणाक्षरन्यायेन 'by happy *chance*.' स मया समापत्तिदृष्टः 'I *chanced* to see him, I accidentally met him.'

स्वभावो दुरतिक्रमः 'nature can't be *changed*.' क्षीरं दधिभावेन परिणमते, दधिभावमापद्यते 'milk is *changed* into curds.'

हस्ते निक्षिप् or समर्पय् 'give in *charge* of'. अयं जनः कस्य हस्ते समर्पितः-निक्षिप्तः 'in whose *charge* has this person been given.'

समाश्वसिहि, धैर्यं निधेहि हृदये 'be of good *cheer*, or *cheer* up, take courage.'

इत्थं or एवं गते-सति 'under these *circumstances*'. 'such being the case'. दुर्गत, दुर्दशापन्न, दुःस्थित 'in bad *circumstances*.' येन केनापि प्रकारेण 'under any *circumstances*', 'any how.' यथावसरं, यथाकालं 'according to *circumstances*.'

अतिभूमिं गतो रणरणकोऽस्याः 'her anxiety has reached its *climax*', or the highest pitch.

निमिमील नरोत्तमप्रिया 'the king's beloved *closed* her eyes in death.' अद्य निवार्तं नभः 'it is *closed* to-day.'

मृत्युमुखान्मुक्तः 'rescued from the *clutches* (jaws) of death'.

यद्भावि तद्भवतु '*come* what may.' यद्भावि तद्भवतु शुभमशुभं वा '*come* harm, *come* good.' प्रकृतिमापद्, संज्ञां-चेतनां-लभ् or प्रतिपद्, प्रकृतौस्था '*come*

CON.

to oneself, regain consciousness, to come to one's senses'. आगामिनि सोमवासरे on the *coming* Monday.'

तां सुखशयितं पृच्छ 'ask her whether she has had a *comfortable* sleep.' रात्रावपि निकामं शयितव्यं नास्ति 'I can't sleep *comfortably* even at night.'

दीर्घिकावलोकनगवाक्षगता 'sitting at a window *commanding* (the view of) a well'. आकृतिविशेषेष्वादरः पदं करोति 'good forms *command* respect.' पदं हि सर्वत्र गुणैर्निधीयते 'merits *command* notice or attention.' तनुवाग्विभवोपि सन् 'though I have no *command* of language' (though possessed of scanty powers of speech or description). तं वाग्वश्येवानुवर्तते 'he has *command* of language.'

इदं वृत्तं लेख्यं-पत्रं आरोपय पत्रे निवेशय '*commit* this matter to writing'.

अस्माभिः सहैककार्याणां 'who have made *common* cause with us.'

सहाध्यायिन् 'a *companion* at school', 'a fellow-student.' समदुःखसुखः 'a *companion* in joy and sorrow.'

अहमहमिकया प्रणामलालसाः 'a *competing* with one another to salute first.'

अभिनंद्य ब्रवीति 'says or writes after presenting *compliments.*' च्यवनाय मां प्रणिपातय or मदीयो नमस्कारो वाच्यः 'give my *compliments* to Chyavana.' उपचारपदं 'a *complimentary* saying.'

स नाद्यापि पर्यवस्थापयति-संस्तंभयति आत्मानं 'he does not yet *campose* (collect) himself.'

महदपि राज्यं न मे सौख्यमावहति 'even my large kingdom does not *conduce* to my happiness.'

अपि रक्ष्यते त्वया रहस्यनिक्षेपः 'have you kept the secret *confided* to you.' विश्वास-विश्रंभ-भूमिः स मम 'he is my *confident.*' विश्रंभस्थाने मन् 'to take into *confidence.*'

प्रसवकालः, प्रसवावस्था '*confinement* of a woman'. प्रसूता or प्राप्तप्रसवा तद्भार्या 'his wife is *confined* (is in child-bed).'

दिष्ट्या सुतमुखदर्शनेन आयुष्मान्वर्धते 'you are to be *congratulated* upon seeing your son's face,' or 'I *congratulate* you upon seeing' &c.

ORE.

प्रसन्नः-उपपन्नः-ते तर्कः 'your *conjuncture* is clear (you have rightly *conjuctured* or guessed)'.

अग्निसात्कुरु, ज्वलनाय समर्पय '*consign* to the flames'.

तस्याचरणं वचसा न विसंवदति 'his conduct is not *inconsistent* with his words'. स्वार्थाविरोधेन '*consistently* with their own interest'. अभिरूपभूयिष्ठा परिषद् 'an assembly mostly *consisting* of learned men

तस्य वचसि दुराशयं मा कल्पय-आरोपय 'do not put a bad *construction* upon his words'.

तत्परतयैव वेदांतवाक्यानि योजयंति '*construe* Vedântic sentences as referring to it'.

जनहितमपि तावत् त्वया चिंतनीयं-मनसि कार्यमेव-अवेक्षणीयं 'you must also *consult* public good': स्वहितपरायणो मा भूः 'do not *consult* (be intent on) your good alone'. सांवत्सरिकैः संवाद्यताम् 'let astrologers be *consulted*'.

गुरुः प्रहर्षः प्रबभूव नात्मनि, वपुषि न ममौ 'he could not *contain* his great joy'.

तेन ह्यस्य गृहीतार्था भवामि 'if so, I shall know its *contents.*'

यथावकाशं, कार्यांतरांतरायमंतरेण 'when it suits one's *convenience.*' अन्यकार्यातिपातमंतरेण-कार्यांतराविरोधेन-भवान् कदा मया द्रष्टव्यः 'when may I *conveniently* see you'.

अनभ्यंतरा वयं मदनगतस्य वृत्तांतस्य 'we are not *conversant* with love matters.'

प्राणव्यये नापि 'even at the *cost* of one's life.'

त्वद्वचनप्रत्ययात् '*counting* upon your promise.'

आ-समा-श्वस् 'to take *courage*,' धैर्यं आस्था, धैर्यं अवलंब् or अवष्टंभ्, धैर्यावष्टंभं कृ 'to summon *courage.*'

कथाप्रसंगेन, कथायोगेन 'in the course of conversation.' कालक्रमेण, गच्छता कालेन, दिनेषु गच्छत्सु, गच्छति काले 'in *course* of time.' गत्यंतराभावात्, अनन्यगतिकत्वात् 'there being no other *course*.'

स त्वत्तो लब्धोदयः 'he is your *creature*' (owes his rise to you).

DEL.

एते संकल्पा मम प्रादुरासन् or आसीत्-समभूत् मे मनसि 'these thoughts *crossed* my mind (occured to me)'. मम दर्शनपथमागतः, नयनविषयमवतीर्णः 'he *crossed* my sight.' व्यत्यस्तभुजः 'with the arms *crossed.*' व्यत्यस्तपादः '*cross*-legged'.

सर्वेऽस्य प्रयत्नाः सफलतां ययुः—फलिताः 'his efforts were *crowned* with success.'

आचारपुष्पग्रहणार्थं 'to take flowers as is *customary*'. आचारं प्रतिपद्यस्व 'make the *customary* bow (salutation)'.

मर्मच्छिद्-भिद्, मर्माणि कृंतत् '*cutting* to the quick'. मद्वचनमाक्षिप्य '*cutting* short my speech'.

D.

तस्योत्साहभंगं मा कृथाः 'do not *damp* his energy.'

आतुरो जीवितसंशये वर्तते 'the patient is in a *dangerous* state.'

अंधं तमः, सूचिभेद्यं तमः 'pitchy (blinding) *darkness.*' संतमसं 'all-pervading *darkness.*'

हाहानिनादेन दिशो बधिरयंतः '*deafening* all directions with cries of *alas.*'

स्वासुभिर्भर्तुरानृण्यं गतः 'He paid off the *debt* of his master with his life'.

पश्चिमे वयसि, परिणतवयसि 'in the *decline* of life', 'in *declining* years.'

दूरगतमन्मथा सा, अंतिभूमिं गतोस्या अनुरागः 'she is *deep* in love, far gone in love.'

मम विकारः परिच्छेदातीतः 'my anguish transcends *definition*.'

एकस्य मूल्येन व्ययः शुध्यति, सर्वा व्ययशुद्धिः संपद्यते 'all expenses are *defrayed* out of the proceeds of one'.

वैद्ययत्नपरिभावी गदः 'a disease which *defies* medical efforts'

दीर्घसूत्री विनश्यति '*delay* is dangerous.'

वसुधां तस्य हस्तगामिनीमकरोत् '*delivered* the earth to him.' लेखं तस्य हस्तं प्रापयिष्यामि 'I shall *deliver* the letter into his hand'.

DIS.

सर्वं दैवाधीनं-आयत्तं 'everything *depends* on fate'. मया प्रायोपवेशनं कृतं विद्धि '*depend* upon it, I shall starve myself to death'. असंशयं, नियतं, नूनं, खलु, '*depend* upon it', 'to be sure'. निमित्तसव्यपक्ष '*dependent* on a cause'.

विषण्ण, मुक्तावयव '*depressed* in spirits,' 'dejected.'

सर्वं जनस्योपहास्यतामुपयांति 'are *derided* by all', 'become the laughing-stock of all'.

तस्याः श्रीर्वचनानामविषया 'her beauty can't be *described.*'

सविस्तरं, सविस्तरेण, विस्तरतः-शः, सुविस्तरं 'in *detail*, at length, exhaustively.'

सा पुपोष लावण्यमयान् विशेषान् or मनोहरं वपुः, प्रचीयमानावयवा 'she *developed* her lovely limbs.'

क्षुण्णाद्वर्त्मनो रेखामात्रमपि न व्यतीयुः 'did not *deviate* even a line (in inch) from the beaten path.'

नाहमात्मविनाशाय वेतालोत्थापनं करिष्यामि 'I shall not raise a *devil* for my own destruction.'

पुत्रसंक्रांतलक्ष्मीकाः, गुणवत्सुतरोपितश्रियः 'having *devolved* their property upon their sons.'

लुप्तार्थं वचनं 'a *dead* letter.' अशाम्यं वैरं '*deadly* enmity.' स लोष्टघातं हतः 'he was pelted to *death.*'

अव्यतिरिक्तेयमस्मच्छरीरात् 'she is not *different* from my body (myself).'

विषमपदविमर्शिनी टीका 'a commentary explaining *difficulties.*'

आत्मन्यप्रत्ययं चेतः 'the mind feels *diffident* of itself'.

अलमप्रासंगिकेन or अप्रसंगेन, प्रकृतमेवानुसंधीयतां 'enough of *digression.*'

चक्षुर्विषयातिक्रांतेषु-नयनपथातीतेषु-अंतरितेषु-अदृष्टिगोचरेषु-अंतर्हितेषु-कपोतेषु 'the pigeons having *disappeared*.'

कर्तव्यानि दुःखितैर्दुःखनिर्वापणानि 'the afflicted should *disburden* (ease) their grief.'

DRA.

शिष्य उपदेशं मलिनयति 'a pupil spoils, brings *discredit* on, the instruction (given to him).'

प्रकृतं प्रस्तुतं अनुसृ or अनुसंधा 'to turn to the subject under *discussion.*' प्रस्तावः, प्रस्तुत-प्रकृत-विषयः, प्रस्तुतं, प्रकृतं 'the subject under *discussion.*'

तपस्विव्यंजनोपेताः, तापसच्छद्मना, तापसरूपधारिणः 'disguised as ascetics.'

निष्कारणो बंधुः 'a *disinterested* friend.'

मम द्रव्यस्य कथं त्वया विनियोगः कृतः 'how have you *disposed* of my money.' अहं त्वदधीनोऽस्मि 'I am at your *disposal.*' अयमर्थस्त्वदायत्तः, अत्र भवान् प्रभवति 'this matter is at your *disposal.*' कलहशील, कलहकाम '*disposed* to quarrel.'

किं वो विवादवस्तु 'what are you *disputing* about', 'what is the matter at issue.' वादग्रस्तोर्थः 'a *disputed* point.'

अतिथिविशेषः 'a *distinguished* guest.'

एवं तावदाक्षिपामि, अन्यतः संचारयामि 'I shall thus *divert* his thoughts.'

अंतर्भेदाकुलं गृहं 'a house *divided* against itself.'

अपि कुशलं शिवं भवतः 'how do you *do,*' 'are you *doing* well.' त्वां सुखं-कुशलं पृच्छति 'asks you how you *do.*' देवीं सुखं प्रष्टुमागता 'she came to ask the queen if she was *doing* well.' अलं निर्बंधेन 'have *done* with, enough of, your importunity.' किमस्माकं स्वामिचेष्टानिरूपणेन 'what have we to *do* with watching the movements of your master.'

मनो मे संशयमेव गाहते or आशंकते 'my mind is still in *doubt.*'

नतोन्नतभूमिभागः, उत्खातिनी भूमिः 'ground having ups and *downs,*' 'uneven ground'. पातोत्पातः 'ups and *downs.*' नीचैर्गच्छत्युपरि च दशा चक्रनेमिक्रमेण 'there are ups and *downs* in our condition (in life) as in the course of the wheel.' निपात्यतां-उच्छेद्यतां-असौ प्रजापीडकः '*down* with the tyrant.'

परिणतप्रायमहः 'the day is *drawing* to a close,' 'it is about sun-set.' त्वया स्वहस्तेनांगाराः कर्षिताः 'you have *drawn* down ruin upon yourself with your own hands.'

EFF.

द्वीपिचर्मपरिच्छन्नः गर्दभः 'an ass *dressed* in a tiger's skin.'

चापलाय प्रचोदितः '*driven* to do a rash act.' अविरलवारिधारासंपातः, पटुधारासारः 'a sharp *driving* shower.' किमुद्दिश्य भवान्भाषते 'what are you *driving* at.

मा भवानंगानि मुंचतु 'let not your spirits *droop* (flag), do not despair.' मुक्तैरवयवैरशयिषि 'I slept with *drooping* limbs.' स्रंसते देहबंधः 'the whole frame *droops* down.'

जलबिंदुनिपातेन क्रमशः पूर्यते घटः 'small *drops* make a pool.'

संह्रियतामियं कथा 'let this matter (story) be *dropped.*' अवसन्नप्रायाणि मे गात्राणि, सीदंति मे अंगानि, 'I feel ready to *drop* down.'

शिखी केकाभिस्तिरयति मे वचनं 'the peacock *drowns* my voice with his cries.'

E.

श्रवणगोचरे तिष्ठ 'be within *ear*-shot.'

महति प्रत्यूषे '*early* in the morning.'

न परिहसामि, नायं परिहासस्य समयः 'I am in earnest,' 'I am not joking.' परमार्थेन ग्रह् 'take in *earnest*.'

लब्धं स्वास्थ्यं मया, अहं निर्वृतः, वीतचिंतः 'I am at *case*.' जातो ममायं विशदः प्रकामं अंतरात्मा 'this my soul is completely at *ease*.' यथाकामं, पर्याप्तं, प्रकामं 'at one's *case*.' सुखसुप्त 'sleeping at *ease*.'

दंतहर्षः 'setting the teeth on *edge*.'

फल्, मूर्च्छ् (1. P.) 'to take *effect*,' मारुतस्य रंहः शिलोच्चये न मूर्छति 'the velocity of the wind has no *effect* on (prevails not against) a mountain.' मूर्छंत्यमी विकारा ऐश्वर्यमत्तेषु 'such changes of purpose take *effect* (grow strong) in persons intoxicated with sovereign power.' निशि मूर्छतां तमसां 'of darkness thickening at night.' वज्रं तपोवीर्यमहत्सु कुंठं 'the thunder-bolt has no *effect* on those who have practised austere penance.' इति, एतदभिप्राय 'to this *effect*.' अर्थतः, वस्तुतः 'in *effect*.'

EXC.

नृपस्तस्यां बद्धभावः, कृतानुरागः प्रीतिं-भावं बबंध 'the king was *enamoured* of her,' 'fixed his love on her.'

शृणु मे सावशेषं वचः 'hear my speech to the *end* (hear me out).' कल्याणोदर्कं-स्वंतं-भविष्यति 'it will *end* in good.'

अलमतिविस्तरेण '*enough* of prolixity.' अलं-कृतं-परिहासेन '*enough* of joking.'

कुतूहलेन तस्य चेतसि पदं कृतं 'curiosity *entered* his heart.'

मानमर्हति, मान्यः, पूज्यः 'he is *entitled* to respect.' स पुरस्कारमर्हति 'he is *entitled* to precedence.'

परसुखासहिष्णु '*envious* (jealous of) another's happiness.' ते परस्पर-यशःपुरोभागीः 'they are *envious*, jealous, of each other's fame.'

तुलया धृ 'to consider *equal*.' तत्कार्यं साधयितुमलं सः 'he is *equal* to the task.'

प्रतिशासनं 'sending on an *errand*.'

बंधनभ्रष्टो गृहकपोतश्छिलाया मुखे पतितः he has *escaped* one danger only to fall into another (has *escaped* Scylla to fall into Charybdis). कथं कथमपि मुक्तः 'he narrowly *escaped*.'

सुरक्षितां तां प्रेषय 'send her a good *escort*.'

अत्यंतविलुप्तदर्शन 'disappeared for *ever*.' एकांतनष्ट 'lost for *ever*.' असन्निवृत्त्यै गत, अत्यंत गत 'gone for *ever*.' अप्रबोधाय सा सुष्वाप 'she slept not to *ever* wake again (to wake no more).'

अब्रह्मण्यं, अत्याहितं 'Oh ! an *evil* has befallen;' alas, woe me.

स सत्कारो मम मनोरथानामप्यभूमिः 'the reception *exceeded* even my expectations.'

उत्सर्गाः सापवादाः 'rules have *exceptions*.' अपवादैरिवोत्सर्गाः कृतव्यावृत्तयः 'as general rules are limited by *exceptions*.' अव्यभिचारी तद्वचः, इति लोकवादः न विसंवादमासदायति 'that saying has no *exceptions*.' प्रतिप्रसवः 'a counter-*exception*.'

शिरः शूलस्पर्शनमपदिशन् 'pleading an *excuse* of head-ache.' अनामयापदेशेन 'under the *excuse* of illness.'

FAR.

स्वनियोगमशून्यं कुरु, अनुतिष्ठात्मनो नियोगं '*execute* thy business', 'do thy duty.'

असौ क्रमाद्यौवनभिन्नशैशवः 'his boyhood gradually *expanded* into youth'. हर्षोत्फुल्लनयनः 'with his eyes *expanded* with joy'.

त्वयात्मा क्लेशस्य पदमुपनीतः 'you *exposed* yourself to trouble.' स कातर इति वाच्यतां गतः 'he was *exposed* to the charge of cowardice'. सा तंडुलान् सूर्यातपे दत्तवती, आतापायोज्झितवती 'she *exposed* rice to the sun'.

कियताप्यंशेन, ईषत्, मनाक् 'to some *extent*.' सर्वथा 'to the fullest *extent*.'

लोकदृष्ट्या 'in the *eyes* of the public'. अक्षिगतोहं तस्य 'I am an *eye*-sore to him'.

F

मुखामुखि, संमुखं '*face* to *face*'. पूर्वाभिमुखं गृहं 'a house *facing* the East.'

वस्तुतः, तत्वतः 'in *fact*.' वस्तुवृत्तेन, परमार्थतः, तत्त्वतः 'as a matter of *fact*'.

संकटेष्वविषण्णधीः 'his talent *fails* not in difficulties.' फले विसंवदति '*fails* to give the fruit'. रमणीयोऽत्रयिर्विधिना विसंवादितः 'a good appointment was made to *fail* by Fate'. तस्य धैर्यं न हीयते, न स्खलति 'his courage does not *fail* him'. पुत्राभावे '*failing* male issue'. तस्य स्मृतिलोपः संजातः 'his memory *failed* him'. संततिविच्छेदः-लोपः '*failure* of issue'.

अनिर्वेदः श्रियो मूलं '*faint* heart never won fair lady'

सुदिनं 'a *fair* day or weather'.

पातोत्पातौ, व्यसनोदयौ 'rise and *fall*'. स लक्ष्यच्युतसायकोभूत् 'his arrow *fell* short of its aim.' नव महिमानमुत्कीर्त्य वचः संह्रियते 'words *fall* short in describing your greatness'.

लुप्तप्रतिज्ञ, असत्यसंध, भग्नप्रतिज्ञ '*false* to one's promise'.

अतिपरिचयादवज्ञा '*familiarity* breeds contempt'.

को वृत्तांतस्तत्रभवत्याः 'how *fares* it with her ladyship'.

GET.

नात्र मुनिर्दोषं ग्रहीष्यति 'the sage will not find *fault* with this'. दृष्टदोषा मृगया 'chase is found *fault* with'.

सहृदयः, सचेताः 'a man of *feeling*'. स चेतसः कस्य मनो न दूयते 'what man of *feeling* is not affected at heart'.

आत्मानं मृतवत्संदर्शयामास 'he *feigned* himself to be dead'. कृतकं कोपं कृत्वा '*feigning* anger'. प्रसुप्तलक्षण, व्याजसुप्त, लक्षसुप्त '*feigning* sleep'.

पर्याप्तमाचामति 'drinks (his) *fill*.'

तैः सोपराधी स्थापितः 'they *found* him guilty'.

उदारः-प्रथमः कल्पः 'a *fine* or fair proposal'.

सुश्लिष्टमेतत् 'this *fits* well'.

मन्मुखासक्तदृष्टिः 'with his eyes *fixed* on my face'. आसक्त-बद्ध-दृष्टि 'having the gaze *fixed*'. स्तिमित-अनिमेष-लोचन 'with a *fixed* look'. मनो निष्ठाशून्यं भ्रमति 'the mind devoid of *fixedness* rambles'.

रन्ध्रान्वेषिन्, छिद्रान्वेषिन् 'seeking or finding *flaws*, or picking holes'.

सप्तभूमिकाः प्रासादः 'a palace having seven *floors*'.

हस्तौ समानीय, अंजलिं बद्ध्वा, कृतांजलिः, सां (प्रां) जलि '*folding* his hands together.' भुजाभ्यां तामापीड्य '*folding* her in his arms'.

महतां पदमनुविधेयं '*follow* (in) the foot-steps of the great.' पदवीं प्रतिपद्य *following* the path'. पुरस्कृतमध्यम क्रमः '*following* a middle course'. दुःखं दुःखानुबंधि, विपद्विपदमनुबध्नाति 'one misfortune *follows* another'. अतः किं प्राप्नोति 'what *follows* from this!' परस्तादवगम्यते 'what *follows* is understood'. ततस्ततः 'what *followed* next,' proceed. तद्यथा 'it is as *follows*'.

शांतं पापं, प्रतिहतं अमंगलं 'God *forbid* (forfend)'.

स्वनामत्यागं करोमि 'I shall *forego* my name'.

तीर्ण-पूर्ण-प्रतिज्ञः, पालितसंगरः सत्यप्रतिज्ञः, सत्यव्रतः-संधः 'who has ***fulfilled*** his promise'.

G.

अधुना मुंच शय्यां '*get* out of (leave) bed now'.

HAN.

युद्धाय संनद्धाः or बद्धपरिकरास्ते 'they have *girded* up their loins for battle.'

शुचो वशं मा गमः, शोकाधीनः मा भूः, वैक्लव्यं मावलंबस्व 'do not *give* way to grief.'

ज्वलन्निव ब्रह्ममयेन तेजसा 'as it *glowing* with Bráhmanic lustre'.

इति ख्यातः, कृतनामधेयः, दत्तसंज्ञः 'he *goes* by the name of'. उमाख्यां सा जगाम 'she went by the name of Umá.'

किं तया दृष्ट्या, कोऽर्थस्तस्या दर्शनेन 'what is the *good* of seeing her.' अलं परिदेवनेन 'what *good* do you get by weeping'.

मृत्योर्मुखे वर्तते, कालालीढः, मृत्युगोचरं गतः 'he is within the *grasp* of death' इदं च अशेषविद्याग्रहणसामर्थ्यं 'and this *grasp* of every (kind of) learning'. ममाशयं सम्यग्गृहीतवानसि 'you have well grasped my meaning.

आनंदस्य परां कोटिं काष्ठां अधिगतः 'he was *greatly* delighted'.

रोषात् दंतैर्दंतान्निष्पिष्य '*grinding* the teeth in rage'.

यौवनपदवीमारूढः, प्राप्तयौवनः, यौवनदशामापेदे 'he *grew* up to man's estate (attained his majority). वत्सतरः महोक्षतां स्पृहति, महोक्षभावं श्रयति 'a calf *grows* into a large bull'.

तस्याः आबद्धधारमश्रु प्रावर्तत, उद्बाष्पे नयने जाते 'tears *gushed* forth from her eyes in torrents'.

H.

चौर्यवृत्ति 'in the *habit* of stealing'. ज्ञातदुःख, दुःखशील, परिचितक्लेश '*habituated* to distress'.

रेखामात्रमपि 'even a *hair's* breadth.'

सर्वनाशे समुत्पन्ने अर्धं त्यजति पंडितः '*half* a bread is better than no loaf'.

नियुद्धं, बाहुयुद्धं 'a *hand*-to-*hand* fight.' एकतः-अन्यतः, एकंच-अपरंच 'on the one *hand*—on the other *hand*'. तु, तावत् 'on the other *hand*'. सर्वथा, सर्वत्र 'on all *hands*.' दत्तहस्तावलंब 'given a helping *hand*.' परंपरया आगम् 'to be *handed* down'.

HIG.

त्रिशंकुरिवांतरा तिष्ठ '*hang* between' (like Tris'anku).

आवेदयंति प्रत्यासन्नमानंदं अग्रजातानि शुभानि निमित्तानि 'antecedent good omens are the *harbingers* of coming happiness' (*cf.* coming events cast their shadows before.)

अहो दारुणो दैवदुर्विपाकः 'Oh *hard* fate'. प्रबलक्षुधावसन्न 'hard pressed by hunger'.

तव मुखं कमलश्रियमुद्वहति-आहरति-कलयति 'your face *has* the beauty of a lotus.'

संशयित जीवितः 'who *hazards* his life.

धुरि कीर्तनीय or प्रतिष्ठापयितव्य 'to be placed at the *head* of.' स सर्वेषां धुरि-मूर्ध्नि-तिष्ठति 'he stands at the *head* of all.' वसिष्ठाधिष्ठिताः, वसिष्ठपुरःसराः-प्रमुखाः पुरोगमाः '*headed* by Vas'istha.'

व्रणविरोपणं तैलं 'sore-*healing* oil.'

सुस्थोसौ, कुशलमस्य 'he is in good *health*.' पूर्ववत्-प्रकृतिस्थः समाजायत 'became as *healthy* as before.'

किमस्मान् संभृतदोषैरधिक्षिपथ 'why do you *heap* accusations (calumnies) upon us.'

इति कर्णपरंपरया श्रुतमस्माभिः 'we know it by *hearsay*.'

सोत्साहं, सर्वात्मना 'with all one's *heart*.' सर्वात्मना तस्मिन्कर्मणि स व्यापृतः 'he has applied himself to the work, *heart* and soul.' यथेच्छं, पर्याप्तं, प्रकामं निकामं 'to one's *heart's* content.'

दीर्घं स्थूलस्थूलं निश्वस्य '*heaving* deeply.'

भूस्वर्गायमानमेतत्स्थलं, भूलोकगतः स्वर्गः 'this is a *heaven* on earth.'

अहमनुपदमागत एव 'I shall be close upon your *heels*.' 'I shall just follow you. जंघामवलंब 'to take one's heels.'

विना पुरुषकारेण दैवं न सिध्यति 'God *helps* those, who help themselves.' का गतिः, किमन्यच्छरणं 'I can't help.'

हंत बीभत्समेवाग्रतो वर्तते 'yonder is indeed a *hideous* spectacle.'

स त्वां बहुमन्यते 'he has a *high* opinion (thinks highly) of you.

INC.

इषवः सिध्यंति लक्ष्ये चले 'arrows *hit* a moving mark.'

का कियति मात्रा तेषां मम, तानहं तृणाय मन्ये or तृणीकरोमि 'I *hold* them of no account.' वाचंयमो भव, वाचं नियच्छ, तूष्णीं जोषं आस्स्व '*hold* your tongue.' सर्वगामी-अव्यभिचारी अयं नियमः 'this rule *holds* good everywhere.' मुक्तग्रह 'letting go the *hold.*' रागः शुक्लपटे स्थायी भवती 'red colour takes a firm *hold* on a white cloth.' स लोकस्य मन आददे 'he had a *hold* on the mind of the people (drew the mind of the people towards himself).' लेभेंतरं चेतसि नोपदेशः, अलब्धपदो हृदि 'the advice took no *hold* (was not impressed) on the mind.'

तद्वचः तस्य हृदयमर्मास्पृशत् 'the words went *home* to his heart.

चतुरः शशकान् विश्वासस्थाने धृत्वा 'retaining four hares as *hostages.*'

मानुषीं गिरमुदीरयामास 'uttered *human* accents.'

इति राज्ञां शिरसि वामपादमाधाय 'thus completely *humbling* the kings.'

I

ब्रह्मसायुज्यं प्राप्तः, ब्रह्मलीनः, ब्रह्मभूयं गतः 'becoming *identical* (one) with Brahman.'

दुर्दैवं, दुर्भाग्यं, मंदभाग्यं, दैवविपर्यासः, दुर्विपाकः '*ill* luck.'

अस्मार्तकालात् 'from times *immemorial.*'

स महति जीवितसंशये अवर्तत 'he stood in *imminent* peril of death.'

अलं सेवया (स्नेहभणितेन) मध्यस्थतां गृहीत्वा भण 'away with flattery, speak *impartially.*'

उन्नमत्यकालदुर्दिनं 'an untimely storm *impends.*' अनावृष्टिः संपद्यते लग्ना 'a drought is closely *impending.*'

निर्बंधपृष्टः or पुनः पुनश्चानुबंध्यमानः स जगाद सर्वं 'being *importuned* (pressed), he told all.'

जानकी करुणस्य मूर्तिरथवा शरीरिणि विरहव्यथेव 'Jánakì is the Karu*n*a sentiment or pang of separation *incarnate.*'

वाच्यतां याति, दोषभाजनं-दोषभाक्-दोषपात्रं भवति. 'he *incurs* blame.'

INT.

किं कथ्यते श्रीरुभयस्य तस्य 'the splendour of that pair is simply *indescribable* (what words can describe their splendour).

संभावनीयानुभावास्याकृतिः 'his dignity may be *inferred* from his form.' आकृतिरेवानुमापयत्यमानुषतां 'her very form leads (one) to *infer* her being superhuman.'

अधरोत्तर व्यक्तिर्भविष्यति 'it will be clear who is *inferior* and who is superior'. ओजस्वितया सा न परिहीयते शच्याः 'she is not *inferior* to S'achi is majestic dignity.' न प्रतिच्छंदात्परिहीयते मधुरता '(her) loveliness is not *inferior* to (does not fall short of) that in the picture.'

अमी विनोदनोपायाः संदीपना एव दुःखस्य 'these diversions will only serve to *inflame* grief'.

दर्पाध्मात, मदोद्धत, उत्सिक्त '*inflated* with pride'.

निद्रावश-विधेय 'under the *influence* of sleep.' मूढः परप्रत्ययनेयबुद्धिः 'a fool has his mind *influenced* by the convictions of others.'

पुरुषोत्तमे इति भणितव्ये '*instead* of saying *on Purushottama*'. अध्ययन आरब्धव्ये किमिति क्रीडसि '*instead* of studying why do you play ?' हर्षस्थाने अलं विषादेन 'be not sorry *instead* of being (where you should be) glad.'

परोपकरणीकृत-भूत 'serving as the *instrument* of others.' उपकरणीभावमायात्येवंविधो जनः 'such persons become helping *instruments*.'

चक्रवृद्धिः 'compound *interest*.' सरला वृद्धि, 'simple *interest*' पंचकेन शतेन पंचोत्तरं शतं.' *interest* at five per cent.' दृष्टं युष्माभिः कथारसस्याक्षेपसामर्थ्यं 'you have seen how the *interest* of the story made me digress.' स्वार्थपर, स्वार्थदृष्टि 'looking to one's own *interest*'. अतिरमणीयं कथावस्तु 'the subject-matter of the story is very *interesting*.' पक्षपातितौ आवामनयोः 'we two are (respectively) *interested* in these two.'

न चेदन्यकार्यातिपातः 'if it should not *interfere* with other duties.' अव्यापारेषु व्यापारं स करोति 'he *interferes* in matters not his own.'

मैनमंतरा प्रतिबध्नीतं 'do not *interrupt* him.'

काले काले, अंतरा अंतरा 'at *intervals*.'

LED.

श्रमसहिष्णु, जितश्रम '*inured* to fatigue.'

नायमे कांतो नियमः 'this is not an *invariable* rule'.

रामस्य दैवदुर्नियोगः कोपि 'it was a sad *irony* of fate in the case of Ráma.'

J.

परिहासविजल्पित, नर्मभाषित 'uttered in *jest.*'

अध्वंसजातखेदात् 'on account of the fatigues of *journey.*' उत्थाय पुनरवहत् 'he resumed his *journey.*' सप्ताहगम्यो ध्वा 'it is only a week's *journey.*'

स्वगृहनिर्विशेषमत्र वस 'stay here *just* as in your own house.'

स्वपुत्रनिर्विशेषं संवर्धित 'brought up *just* like one's own sons.'

K.

जानुभ्यां अवनौ गम् or पत् 'go or fall on the *knees.*' जानुदघ्न-द्वयस-मात्र '*knee*-deep.'

भ्रुकुटिं बंध् or रच्, भ्रुवौ संकुच् or भिद् '*knit* the eyebrows.'

बुद्धिर्यस्य बलं तस्य '*knowledge* is power.' तदाख्यया भुवि पप्रथे, तदाख्यां जगाम 'became *known* by that name.'

L.

चिंताशतैर्बाध्यमान-अभिभूत '*labouring* under hundreds of anxieties.'

प्रतस्थे स्थलमार्गेण-वर्त्मना 'proceeded by *land.*'

अलसेक्षण 'with *languishing* looks.'

एष ते जीवितावधिः प्रसादः 'this talk will *last* through life.' कतिपयदिवसस्थायिनी यौवनश्रीः 'the bloom of youth *lasts* for a few days.' कालांतरक्षमा माला 'a garland capable of *lasting* for a long time.'

अर्गलनिरुद्धं पक्षद्वारं 'the postern door was on the *latch.*'

किमिति चिरायितं त्वया, वेलातिक्रमः कृतः 'why are you *late.*'

मुहूर्तं तत् आस्तां, तिष्ठतु तावत् '*lay* it aside for a while.'

विषयप्रसक्तनिरतो जीवितमत्यवाहयत् '*led* a dissolute life.' चित्रकूटयायिनि

LIM.

त्मंनि 'on the way *leading* to Chitrakuta.' अयं पंथा नदीमुपतिष्ठते 'this way *leads* to the river.'

अनुदिवसं परिहीयसेऽङ्गैः 'you are growing *leaner* and *leaner* day by day' (you are gradually wasting away). मदलेखया दत्तहस्तावलंबा *leaning* on Madalekhá's arm.' वामहस्तोपहितवदन '*leaning* her face on her left hand.'

त्र्यवराः साक्षिणो ज्ञेयाः 'there should be at *least* three witnesses.'

अस्मास्ववहीनेषु 'we being *left* behind.' शांते पानीयवर्षे 'when it *left* off raining.'

सुखमुपदिश्यते परस्य 'it is easy to advise or read *lectures* to others.'

लब्धावकाश, प्राप्तावकाश, निर्व्यापार, लब्धक्षण 'being at *leisure*.'

परित्रायस्वैनां मा कस्यापि तपस्विनो हस्ते पतिष्यति 'secure her *lest* she fall into the hands of some ascetic.'

भूमिसात्कृ 'to *level* to the ground.' दरिद्रसमतां नीत-गमित 'reduced to the *level* of poor.'

मनुष्याः स्खलनशीलाः 'man is *liable* to err.'

यदत्रावसरप्राप्तं तत्र प्रभवति भवती 'your ladyship is at *liberty* to do what befits the occasion.' बंधे मोक्षे चाधुना सा ते प्रभवति 'now she is at *liberty* to detain or set you free.'

सर्वथा त्वमेवात्र दोषभाक् 'the fault *lies* with you entirely.' सखीगामी अयं दोषः 'this fault *lies* with my friend.'

प्राणयात्रा-धारणं-रक्षणं 'support of *life*.' साधुवृत्त 'leading a virtuous *life*.' दशांतराणि 'the vicissitudes of *life*.'

अनया दृष्ट्या 'considered in this *light*.'

एवमादि 'this and the *like*.' यस्ते छंदः; यद्भवते रोचते 'just as you *like*. कामचार, स्वछंद, स्वैरिन्, कामवृत्ति 'doing as one *likes*.' कामपूरः 'taking what form he *likes*.' यथाभिलषितं क्रियतां 'do as you *like*.' स न तस्या रुचये बभूव 'he was not to her *liking*.'

अल्पविषय 'of narrow *limit* (scope).' तस्य यश इयत्तया परिच्छेत्तुं नालं 'no (definite) *limit* can be set to his fame.' न गुणानामियत्तया 'not through the *limited* nature of merits.'

MEE.

यावदहं प्रिये 'as long as I *live*.' वन्यफलैः शरीरवृत्तिं निर्वर्तयति '*lives* on wild fruit.' स्मार्ते-काले 'with *living* memory.'

राजकुले-राज्ञे-निविद् cause 'to *lodge* a complaint,' 'to file a suit.' नयनैः-दृष्टिभिः-पा, निध्यै 'to *look* intently at.' तत्साहसाभासं 'that *looks* like wantonness.' जनन्या मे योगक्षेमं वहस्व, जननीमवेक्षस्व-चिंतय '*look* after (look to the well-being' take care of) my mother.'

विगतासुर्बभूव, प्राणैरहीयत 'he *lost* his life.' मित्रैर्वियुज्यते 'he *loses* his friends.' उन्मार्गगामी अभूत् 'he *lost* his way.' च्युताधिकारः, अधिकारभ्रष्टः 'who has *lost* his office.' किंकर्तव्यता-प्रतिपत्तिमूढ 'being at a *loss* what to do.'

उपनम्, उपस्था 'fall to the *lot* of.' तव दुःखमुपनमेत् 'misery will be your *lot*.' कस्यात्यन्त सुखमुपनतं 'to whose *lot* (share) does perpetual happiness fall.'

M.

दोषमपि गुणत्वमुपपादयितुं 'to *make* the best of a bad matter.' लक्ष्यभेदः 'hitting the *mark*.'

अप्रभुरस्मि आत्मनः, न प्रभावाम्यात्ममः, मात्राणामनीशोऽस्मि संवृत्तः 'I am not *master* of myself.' सकलशास्त्रपारंगतः, शास्त्रपारदृश्वा, 'who has completely *mastered* all sciences.' गतोसि सर्वास्वायुधविद्यासु परां प्रतिष्ठां 'you have attained perfect *mastery* over all sciences of arms.'

आवां प्रतिद्वंद्विनौ भवाव 'let us (two) make a *match*.' दैत्येभ्यो हरिरलं 'Hari is a *match* for the demons'. अतीत्य-अतिक्रम्य-वृत् 'to be more than a *match* for'. तुल्यप्रतिद्वंद्वि बभूव युद्धं 'it was a well-*matched* fight.'

यत्किंचित्करमेतत् 'it does not much *matter*.' किं तस्या वृत्तं कस्तस्या वृत्तांतः 'what is the *matter* with her.' किं मम तेन कार्यं-कोर्थः 'what *matters* it to me.' सन्निधानस्य अकिंचित्करत्वात् 'proximity being not *material*.'

परिणतप्रज्ञ, कठोरधी 'of *matured* intellect.'

साकूतं मां निर्वर्ण्य 'casting at me a *meaning* look.'

प्रत्युत् या-व्रज्-गम्-इ 'go out to *meet*.' प्रत्युत्था, अभ्युत्था 'to rise to *meet*.' आपः संप्लवन्ते-संभिद्यन्ते 'waters *meet*.'

NEE,

तस्य हृदयं स्नेहार्द्रीभूतं, स्नेहेनाभ्यष्यन्दत 'his heart was *melted* with affection.'

मेधाविन्. धारणावत् 'having a retentive *memory*.' स्मृतिविषयतां-स्मृतिपथं-स्मर्तव्यशेषं-कथावशेषं गम् or नी pass. 'to remain only in *memory*.'

एको दोषो गुणसंनिपाते निमज्जति 'one fault *merges* in a collection of good qualities.'

चित्त-मनो-व्यापारः-वृत्तिः 'working of the *mind*.' मनसि उत्-इ or वृत्, वृतौ संजन् 'to cross or occur to the *mind*' आस्तां-तिष्ठतु-तावत् प्रथमः प्रश्नः 'never *mind* the first question.'

उत्कंठासाधारणं परितोषमनुभवामि 'I feel pleasure *mingled* with regret.'

मार्गात् भ्रष्टः '*missed* his way.'

गोत्रस्खलितं 'a *mistake* in calling by name.' तस्माद्रर्दभात्-व्याघ्रधिया-बुद्ध्या पशवः पलायन्ते 'animals run away from the ass *mistaking* it for a tiger'.

अलमन्यथा गृहीत्वा 'don't *misunderstand* me.'

आपातरमणीय 'good for the present *moment*.'

खलः सर्षपमात्राणि परच्छिद्राणि पश्यति। आत्मनो बिल्वमात्राणि पश्यन्नपि न पश्यति 'the *mote* thou seest in the eyes of others, but not the beam in thine own'.

तिले तालं पश्यति, अणुं पर्वतीकरोति 'he makes *mountains* of mole-hills.'

अस्मात्स्थानात्पदात्पदमपि न गंतव्यं 'don't *move* even a step further.'

कर्मणो गहना गतिः '*mysterious* are the ways (working) of Fate.'

N.

अपि ज्ञायन्ते ते नामधेयतः 'do you know their *names*.'

अस्य मातरं नामतः पृच्छेयं 'I shall ask his mother's *name*.' नामग्राहं मामाह्वयति 'he calls me by my *name*.' वचनेन ' वचनात् 'in one's *name*.' वाच्यस्त्वया मद्वचनात्स राजा 'say to the king in my *name*.' मामुद्दिश्य तस्मै सभाजनाक्षराणि पातय 'salute him in my *name*.'

मानुषतासुलभो लघिमा 'levity *natural* to mortals.'

दुर्जातबन्धुः 'a friend in *need* (adversity)'. स सुहृद् व्यसने यः स्यात् 'a friend in *need* is a friend indeed.'

OVE.

मालती मूर्धानं चालयति 'Mâlatî *nods* her head.'
ननु शब्दपतिः क्षितेरहं 'I am but a *nominal* lord of the Earth'.
बहुलीभूतमेतत् वृत्तं 'this matter has become *notorious*' (known to all).
यत्नादुपचर्यतामसौ 'let her be carefully *nursed*.'

O.

स्नेहस्यैकायनीभूता 'the sole *object* of one's affection'. किमुद्दिश्य, किंनिमित्तं, किमपेक्ष्य फलं 'with what *object* in view'.

प्रत्यर्थिभूता सा समाधेः 'she was an *obstacle* to meditation'.

श्लाघ्ये गृहिणीपदे स्थिता '*occupying* the honorable position of a housewife'.

इति तस्य बुद्धौ न संजातं, इति यस्य हृदये नापतितं 'this did not *occur* to his mind'. स्मृत्युपस्थितौ इमौ द्वौ श्लोकौ 'these two verses *occur* to our mind'.

कस्मिन्नपि पूजार्हे अपराद्धा शकुन्तला 'S'akuntalá has *offended* some person worthy of respect'. तव न कदापि मया विप्रियं कृतं, प्रतिकूलमाचरितं 'I have never even once *offended* you'. शीघ्रकोपिन्, सुलभकोप 'easily taking *offence*.

च्युत-भ्रष्ट-अधिकार 'dismissed from *office*'.

प्रकाशं निर्गतः 'having gone out into the *open* air'. तत्रोपालंभे पतितास्मि, उपालंभपात्रं जाता 'I laid myself *open* to your taunt'.

गृहीतावसर, लब्धावकाश 'seizing an *opportunity*'.

लोकाचारविरुद्ध, लोकविद्विष्ट '*opposed* to the practice of the world'.

अत्र स्वरुच्या वर्ततां भवान्, यथाभिलाषं क्रियतां 'it is left to your *option*,' or choice.

यथाज्ञापयति देवः 'your Majesty's *orders* will be obeyed'. आनुलोम्यं 'natural *order*'. प्रातिलोम्यं, व्युत्क्रमः, विपर्ययः, व्यत्यासः 'reverse *order*'.

अपह्रिये परिश्रमजनितया निद्रया 'I am *overcome* by sleep caused by fatigue'.

आनंदपरिवाहिणा चक्षुषा 'with an eye *overflowing* with joy'. प्रथमं कुतूहलं सपरिवाहमासीत् 'my curiosity first *overflowed*'.

P.

PLA.

विवर्णभावं प्रपेदे 'grew or turned *pale*'.

शरीरभूता मे शकुन्तला 'S'akuntalá forms, as it were, a part and *parcel* of my body'.

भूमिकाकल्पनं 'assignment of *parts*.'

तस्य नरस्य विशेषं ब्रूहि 'give the *particulars* of the man'.

तेनाष्टौ परिगमिताः समाः कथंचित् 'he with difficulty *passed* eight years'. इदं धियः पथि न वर्तते 'this *passes* conception'. आस्तां तिष्ठतु तदधुना, यातु, किमनेन 'let it *pass* now.' किमर्थमगृहीतमुद्रः कटकान्निष्कामसि 'why do you leave the camp without (taking) a *pass*.' अमुद्रालांछितः 'without a *pass*'. तया हृदयवल्लभोऽभिलिख्य कामदेवव्यपदेशेन सखीपुरतोऽपह्नुतः 'she *passed* off the picture of her beloved upon her friend as that of Cupid.' मध्यमांबावृत्तान्तोऽन्तरित आर्येण 'the account of the second mother has been *passed* over by his honour'.

जालान्तरप्रेषितदृष्टिरन्या 'another *peeping* through a lattice'.

आज्ञा गुरूणां ह्यविचारणीया 'the command of elderly persons (to be considered) *peremptory*', should not be called in question.

नाटकं न प्रयोगतो दृष्टं, प्रयोगेणाधिकृतं न दृष्टं 'the drama has not been seen *performed* (acted) on the stage'.

स्थिरप्रतिबन्धो भव '*persevere* in your opposition'.

आसन्न-शरीर-परिचारकः 'a *personal* attendant,' body-guard. स्वानुभवः '*personal* experience'.

यौवनमंगेषु सन्नद्धं 'youth has *pervaded* the limbs'.

ज्ञायतां कः कः कार्यार्थीति 'ascertain who are the *petitioners*.'

विरहोत्कंठं-हृदयं 'a heart *pining* away in absence'. स गृहं गंतुमुदतान्यत् 'he *pined* for his home.' अंतःपुरविरहपर्युत्सुको राजर्षिः 'the royal sage is *pining* by the separation from his wives.'

पितृस्थाने-भूमौ 'in the *place* of a father,' प्रथमं, प्रथमतः, प्रथमं तावत् 'in the first *place*.' अपरंच, पुनः, पुनश्च 'in the next *place*.'

PRE.

अर्थिन्, वादी, अभियोक्तृ '*a plaintiff*'. प्रत्यर्थी, अभियुक्तः, प्रतिवादी 'a defendant.'

द्वित्राण्यहान्यर्हसि सोढुमर्हन् 'worthy Sir, *please* wait for 2 or 3 days.' यदभिरोचते वयस्याय 'just as my friend *pleases*.' हृदयंगमः परिहासः 'a *pleasant* joke.' सुख श्रव, श्रुतिसुख, श्रवणसुभग मंजुलस्वन '*pleasing* to the ear.'

विहितप्रतिज्ञः-गृहीतक्षणः-अहं 'I have *pledged* my word.' अनयोरेवंत्तेयं प्रतिज्ञा 'they two thus *pledged* their word'. तव विरूपकरणे तेन सुकृतमंतरे धृतं 'he has *pledged* his virtue (honor) that he would not harm you.'

मरणोन्मुख, आसन्नमृत्यु, मुमूर्षु 'on or at the *point* of death'. प्रसवोन्मुखी, आसन्नप्रसवा 'on the *point* of delivery'.

दासी महिषीपदं ग्राहिता, देवीभावं गमिता 'the maid was given the *position* of a queen'.

तदुभयथापि घटते 'it is *possible* in both ways (both sides are *possible*)'.

चिरप्रवृत्त 'being long in *practice*'. सदाचार, सद्वृत्त, साधुवृत्त 'following good *practices*'. कां वृत्तिमुपजीवत्यार्यः 'what profession do you *practise*.' प्रयोगः '*practice*' as opposed to शास्त्रं, आगमः 'theory'.

शासनात् करणं श्रेयः, वाचः कर्मातिरिच्यते 'example is better than *precept*.'

स कथयत्यागामिनमप्यर्थं 'he even *predicts* events'.

वरं मृत्युः न पुनरपमानः 'I *prefer* death to disgrace'.

दौर्हृदलक्षणं दधौ 'she showed signs of *pregnancy*'. कठोरगर्भा 'advanced in pregnancy.'

त्वयोपस्थातव्यं, सन्निहितेन भाव्यं 'you should be *present*'. समतीतं च भवच्च भावि च 'the past, *present*, and future'. अग्निं साक्ष्ये आधाय 'in the *presence* of fire'.

तं वक्षसा परिरभ्य-क्रोडीकृत्य '*pressing* him to the bosom'.

भावितविषवेगः '*pretending* to be affected by poison'. अश्रुतिमभिनयति '*pretends* not to hear'. आर्यध्वजिन्-लिंगिन् '*pretending* to be just'.

साक्षी वाक्यभेदान् बहूनकथयत् 'the witness *prevaricated*'. प्रक्षालनाद्धि पंकस्य दूरादस्पर्शनं वरं '*prevention* is better than cure.'

REA.

द्विषामामिषतां ययौ 'fell a *prey* to enemies.'

प्रथमं वयः, नव-अक्षत-यौवनं 'the *prime* of youth'.

ततस्ततः, ततः परं कथय '*proceed* with your narrative.' प्रस्तूयतां विवादवस्तु '*proceed* with the matter at issue.' प्रवर्त्यतां भगवतो ब्राह्मणानुद्दिश्य पाकः 'you may *proceed* with your dinner-preparations in honor of the worthy Bráhma*n*as.' किंनिमित्तं ते संतापः 'from what cause does the excitement *proceed*.'

क्षुदुद्बोधित '*prompted* by hunger.' स सदा प्रत्युत्पन्नमतिः, प्रबोधननिरपेक्षः 'he seldom wants a *prompter*.'

एष सनिकारं नगरान्निर्वास्यते 'here is this person being disgraced and *proscribed* from the city.'

ब्रुवते हि फलेन साधवो न तु कंठेन निजोपयोगितां 'good men *prove* their usefulness by deeds, not by words.'

अनागतविधाता 'one who provides for the future.' आपदर्थे धनं रक्षेत् 'one should *provide* wealth against times of want.'

स्तूयमाना नोत्सिच्यन्ते or अनुद्धताः 'are not *puffed* up when praised.' दर्पाध्मात, उत्सिक्त, अवलिप्त, उद्धत '*puffed* up with pride.'

चौरदण्डेन दण्डयेत् 'he should *punish* (an offender) as a thief.'

Q.

अनियंत्रणानुयोगस्तपस्विजनः 'ascetics may be *questioned* without reserve.'

R.

मंदोप्यविरतोद्योगः सदा विजयभाग्भवेत् 'slow and steady wins the *race*.'

तद्वचो मम हृदये शल्यं जातं 'those words *rankle* in my heart.' स प्रहारः करालतां गतः 'the wound *rankled*.'

वृत्तांतेन श्रवणविषयप्रापिणा 'by the account *reaching* (her) ears.' इदं प्रायेण तव कर्णपथमायातं श्रुतिविषयमापतितमेव 'this has probably *reached* your ears.'

प्रत्युत्पन्नमति 'having a *ready* wit,' '*ready*-witted.'

परमार्थतः प्रेम 'affection in the *real* sense of the term.'

RES.

धनी उपगतं दद्यात् (धनं) स्वहस्तपरिचिह्नितं 'the creditor shall pass a *receipt* in his own hand'.

दर्शनप्रतिभुवं ददौ 'he entered into a *recognizance* bond.

तदहं विदधे तव स्तवं दमयंत्याः सविधे 'I shall, therefore, *recommend* you to Damayanti.'

नाद्यापि प्रसादं गृह्णासि, प्रसन्ना न भवसि 'you are not yet *reconciled*.' वाक्यानि प्रतिसमादधाति '*reconciles* statements.'

कृतकालोपनेयः आधिः 'a pledge to be *redeemed* at a fixed time.'

आत्मवशं नी, वशी कृ '*reduce* to subjection.' अस्थिमात्रावशेष, कंकालशेष '*reduced* to a skeleton of bones.' अपचितं गात्रं ' a body *reduced* in bulk.'

अत्र पुरावृत्तकथा अनुसंधेया 'a *reference* or allusion is here made to a mythological story.'

भर्तुः प्रतीपं मास्म गमः 'do not show a *refractory* spirit towards your husband.'

नार्हसि मे प्रणयं विहन्तुं 'pray, do not *refuse* my request.'

तस्य मनो मार्दवमभजत, कठिणतामजहात् 'his heart *relented*.' स चानुनीतो मृदुतामगच्छत् 'being appeased, he *relented*.' किमपि सानुक्रोशः कृतः 'he somewhat *relented*.'

दुःखविश्रामं ददाति 'gives *relief* to sorrow.'

हृदि एनां भारतीं उपधातुमर्हसि 'please *remember* (lay to heart) these words well.'

पातालं मामद्य संस्मरयतीव भुजंगलोकः 'this group of gallants as if *reminds* me to-day of Pátála.' अये सम्यगनुबोधितोऽस्मि 'oh ! I am well *reminded*.'

इति जनप्रवादः किंवदंती श्रूयते, इति प्रवादः 'there goes a *report*.'

विश्वासप्रतिपन्न '*reposing* in confidence.'

दोषानपि गुणपक्षमध्यारोपयन्ति, गुणपक्षे स्थापयन्ति '*represent* even faults as merits.'

संवदत्यक्षराणि 'the characters *resemble* one another', agree, coincide.

SAL.

सागरे नद्यो विलीयन्ते 'rivers are *resolved* into the sea.'

वामहस्तोपहितवदना 'with her face *resting* on her left hand.' खुरत्रये भरं कृत्वा '*resting* on the three hoofs.' भाग्यायत्तमतः परं ' further than this *rests* with fate.' सकलरिपुजयाशा यत्र बद्धा सुतैस्ते 'on whom your sons had *rested* their hopes of overthrowing all enemies.'

हरः स्मरं स्वेन वपुषा नियोजयिष्यति 'Hara will *restore* to Cupid his body.'

एवं सर्वतो निरुद्धचेष्टाप्रसरस्य मे 'my actions being thus restricted on all sides (my course being thus hampered).' अपवादः उत्सर्गं व्यावर्तयितुमीश्वरः 'an exception can *restrict* the scope of a rule.'

अतः परं पुनः कथयिष्यामि 'I shall *resume* my story from this point afterwards.'

तस्य चार्थस्य सततं मनसि विपरिवर्तमानत्वात् 'that matter constantly *revolving* in his mind.'

गमिष्याम्युपहास्यतां 'I shall be *ridiculed*.'

अवितथमाह प्रियंवदा 'Priyamvada is *right*.' 'says *rightly*.' न स्त्री स्वातंत्र्यमर्हति ' a woman has no *right* to independence.' तत् देविहस्ते निक्षिपता मया युक्तमेवानुष्ठितं 'I acted *rightly* in delivering it into the hands of the queen.'

ते नाभ्युत्तिष्ठंति गुरून् 'they do not *rise* to receive their elders.' उत्तिष्ठमानः शत्रुः 'a *rising* enemy.'

स्थाने खलु सज्यते दृष्टिः 'it is proper that the eye is *riveted*.

प्रथमं गुणितमिव तवोत्तरं 'your answer is as it were, learnt by *rote*.'

प्रजाः प्रजाः स्वा इव तंत्रयित्वा *ruling* the subjects like one's own children.'

कियदवशिष्टं रजन्याः 'how much has the night yet to *run*.'

S.

सफलीकृत भर्तृपिंडः ' (who showed that) he had not eaten his master's *salt* in vain.'

SHA.

का कथा गणना (with loc.), कथैव नास्ति with प्रति 'what need we *say* of.' जनप्रवादः 'popular *saying*' तथा च लौकीकनामा माणकः 'so runs the popular *saying*,' 'as the proverb goes.'

मुद्रां परिपालयन् उद्घाट्य दर्शय 'open it, preserving the *seal* and show me.'

प्रत्यक्षीकृ 'to *see* with one's own eyes.'

क्रय्य, क्रयार्थं प्रसारित 'exposed for *sale*.'

कृतज्ञता, कृतवेदित्वं '*sense* of obligation.' जरावलुप्तमानावमानचिंतः 'having lost all *sense* of honour and dishonour on account of old age.' यौगिकार्थ 'etymological *sense*.' रूढार्थ 'conventional or popular *sense*.' अन्वर्थ, यथार्थ, परमार्थतः 'in its true *sense*.' अन्यथा एषा वीप्सा न चरितार्था भवति 'else this repetition has no *sense*' (does not become significant).

एकैक, व्यस्त 'taken *separately*' (सर्वाविमयानामेकैकमप्येषा सायतनं, तदस्ति किं व्यस्तमपि त्रिलोचने).

कोपोद्दीपनाय अलं or पर्याप्तमिदं 'this will *serve* to rouse his anger.' उपयोगं व्रज्, स्थाने-भूमौ भू 'to *serve* the purpose of,' '*serve* as.' मरुतः परिवेष्टारः आसन् 'the Gods *served* up food,' इदं पादोदकं भविष्यति 'this will *serve* as water to wash the feet with.'

सर्वांगिका आभारणसंयोगाः '*sets* of ornaments fitting all parts of the body.' रत्नानुविद्ध, मणिप्रत्युप्त, रत्नखचित '*set* with jewels.' पदं कृ '*set* one's foot in.' मनः-धियं-चित्तं बंध् or आधा or संनिविश् caus. or युज् caus. '*set* the heart on.' अनेन समयेन परिणतो दिवसः 'by this time the sun had *set*.' आधीयतां धर्मे धीः '*set* your heart on religious duties.' विनाशधर्मसु विषयेषु मनो मा संनिवेशय '*set* not your heart on transient objects.' अचिरप्रवृत्तो ग्रीष्मसमयः 'summer which has just *set* in.' गुणा विनयेन शोभन्ते 'virtues are *set* off by modesty.'

व्यवस्थापितवाक्, वाचं व्यवस्थाप्य '*settling* what to say.'

इति प्रतिपादितमाकुलीभवेत् 'this position would be *shaken*.'

स्निग्धजनसंविभक्तं दुःखं 'sorrow *shared* by dear friends.' केन वान्येन सह साधारणीकरोमि दुःखं 'with whom else shall I *share* my grief.'

STA.

चर्मिन्, फलकपाणि 'armed with a *shield*. खड्गचर्मधर 'having a sword and *shield*.'

नयनोपांतविलोकितं, साचिवीक्षणं, अपांगदृष्टिः, कटाक्षः 'a *side*-long look.'

विदूषकं संज्ञां लंभयति 'makes a *sign* to Vidushaka.' अर्थवत्, सार्थ, चरितार्थ, अर्थयुक्त, अन्वर्थ '*significant*.'

सीदति मे हृदयं 'my heart *sinks* down' प्रबलपिपासावसन्नानि अंगकानि 'limbs *sinking* down through excessive thirst.' तस्य धैर्यमहीयत, स लुप्त-स्खलित-धैर्यः 'his heart *sank* within him.'

मया रथस्य मंदीकृतो वेगः 'I have *slackened* the speed of the chariot.'

शिथिलितप्रयत्नाः, श्लथोद्यमाः 'who have *slackened* their efforts.'

मंथरविवेकं चेतः 'a mind *slow* to discriminate.' प्रत्यभिज्ञान मंथरः '*slow* in recognizing.'

पराभवो मम हृदि प्रत्युप्तं शल्यमिव, न्यक्कारो हृदि वज्रकील इव मे तीव्रं परिस्पन्दते 'I am *smarting* under the defeat' (the defeat is rankling in my heart).

बधिरान्मंदकर्णः श्रेयान् '*something* is better than nothing.'

वक्तुं सुकरमिदमध्यवसातुं तु दुष्करं 'it is *sooner* said than done.'

तंतुनाभः स्वत एव तंतून् सृजति 'the spider *spins* out its web (threads) from itself.'

सोल्लास, प्रमुदितचित्त 'in high *spirits*.'

मिषतां नः आमिषं आच्छिनत्ति 'snatches away the prey in *spite* of our looking on.'

चारचक्षुर्महीपालः 'the king sees through *spies*.'

उपक्रोशमलीमसैः प्राणैः किं 'what is the use of life *stained* by infamy (ignominy).

संशयस्थं जीवितं तस्य, स संशयितजीवित आसीत्, जीवितं संशयदोलाधिरूढं 'his life was at *stake*.'

वचनीयमिदं व्यवस्थितं 'this will remain a *standing* stigma (on me).' कुंठित-प्रतिहस्त-रुद्ध-गति 'at a *stand*-still.' इदं सोपपत्तिकं न भाति 'this does not

SUP.

stand to reason.' लब्धप्रतिष्ठ 'who has obtained a *standing*. पुलकित, रोमांचिता 'with the hair *standing* on end.'

यात्राभिमुखं प्रवृत् 'to *start* on a journey.' अभिन्नगतयः शब्दं संहते मृगाः 'not *starting* aside the deer hear the sound' सचकितं 'with a *start*.'

अविदितगतयामा रात्रिः 'night, the watches of which *stole* away (imperceptibly glided away).' शनैर्निद्रा निमीलितलोचनं मामकार्षीत् 'sleep gently *stole* upon my eyes.'

ज्वलति चलितेंधनोग्निः 'when the fuel is *stirred* the fire blazes up.'

नैतावता पीडां निष्क्रामति 'the evil does not *stop* here.'

मुखे चपेटां दा 'to *strike* on the face.' चित्ते भयं जनयति '*strikes* fear in the mind.' बद्ध-प्ररूढ-मूल '*striking* deep root.' तस्य हृदयं पस्पर्श विस्मयः 'he was *struck* with wonder.' तद्धि प्रसिद्धतरेण प्रयोगेण शीघ्रं बुधिमारोहति, प्रसिद्धि-बलेन प्रथमतरं प्रतीयते 'being used in its most general sense, it easily *strikes* the mind.'

जर्जरितकर्णविवरः-जर्जरीकृतकर्णपुटः नादः 'a sound *stunning* the ears.'

सा देवीशब्देनोपचर्यते 'she is *styled* (treated as) Queen.'

पितुरनंतरमुत्तरकोशलान्समधिगम्य '*succeeding* his father as sovereign of the North Kos'ala.'

यदि नावसीदति गुरु प्रयोजनं 'if any important duty should not *suffer*.'

खलः करोति दुर्वृत्तं तद्धि फलति साधुषु 'a wicked person commits a fault, and good man *suffers* for it.'

आतपलंघनात् 'from a *sun* stroke.'

पुनरुक्ततां नी 'to render *superfluous*.' अभिव्यक्तायां चंद्रिकायां किं दीपिका-पौनरुक्त्येन 'when there is clear moonlight, torches are *superfluous*.'

अश्वमेधसहस्रेभ्यः सत्यमेवातिरिच्यते-विशिष्यते 'truth is *superior* to thousands of horse-sacrifices.'

कथं जीवितं धारयिष्यामि 'how shall I *support* my life.' न ह्ययं मन्त्रः स्वातंत्र्येण कंचिदपि वादं समर्थयितुमुत्सहते 'this hymn cannot by itself *support* any theory.'

TOR.

नियम्य शोकावेगं '*suppressing* the emotion of sorrow.'

विकारस्य गममीयास्मि संवृत्ता 'I am made *susceptible* of an emotion.' विकारि यौवनं 'youth is *susceptible*.'

धृतद्वैधीभावकातरं मे मनः 'my mind is held in *suspense* and hence anxious.

विहगाः समदुःखा इव चुक्रुशुः 'the birds screamed as if out of *sympathy*.'

T.

भिन्नरुचिर्हि लोकः '*tastes* differ,' 'different men have different *tastes*.'

निर्गंतुं सहसा न वेतसगृहाच्छक्तोस्मि 'I am unable to *tear* myself off from the cane-bower.' विललाप विकीर्णमूर्धजा 'she *tore* her hair for grief.'

गमयति रजनीं विषाददीर्घतरां 'passes the night grown *tedious* on account of dejection.'

शास्त्रे प्रयोगे च मां विमृश '*test* me in theory and practice.'

अनुगृहीतोस्मि, महानयं प्रसादः '(I) *thank* you.' 'thanks.'

द्वावप्यागमिनौ प्रयोगनिपुणौ च 'both are well-versed in *theory* and practice.'

नगरगमनाय मतिं न करोति 'he does not *think* of going to his capital.'

सखीमुखेनोचे 'spoke *through* her friend.'

अपत्यमन्योन्यसंश्लेषणं पित्रोः 'a child is the mutual *tie* of parents.'

अतिपिनद्धेन वल्कलेन नियन्त्रितास्मि 'I am chained down by this *tight* bark-garment.'

समयः स्नानभोजनं सेवितुं 'it is high *time* to bathe and take our meals.' कालानुवर्तिन् 'a time server' नैवं वारान्तरं विधास्यामि 'I shall not do so another *time*.' अनवसरग्रस्तोर्थिभावः 'begging is out of *time*.' अकालक्षेपेण अविलंबितं, अकालहीनं 'without loss of *time*.'

अमुष्य विद्या रसनाग्रनर्तकी, समस्ता एव विद्या जिह्वाग्रेऽभवन् 'learning danced on the *tip* of his tongue.'

धारासारैर्महती वृष्टिर्बभूव 'it rained in *torrents*.'

WAN.

शतसंख्या मामियं स्पृशति 'the number of 100 *touches* me home.' हृदयं संस्पृष्टमुत्कंठया 'the heart is *touched* with anxiety.

मित्राणां तत्वनिकषग्रावा विपत् 'adversity is the *touch*-stone of (the sincerity of) friendship.'

ग्राहकैर्गृह्यते चौरः पदेन 'a thief is *traced* out by his foot-steps.' ब्रह्मशब्दस्य व्युत्पाद्यमानस्य 'when the word *Brahma* is *traced* (to its root).'

क्षुण्णाद्वर्त्मनः 'from the *trodden* (beaten) path.'

परंतपो नाम यथार्थनामा 'Parantapa *truly* so called.' ध्रुवसिद्धेरपि यथार्थनाम्नः 'of Dhruvasiddhi true to his name,' *turuly* so-called.'

उपकारः प्रत्युपकारेण निर्यातयितव्यः 'one good *turn* deserves another.'

U.

असमर्थित, अतर्कित, अतर्कितोपनत '*unexpected*.

समवायो हि दुस्तरः, संहतिः कार्यसाधिका '*union* is strength.'

ज्योतिः शब्दस्तेजसि प्रयुज्यते 'the word ज्योतिः is *used* in the sense of Light. ' ज्योतिःशब्दो ज्वलन एव रूढः 'ज्योतिः is conventionally *used* for fire.' अनुपभुक्तभूषण 'not *used* to ornaments.'

V.

रणधुरां वह्, समरशिरसि वृत् 'to lead the *van*.'

वाचिकं, वाचनिकं, शब्दाख्येयं 'a *verbal* message.'

वाग्व्यवहारः '*verbal* ('oral) discussion.'

लोक-व्यवहार-दृष्ट्या 'from a worldly (practical) point of *view*.'

निर्व्यूढस्तेऽपत्यस्नेहः 'thy parental affection has been fully *vindicated* or shown.'

W.

कालः कश्चित्प्रतीक्ष्यतां *wait* for some time.' सहस्व मासद्वयं '*wait* for two months.'

स्फुलिंगावस्थया वह्निरेधापेक्ष इव स्थितः 'here is fire in the state of a spark (only) *waiting* for fuel..

त्वत्तो न किमपि परिहास्यते 'nothing will be *wanting* to you.'

WIE.

न कामचारो मयि शंकनीयः 'do not suspect me of *wantonness.*

सूर्यातपं सेव् '*warm* oneself (in the sun).' अग्न्यातपं सेव् '*warm* oneself at the fire.'

वृद्धिक्षयौ '*waxing* and waning.'

अंतरा 'on the *way.*' परिपंथीभू 'stand or come in the *way.*' किं, स्वातंत्र्यमवलंबसे 'do you have your own *way.*'

सर्वत्र नो वार्तमवेहि 'know that we are doing *well* in every respect.' युज्यते, बाढं, तथेति उक्त्वा 'saying very *well.*'

छंदोनुवृत्तिः 'acting according to another's *whim*'.

ईश्वरेच्छा बलीयसी, प्रभवति भगवान् विधिः 'God's *will* be done.' बलात्, हठात्, अकामतः 'against one's *will.*'

अयशः प्रमृष्टं 'the ignominy was *wiped* out.'

कुंठितमतिः आसीत्, निरुत्तरीकृतः 'he was at his *wits*' end.'

कष्टमभ्यापन्नः 'in a *woeful* plight.'

नैतच्चित्रं, किमत्र चित्रं 'it is no *wonder,*' 'what *wonder* is there.'

सत्य-पालित-संगरः-संधः 'true to, or keeping one's *word.*'

लघुसंदेशपदा सरस्वती 'a briefly-*worded* message.' सम्यग्ग्रथित-साधुविन्यस्त-पद 'well *worded.*' करुणार्थग्रथित 'pathetically *worded.*'

त्वं मम जीवितसर्वस्वीभूतः 'you are my all-the-*world*' (the all-in-all of my life). लौकिकज्ञ 'knowing the ways of the *world.*'

न तर्हि प्रागवस्थायाः परिहीयसे 'you are not then *worse* off or in a *worse* condition than before.'

अनुरूपभर्तृगामिनी 'having a husband *worthy* of herself.'

वैरसाधनं-निर्यातनं '*wreaking* revenge.'

Y.

बाढं, अथ किं '*yes*'. तथेति उक्त्वा 'saying *yes*'.

वैतसीं वृत्तिं आश्रि 'to *yield* to a superior foe.'

SENTENCES FOR CORRECTION.

अरण्येऽधिवस्तुं यतय इच्छंति।

संन्यासी बहवो दिनान्येकस्थाने नावसेत्।

यद्रामादंतरेणायोध्या शून्या दृश्यते तत्कैकेयीवचनस्य परिणामः।

अस्य गिरेरभितो बहवोऽश्मानः संति।

अस्य वर्त्मनः परितः पलाशवृक्षा दृश्यंते।

हा धिङ् मेऽन्यायाचरणं कुर्वते।

स एवं विचारयन् सकला रात्रिर्व्यतीयाय।

दुर्योधनः पांडवान्नाबिभेत्।

शत्रवे बाणानहं क्षिपामि स तु मह्यं दृशदो मुंचति।

मम वचनं स न विश्वसिति।

सर्वेभ्यः पुत्रेभ्यो गोपालः पितुः श्रेष्ठः

सर्वाभ्यो नदीभ्यो भागीरथी द्राघिष्ठा।

स भोजनादनु बहिरगच्छत्।

संसारसुखानि केवलं दुःखस्थानमस्तीति साधोरंतरेण को जानाति।

इयं नगरी त्रयः क्रोशा आयता।

धनिनं द्रव्यं याचित भिक्षुकैः।

अंभोनिधिं सुधा ममंथे देवैः।

तेषां मे च सख्यमस्ति।

अयं वित्तसंचयस्त एव।

तां वात्रानय मा वा तत्र नय।

हे जगन्नाथ मे सर्वाणि पापानि क्षमस्व।

ताः स्त्रिय आत्मनो निंदंति।

सा युवतिरात्मानं हतप्राणाममन्यत।

क्रुद्धः पुरुषः शिलायामध्यधिशेते।

गोपालो वा रामोऽहं वा त्वं तत्कार्यं करिष्यथेति मां भाति।

पथिके उत्थिते सति तस्य सार्धमहमगच्छम्।

समागतेषु बालेषु तान्फलानि दातुमारभस्व।

तस्मिन् राजनि वसुधामीशाने न कोपि सामंतस्तमभिभावितुं येते

अजाश्च क्षेत्रं नीयमानास्ता ताः शस्यमखादयत्।
भार्यायाः आक्रोशंत्याः सा भर्त्रा प्रतिषिद्धा।
दंभश्च पैशुन्यं च सदा गर्हणीयो।
रूपवतीभार्या सदा प्रीतिपात्रा भवति।
पिता च माता च वार्द्धक्ये परिपालनीयः।
यस्स एवमुवाच तत्तस्य दोष एव।
यत्कौर्यमित्याचक्षते तत्प्रकृतिरेव खलानाम्।
अन्येषां पुत्राणां राम एव पितुः प्रेयानासीत्।
त्वं मम प्राणानामपि प्रियतरा अतस्त्वां सर्वं कथयामि।
अहं तत्र गंतुं न शक्नोमि हि मध्ये नद्यायातवती।
वरं भिक्षां याचितुं न तु परसेवाविधिम्।
अहं वा त्वं तच्चकार।
स गृहं प्रत्यागतो वा नेति मां सत्वरं निवेदय।
राज्ञापराधिनं शता रूपका दंड्याः।
इंद्रः स्वयशः किन्नरमिथुनैर्गापयामास।
प्रासादस्य परितोऽमात्यं भिक्षुकान् स्थापयति राजा।
क्षुधितेन वत्सेन पयः पायय तमन्नं वा खादय।
राज्ञी वनात्पुष्पाणि दासीरानाययत्।
अहं मम मित्रं मा पारितोषिकमपदापयम्।
गुणिषु पूजास्थानं गुणा एवास्ति न लिंगं वा न वयः।
तस्या नार्या अवलोकनस्य पात्रं ते नरा बभूव।
अत्र विषये ईश्वरो न दोषास्पदः।
सा तपस्विनी मत्कृपापात्रं जातम्।
गोविंदस्तस्य भार्या च स्तुत्यचरिते स्तः।
तपो दमो निःस्पृहता च सर्वे अमी यतिषु प्रशस्याः।
ऋते रामं जनकः कमपि नृपं शिवधनुर्भंजायितुं न शशाक।
अयं पर्वतोऽस्य ग्रामस्योत्तरः।
रामस्य पूर्वं गोविंद आगच्छतु।
तं दिवसमारभ्य मम मनः पर्याकुलं जातम्।
पुत्रविवाहस्यानंतरं पिता ग्रामस्य बहिरावसथेऽध्युवास।
स शिष्येणोपनिषदं वेदयामास।
स्वामिना भृत्येन धेनुं पयो दोग्धते।
भिक्षुकं श्रेष्ठिनं धनं याचयति।

स नरः पादस्य खंजः अयं तु नयनस्य काणः ।
स जंबुद्वीपं नावि गतः शकटे च प्रत्यागतः ।
यज्ञदत्तः कुंडिनपुराय प्रेषितः स मासद्वये प्रत्यागमिष्यति ।
रथस्य एव बहु शोभसे तत्कृतमत्यादरस्य ।
हिरण्यकशिपुग्रीवस्य प्राणा आसन् ।
गोविंदो यूयं चैतदकुरुताम् ।
अहं ते वीराश्च शत्रून् पराजयन् ।
त्वमहं गोपालसूनवश्च तत्कृत्यं कुर्युः ।
अयं बटुस्ते ब्राह्मणा वा ग्रामं गच्छतु ।
यूयं वयं वा नदीं गामिष्यथ ।
अतस्त्वां दूरादेव नमः ।
इमां वार्तामहं वयस्य कथयामि ।
यदि स त्वया पाठं नाध्यापयति तर्हि मा तन्निवेदय ।
देवाः स्वभयकारणं ब्रह्माणमाचख्युः ।
तस्मै अहं दूतं प्रहितवान्, किंतु पाटलीपुत्राय न कोप्यद्यापि विसृष्टः ।
अयं नरश्चौराणामतीव बिभेति ।
ममागमनस्य प्रागेव स गतः ।
अलं तं बहु ताडयितुं सोऽस्यशक्तः ।
अस्य पुस्तकस्य रामाय प्रयोजनं नास्ति ।
ये यतयोऽरण्येऽधिवसंति तेभ्यो नृपानुग्रहस्य क उपयोगः ।
भक्तिं देवो रोचते ।
अहं देवदत्तस्य शता रूपका धारयामि ।
स मयि द्रुह्यति नाहं तस्मा अभिद्रुह्यामि ।
न किमपि त्वामधुना प्रत्याशृणोमि ।
राजस्योपरि चंडवर्मा शास्ति ।
अहं शत्रु हत्वा स प्रत्याजगाम ।
रामो रावणं हत्वा विभिषणो लंकाराज्ये स्थापितः ।
त्वया प्रातरेव गां पयो दोग्धव्यमिति तमादिशन् रामोऽत्रागतवान् ।
गौतमीं वर्जं सर्वे निष्क्रांताः ।
अश्मभिर्घातं स शत्रुभिर्हतः ।
रामाय द्वौ पुत्रावास्ताम् ।
प्रभवति निजाय कन्यकाजनाय महाराजः ।
वासुकिः पातालतलस्येष्टे ।

मामग्रे किं तिष्टसि ।
अस्य पर्वतस्य पूर्वं महावापी वर्तते ।
अस्मादुत्तरतस्तु रौद्रं श्मशानम् ।
दिवसे त्रिः संध्यामुपासीत ।
वर्षत्रये दशकृत्वोऽपि मम गृहे त्वं नागच्छः ।
उपवनाद्दक्षिणेनार्त्तरवं श्रुत्वा दुःखितान् शरणं प्रत्यशृणोत् ।
अधुना सुवृष्टिर्भवति चेत्सुभिक्षं सर्वत्राजनिष्ट ।
अपि नाम स राजास्मत्समीहितं संपादयिता ।
अहं ह्यः पथि महांतं भुजंगं ददर्श ।
अत्र विषये तव संदेहो माऽभूत् ।
मा चौरानभैष्ट ।
यदहं तत्र बभूव तदा त्वं भ्रातुः सार्धं मा कलहमकृथा इति तमब्रूयम्
स्वपुत्रं यथा अन्येषां पुत्रेभ्योऽपि प्रीतिः कर्तव्या ।
अशीतिदिवसा यावत्स भृत्यो मामसेविष्ट ।
यावद्धनमीश्वरेणास्मान् दीयते तस्मिन्संतोषो मान्यः ।
ते रथे कुसुमपुराय यातवंतः ।
सा मृतवतीत्याकर्ण्याहं दुःखितो जातवान् ।
शिशुना भाषितं स्मितं च पित्रोरानंदोत्पादकम् ।
अयं मम चिरंतनो वयस्यो भवितव्यः ।
त्वय्यस्माञ्शासति कथमस्माभिरभिभूतं भाव्यम् ।
कुमंत्रिणा नृपसभा न प्रवेष्टव्यम् ।
गोपालो नाम वयस्येन सहागच्छम् ।
जितोसौ मया षोडशसहस्राणां रूपकाणाम् ।
कांचीनाम नगर्यां धनमित्रनाम वणिगवसत् ।
सुवर्णपुरं नाम नगरे द्वौ कोलिकौ वयस्यभावेन आवसतः ।
चंदनमिव शीतले कदलीगृहेऽपि सा निर्वृत्तिं नालभत ।
रामेतिनामा दशरथस्य पुत्र आसीत् ।
उपला इव शत्रुष्वस्मानवस्कंदस्तु वय किं कुर्यामेति न जानिम ।
सुरगुरुमिव प्रज्ञस्यास्य ब्राह्मणस्य दक्षिणां किं न दत्से ।
तव च मे च सख्यमस्ति ।
चेत्त्वं मम कार्यं करोषि त्वामहं मुद्रिकाशतं दास्यामि ।
सा नारी रविरिव भ्राजमानं सुतमलब्धं तु इयं बहुकुरूपम् ।
अश्वमारोढुं मे रोचते ।

त्वामावस्थातुं कथमहमनुमंस्ये ।
अहं त्वामेतत्कर्तुमिच्छामि ।
इमं ग्रंथं वाचायितुं न शक्यते।
इममाम्रवृक्षमधः पातयितुं न सांप्रतम् ।
वरं देशमपि त्यक्तुं न तु नीचसेवां विधातुम् ।
दशरथाय त्रिभार्याभ्यः पुत्रचतुष्टयमुदपादि ।
विजयतु भवान् य एवं जनानानंदयः ।
एनां भवतेऽनुरक्तां किं निष्कारणेन त्यजसि ।
इमं दिवसमारभ्य मासाद्विजयादशमी भवति ।

A GLOSSARY.

Sanskrit-English.

अ.

अंशुमालिन् *m.* the sun.

अकलित *a.* incomprehensible, not known.

अकिंचनत्वं being penniless.

अक्षयत्वं indestructibility.

अगुणः a bad quality.

अगृध्नु *a.* not covetous.

अग्निसात्कृ 8 U. to consign to the flames, burn.

अग्रजन्मन् *m.* a Bráhma*n*a.

अग्रणीः a leader.

अग्र्य *a.* best.

अघं sin.

अंकः a speck, spot.

अंकुरः a sprout.

अंगं a component part.

अंगरागः a scented cosmetic.

अंगुलि *f.* a finger.

अंगुलीयकः-कं a ring.

अचिंतनीय *a.* incomprehensible, inconceivable.

अज *a.* not born.

अंजनं collyrium.

अतिक्रांत *p. p.* past.

अतिगर्हित *p. p.* very blameable.

अतिप्रसंगः excessive rudeness.

अतिभूमिः excess, climax.

अतिमात्रं *adv.* excessively.

अतिमुक्तलता the Mâdhavî or vernal creeper.

अतियंत्रणा over-constraint.

अतिलोल *a.* very frail.

अतिलोहित *a.* very red.

अतिह्रेपण *a.* most shameful.

अत्यादरः excessive respect.

अत्रांतरे *adv.* in the meanwhile.

अदूरवर्तिन् *a.* not distant.

अधिक्षिप्त *p. p.* reviled, traduced, abused.

अधिज्य *a.* well-strung.

अधिराजः a supreme or paramount lord.

अध्वरः a sacrifice.

अनंगः Cupid, bodiless one.

अनतिपात्य *a.* not to be delayed.

अननुदार *a.* having no suitable wife.

अनंतर *a.* contiguous, neighbouring.

अनपायिन् *a.* imperishable.

अनम्र *a.* unbending, haughty.

अनर्घत्वं being invaluable.

अनवगीत *p. p.* not censured.

अनातप *a.* cool, protected from heat.

अनातुर *a.* not stick or fatigued.

अनात्मज्ञ *a.* foolish, sily.

अनादि *a.* having no beginning.

अनायास *a.* easy.

अनामयं health.

अनिर्वृत *a.* distressed, sorry.

अनीश *a.* having no control or mastery

अनुगुणं *adv.* favourably, so as to please one.

अनुचर: a follower.

अनुज: a younger brother.

अनुत्तम *a.* unsurpassed.

अनुत्सेक: absence of pride.

अनुत्सेकिन् *a.* not puffed up.

अनुबंध: course, flow, continuity.

अनुपक्रम्य *a.* incurable.

अनुपधि *a.* guileless.

अनुमित *p. p.* inferred guessed.

अनुविद्ध *p. p.* intertwined, overspread.

अनुवृत्ति *f.* complying or obedient spirit; experience of the past.

अनृतं untruth.

अंतरात्मन् *m.* the inmost soul.

अंतराय: an obstacle, impediment.

अंतरिक्षं the sky.

अंतरित *p. p.* disappeared, departed.

अंतर्लीन *p. p.* latent, hidden.

अंतर्वेदि: the Doab or district between the Ganges and Yamunâ rivers.

अपकारिन् *a.* one who does ill.

अपचार: improper conduct.

अपदेश: a pretext, colour.

अपयशस् *n.* ignominy, ill-repute

अपरिसमाप्त *p. p.* unceasing, unending.

अपवाद: censure.

अपहस्तित *a.* abandoned, thrown away.

अपुनरुक्त *a.* not repeated, new and new every day.

अपूर्व *a.* new, the like of which did not exist.

अपोहनं reasoning power.

अप्रतिभट *a.* unrivalled, having no rival.

अप्रतिविधेय *a.* irremediable.

अप्रतिहत *p. p.* intact, unmarred, unimpaired.

अप्रत्यय *a.* diffident.

अप्रमेय *a.* innumerable, abundant.

अबला a woman.

अब्जभू: the God Brahmâ.

अभिख्या beauty, splendour.

अभिगमनं sexual intercourse.

अभिजनः noble descent.

अभिज्ञानं a token of recognition, souvenir.

अभिनव *a.* new, fresh, blooming.

अभिनिवेशः application, devotion, intentness.

अभिमत *p. p.* liked, dear, desired.

अभियुक्तः a learned man.

अभियोक्तृ *m.* an invader.

अभिरमणीय *a.* very charming.

अभिलाषः a desire, longing for.

अभिव्यक्त *p. p.* clear, very distinct.

अभिषेणय (denom.) to face or encounter with an army.

अभि (ति) संधानं cheating, deceiving.

अभ्यवहार्य food, eatable (lit.) that which is fit to be eaten.

अभ्यागत *p. p.* come as a guest.

अभ्युपेत *p. p.* undertaken.

अमंगलं an evil, an evil thought.

अमर्षित *a.* enraged, exasperated.

अमल *a.* pure, white.

अमानुष *a.* superhuman.

अमानुषी an irrational female.

अमोघ *a.* infallible, unfailing.

अंबुवाहः a cloud.

अयस् *n.* iron.

अरुणः charioteer of the sun.

अरुंधती wife of Vasistha.

अर्जनं acquisition.

अर्थ् *with* **सं** 10 A. to consider, imagine; *with* **प्र** to pursue.

अर्थ्य *a.* significant, not deviating from the sense.

अर्हत *a.* deserving, worthy.

अल्पमेधस् *a.* foolish, dull-witted.

अवकल्प्य *a.* fit to be thought of or conceived.

अवक्षयः destruction, decay, sinking, drooping.

अवकाशः ground, room, scope.

अवगाहनं crushing, treading.

अवपातः a pit for catching game.

अवद्य *a.* fit to be condemned.

अवधूत *p. p.* spurned, disdainfully slighted.

अवमानिन् *a.* slighting, disregarding.

अवयवः a member.

अवलोकिता name of a maid servant.

अवसन्न *p. p.* ended, terminated.

अवसानं close, termination.

अवस्थित *p. p.* settled, remained.

अविक्षत *p. p.* not hurt, safe and sound.

अविधवा a woman not widowed, having her husband living.

अविनीत *p. p.* rude.

अव्यापन्न *p. p.* alive, not dead.

अव्याहत *p. p.* unobstructed.

अशनिः thunderbolt.
अशनं food.
अशरण *a.* helpless.
अशुभं mishap, calamity.
अशेषतः *adv.* completely.
अश्वमुखः a horse-faced creature.
अश्वमेधः the horse-sacrifice.
अस् *with* उत् *pass.* to turn away from; *with* विपरि 4 P. to undergo a change.
असंविदान *a.* ignorant.
असक्त *a.* not over-attached.
असदृश *a.* incongruous, ill-suited, improper.
असार *a.* worthless, weak.
असारता transient state, frail or transitory nature.
असित *a.* black.
असिपत्रं the blade of a sword.
अस्ताचलः the setting (western) mountain.
अहंकारः egotism, pride.
अह्नाय *adv.* quickly, at once.

आ.

आकरः a mine.
आकारः appearance, form.
आकुल *a.* full of; affected by, overcome with.
आक्रंदितं wailing.
आखंडलः a name of Indra.
आखुः a mouse, rat.
आख्यात *p. p.* told, announced.
आगंतुकः a guest, a stranger; °ता the state of being a stranger.
आगमः appearance; bursting out.
आगमिन् *a.* versed in theory.
आतंकः agony, excessive torment.
आतपः heat, sultriness.
आतप्त *p. p.* heated, afflicted by heat.
आतिथ्यं hospitality, hospitable reception; °क्रिया rite of hospitality.
आतुर *a.* afflicted, troubled.
आत्मवत् *a.* wise, intelligent.
आदरः *a.* love, fondness.
आदितः in the very bud.
आत्मीकृ 8 U. to conquer, acquire,
आधातृ *m.* one who imparts.
आधिः *a.* bane, curse.
आधिपत्यं sway, rule.
आंतर *a.* inward, internal.
आनंदनं delight; pleasing to.
आपणः-णं a market, store house
आपतित *p. p.* come to pass, occurred, befallen.
आपन्न *p. p.* distressed.
आप्तः a credible or trustworthy person.
आप्यायना growing fat or stout.
आभोगः envirous, outskirts.

आमंजु *a.* lovely, charming.
आमिषं bait.
आयः gain, acquisition.
आयत *p. p.* long.
आयतनं an abode.
आयासयितृ *a.* giving trouble.
आयुष्मत् *a.* long-lived (one).
आयोध्यिकः an inhabitant of Ayodhyá.
आरंभः an action, undertaking.
आराधनं entertainment, propitiation.
आर्य *a.* polite, courteous, worthy.
आर्यपुत्रः a term used in speaking of the husband.
आर्यमिश्राः worthy or respectable persons.
आलर्क *a.* pertaining to a mad dog.
आली a female companion.
आलोकः sight.
आलोचित *p. p.* thought, considered.
आवरणं obscuring, blinding.
आवलित *p. p.* slightly turned.
आवसथः a dwelling, house, abode.
आविल *a.* turbid, muddy.
आविलय (denom.) to sully, to make turbid.
आवृत *p. p.* surrounded by.
आवेशः influence, subjection.
आशीविषः a serpent.
आशु *adv.* quickly.
आश्रमः a stage or state of life.
आस् *with* **अनु** 2 A. to wait upon, serve.
आसक्त *p. p.* fixed upon.
आसक्ति *f.* attachment.
आस्तरणं a bed.
आस्थानं an assembly; **मंडपः** an assembly-room, hall of audience.
आहवः a battle.
आहारः food.
आहितुंडिकः a juggler.

इ.

इ with **प्रति** *caus.* to convince; *with* **व्यप** to separate, part.
इक्ष्वाकुः one of the kings of the solar line, ancestor of Raghu.
इंद्रियं organ of sense; sense.
इंधनं fuel.
इरावती name of a woman.

ई.

ईक्ष् with **अनु** 1 A. to look after, inquire after.
ईक्षणं eye; sight.
ईप्सित *p. p.* liked, desired.
ईशः a lord, master ; S'iva.

ईश्वर *a.* able; -र: a lord.

ईह् 1 A. to wish, desire.

उ.

उचित *a.* usual, customary.

उच्छ्रित *p. p.* high, raised up.

उत्कर्ष: height; excellence.

उत्कुल *a.* dishonouring or disgracing the family.

उत्क्रुष्टं a loud cry.

उत्खात *p. p.* extermiated, eradicated.

उत्खातीन् *a.* full of hollows, having ups and downs.

उत्तंसय (denom.) to form into an ornamental braid.

उत्तर *a.* latter;-रा (*f.*) Abhimanyu's wife.

उत्तरोत्तर *a.* ever-increasing.

उत्तान *a.* open, unreserved, guileless.

उत्तानित *p. p.* stretched, opened.

उत्पलिनी a lotus-plant.

उत्पीड: a wreath, curl.

उत्सव: festivity, ceremonial rejoicing.

उदंत: account, history.

उदय: appearance, sight.

उद्दामं *adv.* without restraint, violently.

उद्यत *p. p.* engaged in, intent on.

उद्यम: resolve, determination.

उद्धत *a.* proud, high.

उद्बाष्प *a.* shedding tears.

उन्नतत्वं nobleness, sublimity.

उन्नति *f.* eminence, elevation, dignity.

उन्मुख *a.* ready.

उपकंठ: vicinity.

उपकार: doing good, conferring obligations.

उपकारिन् *m.* a benefactor.

उपकार्या a royal tent.

उपघात: destruction, injury.

उपचार: external show, outward form; mode of address.

उपदेश: instruction.

उपद्रव: harm, injury.

उपनत *p. p.* come, befallen.

उपनिपात: occurrence, befalling.

उपपन्न *a.* fit, proper.

उपमा comparison.

उपरत *p. p.* dead.

उपराग: eclipse.

उपरोध: disturbance; damage, injury.

उपलक्षणं characteristic sign.

उपलंभ: ascertaining.

उपवास: a fast.

उपहत *p. p.* doomed, stuck down.

उपस्थित *p. p.* that has drawn near or approached, befallen.

उपहास्यता derision, ridicule.
उपाधी: condition, circumstance.
उपाध्याय: a preceptor.
उपालंभ: a taunt.
उपांशु adv. in private.
उपाश्रय: resorting to, seeking protection of.
उषस् f morning, dawn.
उष्मन् m. warmth, heat.
उष्णिमन् m. heat.

ऊ.

ऊरीकृत p. p. undertaken.
ऊरु: the thigh.
ऊर्जस्वल a great, powerful.
ऊर्मि a billow, wave.
ऊह् with अप 1 P. to remove, destroy.

ऋ.

ऋजु a. not evil, unsinister.
ऋषिकल्प a. almost a sage.
ऋषिकुमार: a young sage.
ऋष्यशृंग: the son-in-law of Das'aratha.

ए.

एकपदे adv. suddenly, all of a sudden.
एकाग्र a. concentrated, fixed on one object.
एकांत a. excessive, ever-lasting, perpetual; with adj. very excessively.
एकैकश: adv. one by one.
एधित p. p. brought up, reared.
एनस् n. a sin.

ऐ.

ऐक्ष्वाक a. descended from Ikshváku.
ऐरावत: Indra's elephant.

ओ.

ओजस्विन् a. splendid, majestic.

औ.

औदरिक: a glutton.
औदासीन्यं indifference.

क.

ककुदं the hump; (fig.) chief or foremost.
कच: hair.
कज्जलं collyrium, soot.
कंठ् with उत् 1 A. to be eager or anxious for.
कतिपय a. some, a few.
कथमपि adv. with great difficulty.
कदली a plantain tree.
कनकं gold.
कंदर:-रं a cave, glen, defile.
कंदल: a mass, collection.
कमलयोनि: Brahmá.
कंप् with अनु to take pity on.

कर्ण् *with* **आ** 10. to hear.

कर्णधारः a helmsman, pilot.

कलकलः an uproar.

कलहंसः a duck or goose.

कलभः a cub, a young elephant.

कला a digit.

कलिका a bud.

कलेवरं the body.

कल्पः a form, mode.

कल्पांतः the end or dissolution of the world.

कल्य *a.* early, prime.

कल्याण *a.* noble, good, blessed. **ल्याणिन्** *a.* blessed.

कष्ट *a.* difficult.

काकपक्षः-क्षकः side-locks of hair.

कांचनं gold.

कामः a desire; Cupid.

कामगम *a.* going at will.

कामतः *adv.* out of lust or passion, sensuously.

कामसू *a.* fulfilling or yielding the desires.

कामिन् *m.* a lover, gallant.

कार्तांतिकः an astrologer, a fortune-teller.

काषायं a red garment.

किन्नरः one of a class of celestial choristers or musicians.

किंवदंति a report, rumor.

किरीटी (न्) Arjuna.

कुटिल *a.* crooked, wily.

कुट्टिमः pavement.

कुटुंबिन् *m.* a family man.

कुतूहलं curiosity.

कुधि *a.* foolish, dull witted.

कुमुदं a lotus.

कुमुदिनी a lotus-plant.

कुशलं welfare, well-being.

कुशलिन् *a.* doing well.

कुशाग्रबुद्धि *a.* of sharp intellect.

कुसरित् *f.* a brook, rivulet.

कृ 8 U. *with* **पुरः** to place in the front; **-अपा** to remove, prevent; **-उप** to do good to, benefit; **-वि** *pass.* to undergo a change, be affected by; **-विप्र** to tease, harm; (*p. p.*) wronged, ill-treated; troubled, harassed, injured.

कृतधी *a.* wise, thoughtful.

कृत्स्न *a.* whole, entire.

कृपण *a.* mean-hearted.

कृश *a.* lean, emaciated.

कृष् 1 P. *with* **वि** to bend, direct (as a bow).

कृषि *f.* husbandry, cultivation.

क्लृप् *with* **परि** (*causal*) fix upon, design; **-सं** (*causal*) intend, settle, aim at.

कृष्णवर्त्मन् *m.* fire.

केतनं an abode, residence.

केशिन् *m.* name of a demon.

केसरिन् *m.* a lion.

कोटरः-रं a hollow, cavity.

कोटि *f.* pitch; extremity, end, point; पराकोटी: highest pitch, climax.

कोशः-षः a bud.

कौतुकं curiosity.

कौपीनं a small piece of cloth worn over the privities.

कौबेरी the northern direction.

कौरव्यः a descendant of the Kurus.

कौलीनं evil report, scandal.

कौर्म *a.* belonging to a tortoise.

कौशिकः Vis'vámitra, son of कुशीकः ०की name of a woman.

क्रकचः a saw.

क्रम् *with* आ to fall upon, seize.

क्रिया work, composition.

क्रीडनीयं a toy.

क्लैब्यं weakness, timidity, unmanly behaviour; being neuter.

क्षणिक *a.* momentary, transitory.

क्षत्रं the Kshatriya or warrior class.

क्षपीत *p. p.* destroyed.

क्षपा night.

क्षम *a.* able, capable; fit, proper.

क्षयः waning.

क्षात्र *a.* belonging to or becoming the Kshatriya class.

क्षारांबुधिः the salt ocean.

क्षितिपः, क्षितीश्वरः } a king, lord of earth.

क्षिप् *with* आ 6 P. to dash against, to seduce, entice; -नि to bestow on, devote to.

क्षुद्र *a.* mean-hearted, base; worthless.

क्षेत्रं a field.

क्षोभः jolting, violent shaking.

ख.

खं the sky.

खंडः breaking, splitting; a fragment.

खल्वाटः a bald-headed person.

खिन्न *a.* fatigued, exhausted.

ग.

गणकः an astrologer.

गणिका a harlot.

गति *f.* recourse, help alternative.

गद्गदं *adv.* falteringly, convulsively.

गंधः odour, perfume.

गंधद्विपः an elephant of the best class (emitting a sweet smell).

गभस्तिः a ray.

गम् *with* प्रत्युद् to go to meet or receive.

गर्भेश्वरत्वं being born rich, getting wealth by inheritance.

गांभीर्यं depth.

गाह् 1 A. to enter, penetrate.

गिरीशः S'iva.

गुणः a good result or effect; credit, merit; use, efficacy.

गुरु a. foremost, chief;—(s.) father; (pl.) elders.

गृहमेधिन् m a householder.

गृहिणी a house-wife.

गोत्रं a family.

गोमायुः jackal.

गौरवं magnitude.

ग्रहः seizure.

ग्राम्य a. vulgar, churlish.

घ.

घट् with सं caus. to unite, join.

घर्मांशुः the hot-rayed sun.

घातकः an executioner.

च.

चक्रवर्तिन् m. a sovereign or paramount ruler.

चक्रवालं the horizon.

चक्ष् with प्रत्या 2 A. to repudiate, caste of.

चंचत् a. shaking about, waving.

चंचूः the beak.

चंद्रकांतः the moon-stone.

चपल a. inconsiderate, thoughtless; fickle, unsteady.

चमू f. an army.

चयः a lump, heap.

चर् 1 P. with वि to roam, wander.

चरः a spy.

चल: a. fickle, unsteady; °चित्तता fickleness of mind.

चलितं a kind of dance.

चातकः the Chátaka bird.

चापलं inconsiderate conduct.

चामरं a chowrie

चारित्र्यं chastity, purity of conduct.

चारुता loveliness, beauty.

चि with प्र pass. to thrive, to grow more ond more;—परि to acquire

चिकीर्षा desire of doing.

चित्र a. strange, wonderful.

चित्रार्पित a. painted or drawn in a picture.

चूडा crest, crown of the head; top; tuft of hair.

चूडामणि a crest jewel.

चूतः a mango tree.

चेष्टा an action.

चेष्टितं course of conduct.

च्युतात्मन् a. of a depraved or corrupt soul, evil-minded.

छ.

छद्मन् n. disguise; pretence.

ज.

जड a. grown dull.

जनता the populace, people.

जंतुः a creature, being.

जन्मभूमि *f.* native land, mother-country.

जयंतः son of Indra.

जलचरः an acquatic animal.

जलदः } a cloud.
जलमुच् }

जलयंत्र a water-engine, artificial water reservoir.

जलाशयः a pool of water.

जातं a child; a collection, brood (of young ones).

जाति *f.* caste.

जाल्मः a rogue, villain.

जीव् *with* अनु. 1 P. to servive, outlive.

जीवनं life.

जीवलोकः the world of the living, the universe.

जृंभ् *with* समुत् 1 A. to endeavour, strive; -वि to appear, to pervade.

ज्या the bow-string.

ज्ञातिः a kinsman; (pl.) kinsfolk.

ज्ञापय (*cause.* of ज्ञा) *with* वि, to say respectfully, beg to say, request;-आ to command, order.

ज्योतिशास्त्रं astronomy.

ज्योतिष्मत् a luminous, brilliant.

ट.

टिट्टिभी a female bird of that naem.

ढ.

ढौक् 1 A. to approach, draw near.

त.

तटिनी a river.

तनु *a.* lean, thin.

तपनः the sun.

तप्त *p. p.* afflicted by heat.

तदात्विन *a.* contemporaneous with that time, living at that time.

तमसा name of a river.

तमिस्रा darkness.

तरंगः *a.* wave.

तरलता fickleness; agitation, perturbation of the senses.

तातः father; a term of endearment (my dear).

तापसः an ascetic.

तालः a palm tree.

तितिक्ष 1 A. (*desid.* of तिज) to forgive.

तिमिरः-रं darkness.

तीक्ष्ण *a.* severe, oven-rigid.

तीर्थं a sacred or holy place; a worthy or fit object, a worthy recipient.

तीर्थोदकं holy water.

तुषार *a.* cool, cold.

तुषारः a thin shower.

तूर्यः-र्यं a musical instrument, trumpet.

तूल: cotton.

तूष्णीं *adv.* silent.

तॄ 1 P. *with* अव to end the course, discharge the contents; -प्र *caus.* to deceive; -वि to grant, impart.

तेजस्विन् *a.* possessed of heroic or martial splendour; -(*s.*) a warrior.

त्वच् *f.* a hide, skin.

त्रयं a collection of three.

त्रिपुरहर: the destroyer of the three cities.

त्रिमूर्ति *a.* having, or existing in, three forms.

द.

दक्ष *a.* clever, wise.

दक्षिण *a.* civil, courtesy.

दंड: stalk (of lotuses).

दम् *with* प्र *caus.* to curb, subdue.

दमनं control, restraint.

दम्य: a young bullock that has yet to be tamed.

दयित *a.* or *s.* dear, beloved; lord.

दरी a dale, valley.

दर्प: pride, haughtiness.

दर्पण: a mirror.

दर्भ: a blade of Kus'a grass.

दलं a portion, bit; small shoot; leaf.

दवाग्नि: conflagration.

दशनं a tooth, tusk.

दार *s.* wife.

दारुण *a.* painful.

दिवसेश्वर: the lord of day, sun.

दिव्य *a.* celestial, heavenly.

दीक्षित *p. p.* ordained, made ready by initiation.

दीन *a.* pitiable, wretched, sad.

दीप् 4. A. to blaze, shine.

दीपक: a light, lamp.

दीप्तिमत् *a.* possessed of majestic lustre.

दु:स्मर *a.* painful to remember.

दुराराध्य *a.* difficult to be propitiated.

दुरितं sin.

दुर्ग *a.* impassable, impervious; (*s.*) a difficulty.

दुर्जनत्वं wickedness, villainy.

दुर्जय *a.* invincible.

दुर्धर्ष *a.* dreadful, inviolable.

दुर्निवार *a.* irresistible.

दुर्भिक्षं famine, scarcity of corn &c.

दुर्लंघ्य *a.* difficult to be transgressed.

दुर्ललित *a.* wayward, unmanageable.

दुश्चर *a.* austere, hard to practise.

दुष्कर *a.* difficult to be done.

दुष्कृत् *m.* an evil doer, a wicked person.

दुष्कृतं a misdeed.

दुष्टाशय } a. wicked-minded.
दुरात्मन् }

दूरीकृ 8 U. to distance, surpass.

दूषणं a fault, defect, weakness.

देवरात: a proper name, father of Mádhava.

देवी queen.

देहभृत् m. } a person, an embodied being.
देहिन् m. }

दैवदुर्विपाक: ill-luck, adverse turn of fate.

द्युति f. splendour, magnificence.

द्रढय् (denom.) to strengthen.

द्रव्यं a material object.

द्रु 1 P. to ooze; to fly.

द्रुम: a tree.

द्विगुणित a. doubled, doubly increased.

द्विज: a bird; a Bráhmana.

द्विजाति: a Bràhmana.

द्विप: an elephant.

द्विरद: an elephant.

द्विरेफ: a bee.

द्वीप: a division of the world.

ध.

धनंजय: a name of Arjuna.

धनेश: the lord of wealth, Kubera.

धन्य a. blessed, happy.

धन्विन्: m. an archer, a bowman.

धर्म: duty, religious merit; propriety of conduct, decorum.

धर्मक्रिया a religious rite.

धर्मपत्नि } a lawful wife
धर्मदारा: }

धर्मारण्यं a penance-grove.

धर्मासनं a tribunal, a seat of justice.

धा 3 U. with अतिसं to deceive; -अंतर् to hide oneself from; -अभि to say, speak; -सं to treat with, make alliance with; to fit (as an arrow).

धातृ m. the creator.

धामन् n. splendour, radiance.

धारणा steady abstraction of mind.

धारावाहिन् a. continuous, incessant.

धारिणी name of a queen.

धीर a. strong-minded, courageous, persevering.

धीरता strength of mind, fortitude.

धुर्य: a leader, chief.

धुक्ष् with सं 1 A. to kindle.

धू with उत् 9 U. to wave, leave fluttering.

धूर्त: a rogue.

धृ 1. 10 P. to support, hold up; with उद् or समुद् to deliver, save, to root up, pull up the roots, extirpate; lift up, extract, take out.

ध्याम *a.* dirty, unclean.

ध्वनत् *a.* roaring, thundering.

न.

नकुल: a ichneumon, a mungoose.

नक्षत्रं an asterism, a lunar mansion.

नग: a mountain.

नंद् 1 P. to be delighted or pleased, rejoice; -अभि to greet, receive, congratulate.

नंदनं the paradise of Indra.

नलिनिका name of a maid-servant.

नलिनी a lotus-plant.

नवीकृ 8 U. to revive, renew.

नह् with सं 4 A. to be ready.

नाट्यं a dance, dramatic representation.

नामग्रहणं calling to mind the name, remembrance of name.

निःश्रेयसं final beattitude, supreme happiness.

निःसत्यता falsehood, telling untruths.

निःस्नेह *a.* cruel, heartless.

निकाम *a.* copious, abundant.

निकष: (-ग्रावन्) a touch-stone, test; mixing powder.

निखिल *a.* whole, entire, complete.

निगाद्य *a.* to be told or mentioned.

निग्रह: chastisement, punishment.

निचुल: a tree of that name.

निज *a.* one's own.

नितरां *adv.* excessively.

नितांत *a.* excessive.

निदाघ: the hot season, summer.

निदानं the first or original cause.

निधनं death.

निबंधनं tie, connecting link.

निमित्तं good omen; a cause; an omen.

निमिष: twinkling of the eye.

नियम: a religious rite.

नियमेन *adv.* invariably; as a rule.

नियोग: order, command, duty.

निरतिशय *a.* unsurpassed.

निरत *p. p.* intent on.

निरपेक्ष *a.*, निरभिलाष *a.* } regardless, indifferent.

निरस्त *p. p.* dispelled.

निराकरणं repudiation, casting off.

निर्गम: an outlet.

निर्गुण *a.* worthless.

निर्झर: spring, waterfall, cascade.

निर्बंध: importunity; pressing.

निर्वाणं complete satisfaction or pleasure, allaying of heat.

निर्वात: still or calm air.

निर्वाद: scandal, evil report.

निर्वापणं alleviation.

निर्वृत्ति *f.* satisfaction, pleasure.

निर्वृत्त *p. p.* become.

निशाचर: a demon, evil spirit.

निषेवित *p. p.* inhabited by, resorted to.

निष्कंप *a.* steady, motionless.
निष्पीडित *p. p.* squeezed or pressed together.
निष्प्रतीकार *a.* irremediable.
निसर्गः nature.
निसृष्ट *p. p.* given, bestowed.
निस्वनः a sound, flourish.
निस्त्रिंश *a.* cruel, ruthless.
निस्पंद *a.* motionless.
नी 1 P. *with* **अनु** to cherish, love; **उप** to invest with the sacred thread; **-समा** to bring together, join.
नीरंध्र *a.* dense, thick.
नील *a.* blue.
नुद् *with* **वि** *caus.* to divert, entertain, amuse.
नूपुरं an anklet.
नैमित्तिकं an effect.
नैषधः a name of Nala; King of the Nishadha.
नैष्ठुर्यं cruelty, harshness of temper.
नैसर्गिक *a.* natural, innate, inborn.

प.

पक्कण (**पक्कणं**) the hut of a Chándála.
पक्षः a side.
पंकच्छिद् *a.* removing impurity or dirt.
पंचालः king of the Panchálas.
पंजरः a cage.
पटु *a.* sharp.
पठ् *with* **परि** *caus.* to teach.
पत् 1 P. *with* **पार** to hover about, wheel round; **-परा** to return; arrive; **-प्रणि** to salute, bow down.
पतंगः a moth; the sun.
पतिंवरा (*f.*) about to choose a husband.
पत्रपुटं a vessel of leaves folded.
पत्रलेखा a proper name.
पत्रोर्णं a garment of wove silk.
पथ्यं well-being, welfare; wholesome diet.
पद् *with* **व्या** *caus.* to kill; **-प्रति** to acknowledge; show, yield; obtain, get; admit, confess; **-उप** *caus.* to bring about, to do.
पदवी path, line of footsteps.
पन्नगः a snake.
पयस्विनी a cow
पयोदः a cloud.
परभृतः a cuckoo.
परमप्रख्य *a.* of great renown, very fumous.
परमार्थः the highest truth.
परमार्थतः *adv.* really.
परंतप *a.* paining or harassing the enemies.
परंपरा a series.
पराक्रमः valour, prowess.
परागत *p. p.* returned.

परावृत्त *p. p.* turned back, returned.

परिगृहीत *p. p.* patronized, favoured.

परिग्रहः espousal.

परितर्पण *a.* gratifying

परिदेवना lamentation.

परिपंथिन् *a.* coming in the way.

परिभवः degradation, humiliation.

परिभाविन् *a.* humbling, degrading.

परिवारः } परिजनः } retinue, train of attendants, suite.

परि (री) वाहः a water-course or drain, an outlet.

परिव्राजिका a female recluse,

परिषद् *f.* audience.

परीक्षित् *m.* name of a king.

परीत *p. p.* overcome with.

परोक्षे *adv.* in one's absence.

पर्यटनं roaming, travelling.

पर्याप्त *a.* able, competent.

पर्यायः regular-rotation or turn, due order.

पल्लवः a sprout, twig.

पल्लविका name of a maid-servant.

पल्लवित *a.* having put forth sprouts.

पवनः wind.

पांसुल *a.* disgracing; कुल° a disgrace to the family.

पांडु *a.* pale, whitish.

पाणिग्रहः marriage.

पातालः-लं the lower or nether regions.

पात्रं an object.

पानीयं water.

पापभाज् *a.* sinful.

पारक्य *a.* hostile.

पारग्रामिक *a.* hostile, inimical.

पारसीकाः the Persians.

पार्श्वः side.

पावकः fire.

पावन *a.* purifying, holy

पिंगल *a.* yellowish reddish-brown, tawny.

पिटः a basket.

पिठरं a pot, pan.

पिपासु *a.* (*desid.* of पा) thirsty.

पिशुन *a.* slanderous.

पिशुनता back-biting, slandering.

पीठं a seat, throne.

पीडित *p. p.* espoused, taken hold of (as a hand).

पीवर *a.* fat, plump.

पुंगवः a bull ; (at the end of compounds) the best or most eminent.

पुण्य *a.* holy, sacred.

पुण्यभाज् *a.* meritorious, blessed.

पुरंदरः a name of Indra.

पुरस्कृत *p. p.* led, headed.

पुराण *a.* old.

पुष् 4 P. to exhibit.

पुष्पित *a.* blossomed, flowered.

पुष्पेषुः Cupid; lust.

पूरोत्पीडः excess or superabundance of water.

पूर्ववत् *adv.* as before.

पृथग्जनः a low or vulgar man, an illiterate person.

पृष्ठं surface; back.

पेशल *a.* clever, skilful.

पोतः a ship; a young one, as in वीरपोतः a youthful warrior.

पौरव *a.* descended from पूरु.

पौरुषं manliness, prowess.

पौरुहूत *a.* belonging to Indra.

प्रकीर्ति *f.* mention of name.

प्रकीर्तित *p. p.* styled, called.

प्रकृति *f.* body of ministers.

प्रकोपः provocation.

प्रकोष्ठः a court in a house.

प्रक्रांतं a valorous deed.

प्रक्षीण *p. p.* annihilated.

प्रगल्भ *a.* bold.

प्रजागरः sleeplessness, being awake at night.

प्रजापतिः the Creator.

प्रणयः love; request, supplication.

प्रणयिता love.

प्रणयिनी a dear friend.

प्रणिधिः an emissary.

प्रतनु *a.* very small.

प्रतापः prowess, valour; heat.

प्रतिनिविष्ट *a.* obstinate.

प्रतिपादित *p. p.* given to; wedded.

प्रतिबंधवत् *a.* attended with difficulties or obstacles.

प्रतिबुद्ध *p. p.* awakened.

प्रतिबोधवत् *a.* endowed with reason, rational.

प्रतिम *a.* like.

प्रतिवाच् *f.* a reply, answer.

प्रतिष्ठा security of position; stability.

प्रतिसक्त *p. p.* fixed on, attached to.

प्रतीकारः } a remedy.
प्रतिक्रिया }

प्रतीत *p. p.* confiding or believing in.

प्रतीप *a.* adverse, contrary.

प्रत्यग्र *a.* fresh, newly-made.

प्रत्यर्थिन् *a.* hostile, opposed to, coming in the way of.

प्रत्यादेशः an obscurer, rival, (lit.) throwing into the back-ground or eclipsing; repudiation.

प्रथित *p. p.* celebrated, well-known.

प्रत्यक् *adv.* to the west.

प्रत्युत्पन्नमति *a.* ready-witted.

प्रदानं giving away in marriage.

प्रदोषः the evening.

प्रद्रुत *p. p.* run away.

प्रबंधः composition work.

प्रभवः source.

प्रभावः power.

प्रभुत्वं power, authority.

प्रमदवनं a pleasure-garden.

प्रमाणं standard, limit, an authority.

प्रमाणीकृ 8 U. to regard as an authority.

प्रमाथिन् *a.* tormenting.

प्रयत *p. p.* pure, purified by austerities.

प्रयाणं marching onwards.

प्रयुक्त *p. p.* contrived; set on; employed, used.

प्रयोग: practice.

प्रलाप: lamentation.

प्रवणीकृत *p. p.* drawn, inclined.

प्रवयस *a.* aged, old.

प्रवातं current of air; windy or stormy weather; °शयनं a bed exposed to the full current of air.

प्रवृत्ति *f.* commencement.

प्रव्रज्या turning out a recluse.

प्रशमित *p. p.* rectified, expiated.

प्रश्चोतनं sprinkling.

प्रसन्न *p. p.* pleased.

प्रसंगत:-गेन *adv.* incidentally, by way of.

प्रसह्य *adv.* perforce.

प्रस्ताव: mention, allusion.

प्रस्तुतं object in veiw.

प्रसूति *f.* progeny, issue.

प्रसूनं a flower.

प्रस्थ: a kind of measure.

प्रहरणं a missile, weapon.

प्रहसनं ridicule, mocking.

प्राक् *adv.* to the east of.

प्राकार: a rampart.

प्राग्रसर *a.* foremost, first.

प्राङ्मुख *a.* with one's face turned to the east, in the eastern direction.

प्राणायाम: suspending the breath.

प्रातराश: the morning meal, breakfast.

प्रांत: the end, margin.

प्राप्तप्रसव *a.* delivered of a child.

प्रार्थना desire, love-suit.

प्रावृष् *f.* the rainy season.

प्राश्निक: a judge, umpire.

प्रिय *a.* dear, beloved.

प्रेषित *p. p.* sent; dismissed.

प्रोद्दीप्त *p. p.* set on fire, blazing.

प्लव (वं) ग: a monkey.

फ.

फण:-णा a hood.

फलं result

फलेग्रहि *a.* fruitful, bearing fruit in season.

ब.

बक: a crane.

बटु: a youth, chap, fellow.

बंदी a captive, prisoner.

बंधुल: a bastard, an attendant in the chamber of a horlot.

बलं army, forces.

बलि: worship.

बलिवर्द: an ox, a bull.

बांधव: a relation, kinsman.

बालिश *a.* or *s.* a foolish person.

बिंब an image.

बीभत्समान *pres. p.* shrinking from, being disgusted with.

बुद्धिजीवन् *a.* employing the reason, rational.

ब्रह्मर्षि: a Bráhmanical sage.

भ.

भग्नोद्यम *a.* foiled in attempts, defeated.

भज् 1 U. to entertain, cherish; practise.

भक्तिमत् *a.* devoted, loyally attached.

भद्र: a title of address, good sir; -द्रा gentle lady; (*a.*) auspicious.

भरणं support, maintenance.

भरतर्षभ: the best or most eminent of the Bharatas.

भर्तृदारिका a princess (daughter of the lord).

भव: birth; S'iva.

भवनं a house, dwelling.

भवितव्यता being destined to happen, destiny, fate.

भागधेयं lot, fortune.

भाग्यं prosperity, good days.

भाजनं a receptacle, reservoir.

भाष् *with* अप 1 A. to abuse, revile.

भाव: feeling or expression of love; incident, occurrence; a learned man, Honourable Sir.

भासुर *a.* shining, resplendent.

भास्वत् *a.* shining; (*s.*) the sun.

भिक्षाशित्वं living by begging.

भीम a. dreadful, terrible.

भुजंग: snake.

भुवनं world.

भू with वि *caus.* to think of, contemplate; to establish, decide; perceive, be conscious of; -सं to be born.

भूतं a created being.

भूतधारिणी earth, supporter of beings.

भूमिका a part, character (in a drama).

भूमिदेव: a Bráhma*n*a.

भूय: *adv.* again.

भूयिष्ठं *adv.* for the most part.

भूरिवसु: a proper name, father of Málatî.

भैक्ष्यं begging.

भोग: enjoyment.

भ्रंश: loss.

भ्रांतिमत् *a.* turning, revolving.

म.

मंगलं auspiciousness; an auspicious; rite, (in compounds)

auspicious; as, मंगलतूर्य: auspicious trumpet; मंगलस्नानं auspicious ablution.

मंजु *a.* sweet.

मंजुल: a kind of creeper.

मंडनं ornament, decoration; embellishment.

मद् with उद् *caus.* to infatuate.

मद: passion, ardent desire; rutting juice.

मदच्युत् *a.* being in rut.

मधु *n.* liquor.

मधुर *a.* lovely, sweet.

मधुमास: the spring-time.

मधुसूदन: Krishna (slayer of Madhu.)

मध्यस्थ *a.* acting as umpire.

मनस्विन् *a.* intelligent, strong-minded; -नी a wise woman.

मनीषिन् *m.* wise man, sage.

मनोभू:
मनसिज: } the mind-born, Cupid.

मंत्र् *with* आ 10 A. to take leave of, bid adieu.

मंत्रकृत् *a.* composing hymns.

मंत्रवत् *a.* attended with incantations or spells.

मन्थर *a.* slow.

मंद *a.* dull, dull-headed.

मंदभाग्य *a.* unlucky, ill-starred.

मंदायमान *a.* lagging behind, tarrying.

मंदीकृत *p. p.* slackened.

मंदौत्सुक्य *a.* depressed in spirits, cast down.

मन्मथ: Cupid.

मन्यु: grief, sorrow.

मरिच: pepper, pepper-shrub.

मरीचि: ray.

मर्त्य: a mortal, human being.

मलयजं sandal juice.

महाजन: the mob, populace.

महाभाग: a fortunate person.

महातेजस् *a.* of great splendour or heroism.

महार्ह *a.* costly.

महीपाल: a king.

महेंद्र: the great Indra.

महेश्वर: a great lord.

महोक्ष: a full-grown bull.

महौषधि *f.* a medicinal drug.

मागधी daughter of the king of the Magadhas, Sudakshiná.

मात: a term of endearment.

मान: pride.

मानिनी a proud woman.

मानुष्यकं human nature.

मारुत: wind.

मालाकार a gardener, florist.

माल्यं a wreath, garland.

मिश्र *a.* an honorific affix, meaning worthy, respectable.

मुक्ताफलं a pearl.

मुग्ध *a.* artless, innocent.

मुद् with अनु 1 A. to second, approve.

मुद्रा seal.

मुरारि: Vishnu.

मुर्छ् 1. P. to take effect on, prevail against; to grow stronger or more intense, gather strength, thicken.

मुसलं a pestle.

मुहुः *adv.* often.

मूर्तिमत् *a.* incarnate, embodied

मूर्धजः hair.

मृगतृष्णिका mirage.

मृणालं a lotus fibre.

मृणालिनी a lotus.

मृद् *f.* clay.

मृदु *a.* soft-minded, weak.

मृष् 10 P. to endure, suffer.

मृशा *adv.* wrongly, in vain.

मृषोद्यं a falsehood.

मेखला a girdle, belt.

मेघनादः a proper name.

मेधा talent, retentive faculty

मेध्य a sacred, holy.

मैथिलेयः son of Maithilî, Kus'a.

मोक्षः release.

मौल *a.* or *s.* one brought up in one's service for generations, an old or hereditary servant (minister &c.)

म्लेच्छः a man of an outcast race; a barbarian.

य.

यजनं a sacrifice.

यत्किंचनकारिता doing worthless things.

यथार्थ *a.* significant, true to its sense.

यथावत् *adv.* according to the proper method, properly, duly.

यदृच्छया *adv.* accidentally, by chance.

यम् *with* नि 1 P. to dissuade; (*caus.*) to regulate, control.

यम *a.* twin.

यष्टि *f.* a necklace, garland.

यस् with आ *caus.* to trouble, torment.

या *with* 2 P. to march on, set out.

याच्ञा mean solicitation.

यातुधानः an evil spirit, a Rákshasa.

यादृच्छिक *a.* accidental.

यावदर्थं *adv.* in all senses.

युज् 7 U. to design, intend, destine; -नि *caus.* to yoke, harness; to unite; -प्र (A.) to act, represent (dramatically). -संप्र *pass.* to be engaged in, apply oneself to, a business.

युध् *f.* fight.

युवराजः an heir-apparent to a throne.

योगः the science or power of concentrating the mind; deep contemplation.

योजनं a distance of 8 miles.

योनिः source, origin.

र.

रंहस् *n.* speed, velocity.

रजनिचरः an evil spirit.

रणरणकं anxiety.

रंज् *with* अप *pass.* to grow discontented with.

रणधुरा the front or van of battle; -रां वह् to lead the van.

रणशिक्षा the art or science of war.

रत्नाकरः the ocean.

रंध्रं a cavity.

रभ् *with* परि 1 A. to clasp, embrace.

रयः current, force.

रश्मिः the rein.

रस् 1. P. to roar.

रसः sentiment.

रसवत्तर *a.* more savoury or tasteful.

रसातलं the nether regions.

रसायनं an elixir.

रसालः the mango tree.

रसिक *a.* graceful, elegant; appreciating.

रहस्यं a secret; the secret (of conduct); °भेदः disclosing or revealing one's secrets.

राक्षसः name of the minister of the Nandas.

रागः passion.

राजन्वत् *a.* governed by a good or just king.

राजर्षिः a royal sage.

राजतंत्रं the science or theory of government.

रात्रिचरी a Rákshasa female.

राध् *with* आ *caus.* to please, humour.

रामगिरिः name of a mountain.

रुजा-ज् *f.* pain, agony.

रुधिरं blood.

रोगिन् *a.* sickly, affected by sickness.

रोषण *a.* passionate, wrathful.

रोषणता angry or passionate temper.

रौरव *a.* made of the hide of the deer called *ruru.*

ल.

लक्ष्मन् *n.* a speck, spot.

लक्ष्मीः beauty, lustre.

लघय (*denom.*) to alleviate lesson.

लप् *with* प्र 1. P. to prate, rave.

लभ् *with* उपा 1. A. to taunt, blame.

ललामं or °मन् *n.* an ornament.

लवंगिका the foster sister of Málatî.

लवणांभस् *m.* the ocean (having salt water).

लाघवं mortification, humiliation.

लांछनं characteristic mark; श्रीकंठपद° distinguished by the name श्रीकंठ.

लिख् with वि 6 P. to implant.

लिखित n. a writing, document.

लुभ् *with* प्र *caus.* to entice, seduce; *with* वि *caus.* to seduce or entice the mind of.

लोध्रः-ध्रं the tree of that name or its flower.

लोल a. eager; eagerly lolling down.

व.

वंश्यः a descendant.

वध्यस्थानं place of execution.

वत्सः a calf.

वत्सतरी a heifer.

वनज्योत्स्ना the Mâdhavî creeper.

वनदेवता a sylvan deity, wood-nymph.

वनस्पतिः a tree.

वन्य *a.* wild.

वप् *with* निर् 1 P. to offer, present.

वप्तृ *m.* a sower.

वम् *with* उत् 1 P. to pour or vomit out, emit.

वयस् *n.* a crow, bird in general.

वर *a.* best, foremost; (रः) a bridge-groom.

वराक *a.* poor, pitiable.

वरीयस् *a.* better, superior.

वर्णः a caste

वर्ग्यः one belonging to a group; (pl.) a group of actors.

वर्णिन् *m.* a bachelor (learned).

वल्कलं a bark garment.

वल्गितं a leap, bound.

वल्मीकः-कं an anthill.

वल्लभ *a.* favourite, beloved; (भा) wife.

वशः subjection.

वशिन् *a.* (a sage) who has subdued his passions.

वश्या a docile and obedient wife.

वस् *with* अध्या 1 P. to inhabit; to enter into.

वसति *f.* residence.

वसंतोत्सवः the vernal festival.

वह् *caus.* to traverse, go over; -निर् *caus.* to perform, manage.

वाच्यं blame, censure.

वाजिन् *m.* a horse.

वादः a report, talk.

वाम *a.* of an opposite character.

वायसः a crow.

वारणः an elephant.

वारयोषित् *f.* a harlot.

वाराणसी Benares.

वारिधरः a cloud

वारियंत्रं a water-wheel, (a fly-wheel for raising water).

वार्तं welfare, well-being.

वार्धकं old age.

विश्रब्धं *adv.* confidently, freely.
विश्रंभः confidence; °स्थानं a confident.
विश्रामः rest, repose.
विश्वंभरा the earth.
विश्वसनीयता power to inspire confidence.
विषण्ण *p. p.* dejected, sorry.
विषम *a.* adverse, difficult.
विषयः scope, province, dominion; object of sense, sensual pleasure.
विषाणः-णं a horn.
विषादः dismay, dejection, sorrow.
विष्टरः a seat.
विसरः a heap, a large quantity.
विसृष्ट *p. p.* dismissed, sent away.
विस्तीर्ण *p. p.* extended over, wide
विस्फारित *p. p.* expanded, dilated.
विहितं a decree, command.
विह्वल *a.* agitated, afflicted, overcome with grief; °ता affliction.
वीज् 10 P. to fan.
वीरसूः mother of a warrior.
वृ 10 P. to ask, beg of.
वृकोदरः Bhíma.
वृज् 10. P. to except; -आ to bend down; -वि (*p. p.*) devoid or destitute of.
वृत् *with* निर् *caus.* to finish ;-परि to revolve; -प्र to spring, arise; to begin, commence; -व्यप to turn back.
वृत्ति *f.* livelihood; behaviour, conduct.
वृध् *caus.* to aggrandize.
वृद्धि *f.* waxing.
वृषलः a S'údra; epithet of Chandragupta.
वृषांकः the bull-bannered God, S'iva.
वृष्टिः *f.* a shower of rain, rain-fall
वेगः speed, force.
वेगानिलः a strong or violent gust.
वेणुलता a bamboo-stick.
वेतसः a reed, cane.
वेदि-दी *f.* an alter.
वेधस् *m.* the creator.
वेशवनिता a harlot.
वेश्मन् *n.* a house, dwelling.
वेष्टनं a turban, a tiara.
वैकृतं an ill-omen.
वैतान *a.* sacrificial, sacred.
वैतानिक *a.* sacred, holy, consecrated in a sacrifice.
वैतालिकः a bard.
वैदेहि Sítá.
वैद्युतानलः the fire of lightning.
वैरिन् *m.* an enemy.
वैहायस *a.* situated in the air, aerial.
व्रतं course of conduct.
व्रीडित *a.* abashed, overcome with shame.
व्यक्ति *f.* manifestation.
व्यक्तं *adv.* evidently.
व्यग्रत्वं being engrossed in.

वासगृहं the inner part of a house; bed-chamber.

विकासित *p. p.* expanded, dilated; spread out.

विकारः malady, illness.

विकारहेतुः a temptation, seduction.

विक्रमः prowess, heroism.

विक्लव *a.* frightened, startled; grieved.

विगुण *a.* bad, worthless

विग्रहः hostility, enmity, strife; a body, form.

विघातः impediment, obstacle.

विचक्षण *a.* learned, proficient, skilful.

विजया (and **जया**) a kind of mantra, which averted the pain of thirst and hunger and gave miraculous powers.

विजिह्म *a.* crooked, turned away.

विज्ञापना a request.

विटपः a branch.

विडंब् 10 P. to imitate.

वितथ *a.* false, untrue.

वितीर्ण *p. p.* descended; given.

विदग्धता skill.

विदेशः a foreign country.

विद्युत्वत् *m.* a cloud.

विद्विष् *m.* an enemy.

विधातृ *m.* the Creator.

विधृत *p. p.* preserved.

विधेयाः a servant.

विधेयज्ञ *a.* who knows his duty, obedient.

विनशनः a country to the north-west of Delhi.

विनिमयः exchange.

विपक्षः an enemy.

विपश्चित् *a.* wise, learned; (a wise man).

विपिनं a forest.

विप्रलब्ध *p. p.* deceived.

विप्लवः adverseness.

विभवः property, wealth.

विभावरी night.

विभुः a lord.

विभ्रमः confusion, loss.

विमनस् *a.* disconsolate, dejected.

विमानित *p. p.* dishonoured.

विमार्गः a wrong road.

वियुक्त *p. p.* separated, love-lorn.

विरत *p. p.* stopped, at an end.

विरागः discontent, dissatisfaction.

विरामः cessation, stop.

विरोधः antagonism; **शाश्वत°** natural antipathy.

विलासः amorous pastime.

विवृत *p. p.* opened.

विवेकः discrimination, judgment.

विश् *with* **अभिनि** 6 A. to enter into; *with* **सं** to sleep.

विशुद्धि *f.* purity.

विशेषः difference; distinguishing feature.

व्यजनं a fan.

व्यतिकर: an incident, occurrence.

व्यपदेश: family; name; race.

व्यय: spending, expenditure; obstacle; loss.

व्यलीकं sorrow, anguish.

व्यवहार: hearing of a case; judicial procedure.

व्यवहारासनं tribunal of justice.

व्यवहित *p. p.* separated.

व्यसनं adversity, need, difficulty; intent or close application.

व्याकुल *a.* deeply or intently engaged in.

व्याल: a serpent, cruel or wicked animal.

व्याध: a hunter, fowler.

व्याहार: } words, speech.
व्याहृति }

श.

शकलं a bit.

शक्ति *f.* a miraculous weapon or missile hurled at a foe.

शक्र: a name of Indra.

शची wife of Indra.

शंकु: a dart, shaft.

शप् 1 U. to abuse, revile.

शबर: one of a wild mountaineer tribe.

शब्द: a title.

शम् *with* नि 4 P. to hear, find; (*caus.*) to subdue, vanquish; -प्र *caus.* to settle, adjust.

शमयितृ *m.* a destroyer

शरजन्मन् *m.* name of Kártikeya.

शरणं a house, dwelling.

शरणागत *p. p.* come for protection, a refugee.

शरद् *f.* a year.

शरव्यं a targate, mark, butt.

शर्मन् *n.* happiness.

शर्वरी night.

शरासनं a bow.

शरीरिन् *m.* a bodied being.

शल्यं a dart.

शश: a hare.

शश्वत् *adv.* forever, perpetually.

शस्त्रभृत् *m.* an armed man, warrior.

शाखामृग: a monkey.

शांत *p. p.* alleviated, removed.

शांति *f.* removal, destruction, expiation; °उदकं soothing water.

शालि: a kind of rice.

शालिन् *a.* endowed.

शाव:,-वक: a youngling.

शास् *with* अनु 2 P. to advise, prevail upon.

शाश्वत् *a.* permanent, everlasting.

शासनं an order, command.

शिक्षा instruction, advice.

शिखा flame.

शिखिन् *m.* a peacock.

शिथिलय (*denom.*) to allow to cool.

शिरोधरः neck.

शिल्पं art, skill.

शिलापट्टः a slab of stone

शिलोच्चयः a mountain; a collection of stones.

शिवं good, blessing

शिष् *with* वि *caus.* to excel, surpass.

शुक्तिः an oyster shell.

शुच् *f.* grief. sorrow

शुद्धांतः royal harem or seraglio; inmates of the harem, *i. e.* queen or queens.

शुश्रूष (*desid.* of श्रु) to serve.

शुभशंसिन् *a.* of good augury, presaging good.

शूलिन् *m.* S'iva.

शृणि *f.* a. goad.

शैलः a mountain.

शैवलं moss.

शोण *a.* red.

शोणितं blood.

शोभा elegance, grace.

श्रीशः Vishnu, lord of S'ri.

श्रुत *p. p.* well-known, reputed.

श्रुति *f.* ear.

श्रेयस् *n.* bliss, good fortune, good; (*a.*) better, more praiseworthy.

श्रेष्ठिन् *m.* a merchant.

श्रोत्रियः a learned Bráhma*n*a.

श्वापदः a beast of pray. wild beast.

श्वेतमान *a.* white.

ष.

षंडः a group, collection, clump.

स.

संयमनं drawing in, holding in.

संयोगः union.

संरंभः turbulent spirit.

संवादः identity.

संव्यवहारः mercantile business traffic.

संविभक्त *p. p.* shared, partaken.

संश्रयः: a resort.

संसर्गः contact, association.

संसारः wordly existence.

संस्तीर्ण *p. p.* strewn.

संस्थापनं establishment.

संस्थित *p. p.* dead ; finished.

संहारः the dessolution of the world.

सकल *a.* entire, unimpaired.

सकाम *a.* satisfied, having the disires fulfilled.

सक्त *p. p.* continued, begun.

संकरः mixture of castes.

संकल्पः a thought.

संकल्पयोनिः the mind-born, Cupid.

संकुल *a.* full of, crowded with.

संकोचः contraction of the limbs.

संगः attachment.

संघः a multitude.

सचकित a. startled.

सज्ज *a.* ready.

सस्यं corn.

सह् *with* उत् 1 A. to dare, venture.

सहकार: a mango tree.

सहज *a.* natural.

सहस्रकिरण: } the sun (having
सहस्रधामन् } 1,000 rays).

सहाय: a companion, friend.

सहोदर: a co-uterine brother.

साक्ष्यं evidence, deposition.

साद: leanness, sinking down.

सादृश्यं likeness, image.

साध् *with* प्र *caus.* to promote, further, advance.

साधनं an army.

साध्वसं fear, timidity.

सानु *n.* summit.

सानुमत् *m.* a mountain.

सानुराग *a.* loyal attached.

सांप्रतिक *a.* proper, right.

सार: strength, power.

सारिका a kind of bird साळुंकी.

सार्थ: a collection, group.

सार्थवाह: a leader of a caravan.

सावधान *a.* with an attentive mind.

साहसकारिन् *a.* bold, audacious.

साहित्यं literary composition.

सित *a.* white.

सिध् *with* नि 1. P. to forbid, prevent.

सिद्ध: a demi-god.

सिंधु: the ocean.

सीरध्वज: a name of Janaka.

सुख *a.* agreeable, pleasant.

सुतीक्ष्ण: name of a sage.

सुधा nectar; स्यंदिन् *a.* dropping honey, mellifluous.

सुभग *adv.* charmingly.

सुश्लिष्ट *a.* well arranged, nicely laid, well-fitted.

सुयोधन: a name of Duryodhana.

सुरद्विष् *m.* an enemy of the gods.

सुहृद्भेद: 'separation of friends; name of the 2nd part of Hitopades'a.

सूक्तं good words.

सूत्रधार: a carpenter.

सृ 1. 3. P. *with* उप to approach, draw near.

सृज् *with* वि *caus.* to send, dismiss.

सेतु: a bridge.

सैंह *a.* of the lion.

सो *with* व्यव 4 P. to attempt, think of.

सोदर्य: a co-uterine brother, brother of whole blood.

सौजन्यं goodness or kindness of disposition.

सौदामिनी lightning.

सौभाग्यविलोपिन् *a.* marring the beauty.

सौहार्दं friendship.

स्कंधावार: a division of an army.

स्तंबकारिता forming clumps or sheaves.

संज् *with* प्र 1 P. to be attached to; -व्यति to link.
संजीवनौषधि *f.* the reviving plant.
सत्केतुः a good banneret.
सत्क्रिया virtue, goodness; hospitality.
सत्वं a being, creature.
सद् 1 P. to sink, drop; *with* वि to be dejected; -उद् to sink, fall into ruin.
सदस्यः an assistant at a sacrifice.
संतति *f.*, संतानः issue, progeny, offspring.
संदिष्ट *p. p.* ordered, commissioned.
संयानं fitting, taking aim.
संधिः a joint.
सन्निकर्षः proximity, vicinity.
सन्निपातः a collection.
सपत्नः an enemy.
सपत्नी a rival wife, co-wife.
सफल *a.* fruitful.
सभाज् 10 P. to pay respects to.
सम्राज् *m.* a paramount sovereign.
समक्षं *adv.* in the presence of, before.
समरं fight; war.
समवस्था state.
समवायः a collection, combination.
समाधिः concentration of mind.
समापत्ति *f.* accident, chance.
समाश्रयः betaking, resorting to.
समिति *f.* fight.
समिद्वत् *a.* fed with sacrificial fuel.
समीपं *adv.* near.
समुन्नति *f.* elevation.
समुच्चयः a collection.
समुत्सुक *a.* over-eager, impetuous.
समृद्ध *p. p.* increased.
समृद्धि *f.* prosperity, affluence.
संपत्ति *f.* excellence of virtues.
संपन्न *p. p.* endowed or furnished with; prepared, made of; become, grown.
संप्रतिपत्ति *f.* admission, confession.
संबंधः a tie.
संबंधिन् *m.* a kinsman, relation.
संभृत *p. p.* collected, gathered.
संभोगः enjoyment.
संभ्रमः fear, confusion.
संमोहः infatuation.
सरणि *f.* mode, way.
सरसिजं a lotus.
सरोषं *adv.* angrily.
सर्गः creation.
सर्वथा *adv.* altogether, entirely.
सर्वदमनः all-subduer.
सर्वांगीण *a.* smeared on the whole body.
सलिलं water.
सशब्दं *adv.* with or producing a sound.

स्तनितं the rumbling of clouds, thundering noise.

स्त्रैणं woman-kind, female sex.

स्थलवर्त्मन् *n.* land-route.

स्थली land.

स्था *with* आ to resort to.

स्थाणुः a name of S'iva.

स्थायिन् *a.* lasting.

स्थिति *f.* stability. permanence; propriety.

स्थिर *a.* firm.

स्थिरीकृ 8 U. to cheer up, console.

स्थास्नु *a.* firm, stable.

स्थैर्यं stability.

स्नातकः an initiated (Bráhma*n*a) house-holder.

स्नानीयवस्त्रं a bathing cloth.

स्निग्ध *p. p.* friendly, affectionate.

स्निग्धदृष्टि *a.* looking intently or with a steadfast gaze.

स्फटिकमणिः a crystal stone.

स्फुट *a.* clearly, visible, distinctly seen.

स्मयः arrogance, pride.

स्यंद् *with* अभि 1. U. to ooze, to be melted.

स्रोतोवहा a river.

स्वच्छंद *adv.* at will, as one likes.

स्वद् 1 A. to like.

स्वभावज *a.* natural.

स्वस्थ *a.* safe, sound.

स्वाधीन *a.* at one's command or disposal.

स्वास्थ्यं ease, tranquillity.

स्वेच्छया *adv.* at will, to one's heart's content.

ह.

हतक *a.* wretched.

हन् *with* अप् 2 P. to destroy annihilate; -प्रति to repel, counteract.

हरिः Indra.

हरिचंदनं a sort of yellow sandal.

हरिणीदृश् *a.* fawn-eyed.

हव्यं an oblation.

हस् 1 P. to clear up, brighten up.

हारीतः a kind of pigeon.

हार्दिक्यः name of a warrior.

हितः a well-wisher, an adviser.

हितवादिन् *a.* or *s.* a well-wisher.

हिमं snow, ice.

हिमवत् *m.* the Himálaya mountain.

हिमरश्मिः } the cold-rayed moon.
हिमांशुः }

हुंकारः the humming sound.

हृ with अभ्यव 1. P. to eat; -उत् to pluck up by the roots, extirpate; -निर् to draw or take out; -सं to drop; curtail, shorten; to withhold; curb, restrain; -व्या to speak.

हृषीकेशः name of Krishna.

हेमंत *a.* cold, wintry.

हैम *a.* caused by snow.

ह्रदः a deep pool of water.

A GLOSSARY.

English-Sanskrit.

A.

Ablest, *a.* पटुतम, प्राज्ञतम.

Absence, in one's परोक्षे, असन्निधाने.

Absent-minded *a.* अन्येहरय॰

Accidentally *adv.* दैववशात्, सहसा.

Accomplishment *s.* सिद्धि *f.*, संपादनं.

Accord, of one एकचित्त, मनस्‌ *a.*

Acquaint *v. t.* बुध् *caus.*, ज्ञा *caus.*

Acquainted *a.* ज्ञ in comp. गृहीतार्थ; परिचित.

Adapt oneself to the will of भावं अनुप्रविश् 6 P. छंदं अनुवृत् 1 A.

Advantage *s.* हितं, लाभः.

Adventure *s.* चरितं, चेष्टितं.

Affairs of state राजकार्याणि.

Affected *a.* पर्याकुल.

Afflicted *a.* पीडित; to be-, खिद् *pass.*

Agony *s.* आतंकः.

All but *adv.* expressed by कल्प or प्राय in comp.; -agreed प्रतिपन्नकल्प.

Ancestral *a.* पैतृक; -property रिक्थं.

Ancient *a* प्राक्कालीन, प्राचीन, पुरातन

Answer *v. t.* प्रति वच् 2 P. -भा 1 A.; उत्तरं प्रतिपद् 4. A.

Anxious *a.* आकुल, सचिंत.

Appearance *s.* दर्शनं, रूपं.

Application *s.* योजनं, विधानं.

Approach *s.* उपस्थिति *f.*, आगमनं.

Appropriate *v. t.* आत्मसात्कृ 8. U.

Approve *v.* अभिनंद् 1. P.

Ardent *a.* पर, उत्कट, गाढ.

Assiduity *s.* तत्परता, निष्ठा.

Assist *v. t.* साहाय्यं कृ. 8 U. or दा 3 U.

Association *s.* संगति *f.*, संगः.

Astonishing *a.* विस्मयावह, आश्चर्यकर.

Attachment *s.* अनुरागः, आसक्ति *f.*

Attendant *s.* परिजनः, अनुचरः.

Attended *a.* सहित, युक्त.

Attract *v. t.* हृ 1. P., आकृष् 1. P.

Auspicious *a.* मंगल, शुभ.

Avarice *s.* लोभः, गृध्नुता.

Averse *a.* पराङ्मुख.

Awaken *v. t.* प्रति बुध् *caus.*

B.

Baffle *v. t.* मोघीकृ 8 U.; पर्यनिवृत् 1 A.

Banner *s.* पताका.
Bard *s.* वैतालिकः; बंदिन् *m.*
Base *a.* अधम, क्षुद्र.
Basin *s.* द्रोणी, जलाशयः.
Become *v. t.* अनुरूप-उपपन्न *a.* भू 1 P. शुभ् 1 A. (gen.)
Befall *v. t.* आपत् 1 P. उपनम् 1 P. (with gen.)
Beginning *s.* मूलं; from the— आमूलात्, आदितः.
Beholder *s.* प्रेक्षकः, द्रष्टृ *m.*
Bent *a.* विहितप्रतिज्ञ, कृतसंकल्प —double with age जरानमितकाय.
Bid farewell *v.* आमंत्र् 10 A. आप्रच्छ् 6 A.
Bit *s.* शकलं.
Boast श्लाघ्-विकत्थ् 1 A.
Break open *v. t.* संदिच्छेदं कृ 8 U.
Brought up संवर्धित, परिपोषित.

C.

Cake *s.* पिष्टापूपः.
Care, with प्रयत्नेन, सादरं.
Carnivorous *a.* क्रव्याद्, पिशिताशन.
Cast off *v. t.* निराकृ 8 U. प्रत्यादिश् 6 P.
Cause *s.* पक्षः.
Censurable *a.* गर्हणीय, निंद्य.
Certain *a.* ध्रुव, नियत.
Certainly *adv.* नियतं, नूनं, खलु.
Chance of failure *s.* असिद्धिसंभवः.
Change (for the better) *s.* विशेषः, विपर्यास; परिवर्तः undergo a—, विपर्यासं या 2 P.
Charming *a.* सुभग, रम्य.
Circuitous *a.* वक्र, विजिह्म.
Citadel *s.* दुर्गः.
Class *s.* वर्गः, सहाध्यायिगणः.
Clear *v. t.* प्र-क्षल् 10 P. प्र-मृज् 2 P.
Clever *a.* बुद्धिमत्, पटुमति.
Close *v. t.* पिधा, 3 U. निरुध् 7 U.
Colour *s.* व्याजः-अपदेशः.
Commendable *a.* प्रशस्य, श्लाघ्य.
Commit *v. t.* आ-चर् 1 P. कृ 8 U.
Communicate *v. t.* नि-विद् *caus.*
Company *s.* समागमः, संगः.
Completely *adv.* निःशेषं; एकांततः.
Compose *v. t.* पर्यवस्था *caus.* संस्तंभ्. *caus.*
Concerning *a.* संबंधिन्, गत.
Conscious *a.* अभिज्ञ, ज्ञ-विद् in comp.
Constitute *v. t.* भू 1. P., अस् 2 P.
Consultation, in-with संमंत्र्य, संवाद्य (instr.)
Contracted *a.* संकुचित, संपिंडित.
Contending *s.* कलहः, विवादः, स्पर्धा.
Conversant अभ्यंतर, अभिज्ञ.
Cost *s.* व्ययः, मूल्यं.
Countryman *s.* स्वदेशजः, देशबंधुः.
Court *s.* सभा; royal-नृप-राज-सभा.
Covered over *a.* आच्छन्न, आवृत.
Cross *v. t.* आक्रम् 1 U.
Crowned, to be—with success फल् 1 P.
Crumb *s.* खंडः, शकलं.

Culprit *s.* अपराधिन् *m.*
Current *s.* रयः, वेगः
D.
Danger *s.* संकटं, आपद् *f.*, कृच्छ्रं.
Dear *a.* प्रिय, कांत.
Deed *s.* चरितं, चेष्टितं.
Deep *a.* अगाध, गंभीर.
Defaulter *s.* दंड्यः, अपराधिन् *m.*
Defeated in one's attempts. *a.* भग्नोद्यम, मोघप्रयत्न.
Definite *a.* विशिष्ट, विशेष in comp.
Delay *s.* विलंबः, कालातिपातः, without-अकालहीनं.
Delighted *a.* प्रमुदित, सानंद.
Delightful *a.* प्रामोदिक. आनंदन.
Deliverer *s.* त्रातृ *m.* रक्षकः.
Demand *v. t.* प्रच्छ् 6 P.
Desist *v. i.* वि-रम् 1 P.
Desolate *v. t.* निर्जनीकृ 8 U. उत्-ध्वंस् *caus.*
Despair *v. i.* निराश *a.* भू 1 P
Detail *s.* विशेषः, विस्तरः.
Deterred *a.* त्रासित, निवारित.
Devise *v. t.* चिंत् 10 P. प्रक्लृप् *caus.* युज् *caus.*
Devoted (to) *a.* आसक्त, तत्पर.
Devotion *s.* भक्ति *f.*
Devolve *v. t.* संक्रम् *caus.* निक्षिप् 6 P.
Devout *a.* धर्मनिष्ठ, धर्मपर.
Dictionary *s.* कोषः, शब्दाभिधानं.
Difficult *a.* दुष्कर, दुःसाध्य.
Difficulty *s.* आपद् *f.*, कृच्छ्रं, दुर्ग with great—कथं, कथमपि.
Dignity *s.* आभिजात्यं, प्रतिष्ठा, गौरवं.
Diligently *adv.* सोद्यमं.
Direct *v. t.* युज्, निविश् (*caus.*)
Directed *a.* आसक्त, अभिनिविष्ट.
Directly *adv.* सरलमार्गेण, अनानागत्य.
Discharged *a.* मुक्त, क्षिप्त.
Discrimination *s.* विवेकः, परिच्छेदः.
Disguised as वेषं परिदधान, व्यंजनोपेत.
Disgust *s.* निर्वेदः.
Disgusted *a.* निर्विण्ण.
Disloyal, to be -वि-अप-रंज् *pass.*
Dismissed *a.* विसर्जित.
Dispelled *a.* निरस्त.
Disrespect *v. t.* अवमन् 4 A.
Disrespectfully *adv.* सावज्ञं.
Distinguished *a.* विख्यात;—guest. अतिथिविशेषः.
Distressed *a.* शोकापन्न, दुःखार्त.
Disturbed *a.* विकृत.
Divide *v. t.* वि-भज् 1 P.
Divine *a.* देव (वी *f.*), दिव्य.
Doomed by fate *a.* दैवोपहत.
Draw near *v. i.* प्रत्या-सद् 1 P.
Dreadful *a.* भयप्रद, भयावहः
Dreariness *s.* शून्यत्वं, निर्जनत्वं.
Dreary *a.* निर्जन, घोर.
Dressed *a.* परिच्छन्न.
Dried up *a.* पीत, उच्छोषित.

Due *a.* देयः.

Dull *a.* मंदबुद्धि, जडमति.

Duty *s.* धर्मः, कर्तव्यं.

E.

Early in the morning महति प्रत्यूषे.

Earnestly *adv.* उत्कटं, प्रगाढं; I hope—इति मे गाढाभिलाषः.

Ease, at, -निर्वृत, वीतचिंत.

Eatable *s.* भक्ष्यं, अभ्यवहार्यं.

Economically *adv.* मितव्ययेन.

Education *s.* अध्यापनं, शिक्षणं.

Effect *v. t.* संपद् *caus.* साध् 5 P.

Elapse *v. i.* व्यति-इ 2 P. अतिक्रम् 1. 4. P.

Elders *s.* गुरुजनः, गुरु *pl.*

Emperor *s.* अधिराजः, चक्रवर्तिन् *m.*, सम्राज् *m.*

Employ *v. t.* प्र-युज् 7. A.

Employment *s.* व्यापरः, उद्योगः.

Enchant *v. t.* विलुभ् *caus.*, हृ 1. P.

Engaging *s.* अभियोगः, व्यापारः.

Engrossed *a.* निमग्न, आकुल.

Enraged *a.* सामर्ष, प्रकोपित.

Entreaty *s.* प्रार्थना.

Envy *s.* मात्सर्यं.

Epithet *s.* विशेषणं.

Escape *v. t.* निर्गम् 1. P. निष्क्रम् 1. 4. P.

Excellent *a.* विशिष्ट, प्रकृष्टतम.

Excessively *adv.* भृशं, नितरां; अतिमात्रं.

Execute *v. t.* अनु-स्था 1. P. सं-पद् *caus.*

Exertion *s.* परिश्रमः, आयासः.

Exhausted *a.* परिश्रांत, खिन्न.

Expectant *a.* ईप्सु, लिप्सु.

Expedient *s.* उपायः, गुणः

Expose *v. t.* पात्रं कृ. 8 U. पदं नी 1 P. or गम् 1 P.

Extend, how far कियदवधिक *a.*

Extensive *a.* विस्तीर्ण.

Extent, to any,-स्तोकांशेनापि.

Extraordinary *a.* अद्भुत, अनन्यसामान्य.

F.

Fail *v. i.* विफलीभू 1. P. मोघीभू.

Failed in attempts भग्नोद्यम, मोघप्रयत्न.

Faithlessness *s.* असत्यसंधता, प्रतिज्ञाभंगः.

Fall in with आसद् *caus.*, दृश् 1. P.—out संपद् 4 A.;—upon आपत् 1 P. अवस्कंद् 1 P.;—a victim आमिषतां गम् 1 P., भक्ष्यस्थाने भू 1 P.

Famine *s.* दुर्भिक्षं.

Fathers *s.* पितरः, स्वधाभुजः.

Fawn (Flatter) upon *v.* चाटुवादैः आराध् *caus.* or उपस्था 1 U.

Favourite *a.* वल्लभ, प्रिय.

Feature *s.* लक्षणं.

Feed (with food) *v. t.* भुज् *caus.*

Feign *v.* अप-दिश् 6 P.
Fickle *a.* तरल, चपल.
Field *v.* क्षेत्र.
Fierce *a.* उग्र, भीषण.
Fiery tempered *a.* कोपन, सुलभ-कोप.
Fine *s.* दंडः; *a.* शोभन, सूक्ष्म.
Finish *v. t.* अव-सो 4 P., समाप् *caus.*
Fix (love) *v. t.* बंध् 9 P.
Follower *s.* अनुचरः, अनुयायिन् *m.*
Fowler *s.* व्याधः
Freed, to be, मुच् *pass.*
Fret (oneself) *v.* परितप् *pass.* क्षुभ् *pass.*
Fuel *s.* इंधनं.
Fulfilled *a.* पूर्ण, सफल.
Fully *adv.* अशेषतः, सर्वात्मना.
Furnished *a.* संपन्न.

G.

Gentle *a.* मृदु, शांत.
Gently *adv.* मंदं मंदं.
Get abroad *v. i.* प्रसृ 1. P., प्रकाशतां गम् 1 P.
Give over सं-ऋ *caus.* (अर्पय).
Glory *s.* यशस्; *n.* उदाहरणं.
Go home (to) *v. i.* स्पृश् 6 P. मर्माणि स्पृश्.
Gratitude *s.* कृतवेदित्वं, कृतज्ञता.
Graze *v. i.* वि-चर् 1 P.
Guard *s.* रक्षिन् *m.*; रक्षकः.
Guardian of the world *s.* लोक-पालः.

H.

Hail-stone *s.* वर्षोपलः, करकाः.
Hastily *adv.* सरभसं, सत्वरं.
Haughty *a.* उत्सिक्त, अवलिप्त.
Haunted *a.* निषेवित, समाश्रित.
Hearing of a case *s.* व्यवहारदर्शनं
Heart-rending *a.* हृदयभेदिन्, अरुं-तुद्.
Heat *s.* आतपः, उष्णं.
Heir-apparent *s.* युवराजः
Helpless *a.* अनाथ, अशरण, दीन.
Hesitate *v.* आ-शंक् 1 A.
Hide *v. t.* गुह् 1 U., प्र-छद् 10.
High *a.* उन्नत, अभिजातः (words) तारतर, कोपगर्भ.
High-mettled *a.* उच्चसत्व.
Hold *v. t.* मन् 4 A.
Honesty *s.* आर्जवं, निष्कापट्यं.
Honeyed *a.* सुधास्यंदिन्, मधुमय, मधुमधुर.
Honorably *adv.* सगौरवं, प्रतिपत्ति-पूर्वकं.
Honour *v. t.* सं-भू *caus.*
House-holder *s.* कुटुंबिन्, गृहमेधिन्, *m.*
House-hold duties *s.* गृहकार्याणि, कुटुंबभरः.
Housewife *s.* गृहिणी.
Huge *a.* स्थूल, विशाल.
Rumour *s.* छंदः.
Hung *a.* अवलंबित, अवसक्त.

I.

Ill *a.* अस्वस्थशरीर.

Illness *s.* अस्वास्थ्यं, विकारः.

Image *s.* प्रतिबिंबं, प्रतिफलं.

Imagination धी *f.*

Immediately *adv.* सपद्येव.

Immodesty *s.* अविनयः.

Immoral *a.* असाधु, अधर्म in comp.

Immortal *a.* अमर, अक्षय, अनश्वर.

Impending, to be closely-उन्नम् 1 P.

Important *a.* गुरु.

Importune *v. t.* अनु-बंध् 9 P. निर्बंधेन प्रच्छ् 6 P.

Impose upon वंच् 10 P. विप्रलभ् 1 A.

Impossible *a.* दुःसाध्य, अशक्य.

Improve *v. t.* उन्नत्ति-श्रेयस्त्वं-नी 1 P. उत्कृष् 1 P.

Improvement *s.* उन्नति *f.*, उत्कर्षः.

Inanimate *a.* अचेतन.

Inauspicious *a.* अभद्र.

Inborn *a.* नैसर्गिक (की *f.*), सहज.

Incarnate *a.* मूर्त, शरीरिन्.

Incur displeasure कोप-अकृपापात्रं भू 1 P.

Independence *s.* स्वातंत्र्यं, स्वैराचारः

Indian *a.* भरतवर्षीय.

Indicate *v. t.* व्यंज् *caus.*, सुत् *caus.*

Indifferent *a.* तटस्थ, उदासीन, मध्यस्थ.

Indigo pot *s.* नीलीभांडं.

Industry *s.* उद्यमः; अध्यवसायः कार्याभियोगः.

Inflicting punishment *s.* दंडनं.

Influence *s.* विकारः.

Inform *v. t.* नि-विद् *caus.*, विज्ञा *caus.*

Innumerable *a.* असंख्य, संख्यातीत.

Inquiry *s.* व्यवहारः.

Inspire (with confidence) विश्वासं नी 1 P., विश्वस् *caus.*

Insignificant *a.* क्षुद्र, नीच.

Insult *s.* निकृति *f.*, मानभंगः.

Intent *a.* पर, तत्पर, परायण in comp.

Intimate *a.* रूढसौहृद.

J.

Jaw *s.* दंष्ट्रा, दशनः.

K.

Keep contented *v. t.* अनुरंज् *caus.*

Kept *a.* स्थापित.

L.

Lady (voc.) भवती.

Laid down *a.* प्रणीत.

Lamb *s.* छागः.

Lavish *a.* मुक्तहस्त.

Leave *v. t.* निक्षिप् 6 P., न्यासीकृ 8 U.

Liberal *a.* वदान्य, त्यागिन्, उदार.

Library *s.* पुस्तकालयः.

Lie *s.* असत्यं, अनृतं.

Liked *a.* कांत, अभिमत.

Limited *a.* अल्पविषय, परिच्छिन्न.
Livelihood *s.* वृत्ति *f.*, जीविका.
Look to *v.* अव-ईक्ष् 1. A. अनुसं-धा 3 U.
Look intently *v. t.* स्तिमितदृष्ट्या प्रेक्ष् 1 A. दृष्टिभिः-लोचनैः-पा 1 P.
Lose त्यज् 1 P. हृ *caus.*; lost one's life अपगतासुर्बभूव.
Loss, at a—to do किंकर्तव्यता-प्रतिपत्ति-मूढ.
Love-lorn *a.* विधुर.
Lovely *a.* चारुगात्र, कमनीय, मधुराकृति; (garden &c.) रमणीय, रम्य.
Lower region *s.* पातालः.
Loyal attachment to throne अस्खलित दृढ स्वामिभक्ति *f.*

M.

Majesty (his) महाराजः, देवः, (her) देवी.
Manifold *a.* नानाविध, बहुविध.
Market *s.* आपणः, पण्यवीथिका.
Mass *s.* जालं, पटलं.
Master completely *v. t.* पारं गम् or दृश् 1 P.
Matter *s.* अर्थः.
Mention, not to—expressed by का-कथा गणना *with* loc., or आस्-स्था *with* तावत्.
Merchant *s.* वणिज्, *m.* श्रेष्ठिन् *m.*
Merge into *v.* निमज्ज् 6 P.
Merit, *s.* गुणः, पुण्यं.
Misdeed *s.* पापं, दुष्कृतं.
Misfortune *s.* दुर्भाग्यं, मंदभाग्यं.
Mistress *s.* भट्टिनी; भर्तृदारिका.
Misunderstand *v. t.* अन्यथा ग्रह् 9 P. मिथ्या संभ्र *caus.* or क्लृप् *caus.*
Modern *a.* अर्वाचीन, आधुनिक.
Morality *s.* नीति *f.* नीतिशास्त्रं.
Mortal *s.* मर्त्यः; *a.* अंतकर, मृत्युजनन, प्राणहर.
Moved to be, (to pity) दयार्द्रीभू 1. P., करुणया विद्रु 1 P.,
Multiplied, to be, बहुलीभू 1 P.

N.

Naked *a.* अशरण.
Narrate *v. t.* कथ् 10 P., आचक्ष् 2 A.
Narrow-minded *a.* कृपणमति.
Naturally *adv.* अवश्यमेव , नूनं खलु; प्रकृत्या.
Next to impossible अशक्यप्राय, दुर्घटकल्प.
Noble *a.* कुलीन;—birth अभिजनः कुले जन्म.
Nocturnal *a.* नैश.
Noise *s.* कलकलः.
Notice *v. t.* लक्ष् 10 P. वि-भू *caus.*
Number *s.* निकरः, संघः.
Nymph *s.* अप्सरस् *f.*, देवता.

O.

Observe *v. t.* निरूप् 10. P. पर्यालोच् 10 P.
Obedience *s.* आज्ञाधारकत्वं, अनुविधायित्वं, आज्ञानुरोधः.
Obey *v. t.* अनुरुध् 4. A. अनुसृ 1. P.

Object (sole) of love; स्नेहस्यैकायनीभूत.

Occasion *s.* अवसरः.

Occupation *s.* व्यापारः, व्यवसायः.

Offend *v. t.* अपराध् 4. P. (loc. or gen.)

Old *a.* वृद्ध, स्थविर, प्रवयस्; चिरंतन, पुराण.

Oppress *v. t.* उपप्लु 1. A. मृश् पीड् 10 P., विप्र-कृ 8 U.

Oration *s.* वाक्प्रबंध.

Overcome *v. t.* वशीकृ 8 U., वशं नी 1. P.

Overtake *v. t.* आ-सद् *caus.*

Owner *s.* स्वामिन् *m*, अधिपतिः.

P.

Painter *s.* चित्रकरः, आलेखकः

Palfrey *s.* वाजिन् *m.*, हयः.

Particular *s.* विशेषः.

Pass *v. t.* गम् *caus.*, नी 1. P., वह् *with* अति *caus.*

Past *a.* अतीत, गत.

Patience *s.* सहिष्णुता, क्षमित्वं.

Pay off *v. t.* शुध् *caus.*, निर्यत् *caus.*

Peevish *a.* पिशुन, दुःशील.

Perforce *adv.* बलात्, बलेन.

Perilous time *s.* जीवितसंशयकालः

Perplexing *a.* उद्वेगकारिन्.

Perturbed *a.* पर्याकुल, पारिप्लव.

Philosopher *s.* तत्त्वविद् *m.*, तत्त्वज्ञः

Picture *s.* आलेख्यं, चित्रं.

Pitchy *a.* अंध, सूचिभेद्य.

Pitiable *a.* करुण, अनुकंप्य.

Pious *a.* पुण्यात्मन्, धर्मशील,

Plain *s.* समभूभागः, समस्थली

Plaintiff *s.* अर्थिन् *m.* अभियोक्तृ *m.*

Plaintive *a.* करुण;—cry आर्तस्वरः करुणपरिदेवितं, विलापः.

Pleasant *a.* सुखावह.

Pleasure-mountain क्रीडाशैलः.

Pollution *a.* कलंकः.

Position *s.* अवस्था, स्थिति *f.*

Possession *s.* वित्तं, विभवः.

Possible, as far as यावच्छक्यं.

Pouring down *a.* वर्षिन्.

Practice *s.* प्रयोगः.

Precinct *s.* उपांतः, परिसरः.

Precipitate *a.* सरभस.

Preferable *a.* श्रेयस्, श्लाघ्यतर.

Preparation संविधा.

Presence *s.* सद्भावः.

Present *a.* संनिहित; to be-सन्निधा *pass.*; *s.* उपायनं, उपहारः.

President *s.* अध्यक्षः.

Prey upon भक्ष् 10 P.

Prime *a.* मूल in comp., प्रधान.

Principle *s.* तत्त्वं, आगमः.

Prisoner *s.* बंदिः-दी *f.*

Proceed *v. i.* उद्-भू 1. P. उत्पद् 4 A. *with* प्रस्तु 2 U. प्र-वृत् *caus.*

Proceeding from *a.* उद्भव, संभूत.

Profess to be one's daughter कन्या नाम भू 1 P.

Proficient *a.* प्रवीण, पारंगत, पारदृश्वन्.

Prompt *a.* उद्यत, तत्पर, दक्ष.

Proper *a.* युक्त, उचित.

Properly *adv.* सम्यक्, यथावत्, तत्त्वतः.

Proudly *adv.* *a* सदर्पं, उद्धतं, सावलेपं.

Provided *a.* उपपन्न, सनाथ.

Provoke revolt प्रजाकोपं,-क्षोभं-जन् *caus.*

Pull down *v. t.* नि-पत् *caus.*, अव-सद् *caus.*

Purification *s.* शुद्धि *f.* परिपूति *f.*

Purifying *a.* पावन.

Put up with सह् 1. A., तितिक्ष् 1. A.

Q.

Qualified *a.* गुणवत्.

Quarrel *v. i.* वि-वद् 1 A.

R.

Rag *s.* चीरं; dressed in tattered—, चीरवासस्, परिहितचीर.

Rainy season *s.* प्रावृष् *f.*, वर्षा (*pl.*)

Rash *a.* क्षिप्रकारिन्, अविमृश्यकारिन्.

Rashness *s.* साहसं, क्षिप्रकारिता.

Rather *adv.* ईषत्, किंचित्.

Rave *v. i.* प्र-लप् 1. P.

Reach the ears कर्णविषयं-या 2 P. श्रुतिपथं आपत् 1 P.

Ready *a.* सज्जीभूत, सन्नद्ध.

Ready-witted *a.* प्रत्युत्पन्नमति, प्रतिभानवत्.

Real *a.* तात्त्विक, परमार्थतः *adv.*

Realized *a.* अनुभूत, प्रत्यक्षीकृत.

Receive *v. t.* प्रत्युत्-गम्-व्रज्. 1 P.

Recover *v. t.* आ-प्रति-पद् 4 A.

Recourse, to have—to अंगीकृ 8 U. आस्था 1 U.

Reduce to ashes *v. t.* भस्मीकृ, भस्मसात्कृ 8 U.

Reed *s.* वेतसः.

Regard *s.* गौरवं, संभावना.

Region *s.* प्रदेशः.

Reign, in the—of मही शासति तस्मिन्.

Relation *s.* ज्ञातिः, बंधुः.

Relent *v. t.* मृदुतां गम् 1 P. काठिन्यं त्यज् 1 P.

Religious *a.* धर्म्य;—action धर्मक्रिया.

Reluctantly *adv.* अकामतः, बलेन अनिच्छत् *a.*

Remedy *s.* प्रति (ती) कारः, प्रतिपत्ति *f.*

Remove *v. t.* अपनी, अपहृ 1 P.

Renowned *a.* विश्रुत, प्रथित.

Repeating *s.* उच्चारणं, उदीरणं.

Reported, to be—expressed by इति श्रूयते, इति जनप्रवादः or किंवदंती-श्रूयते.

Respect *s.* विषयः ; (*v.*) मन् *caus.* पूज् 10 P.

Respectfully *adv.* सादरं, सप्रश्रयं.

Resplendent *a.* देदीप्यमान, भ्राजमान.

Restraining *s.* निग्रहः, संयम.
Result *v. t.* पर्यव-सो 4 P.
Return (to the subject of discussion) प्रकृतं अनुसंधा 3 U. or अनुसृ 1 P.
Revenge, to take-वैरनिर्यातनं-साधनं कृ 8 U.
Revile *v. t.* निर्-भर्त्स् 10 A. उपालभ 1 A.
Rider *s.* अश्वरोहः सादिन् *m.*
Ring *s.* अंगुलीयकं.
Rise against *v.* अभिद्रुह् 4 P. (*acc.*)
Risk *v. t.* संदेहे-संशये-पत् *caus.*
Roam *v. t.* परि-अट् 1 P. वि-चर् 1 P.
Rogue *s.* जाल्मः, धूर्तः, कितवः.
Rout *v. t.* वि-द्रु *caus.* वि-ध्वंस् *caus.*
Ruin *v. t.* नश् *caus.*; *s.* प्रणाशः.
Run a risk संशये (आत्मानं) पत् *caus.*
Rush upon *v.* सहसा अभिसृ 1 P. or आक्रम् 1 U.
Ruthlessly *adv.* निर्दयं, निर्घृणं.

S.

Sacred-ceremony *s.* संस्कार ; शास्त्रविधिः; -learning श्रुतिः, निगमः.
Sacrificial *a.* मेध्य.
Sad. *a.* उद्वेगकर, शोकावह, दुःखप्रद.
Safely *adv.* क्षेमेण.
Sandhyá adoration *s.* संध्योपासना.
Save *v. t.* रक्ष्. 1 P. त्रै 1 A.
Saying *s.* उक्ति *f.*, वचनं.
Scene *s.* स्थानं, दृश्यवस्तु *m.*
Scriptural point *s.* शास्त्रविषयः.
Scheme *s.* उपायः.
Scorching *a.* तीव्र, तिग्म, प्रखर.
Season *s.* समयः, कालः.
Secret *s.* रहस्यं.
Secure *v. t.* जन् *caus.*
Self-respect *s.* स्वाभिमानः.
Sell *v. t.* वि-क्रि 9 A.
Senseless *a.* निःसंज्ञ; अपगतचेतन.
Senses *s.* संज्ञा, चेतना.
Sensibly *adv.* बोधपूर्वं, सचेतनवत्.
Serene *a.* प्रशांत.
Set (mind) *v. t.* युज् *caus.* बंध् 9 P. निविश् *caus.*
Severely *adv.* परुषं, बलवत्.
Sharp *a.* तीक्ष्णमती, कुशाग्रबुद्धि.
Shepherd *s.* मेषपालः.
Ship *s.* पोतः.
Shoot through *v.* निर्-व्यध् 4 P.
Shoulder *s.* स्कंधः, अंसः.
Shy (at) दृष्ट्वा चकित *a.* भू. 1 P. सहसा निवृत् 1 A.
Side *s.* पक्षः
Sight *s.* स्थानं; आलोकः, दर्शनं.
Sign *s.* व्यंजनं, लक्षणं.
Silken *a.* कौशेय.
Silver *a.* रजत in comp.
Single combat *s.* नियुद्धं, द्वंद्वसंप्रहारः युद्धं.
Sinner *s.* पापकृत् *m.*, पापिन् *m.*

Sister's husband *s.* आवृत्तः भगिनीपतिः.

Slaughter-house *s.* वधस्थानं-गृहं

Sleepless *a.* उन्निद्र.

Slight *v. t.* अवधीर् 10 P. अवमन् 4 A.

Snore *v. i.* घर्घररवं कृ 8 U.

Solitary *a.* विविक्त, विजन.

Soundly *adv.* गाढं, निर्भरं.

Sovereignty *s.* प्रभुत्वं.

Spectator *s.* प्रेक्षकः, द्रष्टृ *m.*

Speed *s.* वेगः.

Splendid *a.* शोभन, चारु; उत्तुंग, विशाल.

Spoil *v. t.* मलिनीकृ 8 U.

Sprout *s.* पल्लवः, किसलयं.

Spy *s.* चरः.

Spend *see* Pass.

Stick *s.* यष्टि *f.*, लगुडः.

Still *a.* निश्चल, जड.

Stop *v. t.* प्रति-सिध् 1 P.

Storm *v. t.* अवस्कंद् 1 P.

String *v. t.* अधिज्य-आततज्य *a.* कृ 8 U

Stroke *s.* निर्घातः, प्रहारः.

Strong-minded *a.* धीर.

Student *s.* अध्येतृ *m.*

Subject *a.* अधीन, आस्पदं-पात्रं.

Submit *v. i.* सह् 1 A.

Suitable *a.* अनुरूप, सदृश (शी *f.*)

Sullied with disgrace *a.* अयशोदूषित, अपमानमलीमस.

Sully *v. t.* मलिनीकृ 8 U., दुष् *caus.* (दूषयति).

Superior, to be, अतिरिच्-विशिष् *pass.*

Supplied *a.* संपन्न.

Support (oneself) *v.* वृत्तिं कृ 8 U. जीवितं धृ 10 P.

Surmount *v. t.* उत्-तृ 1 P.

Surpass *v. t.* अति-शी 2 A., अति-रिच्-विशिष् *pass.*

Survive *v. t.* अति-अनु-जीव् 1 P.

Suspicion *s.* आ-शंका.

Sustain *v. t.* धृ 10 P. अवलंब् 1 A.

Swarm *v. t.* मिल् 6 P. संघशः संपत् 1 P.

Swear *v.* शप् 1 U.

Sweep away *v. t.* अप-वह् *caus.*

Syllable *s.* अक्षरं

T.

Taking food *s.* आहारसेवन, अन्नास्वादनं.

Tall *a.* तुंग, उच्छ्रित, प्रांशु.

Tamely *adv.* क्लीबवत्, नष्टवीर्यवत्.

Tarry *v. i.* चिरायति (*denom.*), वि-लंब् 1 A.

Taunt *s.* उपालंभः.

Temple *s.* देवतायतनं, देवालयः.

Temporary *a.* अचिर, क्षणिक.

Temptation *s.* प्रलोभनं, विकारः.

Theory *s.* आगमः, शास्त्रं.

Think of मतिं कृ 8 U. (with Dat.)

This and the like *a.* एवमादि.
Thought *s.* संकल्पः, चिंता.
Threshold *s.* देहली.
Through *prep.* मुखेन in comp.
Thrown down *a.* निपातित.
Tired *a.* क्लांत, श्रांत.
Tidings *s.* उदंतः, वृत्तांतः.
Tortoise *s.* कूर्मः, कमठः.
Touchstone *s.* निकशः.
Transformed, to be भावेन परिणम् 1 U. भाव आपाद 4 A.
Treading in the footsteps पदानुसरणं, पदानुविधानं.
Treat *v. t.* व्यवहृ-आचर 1 P., वृत् 1 A. (with loc.); with संधा 3 U.
Tributary prince सामंतः, करदः.
Tribute *s.* करः, बलिः.
Trifling *a.* क्षुद्र.
Troop *s.* सैन्यदलं, अनीकं.
Trouble *s.* क्लेशः, दुःखं.
Troublesome *a.* कष्टप्रद, क्लेशावह.
Truthfulness *s.* सत्यवादित्वं.
Tutelary deity *s.* कुलदेवता.
Turn *s.* पर्यायः, वारः.

U.

Umbrella *s.* आतपत्रं.
Uncommon *a.* असाधारण, लोकोत्तर.
Undertaken *a.* अभ्युपेत, अंगीकृत.
Undertaking *s.* आरंभः.
Unending *a.* अनंत, शाश्वत, सनातन.
Unfathomable *a.* दुरवगाह्, दुर्बोध.
Unfortunate *a.* मंदभाग्य.
Uninterruptedly *adv.* निर्विघ्नं.
United, to be संगम् 1 A. संयुज *pass.*
Unparalleled *a.* अनुपम, अप्रतिम.

V

Value *v. t.* बहु मन् 4 A.
Vanquish *v. t.* वशं नी 1 P. मूर्ध्नि पादं निधा 3 U.
Vary *v. i.* भिद् *pass.*; varies as the nature of the work प्रयोजनापेक्षितया चलं.
Vaunter *s.* विकत्थनः, आत्मश्लाघिन्.
Verdant *a.* हरित, शाद्वल.
Vernal season *s.* मधुमासः, वसंतसमयः.
Very *a.* परम, or expressed by अपि.
Vie *v. i.* स्पर्ध् 1 A.; तुल् 10 P.
Violently *adv.* प्रसह्य, प्रसभं, वेगेन.
Virtue *s.* धर्मः; सत्पथः.
Virtuous *a.* साधुवृत्त, धर्मशील.

W

Wait *v.* प्रतिपाल् 10 P. प्रति-ईक्ष् 1 A.; —upon *v.* उद्-स्था 1 U.
Walking *s.* पर्यटनं, विहारः.
Want *s.* अभावः.
Wanting, to be परि हा *pass.*
Warlike *a.* विक्रांत, शूर;—deeds पराक्रमः वीरविजृंभितं.
Warning *s.* प्रबोधनं.
Wicked *a.* दुरात्मन्, दुराशय.

Wild *a.* वन्य, मत्त.

Will *a.* इच्छा, कामः ; against one's —बलात्, बलेन, अनिच्छतोपि, तस्य; at —स्वैरं, स्वेच्छया.

Win over *v. t.* वशं नी 1 P., ग्रह् 9 P.

Wolf *s.* वृकः.

Wonder *s.* आश्चर्यं ; it is no—नेतत् चित्रं, किमत्र चित्रं.

Wonted *a.* सहज, नैसर्गिक.

Wood-cutter *s.* काष्टच्छिद्, काष्टतक्ष् *m.*

Work, cease to, व्यपारात् विरम् 1 P.

Working *s.* व्यापारः, चेष्टा.

World, my all the जीवितसर्वस्वीभूत *a.*

Worthy *a.* अनुरूप, सदृश.

Wretched *a.* दुष्ट; -man नरापसदः, नरहतकः.

Z.

Zeal *s.* भक्ति *f.* ; उत्साहः.

INDEX.

*** The figures refer to the section (§) not to the page.

अग्रे 112
अंग 243
अथ 244; -किं 245
अद् *caus.* 45 (*b*), 344
अधः 112
अधिकृत्य, उद्दिश्य 246
अधीतिन् 99
अधोधः } अध्यधि } 33
अनंतरं 82
अनु 37
अनुरूप 117 (*a*)
अतरा 35 (*a*)
अंतरं 106 (*a*)
अंतरेण 35
अंतिक 112 (*b*)
अन्य 81
अपि 135 (*a*); 247
अभितः 34
अयि 248
अये 249
अर्थ 59, 111
अर्ह् 180
अलं 57, 67, 177
असाधु 99
असूय् 63
अहह 250
अहो 251

आ.

आ 84; 252
आं 253
आः 254
आत्मन् 140
आयुष्यं 111
आरभ्य 82
आरात् 81
आस् with अधि; 31
with part. 145
आसक्त 100

इ.

इ with अधि; 113;
(*caus.*) 44
इतर 81
इति 255, 256
इदं 131
इव 257

ई.

ईक्ष् 71
ईर्ष्य् 63
ईश 113

उ.

उत 258, 259
उत्तरतः 112
उत्तरेण 112(*a*)
उत्सुक 100(*a*)
उपरि 112
उपर्युपरि 33
उभयतः 33

ऊ.

ऊर्ध्वं 82

क्लृप्

ऋ.

ऋते 81

ए.

एक-अपर 137,138
एतद् 131
एव 260
एवं 261

ओ.

ओम् 262

क.

कच्चित् 263
कथ् 68
कदाचित्, कश्चित् 135
कामं 265
कार्य 59
कितव 100
किं 59, 266, 267
किल 268, 269

कुशल 100
कुशलं 67 (*d*); 111
कृ 338 ;—अधि 339 ;-वि 340;-अनु 118 (*a*)
कृ *caus.* 45(*f*)
कृत 57
कृते 116
कृष् 39
कृ with अप 332
कॢप् 66
केवल 270
क्रम् 310
क्री with वि, अव, परि 341—परि 71
क्रुध् 63
क्रीड् 311
क्व 264
क्षिप् 98

ख.

खलु 271
खाद् *caus.* 45 (*b*,
ख्या 68

ग.

गम् with सं 312
गुणः 59
(जुगुप्सते) 76
गृहीतिन् 99
गृ 333

घ.

घ्रा *caus.* 45 (*d*)

च.

च 272,273
चक्ष् 68
चर् 313
चि 39

ज.

जन् 77
जातु 274
जि 39;—with वि & परा 314;—परा 79
ज्ञा 342;—with सं 59

त.

ततः 276
तथा 277
तद् 132;275
तप् 315
तावत् 278
तु 279
तुल्य 117
तॄ with वि 97
तं, त्व 127
त्रप् 146
त्रै 78

द.

दक्षिणतः 112
दक्षिणेन 112(*a*)
दह् 39
दय् 113
दा 329
दिव् 59, 119(*a*)
दिष्ट्या 280
दुह् 39
दूर 112 (*b*)
दृश *caus.* 45 (*e*)
द्रुह् 63

ध.

धा *with* अंतर 85
धिक् 33
धूर्त 100
धृ 10 cl. 62

न.

न 281
ननु 286
नः, ना 127
नमः 67
नम् with प्र 67 (*c*)
नमस्कृ 67 (*b*)
नह् with सं 330
नाना 83
नाम 282-4
निकषा 34
निपुण 100
नी 39, 316; *caus.* 45
नु 285
नूनं 287

प.

पच् 39
पटु 100
पंडित 100
पण् 119
पत् with प्रणि (*c*) 76

पर-पर 136
परं 82
परितः 34
पश्चात् 112
पुनः 288
पुरः 112
पुरस्तात् 112
पुरा with pres. 190
पूज् 154
पूर्वेण 112 (a)
पृथक् 83
प्रच्छ् 39; with आ 334
प्रति 33,86
प्रभृति 82
प्रयोजनं 59
प्रवीण 100
प्रसित 100 (a)
प्राक् 81
प्रायः,प्रायेण 289
प्रिय 106

ब

बत 290
बलवत् 291
बहिः 82
बुध् 154
ब्रू 39

भ.

भक्ष् 45 (c)
भद्रं भद्रं 111
भवत् 128,129
भवितव्यं, भाव्यं } 157 (a)
भी 78
भुज् 326
भू 77
भू with प्र 67 (a), 113

म.

मद् with प्र 76
मध्ये 104 (c)
मन् 70,154
मंत्र् with आ 345
मंथ् 39
मा, मे 127
मुच् 98
मुष् 39
मुहुः 292

य.

यत् 293
यतः 294
यत्सत्यं 295
यज् 60 (a)
यथा 296-7
यम् with आ 317; उप 317 (b)
याच् 39
यावत् 190;298-9, and 300
युज् 96, 337
युक्त 117 (a)

र.

रंज् with अनु (pass.) 94,
रम् with वि, आ, परि 76, 318
राध् 71;—with अप 100 (a) note.
रुच् 61
रुध 39

ल.

लज्ज 146
ली with नि 85

व.

वद् 319;-अभि caus. 45 (f)
वरं-न 301
वस् with उप, अनु, अधि or आ 32
वह् 39;–caus. 45 (a)
वा 302-3
वां, वः 127
विद् with नि caus. 68
-with सं 326
विना 83
विश् with अभिनि 31 (a);-with नि 335
विशेषः 106 (a)
वृ caus. 78
व्यग्र 100
व्यापृत 100

श.

शंस् 63
शास् 39;-with आ 327
शी with अधि 31
शौंड 100
श्रद्धा 98(a)

श्रु with आ or प्रति 64
—सं 1
श्वस् with वि 98 (a)

स.

सदृश 117
सम 117
समक्षं 116
समया 34
सर्वथा 33
सह, साकं, समं, सार्धं 58
साधु 99
सुख 66 (b), 111
स्था 320;—अधि; अव,
सं, प्र 320 (a); आ (b),
उत् 321;—उप 322-3.
स्थाने 304
स्निह् 94
स्पृह् 62
स्मृ 113
स्मृ *caus.* 45 (d)
स्व, स्वीय 139
स्वयं 139 (a)
स्वस्ति, स्वाहा, स्वधा 67
स्वागतं 67 (d)

ह.

हन् 328
हंत 305
हा 34,306
हि 307
हित 66 (b). 111
हृ 39
हृ *caus.* 45 (f),
—अनु 324;—व्यव 119
ह्री 146
ह्वे 325